THE PALAEOLITHIC SETTLEMENT OF EUROPE

BRIDGET AND RAYMOND ALLCHIN *The Rise of civilization in India and Pakistan*
DAVID W. PHILLIPSON *African Archaeology*
CLIVE GAMBLE *The Palaeolithic Settlement of Europe*
ALASDAIR WHITTLE *Neolithic Europe: a Survey*

CAMBRIDGE WORLD ARCHAEOLOGY

THE PALAEOLITHIC SETTLEMENT OF EUROPE

CLIVE GAMBLE

Department of Archaeology
University of Southampton

The right of the
University of Cambridge
to print and sell
all manner of books
was granted by
Henry VIII in 1534.
The University has printed
and published continuously
since 1584.

CAMBRIDGE UNIVERSITY PRESS

CAMBRIDGE

LONDON   NEW YORK   NEW ROCHELLE

MELBOURNE   SYDNEY

Published by the Press Syndicate of the University of Cambridge
The Pitt Building, Trumpington Street, Cambridge CB2 1RP
32 East 57th Street, New York, NY 10022, USA
10 Stamford Road, Oakleigh, Melbourne 3166, Australia

First published 1986

Printed in Great Britain at the University Press, Cambridge

British Library cataloguing in publication data
Gamble, Clive
The Palaeolithic settlement of Europe. –
(Cambridge world archaeology)
1. Palaeolithic period – Europe   2. Europe
– Antiquities
I. Title
936   GN772.2.A1

Library of Congress cataloguing in publication data
Gamble, Clive.
The palaeolithic settlement of Europe.
(Cambridge world archaeology)
Bibliography: p.
Includes index.
1. Palaeolithic period – Europe.   2. Europe –
Antiquities.   3. Anthropology, Prehistoric – Europe.
4. Archaeology – Methodology.   I. Title.   II. Series.
GN772.2.A1G36   1985   936   85–15177

ISBN 0 521 24514 1 hard covers
ISBN 0 521 28764 2 paperback

WV

CONTENTS

List of illustrations   vii
List of tables   xi
Foreword by Lewis R. Binford   xv
Preface   xvii

1 European palaeolithic studies: history and
   approaches   1
2 Hunter-gatherer regional systems   28
3 Pleistocene environments and resources   69
4 Technological, typological and experimental
   approaches   116
5 The palaeolithic record of Europe   137
6 Space and subsistence   250
7 Demography and style   305
8 Society, sediments and settlement   343
9 The palaeolithic settlement of Europe   384

Appendices   394
Bibliography   411
Site index   460
General index   463

ILLUSTRATIONS

1.1	Organic model of cultural evolution	11
1.2	Formation processes	19
2.1	Ecological and social systems	31
2.2	Changing role of storage	37
2.3	Complexity in hunter/gatherer technologies	39
2.4	Tlingit subsistence organisation	44
2.5	Local groups in the sub-arctic	48
2.6	Hunter-gatherer population densities	49
2.7	A model of local group organisation	52
2.8	Regional organisation among the Chipewyan	55
2.9	Changes in settlement signatures due to ecology	64
3.1	Regional model of Europe	72
3.2	Contemporary vegetation in Europe	73
3.3	Deep sea core V28–238	76
3.4	Interglacial-glacial cycle in loess deposits	80
3.5	Upper pleistocene in core RC 11–120	83
3.6	Upper pleistocene correlations	84
3.7	Chronostratigraphy of Périgord rock shelters	86
3.8	Last glacial in northern Europe	89
3.9	Climatic regions at glacial maximum	90
3.10	Changing water masses in the north Atlantic	91
3.11	Late glacial evidence from beetles and pollen	95
3.12	Climatic division of the middle and upper pleistocene	96
3.13	Climatic and vegetational transect: NW, Alpine, MC	98
3.14	Climatic and vegetational transect: NE, SE, ME	99
4.1	Levallois flake, blade and point production	118
4.2	Reduction strategy for blades and bladelets	121
4.3	Variation in handaxe shape	123
4.4	Middle palaeolithic artifact types	124
4.5	Comparison of lithic assemblages by cumulative percentages	125
4.6	Micoquian artifact types	128
4.7	Implement morphology and use wear	131
4.8	Secondary retouch on flint artifacts	133
4.9	The *Typologie Analytique*	134

5.1	Handaxes from pre-stage 5	142
5.2	Retouched flake tools	143
5.3	Chopping tools, flakes and denticulates	145
5.4	Markkleeberg environment	148
5.5	Fossil crania	148
5.6	La Micoque	151
5.7	Isernia La Pineta	155
5.8	Torralba settlement system	159
5.9	Aschersleben See profile	162
5.10	Leaf points	164
5.11	Middle palaeolithic assemblages	166
5.12	Settlement on the Swabian Alb	167
5.13	Érd site distributions	170
5.14	EUP artifact types	184
5.15	Carved figure of mammoth ivory	187
5.16	Pavlov collar	188
5.17	Morín grave	198
5.18	Paglicci burial	204
5.19	Les Etiolles distributions	208
5.20	LUP artifact types	209
5.21	LUP artifact types, points	211
5.22	Recolonisation of central Europe	213
5.23	Group movements in the late glacial	215
5.24	Gönnersdorf engraved slab	217
5.25	Cantabrian sites	224
5.26	Laufen and Delemont sites	225
5.27	La Marche engraving	226
5.28	Laugerie-Basse spear throwers	228
5.29	Painting styles	229
5.30	Lascaux plan	233
5.31	René Clastres gallery	234
5.32	Seasonal mobility in Epirus	240
5.33	Central Italy settlement	241
5.34	South-east Spain settlement	243
5.35	Parpalló engraved slab	244
6.1	Flake scatters	253
6.2	Bénagu flint scatter	254
6.3	Les Tarterets conjoins	255
6.4	Structure at Ripiceni	256
6.5	Seating plan model	257
6.6	Bone and stone distribution	259
6.7	Drop and toss zones	261
6.8	Lazaret distributions	262

6.9   Mezhirich structure   266
6.10 Mezin structures   267
6.11 Barca II structures   267
6.12 Plateau Parrain pavement   269
6.13 Achenheim distributions   271
6.14 Factor specific items at Torralba   274
6.15 Le Flageolet distributions   276
6.16 Low energy tools   278
6.17 Model of stone tool variation   280
6.18 Bone needle manufacture   285
6.19 MGUI for Stellmoor and Abri Pataud   295
6.20 Settlement system model   302
7.1   Combe-Grenal fauna   315
7.2   Venus figurine distribution   326
7.3   Venus figurine analysis   327
7.4   LUP harpoons   328
7.5   LUP female engravings   329
7.6   Handaxes and raw material   332
7.7   EUP raw material   333
7.8   Pyrenees raw material transfers   335
7.9   Holy Cross raw material   337
8.1   Abri Caminade plan   346
8.2   Sedimentation at the Abri Pataud   351
8.3   Parpalló and Les Mallaetes sedimentation   352
8.4   Upper palaeolithic assemblage size, France   355
8.5   Upper palaeolithic assemblage size, England   355
8.6   Upper palaeolithic assemblage size, Europe   355
8.7   Périgord retouched tools   356
8.8   Research triangle   357
8.9   Périgord and Germany compared   375
8.10 Settlement record model   377
8.11 Technology at 128 Kyr?   379
8.12 Technology at 8 Kyr   380

ACKNOWLEDGEMENTS

Acknowledgement is due to the following for permission to reproduce illustrations:

Academiae NAUK, Moscow **6.9**; Academic Press Inc. **5.5**, **5.12**, **7.9**, **8,3**; Académiai Kaidó, Budapest **5.11**, **5.13**; reproduced by permission of the Society for American Archaeology from *American Antiquity* 43, iii (1978) **6.5**; John Baker Ltd **4.3**; C. H. Beck'sche Verlag, Munich **5.28**, **5.35**; Böhlau Verlag, Cologne **4.6**, **5.15**, **6.12**; Herman Böhlaus, Weimar **6.18**; Centre Nationale de la Recherche Scientifique, Paris **1.1**, **4.8**, **5.19**, **5.22**, **5.24**, **5.30**, **6.3**, **6.6**, **6.13**; Council for British Archaeology **8.12**; Dümmlers Verlag, Bonn **3.9**; Editions d'Art Lucien Mazenod, Paris **5.29**; Habelt Verlag, Bonn **5.24**; Instituto para Investigaciones Prehistóricas, Santander **5.18**; reproduced from the *Journal of Field Archaeology* with the permission of the Trustees of Boston University **6.1**; Dr Stefan Kozlowski **4.2**; Landesmuseum für Vorgeschichte, Halle **5.9**; Mouton Publishers, Berlin **6.14**; reprinted by permission from *Nature*, Vol. 226, pp.722, 724, copyright © 1970 Macmillan Journals Ltd **5.17**; Oxford University Press **6.7(a)**, **5.32**; Dr Léon Pales **5.27**; Peabody Museum of Archaeology and Ethnology, Harvard **8.2**; Routledge and Kegan Paul Ltd **6.20**; Royal Anthropological Institute of Great Britain and Ireland **7.2**; Société Préhistorique Française **4.1**, **5.31**, **6.2**, **6.8**, **6.19**; reproduced by permission of Professor D. de Sonneville-Bordes from *Science* Vol. 134, 803–40. Fig.2, copyright © 1961 American Association for the Advancement of Science **8.11**; University of Chicago Press **6.10**; University of Washington Press **2.4**; Vydavatel'stvo Slovenskej Akadémie Vied, Bratislava **6.11**.

TABLES

1.1	Coverage in *La Préhistoire Française*	7
1.2	Factor groupings for the mousterian	14
1.3	Density of materials on camp sites	21
1.4	Descriptive classes and behavioural classes	25
2.1	Hunter-gatherer subsistence by latitude	35
2.2	Community structure and hunter-gatherer adaptation	36
2.3	Settlement pattern and effective temperature	38
2.4	Some correlates of K and r selection	41
2.5	Strategic and tactical decisions for hunters and gatherers	45
2.6	Regional archaeological signatures	65
2.7	A hierarchy of analytical units	67
3.1	The regions of palaeolithic Europe	73
3.2	Pleistocene correlations	75
3.3	Correlation chart for the European pleistocene	78
3.4	Pollen analysis and interglacials	81
3.5	The last interglacial/glacial cycle	82
3.6	The date of glacial interstadials	88
3.7	Last glacial correlations within Europe	93
3.8	Production and biomass of world vegetation units	100
3.9	Animal communities and biotopes	104
3.10	Attributes of herd species and predator selection	105
3.11	Faunal communities in central Europe	107
3.12	Selected attributes of four key animal species	108
4.1	Levallois reduction sequence	119
4.2	Technological classification of flint material	122
4.3	Mousterian assemblages in south-west France	127
4.4	'Blind test' experiments on stone tool use	129
4.5	Lower palaeolithic tool use	130
4.6	Functional groupings for artifacts	130
4.7	Typological groupings for the upper palaeolithic	132
4.8	A four part division of palaeolithic Europe	136
5.1	The 'key site' approach in palaeolithic studies	138
5.2	Absolute dates for period 1 sites, northern province	140
5.3	Pre-neanderthal and neanderthal finds	153
5.4	Fossil remains from Krapina	173

5.5   Neanderthal remains from Hortus   176
5.6   *Homo sapiens* grade system   179
5.7   Kostenki/Borshevo stratigraphy and chronology   182
5.8   Aurignacian and perigordian traditions   190
5.9   C14 dates for the mousterian and EUP   191
5.10   Assemblage variation in the Périgord   192
5.11   Chronology of perigordian V assemblages   193
5.12   Grimaldi burials   203
5.13   Chronology of LUP technocomplexes   206
5.14   Périgord correlation chart for upper palaeolithic   219
5.15   Settlement data from SW and NC regions   223
5.16   Leroi-Gourhan's main art styles   227
5.17   Analysis of art sites by style and topography   230
5.18   Upper palaeolithic in the MW region   237
6.1   Torralba groupings   273
6.2   Implement frequencies in mousterian assemblages   281
6.3   Use of quartzite in solutrean assemblages   282
6.4   Bacho Kiro raw material   282
6.5   Flake debitage analysis   283
6.6   Antler and bone points from central and eastern Europe   285
6.7   Broken material from the Bockstein   287
6.8   Broken material in solutrean assemblages   287
6.9   The Modified General Utility Index for caribou   292
6.10   Reindeer from Abri Pataud and Stellmoor   294
6.11   Reindeer faunal assemblages compared   298
6.12   Settlement system models and their correlates   300
6.13   Palaeolithic assemblages from the Lot and Garonne   303
7.1   Herbivore and carnivore representation in open sites   308
7.2   Herbivore and carnivore representation in cave sites   309
7.3   Early last glacial faunal assemblages   312
7.4   Mid last glacial faunal assemblages   313
7.5   Full and late glacial faunal assemblages   314
7.6   Occurrence of carnivores in cave deposits   315
7.7   Faunal assemblages in the southern and mediterranean
       provinces   316
7.8   Faunal assemblages in the northern province   317
7.9   The occurrence of cave bear by region   318
7.10   The fauna from Érd   319
7.11   Female figurines from the EUP   325
7.12   Raw material usage in the Moravian upper palaeolithic   334
7.13   Design elements on engraved bones   341
8.1   Densities of excavated materials from Asprochaliko and
       Kastritsa   348

8.2	Time density estimates for Kastritsa and Asprochaliko	349
8.3	Accumulation rates for materials at Parpalló	352
8.4	Mousterian industries at Pech de l'Azé IV	354
8.5	Assemblage counts from La Ferrassie	358
8.6	Assemblage counts from the Ilsenhöhle	360
8.7	Artifact counts from the Sesselfelsgrotte	360
8.8	Artifact counts from Grotte de l'Hyène	361
8.9	Assemblages from the Cueva Morín	362
8.10	Artifact counts from Bacho Kiro	363
8.11	Artifact counts from Molodova V	365
8.12	Artifact counts from Willendorf II	366
8.13	Ipswichian and Flandrian faunas	368
8.14	Findspot frequency for southern Germany and south-west France	373
8.15	Site density in southern Germany and south-west France	373
9.1	Three interpretative models of the European palaeolithic	385

FOREWORD

In one sense this book represents the realisation of goals which some of us imagined years ago. When one began to argue about the way archaeologists approached the task of giving meaning to the archaeological record one looked forward to the day when the palaeolithic would be presented as something other than a descriptive synthesis of archaeologically recovered things. In this sense this book is a dream come true. It is a serious discussion of how to use the archaeological record as a bridge to understanding the past. It is a demonstration that patterning at the regional level, while being important and fascinating, is also a necessary empirical framework in terms of which we must approach the task of learning about the past. It both opens up archaeology to new dreams of things to be accomplished and broadly outlines some very new challenges.

By shifting the perspective Gamble changes the framework for synthesis. The book is punctuated with new ways of organising old facts. In turn these new organisations produce new facts. To put it another way, Clive Gamble has carried out some very provocative pattern recognition studies in demonstrating his approach. These new facts cannot help but change the way archaeologists think about the past. At the same time they present us with a new past – one not previously suggested by archaeologists. This type of provocation cannot help but draw criticism and produce controversy.

Scientists realise that growth in understanding is largely proportional to the degree to which we can solve specific problems. Such problems are recognisable only when ideas are in conflict over facts. We might say that real progress derives from the successes enjoyed by scientists in bringing different perspectives to bear on similar facts, and this is what Clive Gamble has achieved. His approaches tease very different views of the past from the archaeological record, and his book is not only successful now, but will also play an important role in shaping palaeolithic archaeology in the future.

There is much here to cheer and relish as well as to argue about and investigate. I expect other readers will feel a similar reaction on their initial reading of the book. Gamble's book should be appreciated for its overarching message and picked to pieces only when the issues are clear and the relevance of contentious points clearly established. For instance, the models of the past presented in the final chapter can easily be attacked if the reader dismisses the arguments presented in the earlier chapters. On the other hand, criticism advanced in terms of the earlier aguments is not so easy. If a critic can accomplish the latter in a well founded manner then he or she can certainly write the book that will replace this one. My guess is that such a constructively critical book would be even further away from the content of the old style palaeolithic archaeology books which fill our shelves at this time. This book is new and different. What it stimulates will likewise be new and different.

LEWIS R. BINFORD

Bordeaux, France
February 1984

PREFACE

The European palaeolithic is well represented by general works. When compared with other technological periods (neolithic, bronze and iron ages), there is a positive embarrassment of national, continental and even world-wide syntheses. This has obvious advantages to anyone embarking on a similar venture since not only is the market able to accept such a general approach but much of the hard work has been done by others! The opposite side of the coin however is that the potential readership already has a picture of what they expect, and indeed want, from yet another general work. While it would be easy to break the mould of iron age studies with a European synthesis, since none exists, any novelty in an approach to the palaeolithic must first chip away at a substantial nodule of tradition and expectation.

In this book I have chosen the soft rather than the hard hammer approach to this task of reduction by asking two questions: is the European palaeolithic worth studying, and if so, how should it be studied?

The size of the book that follows shows that the first question received a positive answer although not the cosily parochial reply that European archaeologists often expect. The second has been answered by contrasting what I see as two very different ways of investigating this segment of prehistory. The contrast is not unfamiliar to archaeologists since it follows directly from the earlier Bordes/Binford debates about the mousterian, where, in a scenario worthy of Henry James, European experience met the insatiable New World appetite to know. An integral part of phrasing an appropriate answer has been to devise an analytical framework for past behaviour that has survived the pleistocene mincer in the form of robust chunks of material culture. It has always been my view that the palaeolithic is the worst archaeological data base from which to attempt the reconstruction of culture history. We are dealing not only with early forms of *Homo sapiens* but also with mobile lifestyles that are as far removed as possible from the application of common-sense interpretations derived from the cultural experience of the archaeologist. While these have been liberally applied with some success to later prehistory they have merely trivialised our understanding of the complexities and potential of palaeolithic data to inform us about past lifestyles for which there are no contemporary or historical analogues. In this book I have taken the view that the same data base offers immense scope for investigating the interface between ecological and cultural systems since the constraints of the former on the latter are at their most pronounced with such highly mobile groups. As a result it becomes an opportunity to confront that hardest of archaeological challenges – putting the data and the theory together – in order to replace speculation about our common past with an understanding of why we ever bothered to ask questions in the first place.

The palaeolithic is moreover at an exciting point of transition. The explosion in ethnoarchaeological studies has fundamentally challenged our models and interpretations amongst all classes of data and at all spatial scales of analysis. Furthermore the traditional concerns of dating and quaternary studies have also passed through their own revolutions and palaeolithic archaeology is the direct, albeit on occasion reluctant, beneficiary.

These challenges have been presented to me by many people. Eric Higgs fired my imagination with his broad 'Whooosh!' view of prehistory while Charles McBurney, himself an advocate of a broad geographical picture, would not let me forget those nasty little facts which have to be accounted for in the palimpsest that is the palaeolithic record.

The critical challenges from Robin Dennell, Geoff Bailey, Rob Foley, John Gowlett, Iain Davidson, Bill Boismier, Paul Mellars, Helen Higgs, John Pfeiffer and especially Robin Torrence, who either read drafts or discussed ideas and still talk to me were more helpful than they can imagine. Both colleagues and students at Southampton provided, over the years, that altogether necessary sceptical trampoline on which lead balloons and kites could be dropped and flown without too much damage, and I hope that this book will finally allay some of their misgivings about monkey-men.

A special debt is owed to Pat Carter, who put up with more than his fair share of initial interpretations and eventually told me to stop worrying about what other people might think and just write the thing. Every author at some time needs a clear command like that.

I should also like to thank Robin Derricourt, who first suggested the book and has been a constant source of calm concerning early drafts and disappearing deadlines. The original drawings are all by Fiona Gale and I will never know how she found time to do them! The flint drawings are all by Paul A. Crake. Martin Oake, Nick Bradford and Joy Robinson all helped in producing the final manuscript. Clare Tolmie expertly compiled the index.

Elaine Morris did much of the word processing under the dubious inducement that the book provided an excellent opportunity to learn such important skills. Without her unstinting interest and continual advice over so many years this book would never have been finished.

Finally I would like to acknowledge a particular debt that this book owes to Lewis Binford, who shifted my intellectual anchors at the right moment by pointing out that Big Pictures are all very well in archaeology but what matters is how you direct the supporting cast. Without his enthusiasm and willingness to share the experiences of his archaeological and ethnoarchaeological work there really would not be a book about the palaeolithic settlement of Europe but rather just some dead clips of film on the cutting room floor still waiting for someone to call ACTION!

Southampton, England
December 1983

CHAPTER I

EUROPEAN PALAEOLITHIC STUDIES: HISTORY AND APPROACHES*

> Archaeological 'facts' take their meaning from their conceptual arrange-
> ment and the adequacy or inadequacy of that arrangement, model, or
> hypothesis accounts for the amount of information made available to the
> archaeologist.
>
> David Clarke, *Analytical Archaeology* (1978:9)

Introduction

The palaeolithic of Europe is a record of observations and a register of ideas.
These studies emerged as a component of prehistory and gained respectability as
a concept amid widespread and fundamental social change in the nineteenth
century.

   This change involved the transformation of society under the continuing
impact of the industrial revolution that was well under way in England by the
last two decades of the eighteenth century. The 'European Century' (1815–1914)
witnessed the culmination of three longer term processes: the full development
of a world economy, the creation of the apparatus of the modern state and the
rise of science. The potential and practical advantages of this last development
depended upon a radical shift in the way that nature was conceived, investigated
and utilised. The development of archaeology as an intellectual discipline is
inextricably linked with this wider movement that also saw the foundations of
geological and evolutionary studies.

   At the same time the creation of a world market led to a restructuring of
relations between human societies and to the formation of new class interests
within societies. The period saw the creation of wealth on a previously
unparalleled scale and the rise to prominence of a middle class in all the states of
Western Europe. It is no coincidence that the study of prehistory can trace its
origins to this same period when the social fortunes of the middle class were in
the ascendancy.

   The creation of the wealth from which their influence and power was derived
also involved the exploitation of natural resources and the intensification of
agriculture to support a rapidly expanding work force. Gravel and clay pits were
dug to provide building materials; canals and railways involved civil engineer-
ing works on an ambitious and massive scale; the expansion of cities resulted in

---

* Throughout the book Kyr represents thousand years before the present (bp).

land being converted to different uses; and agriculture, while taking in more marginal land with improved techniques, bit deeper into the surface of the earth. In the process, a vast quantity of archaeological materials was yielded up. The fact that most of these developments were achieved by manual labour also provided favourable conditions for the recovery of objects that lay buried at various depths in the landscape.

These objects had no significance in themselves. In this sense the prehistoric past was not so much discovered, as is commonly portrayed, but *invented* to meet the particular requirements of this same social class. Following the creation of a conceptual framework the material objects came to acquire significance and meaning whereas previously, when found, they had attracted no more than idle curiosity. In particular, prehistory came to serve the ideologies of progress and nationalism in the cause of class identity. The discovery that change was a feature of the past and so part of the natural order admirably suited a nineteenth-century view of the world. Indeed the lesson of prehistory confirmed and comforted the contemporary opinion that progress was inevitable and civilised. In the same way, national history provided a strong ideological framework that helped legitimise economic and political positions. For example, the middle class of Denmark utilised prehistoric archaeology to provide a link between themselves, the cultural heritage of the nation and the 'people'. Moreover, they stressed that national identity was a necessary precondition for continued progress and the goal of sovereignty (Kristiansen 1981).

Prehistory and the concept of a past were not the only means by which the middle class legitimised its new found position and coped with the problems of adjusting to such radically altered conditions in the state of human affairs. Comparable developments took place in the choice of earlier gothic architectural styles with which to build 'new' buildings such as factories, railway stations, museums, and in England, the Houses of Parliament. Age and antiquity became general criteria by which social value was attributed to objects and events, and by enveloping new institutions and activities in a cloak of older material traditions, a new order was confirmed.

As a result, the 'old stone age' that dealt with human origins and the earliest cultures came to be seen as a scientific study of progress in prehistoric times (Trigger 1981:142). So much so that de Mortillet dramatically declared in his guide to the prehistoric antiquities exhibited at the Paris Exposition of 1867 that 'it is impossible any longer to doubt the great law of the progress of man' (Daniel 1964:57). The years that followed this statement saw the corruption of biological evolutionary theory into an account of social development by linking levels of cultural development to notions of primitiveness and different intelligence. This view was apparently confirmed by the study of contemporary hunters and gatherers, as indicated in Sollas' book *Ancient Hunters and Their Modern Representatives*, published in 1911. Here the palaeolithic period followed the division into lower, middle and upper stages. In Sollas' book these were paralleled by the Tasmanians and Australian Aboriginals for the lower and middle stages respectively and by Bushmen and Eskimos as representatives of the upper palaeolithic stage. Elsewhere the palaeolithic was referred to as a stage of savagery, and barbarism and civilization completed the social three age system devised by Morgan (1877) and which has seen a long history of use in prehistoric studies (Clark 1946; Childe 1951; Wymer 1982). Progress throughout savagery was achieved by advances in intellect that were manifest not only in the changing shapes of fossil crania but more importantly in the changing shape of stone tools.

While many of the original circumstances have altered, it is still reasonable to expect that prehistoric studies continue to reflect in their aims, goals and presentations the changing social fortunes of that class which the concept of prehistory serves. The reflections may not be very clear to us but the important point is that we should not assume that archaeology is a neutral subject – either that it can be studied 'objectively' without any reference to its social context, or that the archaeological record exists as a body of facts that can, if prompted by the act of discovery, tell their own story.

The record of observations and the register of ideas that we now know as *The Palaeolithic* is the result of a series of inward-looking *regional traditions* of research which, taken together, constitute our understanding of this segment of the past. These researches have been conducted in an atmosphere of different yet linked intellectual traditions of Western thought. As a result the product of the past bears the unmistakable stamp of the intellectual concerns of the West. These are, of course, the concerns of a mosaic of societies, that in the process of transforming themselves from pre-industrial to industrial states, undermined and rejected their own traditional cultures (A. M. Gamble 1981). It is an irony of prehistoric studies that the subject was created in order to fill a void that resulted from society severing the links with its recent traditions, values and ways of interpreting the world.

In this book I accept these regional traditions and the wider intellectual system to which they belong as the inspiration and organisation of the palaeolithic record of Europe. However, what follows is not a social history of palaeolithic archaeology. The main aim of this book is to propose an alternative regional framework based on an examination of the properties of the palaeolithic record, employing different measures and directed towards other goals. My main contention is that the European palaeolithic can no longer be studied for its supposed intrinsic qualities alone. Instead we must utilise this large data base and place it within a global perspective on palaeolithic studies. I shall show in later chapters that as we alter the scale and dimensions of our perspective with this set of data so we can come to appreciate a different significance in the findings of the regional and national traditions of research into the 'earliest Europeans'. This significance will appear very different, when compared to the traditional roots of the subject. It is therefore to these views, assumptions and achievements that we must first turn since they provide the foundations for all later developments.

Ladders and layers

There are two views which have held considerable sway in the investigation and presentation of European palaeolithic data. The first was supplied by the American anthropologist Lewis Henry Morgan in his book *Ancient Society* published in 1877. Here he described the condition of early man in the following memorable terms:

mankind commenced their career at the bottom of the scale and worked their way up from savagery to civilization through the slow accumulation of experimental knowledge. . . An attempt will be made . . . to bring forward additional evidence of the rudeness of the early condition of mankind, of the gradual evolution of their mental and moral powers through experience, and of their protracted struggle with opposing obstacles *while winning their way to civilization.* (*ibid.*: 3 (my emphasis))

This sketch was echoed in many other accounts and provided a clear basis for understanding the nature of human evolution. This stated that progress, although slow, was inevitable and ultimately attained the state of civilisation. It therefore followed that the process of evolution, which served progress, was goal orientated. This purposive view, wherein evolution had its own pre-set internal motor and only human mental capacity acted as a brake, did not require an investigation of the forces of selection working on hominid culture and biology. Instead, this view required that archaeology provide nothing more than a timetable of when civilised traits, such as tools, fire, shelter, burials, art and ornaments first appeared.

This scheme proved immensely flexible. It provided a unifying framework which made sense of data coming from a number of regional traditions while later accommodating discoveries from other parts of the world. The insistence on the slow, gradual nature of change was in keeping with Darwin's views on species change and meant that explaining *why* evolution took so long was not a central problem requiring urgent examination.

'While winning their way to civilisation' summarised an expectation of the goal of the prehistoric and palaeolithic past. Moreover the phrase emphasises the competitive spirit that was so keenly felt in the European regional traditions which were busily assembling evidence of 'our earliest ancestors' or 'the first Englishman'.

While this view dealt with the concepts of evolution and change, a second was firmly rooted in some common sense opinions. It provided explanatory concepts that could be readily grasped by all participants in the regional traditions of Europe. These confirmed the view that the continent was naturally a place of different peoples and cultures and that therein lay the reasons for its dominance in contemporary affairs. We learn in a landmark paper on upper palaeolithic systematics, by the Abbé Breuil, that

Il devient de plus en plus évident que ce qu'on a pris d'abord pour une série continue, due à l'évolution sur place d'une population unique, est au contraire le fruit de la collaboration successive de nombreuses peuplades réagissant plus ou moins les unes sur les autres, soit par une influence purement industrielle ou commerciale, soit par l'infiltration graduelle ou l'invasion brusque et guerrière de tribus étrangères. (1912:9)

The competitive European spirit was here translated back into the past by recognising cultural traditions among palaeolithic materials with which to draw up the political map of prehistoric Europe. The mechanics of the process was perfectly captured by Breuil with the following image,

Notre monde européen, et surtout sa partie occidentale, est un cul-de-sac vers lequel les vagues humaines, arrivées de l'est ou du sud sous les impulsions inconnues, sont venues mêler et superposer leurs sédiments. (*ibid.:9*)

This aquatic model, dealing with tides in the affairs of early European man, summarises a great deal of otherwise implicit, and therefore silent, interpretation in palaeolithic studies. Breuil stated that we do not know what forces drove prehistoric peoples up the European cul-de-sac in successive waves. It is the record of their presence rather than the understanding of their purpose that forms the basis of traditional regional investigations in European palaeolithic studies.

An important regional tradition

This concern with documenting and describing the material record of the past, rather than with explaining the many forms it takes, attaches particular significance to the fact of discovery. Some of the more notable events are presented in appendices 1 and 2, and many of these refer to a single regional tradition from France.

The importance of the French tradition rests on the energies of a number of early workers – Boucher de Perthes (1788–1868), Edouard Lartet (1801–75), Gabriel de Mortillet (1821–99) – who utilised the rich discoveries of flint, bone and antler artifacts to organise and partition the palaeolithic record of the country into what became the classic sequence for this archaeological period. The descriptive terms they employed have been used and copied throughout much of Europe and later were employed in Africa and Asia. The foundations that were laid in the second half of the nineteenth century bore rich fruit at a later date with the immensely intricate regional perspectives provided by Denis Peyrony (1869–1954) and the international spirit of Breuil (1877–1961) and later by Bordes (1919–81) who all served as major influences on the direction and interpretation of regional sequences from many other parts of the world.

The development of a French regional tradition can be divided into three broad periods as summarised by Sackett (1981).

> 1   *The heroic age.* before 1870 and until 1900. This period saw the discovery and acceptance of cave art as the work of palaeolithic man. The high

antiquity of man was also demonstrated (Breuil 1945), and de Mortillet provided a classification based on stone tools that recognised the acheulean, mousterian, solutrean and magdalenian. During this period the principles of stratigraphic excavation were worked out and a chronology established by reference to the early quaternary studies of Agassiz and Penck, and the presence of cold climate mammals associated with the stone tools.

2 *The traditional foundations*. after 1900 until c.1950. The earlier schemes of de Mortillet were revised and expanded in the light of accumulating information. The 'battle of the aurignacian' was won by Breuil (1912) adding an earlier upper palaeolithic phase before the solutrean and after the mousterian. In 1933 Peyrony subdivided the aurignacian into two traditions, aurignacian and perigordian.

3 *Chronostratigraphic developments*. c.1950. Microstratigraphic observations have led to the revision of many of the traditional cultural frameworks (Laville *et al.* 1980). This has been combined with standardised typologies (Bordes 1961a; de Sonneville-Bordes and Perrot 1954–6) which have assisted the objective description of excavated assemblages of lithic materials. However the debate about why stone tool assemblages of the same industrial tradition vary has been accepted by many as proof that this greater observational rigour has enhanced rather than undermined the explanations of the traditional foundations (Bordes and de Sonneville-Bordes 1970).

Two regions within France have provided a great amount of data and received correspondingly greater attention during this tripartite development. The first area is the river terrace system of the Somme and Seine in the north of the country, while the second centres upon the cave and rock shelters (abri sous-roche) of the Périgord region contained within the modern administrative Department of the Dordogne which occupies the heartland of Aquitaine. In particular, the sites that cluster in the rock shelters around the village of Les Eyzies on the Vézère river, a tributary of the Dordogne, have a significance for the development of palaeolithic studies that goes beyond their immediate regional importance. Within a few kilometres of this small village lie many famous excavated sites: Le Moustier, La Madeleine, La Ferrassie, Laugerie-Haute, Abri Pataud, Combe Grenal – which have provided important stratified sequences of changing lithic assemblages.

The complexity of the French regional tradition is well illustrated in the monumental two volumes of *La Préhistoire Française*, edited by H. de Lumley (1976a). The 1,531 pages contain 233 articles on palaeolithic and quaternary studies by 218 regional experts. The second volume dealing with the palaeolithic industries presents the material by period – lower, middle, and upper palaeolithic – and by administrative region. Some impression of the coverage can be gained from table 1.1.

The French regional traditions have more often than not looked to the intrinsic qualities of their areas in order to account for change and variation in the palaeolithic record. For example, Peyrony, writing in 1933, interpreted the

Table 1.1. *Palaeolithic coverage in* La Préhistoire Française *vol. 2*
(H. de Lumley ed. 1976a).

	Number of regions detailed in each section	Number of articles
Earliest industries	9	8
Lower palaeolithic	22	20
Middle palaeolithic	22	21
Upper palaeolithic	27	25

successional history of two upper palaeolithic traditions around Les Eyzies by
stating that this area would have been a *coin privilégié* (*ibid.*: 557). In his view it
formed a sort of Garden of Eden which was competed for by different human
groups each of which was differentiated by distinctive stone tools, which the
winners dropped, as a record of their success, in the rock shelters. A comparable
point of view was expressed more recently by Bordes (1973:222) to account for
industrial variability in this same area during even longer time spans of the
palaeolithic.

It would be possible to accuse Peyrony of excessive regional favouritism. He
did after all live in a house that sits on the central portion of the deposits in the
Laugerie-Haute rock shelter! However, what his work brilliantly demonstrates
is the success of the regional tradition which, through patient research and
immense knowledge, built up a pattern of sequence and change in palaeolithic
materials. Without such local commitment there would be precious little
understanding today of the complexities of palaeolithic data, so that while we
may now regard some of the explanations of their findings as parochial we shall
probably never again rival their involvement with this material.

Elsewhere in Europe the regional traditions followed the lead and the pattern
supplied by France. As a result a great many accounts exist dealing with the
palaeolithic from other countries and regions. (Many of these form the basis of
Chapter 5.) With the accumulation of larger data sets it has also become more
common to find broader geographical treatments of particular industries and
lithic traditions, as with the middle palaeolithic (Gábori 1976), aurignacian
(Hahn 1977), gravettian (Otte 1981), tanged point assemblages (Taute 1968), and
traditions associated with the late glacial (de Sonneville-Bordes (ed.) 1979).
These studies fit well into stage three of the development of the French tradition
(Sackett 1981). From an earlier period we can see in the work of Zotz (1941) in
central Europe how the regional approach that transcended administrative
boundaries was largely dependent upon political expansion suggesting an
appropriately enlarged regional study unit for the archaeologist.

Within the third period there have been two significant developments which
have had great repercussions for European palaeolithic studies. The first has
been the development of a continuous pleistocene stratigraphic record based, as

we shall see in Chapter 3, on cores drilled into the ocean floors (Bowen 1978). This has revealed no less than eight glacial/interglacial cycles in the past 700 Kyr, thereby completely undermining the ice age model established by Penck and Bruckner in 1909 from work in southern Germany and the Alps, and which identified only four main glacial episodes in the whole of the pleistocene. The deep sea core findings have still not been fully assimilated into the regional quaternary sequences of Europe, but as this happens and is backed by absolute dates, many revisions concerning the age and relationship of lithic assemblages will also appear.

The second development stems from the wealth of finds that have come from fieldwork in Africa. These have demolished the earlier notions of Europe as a cradle for mankind. J. D. Clark (1975) has spelt out that Europe no longer holds a monopoly on the prehistory of mankind and also that the roles of paramount and periphery have been reversed in terms of the relation between Europe and Africa as continents for research into early man.

This raises the question of whether the European palaeolithic is really only of interest to European palaeolithic archaeologists and their parochial concerns? As questions such as the origins of the European upper palaeolithic have come to occupy less of the centre stage in world prehistory it now has to be asked what else can be done with this rich and well researched data base within the developing concept of global palaeolithic studies? The question may reflect in small measure the changed place of Europe in the second half of the twentieth century. However, we must also look in more detail at the major intellectual challenges within the subject itself, which are forcing a re-think of the ways in which we approach the European data.

Two paradigms and two models

The European palaeolithic can be discussed in terms of two paradigms. The first reflects the inward-looking regional traditions. This is the culture history paradigm that has for a long time been the dominant force in directing all archaeological research (Flannery 1967). The second paradigm views culture as an adaptive system. From the perspective of the European traditions this is an external introduction, strongly influenced by developments in archaeology and anthropology in the United States.

The interest in these competing paradigms lies not in deciding whether one is right and the other wrong but in seeing, through their polarised positions, how their respective assumptions and goals are translated into basic operations in the form of models, concepts and the division of the data base into units of classification. They are opportunities to observe archaeologists doing archaeology.

(a) culture history

The practitioners of this approach take as their goal the elucidation and fine resolution of regional sequences based on sound stratigraphic observation. The comparison and analysis of artifactual material is based on the recognition of patterns of likes and unlikes in artifact shapes and assemblage composition. The examples from the previous section would all fall under the umbrella of this paradigm. The achievements have been considerable in documenting cultures from the human past which differ fundamentally from any that can be found either in historical accounts or in the contemporary world (Dunnell 1978:193).

This paradigm also supports the commonly held opinion that the palaeolithic record is piecemeal and preserved on a selective basis so that what is always needed is more data before any prehistory can be written. According to this standpoint the time is never ripe for moving from data collection to historical analysis (Brodar 1979:28; Roe 1981:268).

Sackett (1981) has characterised this approach as 'straight archaeology'. The caution of the practitioners is commendable but does not rest on any solid theoretical basis. In fact, the theoretical content of the approach is determined, as Dunnell (1978) has pointed out, by the fact that, since the terms and classifications used to enshrine observations are framed in language, they implicitly derive significance and meaning because of the way in which language works as a framework for communication. This common-sense, or straight, approach to the data is nothing more than an outcome of using language. This means that interpretative schemes can be put forward, changed and discarded with little or no recourse to any explicit body of theory about the past.

This is particularly evident if we consider the basic terms of the culture history approach and their definitions as proposed by various authorities.

> Assemblage – a collection of artifacts from a specific segment of an archaeological site.
>
> Industry – a distinctive complex or configuration of artifact types and type frequencies that recurs among two or more assemblages.
>
> Tradition – a group of industries whose artifactual similarities are sufficient to suggest that they belong to some broader culture-historical block of technological ideas and practices (Laville *et al.* 1980:13–14).
>
> Technocomplex – a group of cultures characterised by assemblages sharing a polythetic range but differing specific types of the same general families of artifact types, shared as a widely diffused and interlinked response to common factors in environment, economy and technology. A negligible level of affinity, perhaps 5 per cent or less, uniting the group in terms of shared specific types but a residual medium level affinity, perhaps 30–60 per cent, uniting the group in terms of type families (Clarke 1978:495).

> Civilisation – un tout complexe qui implique la possession de techniques
> pour l'obtention d'outils, une vie sociale organisée, une langue même
> rudimentaire, des traditions communes et vraisemblablement le sens
> de la beauté qui apparaît dès l'aube de l'Humanité dans la symétrie et la
> régularité de certains outils et le choix de la matière première (H. de
> Lumley 1976b:xvi).

> Culture – a polythetic set of specific and comprehensive artifact-types
> which consistently recur together in assemblages within a limited
> geographic area (Clarke 1978:490).

It must be stressed that the definitions given here are not universally agreed, and indeed few archaeologists set down exactly how they are using terms. An assemblage, for example, may be used to describe a collection of artifacts from one area of a site, from the whole site, or from a stratigraphical unit within a site without reference to any spatial dimensions or other external reference points. We learn that 'the unit of culture grows geographically with civilization' (Bordes and de Sonneville-Bordes 1970:67) and yet apparently the term 'technocomplex' knows no spatial boundaries (Clarke 1978). As a term it is fitted around a geographical distribution of similar artifact forms. In other words it forms a description *after* the business of pattern recognition among palaeolithic materials has taken place.

It is easier to see how these fuzzy building blocks are incorporated into schemes of meaning and interpretation. The final construction can be described by means of an *organic* model that was originally borrowed from the disciplines of geology and palaeontology (Sackett 1981). The basis of the model resides in the concept of type fossils (French: fossile directeur; German: Leitformen) that describes a collection of artifacts. The use and application of the term is again very variable but basically comes down to the judgement of the typologist over what is indeed a significant and distinctive element within an assemblage. The type fossil approach was used with great success in palaeontology to characterise whole geological strata by particular fossil species. The prehistorians accepted this same view of relationships between evolving fossil species in accumulating strata and adapted it to the study of chipped stone tools. In geology, this relationship, due to the nature of the data, could be related to biological, hence organic, relations. Stone tools were never living organisms in the way that fossils were, and yet they came to be viewed as such, with the result, as Sackett remarks (1968:67), that some uses of the current terminology hint that they might almost be capable of sexual relations!

An example of this organic approach is shown in figure 1.1 with H. de Lumley's phylogenetic account of middle palaeolithic assemblages from southern France. This particular presentation incorporates the analytical advances proposed by Bordes (1953a, 1961a) who argued against the use of *fossiles directeurs* and in favour of an approach to classification through assemblage analysis. This method is described in Chapter 4. Through his

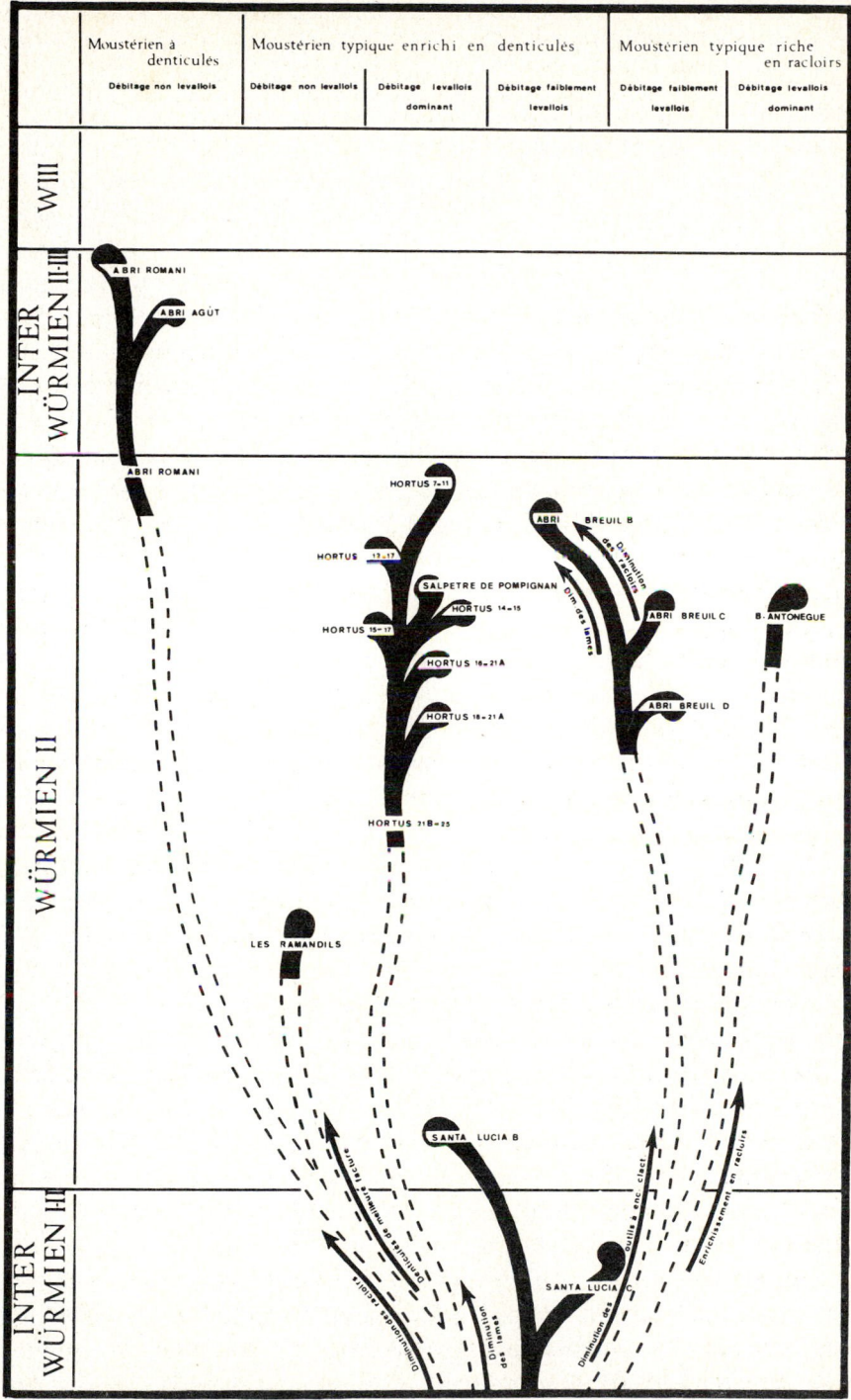

1.1 An example of an 'organic' model applied to the evolution of middle palaeolithic industries in southern France (H. de Lumley 1976c:1025, fig. 16).

analyses of many middle palaeolithic assemblages from the caves and rock shelters of southern France, Bordes isolated a minimum of five recurrent groupings (1981). This surprised him since he had expected his research to reveal a continuous spectrum of assemblage variation based on the proportional representation of 63 artifact types (Appendix 3). In his view, this confirmed earlier interpretations that stone tool assemblages were the durable visiting cards of palaeolithic groups. As a result Bordes explained away his findings as the product of five Neanderthal tribes who inhabited the Périgord region and alternated in their use of the desirable rock shelters that the region contained.

The basis for this interpretation is the premise that similarities in the form of material culture stem from a community of cultural tradition (Collins 1969). This judgement has always been regarded by the consensus view as a self-evident fact. According to this view, 'the objects *share* that feature because the people responsible *shared* the same idea' (Dunnell 1971:194 (my emphasis)).

This classic normative view of culture acts as an explanation of why cultural traditions are either similar or different. It is achieved by the almost imperceptible transition from what at one minute are nothing more than descriptive classes for patterns spotted in palaeolithic materials, and then at the next are spoken of as cultural classes; the fossil material remains of a once living people. Once this transition has been made it is easy to see why the organic model suits the purposes of the culture history paradigm in dealing with change through time.

The culture history paradigm is the way the palaeolithic record of Europe has been presented. It has concentrated upon stylistic variation in stone tools as seen in the shapes and forms they take. The nature of this variation suits an approach which is concerned with the correct placing of excavated assemblages within an array of chronological pigeon-holes. The results have been impressive in ordering data into chronological sequences and, to a lesser extent, into geographical units (Chapter 5).

The drawbacks are that much potential information has been ignored in concentration upon the retouched tools and type fossils. Chipping debris, animal bones, burnt rock and their spatial relationships within sites are some of the other categories of material and information that have to a large extent been regarded as ancillary to the main preoccupation of the paradigm. This over-tidy approach has over-simplified the complexities of the archaeological record and the potential it has to inform us about past behaviour that operated at many levels and scales. As a result, the theoretical content of the paradigm is quickly exhausted. It is salutary to read the interpretations and opinions of Lartet and Christy written over a century ago, based on their excavations in Aquitaine, and find recurrent echoes in the latest interpretations and opinions expressed by their direct intellectual descendants. Although standards of excavation, recovery and observation have improved out of all recognition, the conclusions and insights into past behaviour are all too familiar.

(b) culture as adaptation

This paradigm deals in explicit assumptions and statements of intent. The view of culture is entirely different to that put forward in the culture history paradigm. It is defined in Leslie White's (1959) phrase as man's extra-somatic means of adaptation and is a result of man's unique ability to symbol. Through this ability, events and objects are created and infused with meaning and this can be appreciated, decoded and understood. According to this definition culture is *participated* in rather than *shared* by human beings (Binford 1965). This participation is not however equivalent at all times and places, for reasons that we shall examine later, and from this springs variation in those material culture residues which form our data on the palaeolithic.

One way to understand this paradigm is to compare its application to a body of data with that of culture history. I have already briefly examined the notion that the five assemblage variants identified by Bordes in the mousterian of south-west France reflect five Neanderthal tribes. This account of the observed variation has been rejected by Binford and Binford (1966, 1969; Binford, 1973, 1983). Instead these authors claimed that assemblage variation is a measure of the different ways in which technology was organised to perform different tasks. These activities involved maintenance tasks, where food was consumed and distributed and raw materials converted into tools, and extractive tasks where food resources and raw materials were procured from the environment. The Binfords argued, using a settlement system model, that these tasks would take place at clearly differentiated localities; base and work camps respectively. Since stone tools were designed to perform these tasks, this should be reflected in different assemblage types. Their analysis involved assigning likely functions to each of Bordes' 63 artifact types; then by means of a factor analysis they measured the degree of dependency amongst all the tool types from some 17 lithic assemblages. This produced five clusters of associated artifact types which were regarded as functionally interdependent tool kits (table 1.2).

With hindsight, we can see that the analysis relied too much on educated guesses for dividing up the type list into functional categories and played down the problem of artifacts being thrown away at some other location than where they were used. This functional argument, in what has come to be known as the mousterian debate (see Mellars 1969, 1970; Collins 1969, 1970; J. Guichard 1976; Rolland 1981), drew forth some explicit criticisms from Bordes and de Sonneville-Bordes (1970; Bordes 1973). They raised two major objections. In the first place it seemed inconceivable to them that a covenant would have existed among mousterian people which laid down, as if by charter, that particular cave sites were reserved either for use at set seasons of the year or for carrying out a very specialised set of activities. This sort of formal agreement between the tribes was something they felt would be needed if patterning were to result in the form of the five assemblage variants as modelled by the Binfords. Only in

Table 1.2. *Summary of the Binfords' (1966) study of assemblage variability in the mousterian. The five factors represent five groups of statistically interdependent artifacts among mousterian assemblages and it is suggested that these differences can best be understood by considering the assemblages as tool kits which performed different tasks.*

Factor	Artifact types from Bordes list	Suggested activity	Type of activity	Analogy to Bordes variants
I	borers, scrapers, burins	manufacture of tools from non-flint materials	base camp, maintenance tasks	Typical mousterian
II	points and scrapers	hunting and butchery	work camp, extractive tasks	Ferrassie
III	flakes and knives	cutting and incising, food processing	base camp, maintenance tasks	MTA
IV	utilised flakes, denticulates	shredding and cutting of plant materials	work camp, extractive tasks	Denticulate
V	point, blade, scrapers	killing and butchering	work camp extractive tasks	Ferrassie

this way could they understand, for example, the repeated interdigitation of the five mousterian variants throughout the 55 stratigraphic units at the site of Combe Grenal (Bordes 1972). Their second objection pointed out that in neighbouring areas of France some of the variants which were common in the caves of the Dordogne were entirely lacking (H. de Lumley 1965). They asked what sort of activities were special to the Dordogne which required such a tool kit and yet were apparently unnecessary only a few kilometres away in an area of similar climate and conditions?

These criticisms were answered at length by Binford (1972, 1973, 1983). In many respects the heart of the matter, like so many of the changing perspectives on archaeological aims and practice in the 1960s (Binford and Binford (eds.) 1968), can be summed up by seeing the functional argument as a closely reasoned statement that *we do not know all the causes of variability in the archaeological record.* This simple reality was delivered as something of a plea against the consensus view, which maintained that nearly all variability *can* be accounted for by a view of culture which explains patterning in material culture as the product of shared ideas and cultural norms.

The functional argument put forward by the Binfords pointed out that it was premature to put up the shutters on this question. The culture historians expected to find that all variation was a measure of different people wanting to express that they were different groups of people. When pressed the proponents of such a view will often draw comparisons between assemblage patterning and supporters of rival teams at a football match (Newell pers.comm.). They see the functional argument, with its emphasis on culture as an adaptive strategy, as a challenge to what is to them a self-evident truth about social existence and which requires only the application of the right sort of investigative procedures to the palaeolithic record to become a prehistoric reality. While they can see assemblages of stone tools as different cultures or ethnic groups, they cannot see them as part of an integrated adaptive system. However, while evolution may favour the team with the best away record, this is won by means of a *strategy* designed to achieve that result rather than by a *belief* in the invincibility of the coloured shirt the team wears.

This debate, which engendered many important archaeological discussions on the interpretation of variability, should not be seen as a straight fight between ethnicity and function as an explanatory principle. Instead, it is a debate about *how the archaeological record is formed.* According to one view, assemblages are generated by a shared set of experiences and deposited as a record of that fact. The other maintains that in the course of successful adaptation the cultural system leaves behind a differentiated record of that strategy.

This latter paradigm uses a *multidimensional* model in order to investigate the significance of patterning and variation in palaeolithic materials (Binford 1972:131–5). Since resources are not uniformly distributed within the environments occupied by human groups, energy must be expended in collecting and gathering them. There is, moreover, no single strategy best suited for meeting all the different situations that result from variation in the structure and nature of resources within environments. This variation can be regarded as differing degrees of risk for the survival of human groups and has to be minimised by their adaptive strategies (see Chapter 2 for discussion). Problems arising from the spatial location of resources are dealt with by positioning personnel and planning ahead for future moves. Those risks which stem from the different times at which resources become available or abundant are minimised through strategies which use the potential of technology and the properties of storage. The blueprint for the strategy is contained in the schedule which specifies how the available resources are best exploited to achieve this goal of minimising risk. The tactics by which this is achieved utilise the mobility of human groups and their flexible organisation to partition them into units of different sizes, membership, duration and purpose (Jochim 1976).

This model of adaptation raises expectations concerning the formation of cultural residues in the landscape. We must expect that activities will be differentiated in time and space and that this is due to variation in the distribution and organisation of energy. In other words we should expect the palaeolithic record to vary as a result of past behaviour related to adaptive strategies. Moreover, we must expect that behaviour associated with these strategies is continuous across these landscapes (Foley 1981a). Therefore, we cannot sample at a single point and use the data recovered there to typify the entire adaptation. This leads us to identify the region as the unit of analysis for studying palaeolithic adaptations.

The formation of the palaeolithic record will, according to this model, reflect the dimensions of space and time and their variable impact on human adaptive strategies. From the synchronic viewpoint, we must expect the differential distribution of activity within the landscape. We therefore need measures of the tactical outcomes of mobility, site location, demographic arrangements, storage functions and the organisation of technology. With a diachronic perspective, where we are concerned with long term changes in adaptive strategies, we need measures of selection pressure operating on these same strategies as well as measures of relative increases in survival success. Some basic definitions for this approach are as follows:

> Adaptation – as defined in evolutionary biology is any structure, physiological process or behavioural pattern that makes an organism more fit to survive and reproduce (Wilson 1975:577). A strategy for survival and reproduction.
>
> Adaptedness – the status of being adapted and the ability of an organism to survive and reproduce in a given environment (Kirch 1980:103).
>
> Adaptability – the capacity to become adapted (Kirch 1980:103).
>
> Selection pressure – any feature of the environment, both physical and social, that results in natural selection (ie. food shortage, predator activity) and can cause individuals of different genetic types to survive to different average ages, to reproduce at different rates, or both (Wilson 1975:594).
>
> Natural selection – the differential contribution of offspring to the next generation by individuals of different genetic types but belonging to the same population (Wilson 1975:589).
>
> Behaviour – the dynamics of adaptation (Binford 1972:133).

It should by now be clear just how this multidimensional model differs from the organic model of the culture history paradigm. The latter is concerned with discovery, description and classification, the former with the explanation of change and variation via the examination of the behavioural content of the same material residues. In order to achieve this we need to look more closely at the nature of the palaeolithic record as a step in devising appropriate analytical frameworks and units of measurement.

Properties of the palaeolithic record

I have already referred to the palaeolithic as a record of observations. This record consists of items of spent energy, pieces of stone, bone and other populations of materials both artifactual and ecofactual. It also includes populations of features such as pits, post holes, hearths, boulders and rock shelters, and at a wider scale of analysis, it includes the events and processes of quaternary geology.

These materials are arranged in a three-dimensional matrix which can be described in terms of its spatial attributes. In sum, 'the archaeological record is a structure of relationships between the distribution and form of matter as caused by energy sources acting on matter in the past' (Binford 1981:26).

This structure results from the constraints that the properties and arrangement of energy impose upon human adaptations. Ultimately it refers back to the laws of thermodynamics (White 1959:33) and can most vividly be seen in the implications of trophic relationships, environmental productivity and community ecology for human populations (see Chapter 2). While the *structure* of relationships may be traced through this framework, the manner in which it is *organised* is through transfers and exchanges of energy in space. This produces variation, for example, in the zonation of different environments within the latitudes of the globe. This in turn is related to the amount of solar energy and varies according to the position of any one place on the earth's surface and before local factors such as relief or water further affect the transformation of the available energy into matter.

However, while energy provides a structure, and space an organisational framework, this does not allow us simply to pick up the stones and bones and listen to what they have to tell us about past human behaviour. In this sense, there is nothing obvious in the archaeological record. The material residues have to be decoded via a precise methodology if we are to understand their significance in terms of past behaviour. They are not the pages of a well-written instruction manual telling us what behaviour took place in the past. In fact the data consist only of examples for, and the results of, behaviour and not behaviour itself (Wobst 1978:303). That can be observed only in a living system.

The approach followed here assumes that material culture acts as part of an information system which directs behaviour. The messages that are carried serve as signposts to organise action in a great variety of social contexts. One way in which this has been investigated is by relating the information conveyed by material culture to three behavioural realms. These have been described by Osgood (1940:25–9; see also Binford 1962; Sackett 1982:69) in the following terms:

> *behavioural realm*
> *material*   – artifacts coping with the environment,
> *societal*   – dealing with social organisation and behaviour,
> *ideational* – addressing ideas, values and belief systems.

All artifacts cross cut these three realms, although most will appear to us to play a greater role in only a single realm. Take for example the crown a monarch wears. This can serve in all three realms as (1) a hat to keep the head warm; (2) an item of display which communicates social position and status; and (3) a symbol of the concept of monarchy. More recently Sackett (1982:70) has distinguished only two behavioural domains for artifacts. These are the *utilitarian* which operates in the material realm and includes tools, containers, weapons etc., and *non-utilitarian* which are items which we have reason to think functioned primarily as vehicles for expressing social relations and ideas. This would include ritual paraphernalia, artwork, figurines and costume.

However, all items have some information role to play in all three realms and the division is merely a convenience to highlight how material culture *does* provide us with access to a multiplicity of past behavioural contexts. The problem that faces archaeologists lies in decoding this information; to get at the symboling and its adaptive significance as preserved in the form, shape and relationships of material culture.

With ecofactual data, some behavioural codes may be easier to crack. This is because of the properties of biological data, where we know a great deal about the populations from which they are derived. For example, the skeletons of animals are biological givens. We can identify a bone of reindeer that is 15,000 years old with absolute certainty by comparing it with modern specimens. We cannot do this with a stone tool. Moreover we can infer the whole skeleton from this one bone, together with the distribution of meat and marrow across the skeleton. This represented a resource for man, as well as for other carnivores. Behaviour is required to utilise such resources and in that sense a dead animal is like a tin can, it has to be opened to be used. Man and carnivores deal with this problem in different ways. By observing the differential treatment of the skeleton, our biological constant, we can gain some insight into the operation in the past of behaviour by these different agencies. We can measure the form this treatment took by looking in the archaeological record at factors such as the presence and frequency of anatomical parts, the existence of cut marks on bones, the degree of fragmentation of long bones for marrow extraction; and at other factors such as the degree of carnivore gnawing and the survival of dense parts (Brain 1981). This variation then provides us with a potential insight into the set of decisions that were made with regard to unlocking the energy in that animal carcass, and into which agency did the unlocking. These will vary for a great many reasons depending upon the time of the year, group requirements, distance from camp, nutritional status of the animal and so on (Binford 1978a).

This example demonstrates how archaeologists can proceed to know something about the past and the way it was formed. All historical disciplines have to observe the principle of uniformitarianism (Hookyaas 1963) by which the present provides observational data on processes which let us unlock the information contained in the records of the past. Earlier archaeologists such as Evans (Daniel 1964:45) used this principle to demonstrate the high antiquity of man. They drew upon the association of flint implements with extinct elephants to show that human origins were indeed very remote; but they did not use the principle to say anything about human behaviour. When studying past behaviour we require equally strong warrants for making inferences (Wobst 1978) where the theories and models that we construct for the interpretation of the past are tested against actual behaviour (Binford 1981, 1983). In particular the strength of these inferences stems from the use of constants, such as biological materials, which serve as benchmarks and which we can use as units of measurement for investigating past behaviour.

These are properties and problems of methodology that apply to all aspects of the archaeological record. At all times we must be careful to employ rigorous standards of interpretation and procedure (Gardin 1980) if we are not to impose our own view upon the past, rather than proceed to the information that is contained in the structure and organisation of the archaeological record. There are however additional properties of the palaeolithic record which stem from the multidimensional model and which we need briefly to consider.

(a) mobility

All human societies throw things away and in so doing they create residues. While *Homo sapiens* is not the only species to display such behaviour (see below), the residues we create have distinctive attributes due to the durability, variety and quantity of the discarded materials. It is now common to model the paths by which materials were used in the living system (or systemic context) and then passed into the archaeological context (Schiffer 1972, 1976; Gould 1977). Materials are divided into consumables and durables (fig. 1.2) and are subject to differing degrees of recycling.

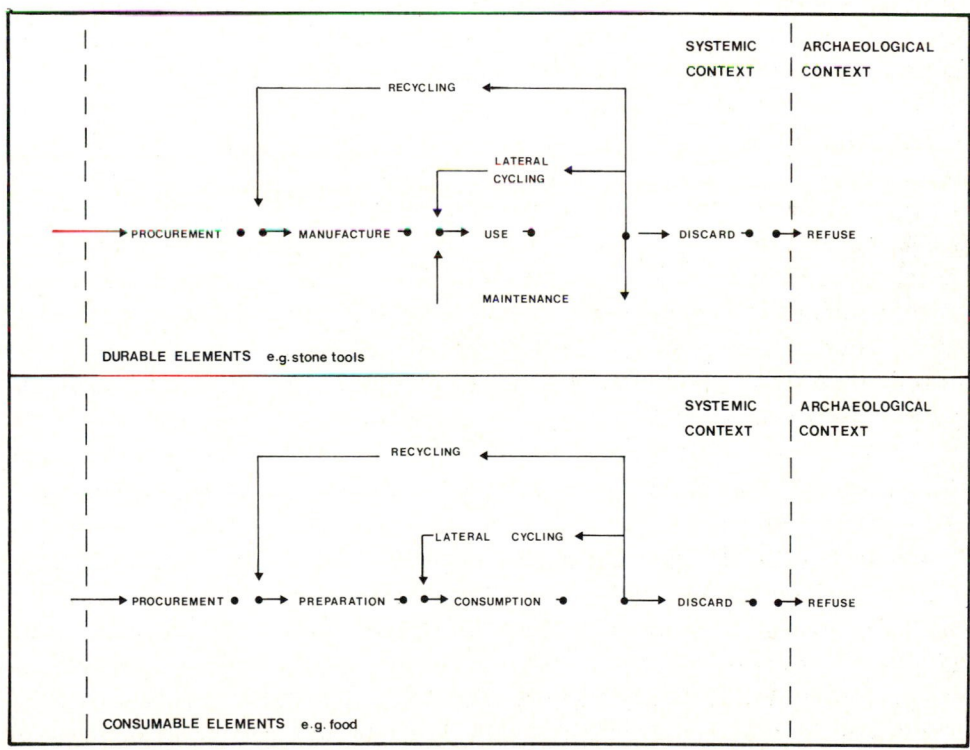

1.2 A model of processes leading to the formation of the archaeological record (Schiffer 1976).

The multidimensional model stresses the importance of individual and group mobility by hunter-gatherers. This may involve many residential moves during the course of a seasonal subsistence round. As individuals and groups move across the landscape foraging for food, so they leave behind material residues that reflect the continuous nature of this large scale, regional behaviour. This is, of course, in contrast to the sedentary pattern of exploitation that is encountered in later prehistory with arable-based agriculturalists. Foley has characterised the archaeological patterns produced by highly mobile groups as off-site archaeology (1981a,b), where the region is the unit of analysis. The choice of this analytical unit is determined by the nature of the adaptation under examination. In particular Foley suggests that we should view these strategies with a home range concept. This may be defined as an area that an animal learns thoroughly, patrols regularly (Wilson 1975:586) and which is shared with other members of an integrated social group (*ibid.*: 256). Off-site archaeology is a developing methodology designed to understand the behavioural information in the regional densities of artifact and ecofact populations. As such it can be contrasted with the more familiar site-based studies (Chapter 2). Its value lies in directing our attention away from an exclusive concern with the patches in the archaeological landscape and towards the scatters of materials that lie between (Isaac 1981a). We shall see in the next chapter that the degree to which a regional pattern of archaeological materials is either clumped or scattered is an important indicator of group adaptation to ecological conditions.

(b) visibility

Hunter-gatherers are generally regarded as depositing ephemeral traces. Either materials do not survive (Yellen 1977a) or technology and food residues consist of such a small number of items that there is hardly anything to recover even after many millennia of occupation (Jones 1977; Deetz 1968).

The Australian Pintupi, studied by Hayden (1979a), use stone tools to make wooden artifacts. The most visible artifact, in terms of size, would be a simply flaked chopping tool which is generally discarded beneath the tree from which the wood was procured. Even at a high density of discard Hayden found that there was only one such implement per $2500 \, m^2$ at such procurement sites. Data on densities of materials deposited at camp sites are also low (table 1.3). Moreover among the Pintupi most hunting kills are of single animals, and these locations are scattered over the landscape. As a result there is little chance for the accumulation, through the repeated use of one hunting location, of artifact patches consisting of scrapers, knives and flakes. Indeed the only places where such accumulations of lithic materials occur are either ritual locations, where wooden masks are made, or look-out posts where hunters manufacture and cache tools while at the same time monitoring the environment for game (see also Gould *et al.* 1971:152–3). These examples show how important context is

Table 1.3. *Density of cultural materials on two Australian Aboriginal camp sites (Hayden 1979a:166) expressed as debris/person/week.*

area m^2	small game bone fragments	chipped stone total	number used as tools
Ngarulurutja			
79–113	54–108	28–57	5–10
Walukaritji			
113	144	7	3

for understanding why there are such variations in stone tool density at different points in the regional landscape. They also point to the sort of problems involved in the survey and recovery of hunter-gatherer traces at a regional scale (Judge 1973). Foley (1981a: 181) has estimated that some four artifacts per annum were deposited in each km^2 of his survey area of 600 km^2 in the Amboseli basin, East Africa. This yields a potential figure of 20,000 artifacts per km^2 which have accumulated over 5000 years of exploitation of this regional environment.

(c) other records

The palaeolithic record is also a palimpsest of many related records. These include the palaeontological record where carnivores, birds of prey and rodents have either added to archaeological materials, or accumulated their own bone deposits. Natural mortalities, such as winter hibernation among bears, and dead fall traps for large mammals have also resulted in significant amounts of materials. These natural accumulations are often associated with archaeological deposits either in caves, river terraces or aeolian sites.

These palaeobiological records have recently received a great deal of attention from palaeontologists who are now concerned with increasing the amount of behavioural information about past environments (Brain 1981; Behrensmeyer and Hill (eds.) 1980). In particular, this has involved a revision of the methodological procedures by which inferences are made from the observation of fossil bones in their depositional context to past living systems. The study of taphonomy, which refers to the laws of burial (Efremov 1940; Gifford 1981), reflects this growing interest. We have already seen a comparable concern amongst archaeologists to improve their methodologies for investigating past behaviour, in what has been referred to as middle range theory (Binford 1977a), transformational procedures (Schiffer 1972) and constructs (Gardin 1980).

The palaeoecologists are also rediscovering the principle of uniformitarianism as a key to unlocking the dynamic study of past environments and the biotic communities that existed within them. These sister disciplines to archaeology have accepted that an understanding of pre- and post-depositional processes acting on faunal assemblages provides the entering wedge into the complexities of past animal ecology. One way this has been achieved is via actualistic studies where present processes are used to sort out the post mortem histories of large mammals (Behrensmeyer and Hill (eds.) 1980). These studies no longer regard these processes as in some way distorting the data or placing bias upon it. Instead the action of such factors as preservation, stream sorting, sub-soil movement and accumulation are all ways by which information about past environments and their dynamic processes, which of course are no longer directly observable, can be investigated (Gifford 1981).

(d) signatures

The importance of these other records, biological and mechanical, for an understanding of the palaeolithic is that they are fellow travellers with the archaeological record. These records, as we shall see in Chapters 6–8, are a source of comparison and measurement for human adaptations. The reason is simple. Many of the elements involved in these records can be observed today and thus form a set of guidelines which help us to investigate past human behaviour which has, of course, no contemporary analogues. It should not, however, be imagined that these guidelines are easily observed. For example, there is no direct analogue for the diverse animal communities (Chapter 3) that inhabited the mid-latitude tundras and interglacial forests of pleistocene Europe. The contemporary observations are at present piecemeal and refer to single elements in this complex biome such as hyenas or reindeer, the effects of frozen ground phenomenon, or the conditions under which loess is deposited. However, as with the case of the reindeer skeleton (see above, p. 18), we can employ some contemporary observations as constants. These would include for example the structure of carnivore jaws and the means by which they tear carcasses and crack bones. In the same way we can employ the distribution of periglacial features to measure the relative intensity of glacial conditions within the continent.

These uses of uniformitarian principles act as limited first steps in discovering which agents were responsible for creating which parts of the archaeological and related records, as well as providing a means of measuring the selection pressures of the environment on adaptive strategies (Chapters 6–8). As taphonomic studies, via these biological constants, increasingly 'defrost' the static character of the past to reveal the dynamic system that produced it, we can expect more sophisticated measures for approaching the study of man. One way to conceive of these measures is as *signatures* (Gould 1980:113). The term 'signature' describes the link between behaviour and distinctive patterns of residue formation. Thus we should be able to speak of different archaeological signatures characterising different adaptive strategies. When we consider a single broad strategy, e.g. hunters and gatherers, we must also acknowledge the importance of ecology in producing predictable variations in behaviour that will be translated into a regional archaeological signature. The advantage of such a concept is that it gets us away from the rigid descriptive categories and classes which have been a traditional feature of archaeological systematics. For example, palaeolithic economies have often been described by the most abundant species found with stone tool assemblages. We speak of reindeer, mammoth, cave bear or red deer hunters (Gamble 1984a) and these descriptive labels are used to characterise widespread palaeolithic adaptations. A signature approach depends less upon such obvious elements to build classifications and instead recognises a wide array of residues and their spatial patterning as the products of variable adaptive behaviour.

One aspect of this approach is to look at particular signatures associated with ecological constraints (Chapter 2). An outcome of this is to view the formation of an archaeological assemblage along two dimensions, integrity and resolution, each of which is reflected in the grain of the assemblage (Binford 1981; Deetz 1968).

The agents which accumulate residues can be varied and include humans, carnivores and other biological and mechanical agencies. These can be built into a model to assess the formation of an archaeological assemblage.

RESOLUTION
(the homogeneity of events and behaviour)

	Low	High	
INTEGRITY (the variety of agents involved in the formation of an assemblage)	(A) Multiple agents responsible for material accumulating at a particular location. Each agent performing a wide range of activities. Multiple re-use of the location where accumulation takes place.	(B) Multiple agents responsible for material accumulating. Each agent performing a single activity. A single episode involving the deposition of material by each agent.	L o w
	(C) Single agent responsible for the deposition of material. Performing a wide range of activities. Multiple re-use of the location where residue accumulation occurs.	(D) Single agent responsible for material accumulating. Single activity performed. No re-use of that location.	H i g h

This matrix considers post-depositional factors, preservation, transportation and sorting, only in so far as they are responsible for materials being brought together. In behavioural terms it is possible to describe such assemblages in terms of their *grain* as follows (Binford 1980, 1981).

Assemblage grain
Coarse grained assemblage – (A, B, C above) where at any one location, the correspondence between an event and the archaeological record it generated is poor. An example of this would be the discard of a broken projectile point at a home base where it was being repaired and not at the kill site where it was used to hunt an animal.

> Fine grained assemblage – (D) where the materials deposited reflect more precisely the activities that were carried out at those locations and in relation to the immediate environment.

This model provides a number of expectations concerning the way by which we can go about making inferences from archaeological assemblages to the behaviour which produced them. Many archaeologists speak of the value of recovering those rare and precious moments (Roe 1981:197) when both resolution and integrity are high. These Pompeii-like moments are all too rare in the palaeolithic (Villa 1982), and most of the time we are dealing with a low resolution between the discarded artifacts and the behaviour which went on at that location, as well as low integrity where many other agents and mechanical processes have added their signatures to the record. However we should not be dismayed by this state of affairs and the coarse-grained signature that is displayed. After all, we cannot change the nature of the archaeological record, but we can investigate it. Rather than give up in the face of such obvious biases of past cultural and post-depositional distortions we should instead recognise them as the consequence of ecological and environmental conditions. (This theme will be expanded in the next chapter.) It is worth noting here that this mode of analysis, via the recognition of signatures, has considerable application within global palaeolithic studies, since their utility as flexible descriptive terms means that they are not restricted to the specific characteristics and contents of local environments. (How, for example, could we compare kangaroo and reindeer economies?) This is mainly due to the fact that these signatures are providing summaries of adaptive behaviour at a regional scale of investigation and therefore within a spatial framework. The complex spectra of variation that must be expected within regions, and which stem from using a multidimensional model of adaptive strategies, require a correspondingly flexible mode of description. Some examples of how this might be manifest in the data from palaeolithic Europe are provided in Chapters 6–8.

Statement of the problem

Data does not speak for itself. I have been in rooms with data and listened very carefully. The data never said a word. (Wolpoff 1975:15)

Our understanding of the palaeolithic record of Europe is based upon the endeavours and achievements of the culture history paradigm. From this base has grown a view of the palaeolithic past that treats descriptive classes as cultural classes and which attaches great importance to regional sequences and evidence for progressive development.

However, by following this approach, we have consistently undervalued the complexity and potential information content in the record. We have examined only some of its most superficial patterns, such as recurrent assemblage groupings and the patterning of stylistic elements through time. These have been spoken of as the work of distinct peoples. On many occasions this has been regarded as adequate and sufficient interpretation of the material. Beyond this, it is often said, lie speculation, guesswork and questions which are not worth asking.

The alternative paradigm discussed above suggests that the restrictions to our understanding of the past are largely of our own making. We should not, according to this view, give up asking questions because we have not yet developed ways of answering them. Instead, the failure to answer these same questions should be taken as a challenge to refine methodologies so as to unlock the information potential that is contained in the archaeological record. The data will never speak to us. Wolpoff is quite right about that. Neither do they speak to the practitioners of the culture history paradigm. They have translated such observations into a now familiar language of peoples and cultures, progress and change. Neither do the data speak to those, myself included, who prefer to view culture as an adaptive system and material residues as the means by which the complexities of past living systems can be investigated.

The central problem that faces this approach is one of methodology. How do we go from observations of the static structure of the archaeological record to an understanding of the dynamic structure, the past cultural system, which produced the material residues that we study? This progress from statics to dynamics (Binford 1981, 1983) involves assigning meaning to the dead facts of the archaeological record. In this case we want to know what they mean in terms of the behaviour which caused them to vary and form the distinctive patterns which we are now so adept at spotting.

It might be argued that this problem could be solved by re-working current terminology and analytical concepts. For example, some approaches have claimed that we should investigate the archaeological correlates of particular behavioural patterns (Schiffer 1976; Renfrew 1973; Hayden and Cannon 1982). An instance of this is provided in table 1.4 where a familiar system of archaeological nomenclature (column a) has been transposed into an apparently dynamic system with behavioural significance (column b). Of course nothing of the sort has in fact happened. The translation of *industry* into *tool kit* suggests that we

Table 1.4. *An artifact based approach to entitation in which descriptive classes are apparently transformed into behavioural classes (after Clarke 1978).*

(a) *Correlate*	(b) *Regularity*
(an attribute)	(an action)
artifact	a cluster of actions
assemblage	repeated cluster of actions
industry	tool kit
tradition	social groups
culture/civilisation/technocomplex	geographically and temporally larger social groups

know what constitutes a palaeolithic tool kit, whereas in fact we do not (Whallon 1978). While the translation is plausible, it is actually no different in kind from the substitution of cultural classes for descriptive classes, which I have already criticised. The use of correlates in order to identify patterns of lithic procurement, or the presence of a chiefdom or corporate group in the archaeological record involves us in a procedure of working towards definitions. We are in danger of being able to investigate the archaeological record only according to the descriptive labels which we can borrow, with apparent certainty, from ethnography.

In that direction lies a possible tyranny of the ethnographic record (Wobst 1978) in closing down our options for understanding the past by focusing only on those examples which happen to be on current display in the ethnographic shop window. Where for example would this approach leave us in the investigation of the society associated with *Homo erectus* and even earlier hominids? We certainly cannot assume that their patterns of social organisation were those which can be found among contemporary hunting and gathering groups. The use of correlates can suggest possible patterns of mobility, foraging behaviour and group size (Isaac 1978) but these remain descriptions of the 'phenotype' and not statements about the all important 'genotype' of social relations which was co-ordinating these factors.

The upshot of this discussion is that we need conceptual frameworks to supply meaning to our observations, and units of measurement with which to probe the archaeological record. In this way we can put into operation a research strategy that is designed to tackle the problems of variation in palaeolithic materials.

The approach followed here will examine the structural and organisational properties of the palaeolithic record. Energy and space will form the two principal dimensions for the observation of variation in palaeolithic materials and act as a means by which interpretation of the patterns thus revealed can proceed. The region provides the main spatial scale for the investigation of past adaptive systems and forms a unit of measurement and comparison. Finally the archaeological materials will be used to measure aspects of behaviour at a variety of scales (see table 2.7).

The regional approach advocated here uses this spatial concept as the primary analytical device to trace the link between the inert facts of the palaeolithic record and the behavioural systems that generated them. It is a framework for research and investigation of both synchronic and diachronic change in pleistocene Europe but it is not a product of the regional traditions of research. It is presented here as an alternative to this traditional approach.

While no conceptual framework can totally escape the problem of partiality, and so present the data in objective fashion, it is incumbent upon an alternative proposal that the information return from a body of data is greater than that supplied by the original method of looking at the past. This can be judged as the book proceeds. In the first instance it is however necessary to investigate further both the basis for selecting a regional framework, with a variety of spatial scales, to study palaeolithic systems, and the claim that this provides a link between the products and an understanding of the behaviour which produced them.

CHAPTER 2

HUNTER-GATHERER REGIONAL SYSTEMS

Having equipped the hunter with bourgeois impulses and palaeolithic tools, we judge his situation hopeless in advance.
Marshall Sahlins, Notes on the Original Affluent Society (1968:86)

Introduction

The archaeological record contains evidence for the study of long term processes, including both adaptation and change. The problem is, how can we gain access to this information?

We have already discussed some of the properties of the palaeolithic record that are a consequence of small-size, mobile societies. It is not therefore surprising that contemporary hunter and gatherer societies have been used to furnish archaeologists with appropriate analogues for the investigation of palaeolithic systems. These are the living systems which we believe are most relevant to understanding the patterning in palaeolithic materials. But once the wheels of archaeological investigation have been set in motion, with this suitable prod from the contemporary world, we have to be careful that our headlong flight back to the statics of the archaeological record does not come full circle. With increasing frequency it is possible to spot, in current archaeological studies, glimpses of the Nunamiut, !Kung and other groups faintly camouflaged in palaeolithic costume. If we want to improve on the previous use of ethnographic observation (e.g. Sollas 1911) then it is important to understand why we turn to these contemporary societies as a point of departure for understanding the palaeolithic.

The selection of hunter-gatherer societies is yet another instance of an assumption being made about the past. A very reasonable assumption, perhaps, but nevertheless an assumption. At an earlier time we might have justified such a choice by pointing out that contemporary hunters were materially the most primitive groups that could be observed. Since this appeared to be the case for palaeolithic remains when contrasted with those from later prehistory, it therefore seemed logical to link these statics with the dynamics of a living set of 'palaeolithic' examples. Moreover, palaeolithic flint assemblages were associated with the bones of red deer, cave bear, hyena, horse, mammoth and many other species all of which we classify as wild animals and which, therefore, in a European view of the world, were obtained by hunting. The material remains of later prehistory were predominantly found with the bones of animals that we call domestic. Many other traits could be listed: the use of caves rather than villages and houses, the absence of writing, the rudimentary traces of ritual and religious behaviour and the variable size and shape of fossil skulls and the brains they contained, which were all taken to indicate even simpler levels of organisation and ability.

Modern research into several of these aspects has changed many of the details in this picture but the assumption still remains that palaeolithic man was a hunter-gatherer and that the remains from this period should be viewed accordingly. It is not that the assumption may be wrong which matters, but, rather more importantly, the means by which we justify its statement. The concept of primitiveness is a poor warrant for judging that palaeolithic remains are the residues left behind by ancient hunter-gatherers whose modern representatives still exist in out-of-the-way parts of the world. The assumption is not justified because we can still find groups who hunt reindeer, possess simple technologies and paint rock-shelters or because historical and ethnographic accounts provide us with a set of terms and concepts that might be translated back into palaeolithic data.

This having been said, my justification for utilising this same assumption rests on the following two considerations.

(1) The most salient characteristic of hunter-gatherer society is that the pattern of social relations, within and between groups, is based upon the consumption of the resources of the environment rather than upon the economic production of resources. This pattern of exploitation sets these social formations apart from those of agriculturalists. In the latter societies, the varied and complex positions of power, status and rank, as well as the institutions of political organisation, stem from the relationship of people to the land and the patterns of differential access to the products that come from the land. This is not meant to imply that positions of power and prestige are lacking in hunter-gatherer society. It is rather that these positions, and all the other social institutions, are reproduced at the same time as the process of exploiting the environment proceeds. Animals are hunted, plants are gathered and the immediate surplus distributed to close kin and members present in the camp. These gifts are made in full expectation of their return at a later date. Prestige and status may go to the habitually successful hunter but this social position dies with him – that is, his children do not inherit his status.

By contrast the pattern of social relations in agricultural formations uses the product of the land to support and reproduce institutions and roles which are defined by the fact of ownership, inheritance and the transmission of property between generations. Moreover these societies are based on the premise that the products of labour are not equally available to all members of society.

The mode of production is critical in determining the character of the social formation which develops from it (Meillassoux 1972, 1973). The pattern of ecological exploitation among hunter-gatherers carries implications of small group size and mobility over the land in the process of consuming resources. Moreover variations in the numerical composition of groups and the degree of mobility will to a large extent be dependent upon the structure of the environment. As the environment reproduces itself on a seasonal, annual and longer term cycle so too does the hunter-gatherer society that is dependent upon its products.

At this level of analysis there is a clear link between the characteristics of the social formation, the implications this has for aspects of exploitation and the consequences for the formation of the archaeological record. The environment can be described in this first instance as *determinant* in that it sets out what is available for exploitation and how, within broad limits, this will have to be achieved through the manipulation of group size, number of moves, and length and location of residence in any one place. Beyond this lies another level. While the ecological relations may be determinant, the social relations must be viewed as ultimately *dominant* (Ingold 1980, 1981) in specifying how the environment is to be exploited. In other words identical environments might be exploited by either hunter-gatherer or agricultural formations. The environment does not, in most cases, determine which. It is the social system, the modes and relations of production, which lay down the pattern of exploitation, the systems of appropriation and the level of demand for surplus production which are required in the process of physical and social reproduction. These contrasted relations are set out in figure 2.1.

This first consideration is, of course, a model of the workings of a social formation. Models simplify reality, there is no alternative. Their advantage is that they provide a foot in the door once we have realised that the data are not going to speak. They allow us to investigate complex systems.

(2) The second consideration is based on the knowledge that we can understand the past only through the present (Spaulding 1968:37), since there is no way directly to observe palaeolithic behaviour. The very general principles of hunter-gatherer social formations discussed above take the form of many different ethnographic lifestyles. However, these recent hunters and gatherers will not provide palaeolithic analogues in the form of clones whereby situations of identical status are reproduced. The past is not present in the contemporary world and waiting to be discovered if we chance to pick up the appropriate ethnographic stone and look underneath. The present provides the route rather than the destination for approaching a study of the past. At best the recent examples of hunters and gatherers are a means to test and strengthen our procedures of analysis from statics to dynamics. Success in these procedures must not be measured by the goodness of fit between an ethnographic example and a palaeolithic pattern. Success stems from exploring and understanding the relationship between behaviour (dynamics) and its material residues (statics).

Recent hunters and gatherers provide us with an opportunity to examine this

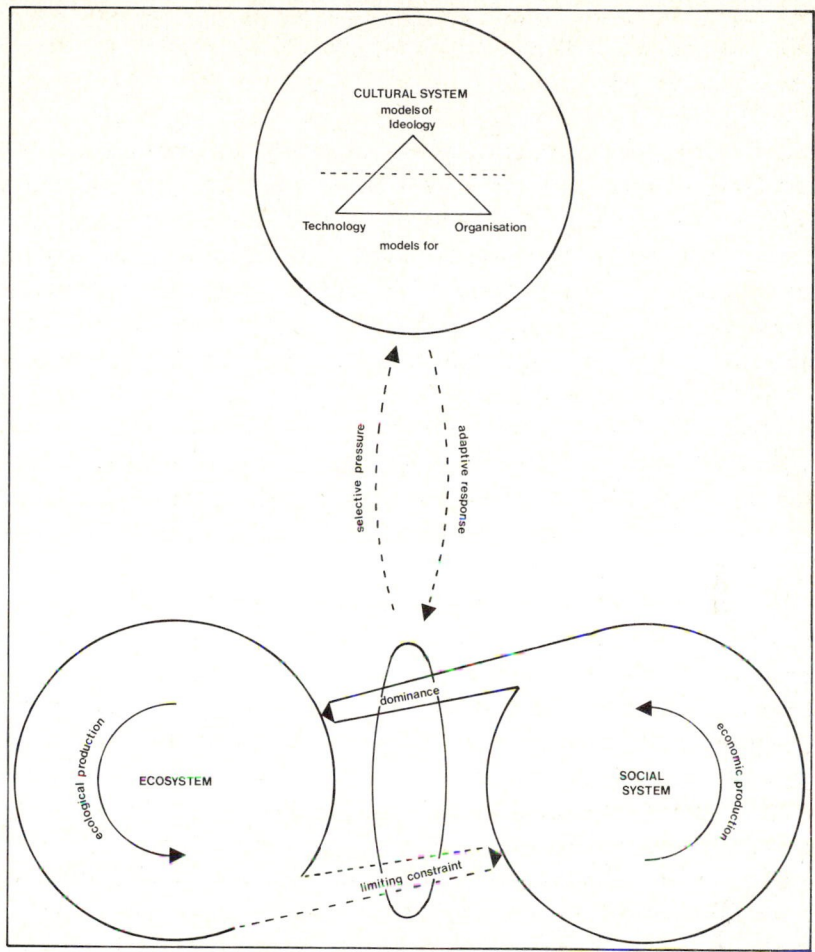

2.1 The relationship between ecological and social systems (Ingold 1981).

relationship, allowing us to think about the causes of variation and how these might be investigated. The immediate lesson we learn is that hunter-gatherer adaptations are highly varied. Understanding the causes of this variation would form a powerful base for prediction and hence the investigation of past situations which must have been every bit as varied.

From these two considerations it is apparent that our unit of analysis must be at a regional scale since this not only encompasses the determinant features of the environment, to which groups must adapt, but also the continual process of social reproduction which specifies that the habitat shall be exploited according to the principles of a hunter-gatherer formation in order to sustain and reproduce social existence.

Man the Hunter: models and approaches

(a) models of hunter-gatherer organisation

Unfortunately most ethnographers and anthropologists have not approached the study of hunters and gatherers from a regional perspective. Instead they have employed the concept of society as a unit of comparative analysis and this is particularly unhelpful in archaeological investigations. Furthermore as Birdsell pointed out some years ago (1958:190), the dominant approach has been to particularise the culture of each people: to resist looking for any underlying uniformities and to refuse steadfastly to pose any questions which might lead to the discovery of general patterns.

The possibilities and advantages of a general comparative approach were finally well demonstrated at the important *Man the Hunter* symposium (Lee and DeVore (eds.), 1968a) and subsequently in a number of volumes dealing with hunter-gatherers from various areas of the world (Damas (ed.), 1969a; Bicchieri (ed.), 1972; Lee and DeVore (eds.), 1976; Smiley *et al.* (eds.), 1980; Leacock and Lee (eds.), 1982). The emphasis on ecology and adaptive strategies has provided a wealth of observation that is relevant to archaeological approaches employing regional concepts as a means of investigating the past.

All of these approaches maintain that ecology forms a major principle in the organisation of hunter-gatherer adaptations. This was first demonstrated in a remarkably perceptive essay by Mauss (1906) that dealt with variation in seasonal behaviour among the Eskimo. Mauss linked the material sub-stratum of Eskimo society with the ecological rhythms of their habitat, and from this total approach he drew conclusions regarding the changing patterns of group composition, settlement form, subsistence activities and the public and private times of the year for Eskimo social life. This large/small group phase, during which a population aggregates and then disperses, is one of the underlying uniformities of all hunter-gatherer systems and is expressed in the principle of fission and fusion.

A second uniformity relates to levels of group organisation. Three levels are generally recognised among all hunters and gatherers and include the family, the local group and the regional population. The local group forms the basic productive unit, as we shall see below. There has however been considerable debate over the characteristics of these local groups and the wider regional populations of which they form a part. Lee (1976) draws up the lists between the patrilocal band model derived from Radcliffe-Brown (1930) and Steward (1936), and championed by Service (1962, 1966), and a bilateral model developed in opposition to these earlier formulations (Hiatt 1962; Leacock 1969). Much of the debate rests on the relationship of the local group to a geographical area, and to other groups in that area.

The patrilocal band model involves marriage outside the group (exogamy), with women moving to another group after marriage: hence the description of patrilocality. Most importantly, the group defends the area it exploits for resources. Set against this is the bilateral model favoured by Lee (1976; Lee and DeVore 1968b:9) where unrestricted access to resources is stressed and where territories, if they exist, form overlapping sets. A distinction is drawn between spatial and social boundaries. The spatial boundaries of groups may not overlap but this does not mean that the movement of personnel will also be restricted. Lee argues that restricted access is rarely found in hunter-gatherer societies where instead it is adaptive to maintain good relations with neighbours and more spatially distant people since this helps to spread some of the risks in the environment. For Lee this principle of open access is a means by which 'the environmental problem has a social solution' (*ibid.*: 95).

Examples can be found from ethnographies to support both models. The nomadic style model developed by Lee and DeVore (1968b:11–12) has enjoyed particular favour in archaeology and the assumptions employed can be seen for example in Isaac's (1978) study of early hominid evolution. Williams (1974) on the other hand has critically examined the postulates of the patrilocal model of band society in the context of the Birhor hunters and gatherers of north-eastern India. He finds that the postulates are justified and proceeds to draw a number of archaeological expectations from the existence of territoriality and the relative closure of social boundaries.

Neither model can serve as a general description for all, or even nearly all, hunter-gatherer adaptations. A confusion has arisen in the debate over the interpretation of variation and the validity of the models used to describe that variation. This was seized upon by Stanner (1965) who is often regarded as a supporter of the patrilocal band model. The basis of his model can be summarised under two main headings:

Basics
(a) some form of exogamous, patrilineal descent group was ubiquitous.
(b) this group had an intrinsic connection, not just an association, with a territory.
(c) there was a marked tendency to virilocality and patrilocality but this was not an iron rule.
(d) the group thus formed was basic to both territorial and social organisation, however concealed by phratries, moities, sections, etc.

Variable estate/range relations
(e) these expressed long term equilibrium under which territorial local groups could survive by nomadic ecology while maintaining a sufficient interaction between band members.
(f) each local group made interaction with a neighbouring set a positive aim.
(g) the fission/fusion principle of group membership and composition.
(h) larger population units (communities) were special cases of unusually favourable conditions which permitted aggregation to take place.

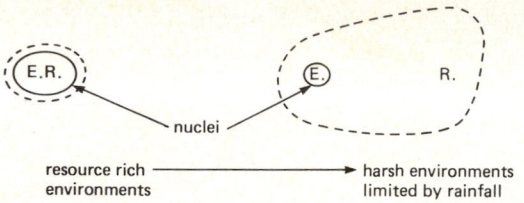

Possible estate (E) and range (R) spatial relations under variable ecological conditions.

It was developed in the specific context of understanding variation in organisation among groups from Australia, the continent of hunters and gatherers, but can be applied more widely. Stanner employed the twin concepts of *estate* and *range* which taken together constituted a *domain* and provided a means of examining variation in the forms of basic group organisation. The estate was a nucleus, a religious core of the territorial group (Strehlow 1970). The range was vital to life and had a subsistence/economic aspect. The territorial estate group roamed over this range as did other estate groups. The degree of variation in overlap between these two spatial/social units depended upon ecological and environmental factors (Stanner 1965:2).

Stanner was therefore proposing a truly ecological approach that expected variation in Australian local organisation to occur along an environmental gradient. In his opinion Australia provided a natural laboratory for such studies which anthropologists had completely ignored. A transect through the natural vegetation zones of the continent would provide a measure of productivity against which estate and range would act as measures of the systematic transformation between social and ecological organisation (*ibid.*: 23–5). To put it another way, variation was considered as a topological surface where the ecological structure of the varied environments throughout Australia pulled and stretched the basic form of the local group model until it was barely recognisable as stemming from the same underlying principles. This approach has found support in the work of Berndt (1976) contrasting territoriality in the Western Desert and Arnhem Land and in discussions by Birdsell (1968) and Peterson (1976a) on the variable patterning of spatial areas associated with groups of standard demographic size.

(b) models at a world scale

Stanner's approach may not have been pursued, as he hoped, in the context of social and spatial organisation, but at a world scale several aspects of hunter-gatherer adaptations have been examined in order to trace this systematic transformation between aspects of ecological structure and behavioural outcomes. These are very relevant to our analysis of hunter-gatherer regional systems.

Table 2.1. *Primary subsistence for hunters and gatherers as measured against latitude.*

The figures refer to the major contribution to the diet by either hunting, gathering or fishing

Degrees from the Equator	Gathering	Hunting	Fishing	Total
60°+	—	6	2	8
50°–59°	—	1	9	10
40°–49°	4	3	5	12
30°–39°	9	—	—	9
20°–29°	7	—	1	8
10°–19°	5	—	1	6
0°–9°	4	1	—	5
	29	11	18	58

Source: Lee 1968: table 6

The basemap for such an approach is provided by the differential distribution of energy throughout the world's ecosystems (Lieth and Whittaker 1975:fig. 2.1). This shows that as a general rule productivity in terrestrial ecosystems decreases away from the equator. The reverse holds true for the productivity of the oceans. The changes in productivity with latitude are most strongly reflected in the composition of hunter-gatherer diets. Lee (1968; Hayden 1981a) has provided a latitudinal transect of hunter-gatherers where their relative dependence upon hunting, fishing or gathering is compared. The results (table 2.1) show quite conclusively, in a sample of 58 societies, that the subsistence base changes with increasing latitude. Lee interpreted the data as indicating a much greater role for gathering in the subsistence economy of these groups than had traditionally been allowed. Hunting formed some 35% of the diet at all latitudes, except those in the high arctic where the proportion is much higher. The greatest variation in the proportional contribution to the diet was between fishing and gathering.

This may not seem very surprising. As productivity in vegetation decreases towards the poles there are fewer plant species available for human consumption. As a result human strategies shift to hunting animals since these have converted the available grasses and plants into energy. By moving to a higher trophic level, man can then inhabit those environments. The fishing strategies of the world (Schalk 1977) display a similar latitudinal distribution where increased importance to man of these marine resources is linked to the increased productivity of the oceans.

On closer examination the relationship between latitude, productivity and subsistence strategy is not so clear cut. Latitude by itself is only a general guide to variation in subsistence. Moreover the oceans are not as productive as the land (Osborn 1977) and the difficulties involved in exploiting marine resources make them a much less attractive set of alternative resources than the productivity map might suggest.

Foley (1982) has shown that the sample Lee used from Africa consisted of foraging groups that inhabit either very dry or very wet environments. In the former environment the strategy of many plants towards the severe and prolonged droughts is to store water and food below the ground. This results in a very productive root crop which is an important resource for Kalahari San groups such as the !Kung (see Lee 1979: plate 6.3). The latter habitats are represented by tropical rain forests where there is a staggering diversity and abundance of fruits, berries and edible vegetable matter. By contrast the animals found in such environments are generally small in size, and do not come together in large herds. It is hardly surprising that hunting, while practised (Turnbull 1966), is not a subsistence mainstay but rather a service supplied to neighbouring agricultural villages.

The intermediate African environments are those where rainfall patterns produce rich grasslands with few plant species that man can eat. These lie between the 500 mm and 1500 mm range of annual precipitation (Foley 1982:399) and are characterised by high figures for large mammal biomass (Redmann 1982:table 4). In other words these large animals, which do form great herds, are prime resources for hunting. They do not however show up in Lee's table since these same environments are also prime grazing lands for cattle pastoralists such as the Dinka, Nuer, Maasai and Samburu who have long since pushed the hunters and gatherers out of these areas.

This example points to the complex patterns of co-variation between ecological factors (table 2.2) and the suitability of resources for hunter-gatherer subsistence strategies. The variation in resource attributes such as body size and herd aggregation are important aspects in determining strategic choices (see below, p. 42).

A different measure has been used by Binford (1980) to monitor variation in both storage strategy and settlement systems. Rather than making a link

Table 2.2. *Co-variation between plant community structure, large mammal biomass and rainfall in equatorial regions, and the predicted hunter/gatherer/pastoralist adaptations (Foley 1982).*

	Mean annual rainfall in mm		
	Below 500	*500–1500*	*Above 1500*
Large mammal biomass	low	large	small
Body size of prey	large	large	small
Aggregation potential of prey	occasional large herds	large	very low
Plant food availability for human groups	high	very low	very high
Predicted strategy	gatherers	hunters/cattle pastoralists	gatherers

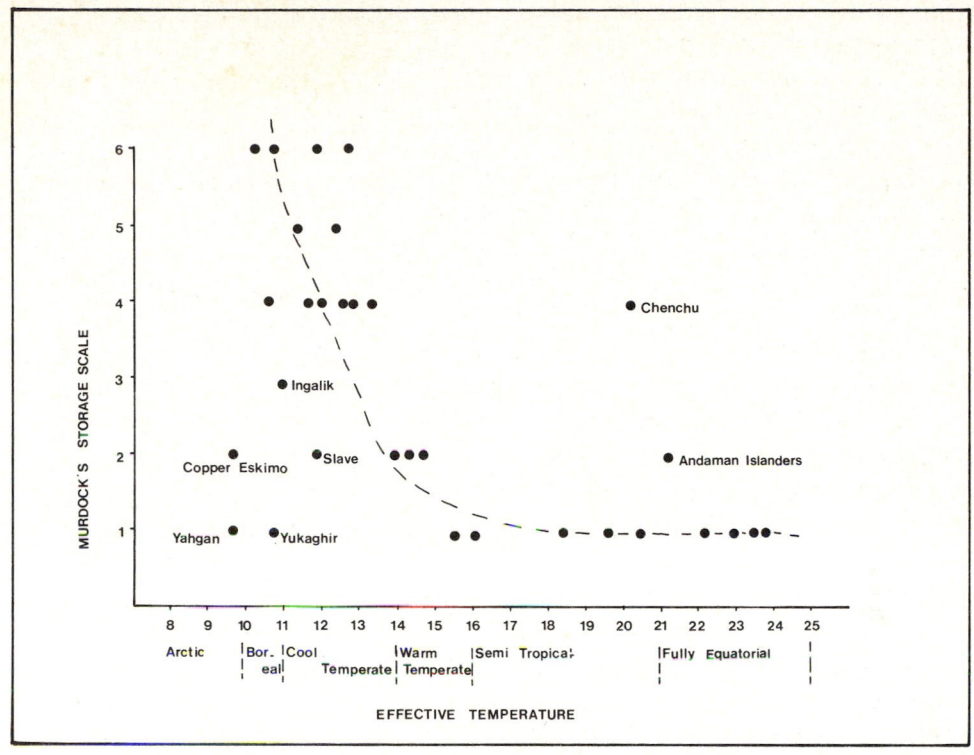

2.2 The role of storage, using Murdock's scale, in food rich and food poor environments as measured by effective temperature (Binford 1980).

between latitude and terrestrial productivity, a measure of *effective temperature* (Bailey 1960) is used to facilitate comparisons between different geographical areas and the resources they contain. In Binford's terms, the higher the value for effective temperature, the greater will be the production of new plant cells *per annum*. Effective temperature is therefore a measure of the length of the growing season. When the degree of dependence among hunters and gatherers on storage is plotted against an increasing scale of effective temperature (fig. 2.2), it can be seen that storage forms a significant aspect of subsistence adaptations only among groups inhabiting environments with a value of less than 15. In latitudinal terms this of course refers to many northern groups, although the measure can incorporate groups from lower latitudes which possess, for a variety of local reasons, lower effective temperature values. Storage is therefore a necessary part of strategies which are primarily dependent for subsistence upon large mammal hunting and fishing and where alternative resources are scarce. This scarcity might be due either to a lack of other usable resources or to factors of timing in these environments with short growing seasons and where several possible resources may come 'on-stream' at the same moment and only for a brief period. Faced with such a circumstance the decision

Table 2.3. *Variations in settlement pattern ranged against effective temperature.*

The sample of 168 hunters and gatherers comes from Murdock (1967)

Effective temperature	Fully nomadic	Semi-nomadic	Semi-sedentary	Sedentary	Total
25–16	18	6	2	0	26
% sub total	(69)	(23)	(8)		
15–8	17	78	29	18	142
% sub total	(12)	(55)	(20)	(13)	
grand total	35	84	31	18	168
%	(21)	(50)	(18)	(11)	

Source: After Binford 1980: table 2

might be to go for the most reliable resource, store it, and so ignore the others.

Effective temperature has also been used to examine variation in settlement patterns (table 2.3). Mobility is highest in the resource-rich areas of high effective temperature in equatorial environments. Moreover high mobility is also common among groups in completely contrasted environments of low primary productivity. Sedentary strategies are most commonly found in the boreal and temperate forest regions and not in those where productivity is highest. We shall return to these observations in a discussion of settlement systems.

Variation in aspects of technology can also be linked with the global distribution of energy. Oswalt (1973, 1976) has devised a system to measure the relative complexity of food getting technologies. This is achieved by constructing scores for items of technology. The number of separate elements that make up a spear, digging stick or bow are counted as technounits. Each individual item of technology is called a subsistant. A high technounit count for the full range of subsistants is therefore a measure of the degree of technological complexity. When this is plotted against latitude (fig. 2.3), we can see a clear relationship between those groups which depend upon animals and the relative complexity of their food getting technologies. However this is not just a simple case of saying that hunting needs a more sophisticated technology. It is also a reflection of the selection pressure that these harsh, resource-poor environments place on survival strategies. Animals will form the key resources but they may be available only for very brief periods during the year. Failure to get these resources would be disastrous since there are few, if any, fall-back alternatives. These constraints pose problems of time for adaptive strategies. This time stress places a selective hone (Torrence 1983) on technology. This involves the sophistication of the equipment used, as well as the way it is organised in terms of planning ahead and anticipating contingencies. As a result technology is

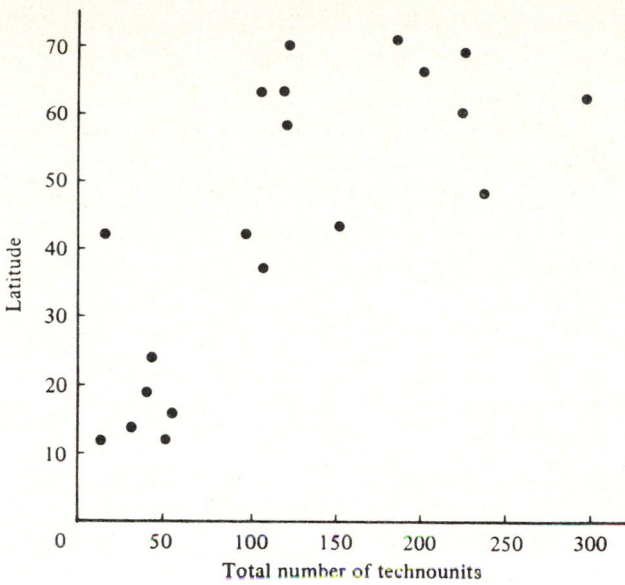

2.3 The varying complexity of hunter-gatherer technologies (Torrence 1983:fig. 3.1).

made as efficient as possible and so helps solve problems of time associated with exploiting mobile resources. A good example of this selection pressure is provided by the exploitation of large sea mammals. Complex gear is required, including boats, retrieval devices and harpoons. The prey are highly mobile and the very brief chances that are presented for their capture require that no opportunity is missed and that success is as assured as possible. Since nothing can be left to chance, it is common to find that the most complex technologies, as measured by Oswalt's technounit counts, are those belonging to groups which rely heavily on hunting large sea mammals (Torrence 1983).

Regional analysis

These examples of variation in aspects of hunter-gatherer behaviour establish a link between energy, ecological structure and adaptive patterns. Their importance lies in the clear demonstration that hunter-gatherer organisation is a systematic transformation of underlying ecological structures. In other words the residues of comparable adaptations that we can spot as patterns in the archaeological record were not derived from random behaviour – the result perhaps of small populations rattling around in a well-stocked larder where choice of action was so great that random behaviour was possible. Neither is the opposite the case: where lack of choice reduced palaeolithic populations to being slaves to their environment. Undoubtedly, during the course of the palaeolithic adaptive strategies underwent change, but this should not be seen as moving man up the ladder from slave to butler and finally to master of his environment. Such a view reduces the study of the palaeolithic to Lamarckian principles where it is human aspirations to do better that determine the course of development and progressive change.

However, one problem with a global or continental approach of this sort is that the conclusions are often too general to be of much use in understanding local conditions and outcomes. After all, we could look at the world productivity map and confidently predict that cereal agriculture would be a non-starter as an adaptive strategy at latitude 70° N. This would be a statement of high predictive power but negligible information content.

The conceptual framework I favour here recognises that in the first instance hunters and gatherers are adapted to local regions rather than to continents. For that reason we need to know what causes variation in their adaptive behaviour at this scale of analysis. The approach is as follows:

(1) spatial – the environmental structure and the patterning of resources is examined in the context of subsistence behaviour;

(2) demographic – the consequence of demographic patterning among groups and the maintenance of breeding networks; and

(3) social – the relations which establish patterns of alliance and contact.

Spatial

(a) simple and complex environments

At a general level we can describe environmental structure in terms of simple and complex systems. The former environments have few animal species (although many individuals of each species) and low plant productivity, and are subject to fluctuations in the abundance of resources. In other words they are unpredictable and consequently any strategy based upon these resources carries considerable *risk*. An extreme example is provided by the arctic tundras where the major herbivores are the small rodents (Pruitt 1970) whose numbers are subject to periodic cycles of rise and crash. Even the large mammals, most notably the reindeer/caribou, are prone to population cycles (Burch 1972). The low primary productivity of the vegetation requires large scale migrations for this species which only contributes further to the unpredictability of the resource for exploitation.

The other end of the spectrum is represented by mature, complex environments. The pattern of interactions in these ecosystems rests on long and complex food chains that result in stability. The sudden rise and crash of animal populations is not common and reflects the greater diversity in the number of animal species. Although the diversity index for species might be high there is much less dominance, when compared to the immature environments, of any single species (McNaughton and Wolf 1970; Redmann 1982:table 4). Tropical rain forests with high plant productivity and biomass and a great wealth of habitats distributed horizontally and vertically through the arboreal canopies

Table 2.4. *Some correlates of K and r selection*

r selection	K selection
favouring rapid rates of population increase, especially prominent in species that specialise in colonising short-lived environments or undergo large fluctuations in population size (Wilson 1975:593).	favouring superiority in stable, predictable environments in which rapid population growth is unimportant (Wilson 1975:587)
Characteristics favoured by selection rapid development; high maximal rate of increase; early reproduction; small body size; single reproduction	slower development; greater competitive ability; delayed reproduction; larger body size; repeated reproductions
Result productivity	efficiency
Length of life short, usually less than one year	longer, usually more than one year
Mortality often catastrophic, non-directed, density independent	more directed, density dependent
Survivorship high rates of early mortality	usually constant mortality or high survivorship to adult stages
Population size variable in time, non-equilibrium; usually well below carrying capacity of environment; unsaturated communities or portions thereof, ecological vacuums	fairly constant in time, equilibrium; at or near carrying capacity of environment; saturated communities
Intra- and inter-specific competition variable, often lax	usually keen
Environment variable and/or unpredictable; uncertain	fairly constant and/or predictable; more certain

Source: After Pianka 1970; Hayden 1981b; table 2

stand as an example of this end of the spectrum. The properties of other environments that lie within this spectrum are discussed by Jochim (1981:569).

This spectrum is of interest since it deals with the structure of environments and the systematic properties they display of stability, complexity, interaction, productivity and risk (Harris 1969; Gamble 1978a; Butzer 1982). Some further characterisations can be made. While a tropical rain forest is an extremely complex ecosystem, held together by an intricate network of interactions, it is at the same time a very brittle environment. Interference, either through clearance of trees or the removal of an animal species, can have far reaching consequences for the organisation of the rest of the biotic community. By contrast, the immature environments, while displaying what seem to be erratic and damaging cycles of dearth and plenty, are in fact extremely resilient habitats where the speed of recovery is high.

These observations have led to a series of correlates that contrast the species in these environments in terms of the selection they undergo (table 2.4). *K* selection is imposed as a function of the carrying capacity of the environment while *r* selection is dependent on the intrinsic rate of increase. A glance at the table shows that the lemmings and the reindeer from a tundra environment are, according to such criteria as body size, maturation rates and rate of population increase, under different selection pressure and yet members of the same environment. This emphasises how K and r selection are strategies employed by species to enhance reproductive success within more general considerations of community ecology (Foley (ed.) 1984). The strategies do not describe whole environments but instead are utilised within the ecosystemic structure. Part of this structure is referable to the history and development of ecosystems and the animals they contain and hence to the subject of palaeoecology.

(b) foraging and diet models

One approach to the study of resources used by mobile human populations has been to characterise exploitation in terms of cost. This is measured by the amount of energy obtained per unit of time spent acquiring it. A balance has to be struck between the expenditure of calories involved in acquiring food and the return, as measured also by calories, from that food resource. These factors have been measured among contemporary foraging groups (Lee 1969; Keene 1981; Winterhalder and Smith (eds.) 1981). Moreover it has been common practice to identify a principle of least effort among hunters and gatherers so that the effort expended in obtaining resources is minimised. At its extreme this has led to a characterisation of hunters and gatherers as the original affluent society where the working week is short and the pickings easy (Sahlins 1968).

Effort minimisation is not however the only goal for such strategies. Reducing the risks inherent in mobile patterns of exploitation and ensuring that larger gatherings of people can meet for ceremonies, marriage and other functions are equally important goals (Jochim 1976:19).

The schedule of resource use forms the all important blueprint for the subsistence strategy. This involves the comparative assessment of resources according to a measured series of attributes (Jochim 1976:23–8). The resource use schedule is based on assessing resources according to the following key attributes:

weight	(w)
non-food yield	(n; expressed as a proportional increase of w)
aggregation size	(a)
density	(d)
mobility	(m)
fat content	(f)

The secure income (goal 1) for any resource can be calculated as wnd/m; the low cost population aggregation (goal 2) can be calculated as wna/m: this emphasises the critical role that the attribute of mobility plays in calculating risk in the subsistence strategy.

The non-food yields refer to furs, skins and antler for raw material. The importance of fat content in meat based diets has recently been stressed by Speth (1983). Another way of assessing resource utility is by supplying measures of ten nutrients which are critical to the human diet and which vary in quantity and accessibility between resources (Keene 1981:181); energy, protein, calcium, iron, phosphorous, vitamin A, thiamine, riboflavin, asorbic acid (vitamin C) and niacin. Once measured in these terms the resources can then be ranked according to their exploitation cost, which involves time spent in travel, search and pursuit together with the handling and processing of resources. From this array a schedule can be drawn up which accommodates the various goals of risk reduction, ensuring group aggregation, and so forth. The costs determine the relative position of a resource in the entire rank of resources. This does not necessarily reflect the abundance of that resource in the environment, but only that in fulfilling a particular goal it represents the least costly solution.

A good example of this last point is provided by Hawkes and O'Connell (1981) who have reconsidered Lee's (1969) study of the !Kung on which the notion of 'an original affluent society' is based. They point out that although the plant resources gathered by the !Kung and Australian groups such as the Alyawara are low cost in terms of travel, search and pursuit time, the costs rise dramatically if handling and processing these foods for consumption are added. This is a feature of small size r selected resources such as seeds and nuts, and helps to explain why, although they are very abundant in the environments of the Alyawara and the !Kung, they are mostly ignored except in times of emergency when less expensive resources are scarce.

Another example where r selected resources are used comes from the north west coast of North America (Oberg 1973). The Tlingit are based in permanently occupied villages from which parties of hunters are sent out into the interior mountains. The main resources come however from the rich salmon streams and from opportunities provided by coastal fishing. These resources are available only for brief moments of the year as the fish migrate up and down the rivers. This factor of scheduling is well brought out by the division of labour in subsistence and other tasks during the year (fig. 2.4). September, for example, is entirely devoted to salmon fishing and storing the catch which will then overwinter the group. During spring, a great deal of time is spent gathering berries and making oil which is used to preserve and store the fruits that have been collected. Here are two examples of extreme time stress where the resources that are most vital to subsistence occur only briefly in the full cycle of the year. The schedule of resource use is based upon the reliability of these species and makes sure that, for example, when the salmon are available, work parties of sufficient size are present in the village.

The Tlingit case raises many questions about the decisions which shape a resource use schedule. This has been modelled by Jochim (1976) as a game against the environment. The environment keeps posing questions such as which resource should be exploited, for how long and by how many people?

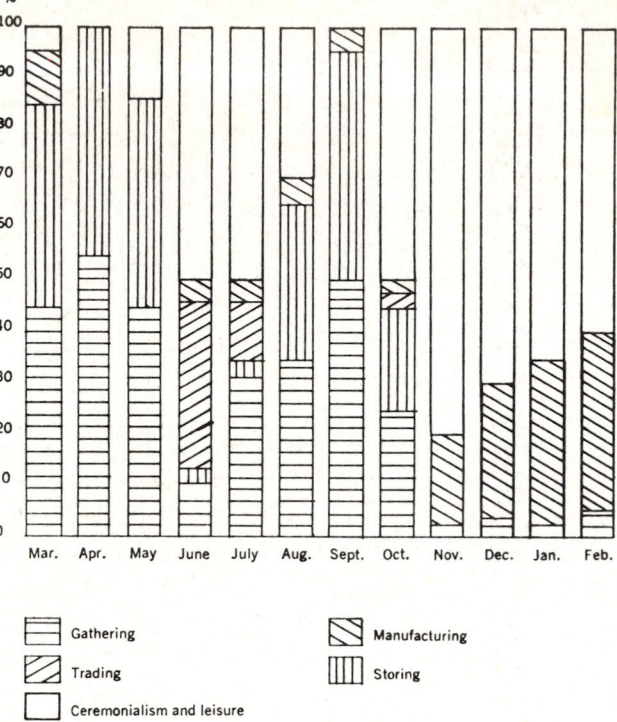

2.4 The relative amounts of time spent each month by the Tlingit on various activities in the annual cycle of production. Note the emphasis on salmon fishing in September, berry picking during spring and summer and hunting at other times of the year.

Future moves in the yearly cycle have to be written into the schedule, as do the implications these hold for moving personnel around the habitat and changing the composition of foraging parties (Silberbauer 1981:249).

The variable, often seasonal, patterns of resource availability and abundance are dealt with by exploiting the strategic options (table 2.5) through a combination of four tactical moves. These deal with the exploitation of space (settlement location and group size) and time (settlement duration and storage). Flexibility in response is the hallmark of the overall strategy and is of course most prominently seen in the pattern of group fusion and fission.

An important aspect of the tactics devised to cope with the spatial exploitation of resources refers to the structure and distribution of resource patches: whether they are clumped and widely separated in space or uniformly distributed (Heffley 1981). An optimal solution to this problem has been devised by biologists studying feeding strategies among a wide array of animal species. In particular these optimal foraging strategies have been developed for birds as in Horn's (1968) classic paper on the Brewer's blackbird. The optimal solution to resource patch size, structure and distribution is, therefore, one that minimises

Table 2.5. *Strategic and tactical decisions among hunters and gatherers*

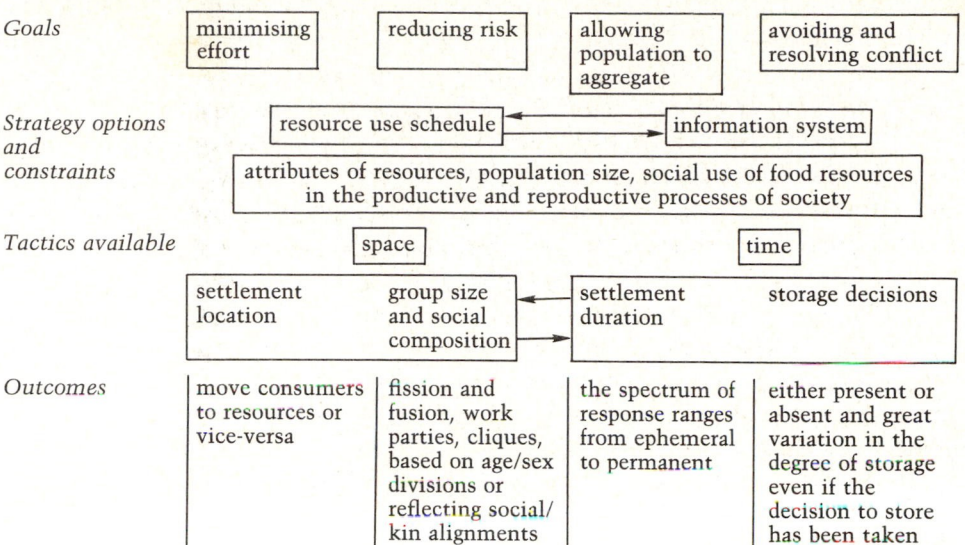

Goals	minimising effort	reducing risk	allowing population to aggregate	avoiding and resolving conflict

Strategy options and constraints

resource use schedule ◄———————— information system

attributes of resources, population size, social use of food resources in the productive and reproductive processes of society

Tactics available — space — time

| settlement location | group size and social composition | settlement duration | storage decisions |

	space			time	
Outcomes	move consumers to resources or vice-versa	fission and fusion, work parties, cliques, based on age/sex divisions or reflecting social/ kin alignments	the spectrum of response ranges from ephemeral to permanent	either present or absent and great variation in the degree of storage even if the decision to store has been taken

exploitation costs and risks by manipulating: (1) the length of time spent travelling to, and exploiting a patch; and (2) the group size and its location either to that patch or to alternative resource patches.

The pay-off for this optimal foraging behaviour is assessed in the context of maximising reproductive fitness. Those individuals who achieve optimal solutions to the problems of foraging for food in the environment will stand to maximise their reproductive fitness either by having more time to search for suitable mates or by controlling feeding grounds for raising offspring. In this context, optimal behaviour can be understood in terms of the adaptive advantages it confers.

Another aspect of such models raises the question of efficiency (E. Smith 1979). This measure arises as an outcome of the selection pressure of the environment. While, for example, the goal of minimising effort in exploiting resources might be interpreted as efficient behaviour, it has not always been clear exactly what adaptive significance this might possess. Smith distinguishes between two environmental structures. In the first, energy is a limiting factor. Selection will therefore favour increased efficiency in energy capture since the result will be to make more energy available. This appears to be a strategy open to subsistence agriculture. The second set of environments, in which most contemporary hunters and gatherers find themselves, are limited both by time and energy since complex decisions concerning the schedule of resource use during the year have to be taken. The Cree who inhabit the boreal forests of North America (Winterhalder 1981) and the !Kung San who exploit the water limited environments of the Kalahari desert (Lee 1979) are two examples. Competing demands as to how time should be budgeted require that the rate of energy acquisition per time is increased. E. Smith (1979:68) notes that in the case of the !Kung San it is inadequate to measure their exploitive efficiency solely in terms of output/input ratios of calories expended for calories recovered (Lee 1969). This would ignore the adaptive significance of any efficiency they might display. If, instead, time is introduced and a measure of net acquisition rates employed then it is clear that the outcome of increased foraging efficiency is to take the pressure off the immediate task of gathering food and to budget the time thus freed to solve other problems. These include obtaining marriage partners and investment in maintaining social networks (Wiessner 1982).

These considerations of the use of resources in space provide a route to understanding the selection pressure that physical and social environments place upon adaptive strategies. This is done by placing a selective hone on human behaviour patterns within a survival strategy. Further examples which have utilised this background can be found (Wilmsen 1973; Jochim 1976; Perlman 1980; Winterhalder and Smith (eds.) 1981), while other examinations of least cost solutions by means of linear programming include those of Keene (1979), Harpending and Davis (1977), and Reidhead (1979, 1980). General discussions are provided by Bettinger (1980) and Durham (1981), and in a biological overview by Pianka (1978).

(c) food management strategies

These models of environmental structure and exploitation patterns emphasise the importance of space in understanding aspects of hunter-gatherer variation. Whereas previously palaeolithic hunters were described by the most abundant species identified in bone assemblages, we can now see that labels such as reindeer, mammoth, red deer or cave bear hunters tell us little about adaptation to the complex matrix of environmental conditions (Davidson 1981). An alternative is to look at variation in subsistence behaviour among hunters and gatherers as a set of *food management strategies*. By using such a concept we can also blur the all-too-rigid division into hunting, gathering and fishing strategies based upon the proportions of sets of species. Food management strategies allow us to concentrate on the crucial composite attributes of the plant and animal resources distributed throughout the environment and how they are procured. At a subsistence level, all food management strategies have a goal that is reasonably characterised as minimising effort in securing returns and reducing risk. The decisions taken will however have very different impacts upon the use of space and the creation of residues.

One way to illustrate this concept of food management strategies is through a recent study by Binford (1980) where he contrasts two settlement systems for hunters and gatherers. The first is a *forager* system where camps are established and parties set out on a daily basis to encounter food. These are common strategies in plant-rich environments. As a result consumers are moved to resources (see Silberbauer 1972:figs. 7–5, 7–6, in an example from the G/wi bushmen). The population is mapped onto the available resources and moulded to the spatial and temporal distributions in availability and abundance. If we refer back to table 2.3, such groups are expected to make many residential camp moves through the year as they pursue this strategy of moving consumers to resources (Silberbauer 1972, 1981; Lee 1979; Lee and DeVore (eds.) 1976; Yellen 1977a; Carlstein 1982). This foraging strategy is well shown by Lee (1969): groups are tethered to waterholes with a foraging radius of ten miles, or two hours walking time, which represents a cost threshold which a daily foraging party is unlikely to cross. The solution would rather be to move the entire residential base and establish another daily foraging radius (see Rogers 1963:79). As a result these settlement systems are commonly associated with only two site types: the *residential camp* and the *location* where the gathering takes place within the leash provided by a foraging radius.

An alternative food management strategy deals with the properties of clumped and highly mobile animal resources. In this *collector* system resources are intercepted. Work parties proceed to known locations within the environment to collect precisely defined resources. Once the animal resources have been collected, they are stored/cached and moved, as parcels rather than as whole animal units, to the consumers when and where they are required. This strategy accounts for the lower incidence of residential mobility among northern groups (table 2.3), even though they are dependent upon highly mobile resources. The settlement system includes not only camps and locations but also *caches*, *field stations*, where the game is monitored (Binford 1978b), and a *field camp* which is the temporary operations centre for a task group operating at some distance from the residential camp (Binford 1980). The accent of collector type strategies is upon planning ahead, thereby solving the logistical problems of temporal and spatial variation in resources. While travelling to these intercept locations to hunt reindeer or to trap beaver, other resources may be acquired. For example, the acquisition of lithic raw materials may be fitted into these patterns of movement in what is described as embedded procurement (Binford 1979; Torrence 1983). In other words, several birds are killed with a single stone. This is a bonus rather than the basis of the strategy as it is with the foragers. The result in spatial terms is to capture energy, fix it through storage at set locations and then distribute it to other points of consumption. Compared with the forager strategy the dislocation in space and time between the capture and the consumption of energy is much greater. This lag effect will obviously have a great impact upon the formation of the archaeological record as measured by degree of resolution (Chapter 1; Chapter 6).

(d) home range and territory size

Environmental structure also affects the spatial extent of the areas over which groups range for resources. The map of tribes in aboriginal Australia compiled by

Tindale (1940, 1974) pointed to an inverse relation between the amount of annual rainfall and the area associated with a tribal grouping. Birdsell (1953) confirmed this impression by demonstrating a high correlation between tribal area and mean annual rainfall, thereby linking the spatial extent of territories with a critical environmental variable. Moreover, as territory size increased group size remained constant. A similar relation can be seen among Athapaskan and Eskimo groups in north Alaska (Burch and Correll 1972:fig. 1) where territory size for regional groups increases away from the coast. This does not however result in comparably larger regional populations but only in variation in population density.

Under most conditions we should expect that home range or territory size will increase as either productivity decreases or unpredictability of a key resource such as rainfall becomes an important constraint. An example from the eastern Canadian sub-arctic is provided by Rogers (1969) where he links the decreasing size of local group territories with increased game densities in a western traverse across the region (fig. 2.5).

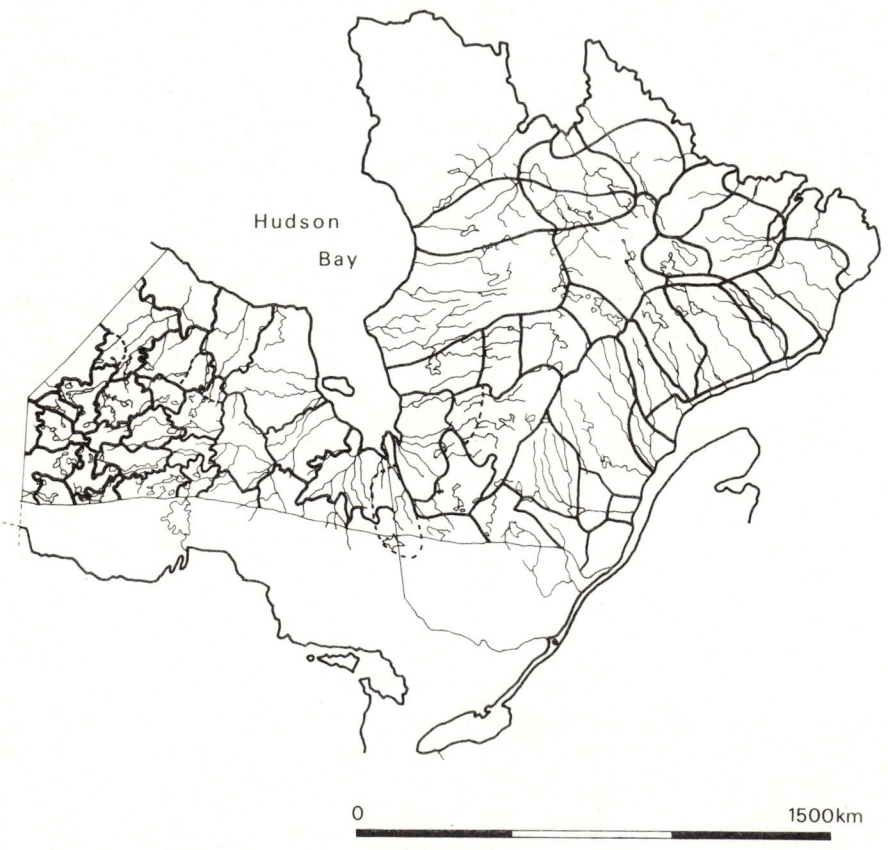

2.5 Local group territories in the eastern Canadian sub-arctic (Rogers 1969).

Further examples of variable territory size can be found in Smiley *et al.* (eds.) 1980, Peterson (ed.) 1976, Silberbauer 1972, Kroeber 1922 and Steward 1938.

However, these observations on the relative productivity of resources and territory size are anticipating the question of the size and recurrence of population units and their demographic arrangement.

Demographic

(a) population density

One of the celebrated asides recorded from the discussions at the *Man the Hunter* symposium was made by an ecologist who pointed out that mice are considerably more productive than large mammals such as deer.

I calculated that if we were capable of utilising the yield of mice, there ought to be (human) population densities of the order of 100 times as great as those that there actually were in such forests. (Deevey 1968:95)

In the present context this ecological comment about an *r* selected resource is important since it points up quite clearly that absolute hunter-gatherer population sizes cannot be accurately deduced from measures of primary productivity or biomass. Neither can these figures be used to predict variation in population numbers, density and distribution (Hassan 1975). At the very least we would need to know whether the adaptation being studied was geared to using the great potential productivity that is available in *r* selected resources or whether resources that are less expensive but also less productive formed the major component of the subsistence strategy.

In fig. 2.6, some population densities among hunter-gatherer groups are shown. The range is very great, with those above one person per square km being

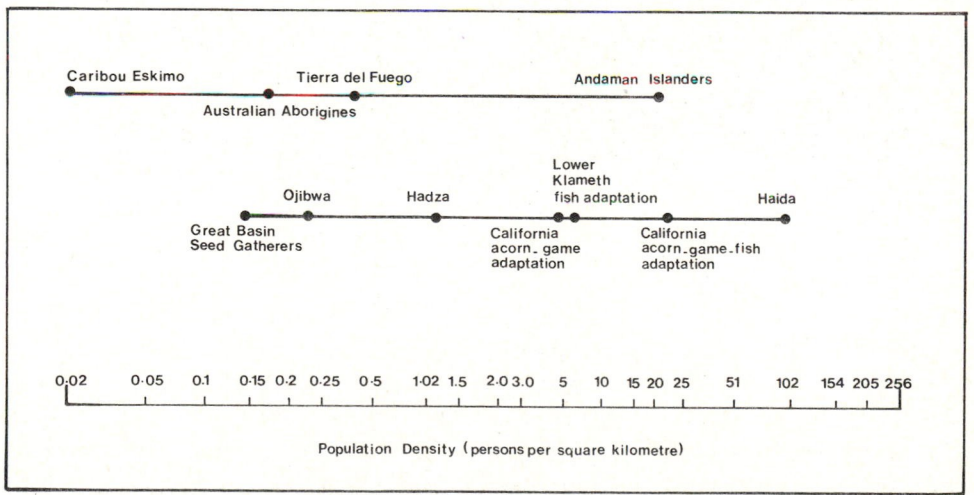

2.6 A sample of hunter-gatherer population densities (Hassan 1975).

dependent upon individually small parcel resources such as fish or a combination of acorns and fish. In these adaptations the resources are clumped in space and predictable. They are also very costly to exploit.

(b) equilibrium models

Demographic analyses have revealed several repeated population sizes among hunters and gatherers that occur irrespective of ecological productivity, territory size or other variables. According to Birdsell (1953, 1958, 1968, 1976) working with Australian data, these central tendencies in population numbers are the outcome of density equilibrium systems where population is adjusted to the carrying capacity of the environment.

The three 'magic numbers' in group size are 25, 175 and 500 persons. The group size of 25 forms the local group or minimum band. In a sample of four continents the range in numbers for such groups was found to be between 20 and 70 (Wobst 1974:170). The local group is the basic productive unit. Most frequently it is named and associated with a territory (Rogers 1969; Damas 1969b).

The next level of 175 persons is a tier of seven such groups. Birdsell regards this grouping as the effective breeding unit (1968), ranging in size between 150 and 200 persons. A study of long term viability of these population sizes has been undertaken by Wobst (1974) by means of a Monte Carlo simulation. The results indicate that the 175 breeding unit is indeed of sufficient size that any member of a local group can be guaranteed, on reaching maturity, a suitable marriage partner from a neighbouring local group. This is defined as the minimum equilibrium size requirement for the assured long term functioning of such demographic units. The simulation also pointed to the effectiveness of the local group minimum band size in being able to ride out any stochastic fluctuations in sex ratios, mortality and fertility so that once again long term survival is assured.

While local group size may be primarily determined by factors of exploitation within a productive unit, the 175 figure represents a minimal solution to the problems of biological reproduction. The system depends upon exogamy where marriage partners are sought outside the local group. Leacock (1969:14) states that exogamy is also essential since it limits competitiveness within a closely co-operating group and so displaces possible social tensions away from the productive unit where they would cause most damage. Exogamy also provides a flexible set of social strategies for forging political alliances (Service 1966:36) and making useful contacts, in an adaptive sense (Wiessner 1982).

The third 'magic number' displays a central tendency of 500. This forms a tier of some 19 local groups. This level has been described as the maximum band (Wobst 1974), regional group (Burch and Correll 1972), connubium or marriage universe (Williams 1974). A good example of this grouping is provided by Rogers

(1969) for the Canadian eastern sub-arctic. Here the marriage universe consisted of a four band unit. Most of the marriages were however contracted within a smaller population unit than the four band unit, which numbered upwards of four hundred persons. Marriage partners were most commonly sought among spatially close groups, and a pronounced movement of women after marriage can also be seen from one lake group to another.

The regional group is not however a political unit. The members may never meet together on a single occasion, and it is more than likely that some marriages will even be contracted outside this unit (Helm 1969:52; Birdsell 1976:97). There has been considerable debate over the correspondence of other traits with this unit. In particular Tindale (1953) and Birdsell (1976) have argued that the unit is also defined by a distinct language dialect, with the result that 85% of all marriages are contracted within such Australian dialect tribes. Critics of the model (e.g. Dixon 1976) point out that dialects rarely act as social barriers (see below, p. 58). However, this same congruence has been noted elsewhere among hunters and gatherers. The Eskimo of the central arctic formed three major groupings (Damas 1969b): Copper, Netsilik and Iglulik, which numbered 450–500, c.800 and c.500 persons respectively. These group-ings were composed at a local level of a number of sealing villages where every winter populations of c.100 persons assembled (*ibid.*:122). Damas refers to these groupings as tribes which were genealogically distinct one from another, since each formed its own marriage universe. Moreover they corresponded to a dialect area and to a cultural sub-area (*ibid.*:131).

Regional groups in north-western Alaska were also defined by distinct dialects, an association with a region and a pattern of yearly movement that set it apart from neighbours (Burch and Correll 1972:21–3). Furthermore these regional groups constituted a marriage universe or *deme* defined as a partially isolated population of individuals which had an intimate social and temporal relation to one another. Population estimates for these 20 regional groups in A.D. 1850 give a range of between 200 and 975 with a mean of 502 persons (Burch 1975:table 2).

The regional group is therefore made up of a number of local groups. It corresponds to a geographical area and forms a population capable of long term survival.

(c) mating networks and demographic spatial geometry

The existence of dialect tribes in Australia depends only upon 'competence in speech (and) mobility on foot' (Birdsell 1968:232). They result from the density of communication patterns between the local groups in either the 175 or the 500 tier. Since no local group is of sufficient size to guarantee long term reproductive success, patterns of contact have to be established with neighbouring sets. The optimal spatial solution leads to groups adopting a hexagonal shape to their

2.7 A model of local group 'packing' so that each group adopts a least cost solution to maintaining contacts with neighbouring groups in either a single (b) or double tier (c) of c.175 and 500 persons respectively. This can be described as a mating network (Birdsell 1958:197).

territories so that contact is made with six neighbours (fig. 2.7). Contiguous boundaries facilitate not only the exchange of marriage partners, information about the environment and resources but also the transfer of raw materials. Ethnographic studies have shown an average of between 5.4 and 5.97 (Birdsell 1958; Wilmsen 1973; Moore 1981) for contiguous boundaries between local groups. An example is provided in fig. 2.5, from which a mean figure of 5.67 neighbours per local group has been obtained.

This social geometry describes a mating network (Wobst 1974, 1976) from which marriage partners are obtained. The position of any one group within the honeycomb lattice (fig. 2.7) will have important implications in terms of the cost of maintaining contacts and patterns of interaction within the network. Those groups at the centre will have an advantageous position compared to those on the periphery. These peripheral groups might opt for an alternative strategy of belonging to adjacent mating networks, thereby introducing some of the fuzziness into the boundaries of the regional group. Such a solution may however seriously weaken both mating networks by reducing the potential number of marriage partners available to either system. This might encourage clearer boundaries enforced through ritual and supported by dialect differences, which turn the allegiance of a peripheral group towards a centre and a single mating network. If this were to happen, then the regional group could be described as endogamous, a closed system in terms of the recruitment and redistribution of personnel, and as a result an autonomous reproductive unit.

Such an outcome is however achieved only at some cost to groups participating in the system.

Low population densities resulting from poor resources also impose costs on mating networks by stretching the size of the systems and the distances over which interaction has to take place. A figure of 300+ km from one edge to the other in a 500 person network is thought by some (Wobst 1976:56) to place additional, and often prohibitive, costs on integration. These costs are expressed in the time that has to be budgeted to maintain face-to-face contacts through visiting and other information exchanges. Furthermore these have to be fitted into already tight schedules of resource use. One consequence might be selection for cultural means such as visual display and ceremony to invest these moments of contact with increased information so that the vital outcomes from these sporadic encounters become doubly sure. Without such mechanisms, the network may fragment and population become locally extinct.

A situation of high population density can pose similar problems of cost in maintaining the smooth functioning of mating systems. Linear arrangements that have to be adopted by groups living along coasts mean that the ideal pattern of six contacts would not be possible. The extra costs of maintaining a linear network might possibly be great enough to prevent the use of the abundant *r* selected resources in such locations until developments in the social strategies which integrated regional groups had evolved and specified how such costs could become acceptable.

(d) geographical boundaries

This section on demography has used several Australian examples to demonstrate the existence of basic units operating under varied ecological conditions. Peterson (1976a:67) has concluded that in the continent there were two main levels of population grouping which arose directly from the pattern of Aboriginal economies and which are explained by the importance of water. The first is the local group and the second the culture-area population. The former is associated with areas circumscribed by drainage basins while the latter follows the major drainage divisions in the Australian continent (*ibid.*:fig. 8). The drainage divisions contain a number of regional groups.

These observations have been noted for the spatial organisation of local groups to geographical areas by a number of authors (Jochim 1976:86–7; Kroeber 1925:160; Heizer 1958:1; Leacock 1969; Jones 1971). Drainage basin divisions also apply to regional groups in north west Alaska (Burch and Correll 1972:fig. 1) and can also be seen in fig. 2.5 for local groups in the Canadian sub-arctic.

The reasons for these natural divisions are various. Watersheds are areas of low productivity and provide obstacles to communication. The rivers and lakes on the other hand not only contain food but also a means of rapid travel through a territory during the summer as well as the winter freeze-up.

Social

(a) alliance

The regional group forms the smallest self-sufficient unit. This autonomy might have been a goal of local groups but it was never achieved:

very few local [north western Alaskan Eskimo] families were large enough to remain totally endogamous for any extended period of time because of incest restrictions. Sooner or later, some members of each unit would have to look elsewhere for spouses. The second limitation was in part a consequence of environmental factors. In most regions, the resource base was too precarious for the members of each local family to persist indefinitely without help from the members of other such units. (Burch 1975:248)

Alliance through marriage or by means of a wide variety of partnerships was therefore a necessary circumstance. An alliance is an achieved social status based to a large extent upon negotiation (Guemple 1972:56). These negotiable alliances provide a means by which the viability of individuals and local groups is achieved within a regional framework. A network of such alliances defines an often diverse set of social relationships where circulation and exchange of persons and goods establishes and maintains ties of variable commitment and duration (Gamble 1983a; Bender 1981).

This viability is achieved by extending links over sufficient social and spatial areas to smooth out any local effects of imbalance in either demography or resources.

According to Yengoyan (1968, 1972, 1976), organisational frameworks, such as the Australian sub-section system, acted as insurance policies for groups inhabiting high risk, unpredictable environments. These policies could be cashed in hard times:

This network of related individuals and groups permits local groups to move into different areas of exploitation, especially during severe droughts and periods of economic hardship. The extension of kin relations via section groupings thus 'insures' for each local group the ability of movement into adjacent areas. (1968:199)

Similar patterns have been observed among the G/wi San of the Kalahari (Silberbauer 1972, 1981) where six local groups were linked together by a variety of alliances which cross-cut patterns of spouse exchange. These alliances served as a mechanism by which commodities were distributed throughout the area. They were stable, lasting at least a generation, and in most cases allies found all they needed from among their partners, thus making interaction with non-allies unnecessary (1972:303).

Among the caribou-eater Chipewyan of the Hudson Bay area of Canada (J. Smith 1978), unpredictability in caribou movements led to the creation of spatially extensive alliance networks between local groups. These were form-alised through exogamous marriage ties, matrilocal residence ties and through visiting which not only emphasised kin relations but also dispensed informa-

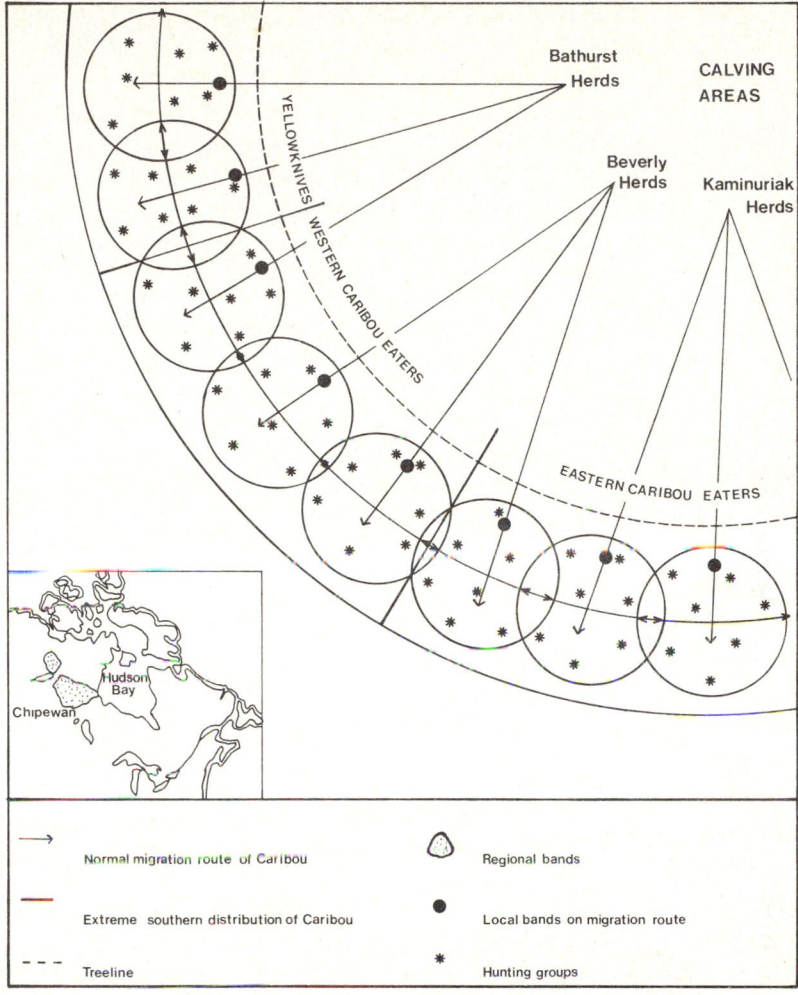

2.8 The regional patterning of Chipewyan local groups to the risks inherent in a caribou based hunting strategy (J. Smith 1978).

tion about faunal abundance or scarcity. If caribou failed to appear in the territory of a local group, then movement to a neighbouring local group was possible (*ibid.*:83). As a result risk was spread over huge distances by using alliances to gather information upon which to base strategic decisions and then, if the resources failed, to provide a further safety net (fig. 2.8) by allowing movement to areas where resources were available.

Unpredictability in resources was not the only area which required an insurance policy. The example used by Yengoyan (1968) allows a local group to call on neighbours for help either by moving into their range or by using resources they had already collected (see Strehlow 1970). However at another level the section system excludes non-tribal members from these all important resources. Closure occurs in the pattern of access and warfare takes over.

In north Alaska it was not possible to rely on strangers for help. In fact it was not even possible to associate peacefully with strangers (Burch and Correll 1972), and as a result maintaining alliances in as many directions as possible was extremely important. These were established through a whole range of partnerships including trade, song and spouse exchange (Spencer 1959), as well as through marriage, and could be seen at such ceremonies as the Messenger feast, at fairs and in the prosecution of military alliances. The existence of these alliances allowed people who were not related to come together peacefully.

The dual nature of Eskimo society – co-operation through kinship ties and alliances but otherwise hostility to strangers – is particularly striking. Burch and Correll (1972:36) make the important distinction that *within* regional groups information exchange, transaction, marriage and all other forms of social relationships were much greater than *between* regional groups. The contact *between* regional groups was the domain of either alliance or warfare. These patterns cross-cut Alaska in what they describe as one great network of social relations. They cross-cut divisions between Athapaskan and Eskimo, dialect divisions and geographical boundaries. They permitted individuals immense scope for movement but only in those directions where a friendly reception could be guaranteed. At this area level the adaptive system relied on rapid restructuring to meet local crises.

(b) information strategies

Information forms a vital resource for hunters and gatherers (Moore 1981). Time will be budgeted to acquire it since it is critical to the implementation of a successful subsistence strategy and information is another option by which the goals in such strategies can be realised (table 2.5). Information strategies are therefore adaptive in that they contribute to survival. They will consequently be subject to selection pressure.

It is now commonplace to define culture as an information system (Clarke 1978) where the messages contribute to survival. The information is acquired as these mobile groups traverse the environment. It is coded into the tribal encyclopedia (Pfeiffer 1982) in the form of dress, technology and material items of display, and disseminated in contexts of ceremony, ritual, visiting and conversation. The information is carried in both verbal and visual modes and serves to inform individuals about society and the environment.

The ethnographic accounts of hunters and gatherers are a testament to the copious extent of hunter-gatherer knowledge about the environment and the many ways in which it is imparted and transmitted from hunter to hunter and from generation to generation. This forms part of a body of social knowledge. Amongst the Eskimo, prestige goes to those hunters with the greatest knowledge (Nelson 1969:373). It not only serves as a means to plan moves in the game against the environment but also acts as a basis for social differentiation. This latter practice is more clearly seen in the levels of meaning associated with items of material culture (Morphy 1977) and in the body of social knowledge contained in ceremony and ritual (Bender 1978). At a regional scale of adaptation, examples can be found where this information is used in coping with emergency situations (Nelson 1973:374), telling the hunt (Blurton-Jones and Konner 1976) and discussing resources within a territory of some 130,000 mi^2 (Binford 1979:257, 272). The information serves to predict moves (Turner in Leacock 1954:5) and, as this example of Pintupi knowledge in the Western Australian desert shows, is vital in coping with critical resources:

So a lifetime of experience, backed by a traditional knowledge, alone enables the people to judge, without having to visit a well that they know, whether it will still contain water, and whether, if dry, with the sides fallen in and the well full of debris, it is worth cleaning out. (Thomson 1962:271)

Yellen and Harpending (1972:fig. 15) have modelled the patterns of interaction in hunter-gatherer society (see Isaac 1972). According to their model the unpredictable environments inhabited by many hunters and gatherers require open access to resources, and this would lead to homogeneity in items of material culture. Closure of the interaction networks would occur only at higher population densities (Wobst 1976), where resources were more predictable. In a recent study of projectile points and items of dress among the San groups of the Kalahari, Wiessner (1983) has shown how group and personal identities are signalled in different ways. The projectile points display an emblemic style, expressing group affiliation, such that a close correspondence exists between language areas and distinctive arrow points associated with them. Assertive style, that addresses individual identity through items of dress and beadwork, was much more spatially varied and dealt with individuals locating themselves within society.

The size of society has been investigated by Wobst (1977). He suggests that an important consequence of communication with socially distant persons will be felt in the cost of such communication. This can be countered by using the visual mode to transmit information via a set of stylistic rules governing convention and design. This extra investment pays off since it regularises contact when it occurs and allows advantage to be taken of infrequent but nonetheless important interaction. If these contacts are not needed, and interaction takes place only among close kin and relatives, then the say-it-in-style use of material culture will be largely superfluous. However, as Wobst points out, once an item of material culture has been used in this way then *all* material culture takes on the role of carrying information whether it carries a specifically coded message or not.

Material culture provides an extremely flexible medium for carrying information about social strategies. While items of material culture may reflect boundary maintenance between groups, it is never a barrier to the movement of personnel since dress and ornament can be exchanged at the frontier (Hodder 1978). Language differences might present more basic checks to such movements. However we have already noted that critics of the Australian dialect tribe model point out that personnel permeated through such linguistic barriers. This occurrence has been studied by Hill (1978) in terms of *area level adaptations* by populations to unreliable environments. She argues that in Aboriginal Australia the complex patterns of linguistic diversity were a feature of the 'insurance' policies of groups in desert environments. Linguistic diversity was based on lexical (vocabulary) rather than phonetic (pronunciation) differences. Phonetic differences, the foreign accent problem, are difficult if not impossible to eradicate whereas new words and patterns of words can be learnt very quickly. As a result when those moments of resource crisis occurred the linguistic barriers were collapsed and groups could move to areas where they could use the resources of other groups. Hill makes the point that the bewildering pattern of diversity among Australian language systems can be understood by considering wider contexts of long term adaptation by regional rather than local groups. These area level adaptations and their linguistic aspects are common to other hunter-gatherer regional strategies, as are patterns of fictive kinship reckoning (Lee 1972).

Patterns of exchange also act to convey information (Wilmsen 1973; Mulvaney 1976). Amongst the !Kung San, Wiessner (1982) has described the hxaro exchange system based upon mutual reciprocity where non-food items are exchanged between hxaro partners who are generally close relatives. These involve trade goods, ostrich egg shell beads and arrows. The 'hxaro paths' extend between camps and over hundreds of kilometres. The hxaro network reduces risks by storing social obligations at a regional scale and these can be cashed at a future date. In this way the viability of the local group is assured by its participation in a regional system.

Wiessner makes the point that once instituted, this social strategy has repercussions for the rest of the social system. The !Kung may not work a very long week, but their 'spare' time is taken up with visiting hxaro partners, keeping alliance options open and as a result guaranteeing the wider system of risk reduction. This is directly relevant to E. Smith's (1979) point, already discussed, that energetic efficiency can be adaptive in freeing more time for social interaction that contributes to, and enhances, survival.

However, while many of the hunter-gatherer adaptations described here may require information strategies servicing alliance networks, we must not make the mistake of regarding the harsh environments in which they are found as the reason why they exist. The pattern of alliances which stress open access to resources in times of crisis may be determined to some extent by the structure of resources. But the pattern of alliances is not specified by the environment. It is rather the case that the flexibility in area level adaptations among so many hunter-gatherer groups is conditioned by principles that specify how environmental problems can be overcome by social solutions. In that sense the social system is dominant (fig. 2.1). In the course of social evolution during the palaeolithic, we must expect developments in these dominant sets of relations such that the determinant effect of the environment on hunter-gatherer settlement and occupation is a constantly rising threshold, as the developing social field specifies the manner of exploitation of varied energy sources.

Archaeological implications

I have dwelt on these examples at some length since they are central to our understanding of the regional scale as the appropriate unit of analysis for hunter-gatherer, and by extension palaeolithic, adaptations. However, this is only a glimpse of contemporary systems and their variation. The 'fit' of any palaeolithic patterns to these examples is in no way a judgement that this was how palaeolithic systems operated or that the range of variation they exhibited is encompassed by these few modern examples. We must be aware, in Wobst's (1978) phrase, of the tyranny of the ethnographic record, where we live in awe of the ethnographer because of his well-focused snap-shots of fleeting human systems.

An example of this possible tyranny is provided by the local group/regional group model. When taken as demographic units, we arrive at the two magic numbers of twenty-five and five hundred persons respectively. It might be tempting to cast round in the archaeological record for some data which appear to fit these modular units. I am sure that data could be found, with for example an excavated camp site with five huts, each judged big enough to house five people, or the spatial distribution of a distinctive artifact type over an area that could quite reasonably incorporate the territories of some nineteen local groups. With diligent searching, this could be, and has been, done for any period of the palaeolithic and mesolithic (Davis 1978; David 1973; Conkey 1980; Freeman 1975; Milisauskas 1978; Campbell 1977:maps 33 and 46), and supported by a whole battery of techniques such as floor area estimates (Naroll 1962; Cook and Heizer 1965; Wiessner 1974), camp site analysis (Yellen 1977a) and stylistic analysis (Clark 1975; Close 1978).

This is an example of ethnography with a shovel (Wobst 1978:303), where the present is reproduced in the form of the past. Modules and models are imposed on 'likely' looking data sets in the belief that the patterning is understood and explained. On the contrary, we should be alert to the fact that while the ethnographer has his finger on the shutter he has very little control over the focus or the quality of the image that is recorded. The freeze-frame images of these rapidly vanishing societies look good as a warrant for understanding the past. That is because they have been composed in the ethnographer's view-finder, where omission, selection and interpretation render them very different from the representative types they are sometimes held to be (Bettinger 1980:192–4).

By contrast archaeology is the discipline whose interest lies in long term processes of adaptation and change and whose data base of material culture provides simultaneous access to all behavioural realms and the multiplicity of variation they contain (Wobst 1978:307). In the context of this book I am, therefore, less concerned with the precise form that variation takes among modern hunters and gatherers than with the observation that these systems do indeed vary with respect to energy and its distribution in space. This is my entering wedge into what is an extremely complex system in which at a basic level we need to increase our knowledge about the nature of the palaeolithic record and how it was formed rather than about the minutiae of organisation among contemporary hunters.

Other entering wedges have been proposed. Butzer (1982) has recently argued that we should approach the past as a study of human ecosystems. He advocates the analysis of human decision making in a contextual framework where the multivarious strands are woven together in the interplay of cultural with environmental systems. A number of conceptual themes are identified for this analytical approach and deal with the properties of space, scale, interaction, complexity and stability of these same past human ecosystems. Measures of these themes would indeed provide an important route to understanding the past and allowing comparisons between systems in time and space to be made. There are still problems however concerning the means by which we establish such necessary measures in the materials of the archaeological record (Gamble 1984a). There is always the danger that we might read into the patterns that have been recovered a degree of stability and a measure of complexity which is in fact only a statement about how we think these parameters ought to vary among the stones and bones of our data base.

With these methodological caveats in mind, what implications can be drawn from the preceding sections on hunter-gatherer regional systems that will be applicable to the study of the past?

It might help to reiterate why this lengthy description has been given. The purpose of pursuing this segment of ethnography was to investigate the appropriateness of a regional approach to a living system and to tie down why we should turn to hunters and gatherers as our starting point for 'thinking' about the past. With these guidelines in mind I would draw the following implications:

(1) Spatial behaviour

Mobility is the key adaptation to the environment. It is the means by which variation in environmental structure and resources can be exploited, risk minimised and information, critical to successful adaptation, gathered. In that sense no movement across the landscape is wasted since even though no food resources might be obtained, information that guides future decisions and so contributes to survival is acquired.

An appropriate unit of analysis at this level will need to incorporate spatial and ecological variables. Such a unit must be larger than any single location where resources are found and must deal with the links and moves between resource patches. The unit has, at the very least, to encompass an annual cycle of movement and exploitation and this should be expanded to include the lifetime areas over which individuals and groups forage. Within such a large scale spatial unit, there will be very varied use of particular locales. Their selection and use by palaeolithic groups can be judged according to measures of cost.

(2) Demographic behaviour

Since no local group can be autonomous when it comes to finding mates and ensuring reproductive success, networks will exist linking local populations together through exogamous marriage rules.

A number of possible mating strategies can exist within the regional connubium. The options of open access to several such networks or rules or closure applied to a single marriage universe will have implications for patterns of demographic adjustment of population to resources. As interaction takes place, in the form of marital and material exchanges, so information flows between units. This may be coded onto material culture or represent verbal communications about resources, rights of access to these resources and the availability of marriage partners. The maintenance of such strategies represents a cost since they have to accommodate variable densities of population. These costs may be traced back to the structure of the environment and the distribution of resources.

(3) Social behaviour

Cost models have the disadvantage of only predicting what resources should, according to a set of assumptions, be exploited and which mating network strategy should be followed. These options, measured by efficiency and related to principles of optimising behaviour in order to maximise particular outcomes, can at all times be over-ridden by the dictates of social relations.

Greater flexibility must be expected in patterns of behaviour. Mating networks and area adaptation insurance policies may predict many links between individuals and groups. The pattern of social alliances will however determine the direction, duration and intensity of such contacts (Chagnon 1977:100–1). As a result the regional systems will consist of an intricate social geography with patterns of shifting alliance as social formations are reproduced. The alliance network is therefore a concept that is socially and spatially larger than any local or regional group engaged in environmental and adaptive strategies. *We must be alert to the fact that local variation is a result of regional and inter-regional processes of adaptation.* These involve coping with environmental structures on a seasonal, yearly and cyclical basis as well as dealing with the constraints this places upon maintaining interactions and recruiting mates from a breeding population.

How can we operationalise any of this in palaeolithic archaeology?

Research design

We cannot dig up an alliance network, a regional adaptation, or a marriage universe any more than we can dig up a chiefdom or a predefined type of settlement. What we usually do is to hang these labels around the necks of the patterns we have discovered, thus showing, in an after-the-event manner, that our conceptual units have empirical reality. The palaeolithic literature is full of terms such as home base, hunting camps, social territories, transit stops, aggregation sites, culture areas and technocomplexes which come and go with fashion, enjoying moments of popularity as 'key' concepts and used briefly to organise quantities of palaeolithic data.

As a result, a dominant approach in palaeolithic archaeology has been to take the site as the principal unit of analysis. This is not surprising, since we can understand the significance of sites and settlements because we live in houses and settlements today. This appreciation makes it easy for us to attach significance to what is otherwise just a pile of chipped rock and features in the soil. At this stage, the reader will probably be surprised that I have not included a lengthy discussion of hunter-gatherer settlement types (Chang 1962; Campbell 1968; Bordes *et al.* 1972; Sklenář 1976; Isaac 1971; Sivertsen 1980). The reasons for such an omission should be very clear by now. Such descriptions would provide yet another instance of working towards definitions supplied from the present and which we believe should have existed in the past. However, we have seen above that behaviour is adapted with regard not to the site but rather to the region. The region is therefore the appropriate unit of analysis. All too frequently, a site-based approach has led to the definition of regions as nothing more than a number of sites falling within a conveniently sized geographical area (Chapter 5).

However, behind the concept of 'a site' lies an enduring unit of observation: the artifact. We often manipulate these units, by means of our analytical concepts, into different combinations and supply the resulting patterns with meaning by calling them sites. For the moment, we should perhaps consider artifacts solely as points of information about past behaviour at a regional scale. This alternative view brings us back to a consideration of archaeological signatures of past adaptive behaviour. At this juncture, they are necessarily signatures at a very large scale and therefore not designed to cope with questions which are interested in small scale, local variation. However, they provide an opportunity to develop flexible descriptions of the variation in the palaeolithic record rather than terms which delight in stressing partitions in a set of data. This flexibility runs counter to many archaeological expectations where partitioning and classification of materials are seen as a primary goal. I would argue that since so many aspects of the behaviour which contributed to the archaeological record are still obscure, it is premature to impose strict partitions on the data set. Consider, for a moment, three simple but basic archaeological questions:

(1) what conditions use-life and replacement rates among stone tools?
(2) how does the form of an artifact reflect either utilitarian function or non-utilitarian messaging through stylistic rules?
(3) under what conditions will discarded materials precisely reflect the activities carried out at a specific location?

The list of questions could easily be extended. I have chosen these three to show at what fundamental level of ignorance we stand in our understanding of the significance of the palaeolithic record in terms of the behaviour which created it. As a result, I think it is too early to insist that the systematics of the culture history approach (reported extensively in Chapters 4 and 5) are the only ones which demand respect for partitioning the data into analytical units.

The patterns we observe in the palaeolithic record are the product of linked, rather than separate, adaptive poses. One way to view these strategies is as a topological surface (Waddington 1978) which is pulled, stretched, pummelled and pinched by the combination of social and ecological factors which condition variation. The surface remains a unity but will exhibit such a variety of distortions and transformations that, if glimpsed piecemeal, as an archaeologist is frequently forced to do, it might be difficult to believe in the underlying, unifying principles and to comment only on the partitions instead (Stanner 1965).

How can the artifact contribute to such a unified approach through the description and decipherment of palaeolithic signatures?

The most comprehensive example is provided by Foley (1977, 1981a, b, c) in an approach termed off-site archaeology. His basic contention is that the archaeological record of mobile peoples 'should be viewed not as a system of structured sites, but as a pattern of continuous artifact distribution and density' (1981b: 163). As individuals and groups move across the landscape foraging for food, so they leave behind material residues that reflect the continuous nature of this regional behaviour. The densities of these residues will vary according to the suitability and advantages of particular resource zones; in other words they will be conditioned by the structure of resources in the environment. Through the use of the ecological concept of a home range, an off-site approach is designed to establish the links between principles of ecological organisation among mobile adaptations as reflected in the past use of space at a regional scale. It provides a methodological investigation of the significance of variable artifact densities. These have been presented as contour densities and serve in Foley's study of the Amboseli basin in East Africa as signatures of long term adaptive strategies that have withstood many environmental changes and taken place within wider contexts of social and political change in this part of the continent.

Foley's observations can be extended to other ecological conditions where the structure of resources is such that patches rather than clines in regional resource productivity and utility occur. This observation lies at the base of Binford's (1980) forager/collector settlement system spectrum. In the latter system personnel are tied to the exploitation of pin-pointed resources such as salmon streams, reindeer drives or sheep salt licks. Under such conditions the impact of ecological structures upon the formation of the archaeological record is to produce clumps and accumulations of material rather than artifacts liberally strewn over large areas. In other words, we have 'sites', but we can now perhaps understand why they might exist in pleistocene Europe as dense pockets of

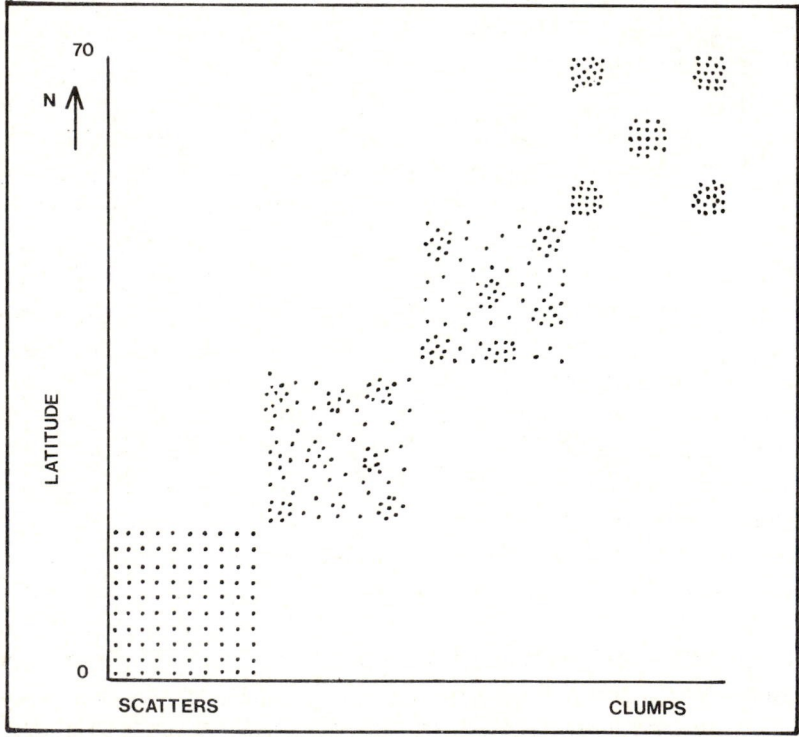

2.9 Changing settlement system signatures from dispersed to clumped residues of material culture. The trend towards dense accumulations of material, what may truly be described as sites, in the northern food poor latitudes represents a transformation of ecological structure into a predictable, distinct signature of past mobile adaptations.

Table 2.6. *Examples of some signatures at the regional scale which are dependent upon mobility and space/energy frameworks.*

Behavioural domains Spatial	Demographic	Social
Signatures settlement system, food management strategies	material and symbolic exchanges	settlement histories; world systems
Examples scatters and patches; degree of dispersion; accumulation of residues in the landscape	open/closed networks intensity; style and morphology of material culture; raw material transfers	presence/absence of settlement; core to periphery relations

artifact accumulation, while in many other parts of the world, e.g. in the Amboseli basin (Foley 1981a), they have much less distinctive formal patterning. An attempt to relate this methodological approach to a larger set of signatures is shown in figure 2.9. The implication for any research design is that the structure of the environment in a given study area carries a number of implications for the density and agglomerative signatures of an archaeological record of mobile peoples.

These settlement system signatures reflect the ordered transformation of ecological structure through past behaviour into the palaeolithic record. As such they serve as a signature for the *spatial domain* of regional systems (table 2.6). A further signature relating to this behavioural domain and indicative of space/energy constraints will be contained in food management strategies. Here patterns of storage, processing, consumption and discard that involve food materials will reflect adaptive strategies to variable ecological conditions. At the present time these signatures have been investigated only to assess the contribution different animal species make to bone assemblages in order to identify the agencies involved (Binford 1981; Brain 1981; Gamble 1983b; Hill 1983). The methodological links between table 2.6 and fig. 2.9 and the signatures in the archaeological record still have to be investigated (Binford 1978a).

Demographic regional networks will have archaeological signatures in the form of variation in patterning of artifact distributions and in the morphology of material culture (Isaac 1972; Yellen and Harpending 1972; Williams 1974; Wobst 1974). The investigation of style (Sackett 1977, 1982; Wobst 1977; Conkey 1978) in material culture represents a starting point in elucidating past behavioural signatures in this *demographic domain*.

The material and symbolic exchanges of this aspect of regional systems will obviously overlap with those from the *social domain*. This is not surprising. The tripartite division is only a means to examine a complex system, and integration must, and does, take place in the social domain. It is only at this level that the units which make up a regional system acquire meaning in terms of an entire adaptation. Examples of two signatures are given here. In the first, the concept of a world system recognises the importance of inter-regional processes upon regional and local outcomes. The impact of world systems on hunters and gatherers can be seen in a number of studies (Leacock 1954; Turnbull 1966; Murphy and Steward 1956; Marks 1976; Leacock and Lee (eds.), 1982) where external demand for furs and ivory and the pressures of surrounding state systems have transformed traditional adaptations. The second signature recognises that the checks to adaptive systems are primarily the result of social forces (Gamble 1983a; Chapter 8). In this context, the record of settlement histories in a region can be traced through standard archaeological procedures of dating and recovery. The signature thus produced measures the systematic transformation of changing pleistocene ecology into a material expression of regional adaptive success. To put it more simply, if artifacts are recovered from a region, then we know that human populations had solved the basic problems of adaptation posed by that regional environment and the resources it contained. The ebb and flow of settlement is therefore a means of monitoring, at a regional scale, the fact of adaptation and the capacity for change. The power of this signature rests on the following proposition:

that the regional environments of pleistocene Europe contained at all times sufficient energy to support mobile adaptive systems.

From this proposition it therefore follows that if settlement histories indicate an ebb at the regional level of adaptation, then the network of alliances and the development of social systems, that specify *how* the structure of resources should be exploited, had not yet occurred. This of course opens the door to an investigation of social evolution (Gamble 1983a) and we will return to a closer examination of this proposition in the next chapter.

This research design is of course constrained by the scale of investigation that has been chosen and the manner in which palaeolithic data are presented. It is impractical in Europe to demarcate 600 km^2 blocks, as Foley has done in the Amboseli study, and sample them in an intensive, systematic manner. Patterns of modern land use and geomorphological processes preclude such a rigorous implementation of a regional sampling design (Cherry and Shennan 1978). Deciding on the dimensions of regions within Europe is discussed at length in the next chapter. It is worth noting here that, by selecting the region as our unit of analysis and the artifact as the basic unit of observation, we can overcome some basic problems inherent in archaeological work. This involves the problem of the sampling paradox (Mueller 1975; Cherry *et al.* 1978) which states that in order to sample in a representative manner it is first necessary to describe the dimensions of the populations being investigated. In archaeology this is very often a case of the blind leading the blind since the purpose of fieldwork is to discover those populations which we first need to be able to describe before we can sample them! The solution to the paradox is to specify spatial units as the

Table 2.7. *Research design based upon a nested hierarchy of analytical scales for the investigation of mobile human adaptive strategies*

This approach is in contrast to the research design (table 1.4) although some of the scales and concepts e.g. artifact and assemblage, may be common to both.

SCALES	UNITS	CONCEPTS
artifact ecofact		*attributes, assemblages*
		lifespace arrangements – the layout of campsites, positioning of personnel within camps, organisation of activities such as butchering animals, sleeping, eating, mending tools
site	TYPE	*exploitation territory* – the area surrounding a site which is habitually exploited by the inhabitants of the site. Its defence is not implied (Vita-Finzi and Higgs 1970) *catchment* – total area from which the contents of a site have been derived. May be greater than the site territory
local region	SETTLEMENT	*site extended territory* – the area that supports resources used by the site's inhabitants, but that lies outside the exploitation territory and is seldom if ever visited. The resources are likely to be mobile (Sturdy 1972)
sub-region		*seasonal territory*
region	SYSTEM	*annual territory* – total area exploited by a group throughout the year (Higgs (ed.) 1975:ix) *home range* *mating network*
inter-regional		*information networks* *lifetime territory* *alliance system and network*

sampling universe and then to sample within them. These regional units can be defined as arbitrary blocks of land or geographical areas so long as they are larger than the phenomenon being studied (Foley 1978). They can of course be specified before fieldwork begins. In this way we can sample within the regional units at a variety of smaller spatial scales for the clusters of artifacts within them. The expected 'site' signature of palaeolithic Europe would produce such artifact clusters. It would be preferable also to have information from survey about the scatters between such patches, but this is not presently available.

Within the regional sampling unit a number of spatial scales are recognised (table 2.7). These in turn are associated with analytical concepts concerning the use of space at a variety of scales (Peterson 1975; Higgs (ed.), 1975; Vita-Finzi and Higgs 1970). This nested hierarchy of scales, units and concepts follows the practice of regional research designs in later prehistory (Clarke 1972; Flannery (ed.), 1976; Renfrew and Wagstaff (eds.), 1982). For example, at the scale of the living space the patterning in materials will be determined by such behavioural factors as the number of people present at that location or the organisation of repeated activities within a defined area. As we proceed up the scale to the region, so patterns of long term adaptive behaviour are reflected in the form and distribution of materials in the palaeolithic record.

The research design therefore has to accommodate existing descriptions and patterns of classification for the European palaeolithic record (Chapter 5). The important point is that these observations on assemblages and sites will be incorporated into a conceptual scheme, based on regional principles, where it is hoped an alternative significance for these groupings can be determined. In the next chapter, I will turn to the question of the ecological base in pleistocene Europe and its regional divisions. The warrant for this line of enquiry has been furnished by the discussion of contemporary hunter-gatherer behaviour at a regional scale and the relationship that variation in adaptation bears to underlying ecological structure as well as to patterns of social relations.

CHAPTER 3

PLEISTOCENE ENVIRONMENTS AND RESOURCES

> In modern terms the total output of energy in savage Europe at any one time probably never exceeded that of a single four-engined bomber.
>
> J. G. D. Clark, *From Savagery to Civilization* (1946:30)

Introduction

The claim that Europe should be regarded as a continent is not always easily supported. It is comparatively small in area and possesses no natural barriers to the east. Europe, instead, is a peninsula of the Eurasian land mass. A cul-de-sac, in Breuil's phrase, where a number of truly continental plates have either come to rest or, in the case of the eastern Mediterranean, are still settling down. The division drawn here to demarcate the continent is a familiar and arbitrary one. The high plateaux and mountains of Turkey, the Caucasus and Iran are considered to lie outside the continent while the eastern limit is set by the Caspian Sea and the Urals. In palaeolithic terms this separates what is a peripheral area (Europe) from a core area (Asia). To the south the Mediterranean acts as a more substantial barrier between the same peripheral area and yet another core (Africa). In these cases core areas would be distinguished by population numbers, productive environments, length of occupation by the human species and constancy of settlement history.

Regional criteria

I have already discussed a number of criteria for studying hunter-gatherer regional systems. In the first place their extensive use of space requires that our regions be large. In this way the possible range of variation can be encompassed. Moreover at this scale the size of the regions must be such that comparisons can be made between them on the basis of variation in the structure and organisation of energy that they contain.

A second point is that we need further concepts, such as home range and annual territory, which allow us to investigate local adaptations to conditions within this larger umbrella framework. Notice how in both cases I have assumed that the continent of Europe is indeed of sufficient size and internal complexity to provide us with a good wedge of environmental variation against which to observe palaeolithic patterns. This can indeed be demonstrated (Gamble 1984a) as I will show below (Chapter 7).

The problem here is one of carving up the European cake into appropriate regional slices. One method might be to take modern vegetation or even maps of reconstructed vegetational conditions during a glacial period and draw boundaries around the floral zones. Another means would be to take three contrasted topographical regions such as coasts, uplands and plains (Jarman *et al.* 1982) and compare the archaeological record that has been recovered from each zone. While this may be useful for looking at restricted aspects of subsistence adaptation among early agricultural formations it is hardly useful for the shifting, restless map of pleistocene Europe where, for example, sea levels repeatedly rose and fell by over 100 m. For the same reason any regional division based upon vegetational zones would be far from adequate since each floral period, as identified by palynologists, would have to have a different regional map. This would make comparison of the archaeological record between periods very difficult indeed since the basemap would always be different!

A third method could take areas of particularly active palaeolithic research, throw a suitably large spatial net over them, say 120,000 km^2, and then compare the contents of one such region with another (Gamble 1983a). This method has many practical advantages but allows the history of research to dictate too strongly in a regional approach. While it may be useful for limited comparisons of settlement histories, it is not appropriate for the long term investigation of mobile adaptive systems where the continuous use of space is recognised as a characteristic feature.

A final example of a method would be to collect data along pre-set transects both north–south and east–west across the continent. These continuous distributions could then be partitioned up into suitable regions depending on where 'breaks' or 'changes' in archaeological materials occurred. This approach would also be entirely unacceptable. The archaeological remains would be used to determine the size and shape of the regions. A procedure such as this runs counter to the purpose of a regional analysis where we want to observe variation in these materials against a space/energy framework and *not* to use them as the basis for drawing up the boundaries of a regional model.

What principles can then be used to construct a regional model and assist in the partitioning of the European continental area? Here is another instance where we need a base of strong inference, or what Binford has aptly termed 'intellectual anchors' (1982) which serve as fixed points of reference in the business of model building and interpretation. There are only three such anchors which pass the test of the principle of uniformitarianism and which can serve in the construction of a regional map of Europe with which to investigate palaeolithic adaptations. These are *latitude, longitude* and *relief.*

At first sight this trio may not appear as very robust reference points, but on our time scale of at least 700 Kyr they are the only certain benchmarks that are available. During this period ice sheets advanced and retreated, oceans rose and fell, animal communities evolved and plant communities suffered progressive simplification. As far as can be judged no single episode of either warm or cold conditions during this period was identical to any other, although we shall see that conditions were often broadly comparable. The parameters of latitude, longitude and relief certainly do not measure the relative severity of one cold phase when compared with another. That can be done only by observation of deep sea cores, faunas or periglacial phenomena. What they do however establish is the relative magnitude of climatic conditions across the continent. In very general terms the combination of latitude, longitude and relief determines the amount of solar radiation reaching a particular location on the earth's surface, as well as determining precipitation budgets. Taken together these condition such factors as the length of the growing season (Lockwood 1974), the productivity (G. Jones 1979) and composition of the vegetation layer (Pianka 1978:fig. 3.21).

During the glacial/interglacial cycle the climatic patterns of Europe underwent many changes that had varied local outcomes. On occasion what we would regard as extremely harsh climates at a continental scale would favour, in terms of the productivity and arrangement of resources, a particular local area. While latitude north, continentality east and the location of an area to upland relief will distinguish major productive regions, this possibility of locally favourable conditions must not be forgotten. In this sense the model is constructed on inflexible benchmarks but expects flexible interpretations at a local scale in terms of useable resources for human groups.

One other factor has to be added. Without it the model will appear monolithically applicable to all periods and adaptive strategies, which it is not intended to be. The dimensions of mobile hunter-gatherer systems have to be worked into the regional model. This will be done by taking the drainage division, drainage basin observations of Peterson (1976a), Rogers (1969) and others as a guideline. The use of such a guideline does not imply that what follows is a regional model based on 'natural regions' each of which might, on examination, be found to contain a distinctive cultural package. The purpose is to construct, in simple outline, a framework against which variation in past human adaptive systems which involved mobility and the consumption of resources can be investigated. The boundaries are not fixed barriers but conceptual aids in the analysis of how the palaeolithic record varies.

The regional model

The regional model for palaeolithic Europe (fig. 3.1) recognises three zonal provinces which are subdivided into nine regions. The effects of increasing latitude north on the length of the growing season are mainly responsible for the zonal partitioning. For example under modern conditions plant growth in Europe requires a mean daily air temperature of 6°C. This results today in a three

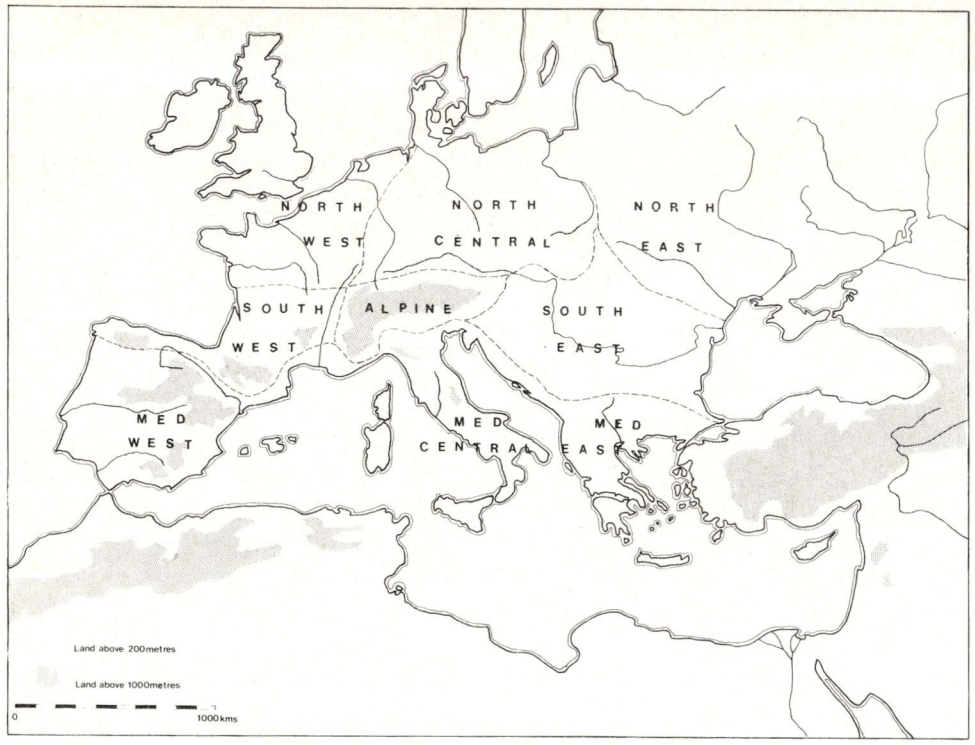

3.1 A regional model of Europe for the investigation of long term survival strategies by mobile populations.

week shorter growing season at latitude 50°N than at latitude 45°N (Lockwood 1974), and this effect can be seen in the zonal distribution of vegetation communities within the continent (fig. 3.2). Moreover the east–west axis of many of the major upland and mountain chains within Europe underscores the primary division of the continent into three provinces.

The regional boundaries are determined by factors of continentality, relief and the pattern of drainage basins within the continent. More precise descriptions of these regional divisions are given in table 3.1. The pattern of present day temperatures, precipitation and vegetation shows that the mediterranean province is principally limited by the factor of summer droughts. Vegetation productivity is also controlled by precipitation in the dry continental regions of eastern Europe, while the oceanic climate of western Europe with high precipitation and generally higher winter temperatures has a marked effect on the northern extension of temperate deciduous woodland. The general outcome of the glacial climates during the pleistocene was to make the whole of Europe much drier and therefore to accentuate these limiting factors on primary plant productivity among vegetation communities.

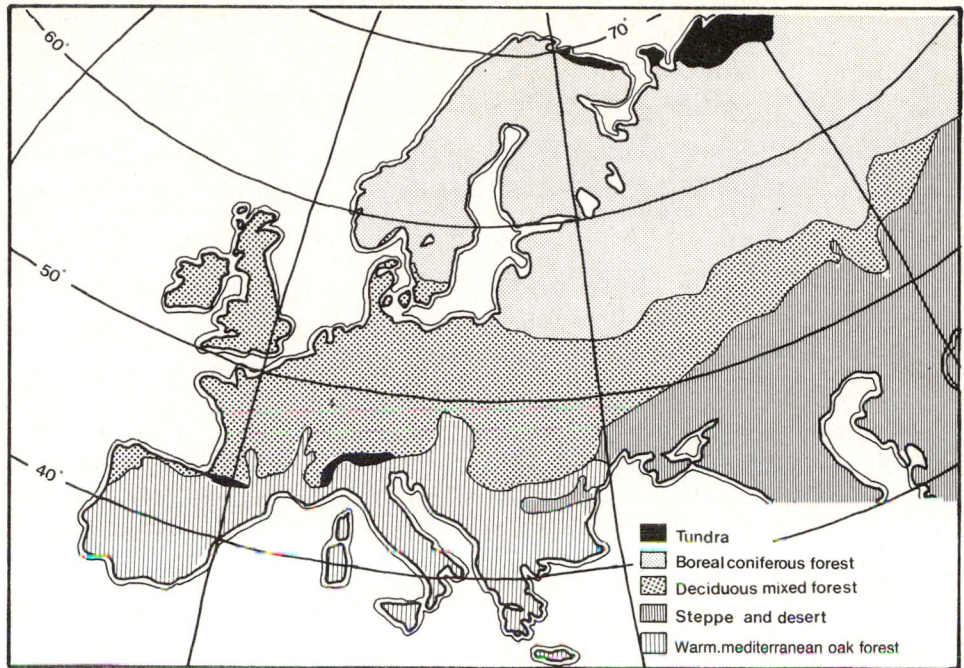

3.2 The present day zonation of vegetation in Europe (Van der Hammen *et al.* 1971).

Table 3.1. *The regions of palaeolithic Europe*

Northern Province
(NW) 1. *North-West*   Includes southern England and the extensive sea bed plain that linked it during times of low sea level with France and the Low Countries. In the east the boundary runs from the mouth of the Elbe and crosses the Rhine at its junction with the Moselle. The Köln basin, Belgium uplands and Vosges mountains are included in this region. The boundary then follows the left bank of the Saone/Rhone corridor.
(NC) 2. *North-Central*   In the east the boundary is traced between Warsaw and the line of the Dniestr river. To the south the regional boundary runs south of the Rhine at Lake Konstanz and the Danube. At Vienna the boundary crosses the Danube. The Hungarian Bükk mountains and the Moravian Karst of Czechoslovakia are included in this region.
(NE) 3. *North-East*   In the west the boundary lies to the west of the Siret and Prut rivers following the watershed of the Carpathians and terminating north of the Danube delta on the Black Sea.

Southern Province
(SW) 1. *South-West*   The boundary with the NW region is the mid-point between the Loire and Garonne estuaries and skirting north of the Massif Central to meet at the Saone/Rhone. This region includes the Saone/Rhone corridor.
(A) 2. *Alpine*   This includes the French Alps to the east of the Rhone. In the east the regional boundary follows the Alps south at Vienna. To the south the regional boundary skirts the north side of the Po valley thus incorporating the Alpine foothills into this region.
(SE) 3. *South-East*   Encloses the Hungarian basin and the Carpathian ring. It is distinguished from the ME region by the watershed of the Dinaric Alps and follows a line between the Morava and Axios rivers and then strikes for Istanbul via Sofia.

Mediterranean Province
(MW) 1. *Mediterranean-West*   The boundary with the SW region runs south of the Cantabrian mountains but encloses the watershed formed by the south east Pyrenees and the Ebro valley.

Table 3.1. – *cont.*

Includes the mediterranean coastal strip around Nice, the Ardèche and the Rhone Delta. Grades imperceptibly with the MC region.
(MC) 2. *Mediterranean-Central*   Includes the Istrian peninsula. No pronounced physical division with the Dinaric coast of the MC region.
(ME) 3. *Mediterranean-East*   Encompasses the Dinaric coast and Greece together with southern Bulgaria and Yugoslavia below the main drainage basin divide of the Dinaric Alps. .

Pleistocene chronology and stratigraphy

Against this static framework we can now observe the processes of recent earth history that took place during the quaternary period of geological time. This consists of the pleistocene and holocene epochs during which occurred, and are still continuing, a restless series of geological, geomorphological and ecological processes. The base of the pleistocene is now fixed at some 1.6 Myr (Haq *et al.* 1977). This falls within a much longer term climatic change toward glacial conditions. Within this epoch shorter term climatic fluctuations have resulted in alternate warm (interglacial) and cold (glacial) episodes.

The causes of climatic change and climatic fluctuations are still not entirely clear. One theory for the origin of ice ages favours variation in the orbital geometry of the earth which would affect the amount and distribution of solar energy reaching the earth's biosphere (Hays *et al.* 1976).

The internal divisions of the Quaternary have traditionally been based upon inferences about climatic fluctuations from the observation of pollen, faunal remains, geomorphological events and a host of other data sources. This has led to classifications of stages and substages within a framework which recognises a cycle of interglacial and glacial periods. For many years this has been based upon a *discontinuous* record derived from the surface of the European continent. Ever since the pioneering work of Agassiz (1840) and the monumental synthesis on Alpine glaciations by Penck and Brückner in 1909, work has been directed toward building up a picture of pleistocene history by piecing together the fragmentary evidence of periglacial features, moraines, glacial tills, river terraces, loess profiles, pollen sequences, molluscan faunas, beetle assemblages and animal bones, particularly of the rodent species. It has not proved possible to find deposits where all these strands are contained in a single entire history of the European pleistocene. Either the passage of ice sheets over the surface of the earth has obliterated earlier evidence or breaks in the deposition have interrupted the build up of a continuous sequence.

The results of these researches led to the classic Alpine chronology of four major glaciations separated by three interglacials (table 3.2). While this has always proved difficult to match with the evidence for glaciations from the north European plain (Butzer 1971; Flint 1971; Woldstedt 1958), this small number of cycles has formed the backbone of pleistocene and palaeolithic chronologies. It continues to do so in many parts of Europe where the familiar terms of Günz, Mindel, Riss and Würm, or their local equivalents, are still

Table 3.2. *Conventional correlations between terrestrial pleistocene sequences of glacial (italic) and interglacial periods (West 1977a)*

British Isles	Alps	NW Europe	European USSR
Devensian	*Würm*	*Weichselian*	*Waldai*
Ipswichian	R/W ?	Eemian	Mikulino
Wolstonian	*Riss*	*Warthe*	*Moscow*
Hoxnian	M/R		Odintzovo
Anglian	*Mindel*	*Saale*	*Dniepr*
Cromerian	G/M	Holstein	Lichwin
Beestonian	*Günz*	*Elster*	*Oka*

applied (Laville *et al.* 1980; Cârciumaru 1980; Quaternary Sistema 1982).

While these schemes are still widely followed, two developments have sounded their eventual demise as the framework for pleistocene chronologies. The developments are: (1) the advent of absolute dates for the entire 1.6 Myr and (2) the stratigraphic record obtained from cores drilled into the ocean floors. Together these developments have revolutionised quaternary geology (Bowen 1978) and the repercussions are now being felt in palaeolithic archaeology.

The marine record

The deep sea sediment cores provide a *continuous* stratigraphic record of pleistocene events that can be fixed at key points by absolute dates. The uppermost sections fall within the range of C14 while the sediments from the cores can be tested for magnetic polarity. Palaeomagnetic studies have shown that at 0.73 Myr the earth's magnetic field changed from reversed to normal polarity. This marker, which was previously dated to 0.7 Myr (Mankinen and Dalrymple 1979), divides the Brunhes epoch of normal polarity from the Matuyama epoch of reversed polarity. Within the Brunhes occur some shorter term events and excursions when the earth's magnetic field reversed for a brief period of time. The Brunhes/Matuyama boundary is a stratigraphic marker of worldwide significance since it can be identified in ocean cores and terrestrial volcanic rocks where it has been dated by K/Ar isotope decay methods. The boundary now marks the division between the lower and middle pleistocene (Butzer and Isaac (eds.) 1975).

With such solid stratigraphic markers it has proved possible to construct a record of pleistocene stratigraphy from many hundreds of cores drilled into the floors of the world's oceans. The coring of the ocean floor produces sediment columns which are made up of the skeletons of small marine organisms or foraminifera. The foraminifera are largely composed of calcium carbonate and when alive these minute skeletons absorb oxygen isotopes. The ratio of two of the oxygen isotopes ^{16}O and ^{18}O is known to vary due to the simple process of evaporation. If evaporation is high, then more of the lighter isotope ^{16}O is extracted leaving the oceans enriched in the heavier ^{18}O. At the time of ice sheet formation, during the glacial part of the cycle, we find that sea levels fall as moisture is drawn off and used to build continental ice caps. At such times the oceans of the world become positively charged with ^{18}O. Since the foraminifera absorb both ^{16}O and ^{18}O in the proportions that were then standard in the oceans it is possible to see that if a column of sediment is analysed for the ratio of these two isotopes in the foraminifera it contains, then an accurate record of continental ice volume to ocean volume can be obtained. The measurement of the ratio is made using a mass spectrometer and expressed in parts per thousand. The curves are not palaeotemperature readings but statements about the size of the oceans. By inference it follows that the cause for oceans becoming smaller and enriched in ^{18}O is the formation of continental ice sheets. In this way the cores are informing us not only about the size of the oceans during the

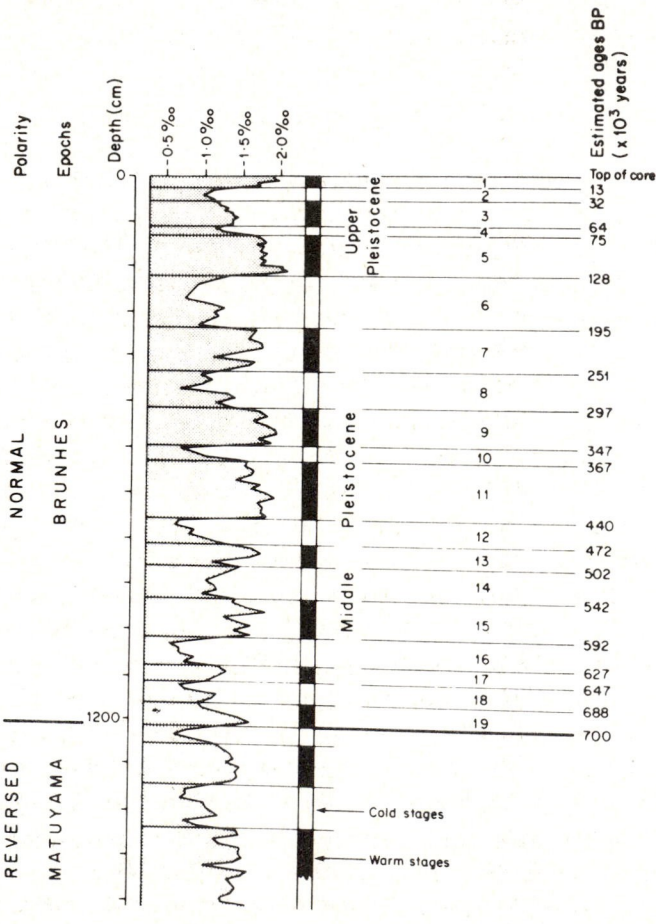

3.3 The stratigraphic record of the Pleistocene as established from core V28–238. The 'saw tooth' shape measures the changing amounts of ^{18}O which indicates the relative size of the world's oceans and ice caps (Shackleton and Opdyke 1973; Gamble 1984b: fig. 2.3).

pleistocene, but also about contemporaneous events on the continental land masses.

The core which is now used as a standard reference for events during the past 0.7 Myr comes from the Solomon Plateau in the Pacific Ocean and is number V28–238 (fig. 3.3) (Shackleton and Opdyke 1973). While this may seem a long way from Europe, it must be remembered that the advantage of deep sea cores is that they record events of local significance, e.g. the European glaciations, at a global scale, and while there are differences in the shape of the curves that are produced from the cores this is due to factors such as the mixing and formation of sediments and not to the differential effect of local climate on local ocean isotopic composition.

The Brunhes/Matuyama boundary occurs in core V28/238 at a depth of 1200 cm (fig. 3.3). Above this boundary, some nineteen stages have been determined in the saw-tooth curve and, by assuming uniform sedimentation rates, the ages for these boundaries have been calculated as a function of depth in the core (table 3.3). These form eight complete interglacial (odd stage numbers) and glacial (even stage numbers) cycles.

Some correlations and cycles

The current aim of quaternary studies is to correlate the evidence from the deep sea continuous record with the more fragmentary data from the land. An excellent summary of present land–sea correlations is provided by Kukla (1977) and Bowen (1978:table 10.1; 1979). It is possible to establish some firm correlations for the middle and upper pleistocene from the observation of profiles in loess deposits. This has been done at Červený Kopec (the red hill) at Brno in Moravia, Czechoslovakia. Here the section consists of wind blown loess deposits up to 100 m in thickness and distributed across five terraces of the Svratka river. Furthermore, it has been possible to establish the position of the Brunhes/Matuyama boundary in the profile. This same chronological marker has been identified in the Kärlich clay pit located in the upper part of the main terrace of the Rhine (Brunnacker 1975, 1980). At both these locations and in other loess sections of central Europe (Kukla 1975), it has been possible to subdivide the deposits above the Brunhes/Matuyama into eight cycles. Within each cycle, there is evidence for soil formation, periglacial features and loess deposition. The cycle is described in greater detail below (pp. 79–82). This pattern of eight cycles at Červený Kopec (CK) and Kärlich correlates well with the eight interglacial/glacial cycles noted in the deep sea cores (table 3.3). A similar series of eight cycles during the middle and upper pleistocene is also recognised through the analysis of the percentages of subtropical and transitional water foraminifera species in core K708–7 (Ruddiman and McIntyre 1976) which provides an excellent check to the ^{18}O isotope values.

The only pollen diagram which provides evidence for this same period of time comes from Tenaghi-Phillipon in Macedonia, Greece (Van der Hammen *et al.*

Table 3.3. *A correlation chart for the European pleistocene*

		Polarity	V28–238 stages	V28–238 estimated ages Kyr	K708–7 Cycles	Loess Cycles	Brno Terraces	Alpine Terraces	Kärlich Succession	Northern Europe	British Isles	Macedonia
UPPER PLEISTOCENE	BRUNHES	Blake	1 2 3 4 5a 5b 5c 5d 5e	13 118	A B	B	CK 1	Würm	J	Weichsel Eemian (Schleswig-Holstein)	Devensian Ipswichian (Trafalgar Square)	Pangaion
MIDDLE PLEISTOCENE	BRUNHES		6 7a 7b 7c 8 9 10 11 12 13 14 15 16 17 18 19	128 251 347 440 502 592 647 730	C D E F G H	C D E F G H I	CK 2 CK 3	Riss-Würm Riss Mindel-Riss Mindel Günz-Mindel	Ja H G F	Warthe Eemian (Northern Germany) Reburgh Eemian (Amersfoort) Saale 'Holstein' Elster Holstein Elster Cromerian Cromerian	Ipswichian Brandon? Wolstonian Ipswichian Ilford Anglian Hoxnian Anglian Hoxnian Cromerian Bestonian Pastonian	Symvolon Lekanis Complex Boz Dagh Complex Phalakron
LOWER PLEISTOCENE	MATUYAMA	Jaramillo Olduvai	20 21 22 23 24	782 900 1.61 Myr		J K	CK 4 CK 5	Günz Donau-Günz	Bb C D E Ba	Cromerian Menapian		

Source: After Bowen 1978: table 10-1

1971). This core is 120 m in depth and yet did not reach the base of the peat deposits. The changing proportions of tree pollen with grass and herb pollen indicate a number of cycles of vegetational change. The core is undated and the correlations necessarily tentative.

The final points of correlation (table 3.3) concern the traditional frameworks of Alpine and north European glaciation. Kukla (1977) has shown that the Eemian marine transgression onto the north European plain consists of at least three separate stratigraphic events correlated with deep sea stages 5, 7 or 9. The possible stage equivalents for the north European moraines which survived later erosion are also indicated in the table. When it comes to correlating the four-part Alpine glaciation based on the river terraces of the Alpine foreland, the problems are equally great. What is quite clear is that terraces form during both interglacials and glacial episodes and not just during the glacial part of the cycle, as earlier stratigraphers had argued. At Červený Kopec the loess covers five terraces back to the Brunhes/Matuyama boundary. The breaks between the terraces occur in deep sea stages 6, 12, 18 and 22 at c.180 Kyr, 450 Kyr, 650 Kyr and 850 Kyr respectively. Kukla has suggested that the Alpine terrace breaks of Riss/Würm, Mindel/Riss, Günz/Mindel and Donau/Günz correspond to the fourfold terrace system at Červený Kopec.

Great care needs to be taken with these correlations. In particular it is easy to become confused by the use of the same terms to describe different phenomena and parts of the pleistocene. For example, the Alpine terminology used in rock shelter studies in France (Laville *et al.* 1980) cannot be assumed to correlate with the deep sea record (table 3.3) just because it happens to use the familiar terms Günz, Mindel, Riss and Würm which elsewhere have been provisionally correlated to a continuous and dated stratigraphic column.

Interglacial/glacial cycle and long term climate change

The study of loess sequences in central Europe has led Kukla (1975) to identify a repetitive pattern of deposits and sediments. These form the basis for the recognition of interglacial/glacial cycles. Each cycle contains a light upper series of poorly developed soils and a lower dark series of well-developed soil horizons. Distinctive marklines allow the stratigrapher to note the transitions and to subdivide the cycle further (fig. 3.4). The two series are divided into three stages. The first two stages occur in the lower series. This begins with a deposit of hillwash loam, followed by the formation of a forest soil of either brown earth or para-brown earth type. Above this, in the second stage, are found less well developed soils of steppe or chernozem type interlaced with distinctive marker horizons and pellet sands. At Červený Kopec the profiles show the large scale deposition of loess during this third stage. The first stage corresponds to interglacial conditions while the second and longest stage saw climatic conditions vary from temperate to glacial. The final stage however represents the

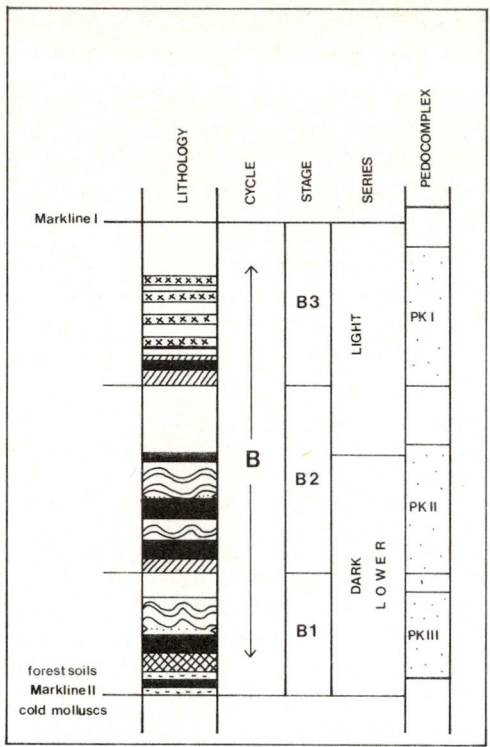

3.4 A single interglacial/glacial cycle as seen in the development of different soil horizons in the loess sections of central Europe (Kukla 1975:116, fig. 3).

glacial maximum in any one cycle. The cycles vary in duration. The last eight have an average duration of 90 Kyr.

Vegetational cycles have been reconstructed from pollen studies. According to these analyses the interglacials, as represented in pollen deposits, proceeded through a four-stage cycle of development and decline (table 3.4) (Van der Hammen *et al.* 1971). There are however considerable problems in correlating these pollen-based interglacials with the pattern of interglacial conditions indicated by the deep sea records.

It has been claimed, using the old chronology, that during the pleistocene, the climate became progressively colder (Frenzel 1973). On the basis of floral evidence Frenzel has argued that the pre-Tiglian cold period in the Netherlands saw annual temperatures lowered by between 8° and 10° C and annual precipitation reduced by some 150–250 mm. By contrast the Weichselian saw annual temperatures reduced by 13° C and precipitation by between 300 and 350 mm. The trend in climatic fluctuations, with each full cycle, was therefore towards a progressive climatic change where the peak of the cold phases became both colder and drier (*ibid.*:181). This, Frenzel maintains, is most convincingly shown in the smaller areas covered by the Alpine and north European ice sheets, and can be seen not only in the position of the moraines but also in the relative

Table 3.4. *Interglacials as recognised through pollen analysis*

(a) General scheme through the four stages of interglacial forest development (M.O.F. = mixed oak forest). (Turner and West 1968)

Vegetational aspect (Early glacial)	Zone	Important pollen types (Herb)	Vegetation (Herb dominated)
Post-temperate	IV	*Pinus, Betula* (higher herb)	Coniferous forest (more open)
Late-temperate	III	M.O.F. genera+ *Carpinus (Abies)*	M.O.F. with other tree taxa not prominent in zone II
Early-temperate	II	M.O.F. genera	M.O.F.
Pre-temperate	I	*Betula, Pinus*	Coniferous forest
(Late glacial)		(Herb)	(Herb dominated)

(b) Zone characteristics of four interglacials established through pollen analysis from England (West 1970) Cr = Cromerian, Ho = Hoxnian, Ip = Ipswichian, Fl = Flandrian. N.A.P. = non-arboreal pollen.

Cromerian	Hoxnian	Ipswichian	Flandrian
CrIV *Pinus, Picea, Betula, Alnus*	HoIV *Pinus, Betula* N.A.P. higher %	IPIV *Pinus,* N.A.P. higher %	—
CrIII M.O.F., *Abies, Carpinus*	HoIII M.O.F., *Abies Carpinus*	IpIII *Carpinus*	FlIII Deforestation affected by human activities low % *Ulmus, Fagus, Carpinus*
CrII M.O.F., high *Ulmus* low % *Corylus*	HoII M.O.F., *Taxus Corylus*	IpII M.O.F., *Pinus Acer,* high % *Corylus*	FlII M.O.F.
CrI *Pinus, Betula*	HoI *Betula, Pinus*	IpI *Betula, Pinus*	FlI *Betula, Pinus*

Source: After Stuart 1982: tables 2.4 and 2.5

values for the isotope curves (fig. 3.3). This trend was accompanied by greater reductions in winter as opposed to summer temperatures and begins in the Elster glaciation when a community of cold tolerant species including reindeer, mammoth, musk ox and bison become established. At Červený Kopec it is noticeable that after stage 13 (loess cycle F) the soils in succeeding cycles show much less mature development than those in the pedo-complexes which preceded this stage (Kukla 1975:fig. 28).

Human adaptations in Europe have to be viewed not only against the repeated fluctuations of climate on a cyclical basis every 90 Kyr but also against the long term climatic change toward drier and colder glacial stadials during the middle and upper pleistocene.

There is, of course, still much to be discovered about the internal characteristics of the eight cycles since the Brunhes/Matuyama boundary. The cores show however that the last warm period (stage 5e) saw the smallest volume of ice for the last 730 Kyr. Furthermore, the relative values of these peaks increase during the last twenty-two stages (fig. 3.3). The cores indicate that the transition from full glacial to interglacial conditions is extremely rapid, giving us the characteristic saw-tooth shape to the curve. Ice and ocean volumes are rarely stable for any sustained period of time. A good example of this is provided by stage 7 which appears in many cores as two warm peaks separated by a sharp glacial episode (Ninkovitch and Shackleton 1975).

The last interglacial/glacial cycle (isotope stages 5–2)

It is now possible to construct a detailed picture for the last interglacial/glacial cycle. This corresponds to the upper pleistocene and will have to serve as a generalised description of the earlier cycles for which there is as yet only fragmentary information.

The upper pleistocene can be divided into four stages (table 3.5), the first three of which are broadly comparable to Kukla's stages (fig. 3.4).

Table 3.5. *The last interglacial/glacial cycle. This corresponds to the upper pleistocene*

Stage	Kyr bp	Deep sea isotope stage	Loess cycle	Proportion of entire cycle %
1. Interglacial	128–118	5e	B1	9
2. Early glacial				
(a) temperate woodland	118–75	5d,c,b,a	B2	37
(b) glacial	75–32	4,3	B2,3	37
3. Full glacial	32–13	2	B3	17
4. Late glacial	13–10	1	A1	—

stage 1: interglacial, 128–118 Kyr

There is now considerable evidence that the last interglacial was of extremely short duration. Shackleton (1969) divided stage 5 in the deep sea cores into five sub-stages of which the first (5e) was significantly different in the isotope record (fig. 3.5). Sub-stage 5e represents the lowest ice volume during the last 730 Kyr and is therefore regarded as the last interglacial. A study of the foraminifera species in a number of north Atlantic cores (Ruddiman *et al.* 1977; Mangerud *et al.* 1979) supports this same division since in 5e low percentages are recorded for a species which has a preference for cold polar waters.

The deep sea record places this interglacial between 128 and 118 Kyr, and a number of absolute dates are now available from raised beaches which confirm this as a period of much higher sea levels than the present day. The Tyrrhenian beach in Italy, some 4–5 m above present sea level, is dated to 129 and 128 Kyr (Brancaccio *et al.* 1978) while on Mallorca Butzer (1975) has dated his Y1 (Hemicycle B) beach, 9–15 m above modern sea level, to 125 Kyr ± 10 Kyr. This high sea level has been dated to 120 Kyr in a number of other beaches around the world, principally in Barbados, Bermuda, New Guinea, Florida and California (Bowen 1978:163).

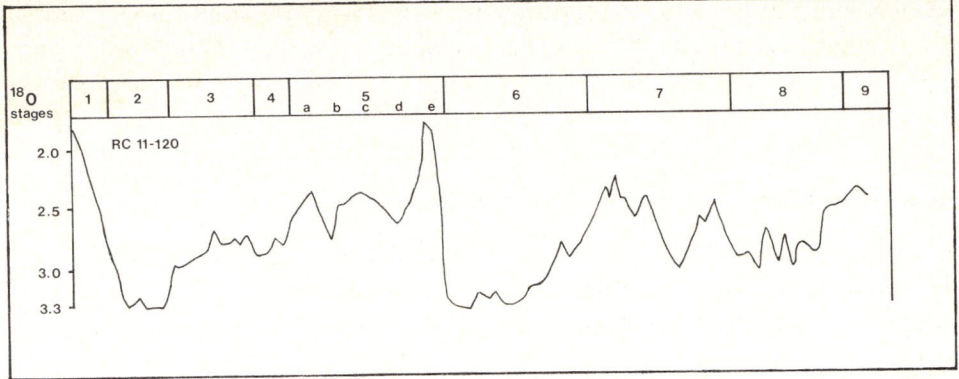

3.5 The upper pleistocene as established from core RC 11–120. The low ice volume in sub-stage 5e, the last interglacial, is very apparent as are the rapid shifts between glacial and interglacial conditions. (Hays *et al.* 1976).

A date of 120 Kyr obtained by 230/Th/234/U on flowstone in the Victoria Cave in England (Gascoyne *et al.* 1981) is associated with a very characteristic interglacial large mammal community that contains hippopotamus. In the Czechoslovakian loess profiles, the forest brown earths with the warmth-indicating snail, *Helicigona banatica*, correspond to isotope stage 5e and fall before the Blake magnetic excursion at 110 Kyr. The two further temperate peaks in the loess glacial cycle B2 (Kukla 1975, 1977) which correspond to sub-stages 5c and 5a, do not have this same characteristic molluscan species. This evidence, backed with absolute dates, substantiates the interpretations of sub-stage 5e as full interglacial conditions.

There is however still considerable debate over this interpretation. Interglacials as identified by pollen analysis (West 1977a) have generally been judged as stages of much greater duration, when a cycle of forest regeneration took place. However, an important pollen profile from Grande Pile in the Vosges mountains of north-east France (Woillard 1978, 1980; Woillard and Mook 1982) provides a very good match with the deep sea core divisions of stage 5 (fig. 3.6). At Grande Pile and Tenaghi-Phillipon in Macedonia, Greece (Van der Hammen *et al.* 1971), the first temperate forest phase is marked by a pollen maximum of deciduous oak mixed forest, and in both profiles this is of greater magnitude and longer duration than the two succeeding temperate pollen phases. Moreover the isotope record from the oceans is supplemented for the upper pleistocene by cores drilled through the ice of the Greenland ice cap (Dansgaard *et al.* 1970, 1971; Johnsen *et al.* 1972). The core from Camp Century is 1390 m in length and the [18]O composition of the ice provides a stratigraphic record comparable to that from the oceans. The main problem lies in dating these cores and that is presently achieved by modelling ice mass formation.

When the fifth stages in these various long sequences are compared (fig. 3.6), we see a repeated picture of three temperate peaks, separated by very short cold phases. Furthermore, the first temperate peak is always the most marked. The

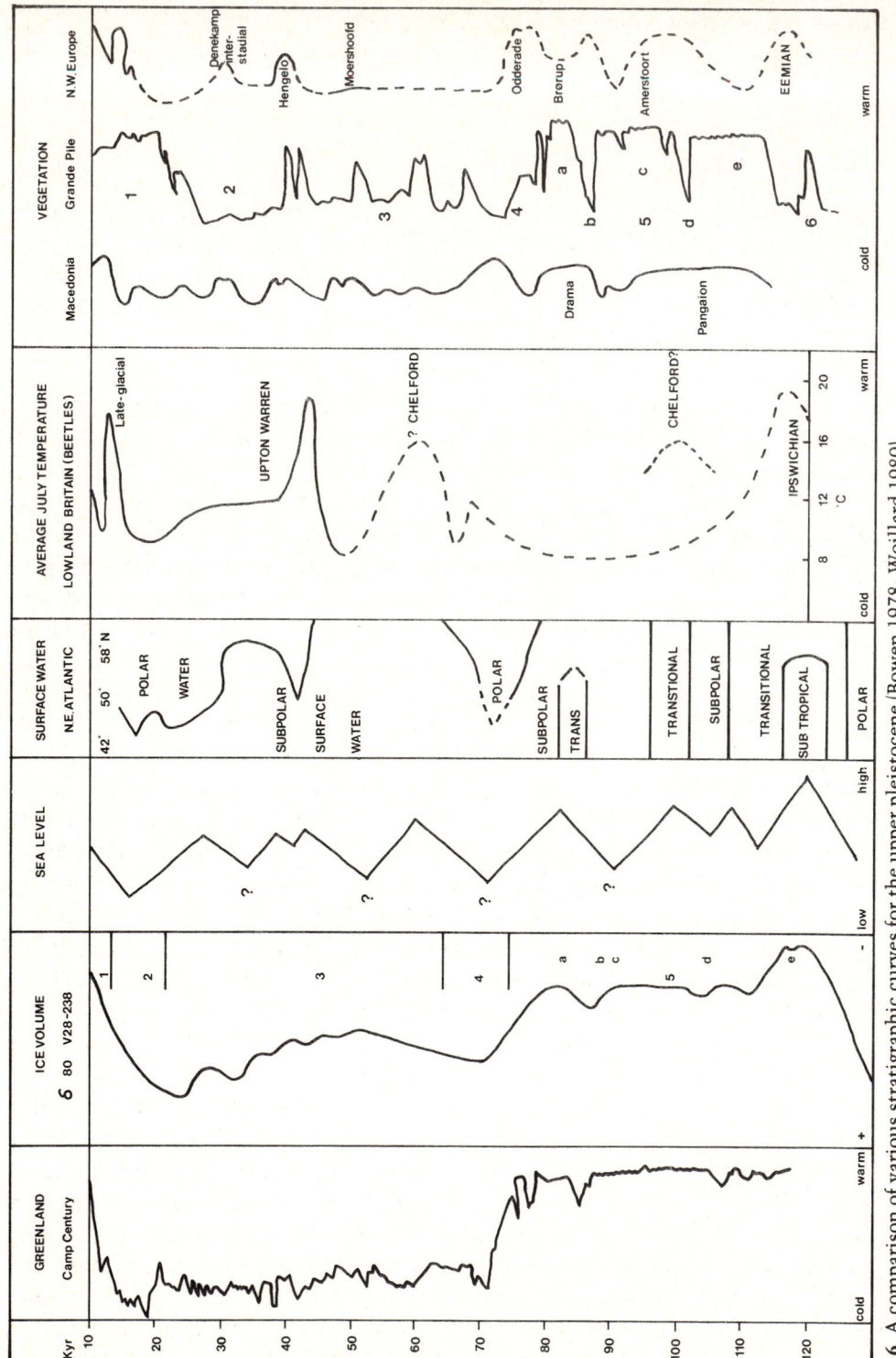

3.6 A comparison of various stratigraphic curves for the upper pleistocene (Bowen 1978; Woillard 1980).

Camp Century peaks have been correlated with the dated raised beaches on Barbados at 125 Kyr, 105 Kyr and 82 Kyr which occur at successively lower levels.

stage 2a, b: early last glacial, 118–32 Kyr

This stage can be subdivided into an early phase (a) with temperate woodland conditions in northern Europe, interspersed by brief periods of intense cold, and a glacial phase (b) with low temperatures and a significant drop in ocean level. The second phase begins at 75 Kyr and is marked, in the deep sea record of core V28–238, by the stage 4/5 boundary.

Sub-stages 5c and 5a are both preceded by short lived but very dramatic cold episodes. These can be seen very clearly in the Camp Century isotope curve and, judging by the pollen profile from Grande Pile, exerted a considerable influence over vegetation (Woillard 1978).

A detailed chronological and climatic record for this entire stage has been constructed by Butzer (1981) from the analysis of cave sediments in northern Spain. His analyses propose a correlation between the cave sediments and isotope stage 5 in the deep sea record. Moreover, he links the cold sub-stages 5b and d in the Spanish cave sediments with sediments that have been classified to the Würm I glacial stadial by Laville (1975: Laville *et al.* 1980) in the classic rock shelter deposits of south-western France.

The method used by Laville is a development from the pioneering work of Lais (1941) into the environmental and chronological information that could be gained from studying the sediments in caves. The rock walls and ceiling of caves are subject to weathering by frost, solifluction and water action. The degree of frost weathering can be determined by differences in the texture of the pieces of limestone that are deposited. The degree to which they have been rounded or retain their sharp edges, their size and the type of sediment matrix in which they are found are all pointers to the amount of moisture and the extent of cold at the time of weathering. On the basis of such analyses, Laville has constructed a detailed local chronostratigraphy for both Würmian and Rissian deposits (fig. 3.7) from selected key sites. His findings have important implications for the interpretation of assemblage variation (Chapter 5).

There are however some difficulties with the scheme that stem from the discontinuous nature of the record being used. Laville's scheme closely follows the model of Penck and Brückner who stated that the Günz, Mindel, Riss and Würm gravel terraces of the Alpine foreland were laid down under glacial conditions and that the intervening interglacials were periods of erosion. Consequently the rock shelter deposits are thought by Laville to be exclusively cold climate in origin. According to his interpretation the increased precipitation during both interglacial and interstadial stages would result in erosion. Therefore breaks in the cave sediment sequences are interpreted as these

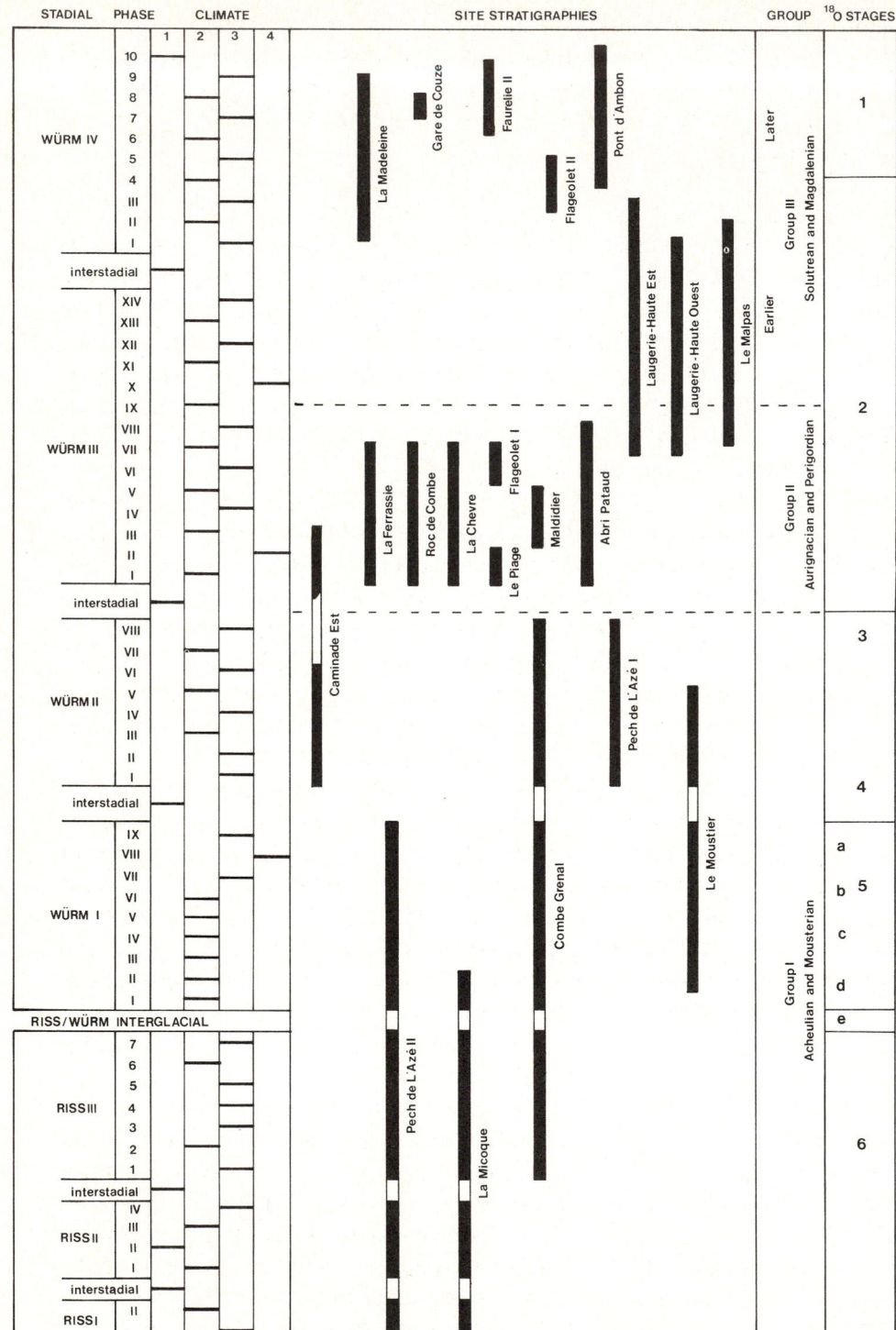

3.7 The chronostratigraphic scheme for penultimate and last glacial rock shelter sites in south-west France. A suggested correlation with the deep sea record for the upper pleistocene has been added (after Laville *et al.* 1980:135, fig. 6.1; Dennell 1983b). Climate states: 1 = temperate; 2 = mild and humid; 3 = cold and dry; 4 = very cold and dry.

temperate stages. This means that hardly any palaeolithic material from the Périgord is dated to either interglacial or interstadial conditions. This might seem strange since these same rock shelters today possess thick layers dating to the post-glacial and formed under modern interglacial conditions. Neither is this view of erosion under temperate conditions shared by Farrand (1975:64) also working in the Périgord, or by Brunnacker and Streit (1966; Brunnacker 1982:128) dealing with cave sediments from southern Germany. Butzer (1981:175) is quite certain that Laville's Würm I stage corresponds to at least the cold sub-stages 5d and b, and Würm II with isotope stages 4 and 3. Neither does Butzer see any difficulty in assigning sediments from the Cantabrian caves to either sub-stage 5e or to the later sub-stages and the less temperate interstadials. Dennell (1983a, b) has recently correlated the C14 dated profile of Grande Pile (Woillard and Mook 1982) with the Würm I and Würm II sequences as recognised in France and his scheme is in agreement with that proposed by Butzer (1981) for the Cantabrian data.

The evidence from the isotope records and pollen diagrams in northern and southern Europe points to a gradual trend towards colder conditions. Tree cover becomes restricted as the drier and colder conditions were established. As a result western Europe became more continental in climate as the moisture bearing winds from the Atlantic were deflected north to begin building the ice sheets (Lamb and Woodruffe 1970). As the moisture became locked up in these ice caps during isotope stage 4, so extensive areas of land in the shallow seas around northern Europe became available for settlement. The cold, but still relatively moist, conditions favoured periglacial activity in a large active layer and it is after 75 Kyr that some of the largest fossil ice wedge casts, pingos and patterned ground features are found. This does not mean that temperatures reached their lowest values during parts of this stage since the size of these features depends on factors such as moisture and the insulating effects of snow as much as on the severity of sub-zero temperatures. Shallow rooted vegetation growing on the surface of the active layer would have provided insufficient check to the movement through solifluction of slope deposits. This would have been a period when erosion of soils and sediments would have been particularly marked, as with the formation of gravel terraces and red bed erosion in the Mediterranean (Vita-Finzi 1969). These ephemeral streams would have extended over large areas, and the lack of vegetative cover would have provided ideal conditions for wind erosion of alluvial deposits. It has been estimated (Starkel 1977) that loess accumulated at a mean rate of 0.07 mm a year during this stage in central Europe. This would have resulted in the episodic build up of loess. Erosion would also have attacked valley slopes with differing effects as those facing south, and so receiving more sun, were subject to greater daily temperature differences and hence more erosion under freeze-thaw conditions. Such conditions would have some impact upon the distribution of resources at a local level. If vegetation could take advantage of the greater solar radiation on

Table 3.6. *The ages of some interstadials in the northern and southern provinces*

	Region	Province		Kyr bp
Lascaux	SW		(1)	16.5–18
Laugerie	SW		(1)	19.2
Tursac	SW		(1)	22–23
Denekamp		Northern	(2)	29–32
Hengelo		Northern	(2)	37–39
Moershoofd/Upton Warren complex		Northern	(2)	43–50
Odderade		Northern	(2)	58 or (3) 73
Brørup		Northern	(2)	61–63.5 or (3) 76–78.5
Amersfoort		Northern	(2)	65–68 or (3) 80–83

Source: (1) Arl. Leroi-Gourhan 1980; (2) Shotton 1977; (3) Kukla and Briskin 1983.

south facing slopes then this would have provided a richer grazing environment. However, the reverse might hold under conditions of poor plant cover with these same slopes consisting almost entirely of eroded scree deposits with little soil cover.

After 75 Kyr the isotope curve at Camp Century shows a change to rapid oscillations leading towards much colder conditions. The period commences with three interstadials recognised in Holland and north Germany at Amersfoort, Brørup, and Odderade (table 3.6). Of these the Brørup is generally regarded as the most significant temperate interstadial (Mania and Toepfer 1973) during which time fir (*Abies*) and spruce (*Picea*) together with birch (*Betula*), pine (*Pinus*) and willow (*Salix*) became established in northern Europe. According to traditional dating, the Brørup interstadial is probably contemporary with the English Chelford interstadial (Coope *et al.* 1971) which is based upon the analysis of habitat tolerances for beetles incorporated in the sediments. We should not expect that these interstadials will be found all over the continent of Europe at the same time since local conditions of precipitation and aridity will have imposed controls over vegetation. Moreover, the age of these early interstadials is still open to debate. Kukla and Briskin (1983) have argued that the Odderade interstadial has been dated some 15 Kyr too young and that it should fall, along with Brørup and Amersfoort, *before* the stage 4/5 boundary at 75 Kyr.

These early interstadials are followed in the Netherlands by lower pleniglacial conditions of treeless polar desert. This is followed by a number of interstadials referred to in the Netherlands as the middle pleniglacial. These are named after the type localities of Moershoofd and Hengelo where the pollen profiles have been dated by C14 (table 3.6). In England a pronounced interstadial based on beetle analysis has been described from Upton Warren (Coope *et al.* 1971).

These north European interstadials are securely dated and the evidence of

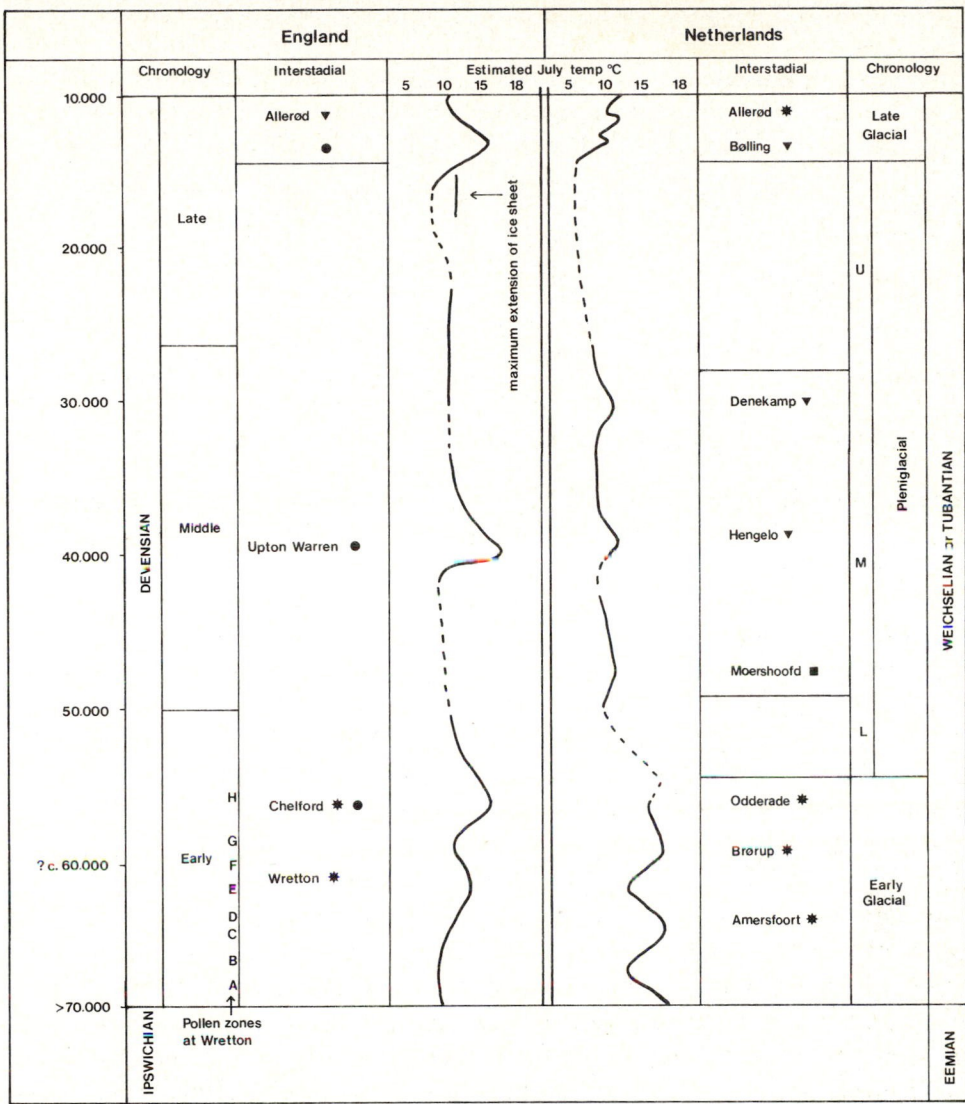

3.8 The last glacial period as recognised from several lines of evidence in parts of northern Europe (West 1977b:236, fig. 2).

either pollen or beetles has allowed temperature estimates to be made (fig. 3.8) for these areas. It is not yet possible to correlate such data over wider areas of Europe. Indeed great caution needs to be exercised with such correlations, as has been discovered with work on loess profiles of central Europe (Fink 1976; Kukla 1977:333).

stage 3: full glacial, 32–13 Kyr

This stage begins with the Denekamp interstadial as recognised in pollen profiles from western Europe, but after 29 Kyr there is a marked intensification of glacial conditions. In central Europe, the annual deposition of loess increased

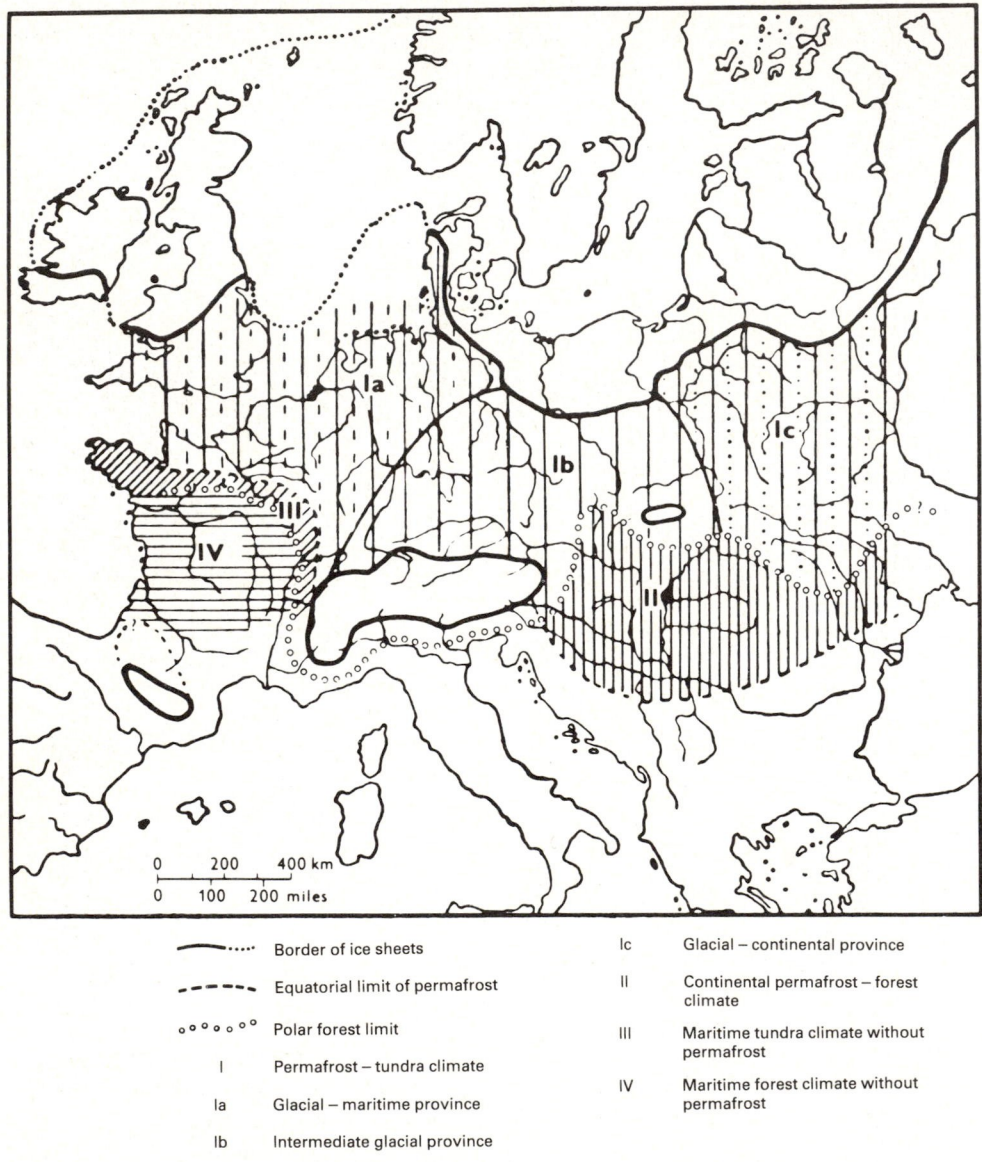

- —————····   Border of ice sheets
- – – – – –   Equatorial limit of permafrost
- ∘∘∘∘∘∘∘∘   Polar forest limit
- I   Permafrost – tundra climate
- Ia   Glacial – maritime province
- Ib   Intermediate glacial province
- Ic   Glacial – continental province
- II   Continental permafrost – forest climate
- III   Maritime tundra climate without permafrost
- IV   Maritime forest climate without permafrost

3.9 The climatic regions of Europe during the last glacial maximum at 18 Kyr (Poser 1948:65, fig. 6).

to 0.4 mm (Starkel 1977) while only poor soils formed during the slight ameliorations to warmer conditions. A rapid expansion of the ice caps onto the north European plain and out from the Alps created an ice free corridor in central Europe (fig. 3.9) where this loess was mainly deposited (Poser 1948). Precipitation after the ice sheet extension appears to have been low and conditions are generally described as extremely cold and dry. A decrease in solar radiation would have resulted in less evaporation so that there would have been many bodies of standing water in the open treeless landscape. This resulted in the Caspian Sea increasing in size at a time when the earth's oceans were shrinking. It has been calculated that the Caspian Sea loses a layer 1000 mm thick through evaporation every year. With a reduction in July temperature of 10° C from present values it is likely that only 400 mm would be evaporated and that even if this coincided with an annual fall in precipitation of between 15%–20% this

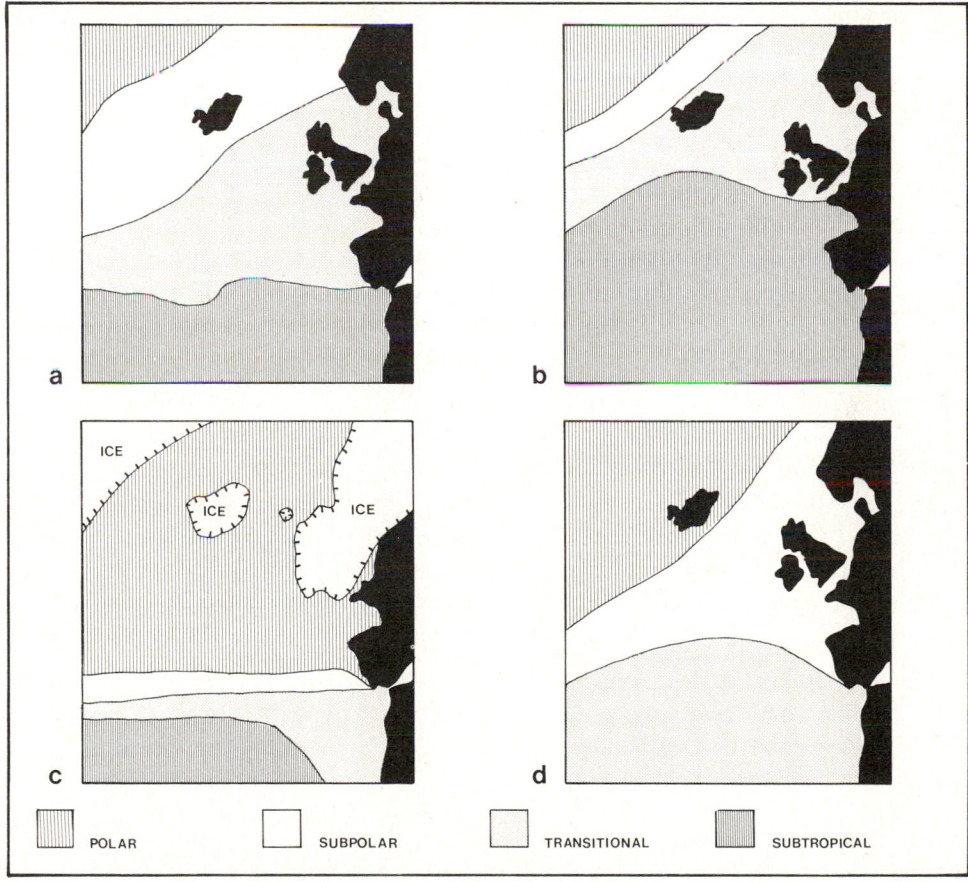

3.10 Reconstructions of the water masses in the north Atlantic at four moments during the upper pleistocene (Ruddiman and McIntyre 1976; Bowen 1978). Key: a = present day; b = 120 Kyr – last interglacial; c = 18 Kyr – the glacial maximum; d = 9.3 Kyr – late glacial/post glacial interface.

would still result in a substantial growth of the area covered by this inland sea (Frenzel 1973).

At the height of this glacial stadial at 18 Kyr (Peterson *et al.* 1979), the earth's sea level fell between 100 and 150 m. Ocean currents were depressed southwards (fig. 3.10) and this resulted in sharp temperature gradients in sea temperature forming below latitude 42° N off the Iberian peninsula (Ruddiman *et al.* 1977). The western Mediterranean also experienced a sharp fall in sea temperature relative to the eastern part of this sea (Thiede 1978; McCoy 1980). Previously this whole basin saw roughly equivalent ocean temperatures.

The sharp fall in sea levels also extended coastal plains in the Mediterranean, creating dry land in the Adriatic (Van Andel and J. Shackleton 1982) and joining large islands such as Sicily to the mainland. In the north, moraines, such as the Dogger Bank, were deposited on what are today submerged landscapes as well as along the north European plain on an east–west axis. An extensive plain linked France with England.

Periglacial features can be dated to this stadial but, due to less moisture and a thinner active layer, they are not so pronounced (Kaiser 1960; Frenzel 1968a, b, 1973; Semmel 1973; Starkel 1977; Velichko and Berdnikov 1973; Cârciumaru 1980). The intense weathering of limestone spalls from the roof and walls of caves (Schmid 1969; Farrand 1975; Laville *et al.* 1980) does provide a measure of the intense dry/cold conditions at this time.

In northern Europe, parts of this stage have been described as polar deserts with severe restrictions on plant growth (Van der Hammen *et al.* 1971). Selected valleys may have provided refuges for small stands of willow but the tree line appears to have been depressed below latitude 42° N. Forests and woodland were also curtailed in the mediterranean area since the lack of moisture resulted in both dry summers and winters. As a result the dominant vegetation in upland areas was *Artemisia* (wormwood) steppe while at lower elevations some scattered stands of pine (*Pinus sylvestris*) are indicated in the pollen diagrams (Bottema 1974; Florschütz *et al.* 1971; Frank 1969). In southern France pollen extracted from a number of cave sediments has shown three short interstadials, Tursac, Laugerie and Lascaux that pre- and post-date the [18]O isotopic maximum at 18 Kyr (table 3.6) (Arl. Leroi-Gourhan 1980).

A great deal of attention has been devoted toward correlating the interstadials of this stage between the regional sequences of Europe. Some of the complexity for Europe north of the Alps can be gauged from a recent compilation by Otte (1981) (table 3.7).

There are two problems involved in making such correlations. In the first place there are the procedures involved in partitioning a set of data into stages (Bowen 1978: chapter 4, fig. 4.7). The same body of data might be divided up at very different points according to the purposes of the study and the way the intervals are recognised. As a result it is not always clear whether similar units are indeed being compared in the procedure of establishing a correlation. The

Table 3.7. Correlations between interstadials and glacial stadial periods during the last ice age
Notice how the absolute chronology for such schemes places the last Riss/Würm 'interglacial' in the later part of stage 5.

Kyr bp	SW and NW (France)	NW (Netherlands)	NC (Rhine)	NC and SE (Austria)	NC (Czech)	NE (USSR)	General Synthesis (Otte 1981)	Deep sea core chronology
15	WIV	Late Glacial	Laacher See tuff				IV Late Glacial	1
20	III/IV							
25			Soil III Eltviller tuff	WIII	WIII	Ostashkov	III/IV Laugerie Lascaux	2
	WIIIb						III Last pleniglacial	
30		Denekamp (Kesselt)	Soil II	II/III = Stillfried B WII	Stillfried B	Mologo-Cheskna	Arcy-Denekamp	
35	WIIIa				WII		III	
40	II/III	Hengelo (Hoboken)	Soil I	Gottweig	Podrahem I/II	(= Briansk)	II/III Les Cottés	3
45	II				Ib	Kalinin		
50	I/II	Moershoofd (?) (Poperinge)		WI	Loopstedt	Verchne-volski	I/II	
	Ib							
55		Odderade						
60								
	Ia			Ia	Kalinin 1	I		
65		Brørup Amersfoort		Stillfried A				4
70								
	Riss/Würm	Rocourt	Metternich tuff			Mikulino	Riss/Würm	
75								
								5a

Source: Otte 1981: table 1, with additions

second problem relates to the very different lines of evidence which are used. An interstadial defined by beetles will differ from one defined by either land snails, pollen or soil horizons. The inference from statics to dynamics, from the environmental sample to the palaeoecological system is just as great as that which faces the archaeologist in the investigation of cultural residues and past behaviour. Moreover these different lines of evidence will not respond uniformly across the continent to changing climatic conditions. They deal with different scales of environmental reconstruction at different time rates (Butzer 1982).

stage 4: late glacial, 13–10 Kyr

An example of this is provided by the fourth stage or late glacial. Polar desert conditions in northern Europe began to ameliorate at 13–14 Kyr and at the same time the isotope record shows a significant change (Dansgaard *et al.* 1971). The rapid passage from glacial to interglacial conditions, known as instant deglaciarisation, was under way by 16 Kyr and by 8 Kyr the melting of the northern ice cap domes was complete (Flohn 1979). The late glacial has been documented in detail from the pollens preserved in the peat bogs of the Netherlands, Denmark and North Germany, and on this evidence, assisted by a chronology derived from melt water varves, and now dated by C14, the following scheme has been established (fig. 3.11). The cold open phases are characterised by *Dryas octopetala* with additional steppe elements. The Dryas phases are preceded and followed by two interstadials, Bølling and Allerød. The former sees the appearance of a park tundra with birch while in the Allerød pine re-established itself in northern Europe for the first time since the Odderade interstadial (Van der Hammen *et al.* 1971).

However, work by Coope (1977) on beetle and insect assemblages from England has shown quite convincingly that the thermal maximum for the Bølling interstadial in fact took place rather earlier than the C14 dates for the pollen interstadials indicate. The beetles respond to changes in temperature and climate at a much faster rate than trees and therefore provide a more precise marker for the interstadial periods. When reference is made to either Bølling or Allerød this usually means that the event being described is the pollen based interstadial rather than the actual period of warmer temperatures during the late glacial.

This may sound confusing. What it highlights is the need for taphonomic studies to improve the power of inferences made by palaeoecologists. Most palaeoecological work is descriptive (Peterson *et al.* 1979:table 1) rather than processual. In other words it deals with static observation rather than with the analysis of dynamic systems. Palaeoecologists have also had to rediscover the principle of uniformitarianism (Imbrie and Newell 1964; Johnson 1960; Fagerstrom 1964; Behrensmeyer and Hill (eds.) 1980) and are currently in the

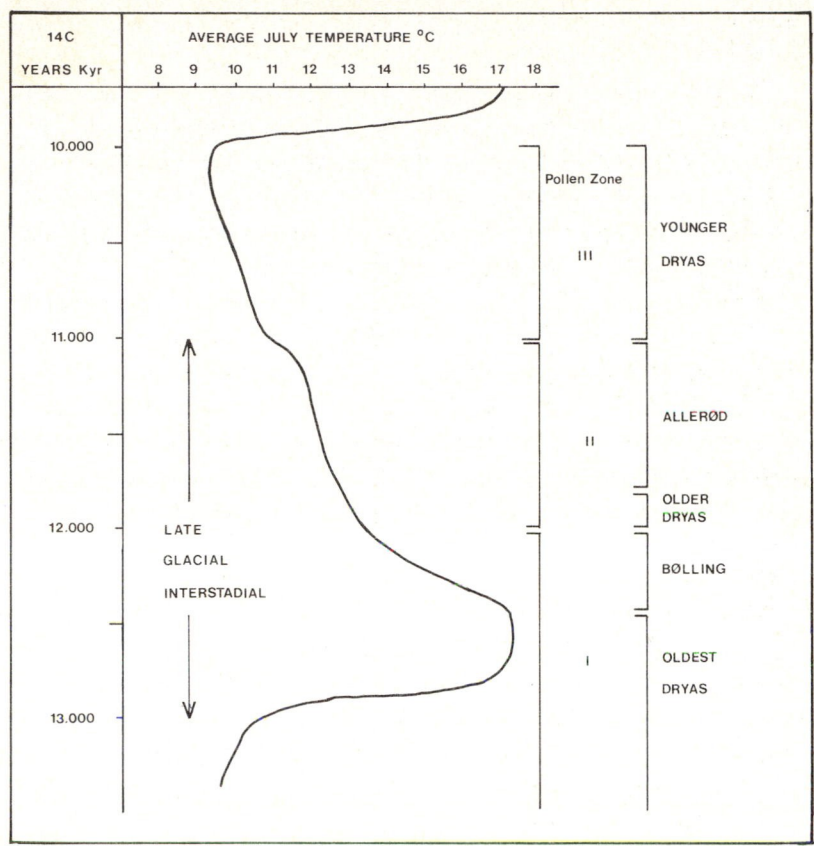

3.11 The late glacial as recognised by coleoptera (curve) and pollen zones (roman numerals) (Coope 1977).

process of investigating the nature of their record of past ecosystems. This is needed particularly in pollen studies to answer the question of *how* palaeobotanical samples are formed.

There is also another, more general level of palaeoecological explanation that requires attention. An impressive example of the integration of results and synthesis leading to explanation is provided by members of the CLIMAP project (Climate:Longrange Interpretation, Mapping and Prediction) where explanations for the maintenance of particular climates in equilibrium were sought by using models of general circulation patterns and compared against palaeoenvironmental data from deep sea cores for the last glacial maximum at 18 Kyr (CLIMAP 1976; Gates 1976; Peterson *et al.* 1979).

Further accounts of pleistocene events and reconstructions can be found in a number of excellent summaries (Butzer 1971; Flint 1971; Frenzel 1973; West 1977a) which build on the earlier works of Woldstedt (1958), Büdel (1951), Firbas (1949–52) and Zeuner (1959).

Synthesis

Up to this point I have provided a regional model of Europe and an outline of pleistocene history. We now have to start asking questions which can utilise this wealth of static palaeoenvironmental data to understand something about past human behaviour as it is coded into the palaeolithic record. Moreover we need to put forward some predictions based on the regional model which can be tested with palaeolithic data in later chapters.

From the perspective of human adaptation, rather than quaternary geology, the divisions of the pleistocene highlight some important long term survival conditions. We have already noted that the three stage division for the loess cycle (Kukla 1975) is an unequal sandwich with the substantial second stage of varied conditions accounting for three quarters of the last interglacial/glacial cycle. Even if this second stage is subdivided, the two subdivisions still account for almost 40% each of the 115 Kyr long cycle (table 3.5). Our knowledge of the earlier seven cycles back to the Brunhes/Matuyama boundary is as yet very sparse when compared to that for the last cycle. However in a schematic fashion I have tried in fig. 3.12 to see whether this same second stage accounts for the majority of the last 0.73 Myr. To do this I have taken core V28-238 and measured the amount of time that falls between sub-stage 5c and above the glacial maximum at 18 Kyr. This does not imply that conditions were entirely comparable within these sections of the curve. But in the absence of more detailed information, this rough guide is the only available evidence for long term conditions.

This analysis shows that some 56% of the last 700 Kyr falls within the second stage. Furthermore the figure shows just how little time was taken up with interglacial conditions comparable to sub-stage 5e and that the full glacial stage 3 accounts for most of the time when stage 2 conditions did not prevail. If we

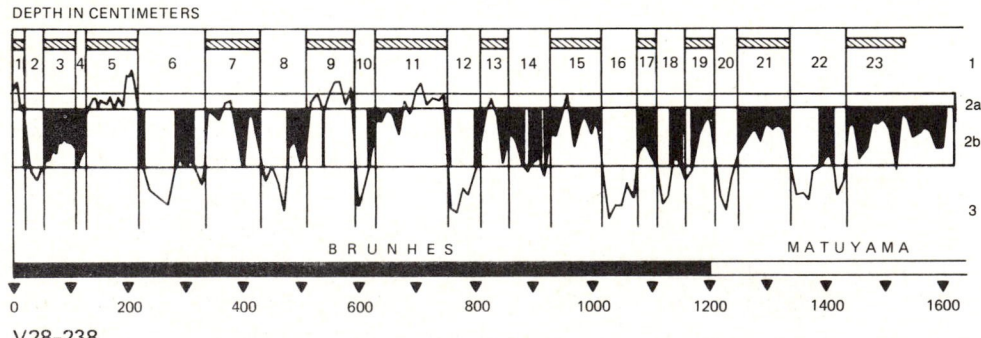

V28-238

3.12   The division of the middle and upper pleistocene according to the three stages of the interglacial/glacial cycle. This exercise is designed to discover which part of the cycle accounts for the majority of the last 730 Kyr and consequently to which long term conditions human groups would have been most advantageously adapted.

further subdivide the stage 2 section at the 4/5 isotope boundary it is clear that some 60% of this stage during the past 0.7 Myr corresponds to the cold, dry and eventually glacial conditions as shown in stage 2b of the last cycle between 75 and 32 Kyr.

We can see from these figures that prolonged occupations of the European continent by palaeolithic groups required a solution to the problems of survival in stage 2 environments. Continuous occupation in the continent would have needed further adaptations to the extremes of interglacial and glacial maxima. It might be suggested from this analysis of the deep sea core record that if colonisation and occupation of the continent occurred only during either stages 1 or 3, it was hardly worthwhile in the context of the long term evolution of the species. No sooner had they become established than populations would have had to retreat since few of the episodes during which these stages figure were of sustained duration.

The key resources during stage 2 of any of the eight interglacial/glacial cycles would be animal, and in particular the large herbivores (see below, p. 103). The acquisition of meat by either hunting or scavenging/foraging and the implementation of storage strategies would have been vital for coping with: (a) the shorter growing seasons of these northern latitudes and (b) the difficulties of finding alternative food sources in either the temperate woodland or open herb phases of stage 2. The regional palaeolithic record should, therefore, be approached according to the models of animal dependent strategies outlined in the last chapter, although I repeat again that this is not an exercise in fitting our data to an ethnographic model. The latter is only a starting point for establishing patterns of variation in palaeolithic strategies.

These predictions do not however take the regional model into account. Neither have I begun to examine what resources were in fact available, and how these vary between the provinces and regions of our model so that further patterns in the formation of the palaeolithic record might be predicted.

Regions and resources

One way to use the regional model is to observe changes in plant productivity along a latitudinal transect. These quickly establish that evidence exists for the differential distribution of plant productivity across the continent. The first transect (fig. 3.13) provides a profile through the NW, Alpine and MC regions and contrasts interglacial with full glacial conditions. In another transect (Van der Hammen *et al.* 1971:fig. 3) which runs between Bordeaux (SW region) and the Hague (NW region), the area around 52° N is characterised by polar desert while at 45° N in the SW region shrub tundra grades into birch forest.

A third transect (fig. 3.14) shows vegetational changes and the southward extension of permafrost in the NE, SE and ME regions. Information is poor for the northern and southern provinces during the early stages of the pleniglacial

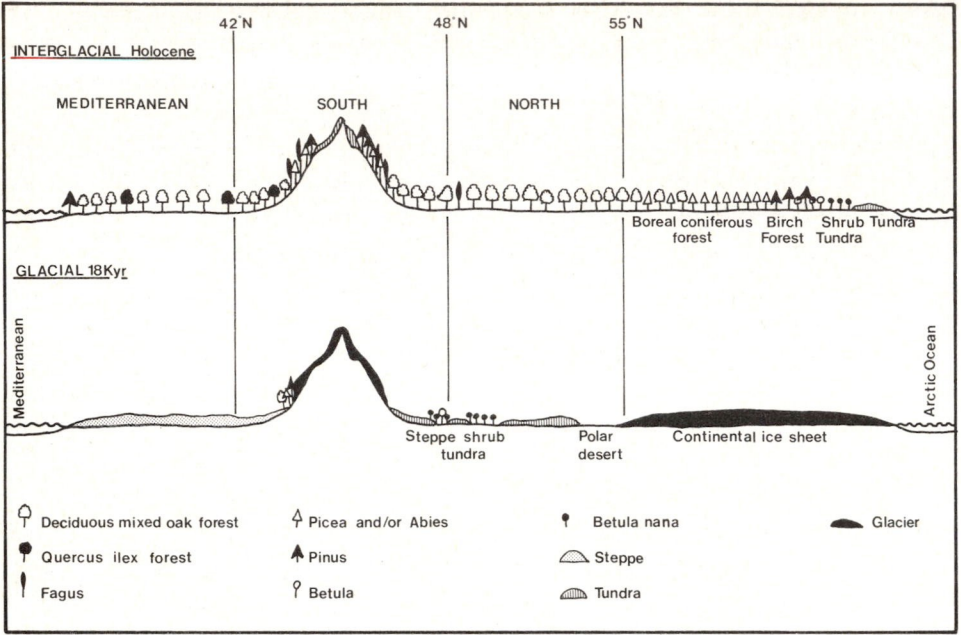

3.13 A transect of climatic and vegetational conditions through the NW, Alpine and MC regions during an interglacial and glacial maximum (Van der Hammen *et al.* 1971).

but we can see that permafrost conditions at this time only just penetrate the southern province. These extend further south during stage 3 when permafrost reaches 45° N at the time of the glacial maximum.

While these transects provide a qualitative assessment of plant productivity between the provinces of the regional model we need to know more about the structure of the environments and the organisation of resources within them. Human adaptive systems are not to be characterised in terms of blocks of vegetation or labelled by a dominant plant species in a vegetation zone, and we need to first look at the potential resource to man that is contained in the primary plant production. Once again the last cycle will be used as a model.

Plant resources

(a) general

Grime (1977) has examined three strategies which plant species adopt to cope with selection factors in the environment. These strategies are linked to factors of disturbance, stress and competition in plant communities. Those plants adapted to factors of disturbance are often *r* selected. In other words they are short lived annual herbs with a great investment in reproduction, as shown by the quantity of seed produced. Periglacial processes in the active layer above the permafrost would contribute to disturbance. Furthermore, low temperatures

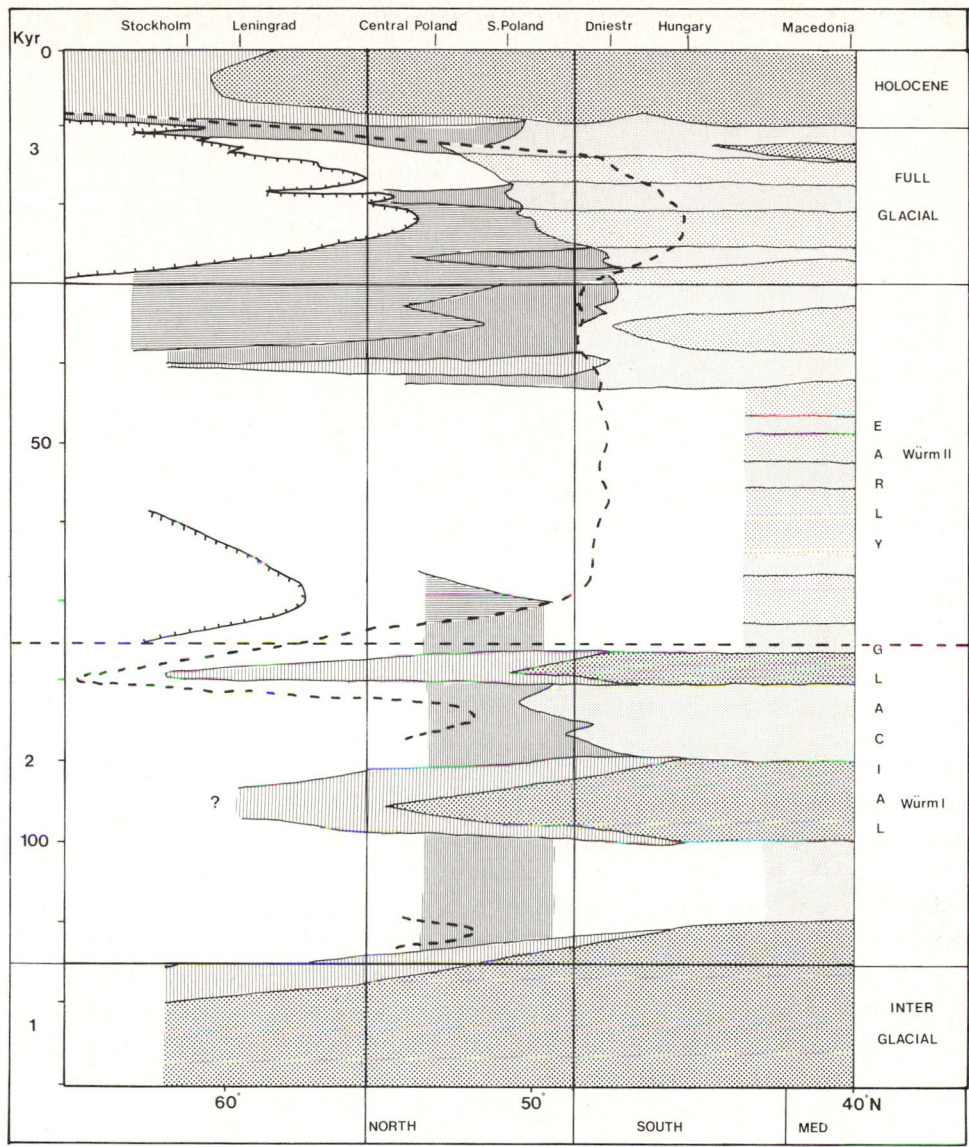

3.14 A transect of climatic and vegetational conditions through the NE, SE and ME regions (Starkel 1977:363, fig. 7).

Table 3.8. *Values for net primary production and mature biomass for world vegetational units (Lieth and Whittaker 1975:tables 10.1 and 10.2), and for range in animal biomass (Redmann 1982:table 4)*

Primary production grams/m^2/year	Mean	Mature plant biomass kg/m^2	Large animal biomass kg/ha^{-1}
Tundra 100–400	140	0.1–3	0.36–4.3
Boreal forest 200–1500	500	20–52	
Temperate forest 600–2500	1000	24	
Temperate grassland 100–1500	500	?–3	9.2–36.4
Mediterranean zone 250–1500	800	26	

would contribute to stress by limiting the growing season and hence production. Environments with low rainfall would also have a comparable influence on plant strategies. Lichens and evergreen shrubs are characteristic of the temperature limited stress strategies while the dry arid environments are characterised by mediterranean species such as the evergreen oak and olive. In Grime's view, these are predominantly *K* selected species where the investment in reproduction is low, life span high, and as a result the vegetation is extremely resilient. It may not be very productive (table 3.8) but the plant base will not fluctuate widely, as can be the case among species coping with disturbance conditions.

Deciduous trees and larger shrubs represent a climax phase of vegetation succession where the competitor strategy has paid off. Here the individual species have captured the available energy and turned it into biomass with in some cases high annual primary productivity.

These contrasted strategies have important implications. There will be little by way of usable food for human populations from the *K* selected stress strategy species unless domestication increases potential yields. The evergreen boreal forests which represent a combination of competitor/stress strategy are likewise *K* selected and produce little for human consumption. Those annual herbs and grasses which are *r* selected to cope with factors of habitat disturbance share common features with other *r* selected species in that size is small but productivity enormous. Very little of this productivity is usable by man unless it has first been converted by animals into protein.

(b) interglacial, 128–118 Kyr (stage 1)

This stage saw the only significant opportunities for the use of plants. The deciduous forests with oaks, beech, hazel and many other shrub species which bear fruits and berries would have provided a rich storehouse of potentially usable energy (Clarke 1976). Moreover, many of the plant resources, and in particular the nuts, could be stored for use on future occasions thus recommending them further as a reliable staple.

However, while these forests are extremely productive in terms of quantities of usable food, it is the size of the package in which the food resource comes that presents problems for exploitation strategies. Each beech nut and acorn has to be opened to extract the energy they contain. In the case of bitter acorns a long and time consuming process of leaching and preparation has to be followed (Gifford 1936; Freeman 1981:110). As a result reliability of the resource has to be offset against the high cost tariffs involved in gathering, preparing and cooking such food. Even though plant foods may be high in nutrient value, they are high in labour costs and consequently may be ignored in a subsistence strategy in favour of less costly resources which contain the same nutrients but in less abundance (Keene 1981).

The same holds for wild fruits and berries. They are available in northern latitudes only during short seasons, which presents problems for their scheduling into the subsistence strategy. A great many have to be collected and stored in a very short time if they are to serve any other purpose than immediate consumption. Storage would have to be an important part of any strategy which used these resources on a large scale (Oberg 1973).

The distribution of these resources in interglacial stages would be in the southern and northern provinces (fig. 3.2), while the boreal and mediterranean forests limited by cold and summer moisture respectively would by comparison have provided very few resources.

(c) early glacial, 118–32 Kyr (stage 2a,b)

This stage consisted of a wide variety of vegetational conditions. The first phase (2a) saw a diminution in the deciduous component of the interglacial forests and woodlands (Woillard 1980) and consequently a reduction in the resources that human groups could use. The glacial sub-stage 2b is recognised as being cold and moist in the southern and northern provinces, and as a result periglacial activity will have disturbed the open herb communities. The interstadials are characterised by larger amounts of herb pollen and some boreal forest elements. In the mediterranean province the open *Artemisia* steppe and herbs are interspersed only by small percentages of pine and birch pollen during interstadial phases.

While there may have been few plants for human groups to exploit during this long and varied phase these environments were certainly extremely productive and exhibited a unique combination of floral and faunal elements (Stanley 1980; Hopkins *et al.* 1982).

(d) full glacial, 32–13 Kyr (stage 3)

This stage saw an intensification of the restrictions on plant productivity throughout all the European regions as climate became dry and very cold. In the northern province and the SE region woodland was restricted to sheltered gallery locations along the major river courses and consisted of dwarf shrubs and willow. Polar desert conditions have been described for the glacial maximum of the Netherlands (Van der Hammen *et al.* 1971). This came about as a result of lower temperatures. It has been estimated on the basis of insect assemblages that temperatures in England were depressed some 7° C below the present July average and 13° C below that for January (Coope *et al.* 1971). This pattern is repeated throughout the northern and southern provinces during the last glacial maximum, with January temperatures falling more than those estimated for July. According to Coope (*et al.* 1971:fig. 2), the reduction in temperature would have reduced the growing season, defined by a mean daily temperature of at least 6° C, from some six months to c.3.5 months in England. This is comparable to the growing season in present day high latitude tundras (Lockwood 1974). In Europe the length of growing season would have increased slightly with latitude S but in the mediterranean province would have been curtailed once again by low precipitation under glacial conditions. Frenzel (1973:158) has estimated that annual precipitation in the steppe areas of the NE, NC, SE and ME regions did not exceed 300 mm per annum, which represents a reduction in the precipitation budget of some 50%. The deposition of loess in NC, NE and SE regions during these arid phases is another indicator of this extreme continentality affecting vegetation patterns. Pollen profiles from Lake Vico (Frank 1969) in central Italy, and Padul (Florschütz *et al.* 1971) in southern Spain indicate arid steppe conditions in this stage. At Lake Vico temperature estimates based upon the pollen analysis give the full glacial July average as 9° C and January as 8.7° C below those of the present day. Moreover, annual precipitation is estimated at 200–400 mm, whereas today at Lake Vico (altitude 507 m a.s.l.) this is 1400 mm per annum. Comparable dry steppe conditions have been reported by Bottema (1974) from the Lake Ioannina area of north-western Greece, ME region.

There was however one region, the SW, which due to a combination of factors enjoyed a more diverse and productive vegetation layer. The region under full glacial conditions was neither too far north to suffer a drastic reduction in growing season nor too far east to feel the effects of aridity that accompanied the glacial advance. Periglacial phenomena are found in the region but are never as marked as those in other southern and northern regions. These conditions combined to produce a comparatively rich vegetational mosaic for grazing species (Paquereau 1974–5).

(e) summary

Many of the descriptions of last glacial environments use terms such as tundra or steppe. In the case of the former this should not be taken to imply conditions that can be found today in the low productivity tundras (table 3.8). Even with lowered temperatures and the presence of ice sheets in Europe the latitudinal position of the continent would have resulted in higher rates of photosynthesis.

The shorter summer growing season would have been extremely productive as plants went through their very rapid reproduction cycles.

This discussion has once again had to concentrate upon conditions during the last glacial/interglacial cycle. These can only act as a guide to possible conditions in earlier cycles. Reconstructions of vegetation during this cycle and for earlier periods can be found in Frenzel (1967, 1968a, b, 1973) and Grichuk (1973). The brief review present here has however shown that plant resources were available in Europe for direct exploitation by man only during the full interglacial stage. However the high labour costs that would have been involved in the use of these resources mean that any strategy which depended on these resources for a significant component of the diet would have had to possess a very high level of exploitive efficiency that is only achieved through intricate time scheduling and long working hours. These cost tariffs are not appreciably reduced by either an improvement or investment in technology. They are a general consequence of plant based subsistence strategies.

Large mammal resources

The conclusion that animals provided the key resource in the colonisation and prolonged settlement of Europe is not novel. Meat has always been regarded as the staple diet of palaeolithic hunters. Stone projectile points, cave art and the abundant animal bones from caves and open sites have supported such a view. The exploitation costs for the plant foods that were available during much of the interglacial/glacial cycle provide another line of argument supporting this traditional view. However, the diverse animal communities of middle and upper pleistocene Europe also contained species with a wide range of exploitation costs and risk. These same resources were also the basis for carnivore strategies, and the use of large mammals in palaeolithic food management strategies has to be considered within this wider community framework.

(a) herbivores

It is not possible to divide the herbivore species into three communities corresponding to the three stages of the interglacial/glacial cycle. Animal species are tolerant of a wide range of environmental conditions and limiting factors. This makes it difficult to associate a particular group of species with a set of climatic conditions inferred from pollen analysis or other sources. At best the large herbivores of pleistocene Europe display a gradient in habitat preference from full interglacial forest conditions to full glacial environments (table 3.9). The mammal community of the pleistocene was unique in its combination of present day arctic species (musk ox, reindeer, wolverine, arctic fox) with sub-tropical carnivores (hyena, leopard, lion), mid-latitude temperate herbivores (red deer, roe deer, aurochs, pig), steppe (saiga antelope, ass) and mountain

Table 3.9. *The major associations of biotope and animal communities as outlined by Hescheler and Kuhn (1949:171)*

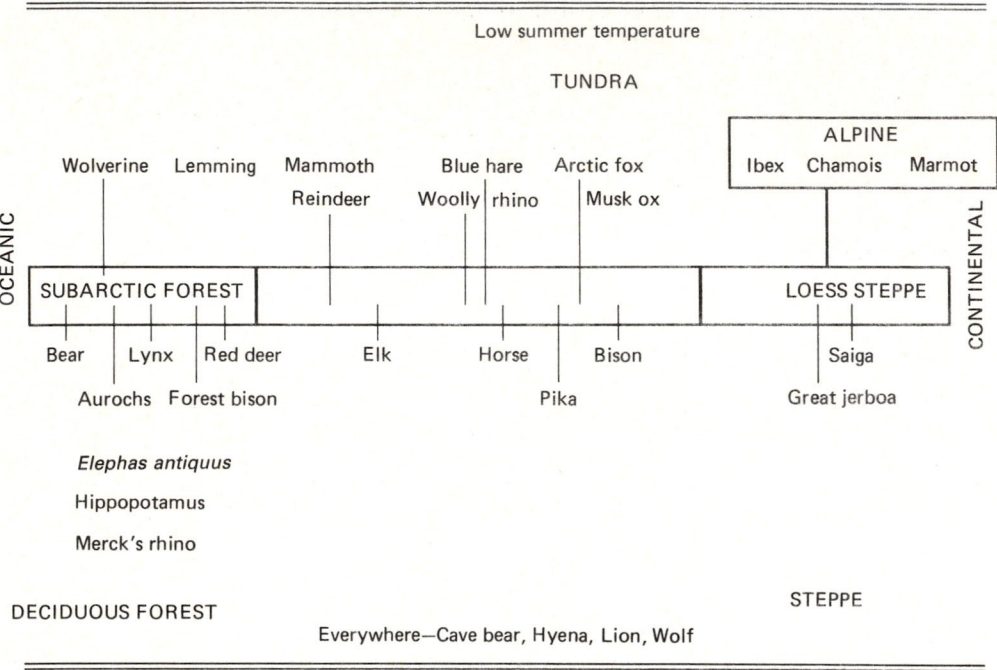

species (chamois, ibex, lynx), and open grassland grazers (bison, horse). To this diverse community have to be added a number of megafaunal species that are now extinct but which included mammoth, woolly rhino, forest elephants and rhinos, hippopotamus and giant deer. Finally two carnivores with extensive contemporary geographical ranges, wolf and bear, were also members of this community.

The geographical range of the cold adapted elements in this faunal community included Europe as well as Siberia and North America. This indicates a highly productive vegetation base for both grazers and browsers during substantial parts of the eight middle and upper pleistocene cycles (Guthrie 1968, 1982; Vereshschagin and Baryshnikov 1982).

(b) attributes

Since there are no direct analogues in modern environments for these mid-latitude pleistocene communities it is difficult to model the complex set of community interactions that would have resulted in variable figures for biomass density and other important factors for human subsistence strategies. In table 3.10a,b a simple model for these communities is set out using the three key attributes of species size (weight), aggregation and mobility (see p. 42). All three

Table 3.10. *Attributes of the main herd species and suggested predator selection in last glacial faunal communities*

(a) size and degree of annual migratory mobility

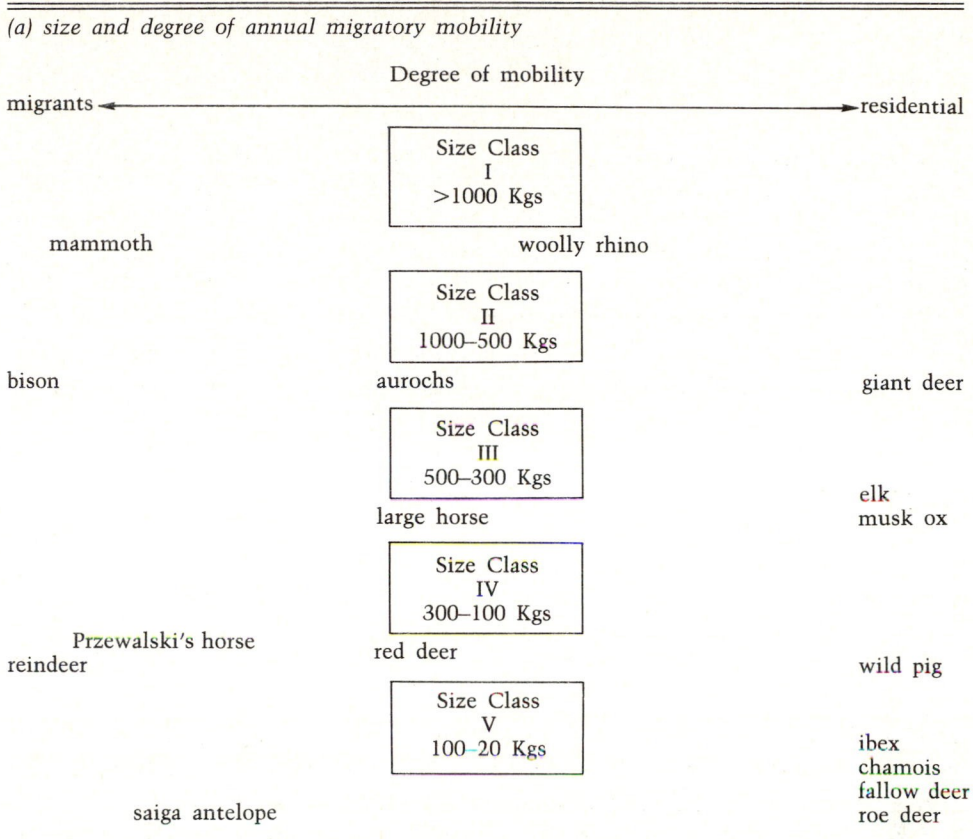

(b) aggregation potential at set seasons of the year
species with high potential – bison, reindeer, saiga
species with medium potential – mammoth, large horse, musk ox, red deer, fallow deer
species with low potential – woolly rhino, aurochs, giant deer, elk, Prezwalski's horse, wild pig, ibex, chamois, roe deer

(c) estimated predator/prey relations

size class	predator
I	juvenile mammoth and rhino killed by lion and hyena
II	migratory bison killed by lion and hyena; giant deer and elk taken by lion and wolf
III	hyena is the major predator on horse while wolf takes musk ox
IV	migratory horse taken by hyena; residential cervids and wild pig taken by wolf and leopard, especially juveniles; migratory reindeer are main prey of wolf
V	saiga antelope is only migratory species and wolf is its major predator; residential species are taken by leopard, lynx and wolverine

Source: From Weniger 1982; Gamble 1978a, b, 1979; Freeman 1973; Heptner *et al.* 1966; Van den Brink 1967; Schaller 1972; Ewer 1973; Kruuk and Turner 1967; Bell 1970; Guthrie 1968

attributes contribute to exploitation risks involving either a single species or a combination of herbivores.

The table can be used to distinguish three groups of animal species which share a number of comparable attributes. At the megafaunal end of the scale are the mammoth, elephant and rhino. These animals have low reproductive rates, are difficult, but not impossible to kill with simple hunting technologies, and would have shown great differences in the amount of annual mobility under different environmental conditions. Although the adults of these species would not have been predated upon by the carnivores, this lack of competition was unlikely to have recommended these same species as resources for human groups. Their main role in the ecology of the animal communities to which they belonged was most probably during the glacial winters when a species such as the mammoth would have cleared snow from vegetation and so opened up the herb and grass layer for smaller species in the community. Indeed competition for winter food in the form of browse or lichens can account for many of the different feeding mechanisms exhibited both by these megafauna and the other large mammal species (Gamble 1978b:table 4.9, fig. 4.vi; Guthrie 1982: fig. 3).

The second group (tables 3.11 and 3.12) consists of only four species (bos/bison, horse, red deer and reindeer) which formed the major elements as measured by numbers and population density in the communities. They show a considerable range in body size and variation in the attributes of mobility, and herd aggregation must also be expected. These are the species around which palaeolithic exploitation strategies were built. They were the solution to the problem of what to eat that faced human populations in the open environments of stages 2 and 3. Their attributes are listed in table 3.12 and indicate the different packages in which these all important resources came.

These same four species would also have been the prime prey species for the large social carnivores – hyena, wolf and lion (table 3.10c). According to Schaller (1972:table 79) the choice of prey by carnivores can be ascertained from such factors as the method of capture, time of hunting, degree of social cooperation and the size of the carnivore involved. These factors point to the wolf as a predator on cervids while lion and hyena are primarily interested in bison and horse respectively (Guthrie 1968). This does not mean exclusive predation on these species. In reality there would have been competition for sex and age classes of the primary prey between the carnivores as well as the inclusion of other species in the carnivore diet. The carnivores would have preyed more frequently upon these large herbivores because of their higher reproductive rates, tendency to herd aggregation at some seasons of the year, and widespread distribution over diverse vegetation communities. These same factors would have been important for human predators but with a further critical dimension. None of the carnivores can store significant amounts of food. That is why their population numbers are so closely tied to the reproductive patterns of the herds upon which they depend. It is also one reason why a kill by one carnivore will

Table 3.11. *Faunas of central Europe during the pleistocene*

The groupings are according to the utility of species to human groups as hunted resources. Carnivores have been omitted and this is not a complete list of pleistocene fauna.

	1	2	3	4	5	6	7	8	9	10
group 1										
Archidiskodon planifrons	+									
Archidiskodon meridionalis		+	+?		+					
Elephas antiquus					+		+		+	
Mammontheus trogontherii					+?	+	+	+	+?	+?
Mammontheus primigenius								+	(+)	+
Dicerorhinus etruscus	+?	+	+?		+					
Dicerorhinus kirchbergensis		+	+?		+		+		+	
Coelodonta antiquitatis						+		+		+
Hippopotamus amphibius		+			+		+		+	
group 2										
Leptobos elatus	+?	+								
Bos primigenius							+	+		+
Bison priscus								+	+	+
Equus stenonsis	+									
Equus caballus			+?			+	+			+
Equus sussenbornensis					+	+				
Equus hydruntinus								+		+
Cervus falconeri	+									
Cervus dicranius		+								
Cervus rhenanus		+								
Cervus elaphus					+	+?	+	+	+	+
Rangifer tarandus						+		+		+
group 3										
Sus strocci		+								
Eucladoceros tegulensis		+								
Sus scrofa					+?	+			+	+
Alces alces									+	+
Megaloceros giganteus							+	+?	+	+
Saiga tartarica								+		+

Key: 1: Pretiglian (cold); 2: Tiglian (warm); 3: Eburonian (cold) and Waalian (warm); 4: Menapian (cold); 5: Cromerian (warm); 6: Elster (cold); 7: Holsteinian (warm); 8: Saalian (cold); 9: Eemian (warm); 10: Weichselian (cold)
Source: After Frenzel 1973

often be used by other carnivores, and through such feeding chains the maximum use is made of the captured energy resource. Through storage strategies human groups are able to budget the use of a resource over a much longer period of time following either a successful hunt or the retrieval of a carcass either killed by carnivores or resulting from a natural mortality. The size of these four species allows this strategy to operate under a number of different circumstances. Animals may be hunted singly or in herd drives (Oswalt 1976; Ingold 1980; Speth 1983). In the latter strategy a large drive and kill is analogous to killing a single elephant or mammoth when measured in terms of the quantity of calories recovered in a single predatory event. Under the former strategy of hunting individual animals, the hunter can process the carcass and create a

Table 3.12. *Selected attributes of the four key species that were utilised in palaeolithic food management strategies*

	Bison (*Bison bonasus*)	Horse (*Equus przewalski*)	Red deer (*Cervus elaphus*)	Reindeer (*Rangifer tarandus*)
Pleistocene forms	steppe *Bison priscus** woodland *Bison schoetensacki** aurochs *Bos primigenius**	caballine forms *Equus bressanus** *Equus mosbachensis** *Equus germanicus** *Equus przewalski* zebrine forms *Equus stenonsis** *Equus sussenbornensis** asses *Equus stehlini** *Equus hydruntinus** *Equus hemionus*		
Gestation (days)	261–83	320–43	238–45	230–46
Weight at birth (kgs)	22–3	25–30	8–11	6.3
Number in birth	1	1	1	1 (sometimes 2)
Interval between births, (years)		2		
Birth season	mid May–June 14	end of April, May, early June	mid June	end May, June
Breeding age females males	3 years 10 years	2–4 years	3 years	3 years
Life span (years)	22	20+	17	15
Breeding life (females)	19 years	16 years		
Adult weight males females	500/850–1000+ kg 330	200–350 kg	100–250 70–150	120–150 80–100
Basic herd size males females	groups of 3–5 + calves 6–10 max 15	5–11 *E. hemionus* 11–20	4–10	30–40 open country mixed sex herds 15–20 in woodland
Feeding classification	grazers with winter browse; multiple stomach ruminant	single stomach grazer	browsers in the winter	grazers and occasionally browsers on willow and birch shoots
Limiting factor	winter forage	winter forage and deep snow	snow depth >50–70 cm	snow depth >60 cm
References	Heptner *et al.* 1966 Vereshschagin and Baryshnikov 1982	Mohr 1971 Heptner *et al.* 1966 Eisenberg 1966	Heptner *et al.* 1966 Van den Brink 1967	Heptner *et al.* 1966 Van den Brink 1967 Pruitt 1970 Spiess 1979

(* = extinct form)

store. Many of these stores can be created in the environment and by doing so one element in a flexible strategy of spreading risk would be produced. This same type of strategy could not however be pursued for an animal the size of a mammoth. The low reproductive potential of this species made it impossible to hunt one at a time with the same frequency as a smaller animal. As a result even though the human predator had a further string to his bow through the tactical use of storage he was still limited by the attributes of his prey in the matter of which animals would be selected for hunting. Regular and sustained mega-faunal exploitation was therefore too risky for the size of predator involved.

The third group of animals in table 3.11 would have presented alternative resources for human groups. They fall into two size classes. The large species have very low reproductive rates and are generally clumped resources within the environment. This is well shown by the musk ox (Wilkinson 1975) which is used by the Eskimo but in emergency rather than normal situations. The small body size species have much higher reproductive rates but often a low popula-tion density as with roe deer, ibex and chamois. Smaller body size is a characteristic of woodland species such as pig and roe deer. The only species which has a high herd aggregation potential and therefore a high population density at certain times of the year is the saiga antelope which is today found in the arid steppes around the Caspian Sea (Heptner *et al.* 1966).

This third group consisted of a mixed bag of species. Either they had comparable attributes to the megafauna for hunting strategies or else they were small in size and hence the human energy expended in hunting them was not adequately returned. Their most important contribution was in providing predictable alternative resources since many of them (musk, ox, elk, roe, ibex and chamois) could be precisely located within the landscape. Their use could be scheduled into a wider strategy based around the four main species since this would have taken some of the pressure off the all important quarry of the main herd animals.

(c) geographical distribution

The two main limiting factors in the environment for any of these herbivores would have been snow cover and the availability of suitable winter food, primarily in the form of browse. Competition between species in the communi-ties would also have provided restrictions on the distribution of some grazing species.

Representatives of the megafaunal group are found throughout Europe. The mammoth is rarely encountered in the mediterranean province but the square lipped woolly rhino, a well adapted grazing species, is found throughout the MW and MC regions (Vereshschagin and Baryshnikov 1982). Hippopotamus is most commonly encountered in the oceanic climates of the NW and SW regions as well as in the MW and MC regions.

The four principal herd species are found throughout the northern and southern provinces. The red deer is restricted in its northern range during the early and full glacial by the lack of woody browse as suitable winter fodder. By contrast, the reindeer which can utilise lichens is well adapted to such conditions. However the reindeer was at all times rare in the mediterranean province. In this same province the aurochs (*Bos primigenius*) were the principal bovid in the MW region where bison was absent (Kurtén 1968). Elsewhere bison, and horse, are found throughout the three stages of the interglacial/glacial cycle.

Among the third group, the elk was found throughout the northern and southern provinces while musk ox and giant deer (*Megaloceros giganteus*), with its remarkable 4 m antler spans, were to be found only in these two provinces. The other species in this group are found extensively throughout the three provinces with the exception of the saiga antelope. This species appears in the NW, NC, and SW regions during stage 3 of the last glacial cycle. During the pleistocene the mountain species, ibex and chamois, occurred at much lower altitudes than today, and thus form a part of many fossil communities in the continent.

The large carnivores are found in most of the regions. Musil (1980–1) has shown that the cave bear (*Ursus spelaeus*), another cold adapted form, had its greatest occurrence in the NC region (Chapter 7). Brown bears were present in those mediterranean regions where cave bear was either rare or absent. The lion, wolf and hyena all had a widespread distribution, although they are rare in the Alpine region. Leopard was generally uncommon in the northern province but is known from the SW region and in the mediterranean province. *Alopex lagopus*, the arctic fox, forms part of the northern arctic community whereas the wolverine, *Gulo gulo*, is also known from the MC and ME regions.

The composition of the animal communities was subject to much variation during the middle and upper pleistocene (Soergel 1943; Toepfer 1963; Kurtén 1968; Maglio 1975; Kahlke 1975; Stuart 1982) and there are still many interspecific details of the palaeo-communities which need examination. In very general terms the animal community which is well known from the upper pleistocene can serve as a model for earlier communities, though it should be remembered that the general trend during the pleistocene is towards more cold adapted and arctic species in the faunal communities (table 3.11).

(d) human exploitation: summary

The four main herd species would have provided an immensely varied platform upon which food management strategies could be built. The local decisions and use of tactical choices (table 2.5) would have depended upon such factors as the timing of large herd aggregation, the physical condition of the prey at various times of the year and the availability of alternative resources and their exploitation costs.

It is clear that the animal species which were available during the interglacial forest conditions were more costly to exploit than those on the open tundras and steppes of stages 2 and 3. The interglacial faunal communities characterised by hippopotamus and straight tusked elephant (*Elephas antiquus*) also had other forest adapted species with small body sizes (roe and fallow deer) and lower population densities. In terms of animal biomass, degree of herd aggregation, animal size and mobility, the faunas of stage 2 would have provided the best conditions for secure hunting. In these environments, the huge primary productivity of the vegetation was converted into animal biomass rather than into the forests and woods of stage 1 interglacial environments (for a further discussion of this point see Phillipson 1973). While the open environments of stages 2 and 3 would have been uncertain when it came to predicting animal movements and cycles of population numbers, they were nonetheless resilient environments that favoured long term adaptation. The cycles of forest regeneration during the interglacials produced a rapid turnover of different environments and consequently alternations in the densities and availability of animal species. The number of large animal species were in fact less than the number which formed the open grazing community. This reduction in alternative prey species was not compensated for by a readily available set of plant resources that could be cheaply exploited.

The picture is beginning to emerge that not only was stage 2 the longest part of the interglacial/glacial cycle but it also contained the most abundant resources for animal based adaptations in Europe. The number of species in the northern and southern provinces was as great and often greater than in the mediterranean. This shows that usable energy was available in all three provinces for most of an interglacial/glacial cycle. Only during the full glacial stage, when polar desert conditions prevailed in parts of the northern province, might animal biomass have been reduced to density levels where hunting strategies were placed at considerable risk due to the paucity of resources.

Hunting is however only one strategy for using animals. The group 1 megafaunal species, as well as the large herbivores, could have been exploited by scavenging. The high frequency of deaths of mammoths, elephants and rhinos by lakes and rivers is well shown by the recovery of palaeontological material from Europe (Kowalski 1959; Kahlke 1975; Toepfer 1963; Dawkins 1869; Vereshschagin 1974). Although these species are too high risk to hunt, unless their non-food products such as ivory offer an incentive (Marks 1976), their scavenged carcasses would provide an alternative supply of food. High frequencies of winter deaths among ungulates might well have provided palaeolithic groups with a secure strategy in the spring of searching the landscape for frozen carcasses as they were revealed by the melting snow. These natural mortalities would, of course, include the four main herd species and competition in the spring to get to them before the carnivores would perhaps have been intense. On the contrary in winter the role of fire in defrosting these carcasses may have been a crucial adaptation in securing the food from an economic niche that was otherwise uncontested at this time of the year. This would have been an unearned resource, encountered in the normal course of individual and group mobility over the environment as the basic food management strategy was followed. The decision whether to use such a resource, or ignore it, would depend upon the interplay of many intricate scheduling factors. While such resources might not be reliable, since it would be difficult to predict exactly when and where they would occur, they might form an important instance of an unearned supply of food that could be used to take the pressure off declining stores or as an emergency in times of real crisis. The third group of localised resources would however normally have filled this requirement since the characteristics of many of these species would allow hunters to know their precise position in the landscape. This reliability would mean that ibex, musk ox, elk and other animals could either be programmed into the regular schedule or used intensively if the main staples of bison, horse, red and reindeer were under pressure. In both cases the group 2 and group 3 species would either be intercepted in drives, hunted in smaller groups or taken singly.

Detailed accounts of animal species behaviour can be found in the following works: Heptner *et al.* 1966; Baumann 1949; Schaller 1972; Kruuk 1972; Mech 1970; Formozov 1970; Pruitt 1970; Van den Brink 1967; Kelsall 1968; Darling 1937; and archaeological reviews in Klein 1969a; Freeman 1973; Higgs, ed. 1972, 1975; Weniger 1982.

Small mammals, shellfish, fish and birds

Another source of alternative resources could have been provided by a group of predominantly *r* selected species. These would have been present in many of the regions and during all three of the interglacial/glacial stages. They are small packages of energy that have high reproductive rates and which can occur at great densities. As Deevey (1968: 95) and Hayden (1981b) have pointed out if human groups can solve the problems associated with exploiting these resources then spectacular population growth is possible.

The problems are however considerable. The lagomorphs (rabbits, hares and steppe pikas) were widely distributed in pleistocene Europe. The varying hare (*Lepus timidus*) is associated with northern regions under glacial conditions while the rabbit (*Oryctalagus cuniculus*) is common under most climatic conditions in the mediterranean. Davidson (1976) has shown however that while rabbits are abundant, they are a relatively expensive food source to exploit. He cites capture rates (Thompson and Armour 1951) of 1.5 rabbits per man hour of searching time under normal conditions, dropping to 0.5 under plague conditions. The meat weight per rabbit is 0.9 kg which yields a calorie return of 1,080 Kcal. Some 2.54 rabbits per day are therefore needed to meet a per person calorie intake of 2,750 Kcal, which is regarded as the mean requirement for an adult living in a habitat where the average annual temperature is 5° C. Therefore in order to subsist solely on rabbits a total of five hours per day per person would have to be spent searching for this resource. Such a figure does not include further processing and consumption time. The result would be little extra time to pursue other resources unless net acquisition rates could be improved drastically. The lack of fat on such small game makes it a nutritionally poor resource (Speth 1983).

When ranked against other resources, the enormous potential yields from shellfish beds are also only won at great expense. Bailey (1975, 1978) has estimated that in terms of calorie return one red deer is equivalent to 52,267 oysters (*Ostrea edulis*). In order to supply mean calorific requirements some 700 oysters per person have to be collected each day. In the case of limpets (*Patella vulgata*) this figure is 400, while for cockles (*Cardium edule*) this rises to 1400. Not only do these resources have to be harvested from the intertidal shell beds, but processed. This adds an extra cost, as Osborn (1977) has pointed out. A single North American white tailed deer is the food equivalent of some 10,593 clams. While this number of clams has to be collected, not all the harvested resource is food. In fact of the 408 kg harvested only 22% is usable – the rest is shell. For the white tailed deer, the ratio of edible meat to carcass waste is at least 50%. Net energy acquisition rates for shellfish resources can therefore be low even though the resources are abundant and highly productive. Further factors that have to be taken into account include the shore topography, tides, sea temperature and the feeding conditions which shellfish require. This places many restrictions on the occurrence of these resources around the coasts of Europe and favours the Atlantic seaboards (Bailey 1978).

The shifting polar front shown in fig. 3.10 would have created rich marine environments at 42° N off the coast of Spain and raises the possibility that inland runs of salmon from the Atlantic would have provided an important resource for parts of western Europe (Jochim 1983). In south-east Alaska, the pink salmon formed just such a rich resource for the Tlingit Indians. Each productive unit or housegroup of c.30 people required at least 5000 kg of stored fish to ensure a food supply for the rest of the year (Schalk 1977:233–4). This amount of fish had to be speedily processed, dried and stored to prevent spoilage. The 5000 kg could be acquired in just under seven days assuming a daily catch of 560 pink salmon and processing by the six women in the housegroup. However, there was little leeway for mistakes. Counts of the migrating salmon indicate that 80% of them passed the counting station in an interval of only 14–26 days while in some years 40% passed in 3 days. Schalk concludes that 'it would be an understatement to say that the productive unit of [the] Tlingit would frequently be hard-pressed to successfully store the necessary amount of fish' (*ibid.*:235).

The small community on the tiny windswept north Atlantic island of St Kilda subsisted primarily on the flesh, eggs and oil taken from the nesting colonies of sea birds. These huge colonies supported a population of 100 people during the first half of the last century (Steel 1975). At this time, the St Kildans took on average 20,000–25,000 puffins, 12,000 fulmars and 5,000 gannets every year. The puffin population was probably in excess of 1,000,000 birds at this time and a capture rate of some fifty birds per man per day was possible. A visitor to the island in 1697 estimated a weekly consumption of 16,000 eggs which had to be collected from precipitous rock ledges. Killing the fulmars for their precious oil and flesh lasted a fortnight (*ibid*.:66) and the harvest was equally divided among the islanders. In this example, the nesting birds formed a high density, reliable resource. Alternative subsistence items could not have supported a population of comparable size. While such dense numbers might have occurred along the coasts and enlarged inland seas of pleistocene Europe, they would have only been one resource in a much wider spectrum of possible subsistence choices. If large mammals formed one of these alternative resources, then the likelihood of birds forming a significant part of the diet and subsistence schedule would be greatly diminished due to factors of exploitation costs resulting from the size of the resource.

The various costs that have been detailed here should not be taken to indicate that, when available, these resources were not utilised to some extent. The examples point rather to the consequences in terms of the effort, time budgeting and scheduling necessary to use the full potential of such resources. Rabbits may be acquired at much less cost if traps are used but the use of such untended facilities (Oswalt 1976) still requires a schedule so that they can be set, inspected and emptied (Nelson 1973), and this schedule has to be balanced against competing demands on limited amounts of time and labour. Set against these observations, we can see not only that the large mammals provide plenty of usable food for human groups but that it comes in the right package size. While small resources can be exploited, this is only achieved through a massive intensification of subsistence effort. The case of the Weagamow Ojibwa (Rogers and Black 1976) in the Canadian sub-arctic illustrates this point. Their staples of fish and hare during the period 1880–1920 were a necessary adaptation after caribou and moose stocks had been severely depleted. The Ojibwa vividly recollect the periodic food shortages and the intense effort that had to be expended in acquiring the small game (*ibid*.:16–17).

Summary

This chapter has provided an extended discussion of the proposition put forward in Chapter 2 (p. 66). We have seen that the availability of energy was not a limiting factor in the regions and provinces during most of the three stages of an interglacial/glacial cycle. Only during the full glacial stage 3 in the northern province might the harsh polar desert conditions have resulted in too little usable energy being available to maintain an adaptive strategy. While the availability of energy was not limiting the structure of resources, the organisation of the environments to which palaeolithic groups had to adapt no doubt imposed constraints. These contrasted habitats were subject to cyclical change that altered the arrangement of resources and which required different tactical solutions. These would have ranged from information sharing to intricate personnel and time budgeting schedules. Patterns of mobility and the maintenance of social networks would also have been very different between regions and provinces as well as between the climatic stages. Consequently, the archaeological record should exhibit variation in the formation of different signatures left on the landscape (table 2.6).

The examination of resources and their variation has also pointed up the importance of animal based food management strategies in adapting to the environments of pleistocene Europe, and in particular to the long periods of time represented by stage 2. These open environments, stocked with large herbivores, were undoubtedly the niche that the early hominids competed for with other carnivores. The long term resilience of these mammal communities and the environments they inhabited would have selected for adaptive change. We shall see in later chapters whether the first colonisers had solved all the problems connected with living between the sheets in ice age Europe.

CHAPTER 4

TECHNOLOGICAL, TYPOLOGICAL AND EXPERIMENTAL APPROACHES

> Moreover, in primitive societies, conservatism is usually very strong, and
> if one supposes that a Mousterian of Acheulian Tradition married a Quina
> woman, she might have well gone on using the thick scrapers to which she
> was accustomed, but we doubt that her daughters would have done the
> same.
>
> F. Bordes and D. de Sonneville-Bordes,
> The significance of variability in palaeolithic assemblages (1970: 65)

Introduction

In my approach to the study of the European palaeolithic, I have so far
recognised, but not confronted, the regional traditions of research. These
traditions have given us a framework of three palaeolithic periods – lower,
middle, and upper – and a myriad of industrial, assemblage and geographical
variation within this tripartite division. The purpose of this chapter is to
establish a general approach to this data by examining the concepts which have
been used to partition and order the fruits of research. This is to be seen as a
preliminary step in the examination of the regional model outlined in the last
chapter. It might be suggested that for our purposes any consideration of the
culture history approach is superfluous since it cannot answer the questions
concerning past behaviour in which we are interested. It is not possible however
to cast off the legacy of 150 years of research so lightly. This inheritance carries
with it a set of procedural obligations which need to be understood if we are to
form any impression of the contents and dimensions of the palaeolithic record.
These obligations include the study of technology, the practice of typological
analysis and the patterning of recurrent groupings in the data against a temporal
framework. They need to be understood if we are to change our approach to the
investigation of the past.

These procedures are heavily weighted towards the examination of the
durable, stone artifacts which have formed the mainstay of investigations into
the regional traditions. While subsistence data and settlement classifications
have been used to provide alternative frameworks, such studies are currently
very much in the minority (Chapter 5).

Technology and two palaeolithics

Differences in techniques of stone tool manufacture were previously used to support the tripartite division of the palaeolithic. It is now possible to recognise only one major distinction in European palaeolithic technology and knapping techniques. This occurs at c.35 Kyr and marks the division between the lower/middle and the upper palaeolithic.

(a) core tool and flake technology of the earlier palaeolithic

The lower and middle palaeolithic were once distinguished from each other by the use of different striking hammers, hard and soft, and the production of core implements rather than flake tools. Experimental studies of stone tool manufacture (Crabtree 1970; Bordaz 1970) have shown that a wide variety of knapping techniques can be used to produce comparable end products. Moreover, the absolute dates now available for these early industries point to an array of techniques at any one time rather than the appearance of one technique after another (Chapter 5). In that sense the application of the terms lower and middle palaeolithic to European data is no longer instructive about the relative levels of technological attainment. If the terms have any significance left this can only be viewed against the longer cultural histories provided by African evidence for early hominid evolution.

Core tools vary in technical sophistication. Chopping and pebble tools can be quickly fashioned from river or beach pebbles with a few blows. The irregular cutting edge may be of less importance than the flakes produced in the process. These can either be used as simple cutting tools or serve as blanks which, with additional retouch, can be turned into implements. The flakes can be struck with hard stone hammers or with softer wooden, bone or antler billets. An even simpler method, that lies within even our own technological competence, is to smash one stone nodule against another. This classic anvil technique produces very thick, irregular flakes with massive striking platforms indicative of the brute force mode of production.

Handaxes form the most distinctive category of core tools where a nodule is successively worked to leave a residual implement. This reduction process has been studied by Newcomer (1971) in a replication experiment designed to document the manufacturing process. In this experiment, the initial flint nodule weighed almost 3 kg and from this a handaxe weighing 230 gm was flaked. In the process, 51 large by-product flakes were produced as well as an additional 4618 small chips and flint chunks. Newcomer's further experiments led him to propose at least a three-stage process to handaxe manufacture. The *roughing out* stage involved the use of a hard hammer to produce a handaxe outline and this resulted in some ten large, thick flakes with massive striking platforms and a large amount of nodular cortex on their supper surface. This was followed by a *thinning and shaping* stage where the hard hammer was exchanged for a soft one. These thinning flakes, of which about twenty were produced, carry the traces of previous flake removal scars on their upper surfaces. Their striking platforms are most commonly thin or shattered and the edges of the flakes irregular. The final *finishing* stage used the soft hammer again and a further twenty flakes were removed to correct the final outline of the handaxe. The flakes were smaller with flatter bulbs of percussion and less irregular edges.

Palaeolithic handaxes were also produced on large flakes struck from carefully reduced nodules. The best known of these reduction strategies, which produced flakes and large blades of desired dimensions, is named after the

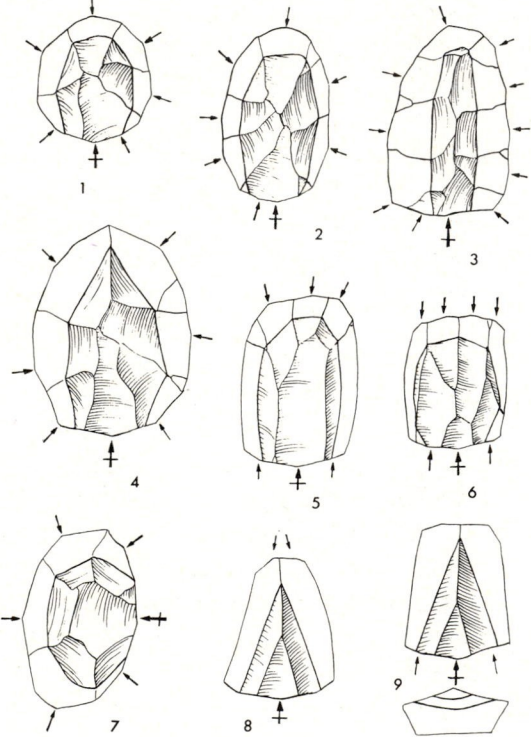

4.1 Varieties of levallois flake, blade and point production (Bordes 1980:fig. 1).
(1) Classic levallois core
(2) Classic elongated levallois core
(3) Classic elongated levallois core for flake/blade production
(4) Classic levallois core with pointed flake
(5, 6) Levallois core with parallel preparation, long and short
(7) Victoria West core
(8, 9) Levallois cores producing triangular points and prepared in two different ways
Flakes/blades are shaded and the arrows indicate the preparatory flaking. The larger arrows indicate the direction from which the desired flake/blade/point was detached.

Table 4.1. *Stages and steps in a flaking experiment using the levallois technique*

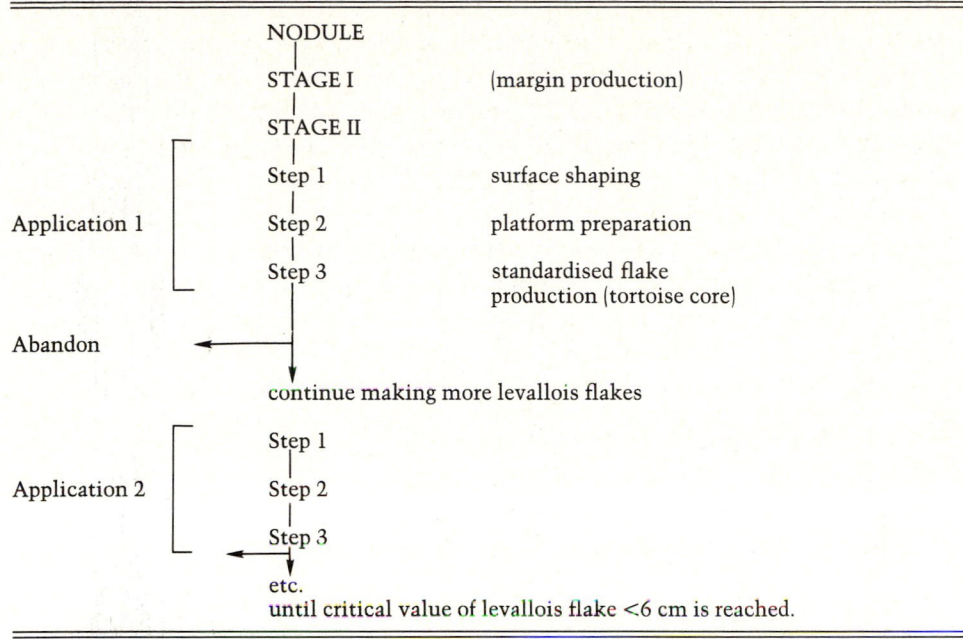

```
                    NODULE
                      |
                    STAGE I            (margin production)
                      |
                    STAGE II
                      |
                    Step 1             surface shaping
                      |
Application 1       Step 2             platform preparation
                      |
                    Step 3             standardised flake
                                       production (tortoise core)

Abandon  ←————————————
                      ↓
                    continue making more levallois flakes

                    Step 1
                      |
Application 2       Step 2
                      |
                    Step 3
              ←———————↓
                    etc.
                    until critical value of levallois flake <6 cm is reached.
```

Source: After Bradley 1977

suburb of Levallois on the Seine river. It is here that the distinctive technique was first noted and where the shape of the flake/blade is predetermined by the careful preparation of the core *before* the flake is detached (Bordes 1980). The levallois technique produces broad flat flakes, large blades and triangular points (fig. 4.1). These blanks display the traces of previous flake removals on their dorsal surfaces and on occasion their striking platforms are faceted as a means of facilitating their removal from the core. The pattern of flake removals has resulted in the description of 'tortoise core' for the discarded core after the flakes have been removed.

In a flaking experiment, Bradley (1977) produced twenty levallois cores on tabular blocks of flint 4 cm thick and 15 cm in diameter. He describes his reduction strategy by means of a stage and step chart (table 4.1) where at each step distinctive flakes are produced. He set a limit of less than 6 cm as the critical threshold for the production of levallois flakes and abandoned the experiment at this stage if flake length fell below this value. On average, 4.35 levallois flakes (range 3–8) were produced per core and an average total of 102 other flakes came from each core.

Another reduction technique results in disc cores where the aim is to remove flakes of varying sizes rather than of specified dimensions. Continuous flaking leaves a residual core of roughly circular shape.

The fracture patterns of the raw materials available to palaeolithic knappers do not seem to have been an important constraint to the use of a particular technique. The levallois technique was employed on quartzites as well as on high grade flint with a crisp conchoidal fracture. Size of raw material nodules was probably more important as a technological constraint (Fish 1979:table 24), but even so the variety of knapping procedures displayed upon small river gravels and large blocks of flint point to a mastery of the technique that was not limited by the available stone resources. Except in extreme cases, the decision to use a technique of flake preparation was not dependent upon the properties of the raw material but rather on the contingencies of the situation for which artifact manufacture was undertaken (Chapter 6).

The only other technological items which have survived prior to 35 Kyr are a few objects made in wood. These include the tip of a yew 'spear' from Clacton (Oakley *et al.* 1977), a yew 'spear' some 2.5 m in length from Lehringen (Jacob-Friesen 1956), and a number of wooden fragments from Torralba (Freeman 1975).

(b) blade cores, bone and antler

Core reduction strategies change quite considerably after 35 Kyr. The techniques of nodule preparation are designed to produce a great many thin, parallel-sided blades. These serve as standard blanks which can be quickly retouched into a variety of implement types. The cores vary greatly in size from the production of very large blades to microlithic bladelet cores.

Core reduction strategies have been studied in great detail for the late glacial in Poland (Ginter 1974; Schild 1971; Kozlowski and Sachse-Kozlowska 1980). The purpose of the reduction strategy was to produce slender, straight sided blades to be mounted as projectile points. High quality raw material sources were utilised and in particular those in the Holy Cross mountains where a distinctive chocolate-coloured flint was quarried (Schild 1971). The sequence of production is shown in figure 4.2.

This resulted in distinctive debris at workshop sites and the production of opposite platform cores (see Chapter 6 for further discussion). At the excavated site of Olbrachcice in south-west Poland, Burdukiewicz (1980) has provided a detailed description of the material based on such a core reduction sequence (table 4.2). The studies have revealed many details about technological sequences and the nature of these extraction and workshop sites. These sites exhibit repeated patterning in relation to densities of material and the presence/absence of parts of the reduction sequence (Ginter 1974).

The trend towards microlithic blade production is particularly marked after 20 Kyr. From this time it is also possible to see new forms of retouch, most notably pressure retouch where heat treatment of the raw material facilitated the removal of very thin flakes (Price *et al.* 1982).

The entire period is however characterised by the exploitation of high grade

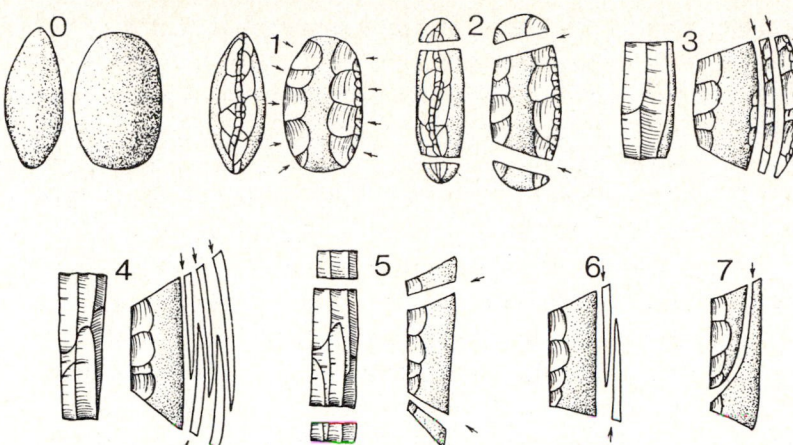

4.2 The sequence of steps in a reduction strategy for the production of blades and bladelets. The examples come from the LUP of Poland (Kozlowski and Sachse-Kozlowska 1976:fig. 3).

Key:

	nodule	0
step 1	testing	0
2	cortex removal	1
3	platform shaping	2
	pre-core	
step 1	preparation of flaking surfaces by trimming flakes	3
	core	
step 1	blade production	4, 6
2	core rejuvenation	5
	worked out core	7

lithic resources and the distribution of these materials over considerable distances. Blades are made in materials other than flint, chert or obsidian, but the development of a microlithic component and the production of many blades from a single nodule favours these raw materials with their predictable fracture planes over the less serviceable quartzites.

The shift to blade production in the upper palaeolithic of Europe is also complemented by the appearance of objects made in bone, antler and ivory. The use of antler and bone to make projectile points, spear throwers, needles and awls is unknown from earlier times as is the use of mammoth ivory to fashion ornaments and figurines. The technology of antler and bone working is not complex (Semenov 1964; Camps-Fabrer (ed.) 1974; Newcomer 1974). Antler can be soaked to make it pliable and more easily worked with stone tools. The density of bone makes it particularly suitable for the manufacture of borers and awls. These properties were well understood by palaeolithic technicians.

The upper palaeolithic blade technology is often referred to as the leptolithic or light stone. Reductions in size and weight were most probably required by developments in projectile points where lightweight components were used either singly or in combinations in the armatures. These included the

Table 4.2. *A technological classification of material from the LUP site of Olbrachcice, NC region*

Class	Description	Numbers		
I	Raw material	121		
II	Core preparation			
	cortical flakes	84		
	cortical blades	18		
	flakes with dorsal preparation	22		
	core trials	3 (started and rejected)		
III	Core exploitation			
	(a) single platform cores	11		
	(b) opposite platform cores	8		
	(c) changed orientation cores	3		
	partially cortical flakes	130		
	partially cortical blades	42		
	flakes from core type (a)	276		
	flakes from core type (b)	22		
	flakes from core type (c)	73		
	blades from core type (a)	89		
	blades from core type (b)	10		
	blades from core type (c)	14		
IV	Core rejuvenation			
	core tablets	25 (removal of striking platforms)		
	blades with rejuvenation traces on surface of the core	10		
V	Cores in final stage of exploitation + undetermined fragments of blades, flakes and chips			
	cores in final exploitation stage	20		
	indeterminate core fragments	31		
		proximal	medial	distal
	fragments of cortical flakes	96	138	80
	fragments of non-cortical flakes	256	237	161
	fragments of non-cortical blades	104	159	117
	indeterminate fragments of flakes/blades	405		
	chips (flakes reaching 1.5 cm in diameter)	2328		
VI	Retouched tools and tool waste	456		
	microburins	20		
	burin spalls	49		
VII	Tools for flint artifact production			
	hammerstones	2		
	bolsters (cracked hammers)	5		
Totals for each class				
	I	121		
	II–III	805		
	IV	35		
	V	1399		
	VI	456 (+69)		
	VII	7		

Source: Burdukiewicz 1980

microlithic elements, the backed blades and bladelets. Barbed and tanged arrowheads, and by inference the bow, are known by 20 Kyr from eastern Spain (Davidson 1974). In the earlier core tool and flake technologies, the projectiles were wooden spears which were either fire hardened to a serviceable point or probably tipped with a triangular levallois flake. While handaxes are not known from the upper palaeolithic, simple chopping tools are still present in assemblages indicating a widely divergent spectrum of input to technology in terms of both energy and technical expertise (see Chapter 6).

Typology and assemblage variation

(a) lower and middle palaeolithic, pre-35 Kyr

Typological approaches provide a means of classification based on the analysis of artifact shape and other attributes such as weight, raw material and retouch. The work of Roe (1964, 1968a, 1976, 1981; Hodson 1971) on the lower palaeolithic handaxes of England takes a single artifact type from lower and middle palaeolithic assemblages and assesses patterns of similarity of these types on the basis of measured attributes. The handaxes are then used as a basis for comparing 38 key assemblages in the search for significant patterning. The nine attributes used by Roe have been increased to thirty-four by Callow (1976) in his analysis of the same material. The aim of such analyses is to discover higher order classifications of recurrent patterning in artifacts and assemblages

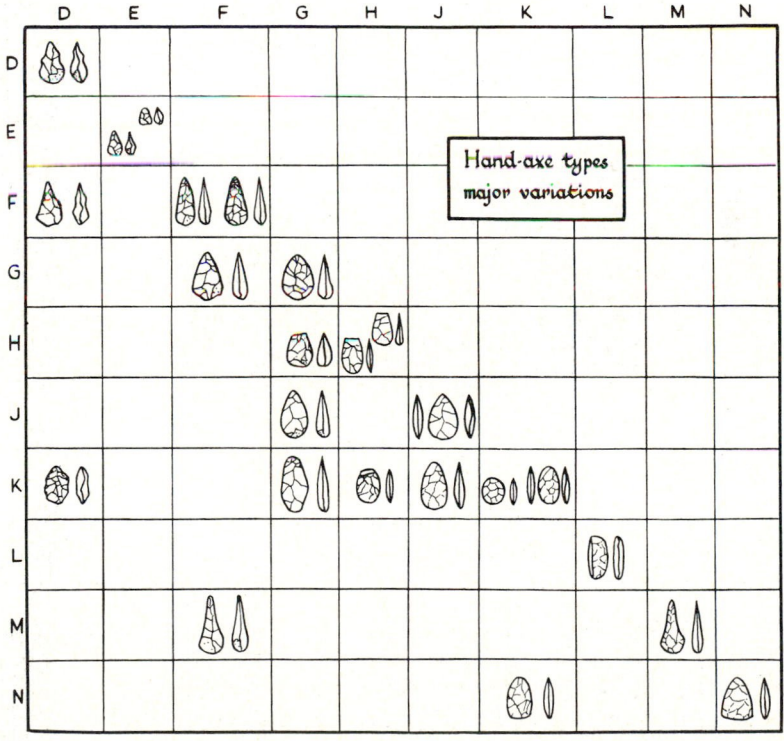

4.3 Variation in handaxe shapes as analysed by Wymer in his study of the abundant lower palaeolithic material from the Thames Valley (1968:60, fig. 27).

in a data set which is often far from adequate in terms of recovery and dating (fig. 4.3).

The context and chronology of material from the caves and open sites of France is generally much better understood. This data was typologised by Bordes and Bourgon (1951; Bordes 1953a; Bourgon 1957), where attention was paid to the entire excavated assemblage. This resulted in Bordes' landmark publication in 1961 entitled *Typologie du paléolithique ancien et moyen*. This assemblage analysis involves a list of 63 artifact types (Appendix 3) together with a further 21 handaxe forms. A very succinct account of how a typological analysis is conducted is provided in Bordes (1972). The assemblage of flint tools is sorted and counted according to these defined types. (A selection of the common forms is illustrated in fig. 4.4.) The resulting data is displayed in the form of a

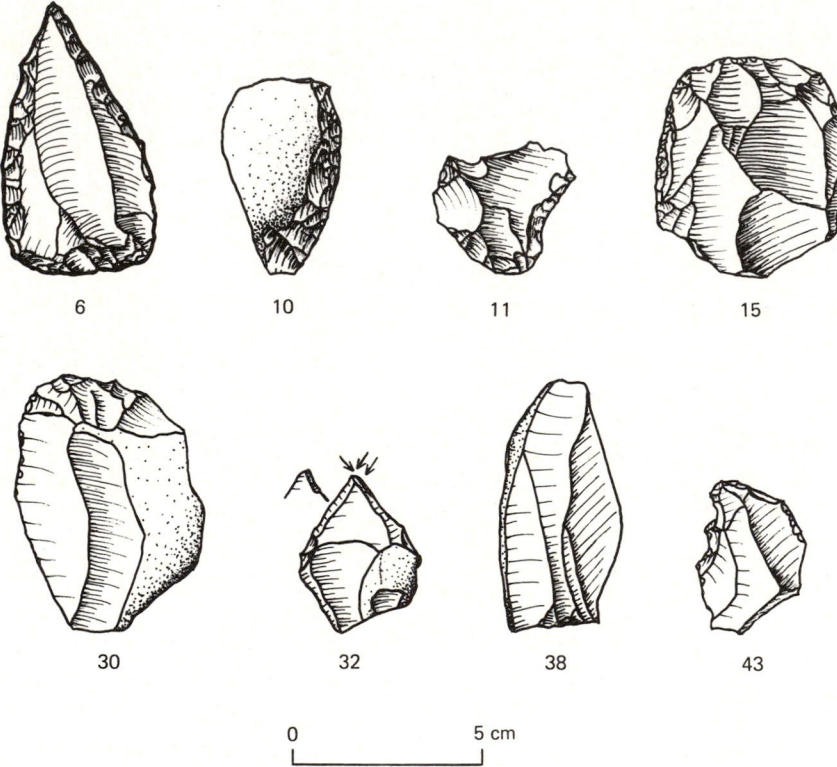

4.4 Middle palaeolithic artifact types. The numbers refer to Bordes' 63 type list (Appendix 3).

    6   mousterian point
   10   single convex side scraper
   11   single concave side scraper
   15   double convex side scraper
   30   end scraper on a flake
   32   burin
   38   naturally backed knife
   43   denticulate

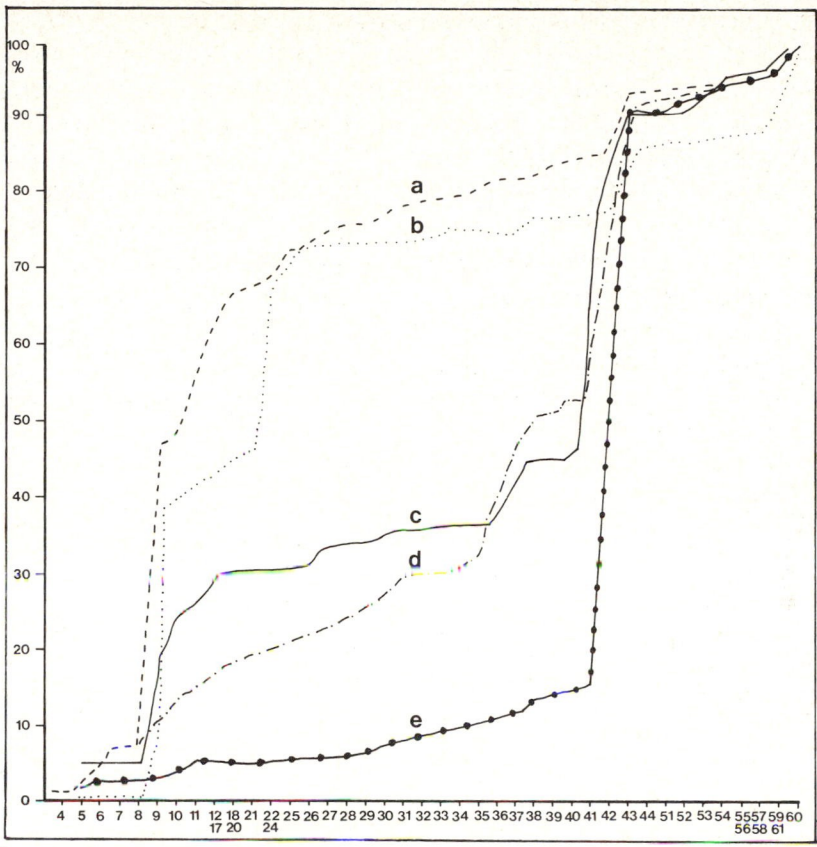

4.5 Cumulative graphs for the five mousterian variants based on the 63 implement type list (see Appendix 3) (after de Sonneville-Bordes 1974–5:fig. 1).
Key: (a) Ferrassie mousterian (La Ferrassie, level C); (b) Quina mousterian (Combe-Grenal, level 21); (c) Typical mousterian (Le Moustier, level B); (d) Mousterian of Acheulean Tradition [MTA] (Le Moustier, level G); (e) Denticulate mousterian (Combe-Grenal, level 14).

cumulative percentage curve (fig. 4.5, and table describing the variants – Bordes 1972:53–4) which provides a visual impression of the composition of an assemblage. Further comparative measures are provided by a number of typological indexes. The scraper index (IR) is the percentage of all the scrapers, numbers 9 to 29 on the type list. The Quina index (IQ) is the percentage of distinctive, transversal Quina scrapers (nos. 22–4) among the whole class of scrapers. The first three types on the list are flakes and points made by the levallois technique but which have not been subsequently retouched. They are also treated as an index (TyLI). For this reason many of the cumulative graphs commence with type 4. The count for the entire assemblage also recognises this. The *real* count includes the entire 63 type list. The *essential* count omits types 1–3 and the slightly retouched category 46–50 since the latter group could be the result of frost action causing natural retouch to the edges of artifacts by crushing them in the sediments or as a result of other forms of spontaneous retouch (Newcomer 1976). The first group is omitted in the essential count to enable more detailed comparisons between assemblages which are rich in unretouched levallois flakes with those that are not.

The 63 list is also examined in terms of four groups: 1–4, the levallois group I; 6–29, the Mousterian group II consisting mainly of different types of scrapers; 30–7 and 40, the upper palaeolithic group III; and 43 the denticulate group IV. These are also expressed as indexes.

Bordes' scheme also takes into account the techniques used in manufacturing the artifacts. These technical indexes summarise the proportional frequency of levallois points, blades and flakes (IL) that are both retouched and unretouched. Information is also noted regarding the faceting of the striking platforms on flakes and blades (IF) while the laminary index deals with the proportions of blades in the assemblage.

Bordes has reviewed his 'Typologie' on a number of occasions (1981; Bordes and de Sonneville-Bordes 1970). The original number of five recurrent groups which his analysis revealed has since been increased to seven for south-west France (table 4.3). Other workers using Bordes' methods have analysed assemblages from other parts of Europe (e.g. Valoch 1967a; González-Echegaray and Freeman 1973).

An alternative scheme has been used by Bosinski (1967) in his study of the German middle palaeolithic. Here he employed an assemblage approach but did not specify a list of precisely defined types. The German collections are generally small and more easily characterised by a distinctive artifact type such as a handaxe or leaf point. While Bosinski considered other associated forms, it is in essence a type fossil approach to assemblage grouping (fig. 4.6). Gábori's (1976) review of the middle palaeolithic in central and eastern Europe is faced with similar problems of small artifact collections that rarely occur in multi-level stratigraphic sequences. This is in extreme contrast to some of the sites in south-west France, where for example at Combe-Grenal (Bordes 1972) there are no less than fifty-five middle palaeolithic levels stratified above nine acheulean assemblages, many of which contain sufficient artifacts to conduct a Bordes analysis.

All of these typological schemes place particular emphasis on the retouched implements. The by-products of tool manufacture, though recorded, are generally regarded as waste. Only the unretouched levallois points are accorded the same typological status as a retouched tool.

Recent developments in the examination of the edges of stone tools, for edge damage and use wear polishes left behind as a result of activity, have however changed this picture (Keeley 1974, 1980; Tringham *et al.* 1974; Odell 1975; Odell and Odell-Vereecken 1980; Anderson 1980). These studies depend upon exactness and rigour in experimental procedures, and over them there is

Table 4.3. *The major assemblage variants in the mousterian of south-west France*

The five main variants are the two subtypes of the Charentian scraper dominated assemblages, typical, denticulate and MTA.

Variant	Levallois Index IL %	Side scraper Index IR %	Upper palaeolithic types Group III %	Denticulates Group IV %	Quina Index IQ %	Handaxe Index IB %
Charentian						
(a) Quina subtype	<10	50–80		low	14–30	absent/rare
(b) Ferrassie subtype	14–30	50–80		low	6–14	absent/rare
Typical	very variable	>50		moderate	0–3	absent/rare
Denticulate	very variable	4–20		60	0	low
Mousterian of Acheulean Tradition (MTA)						
subtype A	very variable	25–45	seldom > 4	common	very low	8–40
subtype B	very variable	4–20	strong	60	very low	absent/rare
Asinipodien	very common	rare	many naturally backed knives	rare		
Vasconien						many cleavers on flakes

Source: Bordes 1953a, 1972, 1981

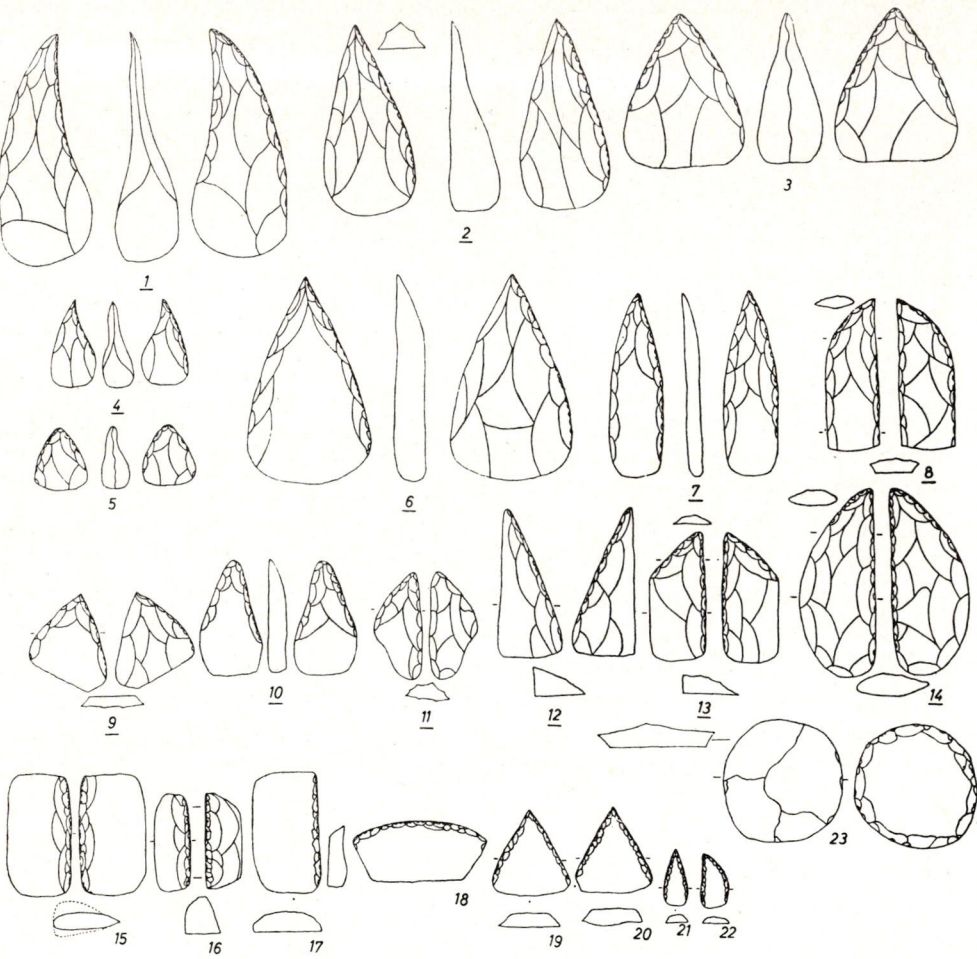

4.6 Characteristic artifact types in middle palaeolithic micoquian assemblages from Germany, NC region (Bosinski 1967:48, abb.7). The type fossils are underlined. (Scale c.1:3).

1–3	Halbkeil	
4	Faustel	very small handaxe
5	triangular Faustel	
6–11	Faustkeilblatt	handaxe made on tabular flint
12	Bocksteinmesser	Bockstein knife
13	Pradnikmesser	Pradnik knife
14	Wolgogradmesser	Wolgograd knife
15		bifacial scraper
16		keeled scraper
17		single scraper
18		broad, convex scraper
19–20		point scrapers
21–22		small points
23		levallois core

Table 4.4. *The results from blind test experiments on the use of stone tools*

Number of specimens correctly identified/sample size

	High power microscopic approach (Keeley and Newcomer 1977)	Low power microscopic approach (Odell and Odell-Vereecken 1980)
Used area of tool	15/17 88%	26/31 84%
Activity	13/17 77%	21/31 68%
Relative worked material	13/17 77%	23/31 74%
Specific worked material	10/17 59%	10/31 32%

considerable debate (Holley and del Bene 1981; Keeley 1981; Hayden (ed.) 1979; *Lithic Technology; Newsletter of Lithic Technology; Flintknappers Exchange; Lithics*). The results of blind test experiments between low power and high power microwear analysis (table 4.4) are particularly encouraging in demonstrating the potential of these approaches and especially in precisely determining which areas of the tool were used.

The high-power approach pioneered by Keeley (1980) identifies a set of six distinctive microwear polishes left on the surface of the flint when it was used to work wood, vegetable matter, bone, hide, meat and antler.

The application of these experimentally derived methods of analysis has produced three major conclusions. In his study of material from lower palaeolithic excavations at Clacton and Hoxne, Keeley (1980) was able to show that:

(a) only a small proportion of the total chipped stone assemblages from these sites bore use wear traces;

(b) *ad hoc* tools were frequently used. These would normally be classified as waste flakes, unmodified flakes or other manufacturing debris; and

(c) the polishes present on the used specimens indicated that a range of materials had been worked at either site and that the same material had been worked by morphologically different tools (table 4.5; fig. 4.7).

It is not yet possible to construct a classificatory scheme based upon the known functions of flint artifacts, both implements and waste chippings. For example a scheme has been put forward by Pradel (1972/3) which provides a classification (table 4.6) but does not tell us how to discover the various functions! Keeley's findings are conclusive in pointing out that the morphology of an implement or piece of flake debitage is in itself a poor guide to the function of that implement. The same artifact type might be used for a wide range of tasks involving several raw materials. Such low resolution between shape and function makes it difficult to infer activity patterns or tool kits from artifact assemblages. However, one advantage of a scheme such as Pradel's, if it were practicable, would be that comparisons could be made between the proportions of similar functional classes in very different technologies. At the moment, for

Table 4.5. *Frequency of various uses as determined by counting edges at Clacton and Hoxne, Lower Saxony*

	Clacton		Hoxne	
	No.	%	No.	%
Wood whittling/planing	10	20	2	5.9
Wood chopping/adzing	4	8.0	1	2.9
Wood sawing	2	4.0	0	0.0
Wood scraping	5	10.0	2	5.9
Wood wedging	1(?)	2.0	5	14.7
Hide scraping	3	6.0	5	14.7
Hide cutting	1	2.0	2	5.9
Meat cutting/butchery	10	20.0	10	29.4
Boring, wood and bone	4	8.0	2	5.9
Plant cutting	0	0.0	3	8.8
Other	10	20.0	2	5.9
Totals	50	100.0	34	100.0
Percentage wood working		50.0		32.3
Percentage use on meat and hides		28.0		50.0

Source: Keeley 1980:159 table 34

Table 4.6. *Functional groupings for artifacts according to Pradel (1972/3)*

The 'functions' are guesses based on an assessment of the use of an implement according to its shape

1. Projectile points	microliths, points, flechettes
2. Cutting tools	short: burins, chisels, knives, blades, bladelets, long: saws, tranchets, large cutting tools
3. Scrapers	end scrapers, side scrapers, planes, steep scrapers
4. Pointed hand-held tools	hand-held points, picks, awls
5. Tools which are not strongly differentiated by function	pebble tools, choppers, primitive side scrapers, Abbevillian bifaces, composite tools, utilised flakes

example, it is not possible to compare the lower and middle with the upper palaeolithic (see also Isaac 1977). Typological and technological systems of analysis very often emphasise differences between collections of stone tools that may however have been used to perform the same tasks.

(b) upper palaeolithic, 35–10 Kyr

Comparable typological schemes to those used for the earlier palaeolithic have been developed for the upper palaeolithic (de Sonneville-Bordes 1960; Tixier 1963; de Lumley (ed.) 1976a; Smith 1966) and have been applied elsewhere in Europe (Valoch 1960; Otte 1979; González-Echegaray and Freeman 1973; de Sonneville-Bordes 1961, 1963a, 1965, 1968, 1969). The original typological scheme used a 92 item type list which has since been increased to 105 elements (Appendix 4). The *lexique typologique* provided by de Sonneville-Bordes and

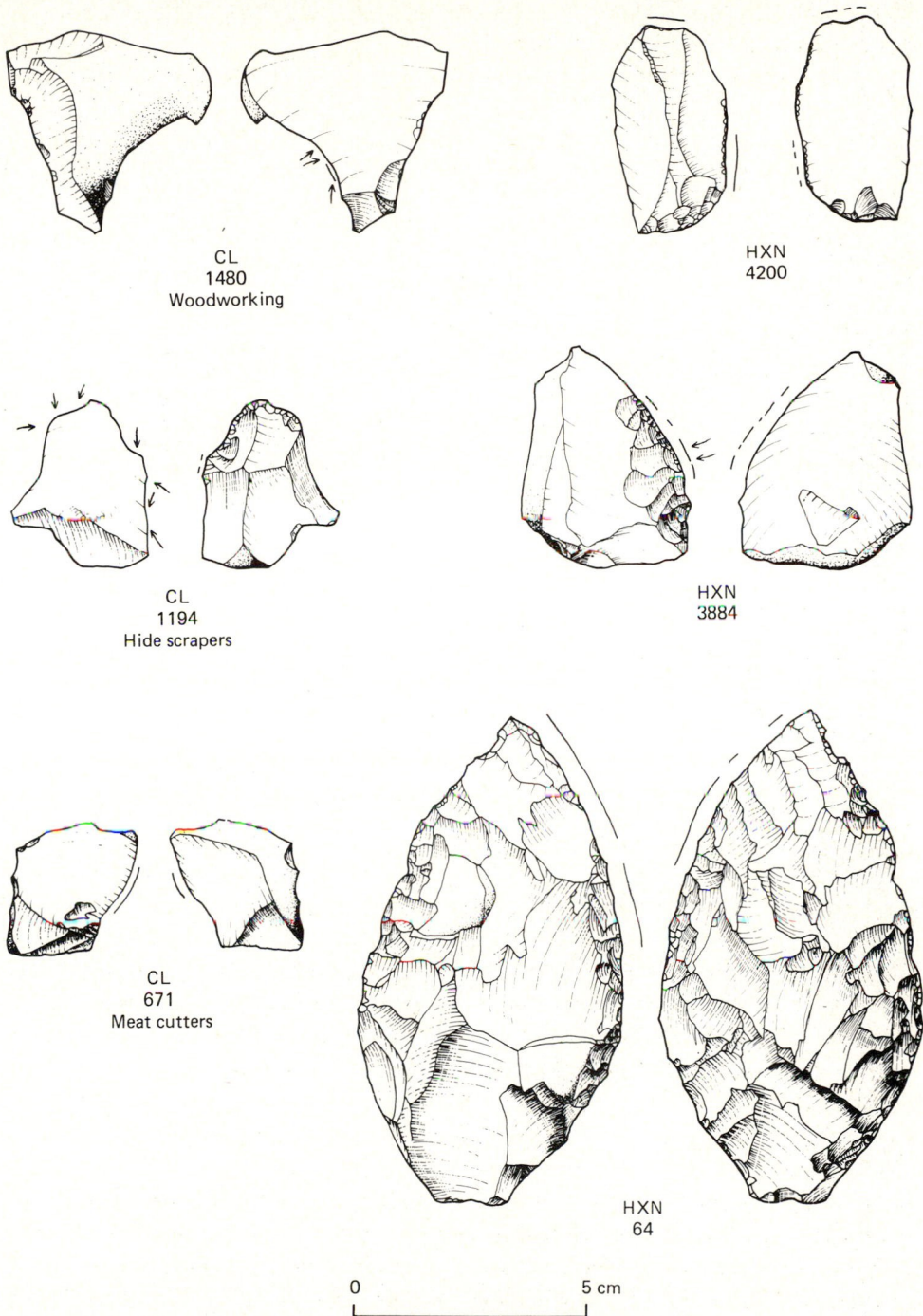

4.7 A contrast in artifact shapes but similar functions as revealed by the study of microwear polishes (heavy lines) on their working edges (Keeley 1980). The arrows indicate damage arising from utilisation. HXN = Hoxne; CL = Clacton.

Table 4.7. *Typological groupings for the upper palaeolithic*

de Sonneville-Bordes and Perrot (1954–5)		Laplace (1966)		Kozlowski and Kozlowski (1979)
Lexique typologique		*Typologie analytique*		
1–92	type list (see Appendix 4)	typological groups	code	typological groups
1–16	Endscrapers	1. Burins	B	A. End scrapers
17–22	Composite tools	2. End scrapers	G	B. Side scrapers and irregular scrapers
23–26	Drills (awls, borers)	3. Truncations	T	C. Burins
27–44	Burins	4. Borers/Zinken	Z	D. Truncated blades
45–59	Backed tools	5. Backed points	PD	E. Retouched blades
60–64	Truncated pieces	6. Backed blades	LD	F. Perforators
65–68	Retouched blades	7. Backed truncations	DT	G. Combined tools
69–72	Solutrean pieces	8. Geometrics	GM	H. Core tools
73–78	Various pieces	9. Flat retouch pieces (Solutrean foliates)	F	I. Leaf-shaped points
79–90	Tools on bladelets	10. Points	P	J. Tanged points and small leaf points
91	Azilian point	11. Retouched blades	L	K. Microliths and other backed tools
92	Misc.	12. Side scrapers	R	L. splintered pieces (Chisels)
		13. Abruptly retouched pieces	A	M. Misc.
		14. Denticulates	D	
		Misc.	DV	

Perrot (1954–5) can be broken down into ten major artifact groups (table 4.7). A lively review of the advantages of this approach and the shortcomings of the 'competition' is provided by de Sonneville-Bordes (1974–5). Type fossils are also incorporated into this typological approach. Useful type fossils are those which have a short and well-defined chronological existence within the wider development of a culture. For the French upper palaeolithic, de Sonneville-Bordes recognises the following artifacts as useful type fossils: aurignacian bone and antler points, noailles burins, Font Robert tanged points, shouldered and pressure flaked solutrean leaf points, stemmed points of the late magdalenian and azilian antler harpoons. Descriptions of these and many other lithic forms can be found in Brézillon's (1968) dictionary of palaeolithic terms and types. The variety of forms that secondary retouch can take (fig. 4.8) also now constitutes an important attribute for describing implements.

The intricate interplay between the assemblage and type fossil approaches based on an immense first hand knowledge of lithic material is perfectly summarised in this following description:

In a test trench, after seeing about ten or twenty tools, or even sometimes flakes, one can tell if a mousterian assemblage belongs to the Quina or M.T.A. facies, even if no Quina scraper or handaxe has yet been found. Before the discovery of the first noailles burin, one can tell if one is dealing with a noailles level by the style of the other burins on truncation. (Bordes and de Sonneville-Bordes 1970:72)

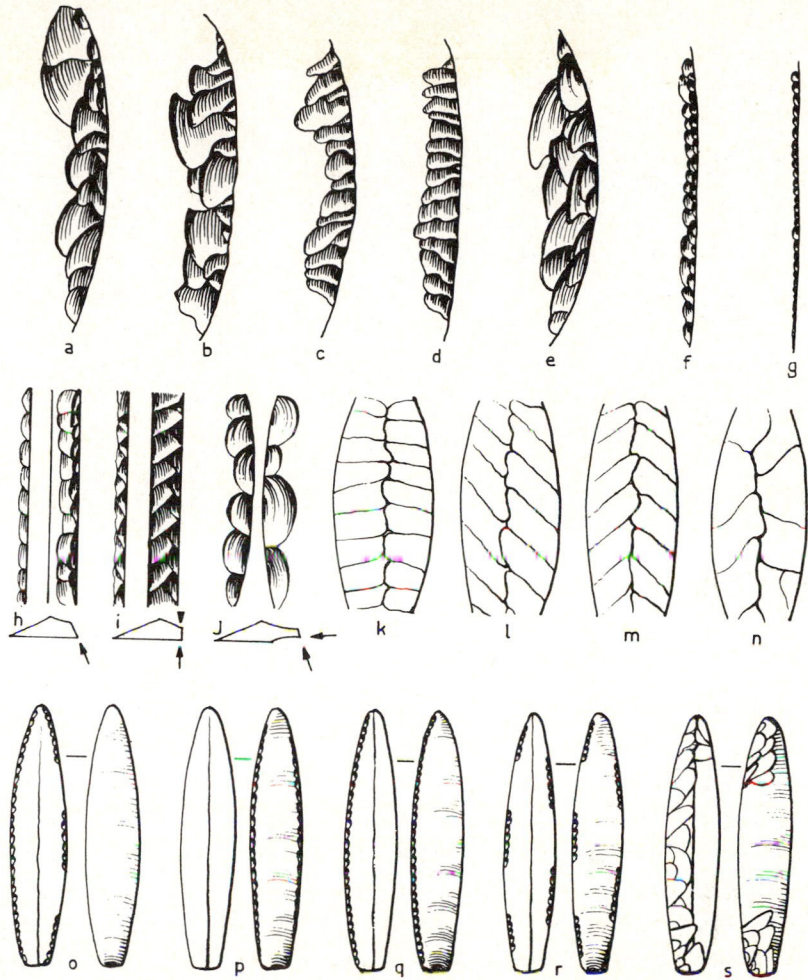

4.8 Forms of secondary retouch in flint artifacts (Brézillon 1968:109, fig. 20). (a, b) scaly; (c) sub-parallel; (d) parallel; (e) scalar (Bordes); (f) aurignacian (Bouyssonnie); (g) abrupt marginal; (h) abrupt normal (blunting); (i) abrupt backing on anvil; (j) plano-convex; (k) transversal and parallel; (l) oblique and parallel; (m) chevrons; (n) flat and irregular; (o) continuous and discontinuous on the proximal medial and distal portions, direct; (p) reverse; (q) alternate; (r) alternating; (s) invasive.

The importance of the Bordian typological schemes has been to transform this acute appreciation of assemblage composition into statements about palaeolithic materials that can be replicated and understood by other workers with less experience and no access to the original data.

An alternative typological scheme used extensively in Italy, southern France and southern Spain is based upon the work of Laplace (1961, 1966). This scheme sets out to establish similarities between assemblages. The *typologie analytique* uses the concept of primary morphological types. These are the basic

4.9 The upper palaeolithic types used by Laplace (1958–61) in his *Typologie Analytique*. These generalised forms are the basis for all upper palaeolithic typologies.

artifact forms. Some sixty primary artifact types are recognised with additional sub-divisions (fig. 4.9). These are then ordered into 14 typological groups (table 4.7) and indexes are calculated for each group and used as a basis for comparing assemblages. This is of course very different from de Sonneville-Bordes' approach where in the cumulative graph every artifact type has an equal weighting. A comparable scheme to Laplace's has been used by the Kozlowskis (J.K. and S.K., 1979) in a wide ranging study of the European upper palaeolithic (table 4.7).

The Laplace typology is an extreme example of the organic model, employing what he refers to as the dialectic method to identify structural process (Laplace and Merino 1979). In his interpretation, the leptolithic assemblages form part of an organic whole and so represent different manifestations of a common polymorphic base. Change occurs through catalysts and mutation and the end result is a purposive goal-seeking evolutionary drive where the stone tools are imbued with their own internal dynamism to evolve. Human behaviour seems very removed from this elaborate, clockwork model of lithic assemblages.

The scheme of de Sonneville-Bordes and Perrot also takes into account the unretouched pieces and records debitage counts. The waste flakes and unretouched categories were not included in Laplace's original study although other studies have devised schemes for typologising this material (e.g. Bagolini 1968).

Use wear analysis of upper palaeolithic material was begun by Semenov (1964) in his study of material from Russia. This has generally used low-power microscopic examination of edges and working facets for evidence of striations. An example of this is provided by Rosenfeld's (1971) study of 34 end scrapers from La Madeleine. Edge abrasion could be seen on the retouched end of the blade and furthermore this working edge still bore traces of red ochre. This observation has been confirmed by high-power magnification (Keeley 1980:171) and an interpretation offered that in this instance the end scrapers were used to rub these mineral pigments into hides to preserve them. Other examples of the low power approach can be found in Leroi-Gourhan and Brézillon (1966) and Feustel (1973). As with use wear studies on earlier palaeolithic material these studies show that specific artifact forms were not used for a single task or restricted to working a particular raw material.

Further temporal frameworks

The technological and typological divisions establish a single clear chronological marker at 35 Kyr. Either side of this marker it is possible to make two further chronological divisions. In the earlier period (table 4.8), I propose to separate material older than 128 Kyr from collections dated between 128 and 35 Kyr. The reasons for this division are twofold. In the first place, there is as yet very little precision in dating material that is older than the last interglacial/glacial cycle,

Table 4.8. *A four part division of the palaeolithic record of Europe*

Period	Kyr bp	technology/typology	Pleistocene division		
4	20–10	blade and bladelet microlithic elements	Upper Pleistocene	4	Late upper palaeolithic (LUP)
3	35–20	blade	" "	3	Early upper palaeolithic (EUP)
2	128–35	flake, core/chopping tool	" "	2 ⎫	
1	>128	flake, core/chopping tool	Middle Pleistocene	1 ⎭	Earlier palaeolithic (formerly middle and lower palaeolithic)

and 'lumping' is therefore unavoidable. Secondly, much of the material after 128 Kyr comes from well-stratified contexts in caves and rock shelters while the earlier material is better represented from lake muds and river terraces. While future work may show that the material from the caves has a much greater chronological depth than presently suspected this division at 128 Kyr is adopted here in order to bring out this contrast in the locations of our findspots.

The division after 35 Kyr falls at the last glacial maximum at 20 Kyr. This marker is not determined by a change in the findspot locations from which our data base comes but by the appearance from this time of microlithic components in ever increasing quantities. These small size elements require sieving and screening procedures if a representative sample is going to be recovered. Consequently the potential for numerically much larger assemblages is enhanced. This chronological division, followed in the next chapter, has been selected in order to take these factors into account.

This brief review of technology, typology and their basic temporal patterning has given us four divisions (table 4.8) for analysing the archaeological material from the provinces and regions of palaeolithic Europe. It is to this picture of culture history that we can now turn to look for patterning in the European palaeolithic record.

CHAPTER 5

THE PALAEOLITHIC RECORD OF EUROPE

Somme toute, à chaque instant de leur évolution, les industries humaines ont été soumises à trois impératifs principaux, interférant les uns avec les autres: (1) le besoin de tel ou tel outil . . . (2) les qualités intrinsèques de la matière première dont les hommes disposaient alors (3) *la tradition technique et la routine, heureusement assez tyrannique pour nous permettre de définir des industries.*

François Bordes, L'évolution buissonnante des industries en Europe occidentale (1950:419)

Introduction

The European palaeolithic has been divided into many space/time groupings using typological methods combined with technological observations. It is difficult to speak of a consensus view since each regional tradition has its own internal complexities, history of research and style of presentation that makes comparison between the data recovered by these traditions a difficult matter. However the purpose of this chapter is to attempt a general picture of variation in palaeolithic materials against the framework of the regional model outlined in Chapter 3. This is intended as an introduction to the complexities of the data base, and where possible the references should be followed, and collections of material studied, in order to gain a first hand impression of the difficulties of describing widespread patterns.

Key sites

The data of palaeolithic Europe are frequently described by a detailed examination of key sites and sections. This core of key sites is considered as a source of prime data points for information about the period. An example is provided in table 5.1, taken from Bhattacharya's (1977) study of palaeolithic Europe, where special attention was paid to central Europe. The discussions and interpretations of the artifactual material contained in these sites and their place in chronological and classificatory schemes form the very heart of traditional palaeolithic discourse, practice and knowledge.

Similar lists of key sites could be compiled from other general works on palaeolithic Europe (Müller-Karpe 1966; Bordes 1968a; Coles and Higgs 1969; Wymer 1982; Gamble 1984b). The importance and hence selection of such sites is generally decided by the following factors:

Table 5.1. *An example of the 'key site' approach in palaeolithic studies*

This list, divided here by province, region and period, comes from Bhattacharya (1977) which placed particular emphasis upon the archaeology of central Europe

		Northern province		
Palaeolithic period	**Lower**	**NW region** Somme terraces, (Abbeville, St Acheul, Cagny); Chelles; Thames (Swanscombe); Clacton; Hoxne	**NC region** Heidelberg; Markkleeberg; Cröben; Zehmen; Reutersruh; Balve cave; Vogelherd; Hannover Döhren; Hundisburg; Bilzingsleben; Sedlec	**NE region**
	Middle	Spiennes; Spy; Ouse; Pinhole cave	Bockstein; Schulerloch; Lehringen; Schambach; Achenheim; Klausen caves; Weinberg caves; Kartstein; Sesselfelsgrotte; Rheindahlen; Balve; Salzgitter-Lebenstedt; Ehringsdorf; Weimar; Taubach; Königsaue; Subalyuk, Kůlna; Sipkă; Nové Mesto; Gánovce; Propst; Byci Skala.	Volgograd; Molodova; Rozhok I; Kiik-Koba; Il'skaya; Starosel'e; Volchij Grot; Achštyvskaya I
	Upper	Arcy-sur-Cure; Feddermesser (Lommel); Hengistbury Head; Creswell Crags (Pinhole; Mother Grundy's parlour)	Federmesser (Rissen; Borneck; Meiendorf; Stellmoor); Bromme; Vogelherd; Ofnet; Kösten; Brillenhöhle; Weinberg caves; Munzingen; Teufelskuchen; Petersfels; Stankowicze; Švédův Stůl; Dolní Věstonice; Tišnov; Předmost; Pavlov; Petrkovice; Pekárna; Willendorf; Szeleta; Istallöskö; Henye; Giengen; Balve; Wildscheuer; Andernach; Gönnersdorf; Ilsenhöhle; Jerzmanovice; Kesslerloch; Maszycka cave; Swidry Mielnik.	Kostenki; Molodova; Gagarino; Avdeevo; Honci; Mezin; Timonovka; Puškari; Sjuren I; Ceahlau; Stânca Ripiceni

		Southern province		
	Lower	**SW region** Pech de l'Azé	**ALPINE region** Wildkirchli; Drachenloch; Laaberg terraces; Wildemannlisloch; Repoulsthöhle	**SE region** Vértesszöllös
	Mid-dle	Le Moustier; La Micoque; Combe-Grenal; Fontéchevade; Pech de l'Azé; Laussel; Castilló	Broion cave; Quinzano; Cotencher; Salzofenhöhle; Gudenushöhle	Tata; Érd; Ohaba Ponor; La Adam; Bacho Kiro
	Upper	Caminade; Les Cottés; Roc de Combe; La Ferrassie; La Madeleine; Isturitz; Laugerie Haute; Castilló	Moosbühl	Arka; Bacho Kiro; La Adam

		Mediterranean province		
	Lower	**MW region** Le Vallonnet; Terra Amata; Torralba	**MC region** Venosa; Torre in Pietra	**ME region**
	Mid-dle	Gorham's cave; Devils Tower	Guattari cave; Basua; Torre dell' Alto; Lower Versillia	Crvena Stijena; Postojnska Jama; Larissa; Kokkinopilos; Asprochaliko
	Upper	Parpalló	Grimaldi caves (Cavillon; Prince; Torre; Enfants; Barma Grande; Mochi); Rommanelli; Castello	Crvena Stijena; Seidi; Potŏcka cave; Kastritsa

(1) chronological information either in the form of an absolute date or a relative age obtained by a geological 'fix';

(2) stratigraphic succession of several artifact assemblages in a single column;

(3) the recovery of enough lithic material per assemblage to conduct a typological analysis; or the presence, in a small assemblage of a 'good' type fossil;

(4) assessment of degree of disturbance of the archaeological material from the desired 'in-situ' state;

(5) associated fossil human material;

(6) associated art works, either portable figurines, engraved plaques or painted caves;

(7) any other unexpected item, e.g. burials, wooden spears, alignments of bones and clumps of stones, exotic raw materials, etc.;

(8) associated evidence of animal faunas, pollen, etc., or features such as huts, hearths, etc.;

(9) the standard of reporting;

(10) problems posed by the excavator prior to excavation and answered by the excavation.

This list points up how the fortuitous act of discovery of an object like a skull or figurine can be as influential in establishing the 'importance' of a site as the questions directing research or the quantities of implements recovered. It must be remembered that according to the requirements of the organic model used in the culture history approach (Chapter 1), only a date, relative or absolute, and the opportunity this provides to observe change in a controlled vertical sequence are essential criteria for interpreting the finds.

It is important to bear this in mind since the descriptions that follow are derived from such a site based, organic, approach. This paradigm has shaped what is regarded as good evidence and this is enshrined many times in text books and general reviews of the subject.

Northern province 1

(a) chronology

The earliest absolute dates from this province point to occupation from stage 9 (table 5.2) at Swanscombe. The number of dates is however very small. The geological context of many of the findspots shows that they are associated with cold climate conditions (Collins 1969:table 12). Moreover there are localities such as the deposits at Westbury-sub-Mendip in England that in all probability pre-date stage 9. A glance at the isotope curve (fig. 3.3) shows that these early 'interglacial'/temperate episodes of the middle pleistocene were periods characterised by much less melting of the polar ice caps than occurred in sub-stage 5e. We are therefore dealing with the equivalent of the first stage of the early glacial part of the cycle. A number of sites in the NW region, including levels at

Table 5.2. *Absolute dates for period 1 sites from the northern province*

Swanscombe	Base of upper middle gravels, skull horizon	$326 \pm {}^{99}_{54}$ Kyr (1)
Clacton	Associated with artifacts	$245 \pm {}^{35}_{25}$ Kyr (1)
Ehringsdorf	Travertine site with artifacts	225 ± 26 Kyr (2)
Bilzingsleben	Travertine, minimum age only. Probable age of 350 Kyr estimated for artifact horizon	$228 \pm {}^{17}_{12}$ Kyr (3)
Pontnewydd	Cave	$170 - 200$ Kyr (2)

References: (1) Szabo and Collins 1975; (2) Cook *et al.* 1982; (3) Harmon *et al.* 1980.

Swanscombe and Hoxne (Wymer 1977) are associated with this segment of the interglacial/glacial cycle.

Early ages have been proposed for sites in Czechoslovakia at Přezletice (Fridrich 1976) where four artifact bearing horizons are known. This site has been dated to the Cromerian (Elster) but exactly where this should be placed on the isotope curve is uncertain.

The cave site of Pontnewydd (Green *et al.* 1981) in north Wales and the open travertine site of Ehringsdorf (Harmon *et al.* 1980; Cook *et al.* 1982) now both have absolute dates which indicate ages of c.200 Kyr. It is difficult at the present time to be precise, but the available evidence suggests a considerable ebb and flow in the settlement of this northern province as the climatic fluctuations of the pleistocene took place.

An important site for understanding the stratigraphic succession of lithic industries is the Barnfield Pit at Swanscombe (Wymer 1968). This multi-level site in the 30m terrace of the Thames (Ovey (ed.) 1964) consists of a series of gravels and loams which contain a number of contrasted artifact assemblages as well as a rich variety of environmental information (Evans 1975; Gladfelter 1975). The other key locations for observing stratigraphic relations have been the terrace systems of the Thames, Seine and Somme (Breuil and Kozlowski 1932; Bordes 1954, 1956; Tuffreau 1976a, 1982; Wymer 1968; Roe 1981). The terraces provide a form of relative dating for the large number of industries contained within their gravel and loess pits. It is now clear however that the earlier schemes of Breuil (1939) which viewed the terraces as chronological steps, each with a distinctive assemblage of artifacts, is supported neither by geological dating nor by our present understanding of the nature of variation in flint industries and assemblages.

The majority of sites from this province at this period are open locations which take a number of forms. These range from lake deposits (Hoxne), gravel terrace sites (Swanscombe, Markkleeberg) to loess/brick pits (Le Tillet, Biache–Saint-Vaast; Rheindahlen). Lower palaeolithic material is also known in a stratified context from the raised beach deposits of southern England (ApSimon *et al.* 1977; Woodcock 1981) and northern France (Monnier 1980). A distinctive group of sites are those incorporated in travertine deposits at Bilzingsleben, Taubach and Ehringsdorf. Travertine is formed under warm, humid conditions as the calcium carbonate in the parent geology is dissolved by warm springs. Occupation was sited at the margins of small lakes (Mania and Dietzel 1980) and these sites should correspond to warm peaks in the isotope curves. At Bilzingsleben (Mania *et al.* 1980) this is thought to have occurred at c.350 Kyr, which if substantiated would place the site within stage 9. A more recent date 228+17/–12 Kyr (Harmon *et al.* 1980) obtained by Th/U dating is on another section of the travertine quarry and must be regarded only as a minimum age for the archaeological deposits.

Artifact material from cave sites is known from Pontnewydd, Westbury-sub-Mendip, La Cotte, which is a coastal cave on the island of Jersey (McBurney and Callow 1971), Hunas in southern Germany (Freund 1978) and Stránská Skála near Brno in Moravia (Musil and Valoch 1968; Fridrich 1976).

(b) industrial groupings

Two major industrial groupings, or civilisations, have been recognised in the province. These are the acheulean, named after St Acheul on the Somme, and the clactonian from the type site of Clacton-on-Sea in eastern England (Singer *et al.* 1973).

The term acheulean is synonymous with its distinctive type fossils which are a wide variety of different shaped handaxes (fig. 5.1; Appendix 3). The many forms they take have been described by a number of attribute analyses (Bordes 1961a; Roe 1964, 1968a; Wymer 1968; Callow 1976). The handaxes form a rich data base. Roe (1968b) has compiled a gazetteer for the handaxes that survive in the museums and private collections of southern England and this consists of some 100,000 implements. To this number must be added an unspecified number of flake implements and debitage which have by comparison been poorly collected and recorded. Three assemblage groupings are apparent – pointed, ovate and intermediate – although it is not clear what significance this finding has in terms of past behaviour which required different shaped and weighted handaxes. It has for example been suggested by Hayden (1979b) that handaxes were only a source for producing flakes. In other words, they are cores which have reached the end of their useful life and have finally been turned into an implement, used once and then thrown away. More microwear studies (Keeley 1980) would help to sharpen some of these speculations.

Recent work at Hoxne (Singer and Wymer 1976), Swanscombe (Waechter 1971) and Biache–Saint-Vaast (Tuffreau *et al.* 1977, 1982) have demonstrated the wide range of ancillary tools made on flakes. This has been known for a long time at other sites, primarily High Lodge (fig. 5.2, o,q) at Mildenhall in eastern England (Marr *et al.* 1921) and in the Atelier Commont at St Acheul (Bordes and

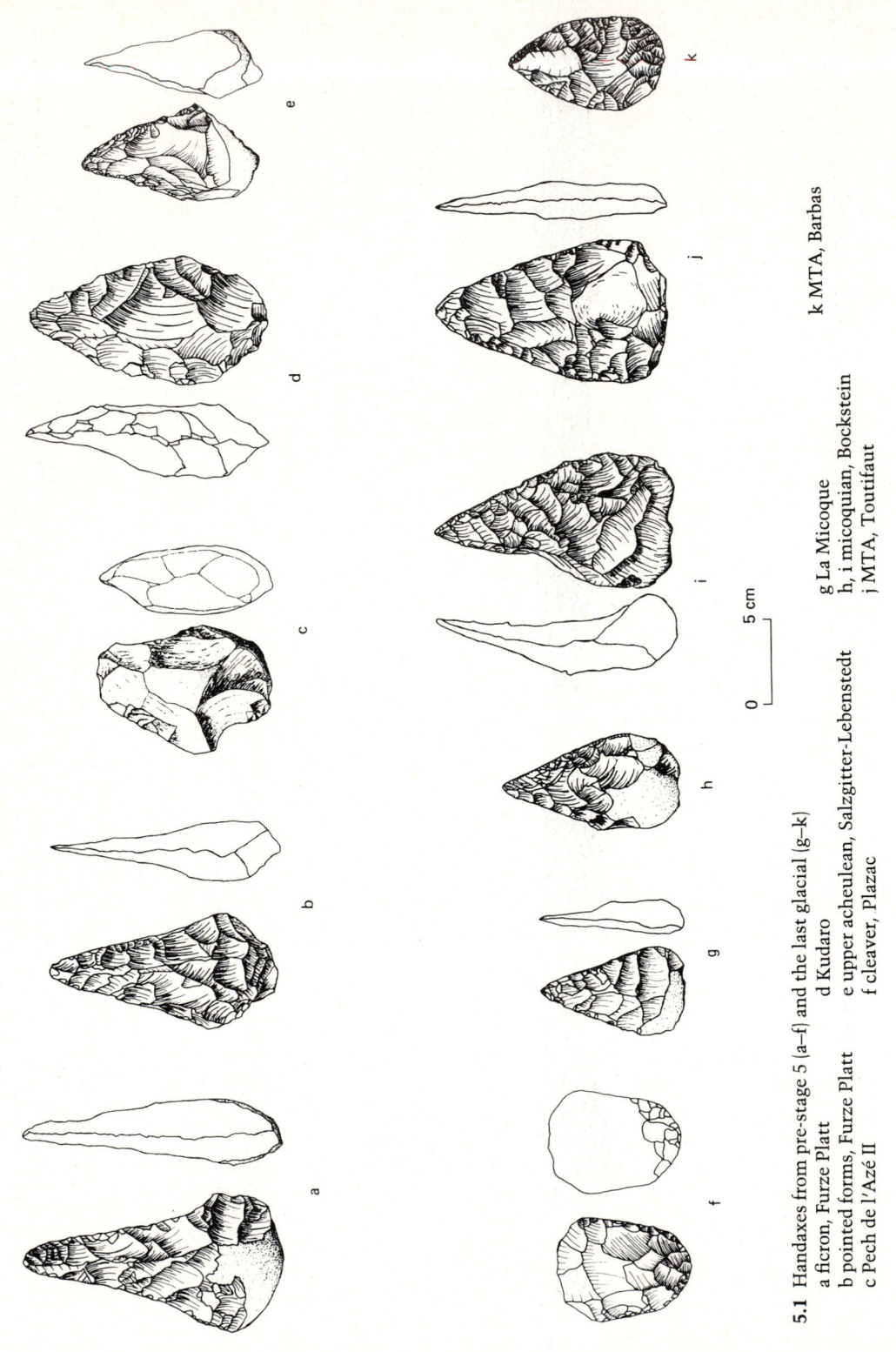

5.1 Handaxes from pre-stage 5 (a–f) and the last glacial (g–k)

a ficron, Furze Platt
b pointed forms, Furze Platt
c Pech de l'Azé II

d Kudaro
e upper acheulean, Salzgitter-Lebenstedt
f cleaver, Plazac

g La Micoque
h, i micoquian, Bockstein
j MTA, Toutifaut

k MTA, Barbas

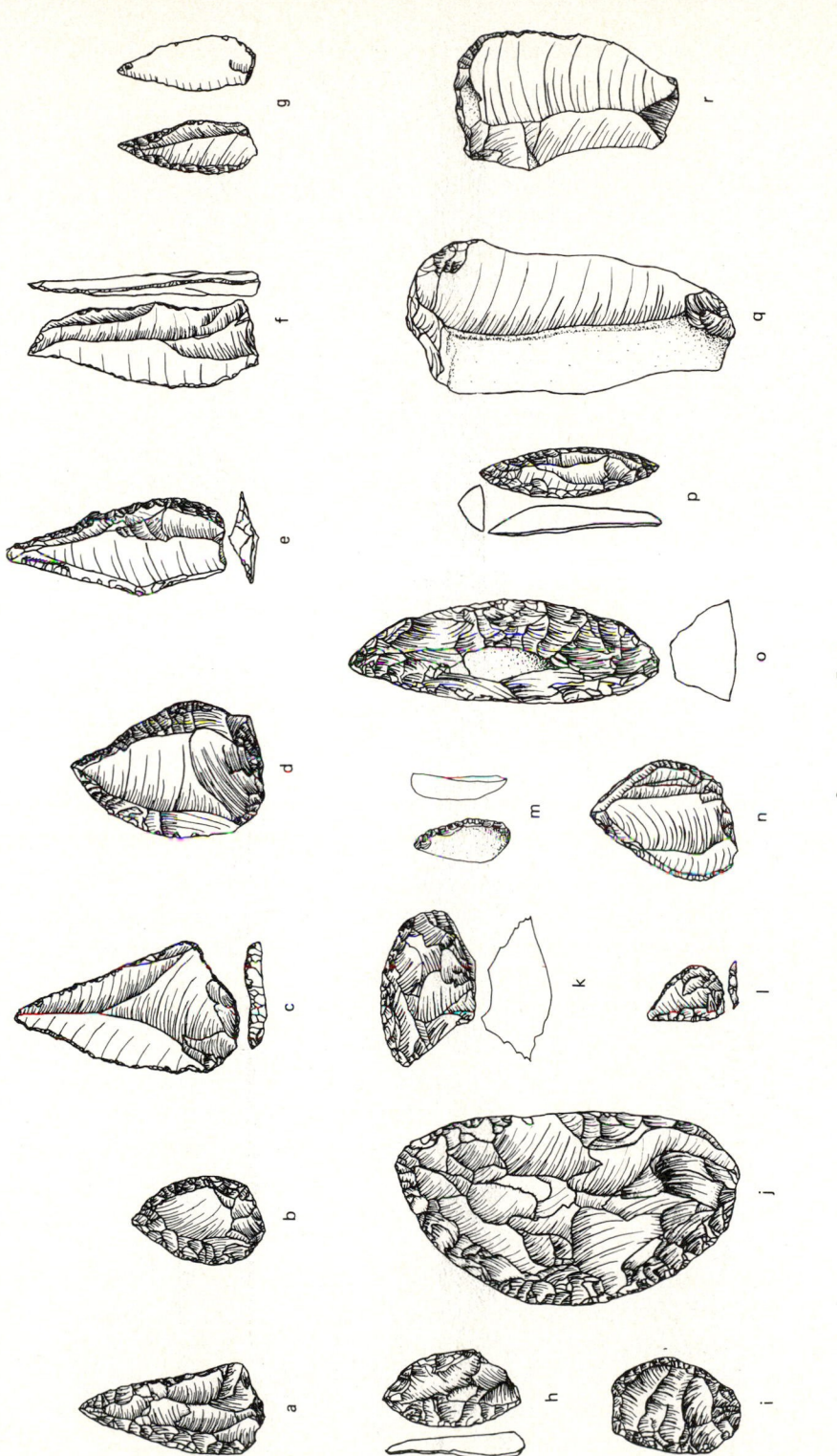

5.2 Retouched flake tools from the earlier palaeolithic of Europe, stages 1 and 2
Points: (a) Pech de l'Azé II; (b) Rheindahlen; (c) Salzgitter-Lebenstedt with faceted platform; (d) Markkleeberg with plain platform; (e, f) Markkleeberg flake/blades; (g) Lazaret; (h) Ehringsdorf
Side scrapers: (i) Ehringsdorf convex; (j) Marsal quina form; (k) Esquicho-Grapaou quina form; (l) Lazaret dejété; (m) Monte Circeo pontinian; (n) Pech de l'Azé II convergent side scraper – note the similarity with point (b) Thick scrapers: (o) High Lodge keeled scraper; (p) Ehringsdorf limace scraper End scrapers: (q) High Lodge flake/blade; (r) Markkleeberg

0   5 cm

Fitte 1953), where scrapers of various forms and other retouched implements such as points were predominant in the inventories of retouched tools.

This flake element is also seen in assemblages using the levallois technique as at Bakers Hole (Wymer 1968) near Swanscombe on the Thames and at Reutersruh in Hesse, West Germany (Luttropp and Bosinski 1971). These are both very rich sites in terms of the quantities of knapped stone debris. The characteristic tortoise cores are found in great numbers even though the raw material is very different. At Reutersruh it is quartzite while at Bakers Hole large nodules of good quality flint were available and used.

The flake assemblages (figs. 5.2 and 5.3) were at one time regarded by Breuil (1939) as a separate phylum to the acheulean with its handaxes. This distinction is no longer meaningful since it is now abundantly clear that the levallois technique forms a variable component of the handaxe industries, and that flake implements have been consistently under-represented in collections. Neither is it possible to see, as Breuil did, the development from coarsely flaked handaxes at Abbeville through to the finely shaped and retouched handaxes of the acheulean. Improved geological knowledge (Tuffreau 1976a; Bourdier 1976) has led to the abandonment of a progressive view of successive artifact types.

The second industrial variant is a core/chopping tool industry known as the clactonian. This industry lacks sophisticated retouched implements and the majority of the flakes are irregular in outline, thick in cross section and have massive striking platforms. This has presented problems for the typologist although recourse has been sought in measuring and comparing the size and angles of the striking platforms (fig. 5.3, e–g) (Collins 1969; Ohel 1977, 1979).

The clactonian is a separate entity from the acheulean. This is shown at Swanscombe (fig 5.3, d) where it occurs below the stratified acheulean levels. Ohel (1979; Ohel and Lechevalier 1979) has however argued that the clactonian of eastern England and northern France was a preparatory stage in the manufacture of acheulean handaxes. Preliminary flaking and roughing out would take place at these 'quarries' after which the blanks would be carried away and turned into handaxes elsewhere. This ingenious scenario does not however take into account the fundamental differences that exist in flint working techniques between these two industries (see comments to Ohel 1979), and the fact that clactonian flaking techniques are ill suited to producing handaxe roughouts.

A further group of flake assemblages are known from East Germany. The material from Wangen and Wallendorf has on occasion been described as clactonian (Toepfer 1970; Collins 1969), which is a comment on the unstandardised lithic forms and the anvil pattern of fracture which results in massive striking platforms. A detailed attribute analysis of the technology of an unstandardised flake industry from Taubach (Schafer 1981), referred to as taubachian by Valoch (1982a), establishes some patterns with other local flake based assemblages. At the site of Bilzingsleben there is a large assemblage of struck flint, c.60,000 pieces. Retouched tools are both rare and small in size (fig.

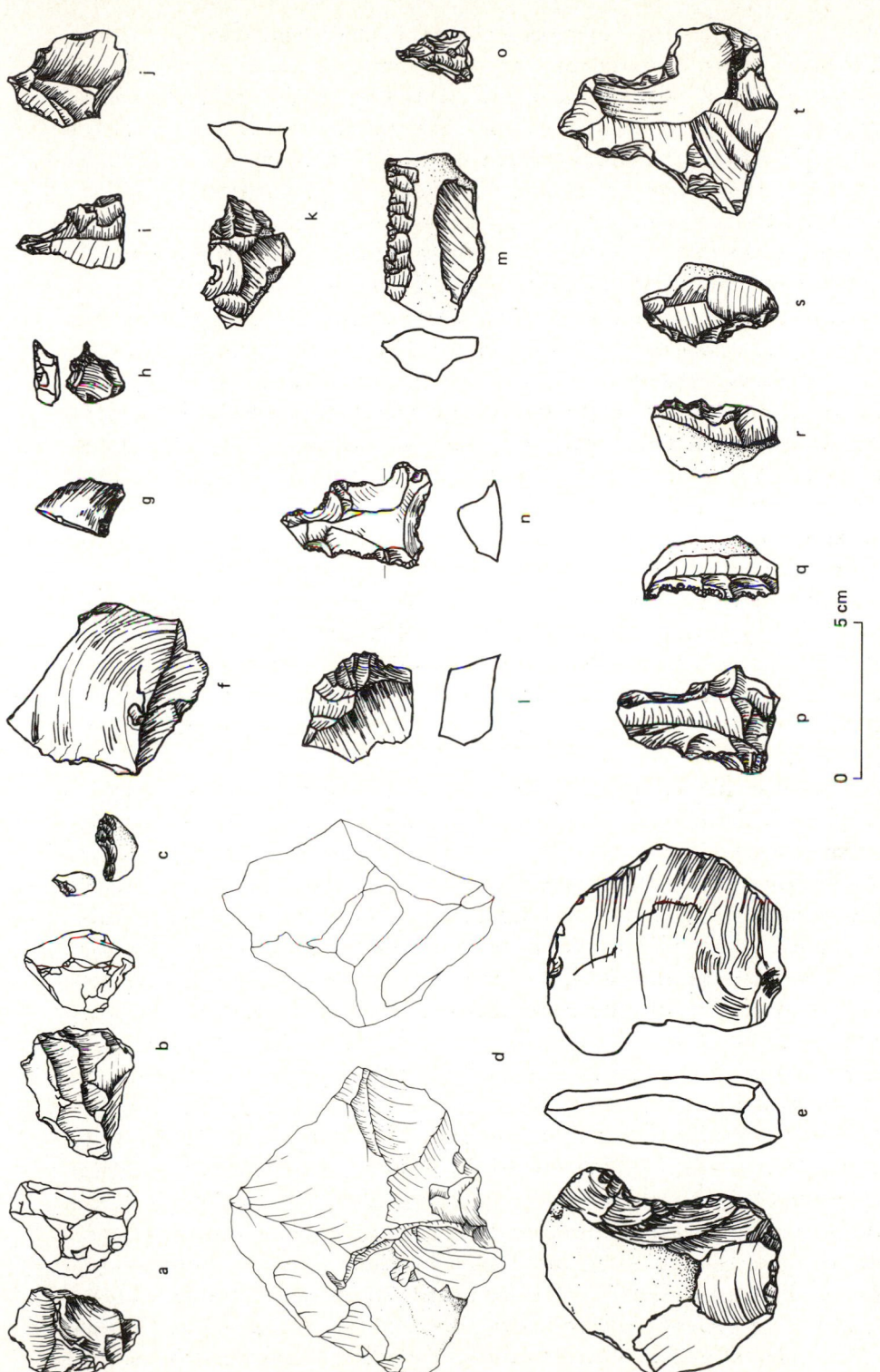

5.3 Chopping tools, flakes and denticulates from the earlier palaeolithic of Europe, stages 1 and 2. Chopping tools and core tools: (a, b) Fontéchevade tayacian; (c) Bilzingsleben; (d) Swanscombe. Flakes: (e) Clacton secondary working produces a bill hook; (f, g) Clacton plain massive platforms. Awls and borers: (h, i) Bilzingsleben; (j) Remenham. Denticulates: (k, l) Hortus; (m, n) Bilzingsleben; (o, p) Isernia; (q, r) Arcy-sur-Cure; Grotte de l'Hyène; (s) Pech de l'Azé II; (t) Remenham with retouch to form scraper.

0   5 cm

5.3, c,h,i,m,n) (Mania 1978). Handaxes are not known. There is however a range of scraper forms, awls, points and denticulates as well as chopping tools (fig. 6.16). As such, the Bilzingsleben material can be described as predominantly a flake assemblage. It is however very different from the material from Ehringsdorf, another travertine quarry site (Behm-Blancke 1960). The implements in the levels at Ehringsdorf were once thought to form a likely 'ancestor' for the mousterian of the last glaciation since they show a high degree of bifacial working into points and scrapers (fig. 5.2, i,p) with a pronounced use of the levallois technique. However, the absolute date of 200 Kyr now rules out such an organic relationship with the industries of the early last glacial. Instead the assemblage forms yet another variant in the complex pattern of assemblage types at this early stage. Two more well documented, but poorly dated, assemblages come from Markkleeberg (fig. 5.2, d-f,r), East Germany (Grahmann 1955; Mania and Baumann 1980), and Salzgitter-Lebenstedt, West Germany (Tode (ed.) 1953). At Markkleeberg, the assemblage is poor in handaxes and some clactonian elements are present. However, there are many well struck flakes, many of them using the levallois technique, and blades are also a feature. Handaxes are very rare indeed. This is not the case at Salzgitter-Lebenstedt which has consistently been dated to the last glaciation (Tode (ed.) 1953; Grote 1978) but which according to Bosinski (1982:166) must be considered as at least penultimate glaciation in age. The handaxes are large and plano-convex in cross section (fig. 5.1, e). The technique of flake manufacture is strongly levallois (fig. 5.2, c). This site forms the type asemblage for Bosinski's (1967) Jungacheuléen (upper acheulean) industry.

In the NW region at Rheindahlen near Köln, a further flake dominated assemblage with well made points and scrapers is known (fig. 5.2, b) (Bosinski and Brunnacker 1973). The assemblage closely parallels the Ferrassie variant of the Charentian scraper mousterian from the SW region (Bosinski 1982a).

The complexity of the industrial groupings is well demonstrated at the multilevel loess site at Achenheim (Wernert 1957) on the Rhine in the NC region. Comparisons have been drawn between the bifacially worked pieces and those from Ehringsdorf (Thévenin 1976), while a coarse chopping tool element is also present (fig. 6.16).

(c) geographical variation

It was noted some time ago (McBurney 1950) that the distribution of handaxes from the earlier glaciations is largely restricted to regions west of the Rhine. McBurney interpreted this as an adaptation to the more genial forest conditions of western Europe which in some way stimulated cultural elaboration. Handaxes which are thought to pre-date the last interglacial period are indeed rare in Germany (Freund 1963). Moreover, they occur as single finds rather than large assemblages. Indeed Bosinski (1982a) regards the appearance of assemblages, such as Salzgitter-Lebenstedt, as indicating a transition between the lower palaeolithic and the formation of discrete, recurrent cultural groupings that have come to be so closely associated with the middle palaeolithic and the mousterian variants.

The dating of many of the assemblages is however very poor. As a result this division into a handaxe and non-handaxe province, with the NW region containing abundant examples of handaxes, may be more apparent than real since there are many handaxes from central Europe, traditionally dated to the last glaciation but which may be much older. In the same way, the appearance of the levallois technique as a feature of middle palaeolithic assemblages during the penultimate glaciation will also require revision as more absolute dates become available. What we can presently see is a number of flake assemblages scattered across the province and showing a wide spectrum in manufacturing techniques. The range is from Ehringsdorf, Markkleeberg and High Lodge (fig. 5.2) to Clacton, Bilzingsleben and Taubach (fig. 5.3). Collins (1969) provides a geographical background to the distribution of acheulean and clactonian material based on the traditional geo-chronology of the pleistocene, and some measure of the complexity of industrial variation can be gauged from his work.

Reconstructions of patterns of land use and subsistence behaviour are rare. Grahmann (1955) suggested that the Markleeberg site lay on a major game trail to the south of the Riss glacial gravels where mammoths and other game migrated in a small tundra corridor between the ice sheets and the arctic waste (fig. 5.4). Mania and Dietzel (1980) have provided a series of reconstructions of the hunters at Bilzingsleben based on the assumption that the bones and chipped stones found in the lake are in large degree the direct result of hunting behaviour.

One region has not received much attention. The NE region is often described as devoid of archaeological material that is older than the last interglacial (see table 5.1). However, acheulean occurs in the Caucasus cave sites at Kudaro I and II (fig. 5.1, d) (Loubine 1980). Chopping core tools have been found in the Oka and Moskva rivers (Valoch 1968), while a middle pleistocene site has recently come to light on the Don river at Mikaelovska (Kuznetsova 1982; Loubine 1981). Handaxes and hence acheulean assemblages are very rare in the Ukraine but sites at Zhitomir and Khotylevo (Zaverniaev 1978a; Valoch 1982a) do point to a presence.

(d) human remains

With the exception of juvenile teeth and mandible fragments from the cave at Pontnewydd (Green 1981, 1984; Green *et al.* 1981), all human fossil material which predates the last interglacial/glacial cycle comes from open locations. The material includes the massive mandible from Mauer near Heidelberg and the Steinheim skull (table 5.3) which is not well dated. This small cranium of a

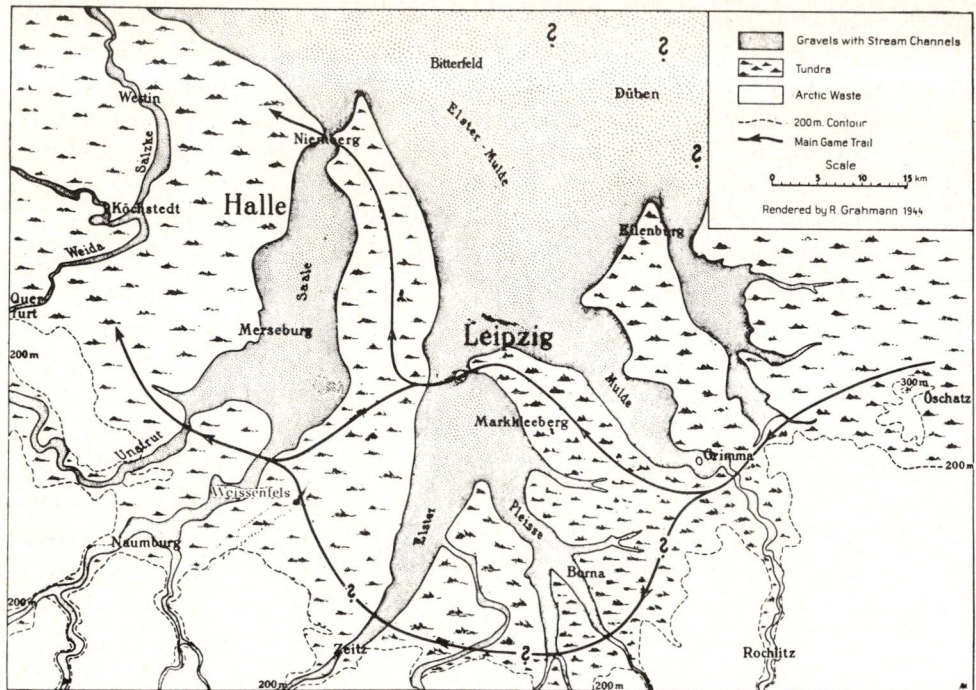

5.4 A reconstruction by Grahmann (1955: fig. 4) of the major game trail that followed the edge of the Riss gravels in the vicinity of Leipzig NC region. The gravel pits around Markkleeberg contain many bones of both mammoth and elephant. Grahmann used these observations on environment and resources to predict where other palaeolithic sites might be located in the Leipzig area, for instance at Grimma, should exposures in the gravels become available for inspection.

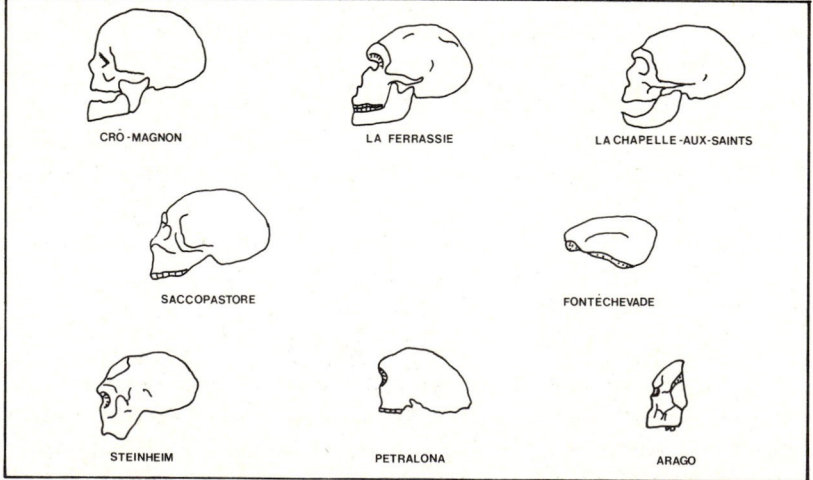

5.5 Fossil crania for the middle and upper Pleistocene of Europe. The specimens are arranged according to their position in a grade (table 5.6) and have been orientated in the same direction for the purposes of visual comparison (after Gamble 1984b).

young adult has a pronounced supra-orbital torus and a flattened cranial dome (fig. 5.5). It is frequently cited as a precursor of later populations. The Bilzingsleben material consists of two occipital, two frontal fragments and one molar (Mania *et al.* 1980). The Swanscombe skull is represented by the occipital and parietals which are very thick and robust. The fragments of an adult calvaria were found at Ehringsdorf in 1925, together with other post-cranial material from the lower travertine. However, the pieces of the calvaria have been re-assembled in two different ways by von Weidenreich and von Kleinschmidt (Behm-Blancke 1958: Taf. 42 and 43), which makes it difficult to assign it to a fossil lineage. In 1915 part of a child's skeleton was found in the same site.

Further references

NW: Wymer 1968, 1982; Roe 1981; Monnier 1980; H. de Lumley (ed.) 1976a; Collins 1969; Howell 1966; Cook *et al.* 1982; Gamble 1984b.
NC: Toepfer 1968, 1970, 1976; H. de Lumley (ed.) 1976a; Zotz 1951; Valoch 1968, (ed.) 1976a, 1982a; Mania 1978.
NE: Loubine 1980, 1981; Valoch 1968, 1982a; Păunescu 1970.

Southern province 1

(a) chronology

There are some claims for very early industries in the SW region. At Chillac (Delporte 1976; Guth 1974) some flaked pebbles have been dated on geological grounds to c.1.8 Myr. The site at Soleihac (Bonifay *et al.* 1976) is dated to c.0.9 Myr principally on the basis of the fauna with which the 50–60 artifacts so far recovered are associated. The earliest absolute date for the province comes from the travertine site of Vértesszöllös in northern Hungary situated in the SE region. A Th/U date on the travertine gives a range between 250 and 475 Kyr. The fauna has been assigned to a stadial within the Mindel (Elster) glaciation. Another absolute date for the province is a U-series date of 146±16 Kyr for level 11 at the Bourgeois-Delaunay rock shelter in the La Chaise complex (France) which contains human fossil remains and artifacts (Debenath 1976).

Important stratified locations are all to be found in the SW region. These include a well known group of cave sites which include La Micoque (fig. 5.6), Combe-Grenal, Fontéchevade, Abri Vaufrey and Pech de l'Azé II (G. Guichard 1976). The Abri Vaufrey has a mousterian or middle palaeolithic assemblage variant stratified beneath a stalagmite floor dated by Th/U to 200 Kyr. This assemblage would previously have been assigned on typological grounds to the last glacial period. Lower palaeolithic assemblages at Pech de l'Azé II, Combe-Grenal and La Micoque have all been dated, on the basis of the sediments they contain, to the penultimate glaciation. In the French scheme this is called Riss after the classic Alpine sequence. At Combe-Grenal there are nine levels of acheulean ranging in size from five lithic pieces in level 64 to 17,432 in level 58 (G. Guichard 1976). At Pech de l'Azé II there are four principal artifact horizons, levels 9, 8, 7B, and 6, which date to stages within Riss I and Riss II, while at La Micoque (fig. 5.6) assemblages described as pre-mousterian in levels E and H, dated to Riss I and II respectively, are succeeded stratigraphically by acheulean assemblages in levels J and L during Riss III (Laville *et al.* 1980).

The Alpine region lacks any definite lower palaeolithic material. Claims have been made for early artifacts in caves such as the Drachenloch, Wildemannliss-loch and Wildkirchli in Switzerland and the Repoulst caves in Austria. These claims however are difficult to assess without absolute dates, and depend to a great extent upon interpreting the simple flakes as produced by primitive, and hence early, industries. Early material has also been noted on the Italian side of the Alps (Fedele 1981) at the Monfenera cave situated at 1000 m.

Open sites are well known from the SW region (G. Guichard 1976:914), although they have tended to be overshadowed by the more famous cave investigations (Bordes 1972). In the SE region, very few sites are known (Valoch 1968). The site of Vértesszöllös was, at the time of its discovery in 1963, the first positive identification of a lower palaeolithic pre-last glacial site in this region (Vértes 1975).

(b) industrial groupings

The acheulean is well represented in the cave deposits of the SW region (fig. 5.2, a,n). The assemblages contain a variety of handaxe forms (fig. 5.1, c) as well as cleavers made on flakes (fig. 5.1, f). Features such as these cleavers and the general rarity of handaxes, when compared with the large numbers and assem-blages from the northern province, led Bordes (1971) to describe the SW material as a meridional variant of the acheulean. The levallois index in these assem-blages is variable and the dominant tool forms are side scrapers, with backed knives, burins, end scrapers and awls. The acheulean is also found in the caves of Cantabrian Spain, within the SW region. In particular the multi-level site at Castilló (Obermaier 1924; Butzer 1981) produced a few points, handaxes and some retouched flakes from at least two stratigraphic levels (Freeman 1975).

A further assemblage variant known as the tayacian comes from Fon-téchevade (France, SW region) (fig. 5.3, a,b) (Henri-Martin 1957) and other sites. This consists predominantly of rough flakes and on occasion a chopping tool/core element. More generally the term tayacian has been used to describe an assemblage of lower palaeolithic age which lacks handaxes but has plenty of flakes. However, many of the 'diagnostic' flake specimens have been severely modified by solifluction action which has ground and crushed their edges, giving them the appearance of being 'intentionally' retouched. This is the case in level 2 at La Micoque which Peyrony (1938) classified as tayacian. Indeed there has

	LA MICOQUE	Laville et al 1980	Bordes 1956	Breuil 1932	Bourgon 1951
					number of specimens
Würm I	N layer 6	MICOQUIEN	6 Micoquien	6 Micoquien	781
Riss/Würm Interglacial	EROSION				
Riss III	L8 L7 L6 L5 L4 L3 L2 L1 ashes layer 5 K3 K2 K1 J ashes layer 5	ACHEULEAN / ACHEULEAN	5 Acheulean	5 Tayacian	901
Riss II/III Interstadial	EROSION				
Riss II	H3 H2 archeo layer 4 H1 G5 G4	PREMOUSTERIAN	4 Mousterian	4 Tayacian	400
	EROSION				
	G3 G2 G1 F				
Riss I/II Interstadial	EROSION				
Riss I	E archeo layer 3	PREMOUSTERIAN	3 Primitive Mousterian	3 Clactonian	2410
	D C archeo layer 2 B	(indeterminate)	2 ?	2 Clactonian	509
	levels I to XIII				
?	A archeo layer 1	(indeterminate)	1 ?	1 Clactonian	a few

5.6 Stratigraphy and industries at La Micoque, SW region (G. Guichard 1976; Laville *et al.* 1980).

been considerable disagreement, as fig. 5.6 shows, over what to call these assemblages from the first five archaeological levels at La Micoque. Breuil (1932) classified the first three archaeological levels as clactonian which were then, in his opinion, followed by two levels of tayacian. Bordes (1953c) regarded the two earliest levels as unclassifiable. The next three levels he classified as primitive mousterian, with an acheulean in level 5. G. Guichard (1976:figs. 2–4) illustrates some flake and core cleavers from level 3 of La Micoque, which is now placed under the generic label of pre-mousterian (Laville et al. 1980:145), without indicating any direct relation between these assemblages and the mousterian which followed at a much later date.

It must be remembered that Breuil placed the tayacian of southern France on one side of his parallel phylum model of industrial evolution. This phylum began with the clactonian and continued through eight stages of the levalloisian. It was considered distinct from the core tool/handaxe tradition with which it was contemporary (Oakley 1969:144). On the contrary, it is now possible to see much more complex assemblage variation, both synchronic and diachronic, among the stratified assemblages from the caves of the SW region (Bordes 1950). The industries into which these assemblages are grouped do not form developmental series where one 'evolves' into another. Moreover, there are many links with assemblages in the northern province, where for example Wymer (1982:121) has drawn attention to the similarity between premousterian (tayacian) assemblages, in the SW region, and comparable flake material from Taubach in East Germany and from Remenham (fig. 5.3) in the Thames valley of southern England.

The artifacts from Vértesszöllös (Kretzoi and Vértes 1965; Vértes 1975) belong to a different tradition. They consist of choppers, chopping tools, side scrapers and many flakes made on small quartzite river pebbles. The technique of manufacture has been described as standardised in manufacture but unstandardised in terms of morphology. In other words, simple percussion techniques were used to flake the pebbles and this resulted in flakes of many different shapes but uniformly small size. Very few of these bear any retouch. The sample mean for the length of the utilised pieces is only 2.4 cm. Large quantities of burnt bone but no hearths were also reported from this multi-layer middle pleistocene site.

Other choppers and chopping tools have been recovered from around Budapest and are known as the Buda industry (Vértes 1965). For the most part these finds are undated.

(c) geographical variation

Handaxes are unknown from the SE region (Valoch 1968:354) and this supplements the pattern of distribution for this artifact type that has already been noted in the NE region. A zone of core/chopping tool industries is sometimes spoken of, which links Clacton with Vértesszöllös. More findspots are needed from the SE region before such claims can be assessed.

In the Alpine region it is difficult to date any material to this period. No doubt the Alps were used, but the active scouring of the caves by ice sheets and periglacial processes has obliterated any traces that might have existed.

The SW region is commonly portrayed as dominated by the well known cave sites but in fact many open locations are known where acheulean artifacts, primarily handaxes, have been recovered. As a general rule handaxes are rare in caves, a fact which has been noted by Rolland (1981) in discussing the middle palaeolithic material from the same region. An example of the wealth of open sites is provided by a survey of the Bergeraçois communes in the Périgord area. Here some 200 findspots with either acheulean or mousterian of acheulean tradition have been recovered. Many of the findspots are open sites and some of these have several levels of acheulean as at Bertranoux in the commune of Creysse (G. Guichard 1976:914).

(d) human remains

The fossil remains from the SW region all come from caves and rock shelters (table 5.3). These include an important series of skull fragments, mandibles and teeth from the Abri Suard and the Abri Bourgeois-Delaunay which form part of the site of La Chaise in Charente (Debenath 1976). Level 11 at the Abri Bourgeois-Delaunay has a U-series date of 146 Kyr. Other fossil material includes cranial fragments from Fontéchevade and an adult mandible from Montmaurin. No fossil material has yet been recovered from Cantabrian Spain

Table 5.3. *Pre-neanderthal and neanderthal fossil remains from Europe*

The pre-neanderthalers, based on age and morphology, are italicised

Riverine deposits		Cave deposits	
		Northern province	
	NW region		
Swanscombe	England/Wales	*Pontnewydd*	La Cotte
	Belgium	Engis	Fond de Forêt
		La Naulette	Spy
Biache–Saint-Vaast	France	Angles	Arcy
Genay		Vergisson	
Hahnöfersand (NW, NC)	Germany	Neanderthal	
	NC region		
	France	*Vergranne*	
Mauer Steinheim	Germany	Stadel	Klaussenische
Ehringsdorf Bilzingsleben		Wildscheuer	
Salzgitter-Lebenstedt Taubach			
Gánovce Sala	Czechoslovakia	Kůlna	Ochoz
Přezletice		Sipká	
	Hungary	Subalyuk	
	NE region		
Rozhok I	Russia	Starosel'e	Kiik Koba

Table 5.3 – cont.

Riverine deposits		Cave deposits	
	Southern province		
	SW region		
	France	La Cave	Chateauneuf
		Petit Puymoyen	La Quina
		St Césaire	Le Moustier
		Roc Marsal	Caminero
		La Chaise	Combe-Grenal
		Fontéchevade	Marillac
		Montmaurin	Pech de l'Azé
		René Simard	Soulabé
		La Ferrassie	Régourdou
		La Chapelle-aux-Saints	
	Spain	Lezetxiki	
	Alpine region		
Quinzano Ca'Verde	Switzerland	St Brais ?	
	Italy		
	SE region		
Vértesszöllös	Hungary		
	Romania	Ohaba Ponor	
	Yugoslavia	Krapina	Velika Pecina
		Veternica ?	Vindija
	Mediterranean province		
	MW region		
Bañolas Forbes Quarry ?	Spain	Devils Tower (Gibraltar)	Cariguela
		D'Agut	*Cova Negra*
		Atapuerca	
	Portugal	Columbeira	Salemas
	France	Baume des Peyards	Crouzade
		Hortus	Macassargues
		La Masque	*Orgnac III*
		Rigabe	*Arago*
		Bau de l'Aubesier	*Lazaret*
		Putride	
	MC region		
Pofi Saccopastore Sedia del Diavolo	Italy	Bisceglie	Uluzzo
		Camerota	Leuca
		Guattari	Fossellone
			Grotte du Prince
	ME region		
	Yugoslavia	*Šandalja I*	
	Greece	*Petralona*	

Sources: Oakley *et al.* 1971; M de Lumley 1973; Mania *et al.* 1980; Day 1977; Cook *et al.* 1982

in the SW region. At Vértesszöllös an occipital fragment has been found together with some deciduous teeth (Day 1978).

Further references

SW: H. de Lumley (ed.) 1976a; Bordes 1972; G. Guichard 1976; Debenath 1976; Laville *et al.* 1980; Gamble 1984b.

Alpine: Bhattacharya 1977; Fedele 1978, 1981; Leonardi and Broglio 1962.
SE: Valoch 1968; Vértes 1960, 1975; Howell 1966; Cook *et al.* 1982.

Mediterranean province 1

(a) chronology

The recent find at Isernia La Pineta, MC region, southeast of Rome in central Italy provides the earliest securely dated artifactual horizon in this province (fig. 5.7). The artifacts come from lacustrine sediments stratified below a volcanic tuff dated by K-Ar to 0.73 ± 0.04 Myr (Coltorti *et al.* 1982). This directly dates the archaeological levels since the subsequent volcanic activity very rapidly covered the archaeological surface with pumice. Palaeomagnetic studies also confirm the K-Ar age for the site since the sediments which contain the artifacts

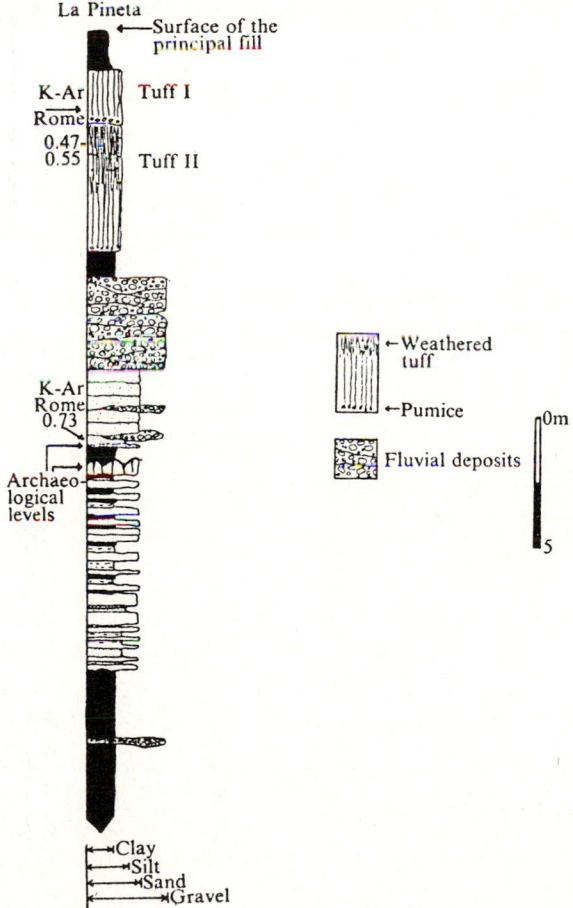

5.7 The stratigraphic position of the cultural horizon at Isernia La Pineta, MC region (after Coltorti *et al.* 1982).

are of reversed polarity and hence of Matuyama age. The large mammals associated with the archaeological material are a classic lakeside death assemblage. They include bison (*Bison* cf. *schoetensacki*), rhinoceros (*Dicerorhinus* cf. *hemitoechus*), straight tusked elephant (*Elephas antiquus*), bear (*Ursus deningeri*), hippopotamus, pig, a goat (*Hemitragus* sp.) and one specimen from a cervid.

Much earlier dates have been claimed for the high sea level cave of Vallonnet near Nice in the MW region (H. de Lumley 1975, 1976d). The sediments are of normal polarity and have been interpreted as belonging to the Jaramillo event dated to 900 Kyr. There is however no reason to suspect such a great antiquity just because the stone tools are of 'primitive' form and a later, middle pleistocene date is probably in order. The associated fauna has been described as very final Villafranchian and the eventual chronological position of this site will depend on the relative dating of these species.

Other dates from central Italy, MC region, are available for archaeological material. At Torre in Pietra (Piperno and Biddittu 1978) A. C. Blanc discovered an acheulean assemblage in fluviatile deposits. It has been stated that this industry is 430 Kyr old (Howell 1966) based on a K-Ar date from the same level, m, as the archaeological material. However the block of black pumice which was used to obtain this date is derived and thus serves only as a *terminus post quem* for the industry, which is probably rather younger than this much quoted date. At Anagni (Biddittu *et al.* 1979) a lower palaeolithic lithic assemblage lies stratified between two volcanic horizons dated by K-Ar to 366 and 458 Kyr respectively (Piperno and Segre 1982).

In Spain, middle pleistocene dates have been claimed for the sites of Torralba and Ambrona (Howell 1966; Butzer 1971) and more recent terrace gravel finds near Madrid at Aridos (Santonja *et al.* 1980) are certainly older than the last interglacial. Freeman (1981:114) is doubtful that any material so far recovered from the Iberian peninsula is older than the middle pleistocene and certainly none of the abundant acheulean material can at the moment be pinned down to a more precise position within this period.

The evidence for early material in the ME region is very poor. Cubuk (1976) has suggested that some primitive looking tools from the island of Kephallinia in the Ionian sea may be of great antiquity due to their position in a high fossil shoreline.

A variety of site types are represented in the province. These include the inland and sea cut waves along the mediterranean littoral of France and Italy in the MW and MC regions. Gravel terrace locations in Spain and central Italy are also rich in material. Lakeside locations are known from Isernia La Pineta and marsh conditions at Torralba, while material interstratified with fossil shoreline deposits is known at Terra Amata (H. de Lumley 1969a, 1975) and in the raised beaches of western Italy (Blanc 1957).

(b) industrial groupings

In the MW region pre-mousterian (tayacian) assemblages are found at sites such as Arago and Baume Bonne (H. de Lumley 1969b, 1971, 1976e, f) in levels dated to the Riss glaciation. De Lumley (1976d:847) has also distinguished a further facies called the evenosien after the gravel terrace type site of Ste Anne d'Evenos. This is contrasted with the local pre-mousterian (tayacian) since it shows a frequent use of the levallois technique.

Pebble tools are known from Vallonnet although the number of implements is very small. A series of acheulean industries has been recovered from the Ardèche (Combier 1967) and in particular from the cave site of Orgnac III. Terra Amata, near Nice, combines both simple pebble chopping tools, flake implements, among which are many side scrapers, and what are described as proto-handaxes. The levallois technique is absent in this multi-level site (H. de Lumley 1976e:823). The cave of Lazaret (de Lumley 1969c) provides a well studied assemblage of pre-last interglacial acheulean material. A great range of artifact types is present including pebble choppers (fig. 6.16), handaxes, finely flaked points and scrapers (fig. 5.2, g,1), dated to a Riss stadial. Acheulean material with many handaxes is abundantly represented from the Manzanares and Jarama gravels around Madrid as at St Isidro and Pinedo (Querol and Santonja 1979) as well as in Portugal around the Tagus estuary (Freeman 1975). Bifaces also form a component of the retouched lithic assemblages for the Torralba and Ambrona sites (Howell 1966). It is often pointed out that the Spanish acheulean contains a significant proportion of cleavers in the assemblages (Jelinek 1977) which links it with Bordes' meridional acheulean from the southern province.

The material from Isernia La Pineta in the MC region is said to number many thousands of pieces which can be divided into two typological groups (Coltorti *et al.* 1982). There are choppers (fig. 6.16) made on limestone river pebbles, and these dominate the assemblage. The second category consists of retouched flint flake tools (fig. 5.3, o,p) of which only a very few are scrapers and the rest denticulates. At Anagni the forty-four tools are predominantly scrapers with one lava biface. At Torre in Pietra an acheulean assemblage contains a number of handaxes exhibiting a variety of different shapes and degrees of finish. Many other acheulean assemblages are known from Italy (Leonardi 1976; Radmilli 1976) and Sicily (Pianese 1968), which was joined to the mainland of peninsula Italy for much of the pleistocene.

A solitary handaxe was picked up at Palaiokastron on the Greek mainland (Dakaris *et al.* 1964) in the ME region. At Šandalja in Yugoslavia (Malez 1976) chopping tools associated with a lower pleistocene fauna represent the earliest occupation in the Istrian peninsula. Other material from the ME region is discussed by Reisch (1982).

(c) geographical variation

Acheulean and non-handaxe assemblages are found throughout much of the province, as indicated above. Several local variants have been described, with the acheulean from the caves fitting in to the meridional acheulean as recognised by Bordes (1971). In Italy, Radmilli (1976) distinguishes no less than three separate facies of clactonian from the type sites of Madonna del Freddo, Valle Guimentina and Venosa. Elsewhere in the province these assemblages would be placed within a pebble tool/flake tradition.

Reconstructions of hunting behaviour have been made at Torralba (Freeman 1975, 1981; Butzer 1982). These authors both favour man as the prime agent responsible for creating the clumps of animal bones associated with stone tools within the excavated sites. Butzer has recently presented an analysis of the site in its local and regional environment which is reminiscent of Grahmann's (1955) reconstruction for the location of Markkleeberg in the NC region. According to Butzer (fig. 5.8) the sites at Torralba and Ambrona are located on important game trails between summer and winter areas where the hunters could prey upon migrating herds in spring and autumn. He refers to this as a special case of a concentrated resource model from which springs a distinctive type of settlement pattern. At other times of the year the hunters would fan out in smaller groups into the surrounding country where a number of ephemeral camps would be created which would be located near to key resources such as water, the position of animal herds and nearness to suitable raw material quarries. This scenario presents a number of expectations for the type of archaeological record created by such patterns of mobility linked to the distribution of resources in these middle pleistocene environments. An alternative view of the associations between the megafauna at Torralba and Ambrona and the stone tools is provided by Binford (1981:16–17) and discussed further in Chapter 6 below.

(d) human remains

The fossil remains from France and Spain have all been referred to as pre-neanderthalers (M. A. de Lumley 1973, 1976a). Among these specimens are skull fragments, mandibles and teeth from Atapuerca near Burgos (Aguirre and de Lumley 1977) and a parietal fragment from Cova Negra. The facial area of the Arago skull (fig. 5.5) was found in a level containing many fragments of mammal bones and is in all probability part of a carnivore created residue. Other material from La Caune de l'Arago (Tautavel) includes two robust mandibles. Orgnac and Lazaret have also produced a few teeth and skull fragments.

Italy at present lacks fossil material of this age. At Šandalja I in the Istrian peninsula an upper human incisor was found in association with a lower pleistocene fauna (Malez 1976). By far the most important fossil material in the

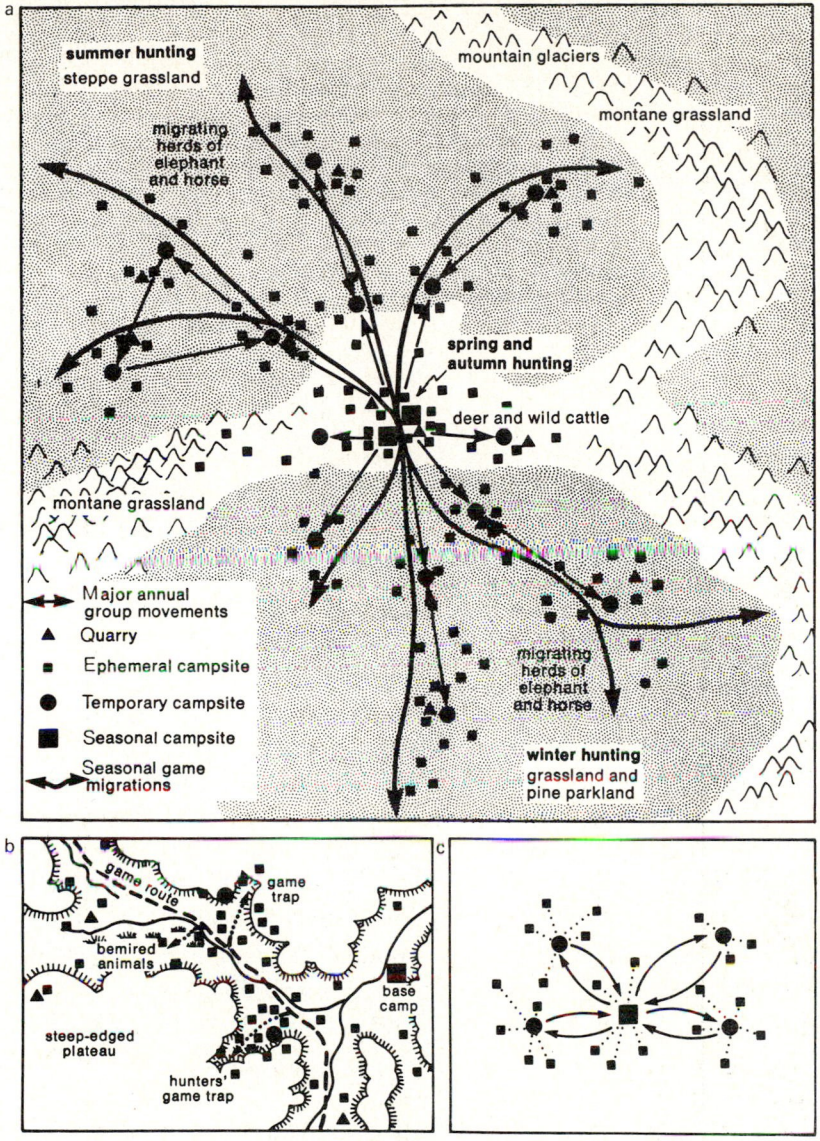

5.8 A seasonal mobility model for acheulean hunter-gatherers in mid-Pleistocene Spain, MW region, based in part on information from Torralba and Ambrona. (a) reconstruction of intercept hunting during spring and autumn; (b) the use of topography to secure game: a possible reconstruction for the Torralba, Ambrona sites; (c) the mobility model used to interpret the archaeological patterns. (Butzer 1982)

ME region is the skull from the cave of Petralona near Thessalonika in north-eastern Greece (fig. 5.5) (Stringer 1974, *et al.* 1979). The estimated ages for this almost complete cranium once ranged between 70 and 700 Kyr. The calcite encrustation on the facial area of the skull has however now been dated by

Electron Spin Resonance (ESR) techniques to between 160 and 240 Kyr (Hennig *et al.* 1981, 1982) which confirms its position as one of the most important, but not the oldest, middle pleistocene skulls in Europe.

Further references

MW: H. de Lumley 1969 b, 1971, (ed.) 1976a; Freeman 1975, 1981; Combier (ed.) 1976, 1967; Howell 1966; Cook *et al.* 1982.

MC: Leonardi 1976; Blanc 1957; Fridrich 1976; Radmilli 1976; Howell 1966; Gamble 1984b.

ME: Reisch 1982; Cook *et al.* 1982.

Northern province 2

(a) chronology

There are no absolute dates which place any archaeological material from this province within the last interglacial, 128–118 Kyr. There are however absolute dates for animal faunas, as at the Victoria Cave in Yorkshire, England, where a fauna containing hippopotamus has been dated by 230Th/234U to 120±6 Kyr. At the cave site of Hunas near Nürnberg in southern Germany (Freund 1978; Brunnacker 1982) last interglacial sediments representing a depositional episode that lasted some 12–15 Kyr contain a few flake tools. However most of the abundant archaeological remains from caves and open sites are associated with sediments which indicate a variety of cold climate conditions. These can now be placed in the early glacial period, isotope stages 5d–a, 4 and 3 and which cover the period from 118 to 35 Kyr (fig. 3.7) (Dennell 1983b). These sediments include loess deposits as in the Seine (Bordes 1954; Tuffreau 1976b), the Somme (Tuffreau 1976c) and Köln basins (Bosinski and Brunnacker 1973) of the NW region, throughout the NC region (Bosinski 1967; Toepfer 1970) and the NE region (Chernysh 1961; Klein 1969b; Goretsky and Tseitlin 1977; Goretsky and Ivanova 1982).

An important section of last glacial deposits comes from the site of Königsaue in the NC region (Mania and Toepfer 1973). The 25 m section consists of sands and gravels which are repeatedly interstratified with peat horizons. From this section, it is possible to reconstruct the climatic history of the area as shown by the expansion and contraction of a small lake, the Aschersleben See. The period begins (fig. 5.9) with cold but moist conditions during which frozen ground phenomena are found in the form of massive fossil ice wedge casts and cryoturbation features. The archaeological materials consist of three lithic assemblages discarded on the banks of the lake. These have been dated to the Brørup interstadial of the early last glacial. This interstadial is regarded by Mania and Toepfer as an important phase of occupation throughout much of the northern province just prior to the polar desert conditions of the early glacial. Other important artifact collections from the Bockstein in southern Germany and the Kůlna cave in Moravia, both in the NC region, may well date to this same interstadial, known from palynological work in the Netherlands. The presence of ice wedges suggests that this profile does indeed fall within stage 4, post-75 Kyr. The stage Ia which they correlate with the Eemian interglacial (fig. 5.9) may prove instead to be part of later stage 5.

The middle Dniestr has been systematically investigated for many years and provides a detailed chronology for the last glaciation in this part of the NE region. The principal sites are found in deep loess sections deposited on the terraces of the Dniestr river. The three most important sites are Molodova V (Chernysh 1961), Molodova I (Goretsky and Ivanova 1982) and Korman IV (Goretsky and Tseitlin 1977). At Molodova V, the section contains twelve major archaeological horizons of which the lowest, XI, XII and XIIa, contain middle palaeolithic material. C14 dates for these levels indicate minimum ages of between 40.3 and 45.6 Kyr and these levels are correlated by Ivanova (1982:234) to the Brørup interstadial. After these levels, solifluxion processes become marked in the profiles at all three locations.

The site of Ketrosy, also on the Dniestr, has mousterian artifacts and is dated to a period when the environment of the Dniestr was a forest steppe. This is placed between the Amersfoort interstadial and the Mikulino interglacial. During the Brørup and Amersfoort interstadials the site was flooded (Ivanova, Bolihovskaja and Rengarten 1982).

Many of the caves in the province have evidence for cold climate sediments and arctic faunal elements associated with middle palaeolithic flake assemblages. Those caves which contain temperate elements such as porcupine (*Hystrix* sp.) and leopard (*Panthera pardus*) have either very few or no artifacts associated with them, as is the case with the Stadel in southern Germany (Gamble 1979:43–4) and the Kálmán-Lambrecht cave in Hungary (Jánossy 1963–4), both of which are in the NC region. It is possible that these faunas date to the later temperate sub-stages of isotope stage 5, and prior to the stage 4/5 boundary of 75 Kyr.

Occupation was not continuous in these regions during the early glacial (Müller-Beck 1957). It is generally lacking during the harsh polar desert stages that occurred after 75 Kyr as well as during the last interglacial (Gamble 1983a, 1984a). A number of sites can however be dated to the interstadial episodes that correspond to the Moershoofd/Upton Warren complex and to the Hengelo. At Bohunice, a large loess/brick pit at Brno, Moravia, in the NC region, C14 dates have been obtained for an assemblage with middle palaeolithic typology and upper palaeolithic technology. These place the artifacts, which occur in a brown soil, between 40.1±1.2 and 42.9±1.7/1.4 Kyr (Valoch 1976b). A re-examination of the sediments in level F of the Weinberghöhlen at Mauern in the NC region (Bohmers 1951; Zotz 1955; von Koenigswald *et al.* 1974) has shown that the

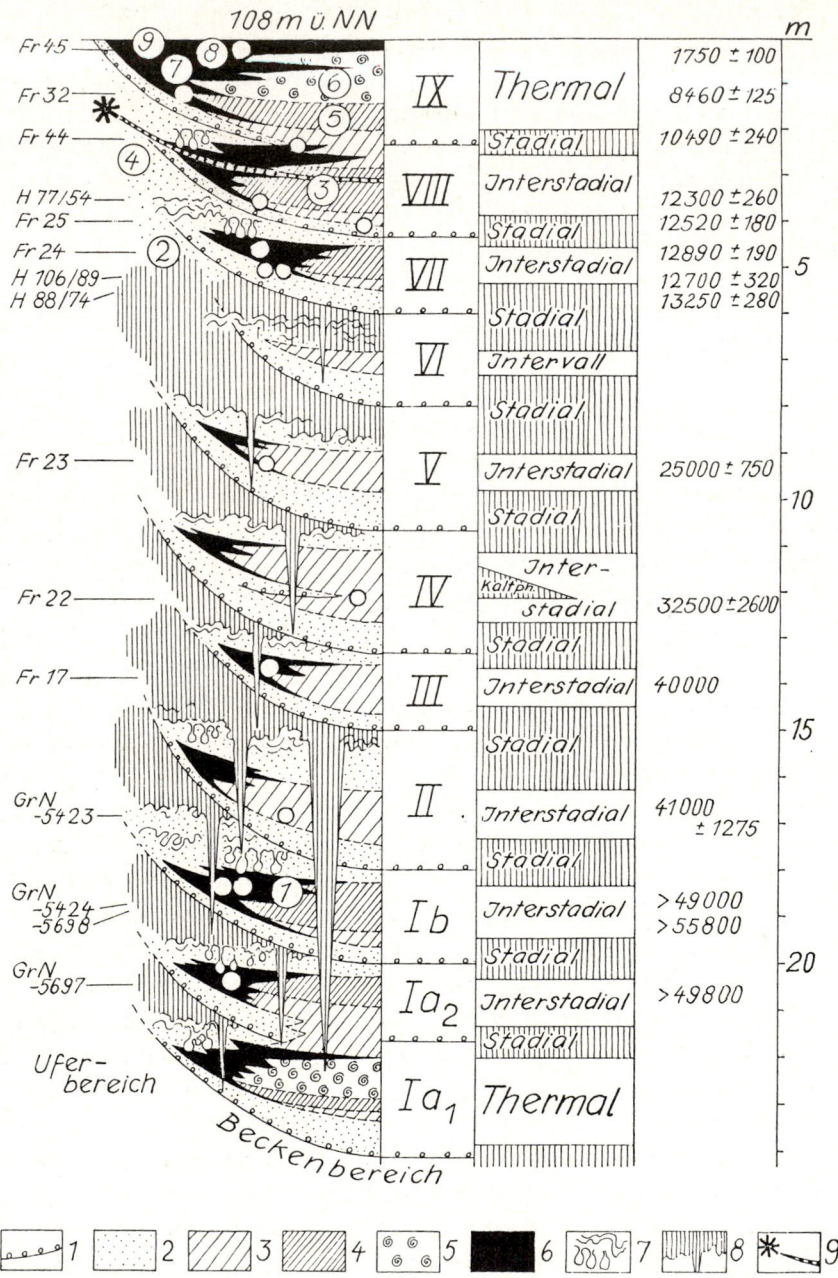

5.9 A schematic profile through the last glacial deposits at the Aschersleben See, East Germany, NC region (Mania and Toepfer 1973:abb. 7). 1. erosion surface, 2. sand and gravelly sand, 3. sand and silts, 4. clay silts, 5. organic silts, 6. peat, 7. cryoturbation, 8. solifluction and fossil ice wedge casts, 9. volcanic ash from the Eifel, Laacher See tuff. Ia–IX sediment layers. C14 dates are all bp. Numbers in circles: 1 = middle palaeolithic horizon; 2 = EUP horizon; 3 = reindeer pick implement; 4 = LUP horizon; 5–9 = mesolithic to Roman.

distinctive middle palaeolithic assemblage, with large bifacially flaked leaf shaped projectile points (fig. 5.10, a), can be dated to the Hengelo interstadial of northern Europe (Müller-Beck 1974:40). A similar correlation is suggested by the C14 dates of 38.3±1.4/1.2 Kyr for the leaf points from Kents Cavern (fig. 5.10, f) in southern England (Campbell 1977) and level 6 in the Nietoperzowa cave at Jerzmanowice in Poland, NC region (Chmielewski 1961), where a C14 date of 38.5±1.2 Kyr is associated with a number of typologically different leaf points in a small lithic assemblage.

(b) industrial groupings

Three major industrial groupings are commonly recognised: (1) assemblages containing handaxes and bifacially worked knives; (2) a highly variable group of assemblages referred to generically as mousterian; and (3) a small group of poorly understood assemblages containing leaf points.

(1) A widespread group is named after the uppermost level 6 at La Micoque (fig. 5.6) in the SW region. The micoquian is characterised by small, pointed handaxes which are found throughout much of the northern province in Belgium, Germany, Poland, Czechoslovakia and western Russia (fig. 4.6). The assemblages come from both cave and open locations (Bosinski 1967; Schwabedissen 1970; Mania and Toepfer 1973:fig. 37; Gábori 1976; Ulrix-Closset 1975). They are generally small assemblages as measured by the numbers of retouched and hence typologisable specimens. The micoquian from the NC region has been divided by Bosinski (1967) into a number of different inventories based upon distinctive assemblages from some of the 'richer' sites. These type sites are Rörshain (fig. 5.10, e) (Bosinski 1973b), Klausennische, Schambach (Bosinski 1967) and the Bockstein (fig. 5.1, h,i) (Wetzel and Bosinski (eds.) 1969). Other important assemblages in the NC region have come from the Speckberg in southern Germany (Müller-Beck 1973a), Kůlna cave (Valoch *et al.* 1969), Wylotne in Poland (Valoch 1968) and Königsaue (Mania and Toepfer 1973). The open loess site of Ripiceni-Izvor (Păunescu 1965) and the cave locations of Starosel'e and Kiik-Koba in the Crimea (Gábori 1976; Klein 1965) have all produced micoquian assemblages from the NE region.

In many instances the handaxes from these assemblages are more aptly described as knives, as in the term 'Bocksteinmesser' that was used by Wetzel (1958) to describe the curved bifacially worked pieces from that site (fig. 5.1, h,i). The pradniks from the caves near Ojcow in southern Poland are also a variant of these bifacial knives. Since they are highly distinctive in shape and vary from local region to local region these type fossils have been used to isolate and discuss industrial groupings (Zotz 1951). The number of retouched pieces in each assemblage is often very small and as a result a Bordian analysis is frequently not possible.

At the Balve cave in the Hönne valley, NC region, a series of excavations

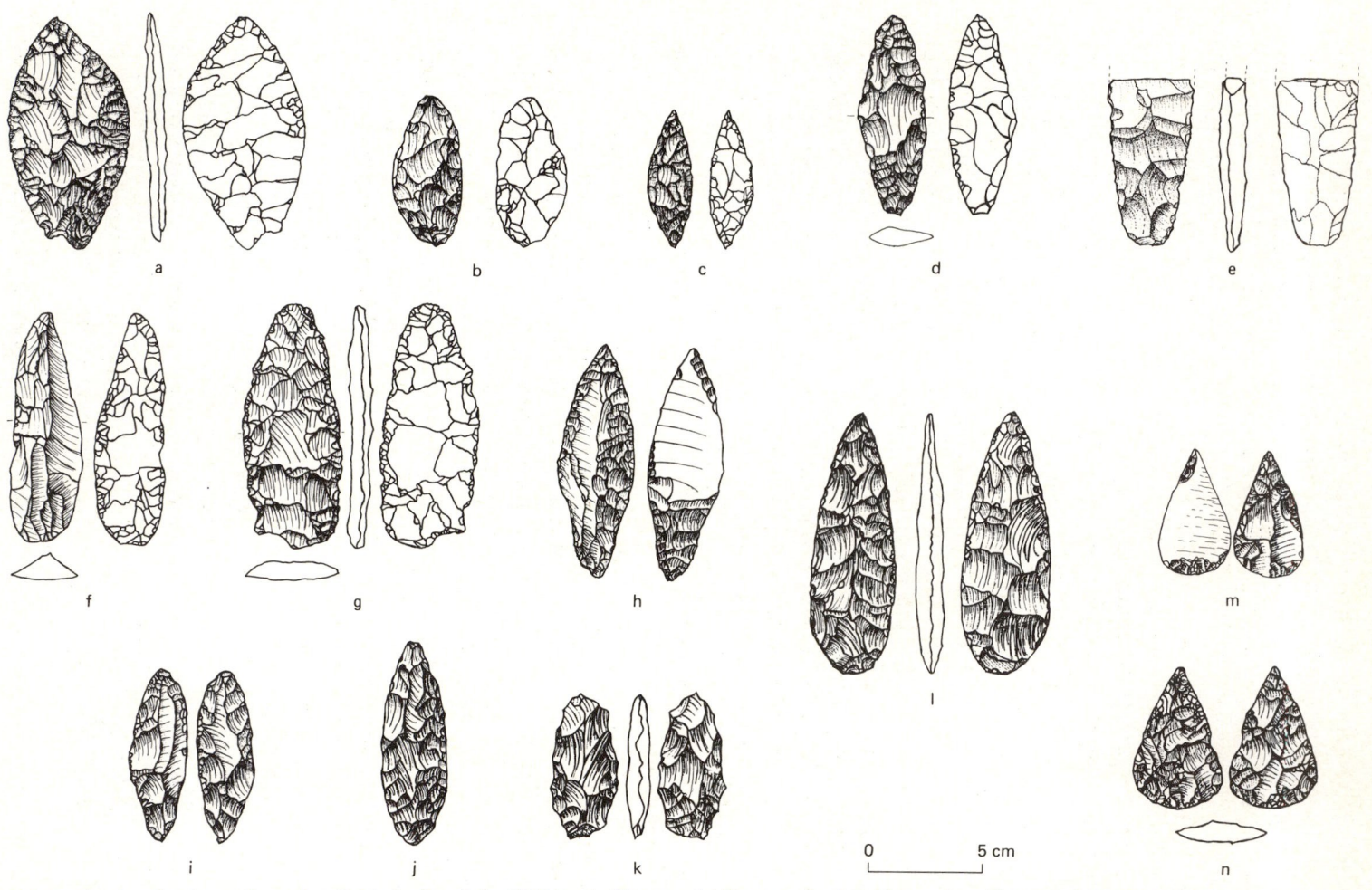

5.10 Leaf points for the earlier palaeolithic (a–f) and the EUP (g–n) of Europe. (a) Mauern; (b, c) Kokkinopilos; (d) Morfi; (e) Rörshain; (f) Kents Cavern; (g) Soldiers Hole; (h) Kostenki Telmanskaya; (i) Jerzmanovice; (j, k, l) Szeleta; (m, n) Moravany.

(Andree 1928; Günther 1964) recovered four main stratified assemblages. This is the only cave stratigraphy in the NC region where it is possible to see the stratigraphic relationship between the micoquian and the upper acheulean, or Jungacheuléen (Bosinski 1967). The latter, assemblage I at Balve, is stratified *beneath* two micoquian assemblages, II and III. Elsewhere in the NC region at Salzgitter-Lebenstedt the upper acheulean is now regarded as penultimate glaciation in date (see above, p. 146).

Other handaxe forms from assemblages in the NW region have been linked with the mousterian of acheulean tradition (MTA) from the SW region. This is the case for material in the Paris basin where the characteristic triangular handaxes occur at the base of the upper loess dated to the last glaciation (fig. 5.1, j,k) (Bordes 1954, 1981). However both micoquian and MTA occur in this area of the NW region (Bordes 1954) as at the loess site of Le Tillet where the levallois technique of flake production was commonly used. The caves of Spy and l'Hermitage in Belgium contain assemblages that have been described as MTA and upper acheulean respectively (Ulrix-Closset 1975). Some finely flaked triangular bout coupé handaxes, often single finds, are usually cited as the principal evidence for a middle palaeolithic in southern England (Roe 1981). These are regarded by Bordes (1981:81) as MTA. Recent work in Brittany by Monnier (1980) has however shown that in this part of the NW region a great number of flake assemblages some with MTA bifaces and others lacking these type fossils and so assigned to a typical mousterian are found incorporated into beach deposits.

(2) Throughout the province are found assemblages which are regarded as typical mousterian. By this is meant a flake based assemblage where the retouched implement classes are made up of variable quantities of points, side scrapers of all types, denticulates and other forms including burins and awls. The use of the levallois technique is a variable feature. Bifacial tools such as handaxes are either rare or absent. For the northern province this industrial attribution usually describes assemblages which are small in size and which lack any diagnostic retouched pieces. Bosinski (1967) recognises three type sites in Germany, Balve assemblage IV, Rheindahlen and Kartstein, which have produced distinctive inventories dating to the early last glacial.

The complex of caves at Arcy-sur-Cure (Yonne, France) in the NW region have produced a number of mousterian horizons. One of these, the Grotte de l'Hyène, contains seven principal levels from which assemblages classified as typical and denticulate (fig. 5.3, q,r) have been recovered (Girard 1976, 1978). Scraper variants analogues to the Charentian of the SW region have been noted in material from Belgium in the same region (Ulrix-Closset 1975; Bordes 1981).

The middle Dniestr sites at Molodova and Korman IV are assigned to a typical mousterian where the use of the levallois technique is often marked (Klein 1970, 1973).

(3) The leaf point assemblages form a poorly understood group (Allsworth-

Jones 1975). They have supplied some of the most distinctive type fossils for this period in the northern province and the association of some of the leaf points, as at Jerzmanovice (fig. 5.10, i) (Chmielewski 1961) and the Ilsenhöhle (Hülle 1977), with upper palaeolithic elements has led to suggestions that they form an important root for the derivation of later industrial traditions (Müller-Beck 1968a). The group of sites centred upon the Altmühl valley in southern Germany, NC region, contains the largest number of these bifacially retouched projectile points, some of which have a hafting notch at the base (fig. 5.10, a). This altmühlian group (Bosinski 1967) is best known from level F in the Weinberg caves at Mauern (von Koenigswald *et al.* 1974). The assemblage is very clearly middle palaeolithic both in typology and in the use of a flake technology. It is stratified above a late micoquian assemblage.

(c) geographical variation

The pattern of distribution for these variants and their further local manifestations can only be described as patchy (fig. 5.11). It must be remembered that these groupings have been arrived at by a number of analytical methods. These include type fossil approaches, observations on technology and assemblage analysis. Which method is used depends upon the size of the lithic assemblage as well as the accepted practice towards classification within a regional tradition. The result is a complex situation of conflicting terms and descriptions that make it difficult to derive any units of culture history from such sparse data (see

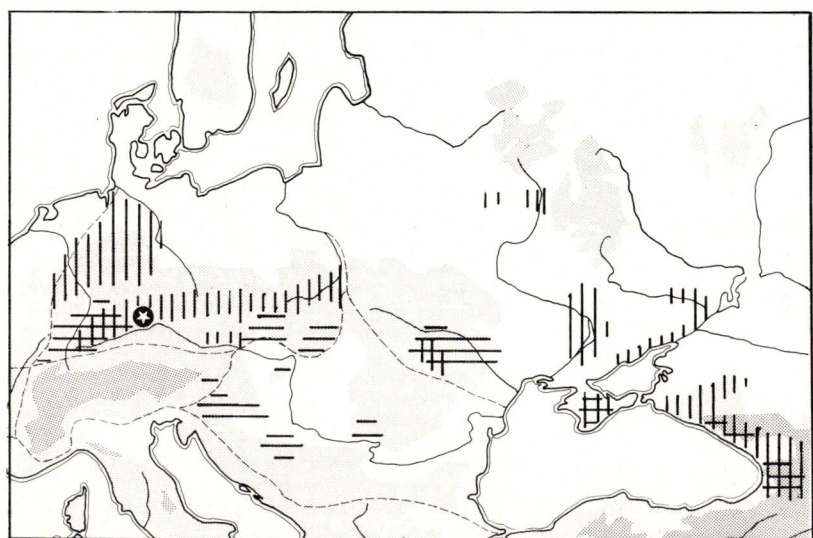

5.11 The distribution of middle palaeolithic assemblages in the NC, NE and SE regions of Europe (after Gábori 1976). Vertical hatching = handaxe assemblages (upper acheulean, micoquian); horizontal hatching = mousterian flake/scraper assemblages; star = altmühlian assemblages.

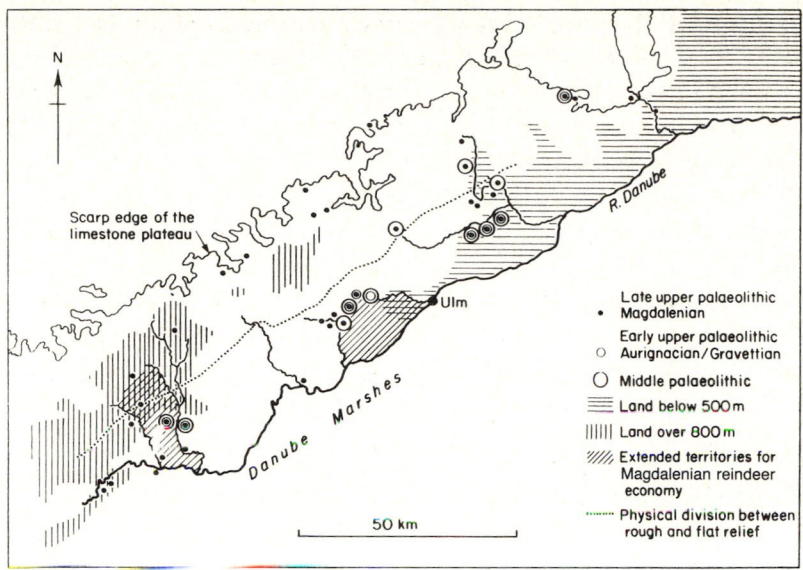

5.12 Long term adaptive strategies on the limestone Swabian uplands of Southern Germany, NC region (Gamble 1984a, b) as revealed by settlement location to resources.

Bhattacharya 1977: fig. 26; Gábori 1976: fig. 62, reproduced as fig. 5.11; Valoch 1968). However we can see that bifacial implements and in particular handaxes/knives are found throughout the province. The upper acheulean, *if* it belongs in time to the early last glacial, is confined to the north European plain (Bosinski 1967:Karte 3), while by contrast the micoquian has a southerly distribution within the province and is especially common in the caves of the central European highlands and the Crimea. The leaf point assemblages are very restricted in geographical focus (Bosinski 1967: Karte 5).

Several regional studies are available which treat these sites as part of a reconstructed settlement pattern in an early last glacial landscape (Klein 1970, 1973; Mania and Toepfer 1973:figs. 37, 40; Gamble 1978a, 1979). The location and catchments of individual sites have also been examined at Königsaue (Mania and Toepfer 1973:chapter 5), Kents Cavern (Campbell and Sampson 1971) and the Stadel (Gamble 1979:fig. 1).

(d) human remains

The find from the Neander valley on the boundary of the NW and NC regions in 1856 has provided us with the characteristic early last glacial human form, *Homo sapiens neanderthalensis*. Neanderthal remains have been found in caves at Arcy-sur-Cure and Spy in the NW region and in the NC region at the Stadel, Klausennische, and Wildscheuer. At Hahnöfersand, an open site near Hamburg, a frontal bone displaying many neanderthal features has been dated by C14 to 36.3±0.6 Kyr (Bräuer 1981). Neanderthal material has also come from the Crimean caves of Kiik-Koba and Starosel'e in the NE region. The nearly complete nature of these skeletons and of those from Spy and possibly Neanderthal itself has led to their interpretation as possible burials (Rowlett and Schneider 1974; Harrold 1980).

Further references

NW: Ulrix-Closset 1975; Roe 1981; Monnier 1980; Tuffreau 1976b,c; Morrison 1980.
NC: Schwabedissen 1970; Gábori 1976; Bosinski 1967, 1976; Müller-Beck (ed.) 1973b; Bárta and Bánesz 1981; Freund 1952.
NE: Klein 1970; Păunescu 1970; Valoch 1968; Vértes 1960; Gábori 1976.

Southern province 2

(a) chronology

The chronostratigraphic framework established by sediment studies in the rock shelters of south-west France provide the most comprehensive account of the early last glacial for the SW region. As we have seen in Chapter 3 there has been some revision of the classic Würm I and Würm II stadials recognised for France (Laville *et al.* 1980). The Würm I sediments with their associated temperate animal faunas dominated by red deer are now equated with sub-stages a–d in isotope stage 5, while the cold faunas of Würm II, when reindeer appear in some numbers, are correlated with stage 4 and part of stage 3 (Butzer 1981; Dennell 1983b). The Cantabrian sediments studied by Butzer have been divided into forty environmental episodes that are equivalent in age with stages 2–5. It is clear from this work that the majority of cave occupation in the Cantabrian part of the SW region occurred during Würm II and therefore after the stage 4/5 boundary at 75 Kyr. Archaeological material that dates to Würm I is very rare indeed (Butzer 1981:table 7 and fig. 17), while no occupation can be associated with the sediments equivalent to sub-stage 5e. The French scheme created by Laville (1975) regards interglacials and interstadials as periods of erosion, so it is not surprising, according to this view, that last interglacial material is unknown from the area. However, this view is also based upon a model of much longer periods of time for the last interglacial than the 10–15 Kyr indicated by the deep sea record (Laville 1982). At the present time, it must be regarded as equally probable that interglacial sediments do exist in the rock shelters of the SW region, as Butzer has shown for Cantabria, but that they contain no evidence for human occupation.

Two absolute dates exist for the province. At Pech de l'Azé (Bordes 1972), Breccia I contains typical denticulate mousterian. This breccia forms a separate stratigraphic unit to the main artifact bearing levels in the cave. It overlies a layer of travertine dated by Th/U to 123 ± 15 Kyr (Schwarz and Blackwell 1983). It is very possible that the travertine corresponds to the last interglacial, sub-stage 5e, in which case the artifacts contained within the Breccia matrix date to a later sub-stage of isotope stage 5 and hence to Würm I. Unlike the Cantabrian part of the SW region, it is clear that in the Périgord occupation was continuous throughout the Würm I stage of the early last glacial.

The second date is also on travertine. This comes from the site of Tata in the SE region, where a middle palaeolithic industry has been dated to c.100 Kyr by Th/U (Schwarz and Skoflek 1982). Elsewhere in the SE region flake assemblages have been assigned relative ages within the early last glacial on the basis of a local geo-chronological scheme that can be compared with climatic frameworks in northern Europe (Cârciumaru 1980). While the French evidence indicates continuous occupation during the early glacial (Gamble 1983a) it is not clear whether this pattern was repeated in the SE region. It is more probable that settlement ebbed and flowed in this more arid area.

(b) industrial groupings

A summary outline of the mousterian variants from the Périgord has already been given in Chapter 4 (fig. 4.5). The discovery of recurrent groupings led Bordes to propose a radically different model for industrial evolution than that proposed by Breuil in the parallel phylum model. This was Bordes' view of evolution as a many headed, ramifying process (1950, 1959). In a later review of his work on the mousterian he remarked that recognising only five types of mousterian had been to err on the cautious side (1981:77) and he proceeded in the same article to add the asinipodien from Pech de l'Azé IV and the vasconien from the Abri Olha in the Pays-Basque region.

These variants could also, in Bordes' opinion, be traced well outside the Périgord and the limits of the SW region (figs. 5.2, 5.3). The mousterian facies at Érd (Gábori-Csánk 1968), an open site (fig. 5.13) near Budapest in the SE region, is comparable to the Quina variant of the Charentian scraper group. The 'monotonous typology' (1981: 78) of the Quina variant is also found at Tata in the same region. The tools are very small at this site and dominated by scrapers (Vértes 1964).

Early excavations at the cave site of Bacho Kiro in Bulgaria, SE region, recovered a small collection of typical mousterian artifacts among which the use of levallois technique is low (Kozlowski 1982:114) but this may be due to the large number of nodule preparation flakes in the assemblage from layer 13. The material is compared with the non-levallois typical mousterian of southern France (H. de Lumley 1969b). A higher levallois index in the next layer, 12/13, suggests comparisons with Samuilitsa cave some 130 km to the north-west of Bacho Kiro, and level 5 at Ripiceni-Izvor in Roumania. The use of levallois

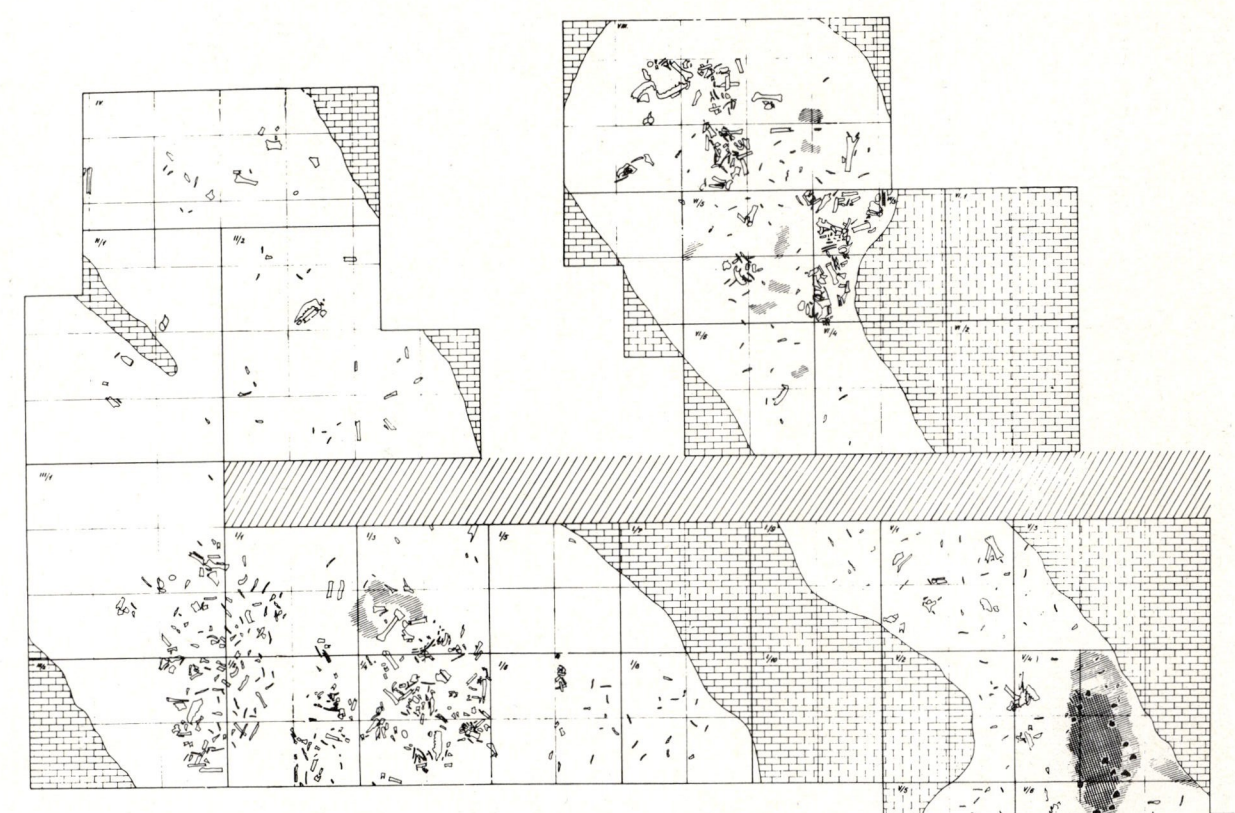

5.13 The distribution of cave bear bones and a hearth at the open air site of Érd, SE region. Two major concentrations of cave bear bones occur in the 'habitation' zone (lower left) and in the little valley (upper right). The hearth (lower right in the little valley) appears to be spatially unconnected with the bear bones which are most probably the result of winter mortalities in this open den site (Gábori-Csánk 1968:fig. 6). Each major square is 16 m^2.

technique is also very rare in the Yugoslavian sites of Krapina, Veternica and Vindija in the same region (Iwanowa 1979). These are scraper dominated assemblages which have also been compared to the Quina variant. Leaf points have been found in a middle palaeolithic assemblage at Muselievo in Bulgaria.

A number of mousterian assemblages are known from the Alpine region. The largest of these comes from the Swiss cave site of Cotencher (Dubois and Stehlin 1933; Müller-Beck 1968b), where quartzite forms the raw material for some poorly retouched pieces. On the Italian side of this region and in the Alpine foothills is found the multi-level site of Broion cave (Leonardi and Broglio 1962) where a denticulate mousterian level has been dated by C14 to 46.4±1.5 Kyr, while the Abri Messena has an assemblage described as typical mousterian and manufactured with the levallois technique.

(c) geographical variation

At one time it was possible to talk of an alpine palaeolithic based upon evidence for hunting cave bears and for ritual activities involving the arrangement of cave bear skulls and bones in caves (Bächler 1940). These interpretations have now been generally discarded (Jéquier 1975) and the poorly retouched artifacts which comprised the alpine palaeolithic from a number of caves in Switzerland and Austria are now regarded as the product of cryoturbation processes, rather than as representative of a separate facies. According to Fedele (1978, 1981) the mousterian locations in the Alps were situated to exploit ecotone contexts and few inroads were made into exploiting areas above 1000 m (1981:69).

The diversity of habitats and economic niches in Cantabrian Spain apparently made it the richest area for resources in the Iberian peninsula (Freeman 1981:136). This accounts in Freeman's view for the higher density of mousterian sites in this area than elsewhere in the MW region of Iberia. However no mousterian open sites have so far been recovered from Cantabria (Butzer 1981:179) and only the denticulate, Quina and typical variants are present in this part of the SW region (González Echegaray and Freeman 1971, 1973; Freeman 1981). The animal bones associated with these lithic assemblages point to a wide diversity of species. Straus (1977a:49) comments that this evidence shows a lack of resource specialisation at this time. This observation is apparently supported by the location of the mousterian caves which are interpreted as regularly reoccupied base camps. These were selected in accordance with the pattern of local relief so as to permit easy access to this faunal diversity (Freeman 1973:39). In particular, human settlement clustered in the coastal plain.

The increase in the number of find spots of mousterian assemblages compared with period 1, combined with the opportunities presented to the typologist by the packaging of the collections in cave and loess sediments, has led to a kaleidoscopic array of variants within the local traditions. Some measure of this can be gained from *La Préhistoire Française* (H. de Lumley (ed.) 1976a:989–1144) for the French area of the NW, SW and MW regions. J. Guichard (1976) supplies an informative summary of the all important Périgord sequence. It must also be remembered that the explanation for this intricate patterning at a sub-regional level stems directly from the model of five Neanderthal tribes. According to this model these lithic assemblages are long run cultural entities preserved over the millennia by the iron hand of custom and tradition (Bordes 1950).

Alternative interpretations of the patterning are possible (e.g. Binford and Binford 1966) but have little chance of embracing quite so much data while retaining allegiance to a single, simple concept. The notion of ethnicity encompasses all the data and although it explains nothing, it does prove extremely resistant to counter-arguments since these usually leave some loose ends free for further analysis. However, if we look at the Périgord data from the point of view of the scale of land use as exhibited by recent hunters and gatherers, it then becomes possible to see the relations between different assemblages from different sites in another light than that of tribal tradition. Binford (1983:figs. 50, 51) has shown how five Nunamiut Eskimo families covered the same amount of space as the entire Dordogne Department, which would of course include all the key sites (La Micoque, Combe-Grenal, La Ferrassie, Le Moustier, etc.) that according to the culture historians were occupied successively by five stand-offish tribes.

This raises the possibility that the variants are linked to a seasonal round of different exploitation activities and that the creation of different lithic assemblages in rock shelters and open sites is linked to this facet of adaptive behaviour.

(d) human remains

Table 5.3 shows that human remains are common in the SW and SE regions, where they come exclusively from caves and rock shelters. A great range in the completeness of skeletal material is displayed. The more complete skeletons from St Césaire, La Ferrassie, Le Moustier and La Chapelle-aux-Saints (fig. 5.5) have been claimed as intentional burials, although the conditions of recovery are such that it is sometimes difficult to judge these claims. The recent find at St Césaire (Lévêque and Vandermeersch 1980) therefore has an added importance in deciding on these questions.

A funeral pit has been identified by Bordes (1972:135) in level 50 at Combe Grenal. It contained no bones, although the excavator suggested that these would have been of a child and so more prone to decay. Peyrony (1930) found a similar sized pit with some human bones at Le Moustier.

The material from the SE region consists of many skull and mandible fragments from the caves of Krapina (table 5.4) and Vindija (Wolpoff *et al.* 1980).

Table 5.4. *A summary of the human fossil finds from Krapina*

teeth	180
skull fragments	135
phalanges	84
vertebrae	55
ribs	33
mandibles	28
scapula	21
humerus	20
clavicles	17
patella	15
fibula	14
metatarsal	12
astragalus	12
ulna	10
maxillae	6
metacarpal	5
femur	4
tibia	4
carpals	2
tarsals	2
pelvis	2
calcaneus	1

Source: Oakley et al. 1971

The highly fragmented state of the Krapina material has led to claims of cannibalism (Gorjanovic-Kramberger 1906), but it is more probable that the attrition is a result of carnivore activity resulting in the survival of the hard, dense elements of the skeleton.

In the Alpine region, open locations at Quinzano have produced an occipital bone while a frontal fragment has come from Ca'Verde near Verona.

Further references

SW: H. de Lumley (ed.) 1976a; Bordes 1981; Laville *et al.* 1980; J. Guichard 1976; Bourgon 1957.

Alpine: Müller-Beck 1968b; Jéquier 1975; Fedele 1978, 1981; Leonardi and Broglio 1962.

SE: Vértes 1960; Pâunescu 1970; Iwanowa 1979; Gábori-Csánk 1968; Gábori 1976.

Mediterranean province 2

(a) chronology

There are as yet no absolute dates for the early part of this period. A TL date on burnt flint from Cariguela in Granada, Spain (MW region) gives an estimate of

48–28 Kyr, while C14 dates of 49.2±3.2 Kyr and 47.7±1.5 Kyr have been obtained from the mousterian level G at Gorham's Cave, Gibraltar (Freeman 1981).

The sites in the French mediterranean littoral of the MW region are dominated by rock shelter deposits, although some extensive open sites such as the sixty hectare site of Trecassats (H. de Lumley 1969b) have been found. The sediments in the rock shelters are divided, as in the SW region, into Würm I and Würm II sediments (Miscovsky 1976). A survey of the animal faunas from this region by Pillard (1972) emphasises the temperate conditions of Würm I when red deer is common in the caves and rock shelter deposits, while Würm II saw the onset of harsher conditions and an increase in the occurrence of horse and ibex in the faunal remains. At the cave of Hortus (H. de Lumley 1972) the sediments span the Würm II stadial and contain a fauna dominated by ibex which is in part a reflection of the site's location beneath a high cliff edge. The cave sediments at Orgnac III in the Ardèche (Combier 1967) are thought to indicate a human presence in the Riss-Würm, but whether this corresponds to the last interglacial sub-stage 5e in the deep sea cores is not certain.

The abundant industries in Italy, MC region, from both cave and open locations are most commonly associated with early last glacial sediments (Piperno and Segre 1982). In Greece, ME region, middle palaeolithic artifacts have been found incorporated into red-bed sediments at Kokkinopilos, Epirus (Dakaris et al. 1964). These are thought to have been deposited during some part of the early last glacial (Vita-Finzi 1978).

(b) industrial groupings

These are every bit as varied as the groupings previously reported for the SW region. The French part of the MW region has all of the five Périgord variants except the MTA which according to Bordes (1981:81) is lacking. The denticulate mousterian is common as at the multi-level site of Hortus (fig. 5.3, k,l). Typical mousterian assemblages have been identified at the caves of Rigabe (H. de Lumley 1969b) and La Calmette (H. de Lumley 1976c:1007). Scraper dominated assemblages are also common in the well documented assemblages from this part of the MW region (fig. 5.2, k) (H. de Lumley 1969b, 1971) and an impression of the diversity can be gained from fig. 1.1.

Lithic assemblages from Iberia have also been classified according to Bordes' method (Freeman 1981), and the collections have been compared to the Charentian group and to the typical and denticulate mousterian variants (Bordes 1981). A summary of abri and open sites in the Valencia region, provided by Pérez (1974), points to the rich data base that is now becoming available for further study.

A small facies mousterian is known from Latium in central Italy (Taschini 1972). This is made on small river pebbles and is called pontinian (fig. 5.2, m).

While the raw material gives it a distinctive form it provides yet another example of the 'monotonous typology' of the Quina variant of the Charentian group which we have already noted at Érd, Tata and Krapina in the SE region. Mousterian levels have been excavated at Torre in Pietra, level d (Piperno and Biddittu 1978), Torre Nave in Calabria (Bulgarelli 1972) and at Torre dell'Alto (Borzatti von Löwenstern 1966) while the early work of Blanc in the coastal Ligurian cave sites (1957), and in the Monte Circeo complex of caves (Blanc 1942, 1958; Blanc and Segre 1953) south of Rome, again demonstrates the large quantities of multi-level stratified sites in this region of the Mediterranean province.

The ME region has assemblages described as micro-mousterian as well as a flake/blade variant. These come from the rock shelters of Asprochaliko in Epirus, north-western Greece (Higgs *et al.* 1967; Bailey *et al.* 1983a,b) and at the cave site of Crvena Stijena which has eight mousterian levels (Brodar 1958–9) in Yugoslavia. A few kilometres south of Asprochaliko is the open, red-bed site of Kokkinopilos where excavations discovered an assemblage containing finely flaked leaf points (fig. 5.10, b,c) and using the levallois technique (Mellars 1964). These have been compared to assemblages with leaf points at Muselievo in southern Bulgaria (Iwanowa 1979; Kozlowski 1975) in the SE region.

(c) geographical variation

Freeman has divided the Iberian mousterian of the MW region into four major geographical patterns (1981:125). These are the Andalusian, Suboriental (Valencian/Levantine), Catalan and Mesetan patterns. According to Freeman's synthesis of the available data on animal faunas, and by inference palaeolithic diet, the middle palaeolithic diet differed from pattern to pattern while at the same time the regional diversity among the flint assemblages became more finely focused than it was in the earlier acheulean (*ibid.*: 142). The mousterian populations apparently expanded into previously unoccupied areas such as the southern mediterranean coast of Iberia where it seems they tapped the resources of the sea shore. The evidence for the use of marine molluscs at Gorham's Cave (Waechter 1964) is however very scanty and it is very unlikely that they formed the basis for any long term subsistence strategy.

The middle palaeolithic occupation of central Italy has been studied by Barker (1975, 1981). The mousterian sites are mostly located in the coastal lowlands where a diverse animal community of red deer, horse, elephant, rhino and hippopotamus was available for potential exploitation. Barker describes the subsistence economies, as reconstructed from the animal bones found in the rock shelters and open sites of Lazio, as systematic but generalised. In other words a wide array of prey species were taken in a non-random hunting strategy.

An informative study based upon the detailed analysis of the contents of one site is provided by de Lumley's (1972) account of the Hortus cave. A changing pattern of seasonal use for the cave is deduced from the correlations between quantities of tools, age at death of the ibex bones, environmental evidence from pollen work and the neanderthal remains. According to these lines of evidence there was an increase, during Würm II when the cave was used, in the length of time each year that the cave was inhabited as well as in the number of people who regularly visited this facility during the spring and summer seasons.

(d) human remains

The site of Hortus has produced a large number of neanderthal remains (table 5.5) and the fragmented nature of these remains bears comparison with the Krapina and Vindija material from the SE region.

Neanderthal remains are also common in caves from Italy (table 5.3). One of the best known examples comes from the Grotta Guattari in the Monte Circeo complex. Here Blanc (1958) discovered an upturned neanderthal skull lying on the surface of the cave floor. This has often been interpreted as indicating some ritual activity that involved headhunting or cannibalism. However the carnivore remains from the same level (Piperno 1976–7) make it much more likely that the site is a classic hyena den and that these animals are responsible for introducing the skull.

From the clay pit at Saccopastore, but unfortunately still not securely dated, came two skulls (fig. 5.5). The complete specimen is an adult female and is thought to be last interglacial in date (Blanc 1942).

Table 5.5. *The neanderthal remains from Hortus*

These represent a minimum of 20 individuals and a maximum of 36 as indicated by age and sex data from the bones and their relative stratigraphic positions

cranial fragments	2
maxilla fragments	12
mandible fragments	7
clavicle	1
vertebrae	2
pelvis	1
humerus	3
radius	1
hand bones	12
femur	3
patella	1
foot bones	4

Source: M. de Lumley 1976b:569

Further references

MW: H. de Lumley 1969b, 1971, (ed.) 1976a; Freeman 1981; Perez 1974.
MC: Barker 1973, 1981; Blanc and Segre 1953; Taschini 1972.
ME: Kozlowski 1975; Iwanowa 1979; Higgs *et al.* 1967; Dakaris *et al.* 1964;
Bailey *et al.* 1983a, b.

Summary for periods 1 and 2

(a) chronology

The site of Isernia La Pineta at 730 Kyr provides the earliest, most securely dated occurrence for human populations in the continent. The combination of K-Ar and palaeomagnetic determinations provides corroborative evidence for an early date and must stand as a yardstick against which to judge other claims for early finds. Human groups are certainly in Mediterranean Europe during the very late lower pleistocene and early middle pleistocene. The absolute dates indicate that by at least 350 Kyr all the regions except the Alpine and the NE had been colonised, although I would not be surprised to see early occupation in the latter region confirmed by absolute dates. The major evidence for late colonisation of the Russian plains is based on the lack of handaxes, an observation which now provides a poor warrant for drawing such a chronological conclusion. There is not much evidence which allows us to comment on the nature of the settlement histories in these regions but a pattern of settlement ebb and flow as discussed in Chapter 3 is expected. Testing such a model provides us with a fresh reason for acquiring more absolute dates on these early sites since they are a route to answering behavioural questions about the past rather than merely aids in documenting antiquity.

Last interglacial sites, as expected (Chapter 3), are either very rare, or non-existent. This of course depends upon the calibration of the last interglacial with sub-stage 5e and placing the remainder of that stage in the early glacial, Würm I stadial. Here we find intra- and inter-regional variation in settlement histories: Cantabria compared with the Dordogne and the NC compared with the SW region. It is difficult to be precise about the settlement histories in the Mediterranean province but the indications from MC are that continuous occupation during the early glacial period was maintained.

Finally, many more sites are probably pre-last interglacial in age, as absolute dates for the Abri Vaufrey, Ehringsdorf and Pontnewydd are beginning to show.

(b) industrial groupings

Evolutionary schemes which traced the organic development of one industry from another have been supplemented with the discovery of recurrent groupings of particular assemblage types. Techniques of flake production, the degree to which nodules are reduced in a systematic and standardised fashion, and the patterns of secondary retouch to form implements have all been used as a means to search for higher order patterns and classifications in the lithic material. Two major groups emerge. On the one hand are assemblages and industries with simple reduction strategies (fig. 5.3) – clactonian, tayacian, pre-mousterian, denticulate, taubachian, Buda – commonly described as a core/flake/chopping tool complex. On the other hand are assemblages with more complex lithic reduction processes, great internal variety expressed in many styles of retouch, techniques of flaking and assemblage composition (figs. 5.1, 5.2) – acheulean, abbevillien, micoquian, altmühlian, charentian, pontinian, typical, MTA, evenosien. I see little point in dividing this material into the traditional constellations of lower and middle palaeolithic although many archaeologists still use such a classificatory framework (e.g. Ronen (ed.) 1982). Middle palaeolithic has been used here as a shorthand to indicate material that is thought to date to the early last glacial. As absolute dates become available we are beginning to see that the assemblages from the middle and early upper pleistocene of Europe have little temporal ordering and resemble nothing so much as a well stirred minestrone soup of types and techniques that coagulate into industries on the end of the taxonomist's spoon.

(c) geographical variation

The validity of any geographical patterns among this data depends upon the dating of sites. However at the moment it is possible to see that the NW and SW regions and the mediterranean province dominate in terms of (1) the overall quantities of lithic material; (2) the occurrence of repeated assemblage types in stratified contexts; and (3) the relative numerical size of assemblages of retouched implements. As a result there is more emphasis upon the use of type fossils in NC, NE, SE and Alpine to build culture history. This reflects a significant pattern in the archaeological signatures (Chapter 8) of the regions. It will, I believe, prove a significant observation that links variation in lithic material to a geographical basemap.

Few locational studies have been undertaken. Statements about subsistence generally take a face-value interpretation of the identified bones to produce descriptions of mammoth, red deer or ibex hunters.

(d) human remains

The sparse and fragmentary fossil material is the subject of much debate when it comes to comparing and grouping material. Vlček (1978) for example sees *Homo erectus* (Petralona, Vértesszöllös and Bilzingsleben) inhabiting central and eastern Europe at the same time during the Holsteinian interglacial as *Homo sapiens* (Swanscombe and Steinheim) was present in western Europe. This

Table 5.6. *A grade system for classifying the* Homo sapiens *fossils from Europe*

A grade has no chronological significance and orders the fossils on strictly morphological criteria, in this case the shape of the skulls and mandibles

Grade	
3b	Crô Magnon
3a	Neanderthal, La Chapelle-aux-Saints, Monte Circeo, Spy, La Ferrassie, Krapina, Régourdou
3a or 2	Krapina
2	Biache–St-Vaast, La Chaise, Ehringsdorf, Fontéchevade, Saccopastore, Salzgitter-Lebenstedt
2 or 1	Atapuerca, Steinheim, Swanscombe
1	Arago, Mauer, Bilzingsleben, Petralona, Vértesszöllös

Source: After Trinkaus 1982: 309; Stringer *et al.* 1979

scheme requires rather greater accuracy in dating than is currently possible from the discontinuous record. For example, which Holsteinian interglacial are we talking about (table 3.3)? Moreover the attribution of these three fossils as *Homo erectus* is not generally accepted. An alternative scheme based upon morphoclines in cranial shape (Stringer *et al.* 1979) groups the fossil material into grades (table 5.6). Whether these grades can then be used as units of measurement in evolutionary studies depends upon the temporal modes (Gould and Eldredge 1977; Cronin *et al.* 1981) that govern the rate of change under different conditions of natural selection. However we can be quite clear on one point. No correlation can be drawn between a grade and the ability or inability of the fossil representatives it contains to manufacture a particular lithic industry.

The upper palaeolithic is now commonly divided into two groups of industries – an early upper palaeolithic (EUP), and a later upper palaeolithic (LUP) (Campbell 1977; Otte 1979; Freeman 1981; Clark and Straus 1983). In France these have recently been classified into a Group II (EUP) and a Group III (LUP) scheme based on detailed sedimentological investigations (Laville *et al.* 1980). These correspond to divisions 3 and 4 (table 4.8) and recognise a significant change in assemblage composition and technology after 20 Kyr.

Northern province 3

(a) chronology

The transition from the middle to the upper palaeolithic took place very rapidly and apparently simultaneously across the continent. In geological terms this occurred during or just after the Würm II/III interstadial (table 3.7) and in C14 chronology after 35 Kyr.

Within the EUP there are a number of chronologically early industries. One of these is associated with leaf points and is found in the NW region at Kents Cavern, England (Campbell 1977; Campbell and Sampson 1971), and in the NC region in Hungary and Czechoslovakia. These assemblages are not thought to be connected in any way. There may, or may not, be a connection with the earlier leaf point material from the NC regions at the Ilsenhöhle (Hülle 1977) or the material at Jerzmanowice in Poland.

The type site for the NC leaf point assemblages is the Szeleta cave (Vértes 1955a), in the Bükk mountains of Hungary, where a variety of leaf point forms were found. The assemblages which contain them are referred to as szeletian (Freund 1952; Allsworth-Jones 1975). Comparable material has been found at Transdanubian sites in Hungary (Vértes 1960) and in the loess along the river valleys of Moravia and Slovakia, notably the Váh (Zotz 1951; Filip 1966; Bárta and Bánesz 1981).

Contemporaneous with this material are aurignacian assemblages, for example at the Istállöskö cave, also in the Bükk mountains. Here two stratified aurignacian levels have C14 dates of 31.5 Kyr for the lower and 30.6 Kyr for the upper level (Gábori-Csánk 1970).

The aurignacian is now well dated by C14 in the southern German area of the NC region (Hahn 1977, 1981a). The Swabian Alb cave sites of the Stadel, Vogelherd and Geissenklösterle indicate aurignacian assemblages between 30 and 32 Kyr. Even earlier dates are now available from the Geissenklösterle where level III, the earliest aurignacian level in the site, is dated to between 34.1 and 36.5 Kyr. Further north near Köln the open air loess site of Lommersum (Hahn 1974) has C14 dates for level IIc of 31.8–33.4 Kyr.

An important stratigraphic sequence in the NW region has been excavated by Leroi-Gourhan in the Grotte du Renne at Arcy-sur-Cure (1961; and Arl. Leroi-Gourhan 1964; Movius 1969). Here there are six EUP levels. The upper palaeolithic part of the sequence commences with two levels, X and IX, which contain chatelperronian material. This is regarded as the earliest upper palaeolithic industry in the SW region. In level VIII is an assemblage of final chatelperronian/lower perigordian dated by C14 to 33.8–33.5 Kyr. Level VII contains an aurignacian assemblage dated to 30.8 Kyr. The chatelperronian/ perigordian II level at Les Cottés has been dated to 33.3 Kyr, and is mostly separated from an early aurignacian level of 31.2 Kyr by a sterile layer (Pradel 1961). Further typologically early aurignacian assemblages are found in northern France and Belgium, as at the Grotte de la Betche at Spy (Otte 1976a, 1979).

The earliest upper palaeolithic industries in the NE region are found in the intensively researched areas of the middle Dniestr and along the Don rivers. At Molodova V the first upper palaeolithic horizon, X, occurs in level 9. Horizon IX above is dated at 28–9 Kyr (Ivanova 1982). A recent redating of the Kostenki sites on the Don river (Praslov and Rogachev (eds.) 1982) has revised the earlier C14 determinations which consistently gave ages that were considered younger than the indications from the stratigraphic and geological evidence. The oldest upper palaeolithic material occurs in the second terrace at Kostenki XVII where the lower occupation, stratified below volcanic ash, has been dated to 32.2 Kyr (table 5.7). Level Ia at Kostenki 12 is dated to 32.7 Kyr, although this lies above the same volcanic marker horizon.

The gradual development of a C14 chronology for the EUP has led to some revisions of earlier chronological schemes. It was previously believed that the aurignacian was everywhere succeeded by the gravettian. Multi-level sites and sections such as Willendorf II in the loess pits along the Danube in lower Austria, NC region, provided stratified evidence for this replacement (Felgenhauer 1956/9, 1962; Broglio and Laplace 1966). At the site four small aurignacian assemblages are succeeded by five levels with gravettian assemblages. Throughout the NC region the aurignacian was once thought to 'give way' to the gravettian at c.27 Kyr. However the C14 dating of a number of aurignacian and gravettian levels in caves from the limestone uplands of southern Germany (Hahn 1976a,b, 1977, 1981a) points to a chronological overlap between 25 and 22 Kyr for these different assemblages. Upper perigordian/gravettian is dated to 27.9 Kyr for a collection with Font Robert tanged points at the Maisières canal in Belgium, NW region (Otte 1976b). Later upper perigordian thought to date to c.23 Kyr is known from the open site of Plassen-al-Lomm in Brittany (Monnier 1982).

The eastern gravettian is particularly well represented by assemblages dated by C14 to between 26 and 21 Kyr (Otte 1981). These include those from the open settlements of Pavlov and Dolní Věstonice, south of Brno in Moravia (Klíma 1963, 1981), and other sites including Sunghir at 24.4–25.5 Kyr, Kostenki I/1 (table 5.7), both of which are in Russia, and Spadzista Street site B dated to 20.6–23 Kyr in Krakow, Poland (Kozlowski 1974). The principal artifact horizon, VII, at Molodova V is also dated within the same chronological bracket at 23–23.7 Kyr.

(b) industrial groupings

The EUP of this province can be divided into four main groups.

(1) Central European leaf point assemblages (fig. 5.10, j,k,l) which consist of poorly understood collections such as those from the Hungarian caves of Szeleta and Jancovich (Allsworth-Jones 1975). Valoch (1957) has described them as being middle palaeolithic in flint working technique – the leaf points are made on flakes rather than blades – and with a predominance of middle palaeolithic types such as side scrapers. Aurignacian scrapers – keeled and nosed – are present together with some rare antler/bone points. Bárta has argued for the presence of the bow in the szeletian (1974; and Bánesz 1981) because of the small size of some of the projectile points.

The mixed nature of some szeletian assemblages may be due to solifluxion processes mixing the contents of levels. Many of the coarsely flaked leaf points in the lower level of Szeleta are now regarded as cryoturbated artifacts

Table 5.7. *Stratigraphic ordering and C14 chronology for some key sites in the first and second terraces of the Don river at Kostenki/Borshevo, NE region*

The dates are given in Kyr bp.
The stratigraphic position of streletskaya assemblages is indicated by S; C14 determinations are given in parentheses as Kyr bp.

		SECOND TERRACE					Deposit	FIRST TERRACE		
M–G	K I	S II	T	K XII	A II	K XVII		K XXI	K XIX	B II
							CHERNOZEM			1 · 12.3–13.2
	1 · 21.3–24.1							1		2
1					1a · 17.3–19.9				1 · 18.9	3
	2				1b		COLLUVIAL	2 · 19.1–22.9		
					2 · 15.2–21.8		DEPOSITS			
								3 · 21.2–22.2		
			1 — —		3 · 16 —					
	3						LOESS-LIKE LOAM			
	4		2 · 27.7	1 · 32.7	4	1 · 26.7	UPPER HUMIC BED			
2 · 26.4–28.2										
3 · Burial			3 · S							
							NON-HUMIC BED			
							VOLCANIC ASH			
							NON-HUMIC BED			
	5 · S	1 · S		2	5 · S	2 · 32.2	LOWER HUMIC BED			
4			3 · S							
			ALLUVIUM							

Source: Based on Rogachev 1961; Klein 1969a; Praslov and Rogachev (eds.) 1982

Key:
- M–G — Markina Gora (= Kostenki XIV)
- S — Streletskaya (= Kostenki VI)
- A — Anoskova (= Kostenki XI)
- K — Kostenki
- T — Tel'manskaya (= Kostenki VIII)
- B — Borshevo

(Allsworth-Jones 1975) and hence their 'primitive' appearance is due to mechanical rather than human action.

Finely worked, small bifacial leaf points with rounded bases have been found in a clear association with an upper palaeolithic inventory at Moravany nad Váhom-Dhlá (fig. 5.10, m,n), an open loess site by the Váh river in Slovakia (Bárta 1965; and Bánesz 1981).

(2) The aurignacian material (fig. 5.14, a–i) is comprehensively described by Hahn (1972a, 1977; Otte 1979; Bánesz 1976). The lithic inventories are generally small. Three of the largest collections from the NC region are Breitenbach, an open site in East Germany (Toepfer 1970), the Vogelherd cave in southern Germany (Riek 1934) and the loess pit excavation at Krems Hundssteig in lower Austria (Laplace 1970). The assemblages are characterised by end scrapers made on thick blades and flakes (fig. 5.14, c,d,e) and blades with flat retouch that often extends around the entire perimeter of the implement (fig. 5.14, f). A number of assemblages from the NC and NE regions also contain large quantities of small bladelets with fine alternate blunting retouch. These are very common at Krems Hundssteig (Hahn 1977). These bladelets are known as lamelles Dufour (fig. 5.14, h,i) (Brézillon 1968).

Aurignacian assemblages are rare in the NE region, but Hahn (1977) regards the material in Kostenki I/2 and 3 as belonging to this technocomplex (Praslov and Rogachev (eds.) 1982:fig. 22). An important loess section on the Prut at Ripiceni-Izvor (Păunescu 1965) has three small aurignacian collections stratified above middle palaeolithic assemblages and below four gravettian horizons.

The small size of the inventories can be seen at the Istállöskö cave (Vértes 1955b) where in the lower level bone tools formed 71% of the combined lithic and bone tool inventory of only 159 pieces. The split base (fig. 5.14, b) and solid base projectile points made in antler, bone and occasionally even ivory are a marked feature of aurignacian assemblages from caves (Albrecht *et al.* 1972) but are very rare indeed in open aurignacian sites.

(3) Gravettian assemblages in the German part of the NC region and in the NW region are few in number (Otte 1981; Klíma (ed.) 1976a; Desbrosse and Kozlowski (eds.) 1981; Hahn 1969). They are dominated by end scrapers on long blades, burins and slender points with blunting retouch down one edge (fig. 5.14, m). Shouldered points are a noteworthy type fossil (Kozlowski 1976b). In this part of the gravettian range the largest assemblages are known from the Brillenhöhle level VII (Riek 1973), Sprendlingen (Bosinski 1979a), Mauern level C (Bohmers 1951), the Maisières canal, Belgium (Otte 1976b) and Willendorf II/9 (Broglio and Laplace 1966).

(4) In Moravia and Slovakia (Bárta 1967), NC region, and in the NE region are several very large sites (e.g. Dolní Věstonice, Pavlov, Lubna, Avdeevo, Kostenki I/1, Sunghir, Molodova V/VII) with large lithic and bone inventories. These assemblages form the basis for recognising a number of industrial groups (Klíma (ed.) 1976a; Kozlowski and Kozlowski 1979:map 4) among which are the

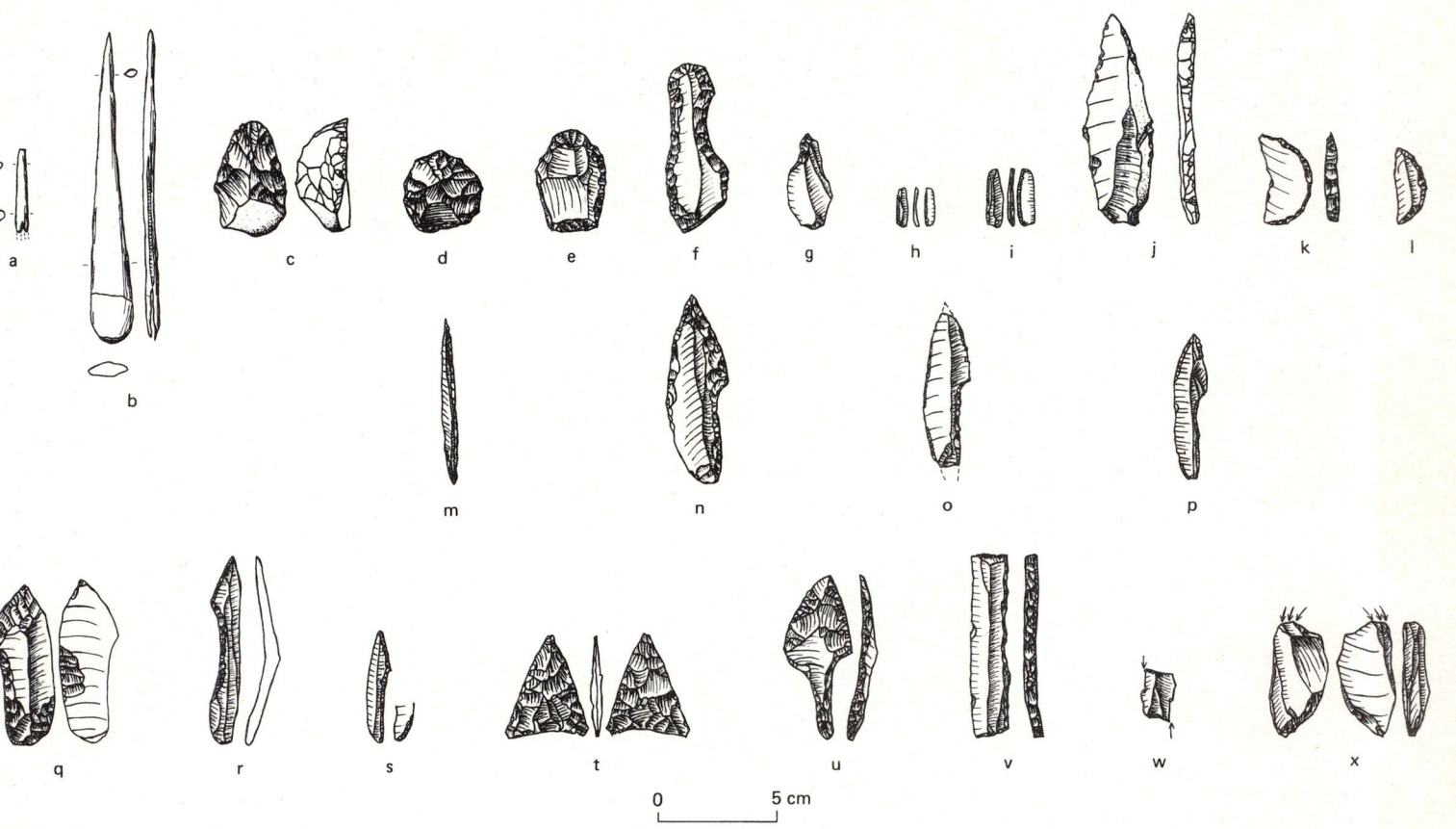

5.14 EUP artifact types: a–i, aurignacian

Bone points: (a, b) split base, Vogelherd V and Istállöskö lower level. Keeled scrapers: (c) Abri Caminade; (d) Vogelherd; (e) Vogelherd nosed scraper; (f) La Ferrassie strangled blade; (g) La Ferrassie busked burin; (h, i) Krems-Hundssteig Dufour bladelets; j–x perigordian/gravettian; (j) Arcy-sur-Cure, Grotte du Renne chatelperronian point; (k, l) uluzzian points; (m) gravette; (n) Moravany Dlhá Kostenki point/knife; (o, p, q) Kostenki knives/points; (r, s) Molodova V/VII shouldered points; (t) Sunghir streletskayan point; (u) Maisières canal Font-Robert point; (v) retouched truncated element; (w) noailles burin; (x) Raysse-Bassaler burin.

pavlovian, molodovian and streletskayan. They can however all be grouped within a general technocomplex description: the eastern gravettian. Distinctive type fossils occur as with the Kostenki shouldered knives/points (fig. 5.14, n–q) that are found in sites on the Don (e.g. Kostenki I/1 and Kostenki XII) and at Avdeevo 300 km to the north-west, but also at Spadzista street B in Poland (Kozlowski 1974), Moravany-Podkovica, Noviny and Nitra among the assemblages in Slovakia (Bárta 1967; and Bánesz 1981), and as far west as Willendorf II/9 in lower Austria (Otte 1981).

Bifacially worked hollow based points (fig. 5.14, t) are a very distinctive feature in the assemblages at Streletskaya (= Kostenki VI), Sunghir (Bader 1978:fig. 86), Kostenki I/5 and Anoskova II (= Kostenki XI) (Klein 1969a; Valoch 1968; Shimkin 1978; Praslov and Rogachev (eds.) 1982). The assemblages at Kostenki (table 5.7) are on stratigraphic grounds much older than the main artifact horizon at Sunghir that is dated by C14.

Many other assemblage variants are known from the Kostenki sites; for example Kostenki XIV/2 (= Markina Gora) with end scrapers on thick blades and a substantial flake scraper element.

Horizon X at Molodova V has a small inventory with some bifacial tanged points. Level VII dated to 23.7–23 Kyr has some 41,500 pieces of chipped stone. Among the 1200 retouched tools burins predominate. Type fossil material is rare but a few, small shouldered gravettian points are present (fig. 5.14 r,s) (Chernysh 1961:table 2).

Ivory, bone and antler tools including clubs, knives, points, pierced staffs, spatulas and many worked objects of unknown function are common on the larger sites of the eastern gravettian such as Předmost in Moravia (Valoch 1982b) as well as in the Russian stations of the NE region (Praslov and Rogachev (eds.) 1982; Klein 1973).

(c) geographical variation

It is striking that throughout the EUP there are no settlements on the North European Plains (Hahn 1977; Otte 1981; Bánesz 1976; Kozlowski and Kozlowski 1979). During this period the ice sheets began encroaching onto part of this plains environment. The open sites of Lommersum and Breitenbach represent two of the most northerly occupations. Settlement in England is also sparse, apparently ceasing altogether after 27 Kyr (Campbell 1977, 2: 207; Jacobi 1980).

A distribution pattern that requires further investigation relates to the aurignacian and szeletian in Moravia (Bánesz 1976:map 1). The distribution of aurignacian settlements forms a ring of sites in the limestone uplands of Moravia and eastern Slovakia, leaving a hollow centre along the Váh and Nitra rivers. It is along these rivers that both cave and open szeletian sites have been identified (e.g. Čertova Pec (= Radošina), Moravany-Dhlá). Elsewhere in the region no such geographical separation between szeletian and aurignacian occurs.

Elsewhere in eastern Slovakia around Kosice (Bánesz 1967, 1968) and at Ceahlau in the NE region (Nicolăescu-Plopşor *et al.* 1966), intensive research has revealed a number of aurignacian sites while the szeletian is entirely lacking.

Hahn has also noted that aurignacian assemblages from the eastern part of the NC and in the NE region frequently contain a few bifacially worked pieces, including fragments of leaf points (1977:tables 1 and 2). These items are however lacking in aurignacian assemblages from Austria and Germany. This emphasises the complete absence of szeletian material in this part of the NC region. A very similar geographical distribution can be seen at c.23 Kyr with the Kostenki shouldered knife/point which is a component of eastern gravettian assemblages.

A number of subsistence and regional land use studies are available for the province. These include the case studies by Klein (1969a, 1973) on the Russian material, NE region, and Campbell (1977) for the English EUP in the NW region. Attention has been paid to the limestone uplands of southern Germany by Gamble (1978a, b, 1979) and Hahn (1981a; *et al.* 1973). Here the principal cave sites, as measured by the quantities of retouched artifacts, are consistently located in the middle of the flat grazing lands along the southern edge of the limestone uplands of Swabia and Franconia (fig. 5.12). The choice of such central locations points to the importance of the large herbivores – bison, horse, red deer and reindeer – for the subsistence economy of these palaeolithic groups and the need to locate settlement centrally to these mobile resources (Wilmsen 1973).

In the eastern half of the province the spectacular nature of sites such as Dolní Věstonice (Klíma 1963; Absolon 1938–45) or Kostenki I/1 (Efimenko 1958) is often attributed to the success of the hunters in killing mammoth (Klima 1976b; Klein 1973; Sklenář 1975).

(d) burial and art

This province has a substantial corpus of art and ornament. Associated with the earliest aurignacian are small animal figurines, carved from ivory, of mammoth, lion, horse and anthropomorphs. These come from the Vogelherd (Riek 1934; Wagner 1981), while from the Geissenklösterle a mammoth has been found in level II and a human figure in level III (Hahn *et al.* 1977; Hahn 1979a; Bosinski 1982b). Finally a human figure (fig. 5.15) carved from a juvenile mammoth tusk came from the nearby site of the Stadel, level IV (Hahn 1970). Scratched signs are also common on aurignacian bone implements (Hahn 1972b).

A greater variety and number of such objects are known from the eastern gravettian area. These include the baked clay animal figurines from Dolní

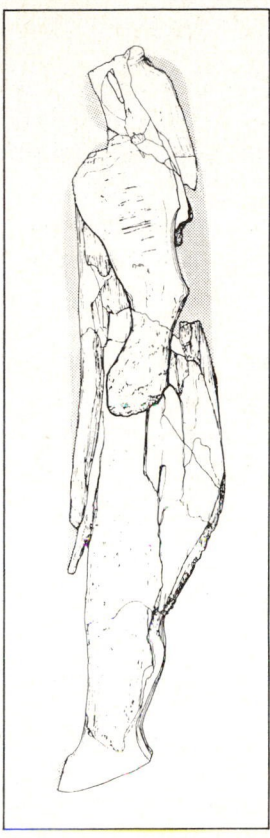

5.15 An anthropomorphic figure carved from a juvenile mammoth tusk, Hohlenstein Stadel, NC region, and dated to 31.7 Kyr (Hahn 1977:taf.16).

Věstonice (Klíma 1963) as well as those carved in ivory from Kostenki I/1 and Avdeevo (Abramova 1967). These are dated to between 26 and 21 Kyr.

A distinctive form of female figurine, the so-called Venus figurines (Delporte 1979; Gamble 1982) are found in these sites as well as many others in the NC and NE regions (fig. 7.2). These include Kostenki I/1, Khotylevo, dated to 23.6 Kyr (Zaverniaev 1978b), both in the NE region, Moravany-Podkovica (Zotz 1968; Bárta and Bánesz 1981) and Willendorf II/9, and possibly Mauern level C (Zotz 1951), the Brillenhöhle (Riek 1973) and Mainz Linsenberg (Hahn 1969) from the NC region. Comparable figurines are known from the SW region but not from the NW (Chapter 7).

A wide range of ornaments including beads of shell and ivory, bracelets of mammoth ivory and pendants (fig. 5.16) are found throughout most of the province although once again they are more commonly encountered in the eastern areas. However the early chatelperronian levels at Grotte du Renne, Arcy-sur-Cure, in the NW region have produced carnivore canines which were pierced for suspension either as pendants or as components in a necklace as well

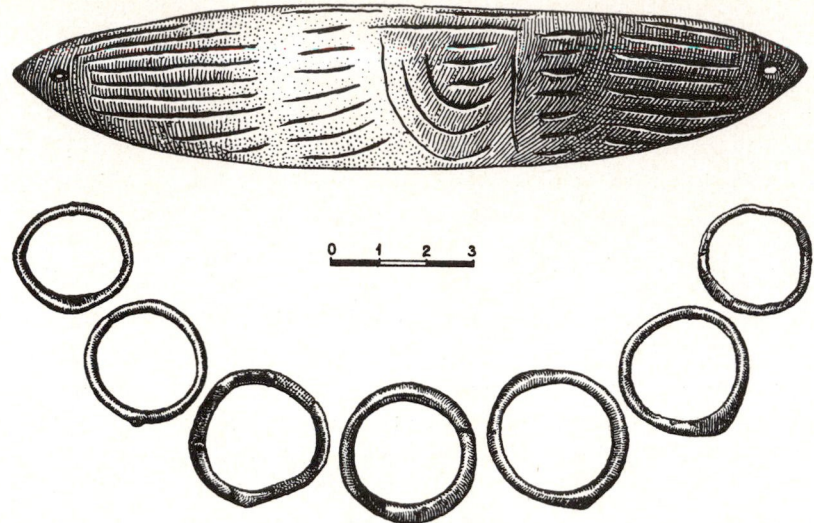

5.16 Engraved ivory collar (top) and bracelets from Pavlov, NC region (Klíma 1957:113, fig. 20).

as a pendant carved in the shape of a fish-tail (Leroi-Gourhan 1961; and Arl. Leroi-Gourhan 1964). An example of the complex nature of material culture at c.23 Kyr in the NE region is well shown in the finds from the excavated burials at Sunghir outside the town of Vladimir some 200 km north-east of Moscow (Bader 1967, 1978). Here two graves have been excavated among the settlement debris. One of them is a double grave of two young boys in which the extended bodies had been laid head to head. Spears of straightened mammoth ivory were placed by their sides together with some stone tools, ivory daggers, pierced antler rods, a disc shaped pendant and small animal carvings; one of which is a horse carved in schematic outline from a sliver of ivory. Both of the bodies, as well as the nearby burial of an adult male, were covered in several thousand ivory beads. The distribution of these beads across the bodies indicated that they had been sewn onto clothes and headgear.

An earlier burial of an adult male is known from Kostenki XIV (= Markina Gora) beneath level 3. This consists of a tightly flexed inhumation without the richness of accompanying material culture.

A large grave pit was found at the loess site of Předmost in Moravia. This contained some eighteen individuals – six males, two females and ten children of various ages (Oakley *et al.* 1971) – found buried beneath stones and mammoth shoulder blades, and associated with gravettian implements. The details of this remarkable find of the late nineteenth century are unfortunately poorly recorded.

From the NW region comes the 'Red Lady' of Paviland found in 1823 in a cave in southern Wales. It was an extended inhumation of EUP date and was found with some ivory rods, perforated shells and two ivory bracelets. The C14 date of 18.4 Kyr from the collagen in the limb bones is thought to be too young (Campbell 1977, 1:144; Morrison 1980:89) and furthermore the skeleton is no lady but instead an adult male c.25 years old. Jacobi (1980) has recently presented convincing arguments that the burial should be regarded as EUP in age and associated with the aurignacian artifacts found in the deposits.

Further references

NW: Campbell 1977; Morrison 1980; H. de Lumley (ed.) 1976a; Otte 1976a,b, 1979; Jacobi 1980.
NC: Hahn 1977; Otte 1981; Klíma (ed.) 1976a; Desbrosse and Kozlowski (eds.) 1981; Kozlowski (ed.) 1976a; Albrecht *et al.* 1972; Bánesz 1976; Bárta 1965, 1967; Bárta and Bánesz 1981; Filip (ed.) 1966; Bosinski 1982b.
NE: Praslov and Rogachev (eds.) 1982; Klein 1969a, 1973; McBurney 1976; Chernysh 1961; Okladnikov (ed.) 1957; Păunescu 1970; Klíma (ed.) 1976a; Desbrosse and Kozlowski (eds.) 1981; Shimkin 1978; Abramova 1967.

Southern province 3

(a) chronology

Information for this province is dominated by the intensive research into the caves of the Périgord area, SW region. Of especial interest are the investigations in the rock shelters in the vicinity of the small Dordogne village of Les Eyzies on the Vézère river (Lartet and Christy 1865–75; de Sonneville-Bordes 1960; Laville *et al.* 1980).

The many excavations in this area by D. Peyrony, and in particular at the site of La Ferrassie (1934), led him to re-define the ordering of the upper palaeolithic as set out in an earlier, classic paper by Breuil (1912). Peyrony (1933) identified two major traditions – perigordian and aurignacian – whereas Breuil had recognised only a single aurignacian cycle (table 5.8). The earliest perigordian/chatelperronian assemblages are dated geologically to after the Würm II/III interstadial since according to French sedimentologists the interstadial deposits themselves are never preserved (Laville *et al.* 1980). In a number of cases however the lower perigordian directly overlies middle palaeolithic horizons. This occurs at La Ferrassie and Le Moustier in the Périgord and outside this area at Gargas, Châtelperron and in the NW region at the Grotte du Renne (Lynch 1966). C14 dates for the late mousterian and earliest upper palaeolithic from both the NW and SW regions of France are given in table 5.9.

The occupation by the lower perigordian of the rock shelters around Les Eyzies was then abruptly terminated, according to Peyrony's scheme, by the arrival of the Aurignacians. This view maintained that the question of who

Table 5.8. *Contrasting views of the aurignacian and perigordian traditions as interpreted by Breuil and Peyrony*

The Laugerie–Haute sequence was not yet known in 1912

SOLUTREAN		
		UPPER PERIGORDIAN La Ferrassie L ....Vc (noailles burins) K ....Vb (truncations) J ....Va (Font Robert points) La Gravette ....IV (gravettes)
UPPER AURIGNACIAN (La Gravette type)	**TYPICAL AURIGNACIAN** (Evolved) Laugerie-Haute West D V	
MIDDLE AURIGNACIAN (Crô-Magnon type)	**TYPICAL AURIGNACIAN** La Ferrassie H'' ....IV (Abri) H' ....III H ....II F I	**MIDDLE PERIGORDIAN** Laugerie-Haute B,B' ....III (obliquely truncated blades, blunted edged blades and bladelets)
LOWER AURIGNACIAN (Châtelperron type)		**LOWER PERIGORDIAN** La Ferrassie E' ....II E ....I (chatelperronian points)
AURIGNACIAN	*TYPICAL AURIGNACIAN*	*PERIGORDIAN*
MOUSTERIAN		
Breuil 1912	Peyrony 1933	

Source: After de Sonneville-Bordes 1960: tableau B

Table 5.9. *C14 dates for the mousterian and early upper palaeolithic in France, NW and SW regions*

mousterian	lower perigordian/ chatelperronian	aurignacian	upper perigordian
Combe-Grenal 1			
39,000±1500			
Combe-Grenal 2			
34,800±500			
La Rochette		*La Rochette*	
36,000±550		28,860±300(4),28,420±320(5c)	
Grotte du Renne 12	*Grotte du Renne* 8	*Grotte du Renne* 7	
34,600±850	33,860±250	30,800±250	
33,700±810	33,500±400		
La Quina		*La Quina*	
35,250±530		30,760±490	
34,100±700			
[a]31,100±400			
Les Cottés	*Les Cottés*	*Les Cottés*	
[a]30,800±500 E1	33,300±500 G1	31,900±430	
[a]31,000±320 E2			
[a]32,300±400 I1			
37,600±700 I2			
		La Caminade	
		29,100±300	
		Abri Pataud	*Abri Pataud*
		31,800±310 level 7	28,150±225 level 5
		29,300±450	27,660±260
		32,800±450	26,660±200
		32,900±700	26,050±310
		32,000±800 level 11	23,350±170
		32,000±550	21,780±215
		33,000±500 level 12	27,060±370 level 4
		31,000±150	23,010±170 level 3
		33,260±425	22,780±140
		33,300±760 level 14	21,380±340 level 2
		34,250±675	20,810±170
		33,330±410	19,650±300

Note: [a] These dates are generally considered to be too young. All dates are Kyr bp.

should live in the Dordogne was a hotly contested issue between rival populations who happened to use different assemblages of stone tools, thereby making their ethnic presence known to archaeologists by wearing distinctive lithic tee-shirts. Bordes (1973:222) summed it up as follows,

As for the upper palaeolithic, it seems that when the Aurignacians arrived in the Dordogne, they swept the Perigordians out for some time, and we find interstratifications at the border (as in Roc de Combe) or evolved Old Perigordian in peripheral places, as in Les Cottés (Vienne) under evolved Aurignacian I. Then the Perigordians came back about the time of the middle Perigordian, and the Aurignacian sites (Aurignacian III and IV) became much rarer in the Dordogne.

This interpretation depends of course on accepting the Dordogne area as a

Table 5.10. *Contemporary assemblage variation during Würm III in the Périgord as determined by sediment studies (see table 3.7)*

Climatic phase	Climate	Roc de Combe		La Ferrassie
Perigord VII	Moderate and humid	1. evolved perigordian VI noailles burins, Font-Robert points, gravette points	L	perigordian V with noailles burins
		2. perigordian V with noailles	K	perigordian V with truncations
Perigord VI	Cold, dry	3. perigordian V with noailles	J	perigordian V with Font-Robert points
Perigord V	Mild and humid	4. perigordian IV with gravettes	H''	aurignacian IV
Perigord IV	Cold, dry	5. evolved aurignacian	H'	aurignacian III
Perigord III	Mild and humid	6. aurignacian II	H	aurignacian II
Perigord II	Cold, dry	7. aurignacian I	F	aurignacian I
Perigord I	Moderately cold and very humid	8. lower perigordian	E'	aurignacian
		9. aurignacian	E	perigordian I
		10. perigordian I		
		mousterian		mousterian

Source: After Bordes 1973; Laville 1976; Laville *et al.* 1980

natural centre, a palaeolithic Garden of Eden, and other areas in France, such as the Lot or Corrèze as a second best choice; a view clearly shared by Delporte (1981:7) and many other archaeologists who have worked in the area.

The sites of Piage (Champagne and Espitalié 1981) and Roc de Combe (Bordes and Labrot 1967) do show assemblage interdigitation in their stratified sections, and elsewhere the fine resolution of chronostratigraphy through sediment analysis (table 5.10) apparently points to contemporaneity between assemblages of different traditions. These observations were used by Bordes (1968a, 1973) as confirmation for his model of why these assemblages were different. In his opinion aurignacian and perigordian were made by different peoples just as the five mousterian variants had been made by five Neanderthal tribes.

A C14 chronology is available for only a few sites (Delibrias *et al.* 1976; Delibrias and Evin 1980). Of these the most important is the Abri Pataud, where a long EUP sequence begins with basal aurignacian in level 14 and ends with a protomagdalenian assemblage in level 2. The absolute dates indicate early aurignacian beween 34 and 29 Kyr, perigordian IV from 28 to 26 Kyr, while elsewhere at the Abri Facteur and La Ferrassie perigordian VI and V assemblages are dated to between 25 and 21 Kyr. Finally the protomagdalenian in level 2 at the Abri Pataud has three dates with a range of 21.3–19.6 Kyr (Movius 1966; Delibrias *et al.* 1976). Rigaud (1978:305) has examined the internal chronology of perigordian V assemblages which on the basis of Peyrony's work at La Ferrassie were classified into three facies. He shows that the chronostratigraphic

Table 5.11. *The correlation of perigordian V assemblages with the climatic sequence of the Périgord as established from sedimentological studies*

The three groups of perigordian V assemblages are *not* the traditional a, b and c divisions as identified by Peyrony on the basis of type fossils found in levels J, K and L at La Ferrassie. In this analysis (Rigaud 1978) the proportions of types and groups of types have been taken into consideration in distinguishing three groups as follows:

Key:

Group I. high % of noailles burins, few plane burins on truncations, gravettes or microgravettes.
Group II. high % of gravettes and microgravettes, few plane burins and noailles burins.
Group III. high % of plane burins on truncation, few noailles, gravettes or microgravettes.

Climatic chronology, Périgord stage	Climatic correlation only	Perigordian V assemblages		
		Group I	Group II	Group III
VII Moderate and humid	Abri Facteur level 8	Roc de Gavaudun level 11		Le Flageolet I level IV
	Abri Facteur level 9			Le Flageolet I level V
		Abri Facteur level 10 Abri Facteur level 11	Le Flageolet I level VI	Les Jambes level 2 level 3
VI Cold and dry	Abri Facteur level 12 Abri Facteur level 13		Le Flageolet I level VII	

evidence points once again to contemporaneity between different perigordian V assemblages rather than the alternative view that they must always succeed each other; a view derived from observations on single sequences such as the La Ferrassie profile showed in successive levels J, K and L. This contemporaneity occurs between the Abri Facteur level 10, Le Flageolet I, level VI and at Les Jambes level 2 (table 5.11).

The interdigitation of assemblages is not apparent in the stratigraphic sequences of the Cantabrian area of the SW region. At the Cueva Morín (González-Echegaray and Freeman 1971, 1973; Butzer 1981) there are eight levels with EUP assemblages of which one is described as chatelperronian, five as aurignacian and two as gravettian (Bernaldo de Quiros 1981). This apparently straightforward stratigraphical succession is however complicated by Butzer's sediment work. A chronostratigraphic scheme for the Cueva Morín, El Pendo and Castilló caves shows some chronological overlap between the chatelperronian and early aurignacian and between the evolved aurignacian and the gravettian (Butzer 1981:168, 177).

The chronology of the EUP in the SE region is, by comparison with the SW, poorly understood, although recent regional syntheses for Roumania by Câr-ciumaru (1980, 1982) are now supplying the information. The cave at Bacho Kiro (Kozlowski 1982) has some five aurignacian assemblages which overlie an earlier upper palaeolithic assemblage from level 11, called the bachokirian, and dated to the middle Würm, Heraklista interstadial. A single C14 date on charcoal from the lower part of layer 11 has given a date of >43 Kyr, while aurignacian assemblages in layers 6b and 6a/7 are C14 dated to 32.7 Kyr and 29.1 Kyr respectively. These early dates could prove of great significance in our understanding of the temporal relationships between the earliest upper and latest middle palaeolithic industries of Europe.

The cave sites of Vindija and Velika Pečina in Croatia have C14 dates of 27 Kyr for EUP assemblages described as aurignacian (Montet-White 1981; Malez 1979).

(b) industrial groupings

The assemblage from layer 11 in the Bacho Kiro cave is dominated by retouched blades. In terms of both raw materials (Chapter 7), technology and typology it forms a complete break with the earlier, middle palaeolithic, assemblages in the cave. The C14 date places it well before any reliably dated aurignacian assemblages. The lack of bone/antler points, the preponderance of end scrapers and the lack of other distinctive aurignacian types has led to the description of the assemblage in layer 11 as bachokirian. This assemblage is as yet unparalleled at any other site.

The perigordian tradition is characterised by backed knives and points. These take a variety of forms, as with the large curved back forms known as chatelper-ronian points/knives (fig. 5.14, j) after the type site in the Allier district, NW region. These are thought to have developed from the earlier middle palaeolithic naturally backed knives found in the MTA B (Bordes 1968a). Certainly these lower perigordian/chatelperronian assemblages, of which La Ferrassie level E is a good example (table 5.8), show variable amounts of middle palaeolithic implements within an essentially upper palaeolithic technology. However, since the crucial Würm II/III sediments are said not to exist in the French caves this in-situ model for upper palaeolithic development will be difficult to test (Rigaud 1976).

Within the NW and SW regions Bordes (1968a) argued for an evolution within the lower perigordian as shown by steadily decreasing proportions of mousterian implements in the assemblages. Perigordian II assemblages contain more well-made blunted backed points named after the NW region site of Les Cottés (Pradel 1961). Chatelperronian assemblages are present in Cantabria as at Cueva Morín level 10 and at open sites in the SW region as at Canaule I (Bordes 1970).

The aurignacian lithic assemblages contain nosed and carinate end scrapers on thick flakes and blades as well as strangulated blades and large blades with continuous flat retouch around their edges. There are a number of other distinctive elements such as the lamelles Dufour (fig. 5.14,h,i), found for example in the earliest aurignacian at La Ferrassie level E' (de Sonneville-Bordes 1973), and busked burins (fig. 5.14,g). However, while the EUP industries of the SW region are now studied by analysing the properties of the lithic assemblages (de Sonneville-Bordes 1960; H. de Lumley (ed.) 1976a), considerable importance is also attached to the judicious use of type fossils when assigning material to particular taxonomic groups. An instance of this procedure is provided by the internal divisions of the aurignacian. At La Ferrassie (table 5.8) Peyrony noted that the four aurignacian levels, F, H, H', and H'', contained very different antler/bone projectile points. These went in stratigraphic order bottom to top, from points with split bases (fig. 5.14,a,b) through those with solid pointed bases, bevelled bases and finally biconical points. It is not possible to identify accompanying changes in the flint assemblages that keep step with these divisions of early (I), middle (II), late (III) and final (IV) aurignacian as defined by the bone and antler projectile points. However a division is often drawn between aurignacian I and II lithic assemblages, with marginal retouch becoming rare and busked burins and nosed scrapers (fig. 5.14, e) becoming more common (Laville *et al.* 1980:221; de Sonneville-Bordes 1973).

The upper perigordian begins with stage IV where many straight backed gravette points and micro-gravette bladelets are found in the assemblages. The three divisions of perigordian V are characterised by the following type fossils – Font-Robert tanged points (Va), pieces on truncations (Vb), noailles burins (Vc) (fig. 5.14, u–w). The last type fossil is a burin on a truncation. However Rigaud (1976, 1978; Laville and Rigaud 1973) has shown that while this type fossil approach has chronological significance at La Ferrassie this is not the case for the four stratified levels with upper perigordian material at Le Flageolet I (table 5.11). Here all four assemblages were described as upper perigordian with noailles burins but also show great internal variation in composition of numbers and typs of burin, including Raysse/Bassaler types – which are flat faced burins on truncations (fig. 5.14, x) – gravettes and microgravettes, as well as Font Robert and even chatelperronian points. In other words there is a mosaic of assemblage types rather than a common gravettian/perigordian industry with different assemblages characterised by significant type fossils. This variability may relate to functional factors (Laville and Rigaud 1973).

Perigordian VI is best represented at Abri Pataud level 3 dated to 23–22.7 Kyr. At Laugerie-Haute a similar assemblage with large numbers of burins is overlain by aurignacian V. The final EUP variant comes at the top of the Abri Pataud sequence in level 2, and at Laugerie-Haute east. Termed the protomagdalenian by Peyrony (D. and E. 1938) others have classified the assemblages as perigordian VII (Bordes and de Sonneville-Bordes 1966), while Movius (1974) regards them as outside the perigordian tradition altogether and refers to them by a new name: the laugerian.

In the Pyrennes and Cantabria there are multi-level sites such as Isturitz (Saint-Périer 1930, 1936; R. and S. Saint-Périer 1952; Clottes 1976), Cueva Morín and Castilló which have standard sequences of chatelperronian/lower perigordian, aurignacian and upper perigordian/gravettian assemblages. At Cueva Morín (González-Echegaray and Freeman 1971, 1973) the chatelperronian in level 10 contains Cottés points and the aurignacian is divided into three stages on the basis of the lithic material.

Elsewhere in the province the retouched tool inventories are often small in number. Two areas in Roumania, in the south-west at the Banat (Mogoşanu 1976, 1978) and in the north at Tara Oaşului (Bitiri 1972, 1976) have been intensively studied. A number of open sites have been found in these areas with stratified sequences including both aurignacian and gravettian assemblages. In the Banat the site of Româneşti-Dumbrăviţa has three levels of aurignacian stratified above two middle palaeolithic assemblages. The final level at the site contains gravettian material. The aurignacian material in the SE region is part of Hahn's (1977) eastern aurignacian group. At Bacho Kiro a split base bone point was found in level 9 in an early aurignacian context while the later aurignacian assemblages in the cave are associated with solid base points (Kozlowski 1982).

(c) geographical variation

A number of detailed studies exist dealing with patterns of faunal exploitation, land use and settlement patterns for the EUP of the SW region. These include the research projects into Cantabrian prehistory by Freeman (1973, 1981), Clark and Straus (1983: bibliography) and the faunal work of Altuna (1972, 1979). These authors have drawn attention to changes in the numbers of occupied sites in this area with an increase in the EUP over the middle palaeolithic (Clark and Straus 1983:table 12.4) and a shift in subsistence patterns to the exploitation of a wider variety of resources including for the first time a small shellfish component. Freeman (1981:148) refers to this as a continuation of an opportunistic strategy.

Analyses of territorial exploitation and changing faunal communities in both the Pyrenees and the Dordogne can be found in Clottes (1976) and Bahn (1977, 1983). In these areas it is possible to see an increase in the number of exploited animal species, as shown by the analysis of the faunal residues (Delpech 1976). This is comparable to the EUP evidence from Cantabria.

Of considerable interest are the environmental reconstructions of the Dordogne contained in Movius ((ed.) 1975, 1977). One objective of this work (Movius 1974) was to recover data in order to examine Bouchud's conclusion (1966, 1975) that the remains of reindeer teeth and antler in palaeolithic horizons from the Dordogne caves pointed to human occupation at these facilities at all times of the year, a conclusion that formed a cornerstone in

Bordes' and de Sonneville-Bordes' (1970) refutation of the functional hypothesis. A re-analysis of the Abri Pataud reindeer material by Spiess (1979) indicates a presence at the site during late fall, winter and early spring. This conclusion is based on evidence from studying antler growth, foetal bones, tooth eruption in mandibles and tooth sectioning to determine through incremental growth rings the pattern of seasonality (Gordon 1982). Spiess argues for the use by palaeolithic groups of the steep sided but sheltered valleys round Les Eyzies as over-wintering places for dispersed, small population units during the EUP (1979:234).

The Alpine region was uninhabited during the EUP.

(d) burials and art

The only EUP burials for the French part of the SW region are from the caves of Combe-Capelle and at Crô Magnon. The Combe-Capelle skeleton, of an adult male aged between 40 and 50 years, is an extended inhumation associated with aurignacian implements (Quéchon 1976). The more robust Crô-Magnon skeletons were almost certainly early aurignacian burials, but discovered too early for accurate recording. The rarity of EUP burials is perhaps surprising after the number of claims that exist for Neanderthal burials (Bouyssonie 1954; Vandermeersch 1976; Harrold 1980). Excavations in the Cueva Morín (Freeman and González-Echegaray 1970; González-Echegaray and Freeman 1971) provide a salutary lesson that some of the traces may well have been missed (fig. 5.17). In level 8 and associated with aurignacian artifacts were found the fragile remains of the contents of two graves. The remains of the bodies in one of the graves (Morín I) were preserved as pseudomorphs in the fine clayey sediments. Painstaking excavation revealed that the body in Morín I was lying on its left side with the arms flexed across the chest. The individual had apparently been beheaded as the head was some 20 cm from its expected position. A quartzite knife was found near the head. The pseudomorph of a curled up, small ungulate, very possibly a roe deer or juvenile ibex, had been placed over the entire head area. The second body in the same grave is the size of a child, while parts of another body were found immediately below. The second grave (Morín II) is small in size and contains no pseudomorphs. The graves were capped by a small mound and are in close proximity to a row of post holes and a shallow rectangular depression measuring 2.6 m × 1.7 m. These delicate traces rely on exceptional preservation conditions as well as expert observation and excavation. Other occurrences may have been missed.

The art of the area associated with early aurignacian assemblages has been catalogued in great detail by Delluc and Delluc (1978). It consists primarily of engraved limestone blocks that have been incorporated in the deposits and hence can be dated. These are engraved with triangular signs that have been interpreted as representations of female genitalia. These blocks come from La

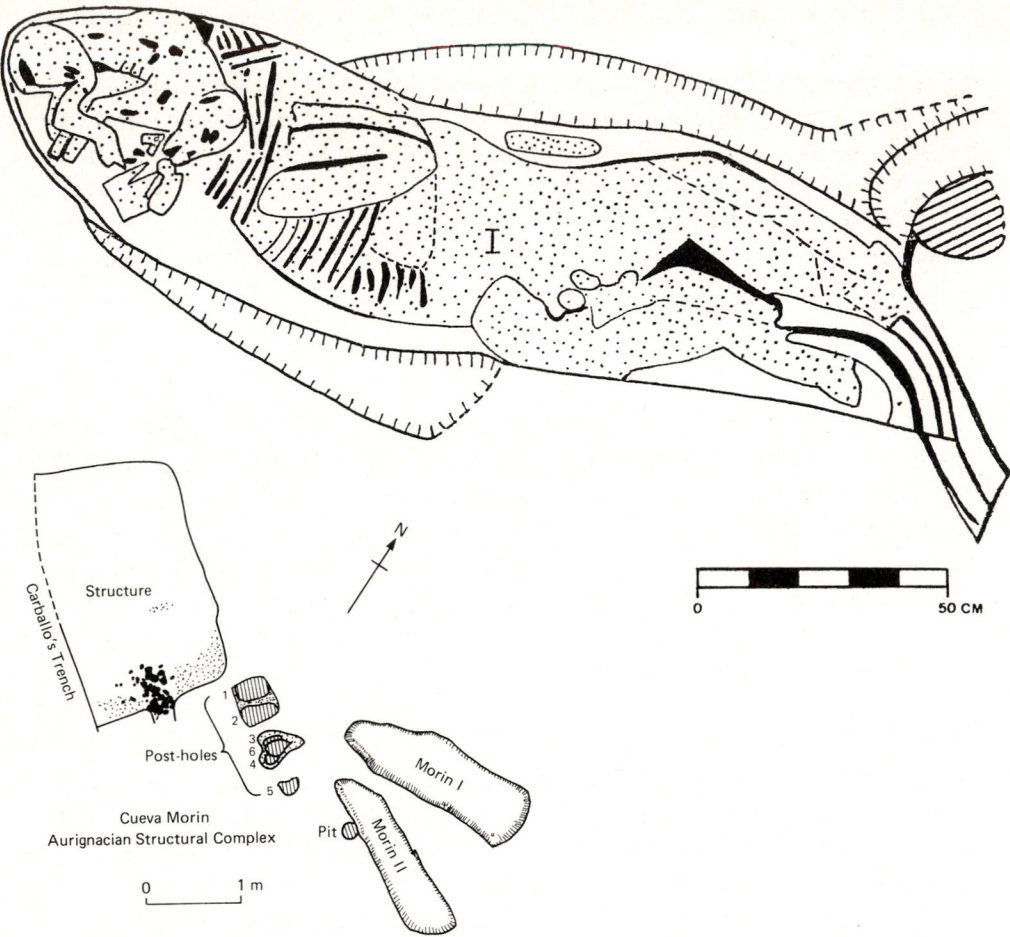

5.17 The aurignacian structural complex and contents of the Morín I grave (Freeman and González Echegaray 1970:fig. 1).

Ferrassie and the Abris Blanchard and Castanet. A low relief engraving thought to be a male profile figure is known from Terme Piliat (Delporte 1979). All of this material is concentrated in the SW region.

Shell, ivory beads and pierced fox canines are common in many sites in the SW region and occasionally encountered in the SE region.

From the upper perigordian and dated at the Abri Pataud and Abri Facteur to 23 and 22 Kyr respectively are examples of female figurines that are often included within the venus figurine tradition (fig. 7.2) (Delporte 1979; Gamble 1982; Gomez-Tabanera 1978). Indeed the first so-called Venus figurines were found at the Grotte du Pape, Brassempouy (Piette 1895), and a further classic representation is known from Lespugue (Graziosi 1960). The Abri Pataud figure is a bas-relief carving on a small limestone block. At the Abri Laussel, and in an upper perigordian context, a number of bas-relief carvings showing the classic exaggerated proportions of the ivory and clay figurines from the NC and NE regions have been found (Lalanne and Bouyssonie 1941–6). There are however no Venus figurines in either Cantabria, SW region, or the entire SE region.

Indeed the rarity of ornaments and engraved objects from Cantabria is striking when compared with the Northern province and the rest of the SW region. In this respect the EUP of Cantabria is very comparable to the SE region where although bone and antler points are known it is only rarely that other uses for these organic materials are encountered.

Further references

SW: H. de Lumley (ed.) 1976a; de Sonneville-Bordes 1960, 1963b, 1973; Laville *et al.* 1980; Freeman 1973; Clark and Straus 1983; Graziosi 1960; Bahn 1983; Clottes 1976.
Alpine: Fedele 1978.
SE: Hahn 1977; Bánesz 1976; Păunescu 1970; Bitiri 1972; Vértes 1960; Kozlowski and Kozlowski 1979; Cârciumaru 1979.

Mediterranean province 3

(a) chronology

The province is rich in sites with multiple occupation horizons. The regional syntheses by Escalon de Fonton (1966; and Onoratini 1976; and Bazile 1976) and Palma di Cesnola (1976, 1981) more than demonstrate the wealth of material that exists, and yet due to the history of research none of the 'classic' stratigraphic sequences, such as Laugerie-Haute, come from this province.

The earliest EUP assemblage in the MC region comes from the heel of southern Italy on the Bay of Uluzzo near Lecce (Palma di Cesnola 1965–6, 1969). Here an assemblage described as uluzzian is C14 dated to 31 Kyr. This occurs in level EII/1, which represents a middle or evolved facies of the uluzzian. Earlier, but so far undated, material occurs in level EIII. Uluzzian assemblages have been dated to 33.2 and 32.7 from two separate levels in the Castelcivita cave at Salerno (Palma di Cesnola 1981; Cioni *et al.* 1979). A date of 31.9 Kyr for a later level at Castelcivita is associated with an aurignacian assemblage that is rich in lamelles Dufour.

A possible aurignacian assemblage, although there are only a few pieces, has been dated to 29.6 Kyr in the Spanish cave of Les Mallaetes in the MW province (Bofinger and Davidson 1977). The gravettian at Gorhams Cave, Gibraltar, in the same region has C14 dates of 27.8 and 28.7 Kyr for material in level D.

Bofinger and Davidson (1977) have carried out a statistical treatment of C14 dates from cave sequences by plotting them against increasing depth. This is to determine sedimentation rates and has been done for the neighbouring sites of

Parpalló and Les Mallaetes. By means of this comparison (Chapter 8) they have shown that the best estimate for the beginning of the solutrean in this area of the MW region is 22.1–21 Kyr. The significance of this is discussed below (p. 236).

In southern Italy there is information about later gravettian assemblages from the important sites of Cala della Ossa (Palma di Cesnola 1971), and the Paglicci cave (Mezzena and Palma di Cesnola 1972). At the former, level Q contains noailles burins as a component of a gravettian assemblage dated to 28.2–27.4 Kyr, which makes them considerably earlier than their occurrence as elements in perigordian Vc assemblages in the SW region. At the Paglicci cave, Monte Gargano, Font-Robert points are dated back to 24.7–24.2 Kyr in level 21 while in level 20 retouched and backed truncations date to between 22 and 21 Kyr. Finally, in levels 19–18 at this site a geometric element appears in the gravettian stone tools, and this falls within the EUP at 20.7–20.1 Kyr.

The Languedoc region of France has been intensively researched by Escalon de Fonton (1966; and Onoratini 1976; and Bazile 1976). A number of temperate oscillations have been recognised on the basis of detailed sedimentological work. During the EUP these are Quinson, Arcy, Salpêtrière and Tursac. The long stratigraphic sequence at the cave of La Salpêtrière in the Gardon valley is essential for understanding the stratigraphic relationships between different assemblages. In the EUP levels at this site, and dating to the Arcy and Tursac interstadials, two aurignacian levels are succeeded stratigraphically by two gravettian/perigordian levels, the most recent of which is described as perigordian V on account of the shouldered points it contains. These are then followed by a further two levels of evolved aurignacian. The earliest C14 dates for upper palaeolithic and aurignacian in this region come from the cave of Esquicho-Grapaou, Gard, with level SLC 1b dated to 34.5 Kyr and SLC 1a to 31.8 Kyr (Bazile 1976, 1981; Delibrias and Evin 1980). At the same site level BR1, containing an early aurignacian assemblage, is dated to 29.6 Kyr (Bazile 1974) while at Salpêtrière the later aurignacian in level 30Ab, which stratigraphically post-dates the gravettian in the site, has a date of 20.5 Kyr which makes it the latest aurignacian in the region.

Elsewhere in the province chronological information is sparse. The multi-level site at Crvena Stijena in Yugoslavia is as yet undated although it contains six upper palaeolithic levels. At Asprochaliko in north western Greece (Higgs and Vita-Finzi 1966; Bailey *et al.* 1983a, b) the EUP assemblages are gravettian in character and dated to 26 Kyr.

(b) industrial groupings

The uluzzian is broadly comparable in both chronological position and typological features to the chatelperronian/lower perigordian of the SW region (Palma di Cesnola 1976, 1981). It is however concentrated in southern Italy. The distinctive element in the assemblages is the curved knife with a blunted back (fig.

5.14,k, l). The technique of flint working is however predominantly middle palaeolithic, with many flakes and a variable use of levallois technique. Side scrapers are the most common artifact type in sites such as the Cavallo cave although end scrapers, burins and other upper palaeolithic forms are also present. Palma di Cesnola (1976) has identified at least three stages in the southern uluzzian assemblages. At the Cavallo cave there is a diminution in middle palaeolithic tool types between level EIII (archaic), EII and EI (middle or evolved) and level D (upper uluzzian). Other uluzzian assemblages are known from sites in the centre and northern part of peninsula Italy. The aurignacian is common only in southern Italy, at the Castelcivita cave (Cioni *et al.* 1979), although distinctive keeled scrapers do occur at an open location, Armailo, in the Ombrone valley (Magi 1973).

A mixture of aurignacian scrapers and gravettian backed pieces is characteristic of the assemblages at Crvena Stijena. The richest level, V, has some of these characteristic aurignacian elements, but the inventory of retouched tools is dominated by small pieces – rods and bladelets – that have been blunted along one or both edges. The EUP assemblage at Asprochaliko in Epirus numbers only 152 retouched pieces for three levels (Bailey *et al.* 1983a, b). Amongst these, backed forms predominate and the assemblage is described as gravettian.

The chatelperronian/lower perigordian is entirely absent in both eastern Languedoc and Provence in the MW region. The aurignacian is moreover very rare in Provence but well represented in Languedoc at cave sites, e.g. Salpêtrière and Esquicho-Grapaou. Aurignacian assemblages are however known from the Grotte des Enfants, hearth K, one of the Grimaldi caves at Mentone where split based bone points were also found.

It appears that regional variation in assemblage composition is very marked in the early stages of the EUP. However, after c.27 Kyr in both MW and MC (and no doubt future research will show in the ME region as well), a widespread upper perigordian/gravettian technocomplex appears with backed blades, points and which also contains the tanged points comparable to the perigordian Va in the SW region. The indications are that the stratigraphic and chronological positions of the assemblages are every bit as complicated as recent work in the Périgord has shown (Rigaud 1978).

The EUP industries of peninsula Spain are not well understood (Cacho 1981) and it seems that the assemblages are dominated by backed elements. Chatelperronian and aurignacian assemblages are rare or absent in the Spanish part of the MW region (Fullola 1979) but upper perigordian/gravettian is common in level VIII at Les Mallaetes.

(c) geographical variation

A selective study of site catchments in the Lecce area has been conducted by Jarman (1972) but a much fuller study of EUP settlement systems in peninsula

Italy can be found in Barker (1973, 1975, 1981). In particular this study focused on the Camerota area with the main site of the Grotta della Cala and associated subsidiary sites. Barker interprets the settlement pattern as small seasonal winter camps located to the distribution of the all important red deer in the local landscape. The relationship between these EUP sites in a small geographical area is therefore determined by a pattern of exploitation geared to a mobile set of resources. At a larger regional scale the EUP settlement pattern of central Italy shows that during this period sites are found for the first time in the high mountain chain of the central Apennines. Barker argues convincingly that during this time there is evidence for the movement of human groups from lowland winter areas, such as the coastal plains of Lazio and Marche, to the upland summer grazing grounds in the high Apennines. This movement by human groups followed that of the principal prey species, the red deer, as the herds searched for suitable seasonal gazing.

The general pattern noted by Barker is comparable to the settlement evidence from Cantabria (Clark and Straus 1983; Freeman 1973) and the Pyrenees (Bahn 1983). In all these areas there is a marked increase in the number of EUP find spots as compared with the settlement evidence from the middle palaeolithic.

(d) burials and art

The complex of caves at Grimaldi, east of Monaco on the Italian Riviera, have produced a number of burials. These are apparently associated both with aurignacian and upper perigordian/gravettian assemblages (table 5.12).

A more recent and well excavated burial comes from the Paglicci cave (Mezzena and Palma di Cesnola 1972). Here a burial of a young male, 12–13 years old, was found in level 21, and associated with an evolved gravettian industry with Font Robert tanged points, dated to 24.7–23 Kyr. The body was placed face up and fully extended (fig. 5.18). As with several of the Grimaldi burials a layer of hematite (red ochre) covered the body. Some thirty pierced deer canines lay around the head and these most probably formed part of a necklace. Eleven flint tools – including end scrapers, a burin and a knife – together with a bone awl, a badly preserved *Cypraea* shell and a large lump of hematite, had also been placed with the body.

The Grimaldi caves also produced some more of the distinctive Venus figurines, although not only is their stratigraphic context uncertain but we do not know from which cave of the complex they were retrieved (Delporte 1979). Undated surface finds of what some regard as Venus figurines have also been made in central Italy at Chiozza and Savignano.

Animal figurines, engraved plaques and other forms of art object which are known from EUP contexts in both the southern and northern provinces are noticeable by their absence throughout the mediterranean province (Hahn 1981a).

Table 5.12. *The burials in the Grimaldi Cave complex at Balzi Rossi (Baousse Rousse), MW/MC region*

Site	Human remains	Position of body if known	Features	Associated lithic industry
Grotte de la Barma Grande	1 adult male, 1 young female, 1 young male	all extended face down or on left side	triple burial strewn with ochre; shell, teeth and bone ornaments; flint knives in left hands of adult male and female	gravettian
	1 adult	extended face down or on left side	covered by stone slabs; shell ornaments	gravettian
	1 adult		laid on hot fire	gravettian
	1 young male	face down	no grave goods	gravettian
La Grotte des Enfants	2 infants		laid on sea shells beside each other	gravettian
	1 adult male	on back	head on an ochre-covered slab; shell ornaments	aurignacian
	1 young male 1 adult female	contracted flexed	double burial; head of youth protected by two upright stones with another laid across; shell bracelet and head ornaments; strewn with ochre	aurignacian

Source: Wymer 1982: table 7.1

5.18 A 'status' burial in the Paglicci cave, MC region. The height of the body is estimated at 1.60 m. (Mezzena and Palma di Cesnola 1972:tav. 1),
A: thirty deer canines pierced for suspension found around the skull.
B: *Cypraea* shell.
C: block of hematite found below the right tibia.
D: bone chisel.
1–11: flint tools including blades, end scrapers, burins and a knife.

Further references

MW: Fullola 1979; Escalon de Fonton 1966; and Onoratini 1976; and Bazile 1976.
MC: Barker 1975, 1981; Palma di Cesnola 1976, 1981; Laplace 1966.
ME: Basler 1979; Higgs and Vita-Finzi 1966; Bailey *et al.* 1983a, b.

A great wealth of data is available for the study of the LUP in Europe (e.g. de Sonneville-Bordes (ed.) 1979). It is now common to identify large geographical groupings, or technocomplexes (Schild 1976; Taute 1968; Kozlowski and Kozlowski 1979), since during this period, 20–10 Kyr, there is a high level of affinity between assemblages, as measured by the proportions of artifact types, techniques of manufacture and retouch, from different sites scattered over large geographical areas. Moreover, since this period lies well within the dating range of C14, it is possible to investigate the changing configurations of these geographical/industrial patterns as the climate went through full glacial conditions at 18 Kyr and then a rapid deglaciation and amelioration in the intricate climatic fluctuations of the late glacial.

Northern province 4

(a) chronology

The NW and NC regions were deserted from 20 to 17 Kyr, and in many areas until well after 16 Kyr (Hahn 1979b; Kozlowski and Kozlowski 1979). In the NE region there is evidence on the middle Dniestr at Korman IV/5, 18.6–18 Kyr, and Molodova V/VI, at 16.7 Kyr, for eastern gravettian sites occurring both at the height of the last glaciation and, in the case of Molodova V/VI, during a local interstadial. Levels 6–4 at Molodova V (Chernysh 1961; Ivanova 1982) point to occupation in the seventeenth millennium bp. On the Seret river, assemblages classified within the wider molodovian tradition (J. Kozlowski 1979) have been dated at Buda-Lespezi V to 18 Kyr, and level II in the same site to 17.6 Kyr. Further north in the Desna and Dnepr basins at Yeliseyevichi an eastern gravettian level has been dated to 17.3 Kyr (table 5.13) (Dolukhanov 1979:874).

As deglaciation began to take place after 16 Kyr (Flohn 1979) the NW and NC regions were re-colonised: for example at Kents Cavern, England, where re-occupation may have occurred as early as 14.2 Kyr (but see Jacobi 1980), and certainly by 12.1 Kyr; and at the open site of the Schussenquelle in southern Germany, 14.1–13 Kyr. Poggenwisch and Meiendorf, which are both sites on the north European plain near Hamburg, can be firmly tied in with the pollen stratigraphy of northern Germany, the Netherlands and Denmark, and placed in zone Ia, known as the oldest Dryas.

A number of cave sites can now be dated to the equivalent of zone Ib, the Bølling interstadial, although the exact correlations between pollen events and climatic events present problems, as we have seen above (Chapter 3). This may help to explain some of the anomalies in dating and associated environmental evidence for either cold or more temperate environments. The sites that fall in the period 13–12 Kyr include the Mendip cave of Sun Hole, NW region (Campbell 1977), dated to 12.3 Kyr, the open site of Gönnersdorf located by the Rhine near Köln (Bosinski 1969, 1979b), at 12.6–11.1 Kyr, and various levels in the Petersfels cave in southern Germany, NC region (Albrecht 1979) dated to 12.9–12.1 Kyr.

The Bølling interstadial is then followed by a brief but very cold spell, zone Ic or older Dryas as recorded in the pollen profiles from northern Europe. The site of Andernach (Bosinski 1979c; Bosinski and Hahn 1973), on the side of the Rhine opposite Gönnersdorf, is placed in this climatic phase, while the cave sites of Kesslerloch and Schweizersbild in Switzerland, and only a few kilometres from the Petersfels, are dated to late Bølling, early older Dryas.

This very brief two hundred year episode of the older Dryas then gives way to the more substantial Allerød interstadial, or zone II. This lasted from 11.8 to 11 Kyr. Further C14 dates from the Petersfels show occupation during this period, 11.7–11.3 Kyr (Albrecht 1979) although the sedimentological evidence points to

Table 5.13. *The chronological ordering of major technocomplexes in late upper palaeolithic Europe; northern and southern provinces.*

Kyr bp.	Palaeoenvironmental chronology and zones	SW region	NW region	NC region North	NC region South	NE region	SE region	
10	III YOUNGER DRYAS		magdalenian	ahrensburgian tanged point/				
11		Late			magdalenian	swiderian	late	D
	II ALLERØD	Group	feddermesser tanged points	bromme/lyngby feddermesser				
12	Ic OLDER DRYAS	III			magdalenian		gravettian	
13	Ib BØLLING		'creswellian' magdalenian			mezinian		
	Ia OLDEST DRYAS			hamburgian	magdalenian			
14		Early Group III						
15							late	C
16	DEGLACIATION BEGINS						gravettian	
17	LASCAUX	Initial magdalenian.				yeliseyevitchian		
18	GLACIAL MAXIMUM	solutrean					sagvarian	B

Source: Laville *et al.* 1980; Jacobi 1980; Schild 1976; Dolukhanov 1979; J. Kozlowski 1979

a cold climate, older Dryas date. The multi-level dune site of Calowanie in Poland (Schild 1976, 1979) is securely dated to this period, as well as another plains site at Rissen, 11.9–11.5 Kyr, in northern Germany, NC region. The latter site has an early assemblage of arched bladelets with blunted backs, known as Feddermesser. Assemblages of this type are widespread on the north European plain. These also occur at Calowanie in levels III and IV where they are dated to the Allerød (Schild 1979).

Tanged points are found higher up in the dune at Calowanie in level IV, dated to zone II, and then continue into level VI. This final assemblage can be dated to pollen zone III, the younger Dryas that is dated to between 11 and 10 Kyr. In the same plains area of Poland the arched bladelet material continues at Witow, levels IV and III, and at Swidry.

The multi-level waterlogged site of Stellmoor in northern Germany, NC region (Rust 1943; Tromnau 1973) has an early level with shouldered hamburgian points dated to the oldest Dryas, zone Ia, and an upper containing tanged points from zone III. Both levels are associated with large quantities of reindeer bones.

The NE region sees several developments during this period. Once again the section at Molodova V is important since it charts the development of the evolved gravettian from 17.1 to 10.9 Kyr between levels VI and I (Ivanova 1982; Klein 1973). From c.13.5 to 11.8 Kyr a group of sites with assemblages comparable to the important site of Mezin (Shovkoplyas 1965; Klein 1973) on the Desna river, NE region, form another major technocomplex.

Tanged point assemblages are found in the LUP of England in the equivalent of the younger Dryas, zone III, as at Robin Hood's Cave at Creswell Crags and during the interface of zones I/II at the open site of Hengistbury Head on the south coast of England. Occupation occurred here when there would have been a Channel river and dry land linking this part of the north European plain to the continent (Mace 1959; Campbell 1977).

The situation in northern France is rather different. Here the magdalenian is well represented, as it is in the upland areas of the NC region, and includes the sites of Pincevent (Leroi-Gourhan and Brézillon 1966, 1972), Les Tarterets (Schmider 1975) and Les Etiolles (Taborin *et al.* 1979), where remarkable preservation of hearths and the surface distribution of stone and bone can be seen (fig. 5.19). At Pincevent C14 dates indicate occupation during zone III at 10.9–10.7 Kyr (Delibrias *et al.* 1976).

Magdalenian assemblages are common in the uplands of East Germany, NC region, and include both open sites such as Groitzsch and several caves around the villages of Ranis and Dobritz, e.g. the Kniegrotte (Feustel 1974). From five of these magdalenian sites a series of some twelve C14 dates provides a range from 13.7 to 10.1 Kyr (Feustel 1979:886) for magdalenian settlement in this part of the NC region.

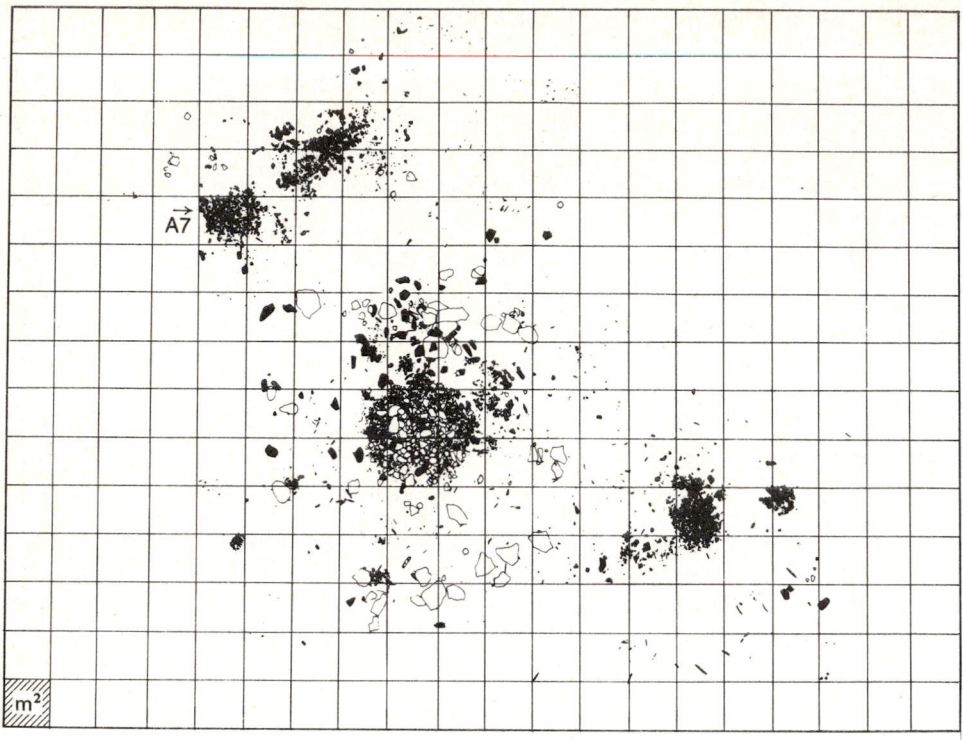

5.19 Plan of central hearth, chipped stone (shaded black) and large stone slabs (unshaded) at the open site of Les Etiolles, NW region. The interpretation of distributions such as these is discussed in Chapter 6. (Taborin *et al.* 1979:774, fig. 1)

(b) industrial groupings

There are three main industrial technocomplexes in the northern province.

(1) The magdalenian is found throughout the Paris basin (Leroi-Gourhan *et al.* 1976), Belgium (Vermeersch 1982) and extensively in the upland areas of central and southern Germany (Bosinski 1979b; Albrecht 1979; Hahn 1981a), East Germany (Feustel 1979; Toepfer 1970), and as far east as the limestone uplands of Moravia and southern Poland (Valoch 1960, 1968). The type site, La Madeleine (Capitan and Peyrony 1928), is in the SW region.

The magdalenian is characterised by a great profusion in some sites of microlithic blunted backed segments, many of them triangular and geometric in shape. Many thousands of these microlithic bladelets (fig. 5.21,k) have been recovered in recent excavations using fine screening at the Petersfels (Albrecht 1979) in the south-west corner of Germany. At the nearby site of the Kesslerloch, but over the border in Switzerland, these same microlithic elements occur within an assemblage containing a standard end scraper/burin component. A diagnostic feature is provided by the antler harpoons. These carry either a single or double row of barbs (fig. 5.20,e–h) (Julien 1982). Another

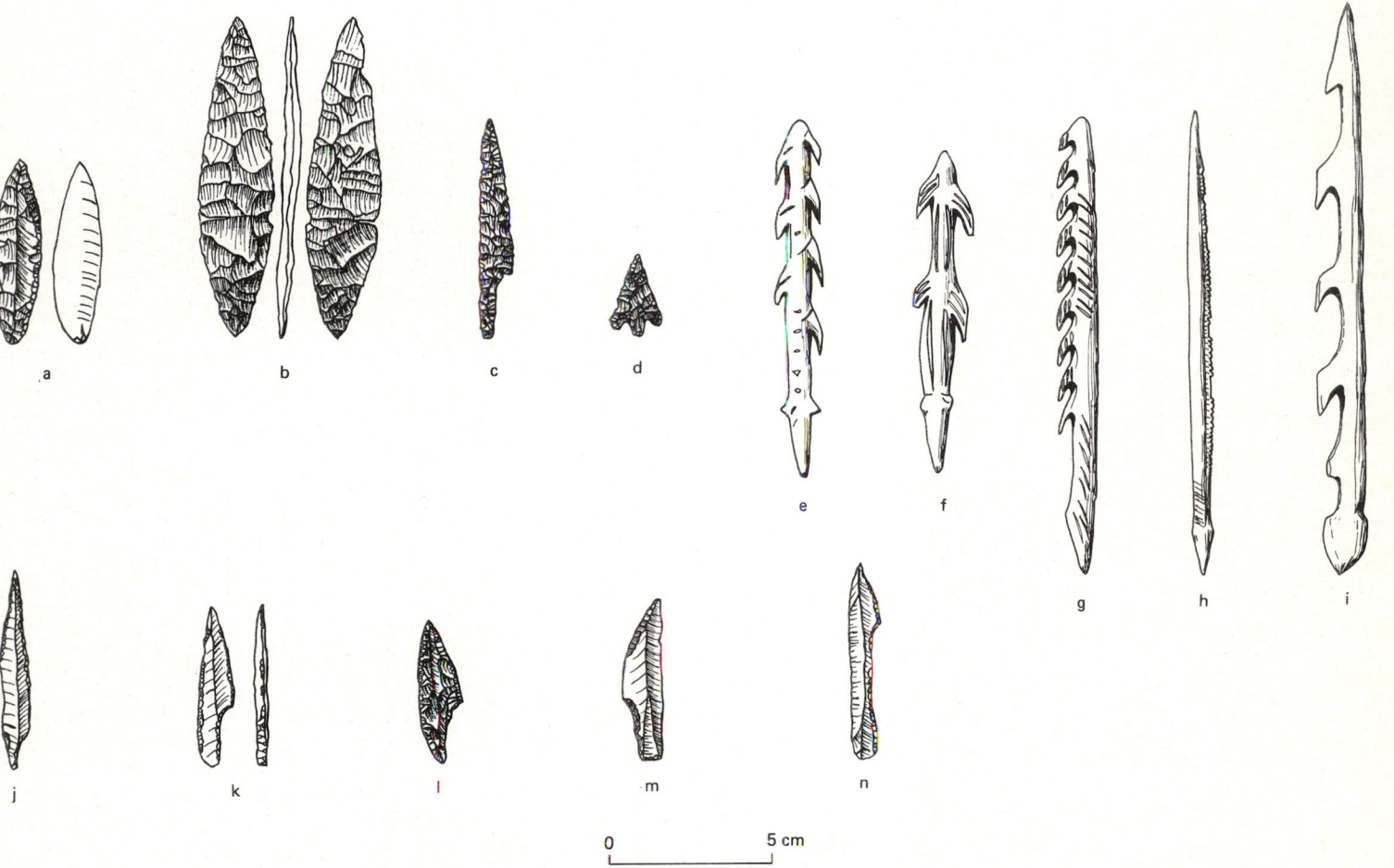

5.20 LUP artifact types: a–d, solutrean; (a) Laugerie Haute unifacial point; (b) Badegoule bifacially pressure flaked laurel leaf point; (c) shouldered point; (d) Parpalló barbed and tanged arrow head. e–h, magdalenian antler harpoons; (e, f) biserial; (g, h) uniserial; (i) Stellmoor ahrensburgian uniserial antler harpoon. j–n, shouldered points; (j) salpetrien MW; (k) epigravettian ME; (l) epigravettian MC, (m) hamburgian NW, NC; (n) magdalenian SW, NC, Alpine.

common feature, known from earlier gravettian assemblages but now assuming particular prominence, is the pierced antler staff, commonly referred to as a bâton de commandement by French archaeologists. A great range of utilitarian bone and antler objects including needles are associated with these assemblages. Many implements of unknown function have also been recovered and these are variously classified as spatula, ornaments and 'cult' objects.

Regional comparisons of the typological composition of magdalenian assemblages have been conducted by de Sonneville-Bordes (1960, 1961, 1963a, 1968, 1969) on lithic material from Belgium, Switzerland and southern Germany. Shouldered points (fig. 5.20, n) are regarded as a noteworthy regional feature in assemblages such as those from the Petersfels (Peters 1930), and contribute to the distinctive nature of the magdalenian in central Europe.

Asymmetrically pointed boring tools, or Zinken (fig. 5.21, c), are found in zone III assemblages at Pincevent as well as in much earlier, non-magdalenian zone I assemblages, from the north European plain.

(2) The second industrial grouping consists of the various late glacial technocomplexes that thrived on the plains of northern Europe after deglaciation had taken place.

The earliest assemblages, characterised by their projectile point material and containing shouldered points (fig. 5.20, m) and Zinken, are dated to zone Ia at Meiendorf, the hamburgian level at Stellmoor, and other open sites on the north German plain, NC region. These backed blade assemblages are later distinguished from each other by the development of regionally distinctive tanged projectile points (fig. 5.21, e–i) (Stielspitzen) and antler harpoons (fig. 5.20, i) (Taute 1968). The main type fossils for these points are ahrensburgian and Bromme/Lyngby points, while other widespread forms are shown in fig. 5.21.

Zinken, tanged and shouldered points also occur in the LUP assemblages of England and especially at the Creswell Crags cave complex in the north and at Cheddar Gorge in the south-west of the country. Two important sites for these areas are Mother Grundy's Parlour and Gough's Cave respectively. The material from Hengistbury Head contains tanged and shouldered points and the 'local', so called, creswell point (fig. 5.21, b), which is a type of backed knife (Morrison 1980:99). Many of these assemblages can perhaps best be seen as variants of the wider Feddermesser complexes of the continental areas of the NW and NC regions (Jacobi 1980).

These assemblages are contemporary with the bromme tanged point complexes of the zone II Allerød interstadial, dominated by small arched bladelets with blunted backs. These penknife-like blades (fig. 5.21, a) are known collectively as the Feddermesser group in East and West Germany, NC region; in the Netherlands and Belgium, NW region, they are known as tjongerian, and in Poland, NC region, as tarnovian, all after the various names of their respective type sites (Schild 1976). Assemblage composition is highly varied.

(3) The eastern gravettian technocomplex of straight backed, blunted edge

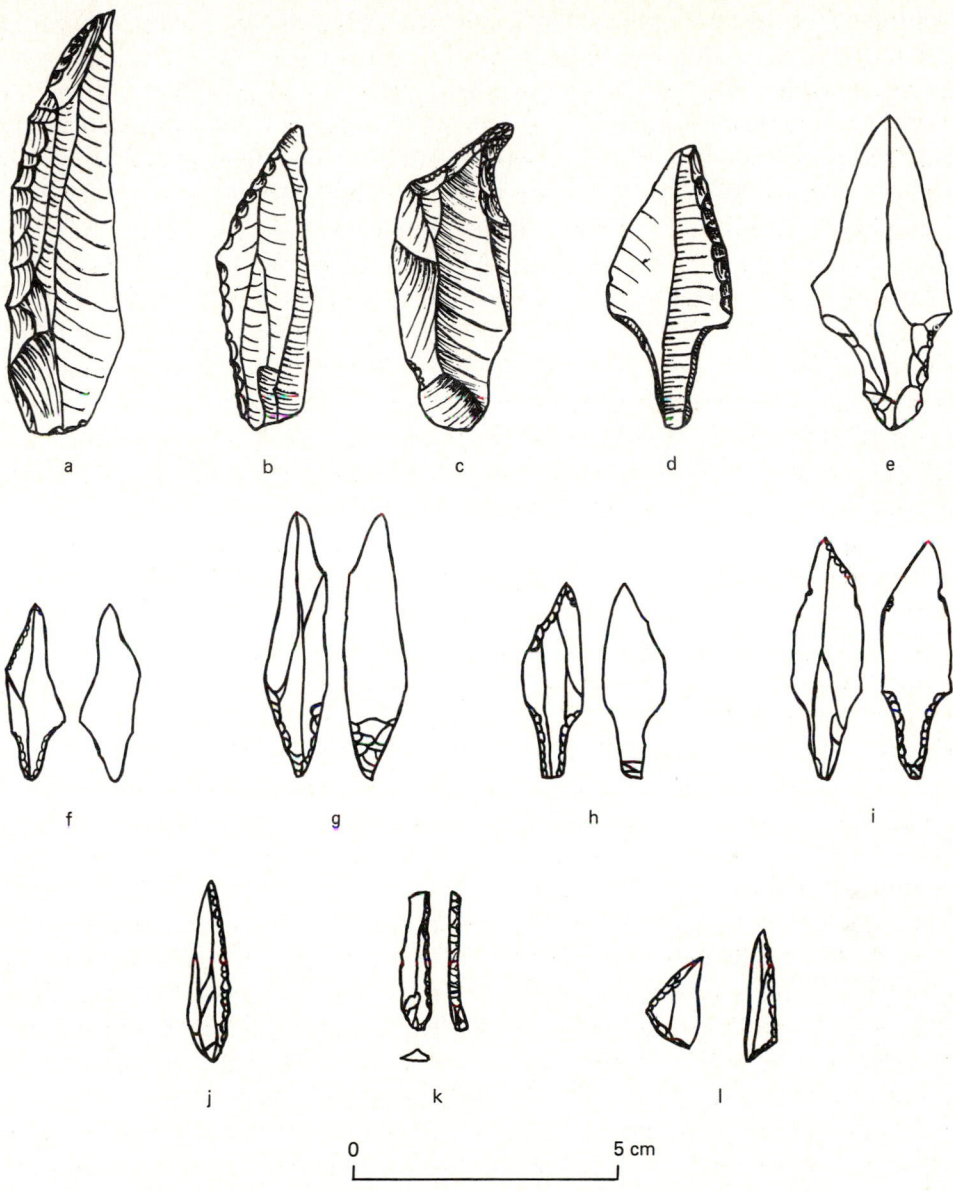

5.21 LUP artifact types: (a) Feddermesser NC; (b) Creswell point NW; (c) Zinken NW, NC. d–i, tanged points; (d) magdalenian SW, (e) Bromme/Lyngby NC, NW; (f) Ahrensburg NC, NW; (g) Swidry NC; (h) Chwalibogonice NC; (i) Hintersee NC; (j) backed rods Alpine; (k) bladelets NC; (l) geometrics NC.

points has been divided into a number of regional groups (Dolukhanov 1979; Kozlowski and Kozlowski 1979). The earlier group, 20–17 Kyr, is termed molodovian in the NE region after the type site on the middle Dniestr river (Kozlowski 1979). This group includes assemblages from Korman IV/5,

Molodova V/VI, and the sites of Buda-Lespezi and Buda-Dealul Viei on the Siruet river. The lithic assemblages from the Desna river sites of Yeliseyevichi and Mezin are used as type sites for wider industrial groupings, identified by Kozlowski (1979); and so too are the LUP sites Lipa and Kostenki. The geographical distribution of these technocomplexes is illustrated in Kozlowski and Kozlowski (1979:map 7, figs. 18–28). These same authors claim that these evolved eastern gravettian groups persist although Dolukhanov (1979:872) reduces them to two major chronological groups: the yeliseyevichian, 17–13.5 Kyr, and the mezinian, 13.5–11.5 Kyr. In his opinion the latter group is contemporary with the hamburgian of the northern plains of the NC and NW regions. The main feature of the mezinian is that more than 50% of the assemblage consists of dihedral burins on truncations (Kozlowski and Kozlowski 1979). This characterisation is, however, based on a sample of only three counted assemblages. The assemblage from Mezin also contains geometric shaped microliths and pierced antler staffs.

Contemporary with the ahrensburgian/Feddermesser technocomplexes are assemblages with swiderian tanged points in the NE region (table 5.13, fig. 5.21, g).

(c) geographical variation and regional case studies

The geographical meeting point for many of these different technocomplexes occurs in Poland (Schild 1975, 1976, 1979) and Czechoslovakia (Vencl 1979). The Allerød sites of Calowanie levels VIa and IV contain tanged points while at Swidry and Witow, level IV, the arched bladelet assemblages are present. A mixture of the two occurs at Witow, levels II and III.

The three regions of Czechoslovakia – Bohemia, Moravia and Slovakia – show a decrease towards the east of magdalenian sites. The last of these occurs in the Moravian karst at the cave sites of Pekárna and Kůlna (Valoch 1960; Filip (ed.) 1966). On the northern side of the Carpathians in Poland the Maszycka cave contains magdalenian while in Austria the Gudenushöhle also has a small collection of magdalenian artifacts. These sites have been used to draw up a major division between the magdalenian assemblages of the central European highlands and the eastern gravettian of Slovakia and the Russian plains (Kozlowski 1971:map 1; Valoch 1968).

The tanged point assemblages are concentrated on the north European plain (Taute 1968) and on the basis of the geographical distribution of the distinctive type fossils they contain have been analysed in terms of a model of social territories (Clark 1975). The type fossils were in Clark's opinion those idiosyncratic items which were used to denote group identity in the past (fig. 5.21, d–i).

The hiatus in occupation in the NC and NW regions from 20 to 16 Kyr must be contrasted with the dense settlement evidence from the SW and NE regions. The Desna, Don and Dniestr rivers of the NE region formed particularly

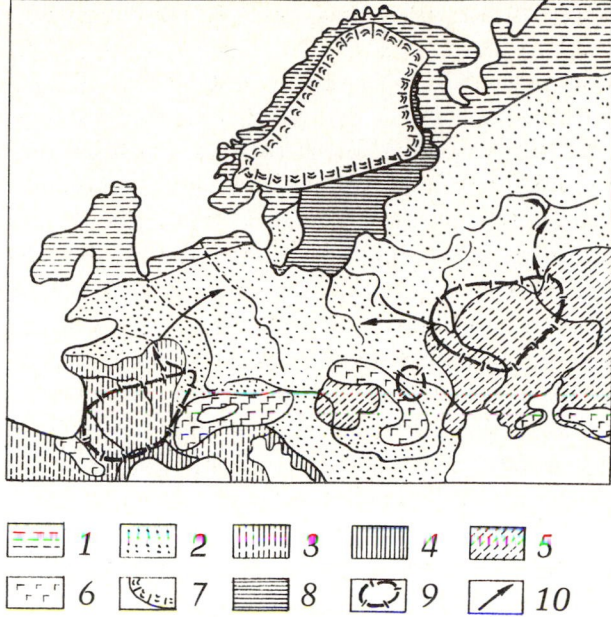

5.22 The recolonisation of central Europe, NW and NC regions after deglaciation at 16 Kyr. The reconstructed vegetation is for the Allerød, zone II, interstadial (Dolukhanov 1979:871, fig. 1).

1. periglacial tundra, 2. coniferous forest, 3. mixed coniferous and deciduous forest, 4. deciduous forest, 5. steppe, 6. alpine vegetation, 7. ice-cap, 8. ice dammed Baltic lake, 9. major population refuges at 18 Kyr, 10. pattern of recolonisation during the late glacial.

important centres during this period of maximum glaciation. After the retreat of the ice sheets from the north European plain this central area was recolonised from these two regional centres (fig. 5.22) (Dolukhanov 1979:fig. 1). This scenario also contrasts the successful reindeer hunters of the SW with the mammoth hunters of the NE region. According to this model recolonisation was part of a process of population expansion that was set in motion as certain environmental constraints were lifted following deglaciation. One result was the establishment of more varied floral communities on the northern plains which could be used by large mammals, principally the reindeer. This was most marked in the Allerød when, it is claimed, groups became more mobile. The evidence for this conclusion is apparently provided by the disappearance of permanent huts and the diversification of the subsistence base to include fishing (Dolukhanov 1979).

Other regional studies of late glacial adaptive strategies are provided by Campbell (1977:map 46) for the LUP of England. Here he employs the concept of a socio-economic buffer zone to explain the large areas without settlement that lay between such intensively used territories as the Mendip Hills and Creswell

Crags, where LUP occupation is abundant. The buffer zone could have acted as a food reservoir.

Sturdy (1975), Hahn (1979b, 1981a) and Weniger (1982) have made detailed studies of the pattern of magdalenian exploitation in southern Germany. The model favoured by Sturdy placed this upland area within a bigger regional picture. He maintained that the only viable late glacial strategy was one where human groups followed the herds of reindeer between the uplands of southern Germany, where they grazed during the summer, and the north European plain in the winter. This would mean an annual migration of some 600 km. He argued that this pattern of exploitation was necessary in order to ensure control over the all important reindeer food resource. Crucial to this argument was Sturdy's contention that there were no other viable alternatives to subsisting on reindeer and that the scarcity of magdalenian sites in the central German uplands showed that groups did not linger in their north–south migrations (fig. 5.23).

Hahn (1979b) has examined the relative merits of a long and short distance movement model. He rejects Sturdy's long distance, herd following hypothesis, by pointing to the winter grazing that was available on the Alpine foreland area of the Danube marshes. He argues instead for short seasonal movements with winter occupation in open air sites such as outside the Petersfels and at the Schussenquelle. The nearby Kesslerloch and Schweizersbild could also be added as winter bases (Weniger 1982). The adjacent Swabian Alb would then be used by small hunting parties while the upper Rhine would be utilised in spring and summer as indicated by the presence of an open site at Munzingen. The patterns of movement have been studied in great detail by Weniger (1982) and a very thorough appreciation made of the available palaeo-environmental information. To support his model Hahn also compares the number of retouched pieces in the magdalenian sites of the area using the assumption that the larger collections, e.g. Petersfels, are indicative of a home base and hence more permanent, all year round, occupation. One idea that his model allows him to reject is Sturdy's claim that the magdalenian/tanged point assemblages of the south and north of Germany respectively were seasonal tool kits of the same human group(s) which moved between the two areas.

These represent important interpretations of a well researched body of palaeolithic data. Some alternative perspectives also need to be considered. For example both of these interpretations assume the recovery of a representative sample of the sites occupied at different seasons of the year, and therefore a complete range of all settlement types in the settlement system. This may not be the case (see Chapters 6–8). Moreover neither model fully considers the alternative of intercept hunting linked to a storage strategy and the implications this behaviour would have on the seasonal information in the form of antler and reindeer teeth obtained from the sites. Finally the models do not consider how the artifact assemblages were created as a result of replacement because of breakage, loss or intentional caching of tools and raw material. This would

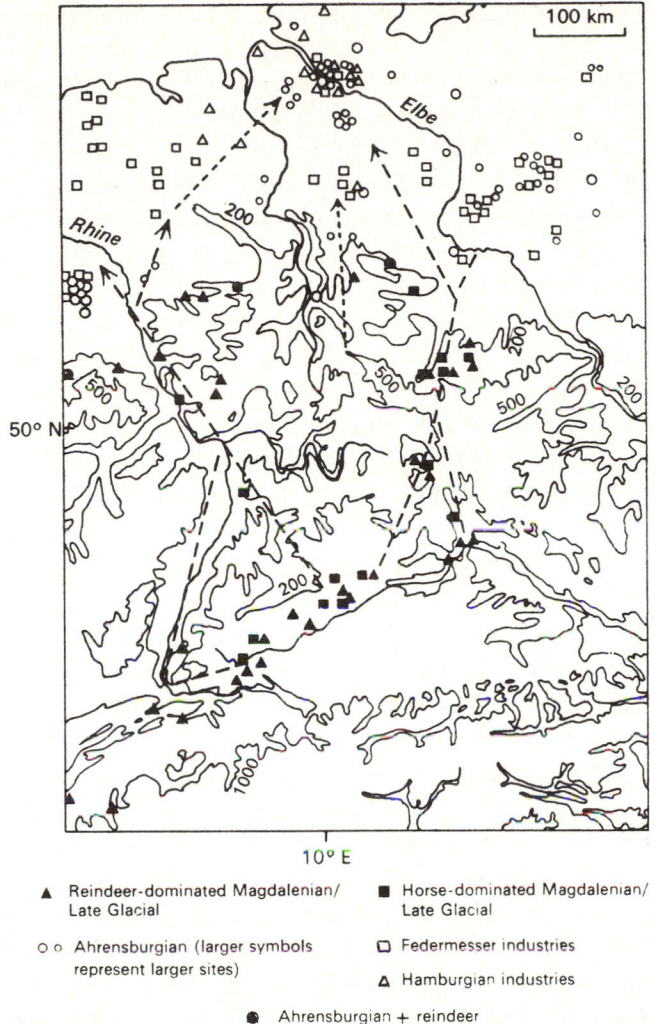

5.23 Hypothetical reconstruction of reindeer migration and human group herd following in late glacial Europe. The arrows indicate the autumn migration (Sturdy 1975:74, fig. 29).

require a different set of observations on the data – breakages, estimates of failure rates among tools, the degree of re-use, microwear traces to determine use – from those provided by a purely typological treatment of the assemblages with which both models are satisfied.

At a smaller scale of analysis the Schaffhausen–Engen group of magdalenian sites, of which Petersfels and Kesslerloch are the two largest, have been interpreted by Sturdy (1975) as positioned so as to take advantage of marsh and rough relief in delimiting the grazing area available to reindeer. Allowing a stocking density of 7.15 deer per km² the area thus enclosed by these sites, 375 km^2, would provide summer grazing for c.2700 deer. The culled annual product from a migratory herd of this size would provide enough food for c.27 people. Comparable site exploitation territories using population distributed around topographic features has also been proposed by Sturdy for valley systems in the Swabian and Franconian Albs but, as previously noted, the site sizes, as measured by numbers of retouched tools, are not as large. However, the estimated population sizes for human groups surrounding these site exploitation territories are very comparable to the Schaffhausen–Engen example and of course closely approximate the size of a minimum band.

(d) burials and art

Cave art, where walls have been either painted, sculpted or engraved, is rare in this province. Engravings of mammoth and other ice age animals have been found in the Grotte du Cheval in the complex of caves at Arcy-sur-Cure (Leroi-Gourhan 1968). These are placed within style IV (see below), and occur in galleries which are very difficult of access. The painted site of Kapovaya in the Urals (Abramova 1967) provides the only example from the NC and NE regions of cave art.

The north European plain is also lacking in representational art with the exception of an engraved plaque from Geldrop III/1 (Taute 1968:210), where a human figure is portrayed. Examples of engraved antler and bone objects are however common throughout much of the province; for example the reindeer engraved on an antler of the same species at Kesslerloch and a row of four horses on the same material at Pekárna (Klíma 1966). Ivory beads are common in most of the sites and a great range of carved objects, many of them probably associated with dress and ornament functions, are also known. Enigmatic objects such as the ivory, foot-shaped 'idol' from the Kniegrotte cave (Feustel 1974), NC region, are attributed to unspecified cult practices. Many geometric designs and rows of diagonal incisions and notches on the edges of pieces are a common feature. An ivory bracelet from Mezin (Klein 1973:fig. 14.6; Abramova 1967) is decorated in this manner with parallel rows of oblique design. Also from Mezin comes a 'painted' mammoth mandible – the colouring being hematite – and a mammoth skull decorated in the same material has been found at Mezhirich (Pidoplichko 1969). This site, together with those from Mezin, Dobranichevka and Yudinovo in the Dnepr and Desna river basins, has produced evidence for large accumulations of mammoth bones. These piles are frequently circular in shape and show evidence for the careful and elaborate stacking of anatomical elements (fig. 6.10). Many of them are interpreted as the remains of huts (Chapter 6), although interpretations as ritual 'objects' have also been proposed.

Our understanding of engraving and art work has been transformed by the excavations at Gönnersdorf (Bosinski 1969, 1979b, 1982b; Bosinski and Fischer 1974) of a magdalenian hut/tent structure. Associated with this structure was a

5.24 Engraved slab from Gönnersdorf, NC region, with mammoths and schematic human representations (Bosinski 1982b:taf. 59).

great mass of cultural debris that included many hundred flat sided schist plaquettes that had provided flooring material and many of which had been engraved with representations of animals and other designs (fig. 5.24). The animals depicted include mammoth, horse, red deer as well as birds, wolf and lion. Perhaps surprisingly the reindeer has not yet been identified, although its bones are present among the remains. On these slabs some 300 profile representations of a highly schematised human body have been identified and generally interpreted as female profile figures (Bosinski and Fischer 1974; Rosenfeld 1977). The slabs resemble scratch pads with many super-impositions and drawings which to our appreciation seem unfinished. The site also produced some small carved figurines that are likened to the female profile engravings (fig. 7.5). Comparable figurines and engravings are also known at the Petersfels (Albrecht 1979), figurines by themselves at Oelknitz and Nebra in East Germany, and an engraved plaque has been found at the Ederheim Hohlenstein in southern Germany (Bosinski 1982b) as well as in the SW region at Roche Lalinde (Delporte 1979).

Further references

NW: Campbell 1977; Jacobi 1980; de Sonneville-Bordes (ed.) 1979; Leroi-Gourhan *et al.* 1976.

NC: J. G. D. Clark 1975; Sturdy 1975; Weniger 1982; Schild 1975, 1976, 1979; Taute 1968; Hahn 1979b, 1981a; Schwabedissen 1954; Bosinski 1982b.

NE: Dolukhanov 1979; Kozlowski, S. 1979; Kozlowski and Kozlowski 1979; Shimkin 1978.

Southern province 4

(a) chronology

There is no hiatus at 20 Kyr in the stratified sites for either the SW or the SE region. In the SW at the massive rock shelter of Laugerie-Haute (D. and E. Peyrony 1938; de Sonneville-Bordes 1960; Smith 1966; Bordes 1978), the late Würm III deposits contain solutrean assemblages above the protomagdalenian and aurignacian V assemblages. The lower solutrean is C14 dated in both the east and west parts of the rock shelter to 20.8 Kyr. The final solutrean is dated in Laugerie-Haute west to 19.7 Kyr and this also dates the Würm III/IV, or Laugerian, interstadial. This is the only interstadial preserved in the cave sediments of the Périgord (Laville et al. 1980). Solutrean material is found just after this interstadial at the beginning of Würm IV in the French sequence (table 3.7), but by 18 Kyr initial magdalenian assemblages, as in levels 18–20 at Laugerie-Haute east, are encountered.

The solutrean in Cantabria (Straus 1977b) is dated between 21 and 17 Kyr (Clark and Straus 1983). Important chronological information has come from the re-excavation of the La Riera cave site (Straus et al. 1981). Here a large series of C14 dates provides a range for the solutrean in levels 4–17 of between 20.9 and 16.9 Kyr.

The initial magdalenian in SW and NW regions of France is known from only a few sites and dates to between 19.6 and 16.7 Kyr. These include the Abri Fritsch, NW region, and the Pégourié cave, SW region, in the Lot district (Hemingway 1980).

Laville (et al. 1980) distinguishes between an earlier and later group III set of industrial assemblages. In the former are found the solutrean and the first three stages of the magdalenian. A date of 13.9 Kyr for levels 2–3 at Laugerie-Haute east marks the end of this phase (table 5.14). In Spain a comparable division is drawn (Clark and Straus 1983) with a lower magdalenian at 17–13 Kyr. The upper magdalenian of Cantabria corresponds to the period of the late glacial in northern Europe and is dated between 15 and 10 Kyr.

The late group III times in the Périgord are represented by the later stages of the magdalenian. These are best known from the type site of La Madeleine on the Vézère (Capitan and Peyrony 1928; Bouvier 1977, 1979). The C14 dates from the site indicate occupation between at least 13.4 Kyr, in level 14, and 12.6 Kyr, in level 7. Other important sections with C14 dates are Le Flageolet II, Gare de Couze and Pont d'Ambon, where the absolute dates contradict the sedimentological dating by Laville (et al. 1980:337).

The magdalenian is very well represented in sites in the Pyrenees at Mas

Table 5.14. *Synopsis of EUP, LUP and Group II/III terminology as applied to the Périgord sequence, SW region*

Group II industries aurignacian, lower and upper perigordian	EUP	Würm III

Early Group III
  solutrean
  magdalenian I–III
	LUP	Late Würm III & Würm III/IV
		Würm IV

Later Group III magdalenian IV–VI	LUP	Würm IV

Source: Laville *et al.* 1980

d'Azil, Isturitz, the cave of Les Eglises at Ussat and Le Portel (Clottes 1976).

The Alpine region around Bern has produced a number of late glacial magdalenian assemblages in the Laufen-Delemont basins. These include St Brais, Kastelhöhle and Kohlerhöhle (Bandi 1969; Müller-Beck 1968b). They have reindeer dominated faunas and most probably date to the equivalent of Allerød or younger Dryas in northern Europe.

The southern Alpine area contains a number of epigravettian assemblages in the alpine foothills of northern Italy. At the Ponte di Veia caves C and E (Leonardi and Broglio 1962) and the Riparo Tagliente, where levels 15–16 are C14 dated at 13.4–13.3 Kyr (Bartolomei *et al.* 1974, 1979).

A chronological summary of the SE region is provided by J. Kozlowski (1979). The period 20–10 Kyr is divided into three, primarily on the associated climatic evidence (table 5.13). Sites during period B include the Hungarian open sites of Arka (Vértes 1964–5), dated by C14 to between 18.6 and 17 Kyr, and two cultural levels at Ságvár, 18.9–17.7 Kyr. A gravettian assemblage at the Ovcja cave in northern Yugoslavia is dated to 19.5 Kyr.

(b) industrial groupings

There are three principal groupings in the southern province.

(1) The *solutrean* is named after the site of Solutré in the Saône and Loire district of France. The classic sequence is however from Laugerie-Haute. This rock shelter is divided into an east and west part with a large block of unexcavated sediment, on which stands Peyrony's house, in the middle. The many stratified layers show a five part division to the solutrean (Smith 1964, 1966) with flat retouch in the proto-solutrean and the appearance of unifacially worked leaf points (fig. 5.20, a) in the lower solutrean. Bifacial pressure flaking marks the appearance of the middle solutrean, at which time the geographical range of known solutrean assemblages increases dramatically. This stage is also marked by the craftsmanship of the slender, finely flaked laurel leaf points to which the techniques of pressure flaking were applied (fig. 5.20, b). The upper solutrean sees the addition of pressure flaked points of willow leaf shape while

in the final solutrean at Laugerie-Haute shouldered points (fig. 5.20, c), still made with pressure flaking, are a feature of the assemblages. The rest of the assemblages consist of pieces with both flat and blunting retouch; end scrapers and burins are the common tool forms. The assemblages also contain a high proportion of flakes. Solutrean assemblages bear little or no relationship to the upper perigordian, and Smith (1966) favours a development from some local, evolved form of mousterian, although no such industry is known that would fit this role of ancestor.

The Cantabrian solutrean can be divided into two assemblage groupings (Straus 1977b). The first is rich in end scrapers, side scrapers, denticulates, notches and solutrean points. The second grouping has far fewer points but many burins, backed bladelets and truncations. These different assemblages correlate with differences in the animal species from the faunal collections with which they are associated (Clark and Straus 1983:133).

It is also noteworthy that eyed needles, made of either bone or ivory, appear for the first time in the solutrean (Stordeur-Yedid 1979).

(2) The *magdalenian* can be divided into two major industrial groupings which are arranged chronologically (Laville *et al.* 1980). In the Périgord scheme the magdalenian is divided into at least six stages (Breuil 1912; de Sonneville-Bordes 1960) with Laugerie-Haute east providing the stratigraphic sequence for the early stages I–III and the classic abri of La Madeleine for stages IV–VI. The early magdalenian has comparatively few antler tools. Common stone tool types are the small raclettes, which are flakes with abrupt retouch, and backed denticulated rods, often of microlithic size. Bladelets are common, as is a variety of borers, among them a star shaped form. Geometric microliths begin to appear in the form of scalene triangles.

The later stages of the magdalenian show an increase in these microlithic forms, especially among the quantities of backed bladelets. These small elements, as Bouvier (1977, 1979) has discovered in his recent excavations at La Madeleine, were often missed in the earlier excavations. A similar set of circumstances was found by Albrecht (1979) in the re-excavation of the dumps at Petersfels in the NC region. As a result the microlithic element in the magdalenian has been underestimated.

The sub-divisions of the later magdalenian were originally based, at La Madeleine, upon the appearance of barbed antler projectile points (fig. 5.20, e–h) (Julien 1982). These are referred to as harpoons. A chronological development is apparent from simple forms, to harpoons with a single and finally a double row of barbs.

The Périgord sequence is not duplicated in all its stages in other areas, for example the Pyrenees, Cantabria or northern Switzerland. Magdalenian I and II are absent in the Pyrenean sites (Clottes 1976), which most probably reflects the hostile environmental conditions in the mountains during the early millennia of the LUP. The later stages are known from many sites in the same area.

The Cantabrian material is grouped into a lower magdalenian with quadrangular section bone points and thick end scraper forms. The sites of El Juyo (Janssens *et al.* 1958; González-Echegaray 1960, 1971) and Altamira, with C14 dates of 15.3 and 15.5 Kyr respectively, place this early group at a comparable age to the magdalenian III in areas of France (Clark and Straus 1983). The upper magdalenian is represented by the assemblage at Tito Bustillo (Moure 1975; Moure and Cano 1976), and in many other sites.

The magdalenian assemblages in Switzerland (Bandi 1969) have been studied by de Sonneville-Bordes (1963a). They are regarded as late in date and comparable in assemblage composition to the Kesslerloch/Petersfels material.

(3) The southern part of the Alpine and SE regions contain LUP assemblages described as *epi-* or *evolved gravettian*. They represent a trend comparable to the magdalenian in that microlithisation is a common feature. Small backed rods are common within a general tradition of blunting retouch on blades to form points of a variety of shapes (fig. 5.21, j). Bone and antler tool types which are so characteristic of the magdalenian are however rarely encountered. Moreover, the frequency with which any tools were made from these organic materials is noticeably much less than in contemporary assemblages from the northern province. The Alpine foothills in northern Italy have only a few of the early and later epigravettian sites, e.g. Trene and Ponte di Veia cave C. More sites are known for the final epigravettian. For example, the Riparo Tagliente (Bartolomei and Broglio 1972) shows a development of truncated pieces and geometric forms and can be compared with a great number of sites from the MC region (Bartolomei *et al.* 1979).

A number of cultural provinces have been proposed by J. Kozlowski (1979; Kozlowski and Kozlowski 1979) for the SE region during the LUP. These are all variants of the evolved gravettian pattern and include, in period B (table 5.13), the sagvarian, after the type site of Ságvár in Hungary, with many end scrapers made on short blades, and a late gravettian with backed bladelets and some shouldered points in the Slovenian Karst at Ovcja and Zupanov Spodmol caves (Osole 1962–3).

The late LUP sites have comparable assemblages as at Kadar, in Bosnia (Montet-White 1979, 1981; Montet-White and Basler 1977) where microlithic shouldered points are a feature of the lithic assemblage, and at Cãlinesti and Remetea-Şomoş in the Ţara Oaşului in Roumania (Bitiri 1972), and the upper levels of the gravettian open site of Arka in Hungary (Vértes 1964–5).

(c) geographical variation and regional case studies

A major research goal has been to place sites and groups of sites within the detailed environmental framework of the period. Many examples using the results of multi-disciplinary investigations into pollens, snails, sediments and animal faunas can be found in H. de Lumley (ed.) 1976a, de Sonneville-Bordes (ed.) 1979 and Laville and Renault-Miscovsky (eds.) 1977. Investigations into site locations have been made by Bouvier (1977, 1979) for La Madeleine, where he has demonstrated that the configurations of the massive shelter wall gave it particular advantages in receiving and retaining heat from the sun. This placed it at an advantage over other locations in the cliffs of the Vézère. West and south facing caves and abris were clearly favoured during these cold periods in both the EUP and LUP. This is shown in the Brive basin, Corrèze district, a more rugged area to the east of the Dordogne department. Raynal (1977) has put forward a model of seasonal use of the Brive area by groups concentrating on particular animal species and possessing permanent settlements in the Dordogne. The numerically small assemblages are indicative of short visits to the Corrèze which might have resulted, in his opinion, from a scarcity of good quality lithic sources in the area.

Evidence for the movement of raw materials – stone and both fossil and marine shells – into Pyrenean sites (Bahn 1982) clearly shows that it was in the LUP that the majority of these transfers took place (fig. 7.8). Although the exact mechanism, exchange or movement of groups, is not yet established, Bahn argues that the patterns indicate seasonal dispersal and aggregation of population centering on two 'super-sites' – Isturitz and Mas d'Azil (Bahn 1982), which 'controlled' the western and eastern Pyrenees respectively.

Both the Pyrenean and Cantabrian data confirm the EUP trend towards a wider resource base (Freeman 1973; Straus 1977a; Bahn 1983). This was first described by Freeman, who regards the magdalenian pattern as a significant break from earlier subsistence/settlement strategies in Cantabria. The magdalenian site locations in his view point to a greater degree of resource specialisation not only upon red deer but upon other species, including a small component of marine foods. Moreover he suggests that the lack of any very big sites, as measured by quantities of artifacts, in the Cantabrian magdalenian might mean that those which are rich in art, such as Altamira, served instead as seasonal aggregation sites. In this way they supplied a focus for a larger regional population (*ibid*.: 40); a suggestion followed up by Conkey (1980).

The work of Clark and Straus (1983; Straus *et al.* 1981) at La Riera leads them to conclude that climatic factors cannot account for the appearance of lower yield but high cost foods such as shellfish in the diet. They instead favour an explanation that a dense population was increasingly facing changes in adaptive strategies to cope with problems of demographic stress. They use the increase in site numbers (table 5.15) in the LUP as evidence for this population explosion.

An alternative explanation by Bailey (1983a) points out that the narrow Cantabrian coastal plain was itself highly susceptible to change under a falling and then rising sea level during the LUP (fig. 5.25). He notes that the major exploitation changes, as revealed by the faunal assemblages from the sites, coincide with the impact of glacial climates on the size of this all important resource zone, and hence the expansion and contraction of the exploitation

Table 5.15. *Settlement data from the SW and NC regions of Europe*

Site sample size is listed in parentheses

	EUP				LUP	
	mousterian	chatel-perronian	aurignacian	gravettian	solutrean	magdalenian
	%	%	%	%	%	%
Pyrenees (169)	15	7	15	10	9	43
Périgord (243)	13	5	18	17	16	31
Cantabria (135)	10	—	13[a]	—	24	53
Southern Germany (123)	34	—	17[a]	—	—	49

Source: Peyrony 1949; Clark and Straus 1983; Bahn 1983; Gamble 1978a,b
[a] Includes all EUP sites in the area

territories around the sites. Bailey rejects the idea of economic intensification occurring independently of environmental change and sees any differences in the archaeological record as reflecting, in this case study, some necessary adaptive adjustments to changed local circumstances.

It should be noted that no open sites are yet known from either the EUP or LUP of Cantabria, so that the cave sites may be a very partial record indeed of the settlement system.

The distribution of caves in 'bottle-neck' locations in the Laufen and Delemont basins, Switzerland (Sturdy 1975) forms an example of site extended territories. In this instance (fig. 5.26) the topographic controls are particularly strong and the location of the sites at intercept locations on the exit routes from these grazing grounds provides strong evidence for Sturdy's land use model. The twin basins cover some 200 km^2 which would allow 1500 reindeer summer grazing at a stocking density of 7.15 deer per km^2. Sturdy estimates that at a low cull rate this size of herd would provide year round food for three families, fifteen persons, so long as they followed the herd north to its winter grazing grounds. The same number of people could presumably be supported if the requisite annual number of animals were killed and stored rather than followed and killed at different seasons of the year. Indeed a more economical explanation might be to view such sites as intercept hunting stations rather than as blocking locations related to close herding, a model which has been criticised as far removed from the ways in which hunters exploit mobile resources (Ingold 1980). This pattern of reindeer exploitation is well documented from Greenland (Meldgaard 1983). At such locations the entire year's supply of meat, rather than just the summer portion, could have been obtained and stored, and thus the long

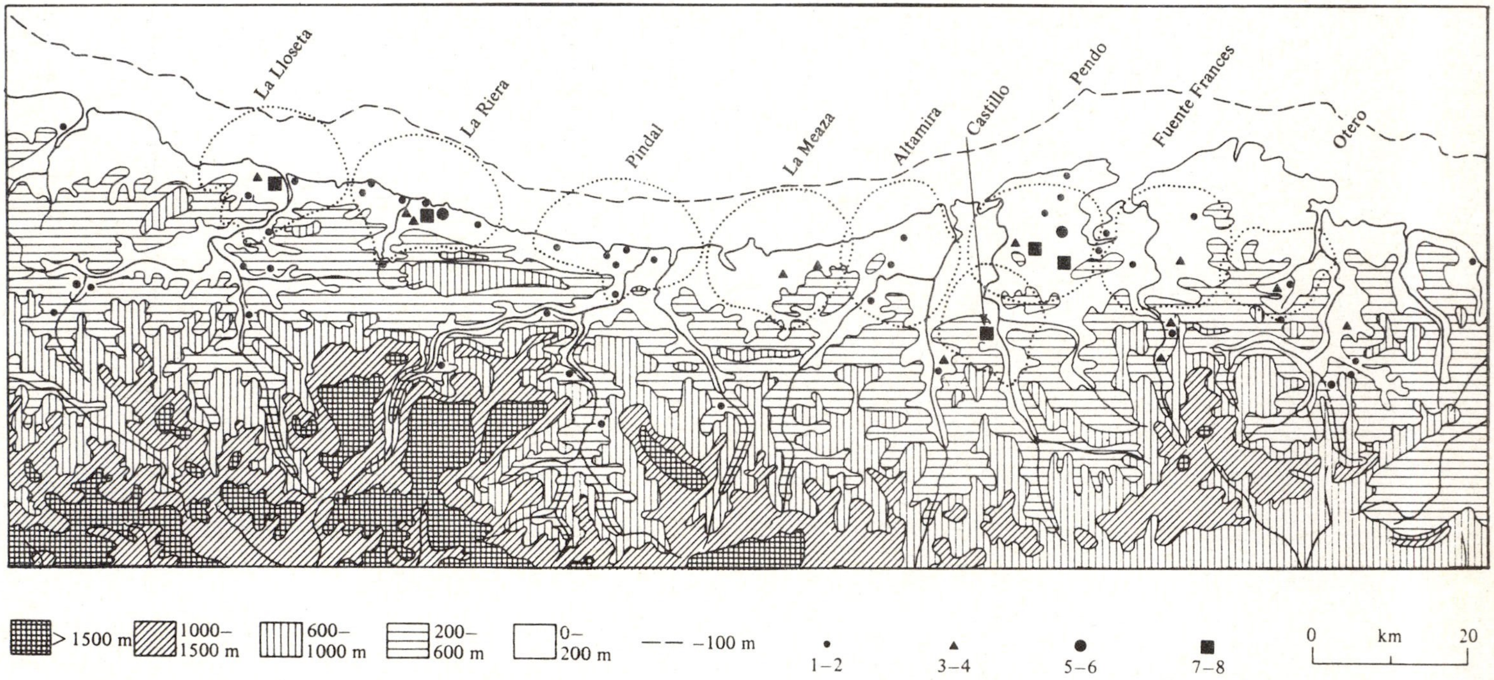
La Lloseta
La Riera
Pindal
La Meaza
Altamira
Castillo
Pendo
Fuente Frances
Otero
> 1500 m
1000–
1500 m
600–
1000 m
200–
600 m
0–
200 m
–100 m
1–2
3–4
5–6
7–8
0
km
20

5.25 Location of palaeolithic sites in Cantabria, SW region. The site symbols refer to the number of periods represented in each site. Many of the sites would have been well located to take advantage of the coastal plain (–100 m contour) that would have appeared under glacial conditions. The dotted lines indicate a hypothetical two hour exploitation territory (Bailey 1983b:fig. 13.1).

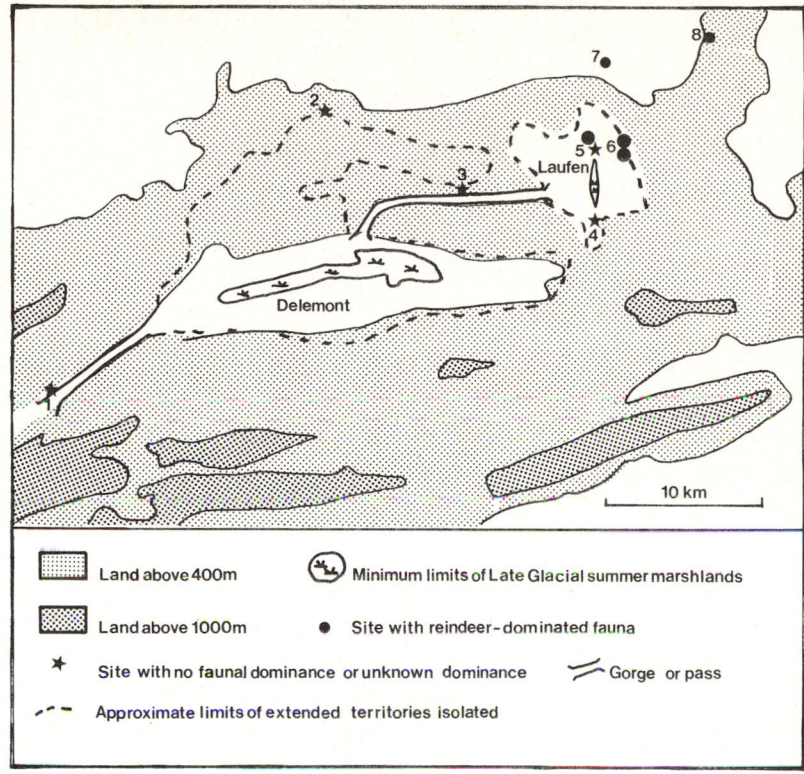

5.26 Site exploitation territories in the Laufen and Delemont basins, Alpine region. The sites act as stop gaps around flat grazing areas defined by rugged relief (Sturdy 1975:78, fig. 22).
1. St Brais, 2. Neumühle, 3. Liesberg, 4. Thierstein, 5. Brugglihöhle and Kohlerhöhle, 6. Heidenküche and Kastelhöhle, 7. Buttenloch, 8. Birseck Ermitage and Hollenberg.

herd-following trek northward avoided. This intercept hunting model, where storage is a key component, has many implications for the formation of the archaeological record and in particular about information concerning the season of site occupation as indicated by the time of year when the animals were killed. However Sturdy's herd following model has found recent support from Vörös' (1982) study of the Ságvár reindeer material from the SE region. The seasonal data from the teeth and antlers point to occupation in autumn and winter and Vörös argues that herd following between the Carpathian Basin in winter and southern Germany in the summer, via the Danubian sites in Austria, is entirely acceptable.

A final striking geographical pattern concerns the presence of bone/antler tools. The needles, pierced staffs, spear throwers and a great profusion of different types of pendants, beads and ornaments (Graziosi 1960) is very much confined to the SW region and the Swiss sites in the Alpine region. In both quantity and diversity of bone/antler implement forms these regions dominate the inventory of such LUP objects from the province (Leroi-Gourhan 1968:chart IV).

(d) burials and art

A very similar geographical pattern can be seen with the distribution of painted caves and major engraving sites. These are confined entirely to the SW region.

(1) engraved slabs. The major engraving sites where small stone slabs were used are La Marche (fig. 5.27; Pales 1976), Limeuil (Capitan and Bouyssonie 1924), Badegoule (Cheynier 1949), Labastide (Clottes 1976) and the Enlène cave in the Volp cavern complex (Clottes and de Begouen 1981). These sites have quantities of engraved limestone plaques and antler objects comparable to Gönnersdorf, NC region, and Parpalló, MW region (Davidson n.d.). The slabs from La Marche show that the human form was a common subject in palaeolithic engraving (fig. 5.27). The Enlène material now consists of almost 600 engraved and scratched sandstone blocks, and smaller numbers of such pieces are known from Isturitz

5.27 An engraved limestone slab from La Marche (Pales 1976: observation no. 30, planche 72). The apparent 'jumble' of scratched lines includes a human head (lower left) with another large partial profile facing it. Above the main head is a complete standing figure drawn upside down to the two profiles. The head and body of a bear can also be untangled in the centre and right of the slab.

Table 5.16. *The major features of palaeolithic art styles as analysed by A. Leroi-Gourhan (1968)*

	Themes	Medium	Quantity	Associated Industries
Style I	sexual symbols; small animal sculptures; human figures	plaquettes or limestone blocks; ivory from mammoth tusks	very few sites and specimens	aurignacian
Style II	animal species defined by set of characteristic details, legs only suggested and extremities rarely rendered, strong sinuous line that defines the neck, withers and back; female figurines	limestone blocks, slabs and ivory plaques; tools of antler and bone; human and animal ivory figurines; use of caves, rock shelters	very few known cave and rock shelter sites with either paintings, engravings or bas-relief carvings; considerable quantities of carved figurines and portable objects	upper perigordian/ gravettian
Style III	animal figures and paintings showing the mastery of style II; elements include high arched horses' necks and shoulders, limbs and extremities are shown in detail, huge low slung bodies, more than one angle of perspective employed, rectangular signs, 'brace' shaped signs	as above with much greater emphasis on caves and rock shelters, several bas-reliefs	a considerable number of examples of this style	solutrean/ early magdalenian
Style IV	animal figures show an extension of style III with outlines closer to a photographic reality, retention of conventions, e.g. bison manes, attitudes and movement of the figures more realistic, signs are regional in character, Périgord=quadrangular and truncated female representations, Pyrenees and Cantabria=claviform and oval; many carved portable objects with animals shown in realistic movement and perspective	as above; majority of all decorated objects (c.80%) can be dated to this style	very many examples	late magdalenian

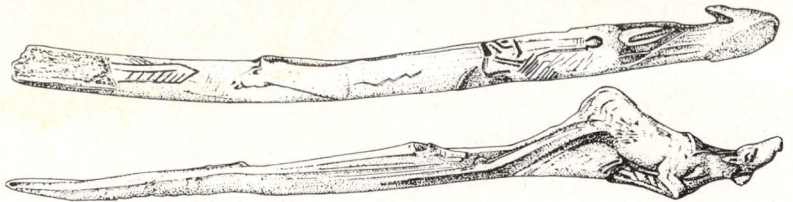

5.28 Engraved and carved antler spear throwers from Laugerie-Basse, SW region (scale 1:3) (Müller-Karpe 1966:taf. 79, 9 and 10).

(Saint-Périer 1936). The scratches and engravings are often superimposed on the same block in an exuberant, plate-of-spaghetti-like manner.

These sites are all associated with magdalenian assemblages.

(2) carved and decorated objects. Engraved antler rods are common in magdalenian sites, e.g. Altamira (Conkey 1980), Isturitz (Saint-Périer 1936) and Badegoule (Cheynier 1949).

Other sites with a great array of decorated objects and frequent examples of animals carved on items such as spear throwers include Mas d'Azil, Bruniquel, Labastide, La Madeleine and Laugerie-Basse (Bosinski 1982b:abb. 12; Sieveking 1976; Graziosi 1960; Leroi-Gourhan 1968). These objects are mostly magdalenian in date and many of them can be more precisely placed within magdalenian stages IV–VI (fig. 5.28).

(3) decorated caves. Leroi-Gourhan (1968) has divided palaeolithic art into four styles (tables 5.16, 5.17, fig. 5.29). The majority of decorated cave walls are found

---

5.29 Chronological and geographical distribution of styles of painting and signs (Leroi-Gourhan 1968:chart XXXV, 5.15)
STYLE I (aurignacian):1–4. Abri Cellier.

STYLE II (gravettian and late aurignacian): 5. La Ferrassie; 6. Castanet; 7. La Ferrassie; 8. Gargas; 9. Isturitz; 10. Kostenki.

STYLE III (solutrean and early magdalenian): 11–13. Lascaux; 14–17. Le Gabillou; 18. Pech Merle; 19. Le Portel; 20–22. Las Chimeneas; 23–27. El Castilló; 28. Altamira; 29. La Pasiega C.

BISON IN STYLE III: 30. Le Gabillou; 31. Pech Merle; 32. Le Portel; 33. La Pasiega A.

STYLE III (early magdalenian, to magdalenian IV): 34. Villars; 35. Lascaux; 36–37. Le Gabillou; 38. Pech Merle; 39–41. Cougnac; 42. Le Portel; 43–48. La Pasiega.

EARLY STYLE IV (magdalenian III – magdalenian IV): 49. Lascaux; 50. Marsoulas; 51. Altamira; 52. La Pasiega; 56. Les Combarelles; 57. Font-de-Gaume; 58. Bernifal; 59. Niaux; 60. Le Portel; 61. El Pindal.

BISON IN EARLY AND LATE STYLE IV; 53. Lascaux; 54. Marsoulas; 55. Altamira; 62. Font-de-Gaume; 63. Niaux; 64. El Pindal; 78. Bernifal; 79. Montespan; 80. Las Monedas.

LATE STYLE IV: 65–69. Les Combarelles; Bédeilhac; 71. Ussat; 72–74. Les Trois Frères; 75–76. El Pindal; 77. Las Monédas.

| PÉRIGORD | QUERCY | PYRENEES | EASTERN EUROPE | |

Table 5.17. *The analysis of cave art sites by style and topographical character*

The table shows that the destruction of paintings has been great in the daylight zones of the caves. At Fontanet the palaeolithic entrance was sealed by a landslide and the paintings preserved. The table also indicates that as a general rule it is only during style IV that paintings are found either at great depth or difficulty of access.

				Easy Access		Difficult Access	
Style	Daylight		Entrance	Average depth	Great depth	Less than 100m	More than 100m
II	Figuier ○	Chabot ○		La Groze ○			Baume Latrone ○●
	Gorge d'Enfer ◑	La Grèze ○		Gargas I ○●			
	Huchard ○	Oulen ○					
	Laussel ◑						
	Oulen ○						
	Pair non Pair ○						
III	Bourdeilles ◑	Altamira I ○●		Altamira II ○	Pech Merle II ●		Villars ●
	Hornos I ○	La Haza ●		Castillo I ○●			
	Mouthiers ◑			Chimeneas ●			
	Roc de Sers ◑			Cougnac ●			
	St-Cirq I ◑			Covalanas ●			
				Ebbou I ○			
				Font-de-Gaume I ●			
				Gabillou ○			
				Lascaux ○●			
				Marcenac ●			
				Pasiega I ○●			
				Pech Merle I ●			
				Portel I ●			

Style IV chart (after Leroi-Gourhan). Sites grouped by period with symbols indicating the presence of engraving, sculpture and painting.

Early IV

- Angles
- Cap Blanc
- Fontanet
- Isturitz
- La Madeleine
- Reverdit
- St-Germaine-la-Rivière

- Altamira
- St-Cirq II

- Bara-Bahau
- Bernifal
- Castillo II
- Commarque
- Ebbou II
- Font-de-Gaume II
- Gargas II
- Hornos II
- Isturitz II
- Marsoulas
- Monédas
- Pasiega II
- Pindal
- Portel II
- Ussat
- Fontanet

- Bédeilhac
- Labastide
- Niaux
- Rouffignac

- Arcy-sur-Cure
- Buxu
- La Mouthe
- Sallèles-Cabardès
- Santimamine

- Combarelles
- Cullalvera
- Etcheberriko
- Pileta
- Montespan
- Trois Frères
- Tuc d'Audoubert

Late IV

- St-Marcel
- Ste-Eulalie
- Teyjat

Source: Leroi-Gourhan 1968: chart XX

Key: ○ Engraving ◐ Sculpture ● Painting

in styles III – Lascaux, Altamira – and style IV – Niaux, Font-de-Gaume, Les Trois Frères, Les Combarelles. These six sites were referred to by Breuil (1952) as the six giants of palaeolithic cave art.

The decorated caves can be treated on a sub-regional basis (Vialou 1976). The greatest number and density occur in the Dordogne and cluster within 30 km of Les Eyzies. The sites in this area include Font-de-Gaume (Capitan *et al.* 1910), Lascaux (A. Leroi-Gourhan and Allain 1979) and Rouffignac (Nougier and Robert 1958). Lascaux is the most important of all the style III sites in the Dordogne area. The site is not only very rich in polychrome paintings of bison, aurochs, horse and deer but also has a great wealth of engravings. An absolute date of 17 Kyr for the Lascaux occupation layer also dates the interstadial that was determined by study of pollens in the sediments. It is assumed that the paintings on the cave walls and this dated occupation level are indeed contemporary.

At Les Combarelles, style IV, engravings of bison and horse dominate the many hundreds of representations in this narrow winding cave (Capitan *et al.* 1924). A further variation in cave decoration can be found at the Abri Cap Blanc, where excavations revealed that the back wall of the shelter had been sculpted into a frieze of large horses (Lalanne and Breuil 1911).

From the Roc de Sers in the Charente (Henri-Martin 1928) came a frieze of sculpted limestone blocks that had been aligned on a ledge along the back wall of the rock shelter. The animals in this 'sanctuary' were bison, horse, ibex and a bird. At Bourdeilles, the Forneau de Diable (Peyrony 1932), limestone blocks with ten low reliefs and two engravings of oxen were presumably arranged within the shelter. The blocks came from an upper solutrean level and are regarded by Leroi-Gourhan as classic examples of style III.

Elsewhere, 'pockets' of decorated caves indicate a small scale regionalism to styles of cave art. This is clearly seen in the similar styles of painting, and in particular the brace shaped signs, from both Pech Merle and Cougnac. These sites are located in the Lot some 35 km from each other and 80 km to the south-east of the Dordogne group.

Another important regional group is to be found around Tarascon sur Ariège with the sites of Niaux, Fontanet and Bedeilhac. Further west in the Pyrenees at the Volp caverns is the large painted site of Les Trois Frères which is part of the same system which contains the Enlène caves and Le Tuc d'Audoubert. In the latter site, which is very difficult of access (table 5.17), are two large bison modelled in clay and lying on the floor of the gallery. Other decorated sites include the large galleries at Gargas, where painted hand signs are very common, and the paintings of horses in style IV black outline at Le Portel.

The Gironde has a few sites, the most important at Pair non Pair which is accorded the status of a style II site and dated to the upper perigordian by Leroi-Gourhan. If this is a correct attribution then these engravings of horse, bison, ibex and mammoth would be rare examples of EUP cave art.

5.30 A schematic plan showing the layout of the axial gallery at Lascaux. The animals include deer, horse, cows and ibex together with rectangular signs on the south wall while on the north wall are much larger paintings of cows, bulls and horses. The plan also shows the position of holes in the rock wall where scaffold poles were placed and ledge sections where the painters could have secured a foothold (Arl. Leroi-Gourhan and Allain 1979:fig. 138).

The Cantabrian evidence is dominated by the site of Altamira. These paintings, and most notably the large painted ceiling with polychrome bison, claviform signs, hinds and boars, are placed in style III. Other sites with engravings and paintings are found in the Monte Castilló caves in the Santander province. Among these are La Pasiega, where painted quadrangular signs, hand prints and rows of dots are a striking feature.

Considerable attention has been paid to the possible meanings of the cave art (Breuil 1952; Laming-Emperaire 1962; Leroi-Gourhan 1968). The detailed examination of wall surfaces and plotting of exactly where the paintings and engravings are found in the caves are now beginning to be published. These studies have followed the impetus provided by Leroi-Gourhan's pioneering synthesis (1968, 1982), where he demonstrated repeated patterning in the choice of subject matter, the pairing of animal species (e.g. horse with bison), and their positioning within the caves and where in his opinion definite locations had been selected (fig. 5.30). This intentionality in layout, in what he termed palaeolithic sanctuaries, had previously passed largely unremarked, and attention had concentrated upon the content of the pictures rather than upon their all important context. Leroi-Gourhan's conclusions have not been without their critics (Ucko and Rosenfeld 1967), but few would deny his importance in initiating a systematic evaluation of cave art in terms of both style and contextual analysis.

General questions are also being asked about why the art only occurs in quantity in the SW region and during the LUP (Jochim 1983), in a series of studies which are investigating the adaptive significance of such behaviour (Conkey 1978, 1980; Gamble 1982, 1983a; Wobst 1977).

(4) group ceremony sites. A number of the deep, decorated caves such as Pech Merle and Fontanet have abundant evidence for the different uses of the various chambers in the cave systems. This can take the form not only of different types of decoration – engraving, painting, scratches and finger tracings in the clay of the floor, walls and ceilings – but also evidence of footprints preserved in the soft clay sediments of the gallery floors. These imprints document the barefoot visits of adults and children to these galleries. The René Clastres gallery, a recently discovered section of the Niaux cave complex (Clottes and Simonnet 1972), produced 500 footprints of at least three children and two adults. These were preserved in a small sand dune in the same chamber as a group of paintings, three bison, one horse and one mustelid. The wooden torch and charcoal that

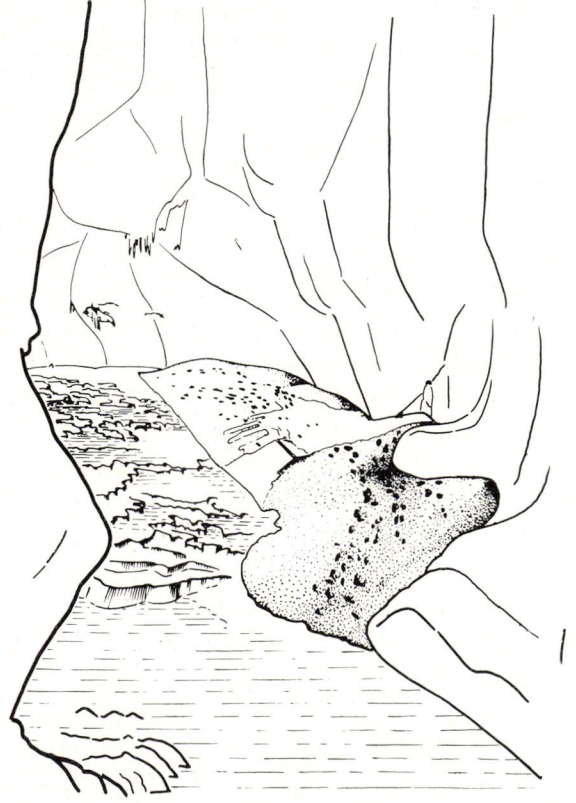

5.31 A sketch of the René Clastres gallery in the Niaux cave complex showing footprints in the dune to the right and paintings on the wall in the far distance (Clottes and Simonnet 1972:311, fig. 18).

the palaeolithic visitors had discarded on the same surface as the footprints gave a C14 date of 10 Kyr for this visit at the end of the last ice age (fig. 5.31).

Pfeiffer (1982) has emphasised the imprinting effect that the often hazardous journeys to these deep caverns would have had (table 5.17). He argues that this aspect would have formed a significant component in initiation ceremonies where coded information vital to the maintenance of palaeolithic society was transmitted to the new members of that society. This was achieved through the art and associated rituals that included the journey and most probably dancing and music.

An example of hitherto unexpected palaeolithic behaviour comes from the magdalenian occupations in the El Juyo cave in Cantabria (González Echegaray and Freeman 1981). As a result of exacting excavation methods a complex construction was uncovered. This had involved the deliberate placement of stone slabs, bone spear points and columns of earth, that incorporated different colours of clay, in a symmetrical rosette like pattern. Beneath this construction was a layer of animal bones interpreted by the excavators as a sacrifice. The excavators found that this same sequence of rosettes and animal bones was repeated as they dug deeper. Other features were revealed including a natural fissure in the rock that had been enhanced with some palaeolithic grafitti to form a face. Taken all together the evidence points to some considerable group participation in construction that in the excavators' opinion lasted several weeks if it was all built in one episode.

(5) burials. The burials from the French part of the SW region are all magdalenian in age (Quéchon 1976). They include the 20–5 year old female from St Germain-la-Rivière (Blanchard *et al.* 1972) who was found tightly flexed in a small stone built chamber and next to a skull of *Bos primigenius*. A necklace of seventy drilled reindeer teeth and red deer canines was found within the chamber. Other flexed burials have come from the Abri Cap Blanc and Chancelade.

From the Alpine region there is a burial at Riparo Tagliente. The top half of the skeleton had been dug away in historic times but enough survives to see that a pit some 50 cm deep had been dug. The body had been placed into this in an extended position and then covered by large rock slabs. Two engraved slabs, one depicting a lion and the horn of an aurochs accompanied the body and the entire feature is associated with an epigravettian flint assemblage (Bartolomei *et al.* 1974).

Further references

SW: H. de Lumley (ed.) 1976a; Laville *et al.* 1980; Leroi-Gourhan 1968, 1982; Pfeiffer 1982; Ucko and Rosenfeld 1967; Breuil 1952; Clark and Straus 1983;

Freeman 1973, 1981; Bahn 1977, 1982, 1983; Clottes 1976; Altuna 1979; de Sonneville-Bordes 1960, (ed.) 1979; Bailey (ed.) 1983b.

Alpine: Bartolomei *et al.* 1979; Leonardi and Broglio 1962; Bandi 1969; Müller-Beck 1968b.

SE: Kozlowski, J. 1979; Kozlowski and Kozlowski 1979; Montet-White 1979, 1981; Vértes 1964–5; Valoch 1968; Bitiri 1972; Vörös 1982.

Mediterranean province 4

(a) chronology

The solutrean is the earliest LUP industry in the MW region. This has now been dated at the cave site of Parpalló, Valencia, in south-eastern Spain, to 20.4 Kyr for the lower and 18 Kyr for the upper solutrean levels (Davidson 1974; Bofinger and Davidson 1977). An earlier date for the lower solutrean of 21.7 Kyr comes from the nearby site of Les Mallaetes and together these suggest that the solutrean in this part of the MW region is at least as early as if not earlier than comparable industries in the SW region, even though, typologically, the Valencian sites lack the proto- and lower solutrean assemblages found in stratigraphically early positions in the Dordogne. An estimated age for the beginning of the solutrean, using sedimentation rates as a control at these two sites, gives dates of 22.1 and 21 Kyr for the earliest solutrean in Spain (Bofinger and Davidson 1977:240). Within this industrial tradition barbed and tanged arrowheads appear at 18.7 Kyr.

Later assemblages described as solutreo-gravettian contain notched points (puntas de muesca). Such an assemblage has been dated at Parpalló to 17.9 Kyr, while the latest date for an assemblage with puntas de muesca is 14.9 Kyr (Davidson 1983; Fullola 1979). The 7.25 m of stratified cultural deposit at Parpalló (Pericot 1942) also contains magdalenian assemblages, while elsewhere in the region epigravettian is found (Cacho 1981).

The chronology of the LUP in Provence and Languedoc, MW region, is set out in table 5.18 (Escalon de Fonton and Onoratini 1976). The key section in Languedoc is from the Salpêtrière cave, Gard (Escalon de Fonton 1966). The C14 dates (Delibrias and Evin 1980) are interpreted by Bazile (1980) as demonstrating a very rapid development from the solutrean to the salpetrien. This latter industry first appears in the site, after which it is named, at 19 Kyr and is replaced by the upper magdalenian between 13 and 12.5 Kyr. However in Provence a different industry, the arenien, is judged to be contemporary with the solutrean in Languedoc (table 5.18) and is firmly dated to the Würm III, just prior to and during the Lascaux interstadial as recognised in the sediments from such sites as Grotte 1 de la Bouverie, in the Var. Lower magdalenian is dated to 16.7 Kyr at the site of Lassac in the Aude district (Sacchi 1976) while upper magdalenian levels are common and a stratified sequence is known from the Grotte de l'Adaouste (Escalon de Fonton and Onoratini 1976).

Table 5.18. *Upper paleolithic industries in southern France, MW region*

Local interstadials	Eastern Languedoc	Western Provence	Eastern Provence
Allerød	azilian	azilian	
	final magdalenian	final magdalenian	bouverien
	magdalenian VI	magdalenian VI	
	magdalenian V	magdalenian V	bouverien
Bølling	upper salpetrien	magdalenian IV	bouverien
	lower salpetrien	arenien	arenien
Lascaux	upper solutrean		
	middle solutrean	arenien	arenien
	lower solutrean		
	aurignacian V	arenien	arenien
Tursac	aurignacian IV	final perigordian	
	perigordian V		perigordian
	aurignacian III		
Salpêtrière	perigordian IV		perigordian IV
	aurignacian II	aurignacian	
Arcy	aurignacian I		aurignacian
Quinson	aurignacian O	?	?

Source: After Escalon de Fonton and Bazile 1976:1164

The LUP of peninsula Italy, MC region, has been intensively researched (Laplace 1966) and a number of C14 dated profiles now exist with which to establish an absolute chronology for the industries. The LUP is divided into three major industrial/chronological divisions (Bartolomei *et al.* 1979).

(1) Early epigravettian: as found at Grotta Paglicci, Cala della Ossa, Romito and Taurisano. The C14 dates for these sites indicate a chronological span between 19.1 and 15.4 Kyr.

(2) Later or evolved epigravettian, dated at Palidoro to 15.5–14.8 Kyr, is also present at the Paglicci cave. The broadest limits as indicated by the spread of C14 dates are 16.1–13.8 Kyr for this phase.

(3) Final epigravettian: as at Romanelli cave in southern Italy, dated to 11.9 Kyr. The C14 dates for this phase range between 15.7 and 8 Kyr with the majority falling between 13 and 10 Kyr (Bartolomei *et al.* 1979:fig. 2).

The ME region also has epigravettian type assemblages, as at Badanj and Crvena Stijena, both in central Yugoslavia. In the Istrian peninsula the site of Šandalia II near Pula has epigravettian assemblages in periods B, C and D of the LUP as recognised by J. Kozlowski (1979) and presented here in table 5.13. Level c at the site is dated post 21.7 Kyr and level b upper to 12.3–10.8 Kyr (Montet-White 1981).

The earliest LUP levels at the cave site of Kastritsa, Epirus, north-west Greece (Higgs *et al.* 1967; Bailey *et al.* 1983 a,b) are dated by C14 to 21–20 Kyr. These levels correspond to a high level for Lake Ioannina which flooded the cave at this time. The stratified deposits contain epigravettian material and span the entire LUP period.

(b) industrial groupings

The proto- and lower solutrean are lacking outside the SW region. It is during the middle solutrean, as defined in the Dordogne sites, that geographical expansion took place and sites such as Solutré on the border of the SW/NW regions, and the Languedoc and Spanish solutrean assemblages in the MW region appear (Smith 1966). We have however already seen above that the lack of these early stages, as defined by typological analysis, does not necessarily mean that the solutrean is chronologically later in these sites. Indeed these typologically late assemblages may well be earlier than the so-called early solutrean of the classic area!

The Parpalló solutrean assemblages begin with laurel leaf points which are considered to be diagnostic of middle solutrean in the SW region. In the uppermost solutrean levels bifacially worked, pressure flaked, barbed and tanged arrowheads (fig. 5.20, d) have been found. These are succeeded by what are described as solutreo-gravettian assemblages with characteristic notched points. Finally at Parpalló magdalenian and epigravettian industries (Fortea 1973), also found at Barranc Blanc and Les Mallaetes, form examples of a widespread technocomplex.

The situation in Languedoc, MW region, is rather similar, although a local early solutrean is recognised in the Salpêtrière cave. Bazile (1980) has emphasised the importance of shouldered points in both upper perigordian, solutrean and later salpetrien (fig. 5.20, j) assemblages in this area. Bifacially worked leaf points are common in the middle solutrean levels. The salpetrien is regarded by Escalon de Fonton (1966) as an episolutrean, a languedocian facies of the terminal solutrean. Shouldered points are present in the earlier phases of this industrial variant, while geometric microliths become more common in the final phases.

The lithic industries in Provence, MW region, to the east of the Rhone are very different (table 5.18) since the solutrean is entirely absent (Escalon de Fonton and Onoratini 1976). Instead of a late upper perigordian facies, the arenien, named after the Ligurian cave of Arene Candide, is recognised. This is seen as a local transformation of a gravettian of noaillian tradition. The assemblages, as at the Grotte Bouverie, include gravettes and shouldered points. The later bouverien industries in eastern Provence are post-noaillian epigravettian with small points and other gravettian features, and without any discernible magdalenian or azilian elements (Escalon de Fonton and Onoratini 1976:1146).

The epigravettian of the MC region also lacks the classic magdalenian and azilian elements (Bartolomei *et al.* 1979). The material from this region was initially subdivided by Laplace (1964). The sequence in the Paglicci cave provides an overview of the general industrial developments (Mezzena and Palma di Cesnola 1972; Palma di Cesnola 1976). A final gravettian in level 18b is followed in levels 18a–17 by an early epigravettian with foliate points. A later stage of the early epigravettian then follows in levels 16–10 where shouldered points (fig. 5.20, l) become the characteristic type fossil. Then comes the evolved epigravettian, and the sequence concludes with the final epigravettian, which is marked by the appearance of backed truncations and triangles. These triangles are a feature of the material from the Romanelli cave and the assemblages of the final epigravettian are broadly comparable to the bouverien of Provence. Other important sites for understanding the final epigravettian in the MC region are the cave site of Arene Candide, Liguria (Cardini 1946) and the very large assemblage at the Grotta Polesini on the Aniene river (Radmilli 1974). This cave has produced 354,000 pieces of struck flint, of which 30,000 are classifiable as retouched tools. These large assemblages are dominated by backed blades, bladelets and points.

Further industrial variation in the Italian peninsula is provided in Bartolomei *et al.* (1979).

At Kastritsa, ME region, the backed bladelets, c.2 cm in length, are also dominant among the retouched tool class. In the upper levels a very few geometric microliths – five triangles, one rhomboid and two trapezes – are present (Bailey *et al.* 1983b). This can be compared with the final LUP in the Argolid site of Franchthi cave (Jacobsen 1976), Greece, ME region, where geometrics are also present but equally rare.

The general trend in the LUP is therefore towards an increase in microlithic backed bladelets as well as the gradual appearance of a variety of geometric shapes. In the earlier phases of the LUP shouldered points and occasionally foliates are found. The bow is presumably present at Parpalló on the evidence of the barbed and tanged arrowheads found in the uppermost solutrean levels. A final feature worth noting is an overall reduction in the size of blades from which the flint tools are made.

(c) geographical variation and regional case studies

The distribution of the solutrean in the mediterranean province confirms that it is an essentially western cultural complex. The magdalenian is likewise concentrated in western Languedoc, Roussillon (Sacchi 1976) and Spain, all MW region, and is not recognised in the MC and ME regions.

A pioneering study of palaeolithic land use and settlement systems was carried out by Higgs (*et al.* 1967; Vita-Finzi 1978) in Epirus, north-west Greece, ME region. This area of high mountains and valleys running parallel to the coast was apparently occupied throughout the LUP, as shown by evidence from excavations at Kastritsa cave (Bailey *et al.* 1983 a, b). This site, located on the edge of a former high level for Lake Ioannina, lies at an altitude of 480 m. It was regarded by Higgs as the summer base camp for a human group that moved in pursuit of the migratory red deer. The equivalent winter base camp was supplied by the rock shelter at Asprochaliko some 40 km south of Kastritsa and located on the Louros river close to the coastal lowlands. It was suggested that the harsher conditions during the glacial period would intensify the environmental differences seen today between the high mountains and the lowlands. Shepherds today use the seasonally available grazing on the Pindhos mountains in the summer, bringing their flocks down to the lowlands in winter (Campbell 1964). It was pointed out by Higgs that the two sites lay close to a present day migration route used by these shepherds. This observation was used to argue that the environmental constraints in Epirus were such that *any* group adopting a mobile strategy would devise a similar exploitation pattern (fig. 5.32). Supporting evidence came from the measurement of cave temperatures (Legge 1972; Higgs and Webley 1971) where it was found that the rock shelter at Asprochaliko was proportionately warmer during the winter, due to the direction it faced and hence the amount of sunlight it received, than Kastritsa.

A re-examination of this seasonal hypothesis and its supporting evidence (Bailey *et al.* 1983 a, b) has shown that the equivalence of the two sites, which is central to the interpretation, is not demonstrated by the evidence they contain. The bone and stone data from Asprochaliko are very small in number by

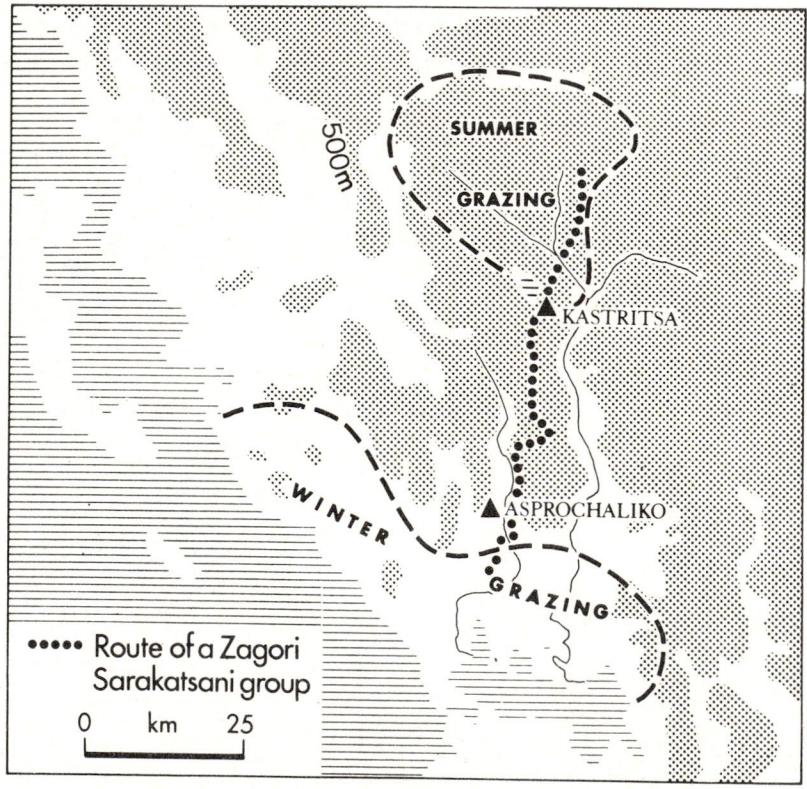

5.32 The seasonal mobility model for Epirus, ME region (Vita-Finzi 1978:fig. 101). The relation of the two cave sites to different seasonal grazing resources, as well as the yearly movement of a modern pastoralist group, is indicated.

comparison with Kastritsa. At Kastritsa red deer does indeed dominate the faunal assemblage, but at Asprochaliko ibex are of equal importance. The two hour site catchment territories are also very different. Asprochaliko is located in a narrow steep sided stretch of the Louros valley and thus well positioned for using local topography to trap game either on the steep slopes or by driving them into the river. Kastritsa on the other hand provides an exceptional observation point over a wide expanse of hunting territory. The re-analysis questions our ability to identify with any degree of certainty a home base in the archaeological record (see Chapter 8). Moreover, the limitation of the original model lay in its insistence on a very simple pattern of seasonal mobility rather than recognising that this aspect of hunter-gatherer behaviour is very variable since it forms their major strategic option in both the short and long term.

A comparable regional model, but employing many more known and excavated sites, was used by Barker (1975, 1981) in an analysis of central Italy, MC region. Here the upland Fucino lake basin, situated at a comparable altitude to Lake Ioannina in Epirus, has a number of sites and a large, well excavated collection of lithic artifacts at the Riparo Maurizio (fig. 5.33). Radmilli (1963) regarded these sites as evidence for all year round occupation of the lake basin by a group of hunters. Barker however points out, using modern shepherd data, that the winters at such altitudes in the Apennine mountains would present serious

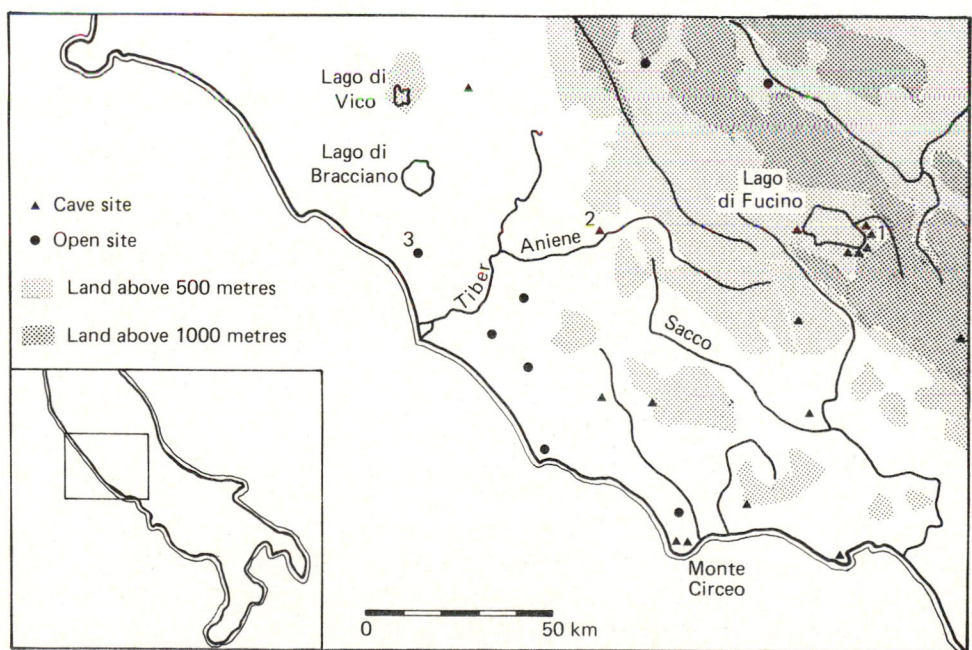

5.33 Settlement patterns around the Fucino basin and Lazio lowlands in central Italy, MC region (Barker 1975:119, fig. 10). 1. Riparo Maurizio, 2. Grotta Polesini, 3. Palidoro.

problems for finding suitable grazing for the red deer upon which these groups depended. He argues instead that in winter both animals and humans would leave the Apennines via the river valleys of the Aniene and Liri and winter on the plains of Lazio. In both upland and lowland areas there are a number of late and final epigravettian sites (Laplace 1964, 1966; Barker 1975, 1981:134–9). The Grotta Polesini is located on the Aniene, and its immediate catchment consists mainly of open plains environment. The large animal fauna is dominated by red deer and the presence of yearlings indicates at least winter occupation. The site is only fifteen minutes' walk downstream from a narrow gorge which could have provided good opportunities for intercept hunting. Barker's interpretation relates two areas within a single economic system and accounts for differences between the lithic assemblages of these areas as related to the different tasks that such seasonal behaviour involved.

Both these case studies employ an integration of on-site data, bones, stones etc., with off-site data, catchments and topography, in order to understand variation in the archaeological record at a regional scale of analysis.

A third case study comes from south-eastern Spain in the MW region, where Davidson (1976, 1980, 1983; Bailey and Davidson 1983) has examined the interrelationships between three cave sites, Les Mallaetes (Fortea and Jordá 1976), Parpalló (Pericot 1942) and Cueva Volcán (Aparicio and Fletcher 1971), within the changing environment and archaeology of a small region in Valencia (fig. 5.34). A consideration of on-site data establishes that Parpalló is the major occupation site in the region as measured by the quantity of stone tools, numbers of occupation horizons, quantities of antler/bone tools and engraved stone plaques. The cave lies at an altitude of 450 m and faces south. The cave at Les Mallaetes is only 3 km distant from Parpalló but lies at 600 m and faces west-south-west, the direction from which blow the cold winter winds (Davidson 1976). The cave at Volcán is located on the present coast.

The on-site seasonality data – antler, ibex mortality information and bird bones – suggests that Volcán and Les Mallaetes were occupied in the summer and possibly spring, while Parpalló was definitely used during the winter. The repeated use of this cave during the LUP is further demonstrated by the great number of hearths within the site, a feature for which there is little evidence at the summer site of Les Mallaetes.

Davidson then uses this three site study to examine the tactical use of particular sites and the exploitation strategy by which they were related. This he does by employing the logistic model of hunter-gatherer mobility (Binford 1980; see Chapter 2). One very clear link emerges between the size of changing regional catchments, due to a lowering of sea levels at 20–17 Kyr, and the impact this has on patterns of regional site density and hence the formation of the archaeological record. Further evidence of the changing regional environment comes from a study of the marine shells found at this inland site. The greatest abundance of these shells comes from levels in the site which correspond to the

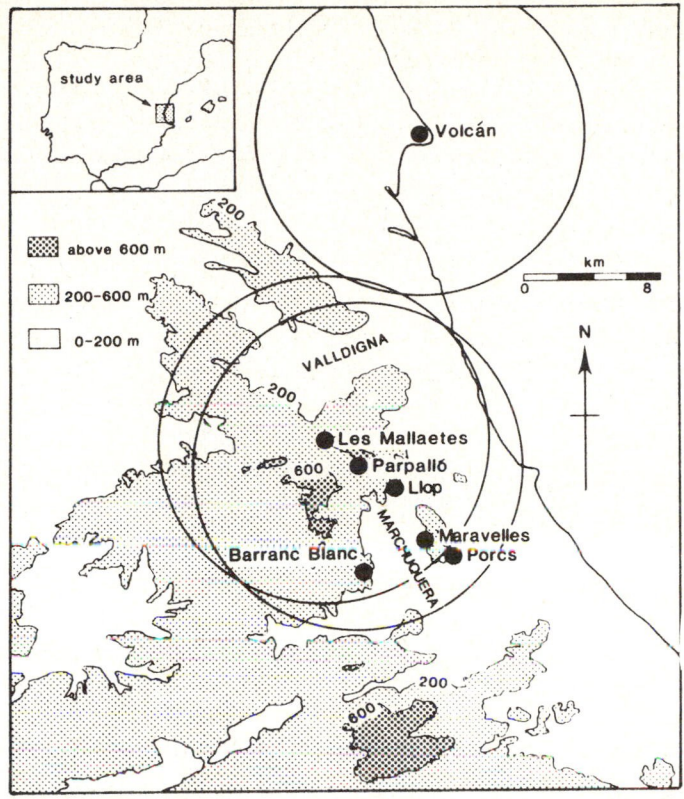

5.34 Settlement patterns in south-east Spain, MW region (Davidson 1983:82, fig. 8.2).

glacial maximum in northern Europe. The changing tactical use of the area by palaeolithic groups and the selection for a logistic strategy at the arid height of the last glaciation can be summarised as follows:

> 30–25 Kyr.　Few sites, and no real integration can be seen between those which have survived.
>
> 25–20 Kyr.　Evidence for the tactical use of sites in a seasonal round with possibly the logistical organisation of activities. This would provide special purpose task sites designed to exploit pinpointed resources in the environment.
>
> 20–15 Kyr.　Extensive visits to a distant sea shore now that the marine regression is at its maximum. The catchment radius of a site such as Parpalló is increased to c.15 km.
>
> 15–10 Kyr.　A reduction in shore visits as sea levels rise even though it is getting closer to the cave. Furthermore there is a reduction in the number of sites as this reduction in site catchment size takes place. Accompanying changes take place in the body part representations of animal species as revealed by the analysis of bone residues and can be interpreted as strategic adjustments to a changing environment and the resources it contained.

(d) burials and art

Parpalló is another site that can be added to the small list of locations with very large quantities of engraved stone slabs (fig. 5.35). These number some 6000 engraved surfaces. By comparison Les Mallaetes has less than two dozen similar artifacts (Davidson 1976, 1983). Small limestone plaques were used at Parpalló, and many are engraved on both surfaces with the sketched outlines of deer, ibex and bovids. Red deer is by far the most common animal depicted on these scratch pads.

The Polesini cave in the MC region has produced a very few engraved pebbles. One very clear design is of a wolf, while a few of the pebbles have also been deliberately coloured. Notched bones, called tally sticks, are also present (Radmilli 1974).

Bone working is known throughout the province and occasionally utilitarian objects are carved and decorated, as with the spear thrower shaped as a mammoth from a middle magdalenian level at Canecaude I, Aude district in the MW region (Sacchi 1976:fig. 7). However, when compared with the profusion of decorated objects from the LUP of the SW and NC regions, the inventory of such objects from the mediterranean province is poor.

Engraved cave walls are known in Sicily. At Levanzo, situated on one of the Egadi islands off western Sicily, a scene involving a number of human figures is depicted. A single engraving has come to light during excavations at the Badanj rock shelter in central Yugoslavia (Basler 1979). It is attributed to the final LUP, since the abri wall on which it was found was covered by epigravettian. The engraving has been identified as a horse and is associated with some signs interpreted as arrows.

Cave paintings occur in Spain, MW region, as at La Pileta (Dams 1978), where fish, a rare subject in palaeolithic art, are to be seen. The site is extremely difficult of access and is some distance from the other cave art sites in southern Spain, located along the Malaga coast. In the high mountains of the south-east of peninsula Spain is the Cueva del Niño (Leroi-Gourhan 1968), with paintings of deer in a shallow abri.

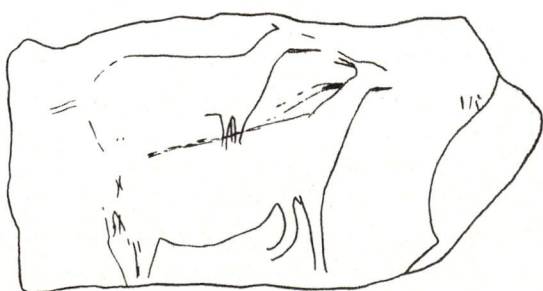

5.35 An engraved limestone slab from Parpalló, level III, showing two hinds (Müller-Karpe: 1966:taf. 161).

Some painted caves are also found in western Languedoc in the Aude river basin, e.g. Sallèles-Cabaradès. Further east, Bayol cave in the Gard district and Ebbou in the Ardèche have important paintings, signs and as yet undeciphered scratches on the cave walls. Ibex, bison, bos and occasionally mammoth, as at Baume Latronne, Gard district, are the most common animals.

Burials are rare. A possible solutrean child burial in a flexed inhumation is known from Le Figuier in the Ardèche (Quéchon 1976). At the Romito cave in Calabria, MC region, three double burials, associated with LUP romanellian/epigravettian flint assemblages have been found (Graziosi 1966). Four burials of similar LUP age are also known from Sicily at San Teodoro (Maviglia 1940; Oakley *et al.* 1971).

Further references

MW: Davidson 1976, 1980, 1983; Bailey and Davidson 1983; Fortea 1973; Fullola 1979; Laplace 1966; Pericot 1942.

MC: Bartolomei *et al.* 1979; Radmilli 1977; Laplace 1964, 1966; Barker 1975, 1981.

ME: Higgs *et al.* 1967; Bailey *et al.* 1983a, b; Brodar 1958–9; Kozlowski, J. 1979.

Summary for periods 3 and 4

(a) chronology

The earliest dates for the EUP came from the northern province at the Geissenklösterle, 36–34 Kyr, for an aurignacian assemblage. Even earlier dates are associated with leaf point assemblages at Kents Cavern and Jerzmanowice. The presence of a strong flake element in these assemblages rules them out as clearly upper palaeolithic collections.

By contrast the earliest C14 dates for EUP assemblages in the other two provinces are all later than 35 Kyr. The single date of >43 Kyr from Bacho Kiro requires confirmation from a full suite of dates.

The aurignacian is widespread by 30 Kyr throughout the northern and southern provinces. It is also found at this date in parts of the MW and MC regions. An early backed blade tradition, chatelperronian/lower perigordian/uluzzian, is found in parts of the NW, SW and MC regions at a comparable date.

Between 26 and 21 Kyr an equally widespread gravettian/upper perigordian tradition is known throughout all the provinces. This has been subdivided into many local and regional facies and sequences.

An important recent finding, confirmed by C14, is that in both the MW and NC regions a number of aurignacian assemblages are found at the very end of the EUP. These findings now give this industrial tradition a chronological range of between 36 and 21 Kyr.

The earliest LUP industries can be dated in the SW and MW just prior to our baseline of 20 Kyr. Within the 10 Kyr of the LUP a significant chronological marker can be seen at c.13 Kyr, corresponding to the advent of the Bølling interstadial in northern Europe and recognised in the division into earlier and later group III sites and industries in the SW region.

(b) industrial groupings

The classic SW sequence from which so many of the typological models and nomenclature are derived has been divided into two main industrial/chronological groupings which correspond to my use here of the EUP and LUP (table 5.14).

Recent work on EUP assemblages has revealed the repeated interdigitation of aurignacian and perigordian assemblages in the SW and MW regions. This is further supported by sediment based dating studies of different sites. One result of this work has been the rejection of earlier models of straight industrial succession which were based on stratigraphic observation alone. These indicated a sequential occupation by the makers of different assemblage types of a small area rather than contemporaneous settlement of those same areas, as recent work has demonstrated.

The gravettian/upper perigordian of 26–21 Kyr, and especially the perigordian V assemblages, contain type fossils which are found widely throughout the three provinces. The extensive geographical areas over which noailles burins, Font Robert points, and, from another tradition, Kostenki knives and hollow based points, are found are symptomatic of the levels of affinity shared by many of the assemblages in these technocomplexes. However from the perspective of the organic model the relationship between these backed blade traditions and the geographically restricted and earlier chatelperronian/uluzzian/lower perigordian assemblages is still debated.

Within the EUP it is worth commenting on the gravettian sites dated between 26 and 21 Kyr. This period sees evidence for elaborate burials – Sunghir, Grotta Paglicci; abundant figurines and carvings of both human and animal figures – Laussel, Dolní Věstonice, Kostenki I/l; large open sites with many thousand pieces of chipped stone – Molodova V/VII, Pavlov, Předmost; as well as rock shelters – Abri Pataud level 3. It is very noticeable that the more spectacular of these sites, in terms of quantities of material, occur in the northern province and the SW region.

The LUP industries display some novel forms of flint working, as with the bifacial pressure flaking in the solutrean. This may have involved heat treating the cores. A further development is the selection of better quality lithic sources, as shown in the increasing use of the flint from the Holy Cross mountains in Poland (Chapter 7).

The trend in lithic reduction strategies is towards economising on the use of these raw material sources. This can be seen in the greater production of small, often backed, bladelets and microliths in the magdalenian and epigravettian assemblages. These elements designed for hafting no doubt contributed to the efficiency of technology by reducing size and weight and making the business of repair and recycling of a bow based hunting technology much simpler.

Throughout the upper palaeolithic bone/ivory and most importantly antler projectile points are found. Many other tools were presumably hafted in either wooden or antler hafts which have since decayed. Needles are definitely found in the LUP.

(c) geographical variation and regional case studies

The north European plain provides a barometer for measuring the ebb and flow of settlement during the 25 Kyr of the upper palaeolithic. The plains remained unoccupied from 35 to c.15 Kyr. Below these northern plains in the NW and NC regions there is a hiatus in occupation between 21 and 17 Kyr. These upland and plains areas were recolonised after 16 Kyr with the onset of deglaciation. The SW and NE regions provide ample evidence for continued occupation during this period of maximum glaciation. Moreover there is evidence from all three mediterranean regions for occupation at the same period. However, even within these areas with evidence for settlement at 18 Kyr, there is also at a smaller analytical scale evidence for local breaks in settlement histories. This can be seen for example in the case study from the Pyrenees.

Several of the case studies I have reviewed point to an increase in the number of sites that are known between the earlier palaeolithic, prior to 35 Kyr, and the EUP. In most instances the EUP site inventory is also smaller than that for the LUP. The increase in known LUP sites is generally interpreted as a rise in population related to the ameliorating conditions linked with deglaciation (but see Chapter 8).

An alternative explanation cites the enhanced survival potential of these later sites, an observation apparently borne out by the remarkable preservation of spatial patterning at sites such as Pincevent and Les Etiolles, NW region. Furthermore the recovery of many more LUP sites in the mountains of the MC and Alpine regions as well as from the Pyrenees may well reflect this factor.

The conclusions from the palaeoeconomic studies often stress that specialisation on particular animals occurred. Horse and reindeer were the two common staples in the northern and southern provinces, while red deer, often combined with ibex, dominates in the mediterranean. This circumstance, shown by the large mammal bones, is accompanied in many regions by an apparent broadening of the subsistence base to include such 'costly' resources to harvest as shellfish, rabbits, snow ptarmigan and fish (Chapter 8).

(d) burials and art

The decorated caves are restricted, with only a few exceptions, to the SW and MW regions. They are predominately LUP in date. Mobiliary art is widespread throughout the continent but examples are much more common in the NW, NC, NE and SW regions. For some items, e.g. Venus figurines, the stylistic conventions which governed their design were very rigid. As a result very similar figurine forms, confined to a comparatively restricted time bracket, have been found over large areas of Europe. A large proportion of the known mobiliary art is also dated to the LUP. Recent finds of sites with many thousands of engraved stone slabs and plaquettes have now modified our views of both the content and the contexts in which palaeolithic art was executed.

Burials are not common. However in the periods 26–21 Kyr and after 13 Kyr there are several which contain both a variety and a quantity of associated grave goods.

A comparison of periods 1 & 2 with periods 3 & 4

The evidence I have discussed above points to the conclusion that however many sub-divisions of the palaeolithic period may be favoured (and being a lumper rather than a splitter I have used only four), there are essentially only two major technological groupings. These contrast an earlier palaeolithic (lower and middle) with the upper palaeolithic. What therefore is different? For the moment I want to concentrate upon the bulk of the evidence, the chipped stone, and how it has been analysed. The other features of the palaeolithic record are discussed more fully in the following three chapters.

One major difference lies in the standardisation of the upper palaeolithic material. There is both a level of affinity in the composition of assemblages and a predictable character to the appearance of type fossils that is lacking in the earlier palaeolithic traditions. The type fossils in the upper palaeolithic do define some sort of chronological position. They can act as a reference point for building culture historical groupings. For example if you pick up a handaxe during fieldwalking the best you can say is that it is earlier than 35 Kyr. The shape and size may lead you to go further and place it either before or after the last interglacial but without much guarantee of chronological accuracy. However if you picked up a Font Robert point it would be possible both to define its chronological position with some precision, just by looking at it, and furthermore to infer the general characteristics of the assemblage from which it came. While the discovery of assemblage interstratification and con-temporaneity has added a further dimension to our understanding of the upper palaeolithic, it is nonetheless still possible to use terms such as aurignacian as a convenient shorthand and know that a chronological period towards the beginning of the EUP is being addressed.

By contrast as absolute dates become available for the earlier material, periods

1 & 2, we find all sorts of erratic patterning; at least as judged by the expectations of the traditional organic model of cultural evolution. For example earlier notions of crudely flaked industries preceding finely flaked during these two periods have now gone by the board. This can most clearly be seen with the blurring and demise of any sensible distinction between the lower and middle palaeolithic in Europe. I would not be surprised to find, as more dates become available, that other cherished chronostratigraphic schemes for the cave mousterian of the early last glacial will also fall victim to the yardsticks now being provided by isotope decay.

The crude/fine model has also been applied to the upper palaeolithic, where judgements have been passed on the qualities of lithic workmanship. Hence the magdalenian has on occasion been regarded as the nadir of flint knapping in the upper palaeolithic, while the solutrean is championed as a golden age. Paradoxically, the achievement of the magdalenian cave artists is often heralded as the true golden age of prehistory, after which the European populations entered something of a cultural trough with the onset of the post-glacial.

These judgements should not be allowed to get in the way of assessing the evidence in terms of variation and differences in adaptive behaviour, even though such assessments are only alternative value judgements. My impression is that the pre-35 Kyr industries do have patterning; but I suspect that very little of this is related to sequential, organic, progressive change as the culture historical models maintain, but rather to the organisation and distribution of population in the landscape.

With the post-35 Kyr industries and assemblages I suspect that what we are looking at is the operation of more constraints on the formation of the archaeological record. This applies not only to the selection and manufacture of stone tools but also very importantly to the places in the landscape where they were discarded.

The difference between the earlier and the upper palaeolithic is therefore not just one of finer chronological resolution due to a shorter time span. The typologies and lithic taxonomies that I have discussed here are picking up significant behavioural differences between the two periods. At the very least they are measuring, through such different shaping of the archaeological record, the degree to which selection was now beginning to hone behaviour. Although this process is still poorly understood, we can see that it led to greater repetition and predictability in such aspects as assemblage composition.

There is nothing new in such a statement. We have now however come as far as the culture history approach, with its intuitive appeal to explanation, will let us. I have examined the space/time framework and the analytical units that people it. Whether we can proceed beyond such a framework and instead of just noting significant changes and guessing at their significance, begin to account for them, is the next problem. The groundwork for tackling such a problem was set out in Chapters 2 and 3 and it is now time to return to it as an alternative framework.

CHAPTER 6

SPACE AND SUBSISTENCE

The history of the . . . galaxy is one of idealism, despair, struggle, passion, success, failure and enormously long lunch-breaks.
Douglas Adams, *Life, the Universe and Everything* (1982)

Introduction

The organisation of the last chapter might have given the impression that the regional model I favour has some impact on all aspects of the palaeolithic record. Should we expect, for example, each province to have a distinctive record of stone tool assemblages, faunal material and site plans? If I had drawn the boundaries 'correctly' would each region then emerge as forming a unique cultural unit which might be claimed as its regional adaptive signature? If this had happened I would have been both surprised and suspicious. The reason is quite simple. My regional model was not designed to make sense of the taxonomies and typologies of the culture history approach that I have reported on so extensively in the last chapter. While any fit between the model and the data I have reviewed might plausibly suggest a causal relationship it has to be remembered that the model was not designed to be measured by data presented in this manner.

However, any such disclaimer for the regional model is hardly necessary. When placed against such a framework the data presents a classic polythetic set (Clarke 1978), with regions sharing traits as measured by type fossils, animal species, figurine forms, fossil evidence and all the other constituent elements of the European palaeolithic data set. The purpose of dividing up Europe into three provinces and nine regions according to ecological principles was done solely to provide a framework for the investigation of past behaviour and not to try and hammer some sense-after-the-event into the systematics that have formed the backbone of the discipline since its inception.

Neither do I expect that there would be a monothetic set of traits which would vindicate the choice of regional units if we were to employ a different set of attributes from the available data. Precise geographical partitioning is not something I expect to occur under the systematic transformation of common behavioural principles and processes by ecological constraints. There will be many aspects of past adaptive strategies that look identical in all nine regions. One such example is provided in the first part of this chapter, where the formation of patterns in camp site data is examined. The questions being asked are very simple: what sort of behaviour generates such repeated patterns and how might we use these observations to understand something about the past?

The second aspect of spatial signatures looks at the concept of tool kits, which has on occasion been regarded as a key concept in a behavioural approach. Food residues are also included within a general consideration of assemblage formation. I would expect that, as our understanding increases of the content and creation of such cultural residues, more patterning against the regional model will become apparent. For the moment the patterning is still obscure, and this section points to alternative attributes to measure rather than providing firm conclusions.

The investigation of settlement systems should also show some clear patterning against the regional model. The case studies mentioned in the last chapter form the basis for discussing alternative sampling strategies and ways of looking at the palaeolithic landscape as suggested earlier (Chapter 2).

Camp sites

Camp site, living site, settlement site are all common descriptions of what basically are dense patches of cultural debris. There may be special features such as pits and quantities of bones which suggest that we are dealing with a clump of material where people lived rather than carried out activities. However, we need to be careful to avoid pre-judging any analysis by the descriptive terms we apply to the material being studied. In the first instance I shall ask the simple question of how these patterned clumps are created, rather than using their different contents to construct any elaborate site typologies.

At one level the question can be easily answered. The dense patches are created by discard behaviour. What is of more interest are the contexts under which such elementary human behaviour takes place. These include activities such as eating, talking, food preparation and manufacturing of tools. None of these activities are restricted to a home base but could and do occur at many different types of site where the principal purpose might be looking for game, collecting plant foods, visiting allies or engaging in group rituals. The number of people involved and the frequency with which a location is visited and these activities occur are obviously critical variables in determining the density of the patches as well as the patterning they show on the ground.

It is worth noting in this context that very little of the spatial patterning of materials among hunters has anything to do with the activity of 'hunting' as generally conceived by archaeologists. Hunting, if it describes anything, describes the mode of production and not what I am interested in here, the mode of discard.

(a) individual patterning

Freeman has provided us with a simple and yet important observation that provides the key to a considerable amount of the patterning in our patches of cultural materials (1978a:113):

A stationary individual can conveniently reach an area of two and one half to three square meters, and this dimension is related only to stature and reach, which vary within a limited range among European populations of genus *Homo, living or extinct* [my emphasis].

The smaller measurement describes the area in front of an individual seated on the ground, while the larger also includes the area that can be reached behind. Adjustments could be made for different height and reach but can then be applied, as Freeman notes, to *Homo erectus*, Neanderthals or even *Australopithecus*, irrespective of other factors such as cranial geometry and the intelligence capacity of the brain thus contained. You can check the dimensions for yourself. While doing so notice how the area that can be easily reached forms an arc due to the mechanics of the arm and shoulder. These mechanical principles serve as a strong constraint on the way residues are, and hence were, created. The result is a spatial pattern with known spatial dimensions that forms an elementary yardstick for measuring and interpreting aspects of the static palaeolithic record. A strong basis for inference is therefore provided.

A further experimental approach has been carried out to observe the spatial distributions of lithic materials (fig. 6.1). This has found that the dispersion of materials follows predictable patterns according to the object being made and the position of the knapper (Newcomer and Sieveking 1980).

The objects being made in this experiment were core axes of neolithic type (as well as the preparation of nodules for blade production). The scatters of lithic debris that these produced were accurately plotted. The knapper either sat on the ground, sat on a chair/low bench, or stood. With each increase in height the resultant scatter pattern became more diffuse (1980:figs. 3, 7, 8). The seated scatters were very small in extent, ranging between 20 cm^2 and 50 cm^2, while knapping an axe from a standing position produced a scatter over 6 m^2 and some of the debris extended even further. When making axes in a sitting position the debris formed a compact circular arrangement (fig. 6.1, a). However, when striking blades a very different pattern resulted. The scatter was less compact and formed an arc around the 45 cm high chair on which the knapper sat (fig. 6.1, b). The blades were placed to the right of the chair and the knapper's leg divides the scatter in half. This reflects the process of nodule preparation where work on the core was done holding it on the outside of the thigh, while platform preparation and blade removal were done holding the core between the legs.

Arc patterns arising from a seated position and of comparable dimensions can be seen in the plans from Bénagu (fig. 6.2) and at the Petersfels (Albrecht 1979:39). Dense scatters associated with seated positions can be seen in M

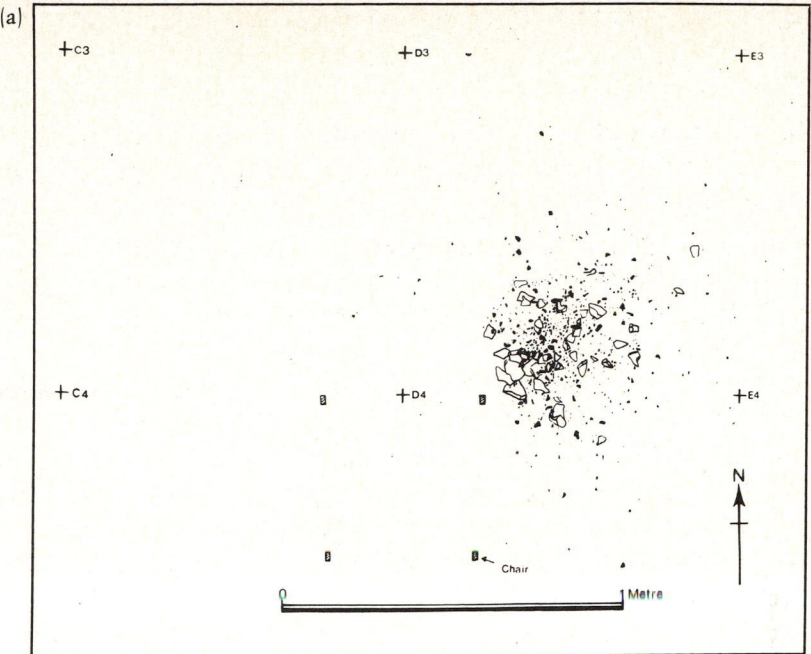

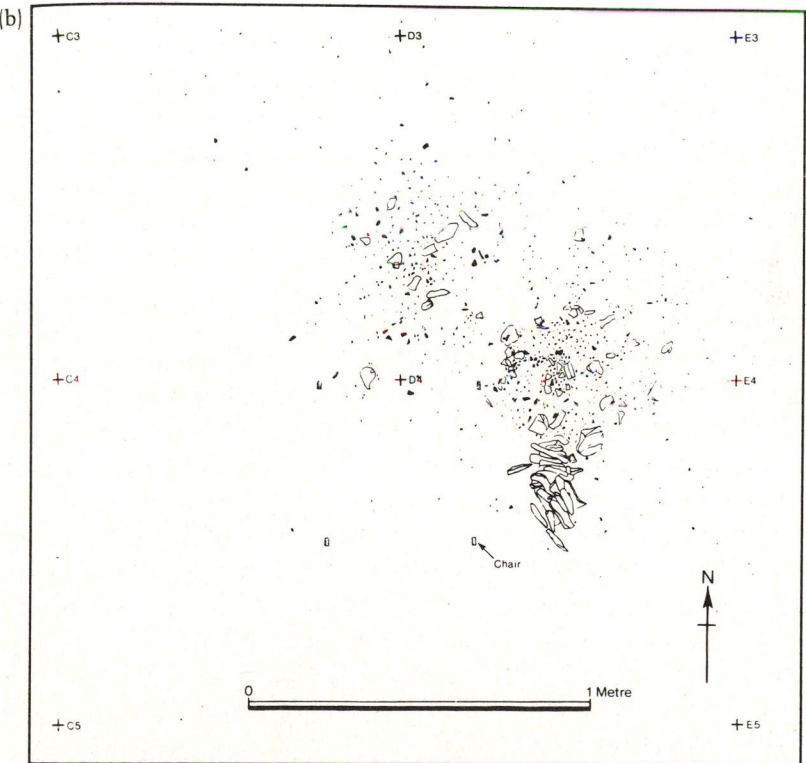

6.1 Flaking experiments. (a) scatter pattern from making an axe roughout using hard hammer only from a 45 cm high chair; (b) scatter pattern from making blades from a 45 cm high chair (Newcomer and Sieveking 1980:347:figs. 3 and 4).

6.2 Chipped stone scatter at the site of Bénagu (Marquet 1975:311, fig. 4). The scatter can be divided into three areas. In the east are cores and large debitage associated with blade production. In the metre square in the centre of the scatter there were retouching flakes from implement manufacture while in the western metre square there was a concentration of burins, apparently made and discarded in that area (black = burins; hatched = cores).

square A7 at Les Etiolles (fig. 5.19) where 3000 flakes and blades were found. These were separated from an arc of cores. A similar pattern can be seen in M square Q13, and both can be compared with the patterns in flaking experiment 4 by Newcomer (fig. 6.1, a).

The use of large stone blocks as seats can be seen in the site plans from Pincevent I (Leroi-Gourhan and Brézillon 1966, 1972) where they were placed next to two of the three hearths (fig. 6.6). Cave B in the Weinberghöhlen at Mauern (Bohmers 1951) has a seat associated with a dense lithic scatter in M square 326. Finally, but from outside Europe, a deflated surface site, D 27B, in the Negev desert, Israel, has some 60 unretouched blades as well as other tools laid out in a neat arc in front of a stone seat (Marks (ed.) 1977:fig. 6.5). The area covered by the scatter is 1.5 m^2.

At the excavated site of Les Tarterets I (Schmider 1975) there are two flint scatters within an area of 40 m^2. The southern scatter is grouped around a hearth and the conjoining flake information reveals only a small dispersal of blades and debitage away from the discarded cores. The northern scatter (fig. 6.3) shows a much greater dispersion and no obvious association with a hearth. One possible interpretation of these different patterns may be that in the northern scatter

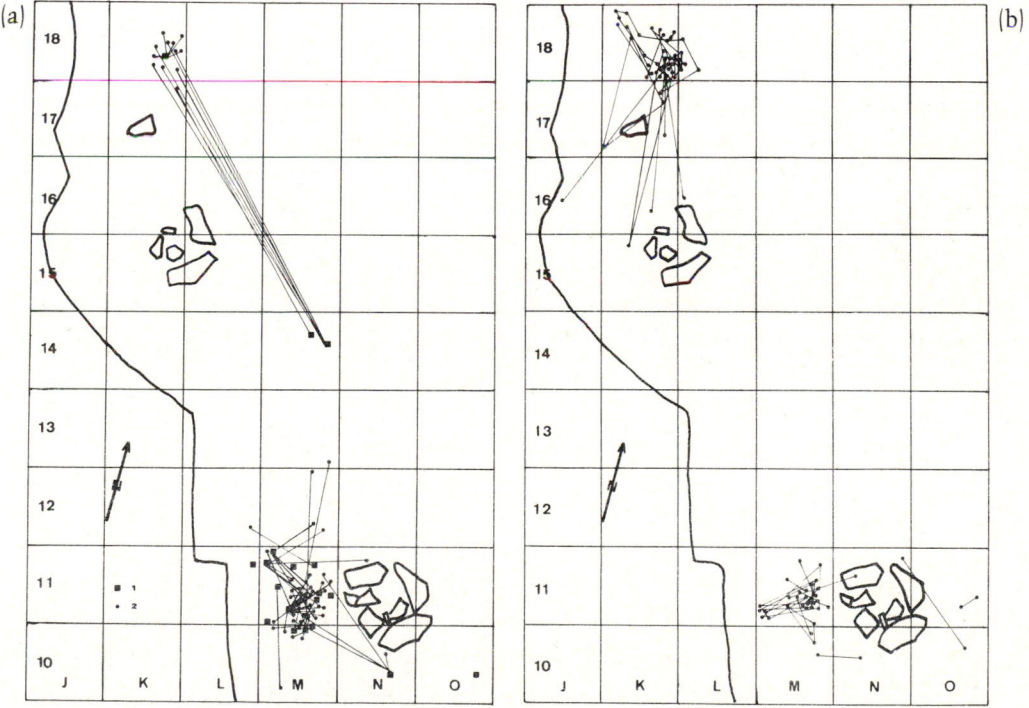

6.3 Conjoining flake patterns at Les Tarterets: (a) distribution of cores (1) and the flakes (2) struck from them; (b) refitting between debitage elements other than the flakes refitted to the cores (Schmider 1975:330, figs. 13 and 14).

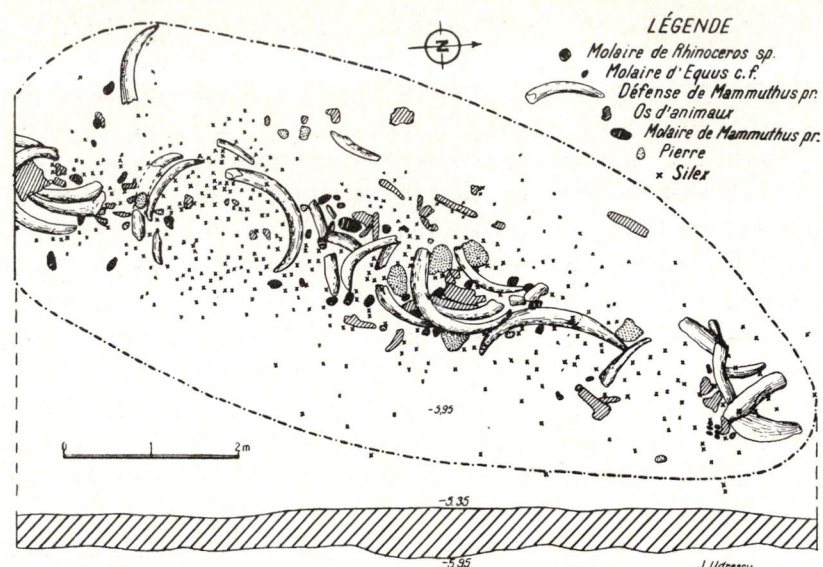

LÉGENDE
● *Molaire de Rhinoceros sp.*
• *Molaire d'Equus c.f.*
Défense de Mammuthus pr.
● *Os d'animaux*
◖ *Molaire de Mammuthus pr.*
◦ *Pierre*
× *Silex*

J. Udrescu

6.4 A possible windbreak on the open steppes of the Prut river at Ripiceni-Izvor. The semi-circular bays are of sufficient size to accommodate a sleeping man. Note that there are no hearths associated with this structure (Păunescu 1965:fig. 19).

knapping took place in a standing position, while in the southern the worker was sitting by the hearth.

The study of flint scatters by refitting the struck pieces back onto the nodules provides a direct measure of the degree of dispersal, as in the above example. Other studies include LUP sites from Poland (Schild 1975, 1976, 1979) and Germany (Reisch 1974) as well as for the earlier palaeolithic at Clacton (Keeley 1980:fig. 60), Rheindahlen (Bosinski 1973a) and Terra Amata (Villa 1982).

The size of the human body also imposes constraints on the construction of windbreak shelters for sleeping behind. A possible example comes from the multi-level loess site of Ripiceni-Izvor in Roumania (Păunescu 1965) where in complex I, interpreted by the excavator as a ritual structure, mammoth tusks and molars had been laid down to form a frame for a windbreak and which allowed for variable wind direction from either east or west (fig. 6.4).

(b) multiple users

The analysis of camp site patterning can very profitably be examined with the help of a seating plan model where a number of people are grouped around a hearth. Once again I would expect such a basic activity to be a feature of sites bearing labels as diverse as hunting sites, ceremonial locations, home bases and overnight transit camps.

One model is provided by Binford's (1978b) study of the Mask Site. This was a hunting stand where Nunamiut hunters gathered to wait for game. Detailed information over a four day period is available and concerns the number of men using the site, the range of activities that went on there, how the space was utilised and the materials left behind. The major activities at this hunting stand were eating, talking, playing cards, sleeping and watching for game. Some craft activities took place, hence the name of the site.

There were five hearths at the site, not all lit at the same time, and advantage was taken of some large boulders to act as windbreaks. The distribution of material left behind can best be understood in terms of a seating plan model (fig. 6.5) where five people were comfortably accommodated around a hearth. Materials were discarded in two main areas. A drop zone right where the person was sitting, and a toss zone where larger objects were thrown. The difference in the sizes of materials between these two zones has obvious implications for archaeologists observing distributions of material on palaeolithic camp sites. Materials in the Mask Site drop zone included small bone chips from marrow

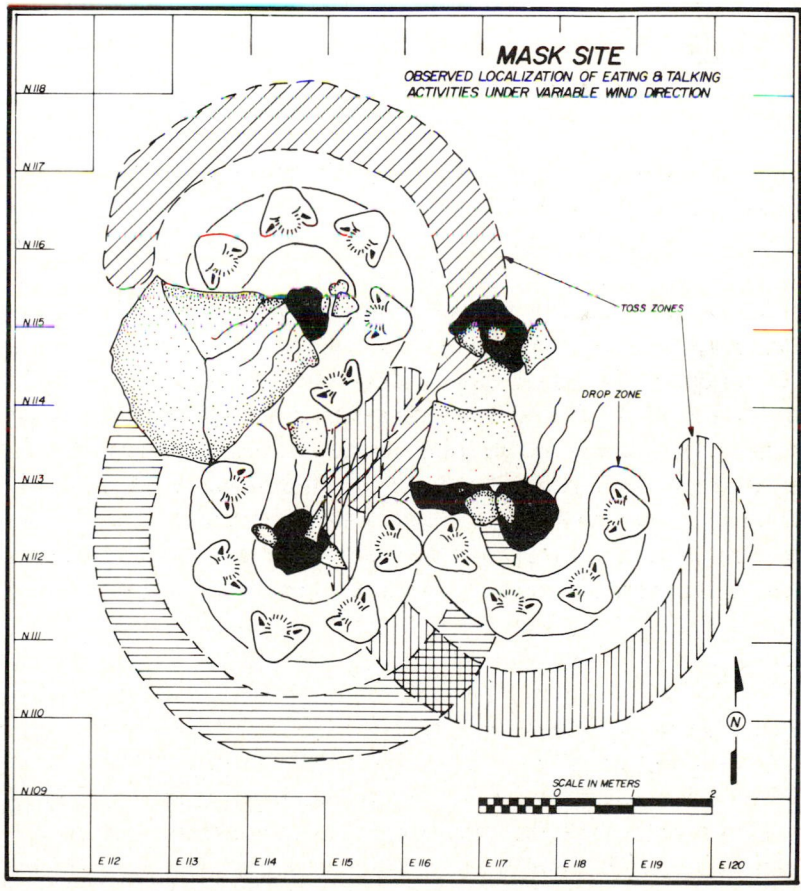

6.5 A seating plan model derived from observations of eating and talking that took place under variable wind conditions (Binford 1978b:340, fig. 5).

cracked bones and wood shavings from working on the masks. The toss zone contained tin cans and the large articular ends of bones. The items of equipment that archaeologists might expect to find in order correctly to classify the site as a hunting stand – rifles, binoculars – were of course taken away. Some rifle cartridges were found, but these were the result of target practice rather than hunting. Other items such as playing cards and a kettle were cached on site for future use. This would be expected, in line with the curatorial principles of Nunamiut technology.

The arrangement of personnel around the hearths combined with the pattern of discard produce very clear semi-circular spatial distributions of residues. The dimensions of these distributions are also important. If we take the hearth as a focus we find that the outermost edges of the toss zone lie some 2.75–3 m from the centre of the hearth, giving an overall diameter of c.6 m. Moreover, the centres of the major hearths at the Mask Site are spaced some 3 m from each other. Both these dimensions can be understood in terms of such simple factors as the size of the human body and the spatial geometry that multiple users of a common facility, in this case a hearth, produce when engaged in the common-place social activities of conversation, eating, passing the time and throwing things away.

Elsewhere comparable dimensions have been noted for seating plans. For example Hayden (1979a:161) also views the hearth as the key with which to break down camp sites into more manageable analytical units. Around the central hearths in his contemporary Australian examples, stone and bone debris was generally scattered within a 5–6 m radius (1979a:166). Wiessner (1974) also records that the !Kung debris scatter was in the order of 3–6 m around hearths.

Archaeological examples of the 3 m spacing rule are common. In all instances the spacing of hearths is accompanied by semi-circular rings of debris (as shown in fig. 6.6, a). The material around the single hearth at Verberie (Adouze *et al.* 1981) shows (fig. 6.6, b) a particularly striking demonstration of a drop zone around a hearth – zones II and III on the plan – while the dimensions of the toss zone strongly suggest that many of the other separate units identified by the excavator – zones IX, IV, VII, VI and V – should also be considered in relation to this feature. Information about the sizes of flint and bone waste between these possible drop and toss zones would help such an interpretation.

The 3 m spacing principle is repeatedly shown in the multi-level site of Molodova V (Chernysh 1961; Fentum 1983). The mean spacing between the

---

6.6 Plans of bone and stone distributions around hearths: (a) Pincevent I showing details of two of the three hearths with clearly marked drop zones. Notice the c. 3m spacing between the centres of the hearths and the positioning of the seat to allow for variable wind direction (Leroi-Gourhan and Brézillon 1966); (b) Verberie, showing detail of area 201–202. Zone I on the plan is the hearth and II the drop zone around it (Audouze *et al.* 1981:109, fig. 7); (c) The interpretation of the Pincevent data as hearths inside tents. This explanation of the patterning is also favoured by the excavators at Verberie (Leroi-Gourhan and Brézillon 1966).

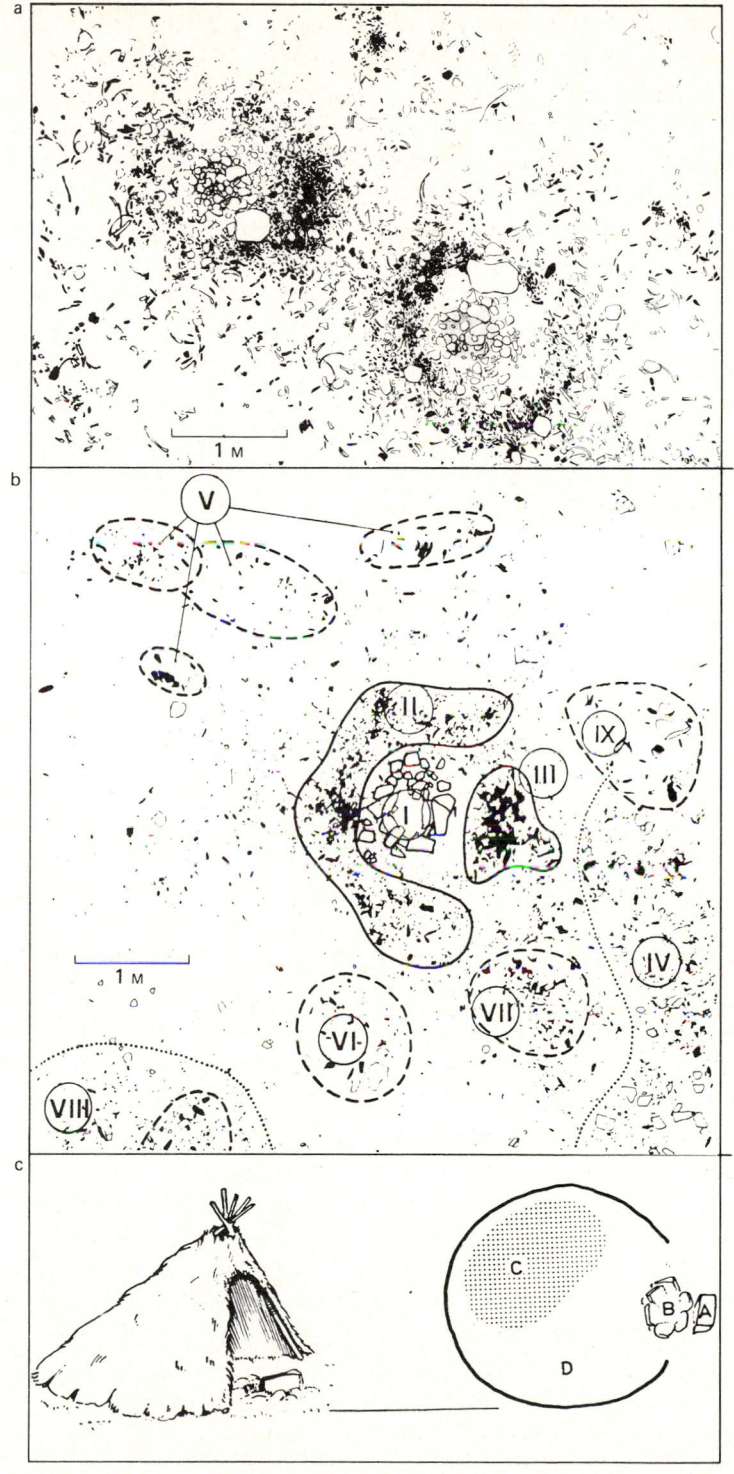

mid-point of hearths in the upper palaeolithic levels is 2.99 m, and an inspection of the site plans reveals that many of the hearths are also associated with semi-circular distributions of bone and stone debris that also conform to the dimensions of the seating model with its toss and drop zones.

Several of the examples I have just cited have been interpreted as the archaeological remains of tents and houses (Sklenář 1975, 1976). The most influential of these interpretations is the reconstruction by Leroi-Gourhan and Brézillon (1966) of circular tents around the three hearths at Pincevent I (fig. 6.6, a). Their interpretation has been followed by many (Simek and Larick 1983) where the excavated patterns have been probed with sophisticated statistical techniques. An alternative interpretation, based on an understanding of the behaviour that produces such patterns in the archaeological record, interprets the same data as indicating outside hearths (Binford 1983:fig. 92) positioned to allow for variable wind direction, a factor borne out by the placing of the stone seats by two of the hearths (fig. 6.6, a).

An example of the influence of the Pincevent model is provided by Campbell's study (1977:73–5, fig. 50) of excavated flint distributions at the LUP site of Hengistbury Head (fig. 6.7). The large stone cores, >200 gm, were interpreted by Campbell as possible tent weights for a circular construction around the two principal hearths. Notice how the mid-points of hearths two and three lie 3 m apart and that the 'ring' of cores/tent weights lies on a diameter of 6 m. In other words the Hengistbury pattern conforms to a seating plan model where the heavier elements are found in a toss zone at some distance away from the hearth. Campbell in fact considered this toss zone explanation but finally decided on an interpretation of deliberate placement for these heavier objects, while maintaining that the smaller lithic debris could be explained as being either placed or tossed *inside* the tent structure.

Further examples of the 3 m spacing principle between hearths can be found in the plans of Kostenki I/l (Efimenko 1958; Klein 1969a), Pavlov I (Klima 1954, 1959), and Lubna II in Poland (Prošek 1961). Several of these hearths are associated with shallow scooped hollows and other features which strongly suggest, as in the case of elaborately built hearths at Verberie, Les Etiolles and Pincevent 36 (Perlès 1976), that these were open-air facilities which were re-used over many years, as indeed was the case with the Mask Site.

Similar repetitive behaviour can be observed in the constrained environments of caves and rock shelters. At Veternica (Malez 1958–9) it appears from the plan that the same place in the mouth of the cave was repeatedly used to position the hearth. The mid-points of the two hearths at Lazaret cave (H. de Lumley 1969c) are 3.5 m apart while the distributions of materials, so well recorded by de Lumley and interpreted by him as evidence for a tent within the cave, could equally be interpreted as semi-circular toss and drop zones around the west hearth (fig. 6.8).

Hearths were also places where many different activities were carried out by

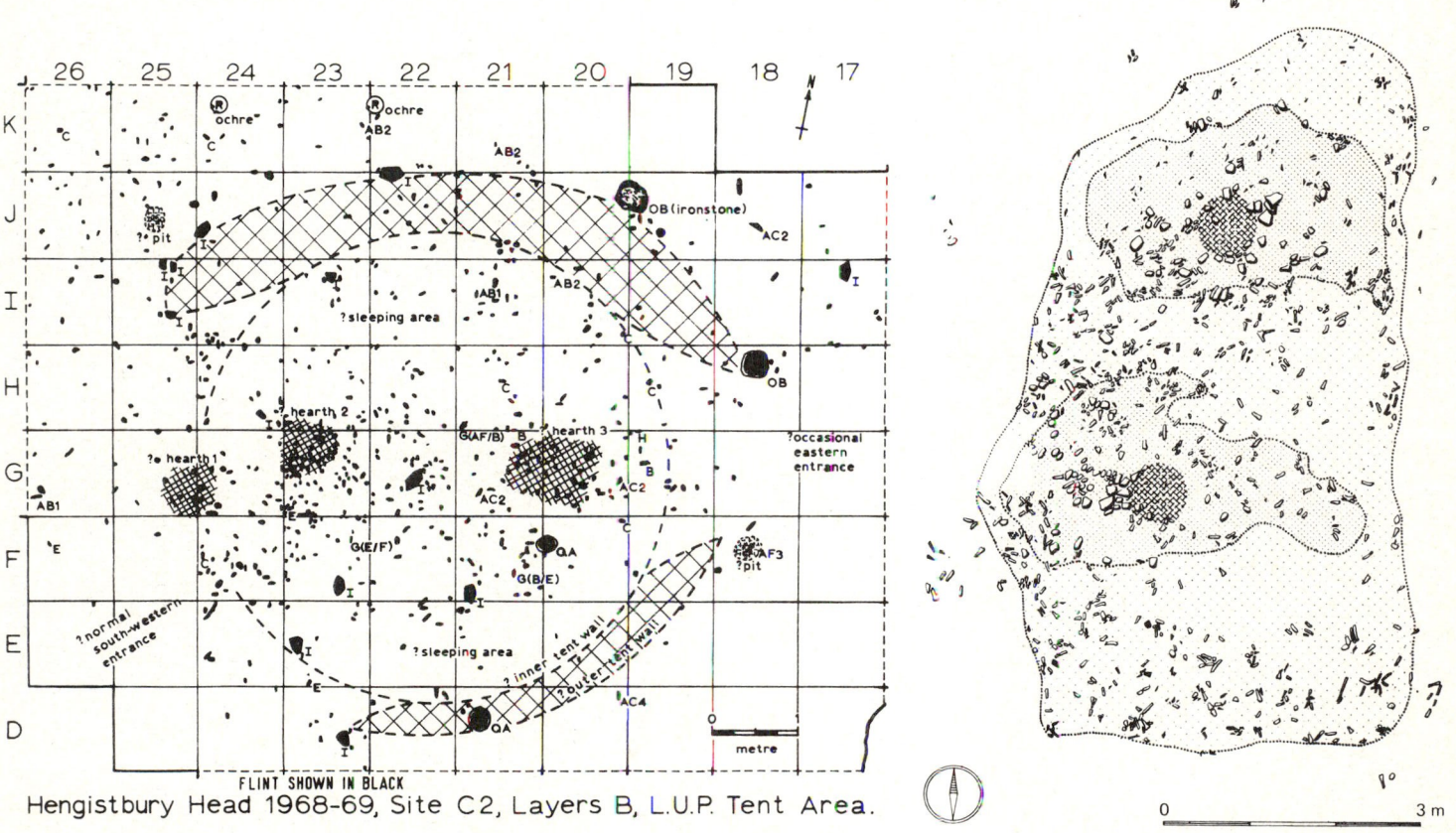

6.7 3 m hearth spacing and associated drop and toss zones of cultural debris: Hengistbury Head (Campbell 1977:fig. 51); Lubna II (Prošek 1961:fig. 90).

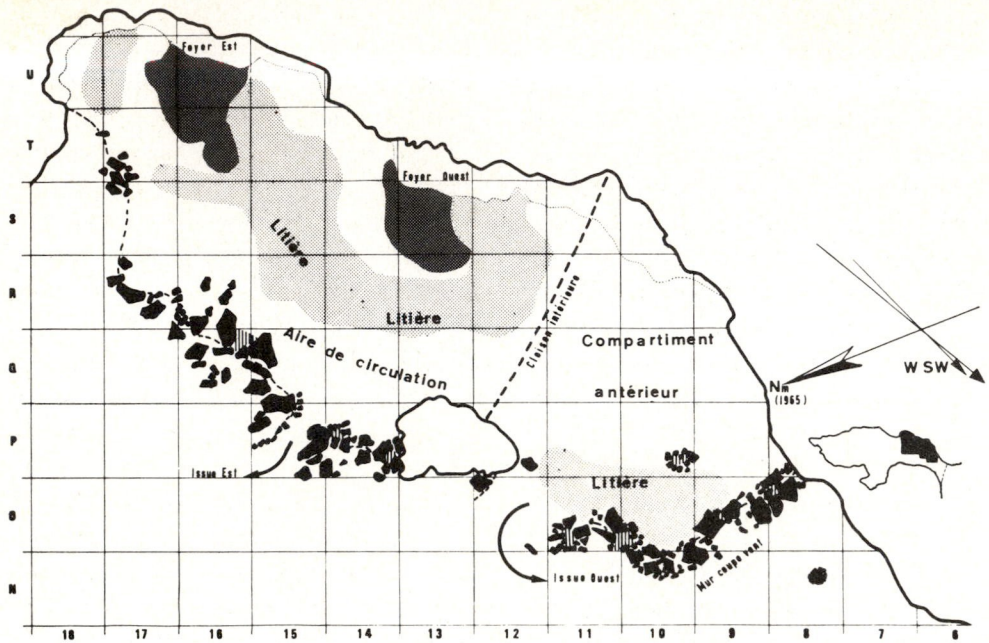

6.8 Distribution of bone and lithic debris around two hearths (*foyer*) in the Lazaret cave, MW region. The hearths are located near the back wall of the cave (H. de Lumley 1969c).

multiple users. The outside working hearth is a case in point. Examples include the excavations at Lommersum (Hahn 1974, 1977), Corbiac (Bordes 1968b), and cave entrances as at Grotte du Renne (Leroi-Gourhan 1961) and Salpêtrière (Escalon de Fonton 1966). The hearth was not only there to keep the worker warm but also on occasion formed an important part of the manufacturing process. This has been shown by recent experimental work on pre-heating flint as a preliminary step for certain flaking techniques such as solutrean pressure flaking (Robins *et al.* 1978; Bordes 1969; Crabtree and Butler 1964; Collins 1973; Price *et al.* 1982). Heating the flint up to 300° C improves the working properties. Changes in the texture and colour of the flint can be detected in archaeological materials.

A further multiple user situation is provided by the use of hearths in sleeping arrangements. The spacing between hearths is generally less than 3 m, as ethnographic examples show (Hayden 1979a; Gould 1968, 1971; Clark and Walton 1962). The dense scatter of closely spaced hearths at Kostenki XI/1a (Praslov and Rogachev (eds.) 1982), Molodova V levels VI and VII, Molodova I/4 (Chernysh 1961; Ivanova and Chernysh 1965; Goretsky and Ivanova (eds.) 1982) is most probably a result of the use of these circular windbreaks of mammoth bones as unroofed sleeping sites. Certainly some of the hearths are located in the walls of the structures, and such positioning would not be expected if this were a house, as many people have suggested. Examples of hearths in windbreak/sleeping sites are shown in Binford (1983:fig. 68).

The patterned distribution of cultural material in caves and rock shelters has long been recognised (Collie 1928). Several arrangements of close packed hearths running parallel to the back wall of the rock shelter may be interpreted as sleeping arrangements with beds placed between the hearths (Binford 1983:figs. 97, 98). An example of this is provided by the excavations in level 3 at the Abri Pataud (Movius 1966, (ed.) 1975, 1977) where five regularly spaced hearths were interpreted by the excavator as the remains of a longhouse, since such regularity was once thought to occur only *within* a structure. Ethnography reveals that this is not the case. Several other tents in caves have been claimed as at Grotte du Renne (Leroi-Gourhan 1961), Lazaret (H. de Lumley 1969c) and the Brillenhöhle (Riek 1970, 1973). No doubt if the sleeping areas and hearths recorded by Clark and Walton (1962) from a rock shelter in southern Africa had been excavated in Europe a tent or hut would have been reconstructed from the regular spacing. The spacing is however to be understood in terms of the spatial requirements of a sleeping person or persons and the micro-climate of the rock shelter which determines where best to put a hearth to maximise heat retention in the rock wall. A further, practical, consideration against finding tents in caves, even in ice age Europe, comes from the Nunamiut who when asked about such behaviour replied as follows:

You go to a cave or rockshelter so you don't have to carry a tent, why go there and climb over the rocks, be away from the willows, and have to carry your water if you have a tent. (Binford 1978a:489–90)

Rock shelters provide excellent facilities for overnight stops. If they are to be visited on a hunting trip then bulky, heavy equipment like a tent can be left behind. The tactical use of such facilities in a mobile strategy strongly suggests that one profitable way to approach their excavation and analysis is as sleeping sites.

(c) huts and houses

So far I have been looking at alternative, and I believe more economical, explanations for the patterning in camp sites excavated by archaeologists. I have shown that in some instances the strong patterning can be understood in terms of simple principles – body size and the way people are seated around hearths. I prefer this approach to understanding patterning in the palaeolithic record to one where the patterns are classified, ordered and interpreted without any reference to the sorts of dynamic behaviour which produced such static residues. Such an approach is presented in Sklenář (1975, 1976), where the published interpretations of huts, tents and houses are accepted uncritically and from which elaborate but useless classifications spring.

However it would be equally unwise to accept the 3 m spacing principle as a sort of palaeolithic 'yard', applicable to all sites at all times. A brief glimpse at a wider ethnography (e.g. Yellen 1977a) reveals many other possible 'magic' distances and spacing relations. Moreover we must be absolutely certain about one point; hearths 3 m apart cannot always be interpreted as hunting blinds! All we can say is that if conversation around hearths combined with throwing things away are common features of behaviour at a hunting blind then the patterning we have looked at should form a component in the archaeological structure of that site. It will also form a component in neolithic, iron age, medieval and contemporary hunting blinds on a Scottish grouse moor, and in many other 'sites' where such behaviour – sitting, talking, discarding – occurred. None of this behaviour is an exclusive property of the palaeolithic, although there may not be too many busked burins and marrow cracked bones in the Scottish example! In the same way I would expect to find examples of the 3 m principle in sites from all nine regions and three provinces in my regional model. However I can imagine that the archaeological signature of camp sites would be very different if we were examining an adaptive human system that had fire but no language. While the semi-circular seating plan is determined by factors such as keeping warm it is also strongly conditioned by the mechanics of small group verbal communication. It is most probably in ways such as these that the archaeological record will inform us about such non-preservable traits as the appearance of language, rather than by trying to reconstruct the voice boxes of fossil hominids in order to infer their relative levels of speech competence (Lieberman and Crelin 1971; Lieberman 1976).

The above discussion may however lead you to think that we are never going to find a palaeolithic tent, hut or winter house even though we strongly suspect that they did exist. There have certainly been many claims. Interpretation is difficult because the presence of such permanent facilities is generally associated with behaviour involving clean-up strategies (Binford 1983). As a result the circular patterns we have encountered in open locations may not be found. Rubbish tends to be dumped rather than dropped or tossed. Moreover, houses are much more than just artifacts providing warmth and shelter. They carry ancillary information about the size and the organisation of family units. Their architectural form is therefore not entirely constrained by utilitarian requirements (Morgan 1965). The contents of the excavated structures may also refer to a phase in their use when they had passed out of service as dwellings and instead served as unroofed locations where rubbish was dumped.

The size of the structure does however provide a possible starting point for stronger inference. Small compact houses insulated with turves and heated either by oil-burning lamps or bone/wood fuel would be an important adaptation to glacial conditions. The construction would also be substantial since these houses would be re-used over many years.

Some impression of size can be gained from the work of Arctic archaeologists working with recent Eskimo and prehistoric sites. Here the findings are that winter houses are often comparatively small in size, 3–9 m^2 (Osgood 1940:303; Binford 1983:fig. 121), and highly variable in construction depending upon the availability of raw materials and especially upon the frequency with which an excavated pit formed part of the house design. Moreover, villages consisting of several such houses and store houses are commonly found (e.g. Oswalt and Vanstone 1967; McCartney and Scholtz 1977).

Larger subterranean winter houses measuring 40 m^2 are described in detail by Osgood (1940:310) for the Ingalik, while Binford (1983) provides information about the excavation of one Nunamiut house which covered 31 m^2 in area. An ethnoarchaeological study of Crow Village, Alaska (Oswalt and Vanstone 1967) plotted five semi-subterranean, square and rectangular plank built houses. These ranged in size from 12 m^2 to 24 m^2. The largest structure in the village was the ceremonial Kashgee that measured 41 m^2 in plan.

These observations should make us cautious in uncritically accepting claims for houses based on the ground plan evidence from such sites as Kostenki I/1, c.46 m^2, and Molodova I/4, at 42 m^2. The interpretation that several of the pits at Kostenki I/1 were indeed habitation pits (Efimenko 1958; Klein 1969a) is more probable according to the single criterion of size. Habitation pit A was dug to a maximum depth of 1 m and covered, albeit in irregular outline, an area of 8 m^2. The contents of the pit included mammoth tusks, scapulae and pelvis bones which it has been suggested formed the collapsed superstructure.

Kozlowski (1974) claims at least two hut constructions made of stacked mammoth mandibles and long bones from Spadzista Street B at Krakow in Poland. Although heavily disturbed by solifluction processes, the circular ground plans of two huts c.2 m in diameter could be reconstructed. He points out that the nature of mammoth bone as a building material limits huts to a maximum diameter of 2.5 m. Some of the bones had been deliberately embedded in the ground and the presence of tusks, interpreted as roofing elements, suggests a height of 1.5 m for these small structures. However, whether they are huts or store houses is still open to question.

The circular pile of 385 mammoth bones at Mezhirich (Pidoplichko 1969) covered a shallow depression containing a hearth and measuring c.5 m^2 in area (fig. 6.9). Similar sized constructions of stacked mammoth bones are found at Mezin hut I, 4 m^2 (fig. 6.10), and Yeliseyevichi, 3–4 m^2 (Pidoplichko 1969). Several larger structures have been examined at Berdyzh, 27 m^2, Dobrani-chevka, 12.5 m^2, Gontsy, 24 m^2 and Tel'manskaya horizon 1, 23 m^2 (Klein 1969a, 1973).

A larger structure which should also be considered is the so-called winter house at Dolní Věstonice (Klima 1963) that was partly dug into the hillside and enclosed at the maximum some 28 m^2. The effective floor area is more in the order of 13 m^2.

A tented structure has been reconstructed at Gönnersdorf (Bosinski 1979b).

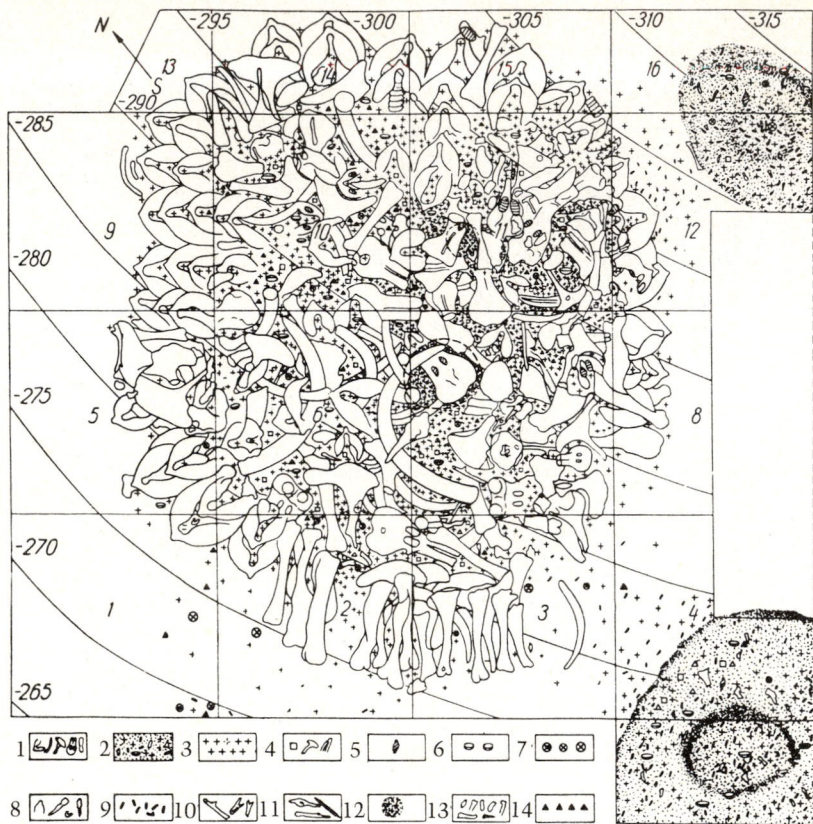

6.9 A possible hut at Mezhirich, NE Region, constructed from stacked mammoth mandibles and long bones and roofed by ribs and tusks. Two outside working hearths are associated with the structure (Pidoplichko 1969:121, fig. 43).

Key: 1. bone ruins of the dwelling; 2. hearth stamping places outside the dwelling; 3. flint articles and flakes; 4. bones with traces of treatment and bone articles; 5. sea shells; 6. stones (granite, flint nodules); 7. pieces of red ochre; 8. bone statuettes for cult purpose; 9. pieces of bone coal; 10. a reindeer antler; 11. bone articles for hunting purposes; 12. a hearth place inside the dwelling (square 7) and grinding place for flint treatment (square 11); 13. bone fragments of the mammoth and other animals in hearth stamping; 14. amber and pieces of amber.

Excavations in 1968 found part of a substantial oval structure of some 20 m². The oval was defined by substantial postholes and the interior was apparently paved with slate slabs, many of which were engraved. This oval area was also covered in red ochre materials which may have been rubbed into the skins that formed the tent covering. Many stone tools and fire cracked quartz lumps were found in the structure and refitting experiments do point to a definite barrier since most of the joins are within the oval. Around the hearth area was a mammoth femur which probably formed a prop on which cooking skins were hung and into which the pot boilers, heated in the fire and now represented by fire cracked rock, were put.

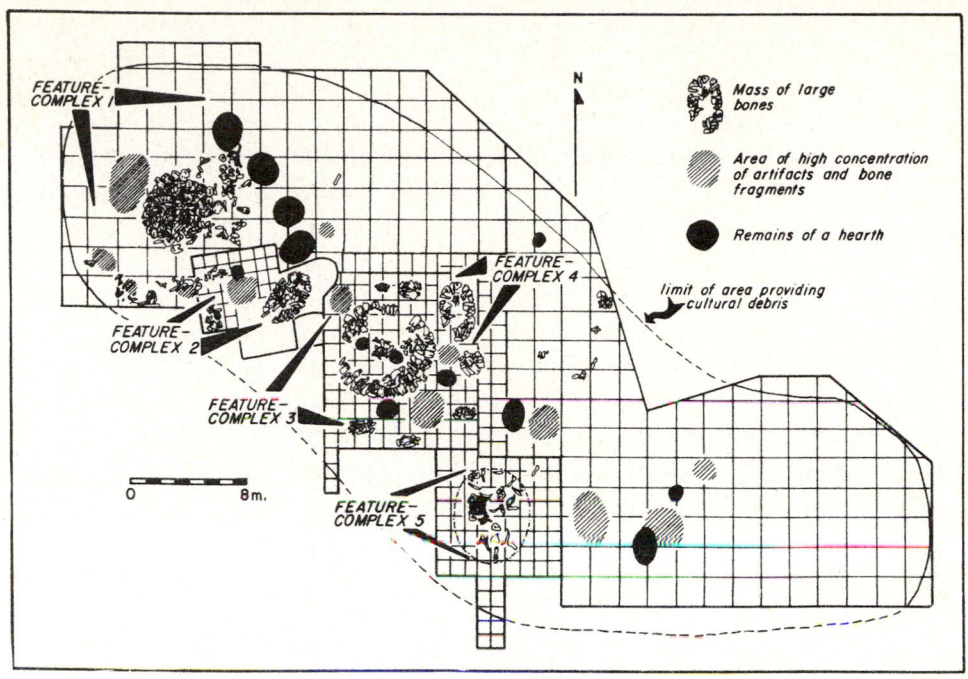

6.10 Mammoth bone structures and hearths at Mezin, NE region (after Shovkoplyas 1965:fig. 15; Klein 1973:97, fig. 20). The association of outside working hearths with the structures can be compared with those at Mezhirich (fig. 6.9).

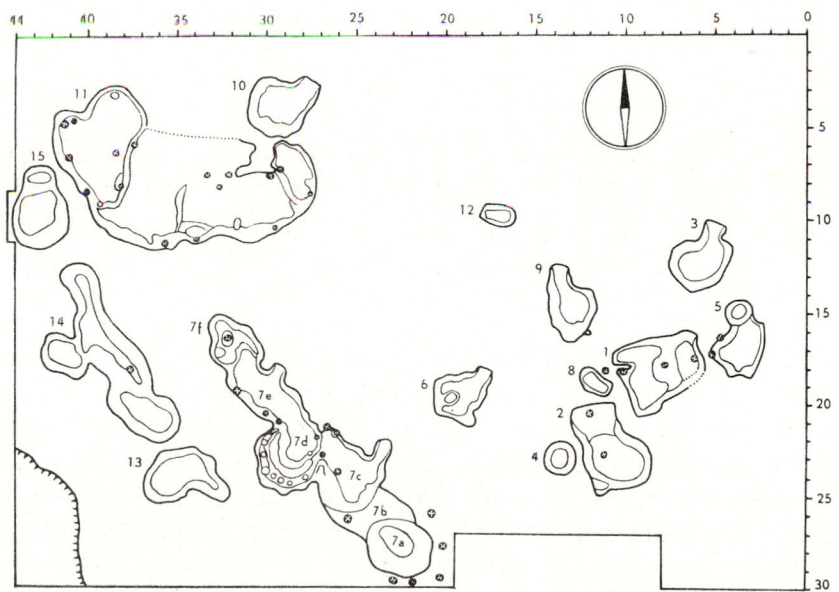

6.11 Pit hollows at Barca II (Bánesz 1968:20, abb. 9). The features have been divided into complexes: I = pits 1, 2, 4, 5, & 8; II = 7; III = 10, 11; IV = 13, 14, 15. Postholes associated with the features are marked.

A further group of dwellings has been claimed at the open sites of Barca (Bánesz 1968), Tibava (Bánesz 1960) and Witów (Chmielewska 1961), where irregular shaped hollows were dug into soft substrates such as loess. Inside these pits are found hearths and small quantities of stone tools. At Barca there are two main excavated complexes separated by 450 m. Barca I has three pits, while the second complex has some fifteen recognised pit features from a total excavated area of 1300 m^2 (fig. 6.11). Pit 7 in Barca II is an irregular feature some 18 m long and between 2.5 and 3.5 m wide. The pit feature was scooped out to a depth of between 40 and 80 cm. Postholes were found both inside and outside the feature. These were of varying depths and surface dimensions. The reconstruction by Bánesz (1968:204) sees a single hut-like structure with two entrances and a number of distinct internal compartments. The quantities of chipped stone within these pit features are very small. Bone was not preserved. There are no traces of hearths in the Barca II hollows although these have been described at Barca I.

The work of Gaussen (1980) has brought to light a number of LUP open sites in the Isle valley, Périgord. These are most notable for the pavements of stone cobbles and slabs which form a variety of shapes. At Le Cerisier the area covered by such a pavement is c.13 m^2 and rectangular in outline. Artifacts have been found along the two long edges of this ground plan and there is an absence of material away from the pavement area. In all cases the area so crisply delimited by the pavements of cobble-stones is small – Guillassou 7 m^2 and 1 m^2, Le Breuil 1, 3.5 m^2, Le Breuil 2, 4 m^2, Plateau Parrain, 12–15 m^2 (fig. 6.12). Gaussen has interpreted them all as the ground plans of tents, though why the interior of the tents should be 'paved' with large round cobbles is not entirely clear. The sites serve as a reminder that the study of settlement archaeology in the European palaeolithic is comparatively recent and much investigation is still needed, since our expectations of site complexity and organisation have also only recently been raised by the input of ethnoarchaeological studies (Binford 1978 a, b, 1983; Yellen 1977a).

(d) other pattern makers

The previous examples are almost all from excavated sites where the integrity of the material is high. A measure of this can be gained by refitting flakes and blades to cores (Audouze *et al.* 1981; Schild 1975). This has been undertaken on many of the sites already mentioned. It is also the case that the majority of these sites are upper palaeolithic in date, which no doubt has contributed to this fact of high integrity since they have not been subject to so many repeated processes of destruction.

Refitting flakes can however be used to test for the integrity of much older material (e.g. Isaac 1981b), as has been done at Clacton (Singer *et al.* 1973). When such observations are combined with the geological evidence for low velocity

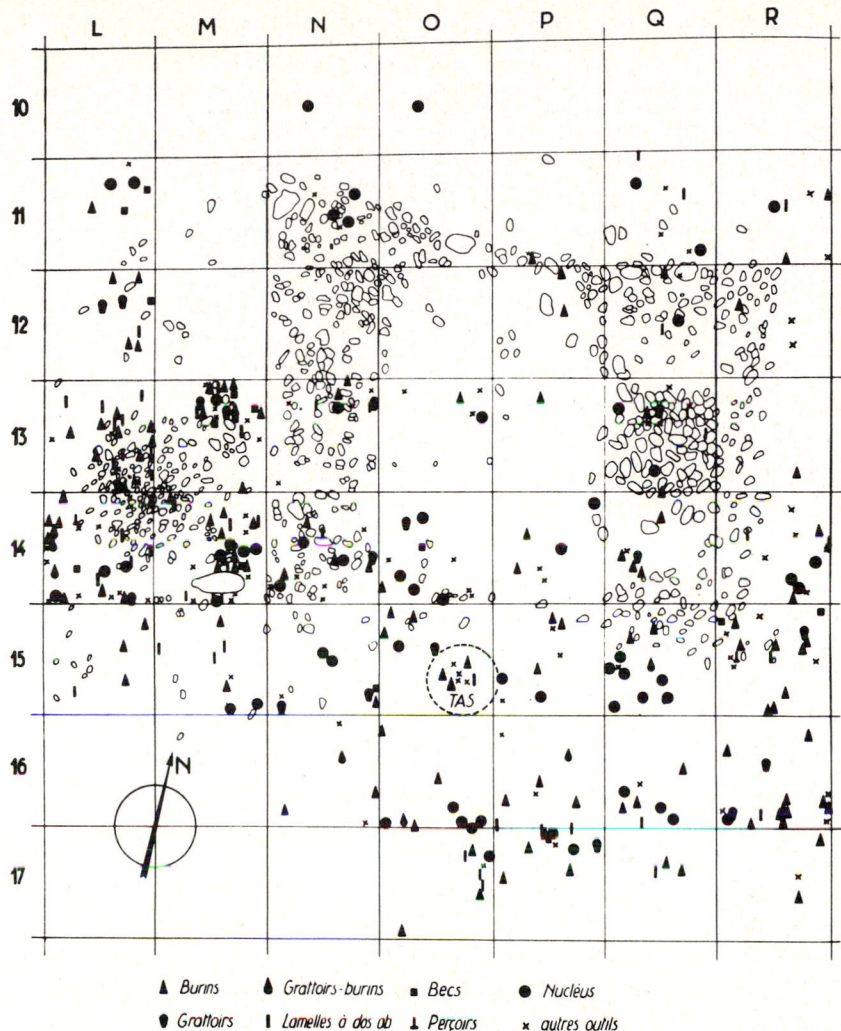

6.12 Plateau Parrain. The stone pavement forms a roughly rectangular shape and the majority of tools lie outside it (Bordes and Gaussen 1970:316, abb. 58).

riverine and lacustrine environments an important measure is provided about the degree of site disturbance. Further indication of these processes can be gained from looking at the degree of abrasion and rolling on artifacts (Wymer 1976). However, the spatial patterns of artifacts from such sites may still be difficult to interpret, and this is due, in part, to our present lack of suitable models to unlock the behavioural significance of such low density distributions.

Relatively undisturbed, high integrity sites from the earlier palaeolithic are rare. It is more common to find, as at the beach site of Terra Amata, that the refitted flakes reveal a site of much lower integrity than initially suspected by the excavator (H. de Lumley 1969a, 1975). In a careful study Villa (1976–7, 1982) has shown that from 232 groups of refitted flakes no less than 40% were refits of flakes found in different stratigraphic levels. In most cases this represented a vertical displacement of 20 cm and raises the general point that the movement of material through sediments due to solifluxion, cryoturbation, animal and earthworm burrowing is often much greater than is commonly allowed (Wood and Johnson 1978). In the case of Terra Amata these considerations call into question the reconstructions of brushwood and reed cabins that sprang from the excavator's conception of the material as lying in situ. In fact the single plan from this multi-level site shows a low density scatter of bone and stone (H. de Lumley 1975, 1976e) that is comparable to a fluviatile deposit such as Torre in Pietra (Piperno and Biddittu 1978), or a scatter of material in a loess deposit as at Achenheim (fig. 6.13) (Thévenin 1976).

Fluvial transport can dramatically affect the clustering and orientation of material, and this has been noted by Kleinschmidt at Salzgitter-Lebenstedt (1953), where reindeer ribs and antlers had been reorientated according to the strength and direction of the stream flow. At the same site a bison skull provided a convenient shelter behind which small mammal bones accumulated. A similar situation can be seen in the stream channel site of Aridos where an elephant shoulder blade provided a break in current with the result that a pocket of microfaunal bones was able to accumulate (Santonja *et al.* 1980:fig. 20). Water sorting may also account for the orientation of elephant bones at Torralba (Howell 1966; Freeman and Butzer 1966). In Villa's opinion we should regard *in situ* archaeological sites as the rare exception and 'unless proven otherwise, layers and soil should be considered as fluid, deformable bodies through which archaeological items float, sink or glide' (1982:287).

These considerations will of course make the archaeological interpretation of spatial patterns more complicated than is sometimes assumed. Research is now beginning into the effects of particular processes (Rick 1976; Wood and Johnson 1978), and palaeolithic applications include Siiriainen's work (1977) on particle movements in rock shelter deposits, and observations on solifluxion and cryoturbation distortion on bones and stone artifacts from Rörshain and Lommersum (Camden and Hahn 1977; Hahn 1976c), while Cheetham (1976) considers in general outline the impact of different hydrological regimes on fragile archaeological sites.

Spatial patterning can also be produced by carnivores. The distribution of bones on the surface of the Grotta Guattari (Piperno 1976–7:fig. 5) might be interpreted as a palaeolithic 'living floor' with ritual overtones, since a neanderthal skull was also found lying upturned on the same surface. However, the gnawed animal bones that also littered this surface and the composition of the anatomical parts of the prey that were represented all argue that this was a hyena den. Consequently, the spatial patterning of the bones, including the skull, should perhaps be interpreted as the result of carnivore behaviour.

A loess site near Basel contains heavily gnawed animal bones and hyena

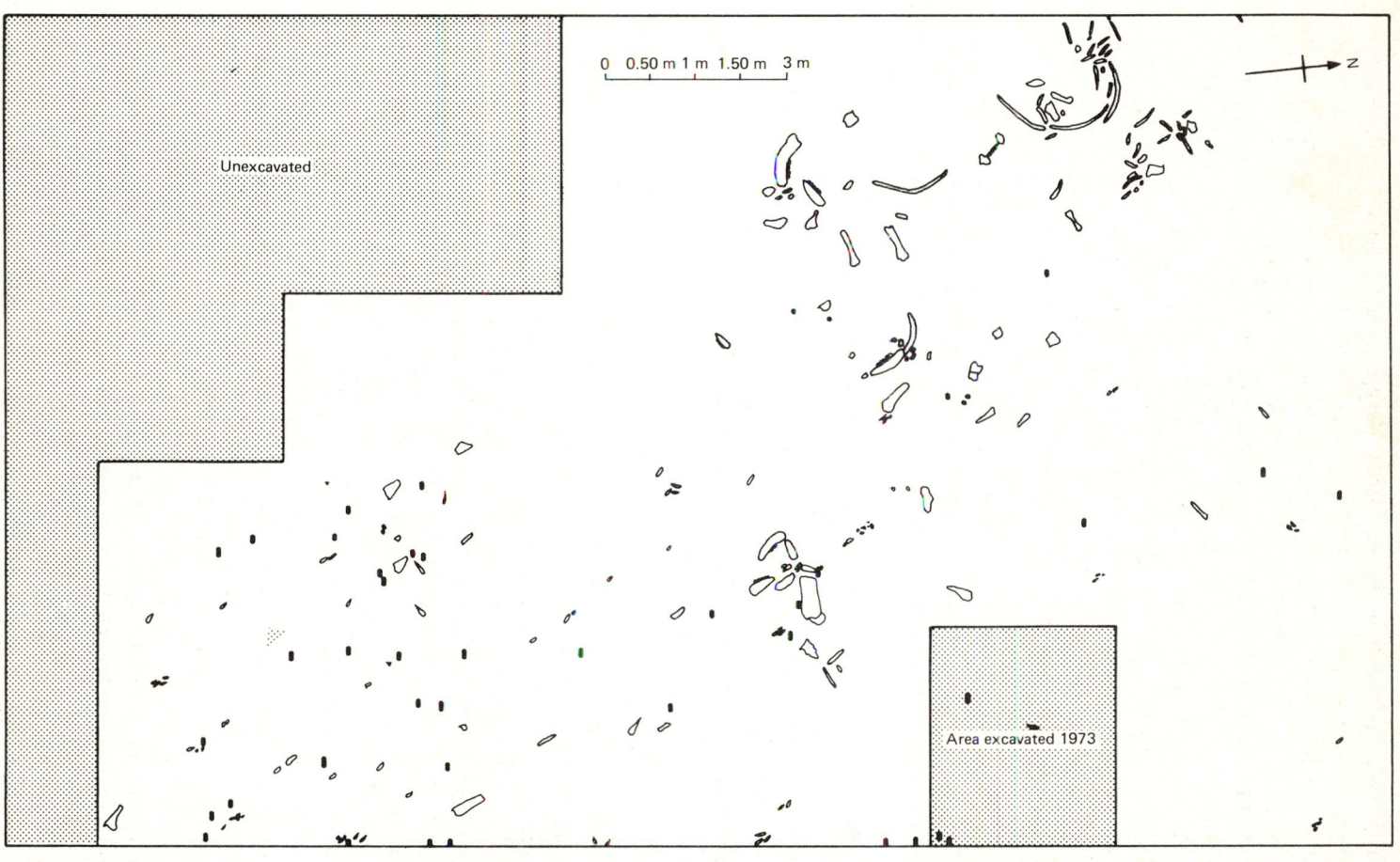

6.13 Low density distribution of bone (horse and rhino) and stone tools in the Achenheim loesses, Sol 74 (Thévenin 1976: fig. 3). The excavators (Thévenin and Sainty 1974) have interpreted this deposit as a butchery site.

coprolites (Schmid 1976). The lack of any human presence in the site left the excavator in no doubt when attributing the hyena as the agent which not only accumulated the bones but also was responsible for their clumped spatial distribution. In other instances, e.g. in caves (von Koenigswald 1975), such distinctions are more difficult to make, since the spatial separation of human and carnivore activity has became blurred in a palimpsest of residues. Indeed many of the accumulations of large animal bones in both loess and fluviatile contexts are probably due to natural mortalities in these localities where bones were covered quickly and hence have a good chance of survival. Examples would include the mammoth 'cemeteries' of Siberia (Vereshschagin 1974) and the many finds of elephant and mammoth from the rivers of Europe (Toepfer 1957; Kowalski 1959; Dawkins 1869; Kahlke 1975).

However, the incorporation in the same deposits of human fossils and artifacts has led to the frequent claim that *all* the material is there as a result of human activity alone. Zeuner (1959) claimed this for deposits at Mauer and Taubach, while recent work at Ehringsdorf (Steiner and Wagenbreth 1971:fig., p. 58) draws similar conclusions between the presence of man and the occurrence of rhinos in the travertine deposits. The association may in many cases be the result of mechanical rather than human activity and needs to be investigated first before conclusions about human behaviour such as hunting preferences are made from such associations.

Tool kits and food residues

So far I have dealt only with the shape of the patterns and not with their contents. A number of techniques have been applied to both the strongly patterned sets (Kintigh and Ammerman 1982; Simek and Larick 1983) and to less obviously structured data (Newell and Dekin 1978). The approaches have been partitioning exercises searching for 'behaviourally meaningful' archaeological units by employing techniques of spatial analysis to search for 'theoretically meaningful patterns in spatial data'. These 'look-see' strategies are matched by studies analysing patterns of covariation in the contents of artifact and ecofact assemblages (McBurney 1968, 1973). The aim here is to look for patterns of association between items which, if found, can then be used as a basis for interpretation. For example, a high correlation between backed points and fallow deer becomes an interpretation that these were the projectiles used to hunt this animal. We shall see below that this is a rather simple conception of how the archaeological record was formed.

The aim of such studies is however to search for statistically robust patterns as a step towards interpretation. This approach to analysis is well demonstrated by Freeman's (1978a) spatial study of assemblages from the Spanish site of Torralba. As a first step he searched the bone and stone tool data with univariate and multivariate techniques to isolate significant *clusters* of material. This

Table 6.1. *Groupings of 'uniquely' determined variables by factor from the occupations at Torralba (Freeman 1978a:Table 5)*

Bifaces (handaxes and cleavers) were found to be partially determined variables associated with factors 1 and 3.

	Interpretation (1978a:86–8)
Factor 1 Perforators/becs Elephant skull fragments	useful sharp-edged probes to get edible material out of cranial passages
Factor 2 Utilized flakes Unretouched flakes Unworked equid limb Bovid footbones	bones possibly used in the production of the unretouched lithics, or residues of operations involving fine slicing with the stone flakes
Factor 3 Denticulates Bovid skull fragments Cervid limb fragments	as Factor 1. The deer bones might have been used as hammers to break open the skulls. (Partially associated handaxes also favoured for this heavy-duty role)
Factor 4 Endscrapers Sidescrapers Elephant teeth Unworked tusk Worked tusk Elephant scapula, pelvis, vertebrae Equid skull fragments, scapulae, vertebrae Cervid scapulae	scraper edged pieces may be the tools used to strip flesh from large bones in the initial butchery stages.

involved a form of factor analysis (principal co-ordinates with rotation). The four factors are shown in table 6.1. The second step in Freeman's analysis is to transfer these observations into a spatial context, to see if the clusters *clump*. The aim is to discover whether items from different clusters also display different spatial distributions (1978a:89). Freeman argues that this would help to determine the existence or not of activity-specific tool kits organised into activity specific areas (fig. 6.14). This appears to be the case for some of the factors in the Torralba occupations where modal values of c.15 and 25 m^2 were found in discontinuous areal distributions (1978a:93). Elsewhere (1975) Freeman has provided a detailed account of activity variation within the excavated area at Torralba using these techniques to provide an objective basis for partitioning the palaeolithic record into units which are apparently of behavioural significance for early man. The study makes the assumption that other agencies – hydrological or carnivore – are not responsible for any of the patterning in this marsh site.

This study is also instructive about the concept of a tool kit and an activity area. The former term came to prominence as a result of the Binfords' (1966, 1969) study of mousterian assemblages where the five variants were analysed in

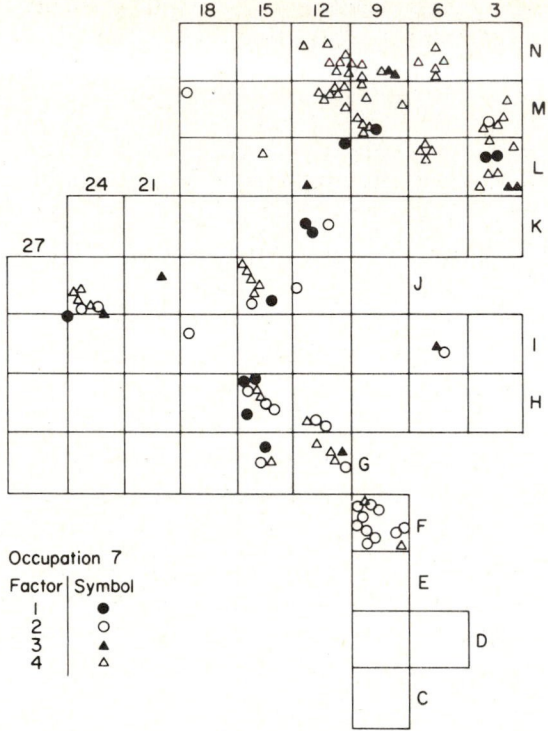

6.14 The distribution of factor specific items in occupation 7 at Torralba. Distance between grid lines equals 3 metres. For key see table 6.1 (Freeman 1978a: 90, fig. 1).

terms of tool kits designed to perform different tasks (Chapter 1). However Whallon (1978) has shown that our expectations of recovering palaeolithic tool kits were much too simplistic. The concept works only if the entire archaeological record is a fine-grained assemblage (see p. 24 above) providing very high resolution and integrity. Activity areas within a location are a far more useful concept, as Rigaud (1978; Delpech and Rigaud 1974) has shown in the analysis of level VII at Le Flageolet I (fig. 6.15). The reason for this is that we need models which deal with how the archaeological record was formed rather than descriptive labels, such as tool kit, to try and tie around the data.

One such model has been put forward by Ammerman and Feldman (1974; Schiffer 1972; see fig. 1.2 above). They view the generation of an assemblage of stone tools as involving at least five elements. These can be described as:

(1) the set of activities;
(2) the number of times that a particular activity from this set is performed;
(3) the set of tool types;
(4) the 'mapping' that exists between tool types and activities. The degree to which either a particular tool type is only used for a specific activity, or the degree to which it is used for a wide variety of general activities;
(5) the dropping/abandonment rates for stone tools.

> The model focuses attention on the crucial element of the correspondence between tool types and activities (element 4). The combinations are as follows: few activities but many tool types; few tool types but many activities; few tool types and few activities; many tool types and many activities.

Element five is important since this points to the very general problem of what exactly leads to the discard of stone tools (Chapter 2), which although it might seem an obvious and fundamental question in archaeology has largely been ducked.

A critical aspect is the degree to which artifacts are recycled in the system (fig. 1.2). This can involve transport away from one location in order that the implement can be used again at a future time as well as carrying away any broken equipment for repair at another location. This treatment provides one distinction between a complete or *expedient* technology where tools are manufactured on the spot from locally available raw materials and then left behind after use, and *curated* technologies where tools are manufactured in anticipation of future use (Binford 1973, 1977b, 1979). In a curated technology tools are repaired and maintained. This investment of effort can be seen in the more complex forms that such implements frequently take (Oswalt 1976; Torrence 1983) and which contrast markedly with the expediently produced artifacts from a complete technology (Ebert 1979: fig. 2.3).

One clear expectation from the archaeological record for a group whose technology is organised according to principles of curation will be the creation of a coarse grained signature (pp. 23–4 above). There will be little correspondence between the location of use and the location of discard of such curated items. Moreover since the important items are often recycled and maintained, the frequency with which they are thrown away and hence enter the archaeological record is in fact inversely proportional to their importance in the technology. If this was the case then a proportional count of tool types from a palaeolithic site would not provide a direct picture of the relative importance of each of those tools within the technology.

Curation is another component in a logistic system of organisation. In such a system it is common to find that raw materials are generally obtained through a system of embedded rather than direct procurement (Chapter 2), and that equipment vital to survival is dispersed in caches around the environment (Binford 1979). These tactics reflect the importance under certain conditions of forward planning and anticipation of future requirements. One element of the embedded strategy means that the recycling and manufacture of tools will generally take place within the context of another set of activities as documented, for example, at the Mask Site or Australian hunting blinds (Binford 1978a, b; Gould *et al.* 1971). An important point is that an embedded strategy saves valuable time. In this sense these activities, raw material procurement and manufacture, are scheduled to fit in with other activities such as moving

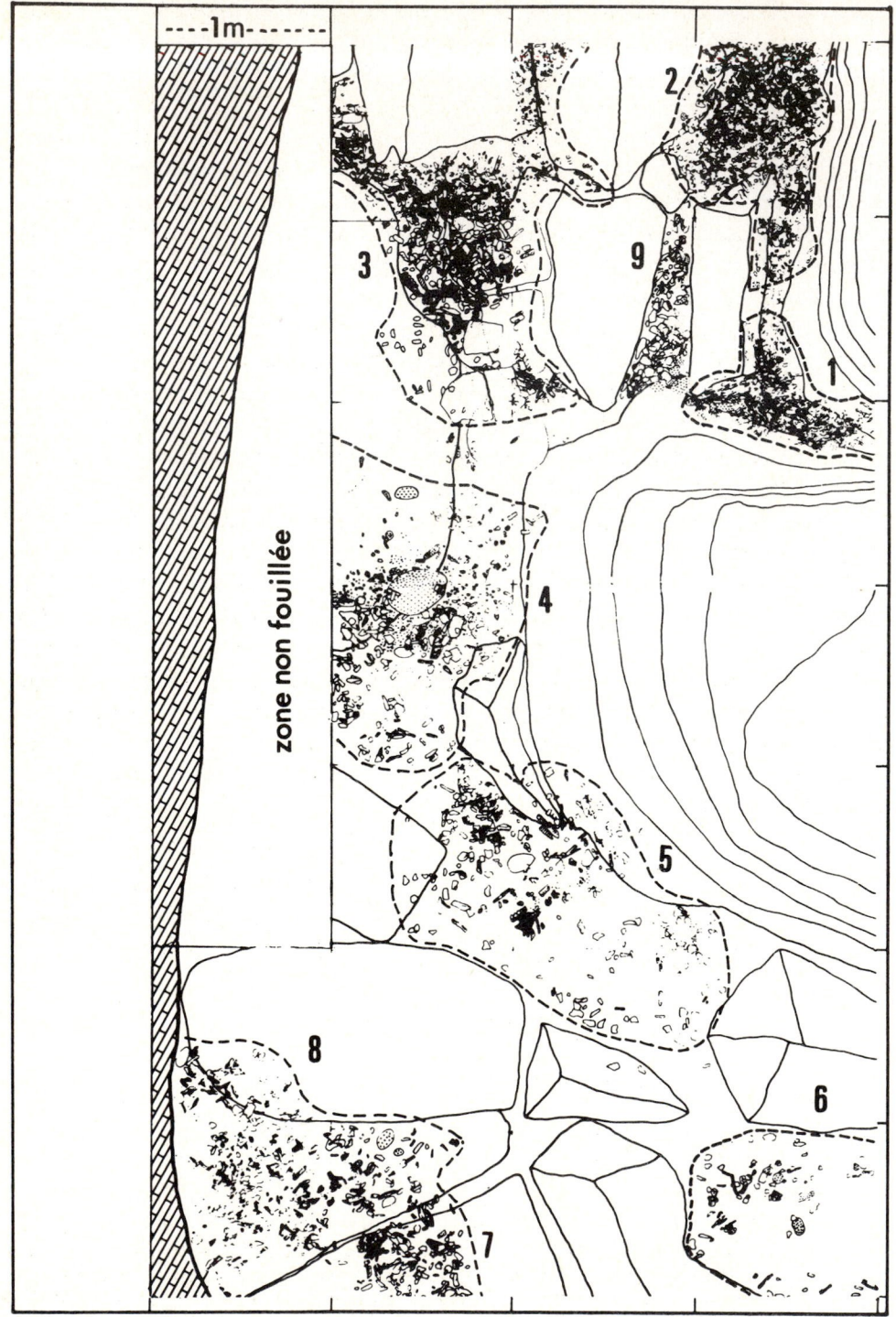

between camps or waiting at hunting blinds. The efficient use of time that results from such behaviour is a further key to successful adaptations in high risk environments (Torrence 1983; Carlstein 1982).

The distinction between expedient and curated technologies should not be taken to imply, within either strategy, that all implements will be *either* expediently made *or* curated. A distinction can be made between personal gear which will be highly curated, site furniture (for example heavy grinding slabs and pounding hammers), which goes with a place, and situational gear, which is a tool kit made for a specific immediate purpose and hence generally of an expedient nature.

These considerations are obviously some way from the approaches I mentioned earlier in this chapter. The different organisational principles and especially the link between a curated technology and high risk, time stressed environments are clearly of interest in a European palaeolithic context. But how can we test any of these models with archaeological data? Can we do any better than just deciding what *we* think are the curated items and making a judgement on, say, MTA B and aurignacian assemblages being either more or less curated than one another?

By asking such questions we are beginning to expose the limitations of the traditional approach to artifact description and classification. The typologies and taxonomies which formed the backbone of Chapter 5 were not designed to answer behavioural questions. The problem is that we lack at the present time the necessary bridging arguments to link such models with the archaeological record (Torrence 1983). What follows is an indication of some of the attributes we need to be recording if we are to begin to assess the behavioural variation that led to the differential composition of stone tool assemblages.

6.15 Distribution plot of level VII at Le Flageolet I (Delpech and Rigaud 1974). There are nine areas defined by large blocks.

1–3	rich in bone and flint remains
4	hearth
5–8	poor in bone and flint remains
9	narrow area between two blocks

bone fragmentation analysis

1	dropping area
2,3	internal activity area (Leroi-Gourhan and Brézillon 1972)
4	hearth
5,6	passageways to 1 and 4
7,8	external activity areas, butchery (Leroi-Gourhan and Brézillon 1972)
9	flint knapping area

The flint analysis revealed differences between the activity areas in terms of relative frequencies of plane burins on truncations, gravettes and microgravettes, denticulates and notches. These were in some instances as great as might be expected between assemblages from different sites or from different levels in the same site.

(a) energy inputs

The concept of curation is based on the premise that a relation exists between the utility of a tool and the amount of energy that goes into its manufacture (Binford 1973). The microwear studies of Keeley (1980) on the earlier palaeolithic sites of Clacton and Hoxne show very convincingly that both 'waste' flakes and retouched implements functioned as tools. What distinguishes the two classes of artifact is the amount of effort that was expended in making them. The curation model would suggest that the waste flakes are situational tools where flakes had been used to perform an immediate task, and that once they were finished with, or the cutting edge became dull, they were thrown away. The implication is that the handaxes from Hoxne had more effort

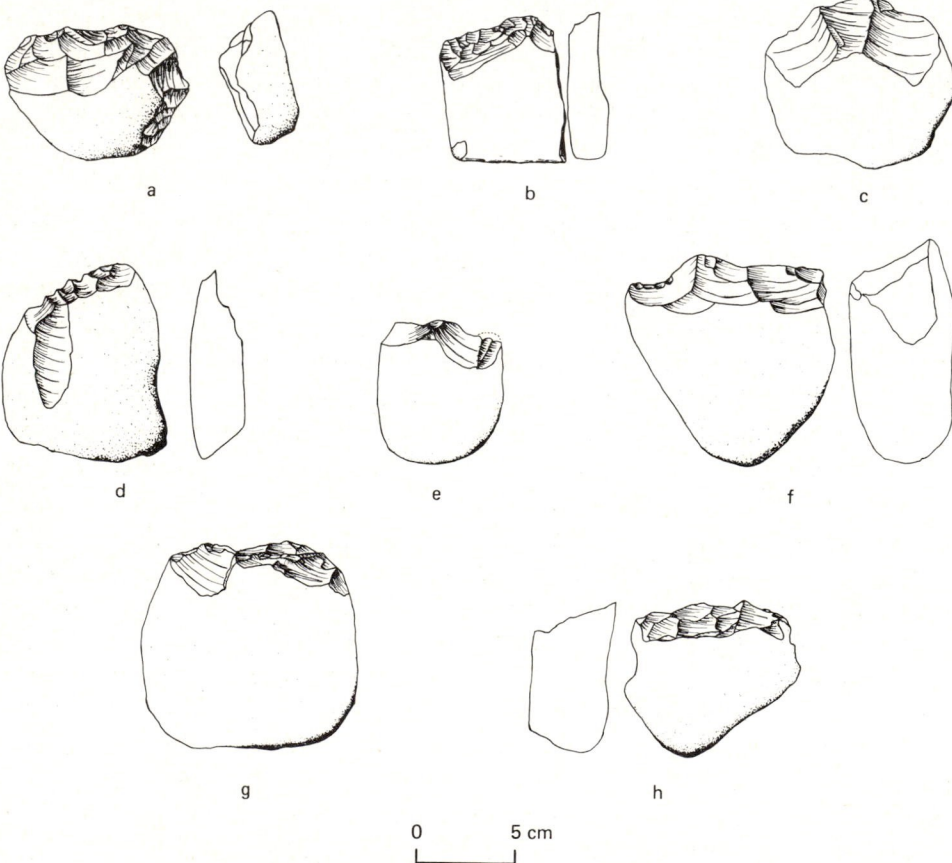

a

b

c

d

e

f

g

h

0   5 cm

6.16 Low energy investment implements. Pebble tools from a varied set of assemblages. Expedient tools of this kind are a feature of all technologies at all times and all places.

Earlier palaeolithic: (a) Isernia; (b) Bilzingsleben; (c) Achenheim; (d) Lazaret; (e) Baume Bonne.

Upper palaeolithic: (f) Abri Caminade; (g) Laugerie-Haute; (h) Voletiny.

expended on their manufacture since this investment was repaid by those implements meeting a number of future requirements and performing the tasks perhaps more quickly and efficiently than a simple flake. However, microwear studies show that both types of stone tools were used to cut meat. The same case holds for pebble-tools, irrespective of their age or the level of technical sophistication shown by the assemblages in which they occur (fig. 6.16).

A method of characterising assemblages through an assessment of the relative expenditure of effort has been proposed by Ebert (1979). He arrives at this assessment by employing a measure of implement size and the number of flake scar detachments on each piece. Together these act as an index of the amount of effort that has gone into artifact manufacture (fig. 6.17). A similar approach has been followed by Wildman (1982) in a study of handaxe assemblages from the Ouse valley in England, NW region. The findings are that the shape of the handaxes serves as a very accurate guide to the relative amounts of effort expended in their manufacture. In a study of mousterian assemblage composition, Rolland (1977, 1981) has demonstrated a significant difference between the five variants that relates to the proportions of retouched implements that they each possess (table 6.2). In this case I have used the proportions of retouched implements as a guide to relative energy inputs.

Other workers have been less enthusiastic about our ability to identify empirically concepts of curation with archaeological materials. At their excavations at Meer, Cahen *et al.* (1979) found that artifacts which would have been judged to have received a good deal of energy investment had been discarded on the site after only minimal use. In their opinion this runs counter to the curation model where such tools, in this case mostly burins and end scrapers made on carefully prepared blades, would be taken away for use at another location. In this way energy investment would be repaid by the continuing utility of the artifact. This is however a rather restrictive view of the concept. In the first place we should be considering the entire assemblage (e.g. Ebert 1979; Wildman 1982) rather than specific tool types. Moreover, technology is a tactical variable. Energy constraints can be broken if it is expedient to do so! While the overall strategy may well have been one where hunters were planning ahead and organising their technology accordingly, this does not mean that they were imprisoned within a behavioural straitjacket. It is also possible, as Marks ((ed.) 1977) has suggested for sites in the Negev desert, that the cores from which the blanks were struck formed the curated element rather than the finished tool. With the higher rates of high grade raw material procurement and sophisticated pre-core and core preparation strategies in the upper palaeolithic (Chapter 4), it may well be that such an interpretation can also be applied to such apparent anomalies as the assemblages left behind at Meer and Pincevent.

Keeley (1982) has also raised the question of hafted elements. These multicomponent tools should be subject to curation, as Oswalt's (1976) work on technounit counts indicates. Elaborate hafting of either bone, antler or stone

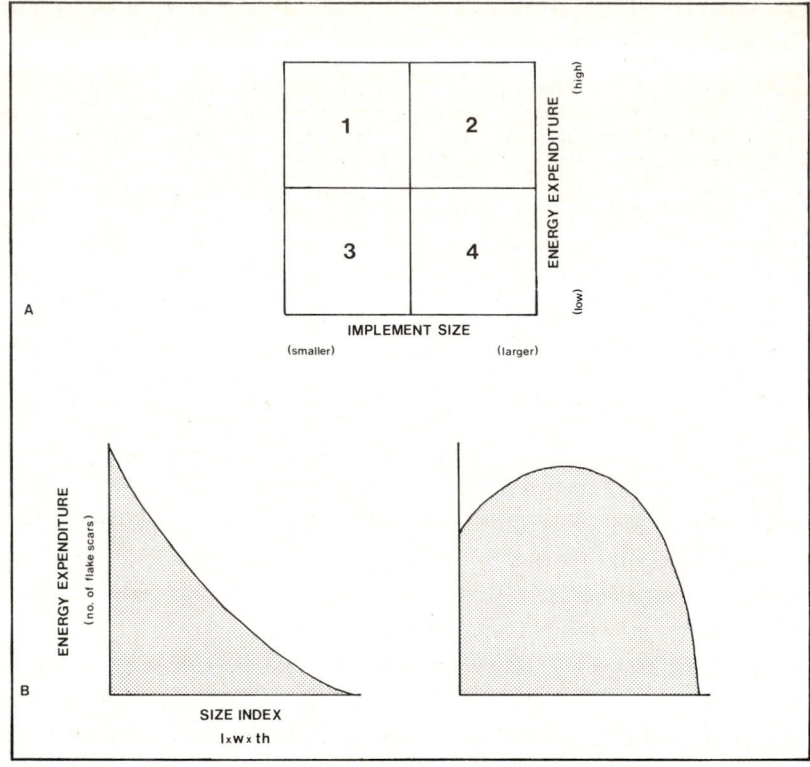

6.17 Stone tool assemblage variation (Ebert 1979). (A) Four box contingency table illustrating the relationship between theoretical linking arguments for points falling in different parts of size energy graphs.

Box 1: curated, small, specific use tools, possibly pieces of a mobile tool kit. Used in jobs or tasks in which a specific set of operations is carried out.

Box 2: specific use or 'specific-job' tools probably not transported as far as those in box 1, but curated. These might also be tools with high symbolic content.

Box 3: expedient, single use, immediately discarded tools; a situation of raw material stress may be indicated because of small size.

Box 4: other things, such as number of working edges, being equal, these should be tools manufactured expediently, used only once, and not transported.

(B) Shapes of limits of the point swarms plotted on implement size/energy expenditure graphs for two Botswana middle stone age sites (1979:fig. 2.5). These represent two assemblage signatures as measured by energy investment rather than implement type.

projectile points has obvious implications for the design, weight and size of these elements. Most important is the archaeologically invisible haft into which they were slotted. Did, for example, disposal of the projectile component take place when the haft broke, or were they refitted to either repaired or new hafts? A complex interaction of artifact use-life, replacement rates and the utility of a tool will obviously have great bearing on the differential creation of the archaeological record (Boismier 1981). Microwear studies designed to ident-

Table 6.2. *Implement frequencies for mousterian variants based on the analysis of 120 assemblages*

Increased implement frequencies are associated with the two sidescraper variants (Quina and Ferrassie). These frequencies may be used as an approximate measure of the greater overall energy investment in these assemblages. Moreover the core/blank ratio shows that greater flake production, and hence energy expenditure, is also correlated with increased tool production.

	Implements	Utilised and blanks	Non-levallois plain flakes	Ratio of cores to flakes and blanks
	%	%	%	
Denticulate	17.1	24.7	57.7	1/20.2
Typical	22.7	26.5	50.8	1/22.5
MTA	25.6	25.4	48.5	1/14.7
Ferrassie	43	21.4	35.4	1/31
Quina	49.8	10.6	39.5	1/33.3
Number of assemblages	120	120	120	94

Source: Rolland 1977: table 2

ify hafting traces on stone tools will contribute towards a necessary first step in getting to grips with such complex behaviour in the archaeological record.

A further measure of energy input is provided by the use of either exotic raw materials or high quality local materials for particular artifact types (see table 7.12). Very little work has been done on this question but Straus' study (1977b) of the solutrean in Cantabria, SW region, raises some interesting possibilities (table 6.3). An analysis of lithic materials in the middle palaeolithic levels of the Bacho-Kiro cave, SE region (Kozlowski (ed.) 1982), shows that, although local volcanic rocks predominate, in the assemblage as a whole there was a much greater use of flint, which is exotic to the Bacho Kiro local region, for retouched tools (table 6.4).

The detailed examination of core reduction strategies in the LUP of Poland (Ginter 1974; Kozlowski and Sachse-Kozlowska 1976; Schild 1971) shows quite clearly that standardised bladelets were produced in a number of steps and at a number of different locations. The chocolate coloured flint from the Holy Cross mountains was mined and knapped into large pre-cores (fig. 4.2). Once this preliminary weight reduction stage had taken place at the sources, the cores were then moved around the landscape as items within a curated technology.

The flint manufacturing waste, or debitage, has received especial attention from Fish (1979) in a study of three earlier palaeolithic assemblages (table 6.5). He recognises primary knapping from nodular raw material by the following criteria – high frequencies of angular flakes, flakes carrying cortex on their surfaces and flakes with cortical platforms.

A further behavioural inference could be made at Pech de l'Azé I, level C–4, and Combe-Grenal level 28. At Pech de l'Azé bifacial retouch was present on

Table 6.3. *Selection of quartzite as a raw material in the manufacture of solutrean projectile points and assemblages*

The table shows great variation in raw material use depending upon the local abundance of good quality flint. The choice of raw material for making solutrean projectile points in Asturias and Santander is very different from the choice for the rest of the assemblage and may well reflect in part the greater energy investment in these bifacially pressure flaked artifacts.

	Total collection	Total of points	Points with concave base	Shouldered points	Rest of assemblage
Asturias region: lacks good flint					
Caldas	177	98	100	—	72
Cova Rosa	217	52	—	64	40
Cueta de la Mina F	584	44	61	18	36
La Riera	143	27	50	0	51
Santander region: flint abundant					
Altamira	522	18	69	0	3
La Pasiega	331	38	83	—	7
Cueva Morín	138	—	—	0	4
Guipuzcoa region: flint very abundant					
Aitzbitarte	332	0	—	0	0

% of pieces made on quartzite

Source: Straus 1977b

Table 6.4. *Different uses of raw material in a middle palaeolithic level from the Bacho Kiro cave*

Note the greater use of flint and flint-like raw materials for retouched tools. Flint is apparently not found within a radius of 100 km from the cave.

Raw material type	Tools	Cores	Flakes blades	Total	Tools %	Cores %	Flakes %	Total %
Flint	22	2	70	94	32	10	11	13
Flint-like	17	1	20	38	25	5	3	5
Volcanic	20	11	491	522	29	55	79	73
Quartzite	2	4	22	28	3	20	4	4
Sandstone	—	—	1	1	—	—	0.1	0.1
Slate	6	2	17	25	9	10	3	4
Dolomitic Limestone	—	—	1	1	—	—	0.1	0.1
Greenstone	—	—	2	2	—	—	0.3	0.3
Mudstone	1	—	—	1	1	—	—	0.1
Totals	68	20	624	712				

Level 13

Source: Kozlowski (ed.) 1982

Table 6.5. *Inferring activity in mousterian lithic assemblages from the analysis of flake debitage*

Site	Level	Debitage sample size	Inferred flaking activity	Angular flakes %	Non-cortical flakes %	Cortical platforms %	Core/flake ratio
Combe-Grenal	14	200	primary flaking	39.5	37	9	1/15
	21	297	flakes manufactured outside provenience	20.5	67.4	5.3	1/108
	27	199	both selection from outside the provenience and primary flaking	15.6	64.3	4.5	1/25
	28	200	no interpretation	26	65.5	2	1/47
	38	195	primary flaking with some selection from outside	31.3	52.3	11.4	1/21
Corbiac	M-1	396	selection from outside and some minor primary flaking	13.6	64	4.7	1/40
Et Tabun	19	129	primary flaking and at least some selection from outside	18.6	49.6	14.8	1/15
Pech de l'Azé I	C-4	200	specialised	23	63.5	7.5	—

Source: After Fish 1979

43% of all debitage, while handaxes and other bifaces formed only 2.8% of the tool count. At Combe Grenal no handaxes were found, although 13.5% of the flakes carried distinctive bifacial retouch. Fish interprets this as evidence for the removal of particular tool categories for use and eventual disposal elsewhere. It would be interesting to know to what extent these flakes could be regarded as resharpening products, since this would provide some use-life measure for these bifacial tools.

Finally these brief considerations of energy inputs might lead us to re-appraise the clumps and clusters noted by Freeman (1978a) for Torralba (table 6.1, fig. 6.14). The factor analysis revealed a significant association between tools with a low energy investment – e.g. perforators and denticulates – and low utility food parts such as skulls and teeth. This may be suggestive of a relationship between the effort invested in tool production, the value of the food return and the reliability of such procurement patterns in the overall food getting strategy.

(b) breakage and replacement

It is still not possible to analyse palaeolithic stone tools in terms of use-life and replacement rates, and until a great deal of experimental work has been done on the performance of raw materials for particular tool types and tasks (e.g. Gould 1980) these very necessary estimates will remain elusive. The purpose of this section is to show that by changing the attributes we record for stone tools we can at least begin to assemble some comparative data on the problem.

I have already discussed manufacturing activities for stone tools, and it should be pointed out that a great deal of information also exists for similar activities concerning bone and antler in the upper palaeolithic. An example in fig. 6.18 shows the use of a horse metapodial to make bone splinters for needles (Feustel 1974:186). Similar examples using reindeer antler to make points using a groove and splinter technique are common (Camps-Fabrer (ed.) 1974; Semenov 1964). These raw materials could well be curated, as has been suggested for the lithic pre-cores in the LUP, by being carried around so that they were at hand when needed. Alternatively they could have been taken from a cache set up at an earlier time to meet such a future eventuality. Either way they are further evidence of forward planning applied to the organisation of technology.

The importance of such forethought comes into focus when we look at breakage rates among bone and antler points. A comprehensive study by Albrecht (et al. 1972) examined these artifacts from 68, mainly EUP, assemblages in central and eastern Europe, NC, NE, SE regions. Their findings indicate that the majority of these points are badly broken (table 6.6), and I would suggest that this occurred as a result of use rather than post-depositional attrition. Almost three quarters of the assemblages are from caves and rock shelters, and moreover *all* the occurrences of split-base antler and bone points were from cave sites such as Istállöskö and the Vogelherd.

Table 6.6. *The condition of antler and bone points from 68 predominantly
EUP assemblages in central and eastern Europe*

Slight damage	Complete/ unbroken	Fragmentary/ broken	Sample size
%	%	%	
14.8	17.3	67.8	277

Source (Albrecht *et al.* 1972)

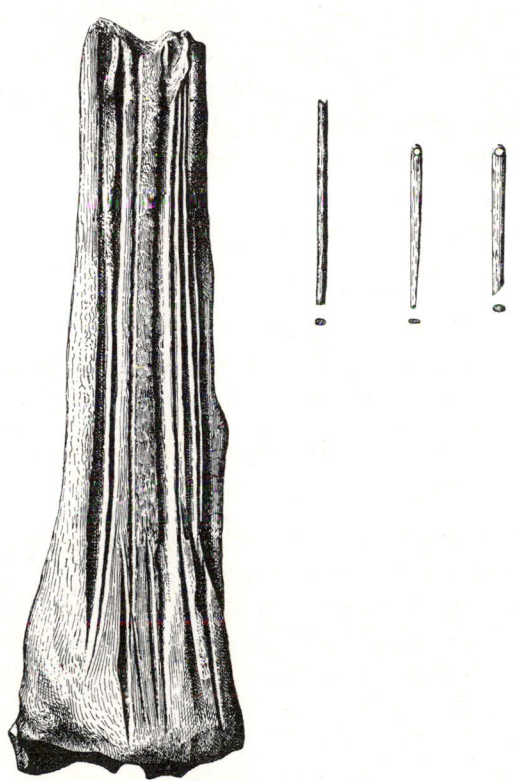

6.18 Bone needle manufacture (Feustel 1974:186, fig. 78).

A study of the distinctive *sagaies d'Isturitz* from level 4 of the Abri Pataud by
Movius (1973) reveals that none of these antler points are complete but that the
group consists of five bases, nine central sections and thirteen tips. The
occurrence of so many broken points strongly suggests that these caves and rock
shelters were used by hunting parties operating away from a home base and that
repairs to the hunting equipment were made at these sites. The tactical use of
these shelter facilities within a settlement system results in higher disposal
rates for broken and worn out equipment. I have already commented (Chapter 5)

that in central and eastern Europe, NC, NE and SE regions, the stone tool assemblages which accompany these distinctive antler points are very small in size and often rather nondescript in terms of typology. The end scrapers, flakes and simple burins were most probably situational items fashioned out of locally available raw materials to execute the task of retooling the all important hunting equipment.

This scenario should not be taken to imply that everywhere we find antler points they will be broken. A study of aurignacian material from Poitou-Charente and Périgord, SW region (Leroy-Prost 1974) records that 68% of a sample 111 split-base points were complete, while 36% of the lozenge shaped types were also unbroken. These higher percentages have to be compared with the generally much larger lithic collections with which such material is associated. One way to interpret this data might be to consider the antler points as caches that were left in known locations for use in emergencies. This provides a further example of planning ahead where the object of such behaviour is to minimise the chances of failure in securing subsistence.

Stone projectile points also provide an opportunity to examine relative breakage rates. The altmühlian level F in the Weinberghöhlen at Mauern (Von Koenigswald *et al.* 1974) produced a number of large bifacially worked leaf points, several of which have a hafting notch at their base (fig. 5.10, a). Of the 49 examples illustrated by Bohmers (1951) and Zotz (1955), 55% are broken. Nearly all of the 114 leaf points at Rörshain in central Germany, NC region (Bosinski 1973b), were also broken (Allsworth-Jones 1975) and may represent manufacturing rejects (fig. 5.10, e). Other examples of small collections of leaf points from earlier palaeolithic assemblages include Torre dell'Alto, MC region (Borzatti von Löwenstern 1966), Baume Bonne, MW region (H. de Lumley and Bottet 1961), and sites such as Kosten, NC region (Freund 1952). In many cases the leaf points that are illustrated are broken, although absolute figures are not available. These very obvious projectile points could, if such counts were available, be compared with alternative projectile material, for example triangular levallois flakes (fig. 4.1, fig. 5.2), not in terms of typology but instead in respect of the energy that went into their manufacture and the incidence of breakage. Other non-projectile point elements in the assemblage may of course show entirely different breakage points (table 6.7).

Assemblages where complete projectile points are common include levels 6, 5 and 4 at Jerzmanowice (Chmielewski 1961) from the EUP of the NC region. Here some 58% of 43 illustrated points are complete. At this and many other sites in the NC region these few distinctive foliate points form the significant focus for typological and taxonomic investigation, since the rest of the lithic industries are very meagre and typologists attempting an assemblage analysis would describe the collections as poor (see Kozlowski 1982:112–13 for a careful discussion of this point). If we begin to consider breakage data, then I believe we can see that the small numerical size of such assemblages is in fact highly

Table 6.7. *Breakage information from the micoquian site of the Bockstein, southern Germany, NC region*

Only the bifacially worked material has been noted from the principal artifact horizon, level III.

	complete	broken	
Bockstein knives	50	7	Bocksteinmesser
Micoquian handaxes	20	7	Micoquiekeile
Plano-convex handaxes	41	10	Halbkeile
Small handaxes	23	2	Faustel
Handaxe flakes	121	13	Faustkeilblatter
Leaf points	4	2	Blattspitzen

Source: Wetzel and Bosinski 1969

Table 6.8. *Breakage proportions in some solutrean assemblages*

The figures in parentheses are the sample size

	% broken				
	Pointe à face plane	Leaf points	Concave base	Shouldered point	Barbed and tanged arrow-heads
Parpalló		41 (34)			43 (30)
Laugerie-Haute Ouest	52 (31)	69 (35)		100 (4)	
Laugerie-Haute Est	44 (23)	67 (31)		100 (9)	
Cantabrian region			97 (88)	72 (138)	

Source: Pericot 1942; Smith 1966; Straus 1977b

significant in behavioural terms (Chapter 8). Indeed we can see that the importance of type fossil rather than assemblage analysis, combined with the incidence of breakage rates among particular classes of stone tools and antler tools, become elements in the archaeological signatures of artifact assemblages within a comparative regional framework.

Even amongst numerically 'rich' assemblages, such as the solutrean of the SW and MW regions, the breakage data suggest that we often ignore much significant patterning to do with past behaviour (table 6.8). The figures indicate different breakage rates for different projectile points, and moreover these vary between sites and regions. Other LUP examples include salpetrien points and shouldered points generally from the south of France, MW region (Onoratini 1978; Bazile 1980), where the illustrated pieces are predominately broken specimens. The shouldered points/knives from Kostenki I/1 (Chapter 5) in the EUP of the NW region would also repay such an analysis. At Spadzista Street B,

NC region, there were sixty-four of these type specimens of which only five were complete and twelve broken a little; of the rest twenty-four were bases, fourteen shafts and nine tips.

These observations only point to alternative ways of analysing and classifying assemblages of bone and stone artifacts where the emphasis is on measuring the behavioural inputs into the creation of an assemblage. The examples are merely illustrative of what could be done, and raise all sorts of questions about which we need more quantitative data: for example, the relationship between such factors as artifact types, raw material choice, use-wear traces, breakage rate and spatial position within a site and settlement system.

A final example of attributes that could be measured and which would contribute to this approach relates to resharpening information. An example comes from the cave site of La Cotte on the island of Jersey, NW region (McBurney and Callow 1971; Callow 1981). Here a specialised technique of resharpening was employed where as much as possible of the retouched edge was removed while retaining the same working edge angle. This results in characteristic sharpening spalls of which c.1000 have been found in the collection. The technique considerably extended the use-life of scrapers. This proved important as rising sea levels progressively restricted access to local higher grade raw materials for use at the site. The La Cotte example provides us with an example of economising behaviour in relation to lithic resources, tool use and assemblage formation.

An example of an efficiency strategy might be provided by some classes of handaxes if we accept Hayden's suggestion (1979a:15) that one of their prime roles in palaeolithic technology was as a source of flakes. If this were so then we should view these artifacts as worked out cores rather than specially fashioned implements. In that case their variety of shapes (Roe 1964, 1981; Wymer 1968; Bordes 1961a; and see fig. 4.3) are a product of the efficient use of raw material rather than the outcome of objects designed to perform special tasks. They were used as tools but probably only at the end of their useful life as a source of flakes. At that moment they perhaps passed from being highly curated raw material objects and became situational gear, used once and then thrown away. When used as tools they would therefore enter the archaeological record in the same way as the flakes struck from them which were then used and also quickly discarded. These intriguing suggestions show that we should not be bound by the traditional conceptions of tools and waste, and consequently predetermine what was important in palaeolithic technology. Instead the questions need to be rephrased to take into account the variable behaviour which created assemblages. We are now fortunate that experimental work on lithic technology and the advent of rigorous microwear studies (Keeley 1980) will make it possible to choose between competing hypotheses.

(c) caches and stores

Caches of raw material, tools and food are some of the most common types of sites found among contemporary and recent northern hunters (Binford 1979). An archaeological example from Banks Island, Canada, is provided by Hahn (1976d). Here a cache of land hunting tools including bow, arrows, knife, drills and snow goggles was cached between stones near to a settlement. A comparable find of arrows is illustrated by Schild (1976:99) for a LUP grave from Lake Onega. A deposit of five very large bifacially flaked core tools in a magdalenian deposit at the Montgaudier cave (Duport 1976:fig. 51) may also represent such a cache, since these exceptionally large pieces are normally found only singly.

Many of the pits in the Kostenki sites have been interpreted as stores of food, furs and raw materials (Efimenko 1958; Klein 1969a), while the two middens of mammoth and rhino skulls and bones at the coastal cliff site of La Cotte, NW region (Scott 1980) may also be a large surplus meat cache from two separate hunting episodes.

One aspect of caching behaviour involves the creation and re-use of facilities. Schild (1971) has illustrated flint mining tools that are found at the extraction sites for chocolate coloured flint in the Polish late glacial. The implements are representative of both situational gear and site furniture and were left behind at these locations for further use. Other mining tools came from pits dug to extract iron oxides, or red ochre, at Lovas near Lake Balaton in Hungary, SE region (Mészáros and Vértes 1955). In this case the finds of giant deer antlers have been interpreted as picks.

Other examples which in Binford's terminology (1979) would be regarded as items of site furniture include the bone anvil standing vertically in pit 75 at Kostenki I/1 (Efimenko 1958:fig. 17) or the mammoth femur used as part of a cooking tripod in the oval hut at Gönnersdorf (Bosinski 1979b). In this same category would fall the ground stone lamps and simple limestone slab lamps found lying on the floor at Lascaux (A. Leroi-Gourhan and Allain 1979) together with fragments of rope and postholes once used for scaffolding (fig. 5.30).

Hearths also formed repeatedly used facilities in many sites and this is shown by their sometimes elaborate construction as at the Abri Pataud (Movius 1966), Verberie (Adouze *et al.* 1981) and Pincevent section 36 (Leroi-Gourhan and Brézillon 1972; Perlès 1976). The focus these facilities provided led to the build up of very robust spatial patterns, as we have already seen above.

Many of these sites from the upper palaeolithic represent large investments of energy at particular locations in the landscape. The 385 mammoth bones that formed the hut at Mezhirich came from a minimum of 95 mammoths which although not hunted had to be collected. The five bone huts at Mezin (fig. 6.10) and the three at Spadzista Street B, Krakow, were assembled from a minimum of 116 and 60 mammoth carcasses respectively (Koslowski 1974). The traces of many small caches will not however have stood up to the attritional forces of post-depositional factors. However, it is possible that some of the dense flint scatters associated with open working hearths, as at Pincevent I and Le Verberie, are in fact raw material dumps. The reason for this interpretation is that many more blanks are found at these sites than were either retouched into tools or used in an unmodified form. Many of the retouched implements bear no micro-wear traces, and the tools, as noted at Meer (Cahen *et al.* 1979), were deposited on the site and not carried away for use elsewhere. One suggestion is that the efficient use of time led to the manufacture of a surplus requirement of blade blanks and implements, and their caching around hearths in known locations. These spare 'tool kits' could then be called upon in times of need when, for example, snow cover made it difficult to find suitable raw materials. The advantage of an upper palaeolithic blade technology as encountered at Pincevent or the Polish late glacial sites is that the blade/blank can be fashioned into all the major, repeated tool forms in the lithic inventory (fig. 4.9). The time consuming part is acquiring suitable raw material for such controlled, standardised blank production, and preparing the core so that blades of different sizes can be struck off when required.

(d) food residues

The investigation of food management strategies through the analysis of food residues from excavations should prove a very powerful component in a signature approach to the study of the European palaeolithic (Chapter 2). The present position is however little advanced beyond the statements about palaeoeconomy that have been presented in Chapter 5. Here for example Klein (1969a) calculated the minimum number of individuals (MNI) to estimate the amount of meat represented by the animal bones at some of the Kostenki sites. This was then divided by the daily calorific requirements of a group of fifty people (ten males, ten females and thirty children). This gives a figure for the number of days that a site was occupied. Whether this occupation was consecutive or took place intermittently over a period of time is a matter of judgement, and Klein warns that such figures are only suggestive.

The Spadzista Street B site excavated by Kozlowski (1974) produced the remains of sixty mammoths, which have been estimated as providing enough food for eight years for the ten to twelve persons living in the three huts. It seems that this is a case where you had to eat your mammoth before you could live in it! The alternative interpretation that the mammoth bones might have been collected from natural-death carcasses, rather than from hunted specimens, is dismissed by Kozlowski, who thinks this unlikely on the evidence that only two of the sixty mammoths had reached an age at which they would have died a natural death (*ibid.*:74).

Ethnoarchaeological studies have shown that instead of thinking in terms of complete animals, as the use of MNI requires (White 1953; Grayson 1978), we should expect the selection of body parts, and their introduction into sites as *food parcels*. It is in this form that bones potentially enter the archaeological record (Yellen 1977b; Binford 1978a; Gould 1967). Amongst the Nunamiut, the locations where animals are killed are rarely those where they are consumed. It therefore follows that the transportation of food parts exerts considerable influence over decisions made at the kill sites. The hunter has to decide which parts to abandon at the kill and which to put into a cache or transport back to the village by either dog, pack or sled. In Binford's analysis these decisions are framed in terms of 'which parts of the animal are best for the greatest variety of uses' (1978a:72). In order to follow the sequence of tactical decisions inherent in this strategy Binford has constructed a General Utility Index (GUI) that assesses the meat, marrow and grease product from different parts of the caribou skeleton. A modified form of this index (table 6.9) also takes into account a number of further anatomical factors. When the Nunamiut butcher an animal they do not deal with it in terms of either single bones or a complete carcass. Instead they dismember it into parcels of meat that contain sets of bones. This results in bones of low utility still being attached to high yield elements, e.g. the hindfeet 'ride in' with the back limbs. The Modified General Utility Index (MGUI) takes this into account by increasing the value of low utility parts in relation to the higher value parts with which they are associated due to their position in the skeleton and to common procedures arising from dismemberment and segmentation for transportation. A knowledge of anatomy, the connectedness of skeletal parts of different values, the sequence by which the carcass is dismembered, are all important if we are to utilise faunal assemblages to discuss past behaviour (Chapter 1; Binford 1981). An assessment of faunal assemblages by means of the MGUI does indeed allow the categorisation of different site types within the Nunamiut settlement system.

At least three types of sites can be distinguished. These are:

> *Kill sites*: faunal assemblages fitted a model of the inverse GUI. In other words the low utility parts were left behind and the higher food utility parts carried away for consumption at residential camps;
>
> *Hunting stands*: the faunal assemblages fitted a model of marrow bone selection. There was variation between assemblages within this class and this was mainly due to the population of bones from which the choice of marrow bones was made;
>
> *Hunting camps*: a cull model accounted for the faunal assemblages from these sites. In particular parts of the animal which were of marginal food value were rare. Variation occurs as a result of other parts introduced as initial provisions, hunting success or the presence of dogs.

The sequence of processing and consumption has been studied in detail by Yellen (1977b:279) for the !Kung. After a successful kill the larger animals are segmented into manageable food parcels. Once the food reaches the consumers, or vice versa, further segmentation occurs as distribution of the kill takes place (*ibid.*:286–9). Up to this stage the skeletal anatomy of the animal has provided a

Table 6.9. *The modified general utility index (MGUI) for caribou*

This estimates the utility of each element in terms of meat, marrow and grease content, while also taking into account the way elements are associated as anatomical sets in the caribou skeleton. Percentages are calculated against femur as 100%

Anatomical part	Caribou MGUI %
femur proximal	100
femur distal	100
tibia proximal	64.7
sternum	64.1
ribs	49.8
pelvis	47.9
tibia distal	47.1
thoracic vertebra	45.5
scapula	43.5
humerus proximal	43.5
humerus distal	36.5
cervical vertebra	35.7
lumbar vertebra	32.1
tarsals	31.7
astragalus	31.7
calcaneus	31.7
mandible with tongue	30.3
metatarsal proximal	29.9
radius/ulna proximal	26.6
metatarsal distal	23.9
radius/ulna distal	22.2
skull	17.5–8.7
carpals	15.5
mandible without tongue	13.9
phalanges	13.7
metacarpal proximal	12.2
metacarpal distal	10.5
atlas	9.8
axis	9.8
antler	1.02

Source: Binford 1978a:table 2.7

blueprint that determines the pattern of dismemberment and separation of elements into food parcels. However, then cooking takes place. In the case of the !Kung this is the moment when most of the human attrition on the bones occurs. They use iron tripod pots with a rim diameter of c.30 cm, and this of course sets the effective limits on the size of meat portions and bones that can be boiled. As a result all the bones are chopped, with steel knives and axes, into pieces 7–10 cm in length.

There is little information on such obvious cut and chop marks from studies of palaeolithic faunal collections. Von den Driesch and Boessneck (1975) have made a detailed study on the location and frequency of cut marks on bones from neolithic sites while Binford's (1981:table 4.03) observations on the incidence of cut marks on aurochs, horse and reindeer from Combe-Grenal indicate that the larger the animal, the more frequently cut marks are found.

It might be possible to use some of these observations in a study of palaeolithic food management strategies. However, we still need to consider those other agencies which have contributed to the faunal record. Evidence for carnivore attrition in the form of gnawing and puncture marks on bones is common (Sutcliffe 1970; Binford 1981; Brain 1981). Von Koenigswald (*et al.* 1974:taf.28) illustrates segments of articulated mammoth vertebra from Zone C in the Weinberghöhlen at Mauern, NC region, which have been clearly gnawed by a carnivore, most probably hyena. While the dentition of the hyena is particularly well adapted to crushing, splitting and gnawing bones, the other large carnivores, lion and wolf, are also capable of inflicting considerable damage on bones. Moreover, they do this in predictable and repetitive ways (Brain 1981). Other species such as the porcupine also gnaw bones and occasionally their highly distinctive chiselled traces can be found on bones from pleistocene Europe (Gamble 1978b:plate I).

Knife cuts and gnawing marks do not necessarily make the task of sorting out *who* collected *what* in a palimpsest faunal collection any easier. Both traces have been found on bones from Olduvai Gorge (Bunn 1981; Potts and Shipman 1981) and in one instance on the same bone where the human trace 'stratigraphically' preceded the carnivore tooth scratch. Moreover, it is often difficult to identify a typical pattern of bone fragmentation that can be used to distinguish bones cracked for marrow by humans from those split by carnivores to get at the same resource (see Brain 1981; Binford 1981, 1983, for a full discussion and possible solutions). As a result it is best to treat with caution the many claims for flake bone tools which abound in the palaeolithic literature (Kitching 1963; Valoch 1980a; Freeman 1978b, 1983; H. de Lumley 1976d; Hörmann 1923). More information is needed in the form of basic descriptive accounts of the frequency of gnawing, the patterns of bone breakage and the size of fragments.

Another route is to examine the composition of assemblages in terms of the anatomical parts they contain. According to this model the assemblages created by carnivores will be very different from those that result from human activity. The carnivores will in many cases consume the choice meat parts at the site of a kill, and transport only the low food parts back to their dens, where the young will feed on them. This is of course entirely opposite to the hunter model, where high MGUI anatomical parts will be transported away from the kill site either immediately or at a later date after a period of storage.

One further factor that needs to be considered is preservation. In a pioneering study of the attritional effects of gnawing on animal bones, Brain (1967,1976) demonstrated that the higher the food value of a bone, the poorer its chances of survival. These findings have been examined in detail by Binford and Bertram (1977) where survival factors for bone elements have been calculated based upon a measure of their density and hence resistance to attrition.

Table 6.10. *A comparison of the reindeer bones from a rock shelter and waterlogged open site*

Anatomical element	Abri Pataud Level 3 (Bouchud 1975)						Stellmoor Hamburgian Level (Krause and Kollau 1943)				
	N	MNI	%	SP	%		N	MNI	%	SP	%
femur p.	6	3	16	40	11		37	18.5	46	115	43
femur d.	1	0.5	3	9	3		35	17.5	44	126	47
tibia p.	0	0	0	0	0		6	3	8	32	12
sternum	not preserved						not preserved				
ribs	224	9	47	188	53		173	7	18	72	27
pelvis	4	2	11	13	4		25	13	33	38	14
tibia d.	6	3	16	22	6		9	4.5	11	15	6
thoracic vertebra	see 'all vertebra'						212	15	38	106	40
scapula	17	9	47	87	25		33	17	43	80	30
humerus p.	0	0	0	0	0		14	7	18	106	40
all vertebra	34	1	5	13	4						
humerus d.	9	4.5	24	41	12		15	7.5	19	33	12
cervical vertebra	see 'all vertebra'						165	33	83	268	100
lumbar vertebra	see 'all vertebra'						107	21	53	108	40
tarsals and carpals	50	3	16	64	18		7	0.3	0.8	3	1
astragalus	12	6	32	89	25		6	3	8	22	8
calcaneus	5	2.5	13	36	10		8	4	10	28	10
mandible	168	14	74	74	21		5	2.5	6	6	2
metatarsal p.	2	1	5	12	3		5	2.5	6	15	6
radius/ulna p.	19	9.5	50	122	35		16	8	20	49	18
metatarsal d.	14	7	37	92	26		11	5.5	14	35	13
radius/ulna d.	3	1.5	8	16	5		10	5	13	26	10
skull	198	17	89	111	31		37	3	8	10	4
phalange I and II	158	10	53	353	100		55	2	5	38	14
phalange III	27	3	16	160	45						
metacarpal p.	2	1	5	1	0.3		25	12.5	31	86	32
metacarpal d.	38	19	100	286	81		24	12	30	86	32
atlas	see 'all vertebra'						40	40	100	141	53
axis	see 'all vertebra'						38	38	95	176	66
sample size	997						1108				

Key: SP = survival proportion as calculated by Binford (1981:table 5.04 column 7), for each bone element. The % is then re-calculated on the most common anatomical element after this survival factor has been applied.

The elements are arranged according to the modified general utility index (MGUI) for caribou (table 6.9).

p = proximal   d = distal

The calculation of survival factors and their linkage to an index such as the MGUI can be described as a study in *economic anatomy*. One such example is presented in table 6.10, where the aim is to model the behavioural decisions that lead to the formation of a bone assemblage. In both examples reindeer is the prey species. The samples come from level 3 at the rock shelter site of the Abri Pataud (Movius (ed.) 1975; Bouchud 1975) and the lower level at Stellmoor (Rust 1943). The preservation at Stellmoor, a waterlogged open site, has always been regarded as exceptional. The data (fig. 6.19) point to a high proportion of high value bones as measured by the MGUI. These include femur, proximal humerus and cervical vertebrae. By contrast the reindeer material in the Abri Pataud (fig. 6.19) has much higher values in the assemblage for the low value parts of the reindeer carcass, phalanges and distal metacarpal, while those bones with a MGUI value of ⟩40 are, with the exception of ribs, very poorly represented. However, apart from drawing a contrast the data are not easy to interpret since these are only two isolated assemblages and should, preferably, be interpreted against a background of similar residues from other sites in their respective settlement systems. Why, for example, at Stellmoor, should the high value

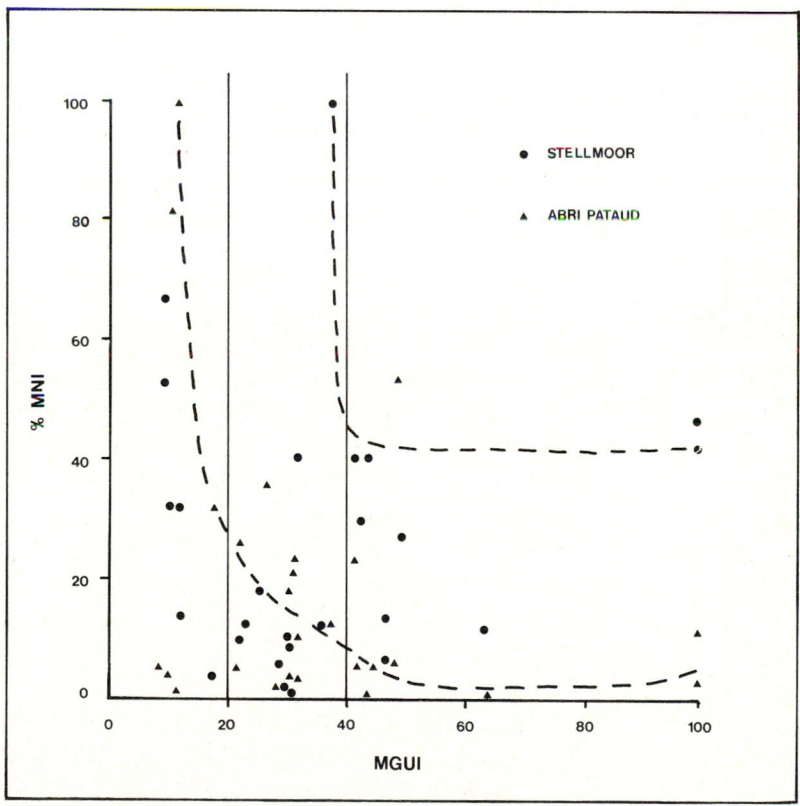

6.19 MGUI calculated for reindeer bones from Stellmoor, hamburgian level, and Abri Pataud, level 3.

bones, many of which were unbroken, be abandoned at the kill site? One answer might be that the assemblage represents hunting episodes designed to obtain primarily non-food items (p. 42) such as skins for clothing, when skins of suitable quality are available only at certain times of the year. Such selectivity has been established in a rigorous study by Speth of a bison drive site in south-eastern New Mexico (1983). An economic anatomy analysis revealed that processing decisions were very strongly conditioned by differential carcass utility. This is most clearly seen in the different treatment of male and female bison and the selection and rejection of anatomical parts. More female than male anatomical parts were abandoned at the Garnsey site, and few of the bones had been broken in processing. The MGUI curve for females revealed that many more high utility parts had been discarded than was the case for male bison (Speth 1983:fig. 31). He was also able to show that at this spring kill site several processing decisions were made because of the higher marrow-fat reserves in the bones of male as opposed to female bison at this time of the year. This detailed study shows how selection of prey by hunters, which includes age and sex classes from the living herd, must also be extended to include carcass selection once the prey has been killed. I would suspect that, where preservation is good at such sites, and consequently where both integrity and resolution are high, analyses such as Speth's will reveal an array of MGUI curves (see Binford 1978a:figs. 2.12–2.18) which reflect the tactical use of herd drives and slaughter to meet a number of seasonal requirements in the annual schedule. In the case of the rock shelter material from the Abri Pataud, the faunal assemblage is a result of carcass parts being brought into the site either as raw material or as food. Resolution and integrity are therefore much lower, but as a result the material will be of use in studies of the long term use of such a rock shelter facility. The high value for ribs is of interest since these may represent small food packages being brought into the site. Otherwise consumption and discard of high food parts, as measured by the MGUI, and allowing for differential survival factors, either took place elsewhere or was so thorough that only fragments, difficult to assign to anatomical part or species, survive. In this case the lowest food value part – phalanges and distal metacarpal – survived because they were not processed so thoroughly, since they had little food value. However, they got to the site since they 'rode in' with other high value food parts to which they were attached. A spatial analysis of the deposits and especially the plotting of size and type of fragment around the hearths that form such a notable feature at the Abri Pataud would be one way to help answer some of the questions this brief analysis has raised.

However it is most probable that the bone residues at these two locations provide a negative image of the types of food management activities that went on there. At the Abri Pataud attrition is very high since this is a consumption site. Here low food parts such as feet and skull, as represented by teeth, were introduced as by-products alongside other bone elements which entered the site not as complete animals but as food parcels. These were subsequently largely destroyed as a result of their food utility. The bone assemblage is, therefore, not a direct reflection of reindeer hunting strategies (Spiess 1979) but rather the dustbin of eating and food management strategies. On the contrary, the Stellmoor assemblage is part of a processing location, where the acquisition of large amounts of meat may not have been as important as some accounts (Clark 1957:fig. 27) have maintained.

One further example is provided by Vörös (1982) for the animal fauna from the Hungarian site of Ságvár, SE region. This site, dating to the LUP, is not in his opinion either a home base or a kill site, even though it has a rich bone and stone assemblage. His analysis (table 6.11), which utilises a simple form of assessing the economic potential of the skeleton, concludes that Ságvár was a processing site, as shown by the high values for low utility parts – skull, teeth and foot bones. A very different assemblage of reindeer bones was bound in the Pilisszántó I rock shelter, where high MGUI bones are more common, although the large numbers of phalanges lead Vörös to suggest that the treatment of hides, still with the feet attached, took place in the cave. Moreover, he believes that the meat may have been introduced into the cave in a filleted condition since scapula, distal humerus, proximal radio-cubitus and femur (except the capita femoris, which had all been chopped off) were absent from the bone collection.

The challenge in European palaeolithic archaeology is to develop these studies of economic anatomy and food management strategies to encompass the wide diversity of animal species that existed. The two examples used here (table 6.10) are primarily single species situations, as indeed are the bison drive studies (Speth 1983; Frison 1975; Reher 1977), and the original work on the Nunamiut (Binford 1978a, 1981). The four main pleistocene herd species, bos, horse, red deer and reindeer do indeed occur with great frequency (tables 7.3, 7.4, 7.5) in many faunal assemblages from the provinces and regions of Europe. One classic example is provided by the changing proportions of animal species at Combe-Grenal (Bordes and Prat 1965:fig. 7.1). However many other species – ibex, chamois, roe deer, giant deer – not to mention the megafaunal elements and the carnivores, are also encountered. While the single species studies may provide another example of an entering wedge into a complex situation, the archaeological study of the entire animal community will almost certainly add new insights to our understanding of what hunters did for a living, and why, that extends beyond any ethnoarchaeological experiences. The result will be an appreciation of resource use and food management that is a long way from the eight year mammoth barbecue.

Settlement systems

The investigation of settlement systems forms another example of the spatial signature of mobile adaptations (table 2.6). In many cases palaeolithic and

Table 6.11. *A comparison of three reindeer assemblages as determined by groups of anatomical elements.*

The groupings are from Kretzoi (1968) and the analysis is by Vörös (1982). The assemblage from Le Flageolet (Delpech 1970) is interpreted as a secondary butchery site with a high proportion of meat bones on site

Anatomical elements	Ságvár		Pilisszántó I		Le Flageolet II Layer IX	
	N	%	N	%	N	%
Head: including skull, mandible, atlas and hyoid	1094	73.5	219	15.6	232	37.1
Trunk: vertebra, sacrum, pelvis	43	3.3	29	2	20	3.2
Meat bearing limbs: scapula, humerus, radius, ulna, femur, patella, tibia	56	3.8	396	28.2	108	17.3
Foot bones: astragalus, calcaneus, carpals, tarsals, metacarpals, metatarsals	232	15.6	333	23.4	211	33.8
Phalanges	58	3.9	425	30.3	54	8.6
Totals:	1488		1402		625	

mesolithic settlement systems have been defined in terms of groups of sites (table 6.12) where particular site types – base camp, hunting camp, transit camp – are defined by quantities of material (Isaac 1971:fig. 6.21) and the spatial size of the patch. The assumption has always been that a high density of occupation represents an important occupation and hence descriptions such as home base (Vita-Finzi and Higgs 1970) have been applied to collections of material. While many of the examples in table 6.12 define their use of such terms, there is little consideration of variation between geographical areas. For example, the density of materials in a cave in the NC region might lead to its classification as a home base and therefore an important node in the investigation of regional settlement systems (Gamble 1978a). However the same site might only reach the status of a small camp in another area, e.g. in the ME region, where the range of material residue densities in sites was much higher (Bailey *et al.* 1983a).

Moreover, base camps, in the form of winter villages, are few and far between among contemporary northern hunters (Campbell 1968:map 1), and I am not convinced that we have as yet securely identified such a class of site in the palaeolithic record of Europe. That does not mean that they do not exist or that there are no strong contenders – Kostenki, Dolní Věstonice, Pavlov, Mezin, Trecassats (H. de Lumley 1969b:401) – for such a title. Neither should we assume that all areas at all times possessed *complete* settlement systems (Chapter 8). If we start with a home base model then certainly we will find 'home bases' wherever we look in palaeolithic Europe. In fact we may be looking at overnight camps used by hunting parties operating at extreme distances from the core areas of their territories where the home bases were located (Gamble 1983a).

This shows only that settlement system models are very open to proving our favourite models right. When it suits us, a thick layer of cultural debris in a site becomes evidence for long and uninterrupted occupation. In other cases the changing presence of carnivores, as revealed by the quantities of their remains, is taken as a measure of changing intensities of use by human groups of rock shelter facilities. Moreover, the excavated contents of a site, and especially the faunal remains, then become the main evidence for explaining why that location rather than any other was selected for habitation. The circular argument between finding red deer bones and deciding that the site was optimally located for their exploitation is often all too apparent (Higgs *et al.* 1967).

An alternative off-site approach (Chapters 1, 2), applied elsewhere (Foley 1981c; Isaac 1981a; Judge 1973), is so far lacking in studies of palaeolithic Europe. However, some guidelines for future work are now available and can be summarised as follows.

(a) Objects that are found together were not necessarily used together. This simple observation is central to understanding the formation of sites and the types of sites we possess in the palaeolithic record of Europe. I expect a basically

Table 6.12. *Some settlement system models and the site types that are defined by various archaeological observations*

Settlement types	Archaeological correlates
Binford and Binford 1966	*Settlement types articulated within a settlement system.* Their use defines the settlement system (p. 269)
base camp	maintenance tasks – preparation and consumption of food and the manufacture of tools for use in other locations (p. 268)
work camp	extractive tasks – lithic procurement, collection stations, kill locations; assemblages dominated by tools used in those specific extractive tasks. The degree to which maintenance activities may be represented depends upon the size and duration of stay of the social unit (p. 269)
transient camp	overnight stay – minimal maintenance activities of a travelling group
Hole and Flannery 1967 seasonal base camps	*Palaeolithic settlement in the Khorramabad Valley* one or two extended families living in a large cave located on an ecotone. Male and female associated artifacts: ornaments, hearths, burials and a wide variety of tool types. Animal bones up to 500 per m³. Wild goat and sheep bones represented by every bone in the body: selected bones only of onager, aurochs and red deer
butchery sites	two to three hunters using small rock shelters with no clear ecological location; task specific tools, no ornaments; less than 100 identifiable animal bones per m³, often no more than 5 per m³. Butchering events particularly of onager, aurochs and red deer, some small game
transitory stations	small groups of hunters; small surface scatters with no bone and no clear ecological location

Winters 1963 (table 77, p. 35)   *Wabash river drainage basin*

	General utility tools	Weapons	Fabricating/ processing domestic tools
settlements	10 + 5%	15 + 5%	75 + 5%
transient camps	15 + 5%	30 + 5%	55 + 5%
base camps	15 + 10%	40 + 10%	40 +5%
specialised hunting camps	25 + 5%	55 + 10%	20 + 10%
generalised hunting camps	55 + 20%	35 + 10%	10 + 10%

Settlement types	Archaeological correlates
Vita-Finzi and Higgs 1970 home base	*Site catchment analysis model* primarily concerned with the exploitation of a site territory. A densely occupied cave (p. 6)
transit site	small chipping floors occurring on probable migration routes (p. 7). American-type 'kill' sites also included in this category
Wilmsen (1970) limited activity locations	*Great plains* located near available resources and would be expected to yield evidence of these resources as the primary activity of the site
multiple activity locations	located in favourable camping areas and would be expected to yield evidence of a variety of activities performed by a relatively large number of people

Table 6.12 – cont.

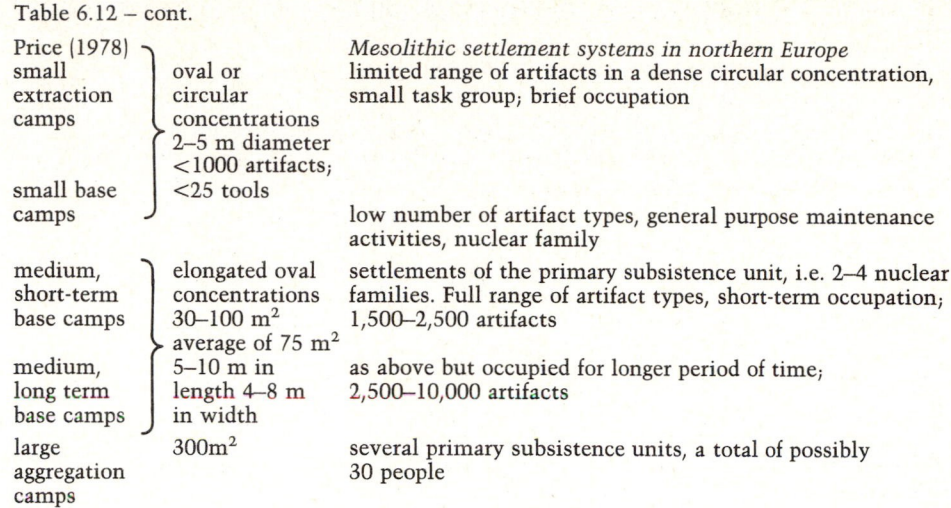

Price (1978)		*Mesolithic settlement systems in northern Europe*
small extraction camps	oval or circular concentrations 2–5 m diameter <1000 artifacts; <25 tools	limited range of artifacts in a dense circular concentration, small task group; brief occupation
small base camps		low number of artifact types, general purpose maintenance activities, nuclear family
medium, short-term base camps	elongated oval concentrations 30–100 m² average of 75 m²	settlements of the primary subsistence unit, i.e. 2–4 nuclear families. Full range of artifact types, short-term occupation; 1,500–2,500 artifacts
medium, long term base camps	5–10 m in length 4–8 m in width	as above but occupied for longer period of time; 2,500–10,000 artifacts
large aggregation camps	300m²	several primary subsistence units, a total of possibly 30 people

coarse grained signature to go with the distinctive patches of cultural materials that are found throughout the continent (Chapter 1).

(b) We need to develop methods akin to those discussed earlier that dealt with seating plans and working positions in order to identify reliably such basic units as residential camp and winter village. One attempt in this direction is Conkey's work on aggregation sites (1980) in Cantabrian Spain, which seems, in part, to have been prompted by the lack of any 'big' lithic artifact sites in the region which would otherwise have fitted the description. As I have shown earlier in this chapter, large quantities of lithic material may not be a characteristic feature of home bases. I would suggest that a more telling characteristic will come from the relation of such sites to the pattern of regional artifact density that surrounds them. The network of hunting blinds, caches, stores, overnight camps, procurement locations and so forth (see Binford 1978a:fig. 5.2) should be much greater within a certain distance from such villages.

(c) If we adopt these models, then a change in scale is required when dealing with palaeolithic settlement systems. We already know that palaeolithic 'sites' can be very considerable in extent. At Borchevo II a trench some sixty metres in length and 800 m² in area was dug alongside the Don river to trace the stratigraphically overlapping settlements (Efimenko and Boriskovskij 1953; Klein 1969a:205). Excavation along the Prut (Păunescu 1970), middle Dniestr (Gorestky and Ivanova (eds.) 1982) and along the Danube in the Austrian Wachau, NC region, at Willendorf (Felgenhauer 1956–9) shows spreads of almost continuous material for several kilometres. H. de Lumley and Boone state that in southern France, MW region, the earlier palaeolithic site of Trecassats covers an area of sixty hectares, with six major concentrations. They describe this site as a palaeolithic village (1976a:649). Between the Jarama and

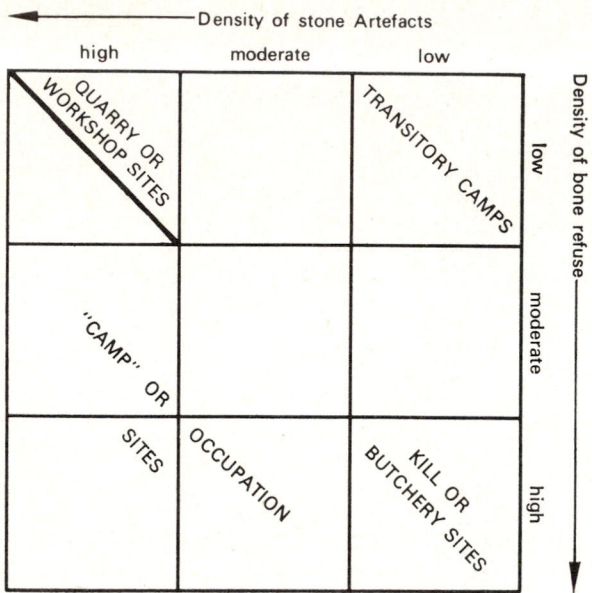

6.20 Classification of quantities of residues on open sites according to a settlement system model (Isaac 1971:285, fig. 10a).

Manzanares rivers in Spain there is abundant evidence from gravel pits of dense earlier palaeolithic occupation (Santonja *et al.* 1980:fig. 1), and the gazetteer compiled by Roe (1968b) for lower palaeolithic artifacts in southern England shows comparable dense spreads of material along and between the major river valleys.

Instead of thinking of 'sites', we should regard such dense occurrences of artifacts as sampling windows into deeply buried past landscapes on which were deposited, at variable densities, robust cultural residues in the form of stone tools. Collections of surface material from the Drahany plateau in Moravia, NC region (Absolon 1935–6; Valoch 1967b:fig. 1), and in Hesse, also NC region, in central Germany (Luttropp and Bosinski 1971), have shown how even unsystematic survey can produce large quantities of material at a local-region scale. The sampling of eroding red bed deposits in Greece (Vita-Finzi 1978; Dakaris *et al.* 1964) produces similar opportunities to gain access to large and otherwise buried landscapes.

The results are not easy to interpret partly because we are still trying to convert the scatters of flints into something we can call a 'site'. A similar problem has been encountered in the study of the mesolithic of southern Britain through fieldwalking (Shennan 1981). In fact the first prerequisite to interpretation may be to abandon such site focused concepts with their connotations of high integrity, high resolution conditions, and instead to document the variable traces of mobile adaptations. As discussed earlier (Chapter 2), the degree of

Table 6.13. *Palaeolithic assemblages from the terraces of the Lot and Garonne and the plateau area between*

	Choppers	Handaxes	Flake tools	Debitage products
Terraces	dominate the assemblages	less common but well made	average represen-tation	common
Plateau	rare/absent	more common, especially cordiforms and amygdal-oids	very common	less important

Source: Turq 1978

clumping or dispersal of materials would be a key descriptive element in looking at these past landscapes in terms of the signatures they contain.

At another level of analysis we can look at the contents of these lithic scatters. In a small study Turq (1978) examined earlier palaeolithic material between the Lot and Garonne rivers, SW region (table 6.13). This small survey is suggestive of important patterning as revealed by differences in the recovery of distinctive artifact types from particular contexts. More studies need to be brought to bear on Turq's findings that expediently made choppers and chopping tools are most commonly recovered from riverside rather than plateau locations. This is certainly the case at the sites of Bilzingsleben, Wangen and Wallendorf in East Germany, NC region, Vértesszöllös and other Buda assemblages in Hungary, SE region, and Clacton, Swanscombe, Northfleet and Thurrock in southern England, NW region. Pebble tools, like large handaxes, are rarely found in caves. Indeed, the descriptive term clactonian that is used to describe chopper tool assemblages and industries in the NW region has *never* been used to describe an assemblage from a cave. While some might argue that this is because the *Clactonians* never lived in caves, or in areas where caves were available for occupation, this is not a convincing explanation. Many other activities went on by the riversides in pre-stage 5 Europe (Chapter 7), and this spatial signature involving a class of artifact forms one small component.

(d) Much of this alternative approach would seem to stand or fall by our ability to demonstrate contemporaneity between sites. This we are unlikely to achieve with an acceptable degree of accuracy for pre-stage 6 material, and even in a period as recent as the LUP the notion of exact contemporaneity between assemblages is spurious. There will always be a standard deviation on the likelihood of such an unlikely event! For many archaeologists, that is evidence of the failure of a regional approach. I would be bound to reply that palaeolithic archaeology is not concerned with those precious moments of time (Roe 1981:197) that can be pinpointed with the accuracy of a digital watch. The patterns of human behaviour we are investigating are both repetitive and accumulative, in terms of the residues they create, over temporal cycles of variable duration. These range from cycles with a wavelength of several decades to those with a wavelength of the order of 100 Kyr or an entire interglacial/glacial cycle (Butzer 1982:table 2.2). Establishing the magnitude of these wavelengths and the accompanying archaeological signatures that characterise human behaviour operating at such repeated frequencies is a very different story from calling for more dates and greater chronological precision of events within these cycles (Chapter 9). I am interested in developing a framework of analysis for palaeolithic studies which deals with processes – ecological, behavioural, social – at a variety of time scales, rather than one which is drawn up to look like a calendar and so ignores the processes over which it is imposed. The central proposition in my approach is that events do not have to be exactly contemporary to be compared, since the object of study is common process rather than shared temporal moments. Although the imagination may beat a little quicker when we gaze on a precious moment of time, such as a mint fresh handaxe with conjoining flakes, this is a misleading model of what the archaeological, and especially the palaeolithic record, consists of.

I have provided pointers in this chapter towards the investigation of the palaeolithic record by means of spatial signatures. It is too early to determine whether the regional model will reveal very different signatures for all the aspects covered here. I think this unlikely in the case of camp site layout. However, I expect that future analysis will reveal inter-regional variation as measured by the signatures from food management strategies. This results from variation in environmental structure, resources and consequently management decisions, and will not be a matter of noting that in different areas different species formed the mainstay of the diet, but rather that variable tactical use was made of storage, scavenging and hunting strategies. It is however still very early days in the investigation of food management strategies, and it is not yet possible to draw any general conclusions. The same is also the case for settlement system studies. One reason for this is the lack of precise methodologies for dealing with the intricate nature of the palaeolithic record that is revealed as soon as we start asking questions about the behaviour that led to its formation. In the next chapter I will expand the scale of analysis and look through the small rather than the big end of the telescope. At this scale of investigation, but with a less precise methodology, the regional model begins to serve as a truly analytical device.

CHAPTER 7

DEMOGRAPHY AND STYLE

Well, I try my best
To be just like I am,
But everybody wants you
To be just like them.
They sing while you slave and I just get bored.
I ain't gonna work on Maggie's farm no more.
Bob Dylan (1965)

Introduction

The variable distribution of population in space has many obvious implications for the formation of the regional archaeological record. It is perhaps surprising then that so little attention has been paid to demographic patterning in the spatial dimension of palaeolithic studies. Instead most of the interest has focused on questions of change throughout time; most notably population growth and decline.

The only significant demographic studies dealing with spatial organisation have concentrated upon the observed ratios between persons and the floor area they occupy (Naroll 1962; Cook and Heizer 1965; Wiessner 1974; Yellen 1977a), as an aid to calculating the number of people who inhabited a site (Jochim 1976:174; Hahn 1977:278). These studies generally take little or no account of the spatial patterns in the data that might for example be produced by a seating model (Chapter 6). They are not concerned with the behaviour that produced the patterns but only with how many m^2 it covered so that the ratios can be applied. This is a good instance where sound ethnographic observations of dynamic behaviour are transferred to an archaeological context without adding any intervening, and yet very necessary, methodological steps. Without the addition of such procedural steps (e.g. fig. 1.2), these observations add only anecdote rather than supplying general principles for understanding the statics of the palaeolithic record. We need to know more about the arrangement of personnel in camp sites and the implications this has for the formation of the archaeological record before such person/floor area ratios are of much use in palaeolithic investigations (Whitelaw, n.d.).

Changes in the annual distribution of palaeolithic personnel have been studied by means of seasonality models, and several examples are provided in Chapter 5. Many of these case studies (e.g. Gamble 1978a; Sturdy 1975; Barker 1981) are truly regional in scale but are considered as economic rather than demographic in approach. One problem with such studies is that their regional terms of reference are all too quickly established either by the distribution of known sites of a certain period, or by the use of a simple common denominator such as reindeer, and lastly by convenient topography to tie it all together in a regional package. As a result the way that a subject for study (reindeer economies) was chosen or an area selected (southern Germany, central Italy) for investigation makes it very difficult indeed to compare between case studies and so use the results of such work in a wider, regional context.

The purpose of this chapter is to look further at regional organisation as a factor in the differential formation of the palaeolithic record. The way has been opened for such an approach by the development of a regional model for the continent in Chapter 3. One reason for constructing this regional model of palaeolithic Europe lay in the link between the dimensions of energy and space for understanding variable adaptive behaviour among mobile groups (Chapter 2). So far in this book I have not tested the ability of the model to act as a framework for the measurement of past behaviour, and it is now time to do so.

What the carnivores can tell us

In order to test the model we need to ask at least two very basic questions.

(a) Is the continent of Europe of sufficient size and environmental diversity to produce variable patterns of human behaviour as a result of selection pressure operating upon adaptive strategies?

(b) How can we measure such variation with palaeolithic residues?

The questions are not easily answered. It might be thought that quaternary studies could be used to establish any differences in selection pressure across the continent. The appearance of ice sheets in the northern province would be an obvious example of harsh conditions which we would expect to have considerable impact on palaeolithic adaptations and hence on the palaeolithic record. The ebb and flow of settlement in this province might be used as a measure of this factor. By contrast, the better conditions in the unglaciated southern and mediterranean provinces might be measured by the more abundant evidence for settlement traces.

While this argument seems very reasonable, it does have a serious flaw. We are once again in danger of setting up a self-fulfilling model where our view of what life was like in the palaeolithic not surprisingly turns out to be exactly correct when we come to examine the evidence! In other words, there is no independent check that our starting assumptions were permissible. I have no doubt that conditions in the northern province were always more severe than elsewhere in the continent. However, such a model needs to be supported by measurements which show that these conditions did indeed affect behaviour rather than by looking at the archaeology and attributing any anomalies or variation we see to these *a priori* interpretations. Otherwise why bother to go to the trouble and expense of examining the archaeology when we can reach the same conclusions by exercising our imaginations?

An independent yardstick that allows us to break out of the possible circularity of such arguments is provided by the carnivorous fellow-travellers who, during the course of the pleistocene, created their own 'archaeological' record (see Chapters 1 and 6). The bears, lions, hyenas and wolves that laid down a faunal record were also subject to variable selection pressure as exerted by environmental constraints. In the case of the bear, the use of cave and rock shelters as winter hibernation dens was conditioned by such factors as the depth of snow cover and the severity of permafrost which prevented digging dens in earth banks. Where snow cover was slight during the arid glacial minima, the alternative method of den construction by digging in snow banks was also prevented since not enough mantle was available for insulating the den. It therefore follows that the use of caves and rock shelters as den facilities by the cave and brown bear will act as a direct measure of selection pressure on an aspect of behaviour.

A similar case can be made for the hyenas and wolves. These species use dens as refuge sites where cubs can be left in safety and where food can be consumed without disturbance by other carnivores. In these instances, the incidence of denning behaviour is a measure of competition between carnivore species, and once again caves and rock shelters will be used under permafrost conditions where alternative methods of den construction are not possible.

These aspects of behaviour have been described as a carnivore coping strategy (Gifford 1981:413), where they utilise a tactic of setting up 'safe-houses'. The behaviour is variable, but where it occurs a tremendous potential exists for the creation of faunal residues. Since this is the case, we can use the distribution and composition of these assemblages to examine critically the relation between the regional model and the production of a variable record of dynamic behaviour in a set of static residues (Gamble 1983b, 1984a).

An impression of how the faunal record acts as an instrument for measuring variable behaviour can be gauged from Kahlke's (1975) survey of upper-lower to upper-middle pleistocene faunas. He divides the continent into three faunal provinces as determined by the types of species found within three large geographical areas. These are a western province (Spain, France) separated from an eastern province (Greece, Yugoslavia, Roumania, Czechoslovakia, Hungary and western Russia) by the Rhine, which he terms a transitional province (table 7.1). The range of animal species, both carnivore and herbivore, is much greater than the basic pleistocene list presented in table 3.11. There are several canid species and instances of antelopes and even camels in the faunal communities. The number of samples is not large, and it must be remembered that these are

Table 7.1. *A comparison of herbivore and carnivore species representation from open sites in western, central and eastern Europe*

Key: ULP = upper lower pleistocene; LMP = lower middle pleistocene; UMP = upper middle pleistocene.

	Site sample size	Occurrence of species		Average number of species per level/site	
		herbivores	carnivores	herbivores	carnivores
Western province					
ULP	16	113	15	7.1	0.9
LMP	6	33	2	5.5	0.3
UMP	2	5	0	2.5	0
Transitional province					
ULP	10	79	32	7.9	3.2
LMP	2	18	7	9	3.5
UMP	4	16	1	4	0.3
Eastern province					
ULP	24	149	78	6.2	3.3
LMP	8	46	10	5.8	1.3
UMP	11	72	35	6.5	3.2

Source: After Kahlke 1975

the important sites from the point of view of producing well preserved, numerically large faunal collections for the purpose of taxonomic analysis. However, a very clear pattern of carnivore representation is produced. The big Rhine gravel pits such as Mosbach and Süssenborn, together with Kahlke's eastern province, have consistently produced higher proportions of carnivore species per faunal collection than is the case for his western province. The information from a very small sample of caves in the same provinces (table 7.2) reveals that considerable numbers of carnivore species did exist in the western province, thereby emphasising the selective deposition of these species in the faunal record of these provinces.

In 1869, Dawkins published a table in which he listed the occurrence of the British pleistocene fauna by its depositional context. There are 112 river deposits in his table which produced only 0.25 large carnivores per fossil locality. By contrast there is an average of 3.6 carnivores per faunal collection in the 36 caves on his list. While Boyd Dawkins' figures cover the entire pleistocene, this variation in carnivore representation certainly echoes and adds to Kahlke's lists for the western province.

This exercise in pattern recognition can be taken further to illustrate how variation in behaviour is important for understanding the formation of part of the human record for the same period. If we return to the distribution of pre-neanderthal fossil remains (table 5.3; M. de Lumley 1973, 1976a; Oakley *et al.* 1971; Cook *et al.* 1982), a very striking pattern that is complementary to the faunal data can be seen. The pre-neanderthal finds in western Europe, as defined

Table 7.2. *A comparison of herbivore and carnivore species representation from cave sites in western, central and eastern Europe*

ULP = upper lower pleistocene; LMP = lower middle pleistocene; UMP = upper middle pleistocene.

	Sample size	Occurrence of species		Average number of species per level/site	
		herbivores	carnivores	herbivores	carnivores
Western province					
ULP	2	12	15	6	7.5
LMP	1	8	11	8	11
UMP	7	48	37	6.9	5.3
Transitional province					
LMP	1	6	6	6	6
Eastern province					
ULP	3	29	33	9.7	11
UMP	8	63	45	7.9	5.7

Source: After Kahlke 1975

by Kahlke's faunal provinces, come predominantly from caves such as Lazaret, Arago, Grotte du Prince, Atapuerca, Cova Negra, Pontnewydd, La Chaise, Orgnac and Fontéchevade. The sample is not large but set against it are the rare finds from open, riverside sites at Swanscombe, Bañolas and Biache. In the areas termed by Kahlke transitional and eastern, the finds are almost exclusively from riverside, lakeside contexts. These include Bilzingsleben, Steinheim, Mauer, Ehringsdorf, and Vértesszöllös. Only the find from Petralona cave in Greece contradicts this pattern. If for the moment we allow that these riverside finds are not the result of cannibalism (Behm-Blancke 1960), but are almost certainly part of carnivore collected residues, then we begin to see a major difference in the formation of the palaeontological record in pre-stage 5 Europe. The tables suggest that carnivores in Kahlke's western province frequently transported food back to their 'safe-houses', where they could be assured of finishing it undisturbed (Binford 1981:221). Since humans were part of the diet, they too were transported and incorporated into the cave deposits, as at Arago (H. de Lumley and Boone 1976b:fig. 8). These figures may well be pointing towards greater competition and selection pressure on carnivore and, by extension, human adaptive patterns in this area. The other provinces recognised by Kahlke could be interpreted as having possibly higher animal biomass with consequently lower levels of competition between carnivores. Hence feeding took place at the site of the kills by the riverside, as Wernert's (1957) astute observations on hyena gnawed bones in the Achenheim loesses testify. The pre-neanderthalers were still part of the carnivore diet in these areas but were rarely transported any distance to safe refuges.

These observations may be extended further to include a comment on the contemporary artifact residues. It is predominantly in Kahlke's western province that we find assemblages containing handaxes (McBurney 1950; Andree 1939; Valoch 1968; Schwabedissen 1970). Whatever the role of these objects in pre-stage 5 technologies (Chapter 6), they represent a greater expenditure of effort than the flake and chopping tool assemblages that are encountered in the transitional and eastern provinces at sites such as Bilzingsleben, Wangen and Vértesszöllös. If we allow that time stress places a selective hone on both the manufacture and organisation of technology, then the greater investment of energy in the acheulean assemblages of the western province reflects the greater competition and selection pressure imposed by the environment on human adaptive strategies. The riverside was a dangerous place to be in this area, but it offered a predictable high density of prey killed either by carnivores or resulting from natural mortalities. These could perhaps be used within a scavenging strategy but would yield returns only if the scavenger/forager was prepared with a suitable tool kit to get at such resources before other carnivores arrived. The same spur to increasing the efficiency of technology and scheduling its use did not exist in central Europe, as at Bilzingsleben, or apparently in some adaptive contexts of the western province, as at Clacton. At both sites the simply flaked chopping tools and *ad hoc* flakes were perfectly sufficient for stripping flesh off bones and cracking them for marrow as scratches on the bones (Mania and Dietzel 1980) and microwear polishes on the tools (Keeley 1980) reveal.

This partial scenario of the middle pleistocene occupation of Europe serves my present purpose since it turns on its head the traditional view of life in the continent. This claimed that the *genial* forest conditions of western Europe led to a *higher* level of culture as evidenced by the abundant finds of handaxes (McBurney 1950). However, if we start to use the accompanying faunal records as an independent measure of variable selection pressure on behaviour, we find instead that the centre of the continent was the area where the 'original affluent society' might have found the living easier. This is of course contrary to what our common-sense view of the differences between stone tools tells us about how well regional populations were doing. The conclusion also highlights my earlier point about needing to measure past behaviour through static residues rather than just by assuming that we understand how the pre-stage 5 world worked. A further conclusion would be that a considerable demographic imbalance existed, with population densities being higher in the centre of the continent than on the western margins. Once again such a conclusion runs counter to the usual way that population estimates are drawn from the numbers of find spots, and yet in this instance can be justified by means of the independent measurement provided by the carnivores.

This sketch obviously lacks fine chronological control and begs its own starting assumptions – for example, that carnivores rather than man are the major agents responsible for the creation of faunal residues in this period of the pleistocene. Moreover, I have broken one of the guidelines laid down in Chapter

3 for deciding on the regional partitions, since the patterns in the data rather than the 'eternal anchors' have been used to frame the discussion. For that reason the two questions which opened this section have not been adequately answered. In order to do so I shall now use the carnivore data from the last glacial, where finer chronological resolution and a unity of depositional context, caves and rock shelters, will provide a more controlled setting for testing the regional model.

Carnivores and herbivores in cave faunas

The cave faunas from the last glacial period have been divided in tables 7.3, 7.4 and 7.5 into three chronological groups. These are the early last glacial, 118–35 Kyr, 35–20 Kyr, and the period dealing with the glacial maxima as well as the beginnings of the process of deglaciation. The material is not continuous across Europe but reflects the pattern of active research and the distribution of karst features. All of these samples are associated with palaeolithic material which has been used to sort the collections into the three chronological groups. The standard of reports is very variable, and as a result the data in these tables have been dealt with only on a presence/absence basis for the major herbivores and carnivores (Gamble 1983b).

The sample areas do provide coverage for most of the nine regions. If we concentrate upon the large carnivore information, the figures from all periods indicate a much greater frequency of occurrence for bear, lion, hyena and wolf in the faunal collections from the regions of the northern province, and considerably reduced frequencies in the southern and mediterranean provinces. These proportional figures have been further compared in table 7.6, where the average number of carnivore species per faunal collection is presented. This table brings out an interesting distinction between the high values for carnivores in the northern as opposed to the southern province. However, the two mediterranean samples from Languedoc/Roussillon (Pillard 1972) and the Istrian peninsula (Musil 1980–1) both give proportionately higher values than those in the southern regions. These figures can be explained by local topography contributing to more marginal conditions and hence the variable character of carnivore behaviour patterns.

These figures may therefore be taken as a measure of variation in past carnivore behaviour. They conform to our expectations that harsher conditions prevailed in the northern parts of the continent, and allow us to see the outcome of variable competitive relationships. The 'intellectual anchors' of latitude, longitude and relief (Chapter 3) can be taken as part of a predictive framework for analysing transformations between energy, the organisation of adaptive behaviour and the creation of variable palaeontological records. Moreover, the indications from the Languedoc/Roussillon and Istrian samples are that the three benchmarks must be taken together if variation is to be predicted, and that

Table 7.3. *The relative occurrence of pleistocene herbivores and carnivores in cave faunal assemblages from the period 118–35 Kyr*

	(1) Southern Germany	(2) Switz- erland	(3) Crimea	(4) S.W. France	(5) Cantabrian Spain	(6) S.France
	%	%	%	%	%	%
mammoth	63	14	69	8	5[a]	7
woolly rhino	79	21	46	15	47[b]	10
bovids	59	36	92	93	58	55
giant deer	30	7	52	—	5	—
elk	—	—	—	—	—	7
horse	93	29	92	89	63	89
E. hydruntinus	—	—	—	2	—	31
musk ox	6	7	—	—	—	—
red deer	61	50	77	39	63	73
reindeer	71	29	23	69	—	31
pig	10	14	15	20	16	23
ibex	24	50	—	13	21	71
chamois	6	64	—	2	11	13
fallow deer	—	—	—	2	—	—
saiga	—	—	92	—	—	—
roe deer	14	—	8	5	21	21
bear	77	93	46	27	26	63
lion	47	21	15	6	11	23
hyena	67	21	77	22	5	42
wolf	67	21	69	22	21	55
leopard	6	7	—	—	5	31
red fox	47	21	46	—	5	31
arctic fox	35	29	62	—	—	—
Vulpes sp.	8	7	—	25	—	—
lynx	8	14	8	—	5	31
wolverine	14	7	—	—	—	2
badger	12	7	8	2	5	—
wild cat	12	7	—	—	—	7
Number of faunal assemblages	49	14	13	59	19	38

Source: (1) Gamble 1978a (2) Müller-Beck 1968b (3) Klein 1965 (4) Mellars 1967; Delpech 1976 (5) Freeman 1973; Straus 1977a (6) Pillard 1972.

[a] *Elephas antiquus*
[b] *Dicerorhinus kirchbergensis*

if this is done the simple units of measurement discussed here are sufficient to monitor, in a rudimentary fashion, selection pressure on past behaviour.

The patterns in the faunal data are very robust. From the multi-level site of Combe-Grenal, SW region, the changing proportions of herbivore bones have been used to document the changing animal communities during Würm I and II (Bordes and Prat 1965). The Würm I faunas are dominated by red deer, while in Würm II reindeer makes a more significant showing, as seen in the number of fragments identified to this species (fig. 7.1). However, against these major fluctuations in the proportional composition of the main large herbivores, the occurrence of carnivores remains very steady. The figures are 0.85 large car-

Table 7.4. *The relative occurrence of pleistocene herbivores and carnivores in cave faunal assemblages from the period 35–20 Kyr*

	(7) England	(1) Southern Germany	(8) Bükk mts. Hungary	(4) S.W. France	(5) Cantabrian Spain
	%	%	%	%	%
mammoth	66	90	30	17	3
woolly rhino	73	55	40	4	19[a]
bovids	66	50	55	87	55
giant deer	60	10	45	7	—
elk	?	—	10	—	—
horse	86	100	65	93	74
E. hydruntinus	—	—	—	26	—
musk ox	—	—	—	2	—
red deer	46	35	40	83	84
reindeer	66	100	80	98	10
pig	—	—	15	39	19
ibex	—	70	15	70	65
chamois	—	25	35	65	55
fallow deer	—	—	—	—	—
saiga	—	10	—	—	—
roe deer	—	—	15	35	48
bear	80	95	100	17	10
lion	53	45	40	7	—
hyena	80	30	85	15	6
wolf	60	70	80	41	26
leopard	—	—	—	—	10
red fox	66	75	70	15	32
arctic fox	?	60	5	2	—
Vulpes sp.	—	—	—	50	—
lynx	6	10	30	9	3
wolverine	6	10	5	—	3
badger	26	10	30	2	6
wild cat	33	—	15	4	10
Number of faunal assemblages	15	20	20	46	31

Source: References as in table 7.3, with (7) Campbell 1977 (8) Mottl 1941.

[a] includes *Dicerorhinus kirchbergensis*

nivore species per faunal assemblage in the 28 levels of Würm I, and 0.82 for the same number of assemblages in Würm II. A similar consistency from a number of sites is apparent from Pillard's (1972) data for Languedoc/Roussillon, MW region, where the Würm I and Würm II division based on red deer and reindeer is also apparent, with the average number of carnivores per assemblage being 3.2 and 2.7 respectively.

Data on the number of specimens identified to each species are rare for the European samples. However, it is possible to see that in those regions with low proportions of carnivores, as measured by presence/absence of these species, the faunal collections are also poor in the number of carnivore remains. A selection of these sites is shown in table 7.7. At the Abri Pataud, SW region, for example,

Table 7.5. *The relative occurrence of pleistocene herbivores and carnivores in cave faunal assemblages from the period 20–10 Kyr*

	(7) England	(1) Southern Germany	(4) S.W. France	(5) Cantabrian Spain
	%	%	%	%
mammoth	15	19	9	6?
woolly rhino	30	19	—	2
bovids	48	38	73	69
giant deer	36	4	3	—
elk	3	6	—	—
horse	63	83	83	85
E. hydruntinus	—	—	4	—
musk ox	—	4	—	—
red deer	30	46	50	98
reindeer	90	81	93	22
pig	—	4	30	13
ibex	6	27	37	72
chamois	—	4	39	54
fallow deer	—	2	—	—
saiga	3	2	17	—
roe deer	—	12	23	44
bear	66	44	24	13
lion	12?	4	—	2
hyena	24	10	3	2
wolf	30	27	47	15
leopard	—	—	—	—
red fox	42	27	1	41
arctic fox	18	34	—	—
Vulpes sp.	—	—	54	—
lynx	15	8	3	6
wolverine	—	4	—	—
badger	15	11	6	13?
wild cat	6	15	10	4
Number of faunal assemblages	33	47	70	54

Source: References as in Tables 7.3, 7.4

Bouchud (1975) identified some 45,000 remains of reindeer from the entire site, and yet only 99 specimens could be attributed to bear, lion, wolf and hyena. Even at Hortus in the Languedoc/Roussillon data set, the bear bones comprise only 9% of the total sample. In a study of the carnivores from Cantabrian sites, Straus (1982:87) draws particular attention to the odd-man-out site of Lezetxiki, where in the mousterian levels cave bear forms between 60% and 92% of the collection. Elsewhere in this sample from the SW region the carnivore data are comparable to the few sites detailed in table 7.7.

These very low figures for carnivore remains are all in stark contrast to sites from the northern province (table 7.8). Here the large carnivores are very commonly the most abundant species as measured by the quantities of identified bones. Cave bear (*Ursus spelaeus*) is frequently the most abundant carnivore but hyena and wolf are both strongly represented by quantities of

Table 7.6. *Carnivore representation in cave and rock shelter deposits during the last glacial*

The figures refer to the mean number of carnivore species per stratigraphic level. The figures in parentheses indicate the number of faunal assemblages from which the mean is calculated

	Middle palaeolithic	Early upper palaeolithic	Late upper palaeolithic
	118 Kyr–35 Kyr early last glacial and pleniglacial	35 Kyr–20 Kyr pleniglacial	20 Kyr–10 Kyr pleniglacial and late glacial
NORTHERN PROVINCE			
England		4.1 (15)	2.3 (33)
Southern Germany	4.02 (49)	4.05 (20)	1.87 (47)
Bükk/Hungary		4.6 (20)	
Crimea	3.3 (13)		
SOUTHERN PROVINCE			
South west France	1.06 (59)	1.6 (46)	1.56 (70)
Cantabria	0.84 (19)	1.0 (31)	0.94 (54)
Switzerland	2.57 (14)		
MEDITERRANEAN PROVINCE			
Languedoc/Roussillon/ Provence	2.89 (38)		
Istria/Yugoslavia		2.9 (13)	

(From Gamble 1984a:table 10.1) *Sources:* Campbell 1977; Gamble 1978a; Mottl 1941; Klein 1965; Delpech 1976; Freeman 1973; Straus 1977a; Müller-Beck 1968b; Pillard 1972; Musil 1980–1.

Note: Carnivores included in the table are: bear, lion, hyena, wolf, red fox, arctic fox, leopard, lynx, wolverine, badger and wild cat.

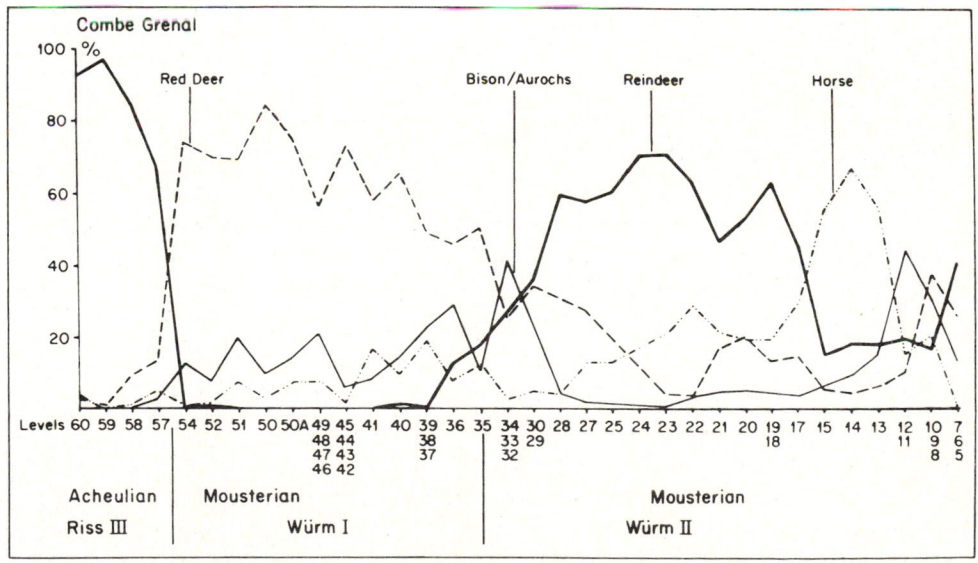

7.1 Changing proportions of the four main herbivores as measured by numbers of identified specimens at Combe-Grenal (Bordes and Prat 1965).

Table 7.7. *Specimen counts from selected assemblages in the southern and mediterranean provinces*

	Hortus (Pillard 1972) MP	Abri Pataud (Bouchud 1975) EUP					El Juyo (Klein *et al.* 1981) LUP	Grotta Polesini (Radmilli 1974) LUP	Palidoro (Bietta 1976–7) LUP
		a	b	c	d	e			
mammoth		1	1		5	3			
rhino	1								
bovids	18	28	71	326	48	41	54	980	235
horse	77	40	66	135	44	79	76	1250	73
E. hydruntinus	1			2		6		2262	352
musk ox					1				
red deer	74	38	19	268	172	108	3917	29,785	532
reindeer		1235	2080	17,302	21,119	3289			
pig			1	1		7	3	3453	65
ibex	1766	36	24	34	26	7	64	362	1
chamois		37	10	44	20	5		694	
fallow deer									
roe deer	1	1	1	47	10	7	120	3167	12
bear	215		1	3	6	1		3	
lion	3	2		3			1		1
hyena					3				
wolf	46	23	4	2	39	12	1	180	4
leopard	68						1?		
red fox	1	6	14	13	161	70	8	872	2
arctic fox									
lynx	59				4			49	
wolverine								3	
badger								241	22
wild cat								208	
Lepus sp.								365	
Aves sp.								850	

Abri Pataud: a = Protomagdalenian; b = Perigordian VI; c = Noaillian; d = Perigordian VI; e = Aurignacian levels 6–14

Table 7.8. *Specimen counts from selected assemblages in the northern province*

+ = ivory fragments

| | (Loubine 1980) Kudaro 1 MP | (Klein 1969b) Starosel'e MP | (Gamble 1979) Stadel communities | | | (Boessneck and Van den Driesch 1973) Brillenhöhle | | (Jánossy 1955) Istállöskö 3 levels | (Sturdy ms.) Kastelhöhle | |
			C UP	B MP	A MP	VIII EUP	IV LUP	EUP	LUP	LUP
mammoth		88	3+	57+	4+	26	1	+		
rhino	1	19	14	116	9				13	
bovids	25	138		101	39	2	6	13	42	62
giant deer		6		7	7					
elk			3						1	
horse		134	74	576	242	77	46	6		35
E.asinus		38,909								
musk ox									1?	
red deer	168	67	8	39	134		3	15	276	26
reindeer		35	142	82	7	101	45	87		1120
pig		1			1			1		
ibex	67					17		22	14	79
chamois	1					2	4	158	2	
fallow deer										
saiga		350				3				
roe deer	12			2	12				68	
Ovis ammon	43								32	
bear	387	1	1819	2069	902	535	15	c.15,000	2232	25
lion			16	40	23			11	10	
hyena		25	38	325	71			13		
wolf	27	32	131	83	60	6	17	152	55	31
leopard	3				4				18	
Cuon alpinus	21									
red fox	116	8				58	1		32	
arctic fox		5				30	42			5
Vulpes sp.			104	32	62	33	20	96		104
lynx				1	2	2	2	15		2
wolverine	20				6				15	
badger	10			1	20			4	8	
wild cat	1		2		8				2	
Lepus sp.	23	9	54	1	3	466	183	265	6	911
Aves sp.	79			no data		575	2095		41	532

Table 7.9. *The proportion (as a percentage) of sites by region which have yielded remains of the cave bear (Ursus spelaeus)*

The sample comprises 792 sites from Musil (1980–1). His survey deals only with *Ursus spelaeus* and other forms such as the brown bear (*Ursus arctos*) are not included

	NORTH	
West	Central	East
4[a]	29	8[b]

	SOUTH	
West	Alpine	East
14	14	17

	MEDITERRANEAN	
West	Central	East
2	4	7

Source: From Gamble 1984a:table 10.2

[a] Musil regards nearly all the specimens from England as arctoid forms, which are common in this part of the north west region.
[b] Sample: mainly from the Caucasus.

identified bones. However, variation is apparent between the regions of the northern province. While the number of carnivore species in the Crimean sample is high per assemblage, the quantities of specimens for each species are generally very low, as shown at Starosel'e in table 7.8.

A further means of looking at different faunal patterning between the regions in the three provinces is to consider the cave bear alone. This is possible due to a comprehensive synthesis by Musil (1980–1) that deals with the occurrence of this species in both palaeontological and archaeological contexts. The distribution of find spots for *Ursus spelaeus* is shown in table 7.9, which brings out the predominant distribution in the NC region. This of course coincides with the higher proportions of identified remains in these same collections. This would include sites such as the Weinberghöhlen (Heller 1955), Stadel (Gamble 1979), Istállöskö (Jánossy 1955), Pod hradem (Musil 1965) and many other cave bear sites. Ehrenberg (1951) has estimated that 99% of the 225,000 bones from the high level cave site of the Drachenhöhle bei Mixnitz in Austria were from cave bear. Comparable large collections are also known from southern Germany, as at the Erpfingen Barenhöhle (Dehm 1966) and the Zoolithenhöhle at Burgailenreuth (Heller 1972). The sample can be extended to include the open air site at Érd, near Budapest in the SE region. This palimpsest site is quite clearly a winter hibernation site for bears, as shown by the presence of neonatal bones. In this instance the bears made use of two small loess-filled 'valleys' in the limestone to dig earth dens (fig. 5.13). The cave bear bones comprise 89% of a total sample of 14,871 identified specimens (Gábori-Csánk 1968). The presence of other large carnivores (table 7.10) as well as hearths and stone tools makes it

Table 7.10. *Identified fragments from Érd*

The site is a palimpsest of behaviour and includes a winter hibernation den for cave bears, a hyena 'safe house' (which probably accounts for the large quantities of horse, rhino and bovids), as well as a place where mousterian people halted. The other large carnivores have also no doubt contributed to this large fauna. The list excludes small carnivores, rodents and lagomorphs. It is unlikely, as the excavator has claimed, that this open site represents a specialist cave bear hunting station.

mammoth	26
woolly rhino	176
bovids	72
giant deer	20
horse	715
Equus hydruntinus	44
musk ox	15?
red deer	55
reindeer	29
pig	1
ibex	9
chamois	1
bear	13,245
lion	24
hyena	281
wolf	105
Panthera sp.	1
red fox	24
arctic fox	4
badger	1

Source: Gábori-Csánk 1968:62–3

strictly comparable with some of the classic *Ursus spelaeus* sites from the caves of the neighbouring NC region.

The last point to comment upon with these carnivore data from caves concerns changes through time (tables 7.3, 7.4, 7.5). The most noticeable feature is the change in the 20–10 Kyr period among the large carnivores. The mean number of species drops quite sharply in samples dated to this period, and it is noticeable that hyena, lion and bear are all poorly represented as measured by the presence/absence data (table 7.5). Changes also occur among the large herbivores, especially mammoth and woolly rhino, which are most probably linked to the reduction in hyena and lion and, by inference, the use by these carnivores of caves as den facilities. In this late period, that is partly associated with the process of continental deglaciation, the wolf is the major bone collecting agent. It is also apparent that in many sites throughout all three provinces (table 7.5), we find at this time an increase in the number of fox bones. Associated with these small carnivores is an increase in bird bones from many different species but often dominated by remains of snow ptarmigan (*Lagopus albus*). This association is clearly seen at the Brillenhöhle and Grotta Polesini (tables 7.7, 7.8). While it may be tempting to see this as another instance of a diversification of the human dietary niche (Freeman 1973; Straus 1977a) that involved a number of small game species at this time, the alternative hypothesis, that this lagomorph/bird horizon in late glacial faunas is due to a change in the carnivores, notably fox, responsible for creating some of these residues, also needs to be looked at.

The changes through time shown in tables 7.3, 7.4 and 7.5 emphasise the large carnivore quartet of bear, lion, hyena and wolf. They are particularly associated with the period between 118 and 20 Kyr when interspecific competition was high due to worsening environmental conditions. This resulted in the creation of the spectacular bone cave residues of the northern province, in which the carnivores themselves form such an important component. This should not be taken to imply that none of the herbivore residues in the southern and mediterranean provinces were created by these same large carnivores. It is noticeable (table 7.5) that the average number of herbivores per faunal assemblage is very consistent between regions and time periods. More work needs to be done on the anatomical composition of species in the assemblages, as well as examination of the bones for gnawing and knife-cut traces in order to determine the relative contribution of man and carnivores to such collections. However, the data presented here do give us a strong basis for saying that we can measure variation in aspects of past adaptive behaviour, albeit carnivore denning behaviour. In other words, we have made that transition from statics to dynamics by examining the variable formation of the palaeontological record as a direct transformation of variation in the selection pressures exerted by environmental conditions on such behaviour. These carnivore residues could therefore give us a positive answer to the two questions on p. 306, and an indication that the regional model is indeed adequate for what it was designed to do. Equipped with this largely independent measure, we can now begin to examine some of the implications of these findings for the formation of the archaeological record.

Humans and caves

The questions at the beginning of this chapter were concerned with human behaviour and with the palaeolithic record. It is not possible to transpose the denning model for the large carnivores directly on to human adaptations. In particular the human use of caves and rock shelters is based upon a very different tactical appreciation of such fixed facilities within a settlement system strategy (Chapter 6). While on occasion caves may have been used as 'safe-houses' for sleeping, as Brain (1981) has argued for the southern African Australopithecine caves, the protection that such locations might afford from other predators was most probably only a minor reason for their use by early humans in Europe. The variable use of caves and rock shelters by humans cannot therefore be taken as a direct measure of variable selection pressure upon an aspect of competitive behaviour, as I have argued above for the carnivores.

An example of this problem is provided by Straus (1982) in his study of the intensity of cave and rock shelter use in the Vasco-Cantabrian area of the SW region. In order to measure changes in the intensity of use, Straus uses the relative occurrence of carnivores recovered from the archaeological deposits. Where carnivores are well represented, this is taken to indicate less intense use by human groups of those same shelter facilities. The data reveal a temporal trend with a move from what he calls 'time sharing' of the shelters by both carnivores and man to 'more full-time occupation' by human groups (*ibid.*: 92). This change is apparently associated with an increase in the trapping of small carnivores for furs in the LUP of the area.

The interpretation is intuitively appealing. However, it is not based on any contemporary observations that the use of caves by humans and carnivores is indeed translated in such an obvious way into a set of static residues. It is more likely that the disappearance of the large carnivores in the LUP (table 7.6) freed the denning facilities for the small fur-bearing carnivores such as fox which appear in some numbers at this time. We must also place the Vasco-Cantabrian data into the wider context of regional carnivore variation at a continental scale. If these data were considered, then all the caves and rock shelters, with the exception of Lezetxiki, would have to be interpreted as sites showing high intensity of human use as compared with areas in the northern province.

The problem is part of a larger domain where we read the palaeolithic record at face value. Examples of this approach include making estimates of population increase through time by counting up the number of sites in a research area (table 5.16) or interpreting the spatial association of an artifact and an animal bone as evidence for hunting and the 'function' of that implement (Chapter 6). The conclusion I would draw here is that we still have a great deal of methodological research to accomplish before we can translate our observations of different categories of data – stones and animal bones – which share a common depositional envelope into such measures as intensity of rock shelter use or the degree to which a faunal collection represents human behaviour. At the present time we are not equipped to read the contents of excavated sites without some sort of methodological dictionary. As a result much significant demographic information lies untouched. In the next chapter I shall return to this point of using the palaeolithic record to measure variation in selection pressure (p. 367ff).

In the present context however, we are still left with our first question unanswered (p. 306). One way to answer it is to consider the impact of regional demographic networks upon the moulding of the information content of material culture (Chapter 2).

Style and interaction

The demographic signatures that I discussed in an earlier chapter used the notion of information as part of a human coping strategy. In particular, this involves the role of material culture within a visual system of communication, where messages are coded in the shape, substance and subject of material objects, and where they derive meaning from the social contexts where they were used.

(a) open systems

The range of such contexts would of course be enormous. They would encompass chance encounters by hunters and planned periodic meetings of the entire social unit. The potential range of messages and meanings carried by all aspects of material culture is also equally vast and, we must assume, dealt with every aspect of social interaction.

For my purpose here, the coping strategy is defined quite narrowly. I am concerned with the impact that high risk environments had on the maintenance of demographic networks which had to operate at low population densities, and where these scattered populations most probably had infrequent moments of larger group aggregation. We have already seen (Chapter 2) that such environmental conditions are characterised by *open systems* of interaction among modern hunters and gatherers. An example of this is provided by Yellen and Harpending (1972:fig. 2) where they present a model of an open (exogamous) and a closed (endogamous) system (see Isaac 1972). They measure the degree of group closure by means of an inbreeding co-efficient which establishes the degree of in-marriage among the group and find that in their sample, the hunter-gatherer populations all had much less group closure than agricultural groups. They further argue that such open systems will be associated with a strategy of rapid information flow designed to cope with uncertain environmental conditions and the need to re-deploy personnel rapidly around the habitat. One consequence of this determined that 'poor and highly variable resources both lead to cultural homogeneity among hunter-gatherers, while rich or uniform resources favour areal differentiation and nucleation' (*ibid.*: 251).

Combined with the problems of coping with uncertain environments are the linked constraints of mating network size and the difficulties of maintaining interaction at an intensity sufficient to ensure biological reproduction (Wobst 1974, 1977; see Chapter 2). The use of material culture to transmit additional information to that dealt with by verbal communication is therefore another string in the adaptational bow for coping with these aspects of existence. The visible messages assist in regulating contact by serving as a support and sanction for action. This guide to action actually heightens the intensity of interaction and so ensures a successful, in the adaptive sense, outcome from infrequent social encounters. This is achieved by providing information links which do not require the back up of precise language descriptions or regular contact between the far flung members of a regional population. I would see the development of information processing in material culture as another example of finely honed adaptive strategies seeking for that little bit extra which helps to minimise risk and which assists in solving the determinant constraints of the environment on a mobile foraging species (Gamble 1982, 1983a).

The problem is that archaeologists have not had great success in cracking the code and getting at the 'hidden' meaning in palaeolithic material culture. We have seen in Chapter 1 how similar assemblages of stone tools have been interpreted as lithic tee-shirts, and the literature on both palaeolithic cave and mobiliary art (Ucko and Rosenfeld 1967; Marshack 1972) abounds with interpretative schemes of varying ingenuity and success in entering the mind of the artists (Leroi-Gourhan 1968, 1982).

An ethnographic example of Australian *Toas*, or direction signs (Morphy 1977), points to the complexity of levels of meaning involved in the interpretation of material objects. These carved and painted sticks are left behind at waterholes to provide information about group destinations, composition and activities for the finder. The information they contain is arranged according to the choice of subject, its depiction and location on the piece. The meaning of these arrangements is derived from the attributes of locality recognised by Aboriginal Australians in their social life of discourse and ritual. This gives the message creator immense scope to stratify the levels of meaning. If the stick is found by a socially distant person they will be able to decode only the most superficial levels of meaning. However, if discovered by a member of the same estate group (Chapter 2), the stick can be interpreted through the shared knowledge of the group rituals which give meaning to an intricate social landscape that is enacted in physical space. In this way significance is given to the form and arrangements of designs on the object, and thus a complex set of instructions and information passed on. As a result a body of social knowledge is created which may not be fully understood by all the people who can potentially find the *Toa*, even though both share common areas of the same range.

It is now common to approach this code cracking exercise armed with a concept of style. This is one of archaeology's most difficult concepts to define, since although archaeologists have always used such a notion as a guide to ordering material the operations by which this has been done have generally remained unstated (Dunnell 1978). I would define the term as the means by which the messages which all material culture carries are made explicit. Style in material culture stems from common encoding and decoding strategies within a system of visual communication (Conkey 1978; Wobst 1977). It is, as Sackett notes (1982:63), 'a highly specific and characteristic manner of doing something which by its very nature is peculiar to a specific time and place'. The same emphasis is given by Lenoir (1975:49) in a thoughtful essay on style and lithic technology (see also Kantmann 1969), while Wiessner opts for a more closely defined expression (1983:256) as applied to items, including projectile points, of the Kalahari San: 'formal variation in material culture that transmits information about personal and social identity'.

In this context I am not so concerned with using a concept of style to identify the existence of social groups in the palaeolithic record (see Close 1978; J. G. D. Clark 1975), but rather with using it to examine the model of open systems. This should be possible since we can use the regional model and its various internal transformations under pleistocene climatic regimes. The exact content of the message is therefore not all that important, but it is rather the number of times it is repeated, and its correlation with environmental conditions, that matter.

An analogy might be drawn with the monitoring of radio transmissions by intelligence services. Where these are very abundant, it proves impossible to listen in on every conversation. The information comes not from the content of the messages, which anyway may be in a secret code, but from noting the variable frequency and number of such transmissions as well as their direction, and in this way a pattern of military movements or personnel locations can be built up (R. Foley, pers.comm.).

(b) figurines

A body of data which provides a provocative illustration of the linkages between style, material culture, information exchange and environment is provided by the so-called Venus figurines (Gamble 1982; Chapter 5). These occur in a narrow time horizon during the EUP (table 7.11) between 25–23 Kyr. They are associated with local variants of either the upper perigordian or gravettian technocomplex and extend in areal distribution over some 2000 km from the SW to the NE regions (fig. 7.2). Several authors (Leroi-Gourhan 1968:96; Delporte 1979; Gomez-Tabanera 1978; Gamble 1982) have stressed the similarity in size and design among the specimens carved from ivory or limestone or fashioned, as at Dolní Věstonice, from baked clay mixed with pulverised bone (fig. 7.3). The famous bas-relief carvings from Laussel can also be included in this group on the grounds of stylistic similarity.

Two points are worth noting. This widespread distribution occurs at a time when conditions were moving rapidly towards maximum glaciation. The environments of the northern province were becoming progressively simplified to the point where between 20 and 16 Kyr several regions in the northern province were abandoned (Chapter 5). The high risk nature of these EUP environments would have resulted in low population densities and the corresponding difficulties associated with maintaining interaction among far-flung members in a mating network. Furthermore, such environments require some social safety nets in order to cushion the effects of local imbalances in resources. In other words, the rapid free flow of personnel and information would have

Table 7.11. *Female figurines from the early upper palaeolithic of Europe*
(After Gamble 1982)

UP = Upper perigordian; G = gravettian

	Complete figurines	Fragments	Heads	Additional figurines	Associated industry	C14 Kyr bp
Group A 'classic Venus figurines'						
1. Brassempouy		3	1	4	UP	
2. Lespugue	1				UP	
3. Monpazier	1				None	
4. Pechialet	1				UP?	
5. Grimaldi	6		1	8	None	
6. Chiozza	1				None	
7. Savignano	1				None	
8. Mainz-Linsenberg		3			G	
9. Brillenhöhle VII		2			G	>25
10. Willendorf II/9	1			1	G	
11. Pavlov		1			G	24.8
12. Dolní Věstonice	1	5	1	2	G	25.6
13. Moravany	1				G	
14. Petrkovice		1			G	
15. Avdeevo	3				G	
16. Gagarino	5	3		1	G	
17. Khotylevo	3	2		1	G	23.6
18. Kostenki I/1	6	c. 47			G	21.3 – 24.1
Kostenki XIII	1				G	
19. Eliseevici		1			G	33
20. Souponevo			1		G	
21. Minevskii Iar	1				G?	
Group B 'more schematic Venus figurines'						
22. Abri Facteur	1				UP(Vc)	23.1
23. Sireuil	1				None	
24. Trasimeno	1				None	
25. Mauern C	1				G	29.1
Group C 'sculpted blocks'						
26. Laussel	3			2	UP	
27. Abri Pataud 3	1				UP(VI)	23

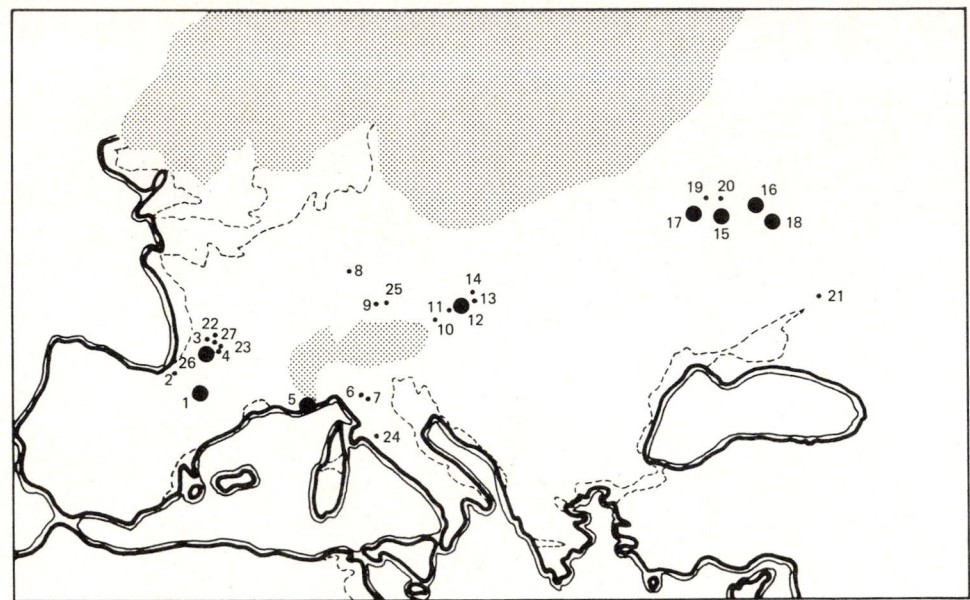

7.2 The distribution of Venus figurines at c.25–23 Kyr. The numbers refer to table 7.11 and the larger dots indicate a number of figurines from one site. The stippled areas indicate the maximum extension of the ice sheets at 18 Kyr (Gamble 1982:96, fig. 2).

been a necessary prerequisite to the successful exploitation of such environments (Gamble 1983a). To this extent the stylistic similarity of these figurines conforms well with the model expectations of an open system put forward by Yellen and Harpending (1972; see above).

The second point refers to the choice of item for such stylistic treatment. These figurines would fall within Sackett's category of non-utilitarian artifact (p. 17) and are hence very suitable for my present purpose since the form they take is not conditioned by any functional requirements that influence the design of a utilitarian tool. Moreover, none of these objects have been recovered from extraordinary locations such as graves or subterranean painted caves. Instead they have come from rock shelters and open sites. The implication must be that these objects could be viewed by anyone at any time (Gamble 1982:98) and hence, that the messages they contained were readily available for decoding. This also implies, as the extent of their distribution indicates (fig. 7.2), that they functioned within a network of regional information exchange where messages were directed at a large target population that included socially as well as spatially distant persons (Wobst 1977).

The Venus figurine data provide an acceptable test for the first question (p. 306). The continent of Europe is indeed of sufficient size and environmental diversity to produce patterning and variation in material residues that can be interpreted as selection on adaptive strategies. The assertion made earlier that

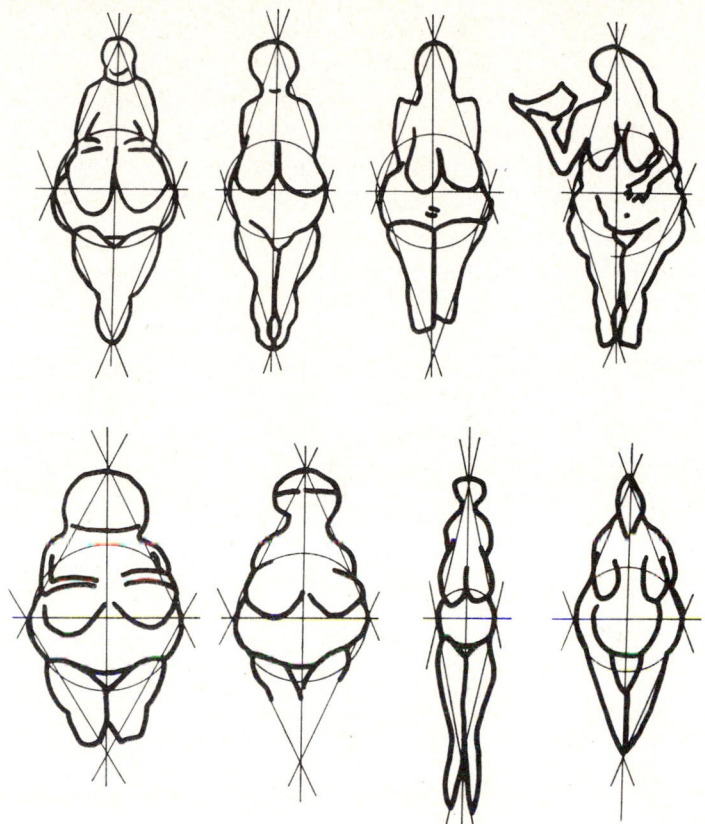

7.3 An analysis of the Venus figurines by A. Leroi-Gourhan (1968:92). Top row: Lespugue, Kostenki, Dolní Věstonice, Laussel. Bottom row: Willendorf, Gagarino (2 examples). Grimaldi.

the north of the continent would always have been a harsher environment has now been measured by this single class of data. At a comparable period it is very noticeable that more southerly areas in the SW region (Cantabria) and the entire Mediterranean province are almost completely lacking in a comparable set of stylistically treated non-utilitarian objects. This makes the unprovenanced figurines from Italy (Savignano, Chiozza and Trasimeno) of considerable interest. Should they be considered in this Venus figurine tradition because of a passing similarity without the all important additional information of stratigraphic context, associated industry or C14 date? In this instance, stylistic similarity alone is not enough to settle the question.

It is also very noticeable that other highly distinctive items of material culture, such as the shouldered stone points from Kostenki I/1, Kostenki XIII, Moravany, Willendorf II/9 and Avdeevo (fig. 5.14, n–q), are associated with Venus figurines. Other sites such as Spadzista Street B also have these utilitarian objects which display very strict stylistic coding (see Chapter 5). There is thus a clear link between the NE and NC regions as indicated by the distribution of these stylistically distinctive items of material culture.

A comparable association between utilitarian and non-utilitarian items of material culture can also be seen in the LUP of the late glacial. In a recent monograph, Julien (1982) has charted the geographical distribution of mag-dalenian antler harpoons. These cluster predominantly in the SW region (fig. 7.4) with outliers in the NC and NW (see Chapter 5). The distribution of mag-dalenian spear throwers, although based on a numerically smaller sample, is also comparable (Bosinski 1982b). These distributions are echoed by the non-

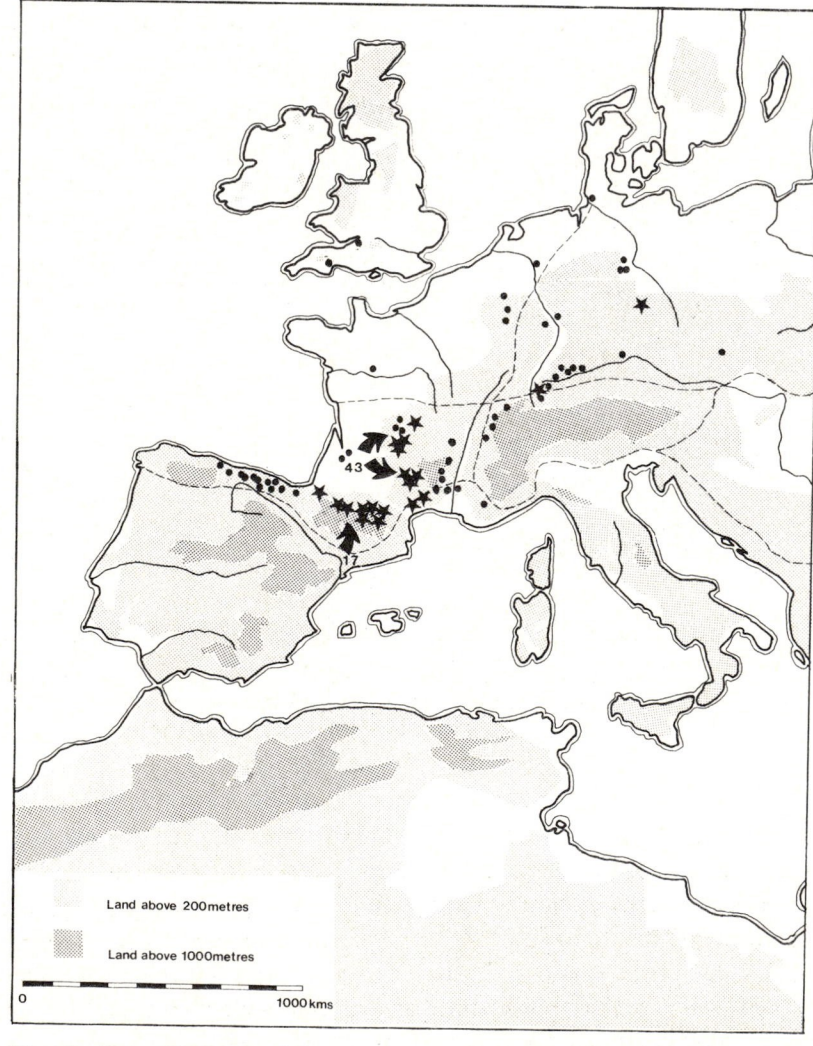

7.4 Distribution of LUP magdalenian antler harpoons (dots) and decorated spear throwers (stars) (Julien 1982:152, map 1, map 2: Bosinski 1982b:54, abb. 12).

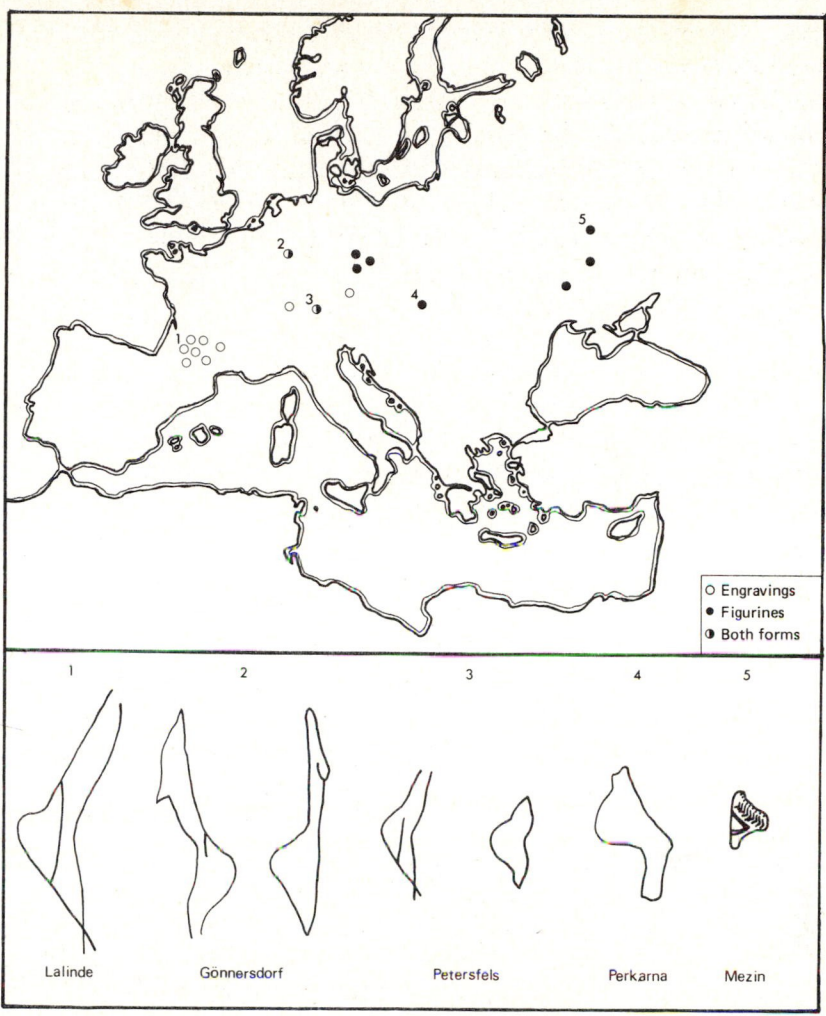

7.5 LUP distribution of schematic female engravings (1, 2, 3) and figures (2, 3, 4, 5). (Bosinski and Fischer 1974; Bosinski 1982b:65, abb. 17).

utilitarian engraved plaques and small carved figurines which have been interpreted as schematic profile figures depicting the female form (Rosenfeld 1977; Bosinski 1982b). The site of Gönnersdorf (Bosinski and Fischer 1974) has provided the largest assemblage of both forms (fig. 7.5). It is also noticeable that the figurine forms are not found in the SW region and none of the engraved representations come from Cantabria. The important point is that during a major phase of recolonisation of the NC region we can find crisp stylistic coding on both utilitarian (harpoons and spear throwers) and non-utilitarian artifacts (engraved slabs and figurines), which corresponds to an expected pattern of open access and information flow.

This does not mean that the messages contained in these two systems separated by some 12 Kyr were exactly identical, or that the social and environmental conditions which prevailed at each time were directly equivalent. There are also many other categories of material culture which carry stylistic messaging and which must have operated in different social contexts and for other adaptive purposes (Chapter 2). These two examples have concentrated upon very obvious patterns of stylistic similarity in order to demonstrate the utility of looking at palaeolithic adaptations at a regional scale of analysis.

There were, of course, many other mediums, such as body painting, wooden artifacts, tent skins and clothing, that could have carried a variety of visual information in the palaeolithic, but these have not been preserved. This does not invalidate such approaches since it has to be taken as a condition of research with such a data base. If an investigator finds such limitations in the data base a major handicap he should perhaps consider an ethnographic or contemporary data base where such factors are not so problematic!

Problems of this sort will undoubtedly be overcome, since the most informative indicators of open regional systems will probably prove to be the durable stone tools. I have already mentioned the Kostenki shouldered points, and many other examples of stylistically distinctive type fossils are provided in Chapter 5. There are however still many methodological steps to be worked out before this potential is realised. For example, at this juncture it might be asked why handaxes or sidescrapers could not be used to demonstrate open systems of information flow in pre-stage 5 Europe? The general problem of style in lithic archaeology has been investigated by Sackett (1982). He points out that the options as to which shape a stone tool can take are limited since, for example, a knife has to perform as a knife. Any stylistic message is therefore added as a supplementary *choice*, since all knives do not have to look exactly alike to be useful as knives. The key point is that in order to make a knife, the artisan has to choose from a wide variety of design patterns what the implement is going to look like. Many other aspects of material culture – pottery, figurines, ornaments – are not bound by such initial starting conditions. Indeed, the handle for a knife would be less constrained in this respect than the functional blade. In these cases, the artisan does not choose the form of the decoration or where it will be placed on the knife handle or pot, but, instead, consciously *selects* the formal elements of variation in material culture which can be invested directly with stylistic messages.

As a result, I think we should be wary about placing the same interpretations on stone tools which are not associated with a wider set of material culture that includes these non-utilitarian objects. The reason for regarding pre-35 Kyr lithic assemblages as different from those of the upper palaeolithic rests on this distinction between choice and selection. Unless both operations are present, as they are with the first appearance in cultural assemblages of non-utilitarian objects such as carved figurines, then we must assume a significantly different approach to the potential properties of lithic materials as a source for information exchange. This does not mean that stone tools prior to 35 Kyr in Europe carried no information in the form of stylistic messaging. They must have carried some, or else the artisans who made them would have been unable to use them since there would have been no significance at all to the variety of shapes! However, the range of meanings and the depth of coding was undoubtedly less, and played no part in open systems of interaction (see Chapter 8).

(c) raw material transfers

One way to illustrate this last point is to examine raw material distributions. The extensive exchange and distribution of a variety of materials by hunters and gatherers has been documented by Mulvaney (1976) where he refers to 'chains of connections' across aboriginal Australia (see also Chapter 2). These have been interpreted by Gould (1980) as indicators of regional insurance policies, where exchange of items promotes interaction and facilitates the movement of personnel at times of food crises. He cites archaeological evidence from the Central Desert of Australia for the use of raw materials exotic to the area, though the tools manufactured from them have poorer performance standards, as determined by experiment, than the same tools made from local materials. However, he points out that in the context of long term adaptation, the existence of such far flung exchange networks, whereby access is gained to basic resources in distant areas (1980:158), is more important than a small difference in the suitability of certain raw material types for particular tools.

The raw materials of palaeolithic Europe have not yet received a systematic synthesis. However a number of geographical and temporal patterns can be seen. In fig. 7.6 the distribution of handaxes in central Europe is plotted. The raw material used in the manufacture of these objects has been compared against the natural distribution of raw material in central Europe. It is very striking that only local raw materials are being used to manufacture these artifact forms. There is no evidence for the long distance movement, by whatever mechanism, of raw materials.

This same observation has been made in other parts of palaeolithic Europe. For example, in Roumania the mousterian at Remetea-Şomoş I (Bitiri 1972), SE region, is exclusively using local raw materials, while the EUP, aurignacian and gravettian, shows significant proportions of central European obsidians and a variety of other raw materials. It is not until the late aurignacian and gravettian that the Ceahlău sites, NE region (Nicolăescu-Plopşor *et al.* 1966), see a marked increase in good quality Prut valley flint. This same pattern is dramatically shown at the Bacho Kiro cave, SE region, where upper palaeolithic chipped stone

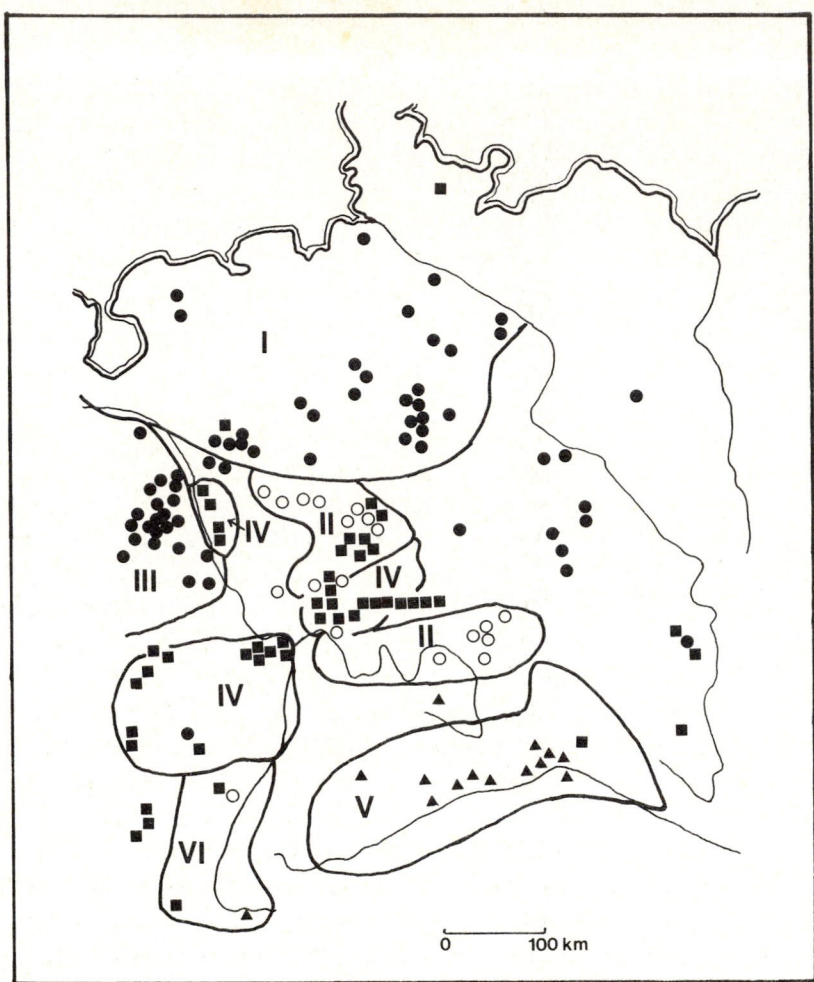

7.6 The distribution of handaxes in the NC region (Schwabedissen 1970).
Raw material zones: I. Baltic flint; II. Kieselschiefer; III. Belgian flint; IV.
Quartzites; V. Hornstein; VI. Hornstein, Kieselschiefer, Quartzite. Filled circles = I
& III. Open circles = II. Squares = IV. Triangles = V.

assemblages are exclusively made of imported flint (Kozlowski (ed.) 1982:159)
from sources 100–200 km away in both eastern and western directions from the
site. This is in contrast to the earlier middle palaeolithic levels in the site, where
local volcanic rocks made up from 67% to over 80% of the chipped stone
assemblages (table 6.5).

It is generally the case that the first evidence for the movement of lithic raw
materials outside their zones of natural occurrence is in the EUP. In central
Europe, this has been documented for both the aurignacian (Hahn 1977:Map 5)
and gravettian (Otte 1981:fig. 15). The most striking distribution (fig. 7.7) in the
EUP centres on a triangle formed by southern Poland, Moravia and Slovakia, in

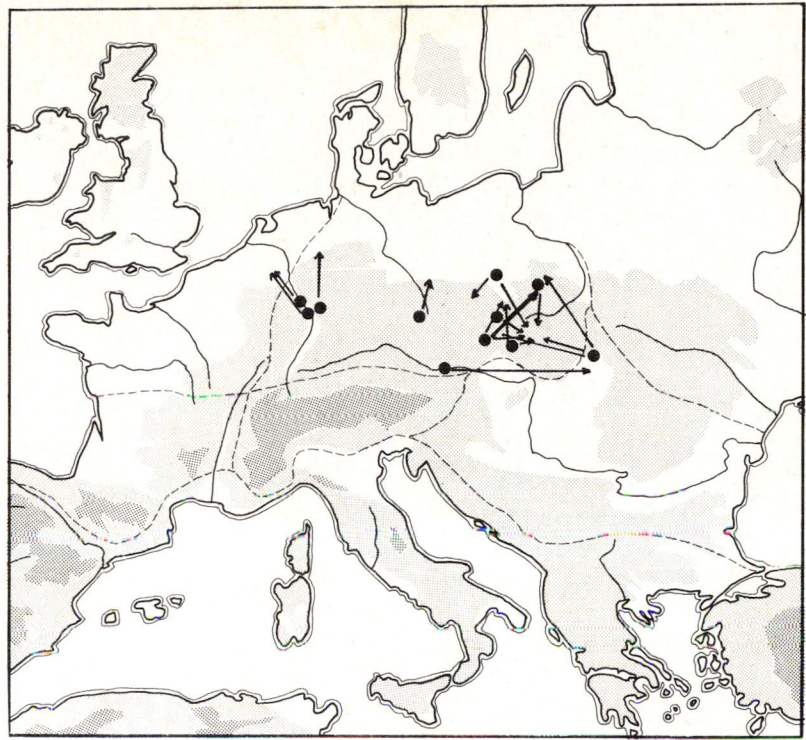

7.7 The EUP raw material triangle in the NC and SE regions (Hahn 1977; Otte 1981).

the NC region (Kozlowski 1961). The Slovakian radiolarite with its highly characteristic red, olive and yellow colours is found in Polish EUP and LUP assemblages even though it is regarded as inferior to the exceptionally fine chocolate-coloured flint of southern Poland (Kozlowski and Sachse-Koslowska 1976). It occurs in small proportions in the Krakow aurignacian assemblages and there are even a few pieces in a late middle palaeolithic site, Krakow-Zwierzyniec I. During the gravettian the few pieces of radiolarite that are found are almost always finished tools. Bárta (1965) has suggested that the radiolarite raw materials from the upper Váh are coming through the Vlara pass in the White Carpathians and so into the Moravian sites. The distances involved are at maximum some 200–300 km for the higher quality flint from southern Poland that is found in the Czechoslovakian sites (fig. 7.7).

Malina (1970) has conducted a detailed study on a number of sites primarily from the Brno area of Moravia, NC region. The findings (table 7.12) show an increase within the EUP of the use of exotic raw materials. Although the sample of sites is small, the gravettian stations dating to the 25–23 Kyr horizon are predominantly using the higher grade lithic resources from outside their natural raw material area. It is interesting to note that in all cases the imported stone resources are used for making tools, while the unmodified flakes and blades

Table 7.12. *Raw material usage in the Moravian upper palaeolithic, NC region*

Site	Totals %		Tools		Blades, flakes		Chips, waste	
	imported material	local material	import	local	import	local	import	local
szeletian								
Hajany	16	84	17.8	82.2	14.6	85.4		
Moravany	44.5	55.5	45.8	54.2	41	59		
Ořechov	34.7	65.3	41.9	58.1	21.1	78.9		
Rozdrojovice	8.4	91.6	35.3	64.7	3.7	96.3		
aurignacian								
Maloměřice-Občiny	18.9	81.1	24.5	75.5	6.9	93.1		
Stránská skála	22.1	77.9	29	71	10.8	89.2		
Maloměřice-Borky II	15.4	84.6	18.2	81.8	9.5	90.5		
gravettian								
Dolní Věstonice	c. 80	c. 20						
Předmostí	87	13						
magdalenian								
Býčí skála	70.8	29.2	72.8	27.2	66.3	33.7		
Ocozská jeskyně	85.7	14.3	90.1	9.9	88	12	82.5	17.5
Hadi jeskyne	54.5	45.5	74.4	25.6	55.4	44.6	44.7	55.3
Maloměřice-Borky I	61	39	62.8	37.2	48.6	51.4		

(*Source:* After Malina 1970: table 1)

show much more use of local material. This is clearly shown in the figures for the szeletian site of Rozdrojovice (table 7.12).

The LUP data continue this trend in Moravia, with much higher proportions of imported material than are known from the EUP. Imported materials for the manufacture of microlithic tools are also known in Bohemia (Vencl 1978). Elsewhere in the NC region a pioneering study by Wiegers (1949/50) located the raw material sources used at the LUP sites of Petersfels and Munzingen in southern Germany. He demonstrated a number of sources for the flints, some of which were up to 150 km away from the Petersfels and 125 km from Munzingen. Bahn (1982) has assembled the available evidence on stone resources in the Pyrenees, SW region, where distances of 40–200 km can be traced. It is interesting that his maps of raw material distributions point to northern, eastern and western contacts for the French Pyrenees but no hint exists of movement of raw materials up from the Iberian Peninsula (fig. 7.8). Moreover,

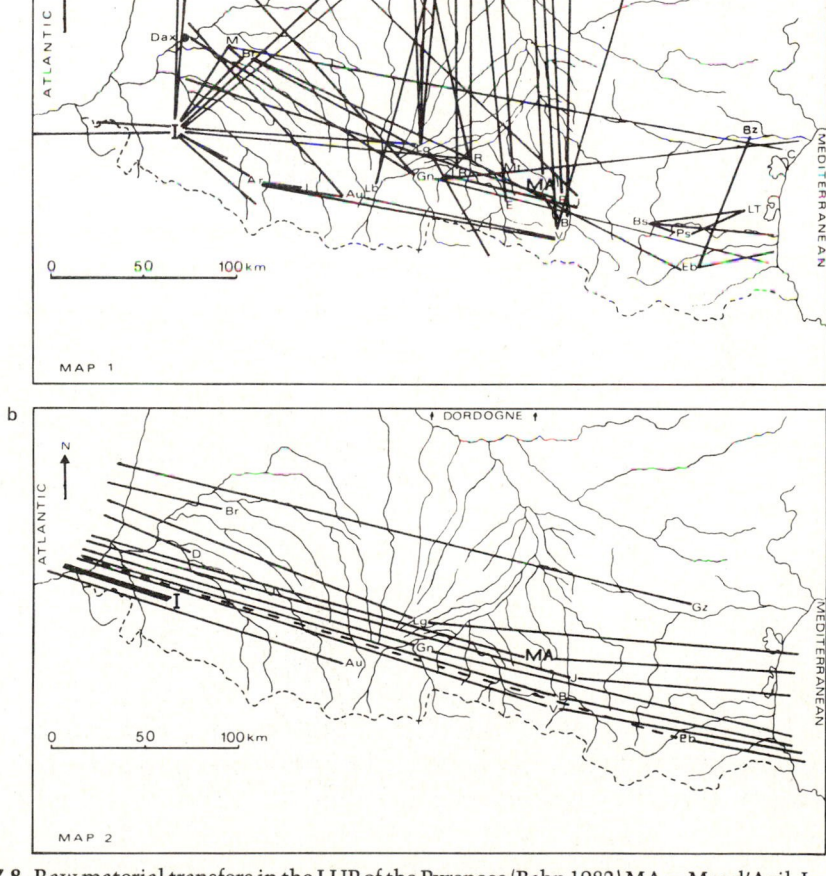

7.8 Raw material transfers in the LUP of the Pyrenees (Bahn 1982) MA = Mas d'Azil. I = Isturitz. (1) lithic/fossil evidence for contacts; (2) marine evidence.

while the pattern of contacts from sites such as Isturitz or Mas d'Azil is to both the Atlantic and Mediterranean coasts, the evidence is overwhelming for greater quantities and frequency of movement to the Atlantic seaboard, and hence *within* the SW region, rather than to the Mediterranean littoral of the MW region (Bahn 1982:Maps 1–3). Other instances of movement of flint resources in the LUP are 175 km in Belgium (Bahn 1977:255), more than 100 km to Gönnersdorf (Brunnacker 1978:245) and a distance of at least 180 km for material found in Swiss sites (Egloff 1979:234).

The Slovakian radiolarites are also most abundantly found in Poland during the LUP (Kozlowski and Sachse-Kozlowska 1980), where the red-coloured variety is commonly found in swiderian assemblages on the northern plains of the northern province. This material travelled a maximum of 300–350 km from source and, it is thought, in the form either of pre-cores or of unworked raw material nodules. Whether the radiolarite was acquired by direct procurement from the Váh river sources or through exchange with groups living in that area is not yet established.

By far the best documented example of traffic in lithic resources comes from work on the distinctive chocolate-coloured flint from the Holy Cross mountains in southern Poland, NC region (Schild 1971, 1975, 1976, 1979; Ginter 1974; Kozlowski and Sachse-Kozlowska 1976). This high grade flint was quarried and is found in the EUP assemblages of Poland, Moravia and Slovakia. The greatest use of the flint comes in the LUP during the Allerød interstadial, zone II, and the succeeding zone III, younger Dryas. Schild (1971) estimates that some 300 sites in the LUP of Poland have flint from this source, and the map in fig. 7.9 is based on 148 sample points. It can be seen from a chronological breakdown of the distribution that during the open conditions of the younger Dryas, the absolute distances over which this flint was trafficked were much greater than during the Allerød interstadial. However, within a distance of 200–300 km from the sources, sites have been found from both zones which have assemblages with as many as 90% of all artifacts made from this raw material. Schild (1971:56) regards the nomadic life on the north European plain as responsible for the distribution of the material. It is certainly interesting from the point of view of the open system model for patterns of interaction that the greatest spatial distributions correlate with the ecologically more specialised conditions of the younger Dryas. This finding does suggest that raw material residues can be used to monitor aspects of regional adaptation and the variable demographic arrangement of personnel in the environment.

The temporal pattern showing the increasing use of exotic, high grade flint sources is now firmly established. The link between the development in the LUP of core reduction strategies to produce microlithic bladelets and, by inference, complex hafting technologies is complemented by this evidence for the selection of higher quality raw materials (Ginter 1974). However, the demographic aspects should not be forgotten: as these raw material transfers

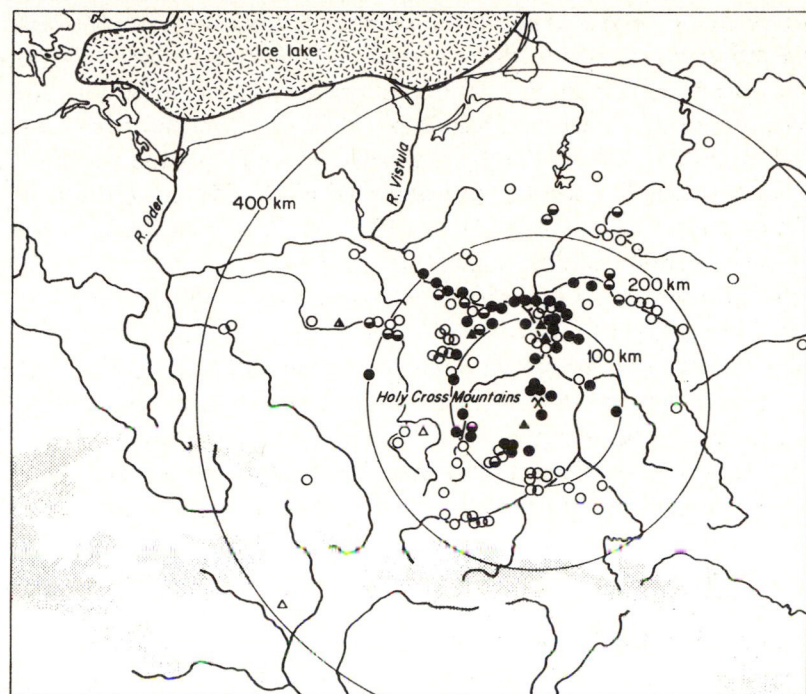

7.9 LUP distribution of chocolate-coloured flint from the Holy Cross mountains, NC region (Schild 1971, 1975, 1976) (reproduced from Champion *et al*. 1984).

took place, rather more than just good flint was obtained as social networks and information flow were promoted (Wilmsen 1973:26–7).

A further strand to this temporal pattern can be seen in the traffic in shells. These came from both marine and fossil sources and were distributed over considerable distances into EUP, but predominantly LUP, sites in the Dordogne (Bahn 1977) and the Pyrenees, SW region (Bahn 1982). Collection from the Atlantic coasts was the most common practice, as shown by species identifications (Bahn 1977:table 1). The Kostenki sites, NE region, contain molluscs which originated on the Black Sea coast, some 500 km to the south (Hahn 1977:map 5). The gravettian open site of Sprendlingen at Mainz-Bingen, NC region (Bosinski 1979a) has two shells, *Cyclope* sp. and *Hinia* sp., collected from the Mediterranean, which is 700 km distant in the most direct line south. The LUP site of Gönnersdorf, NC region, also has shells from the Mediterranean (Brunnacker 1978:232). Fossil shells, whose origin is most probably in eastern England, have been found in EUP assemblages from the Spy cave in Belgium, NW region (Otte 1977). Other gravettian, EUP, finds include Mediterranean shells at Pavlov in Moravia which probably came from the Istrian peninsula, and at Kamegg in lower Austria, also in the NC region, where shells from the Balkans were noted (Otte 1981).

The evidence from shells complements the geographical patterning from the lithic raw materials. The evidence is overwhelming in pointing to extensive chains of connection in the northern and southern provinces. There is no evidence for the circulation of raw materials and fossil shells within the three Mediterranean regions, although there is some indication of interaction between this and the other two provinces. The intensity of interaction, as monitored in the number and direction of these exchanges, was higher in the northern and southern provinces. This would be expected under the environmental conditions associated with the EUP and LUP in these provinces and the necessity for maintaining open systems of interaction and information flow.

These observations provide yet another test for the regional model. Moreover, they demonstrate the importance of approaching the study of palaeolithic Europe with a regional scale of analysis. While the means by which these raw materials were obtained and transferred is still in debate, we might reasonably expect that if extensive interaction had taken place between the Mediterranean and other provinces, then some raw materials distinctive to the latter areas would be found in the Mediterranean province. This strongly suggests that while interaction did take place *between* provinces during the upper palaeolithic, this represented the farthest limits of a regional adaptive strategy. While Europe is by this test an appropriate size for the investigation of past survival strategies, the low intensity of such far flung exchanges indicates that basic survival took place at a smaller, regional, scale. This involved variable levels of intensity in inter-regional rather than continental interaction spheres, as indicated here by the patterning of raw material distributions.

(d) relatively closed systems

At this point it may be asked if there was any alternative to open systems in palaeolithic Europe?

Wobst (1976:55) and Bender (1981) have argued for the development of relatively closed mating networks and social groups at some time in the upper palaeolithic, while recognising that closure of the system would result in much greater costs when maintaining boundaries through symbolling and associated ritual behaviours. By closing down patterns of interaction and associated information flows, the risks involved in successful long term adaptation to the environment might also be increased. These conditions strongly suggest that any degree of closure in the social unit will most probably occur under conditions where the spatial areas it occupies are small and the food supply predictable (Gamble 1983a:204).

(e) why cave art?

These conditions are apparently met in the LUP of the SW region. Jochim (1983:215) has pointed out that at the height of the last glacial maximum, 18

Kyr, a sharp thermal gradient in sea temperatures was formed off the Cantabrian coast at 42° N (Chapter 3, fig. 3.10). These conditions would have favoured offshore feeding grounds for migratory fish, and Jochim has convincingly argued that at 18 Kyr, and during the period of initial deglaciation, salmon would have been a critical resource as they formed an important component of the riverine faunas of the Dordogne, the Pyrenees and Cantabria. This resource would of course link these inland areas with the Atlantic seaboard, and as we have seen above, there is additional support from the shell evidence to show that this was indeed the case (Bahn 1977, 1982).

However, this rich *r*-selected resource must have been available at many other times during the pleistocene, and yet it is only during the LUP that there is any evidence that salmon were exploited. Jochim argues that the abandonment of large areas of northern Europe at 18 Kyr led to the SW region becoming a refuge zone for population. This increase in effective population pressure required alternative, and in this case novel, food resources to be tapped. The logistics of salmon exploitation result in a spatial focus on certain streams and rivers for this predictable, but temporally ephemeral resource. It is also highly probable that this formed one element in a complex schedule that also involved the seasonal exploitation of migratory reindeer and red deer as they passed through the Dordogne and Cantabrian areas. As a result, the strategies that were devised may well be described as super-logistically organised (Rowley-Conwy 1983), in that absolute annual mobility within a territory was high, but residential camps were rarely if ever moved. It therefore follows that group territory size was small. Furthermore, time budgeting, the proliferation of special work camps and the precise deployment of every available food getter were very marked as would be expected when exploiting an *r* resource. This meant that population density was high and sedentism, in terms of a fixed home base, was a prominent feature. A further consequence was however that sedentism led to territorial claims on the all important streams where such key resources were to be found.

Against this background, Jochim (1983:217) interprets the painted cave sites that date to the LUP as territorially based ritual sites acting as land claims. The model he is using traces the consequences of *packing* a rich resource area with a larger population and using social mechanisms, enhanced by art and its communication potential, to overcome any possible conflict that might ensue by providing a means for integrating such close packed populations. Under these circumstances of high population density there would also have been ample opportunity for overlapping mating networks (Wobst 1976) with the attendant problems of ensuring affiliation to any one particular network by groups located on the outer ring of the tier (fig. 2.7). Society specific rituals which focus the members of a mating network on a social centre might well be advantageous in such situations, and Pfeiffer (1982) has discussed the ways in which this all important imprinting took place. In Jochim's words (*ibid.*: 219) the result led to 'relatively closed social networks'.

The model once again emphasises the importance of analysing palaeolithic adaptive strategies on a regional basis cast at a continental scale. The restricted distribution, in both time and space, of painted caves (Chapter 5) here takes on an important role for measuring the success of the strategies which permitted population to remain in the area. It is not the case that the SW region formed a Garden of Eden with leaping salmon and running deer, thus allowing LUP populations to lie back in their rock shelters and pass the time by painting them. On the contrary, the cave art serves as a measure of the intensity of competition between these populations and their physical and social environments. There is absolutely no implication that the SW region was a privileged place to be, but rather that the vivid use of art in display and ritual points to problems of integration among units (Johnson 1982) and a constant alertness to the vagaries of a high risk, unpredictable environment. It is noticeable that these territorial markers are not found in these same areas during the environmentally 'softer' post-glacial.

For these reasons, I would disagree with Jochim when he characterises the SW region with its abundance and variety of game as providing 'richness and security for human habitation' (*ibid.*: 215). This may be true in a relative sense if a comparison were made between the SW and NC regions at 18 Kyr. The structure of the faunal communities wrought by changes in pleistocene climate may have made it possible to inhabit this SW region rather than the Alpine, NW or NC regions, but this was only achieved at considerable exploitation costs and with appropriate social developments (Chapter 8). Far from providing a refuge for populations retreating from the north of the continent, the explosion in cave art, ornament and stylistically coded solutrean flint projectile points (Straus 1977b; Smith 1966) should be regarded as part of an intensification strategy to meet current resource conditions by a resident population. With this model we must concern ourselves with the *demands* placed upon subsistence strategies. These, we shall see in the next chapter, are determined by a set of social relations rather than precipitated by population pressure (Bender 1981).

A further example of measuring the investment in integrating regional populations living at higher population densities is provided by Conkey's (1980) study of engraved antler rods from Cantabria, SW region. These are dated to magdalenian III in the LUP. From an analysis of 1200 such objects from 27 different magdalenian sites, Conkey developed a set of attribute categories that deal with the design elements and the structural principles which were used to arrange such elements on the rods (table 7.13). In a study of five of the largest collections, she showed that those pieces from the well known cave site of Altamira have a greater diversity both in the number of design elements and in structural principles when compared with the four other sites of equivalent age. This diversity fulfilled the expectation that if Altamira acted as a seasonal aggregation site (Freeman 1973:40) for a regional population of hunters and

Table 7.13. *Design elements and structural principles on engraved bones and antlers from five Cantabrian magdalenian sites*

	Design Elements				Structural Principles		
	Number of engraved pieces	Number of instances	Number of different elements used	Average number of uses per element	Number of instances	Number of different principles used	Average number of uses per principle
1. Altamira	58	152	38	4.00	48	13	3.69
2. El Juyo	25	53	19	2.79	13	9	1.44
3. El Cierro	11	35	15	2.33	9	5	1.80
4. Cueto de la Mina	36	69	27	2.55	27	8	3.37
5. La Paloma	22	23	12	1.92	12	7	1.71

Source: Conkey 1980: table 2

gatherers, then it should contain material culture that encompasses the range of forms shown elsewhere in the region.

Understanding the relative diversity between assemblages (Conkey 1980:612) is in this instance the key to assessing the possible function of a site in a regional framework. I would not however share the view espoused by Hayden (1980:623) that this analysis of relative diversity shows that Altamira and Cueta de la Mina represent two focal points, separated by 60 km, for two maximal bands which were self-perpetuating, endogamous and living in relatively rich environments! All that a study of design elements does is to reveal a possible use of material culture to assist in integrating sections of a dispersed regional population. I can see no case for making a further set of inferences between the descriptive label of aggregation site favoured by Conkey and the other descriptive label of maximum band that Hayden wishes to turn this data into. We have seen repeatedly in this chapter that this is not the way that dynamics are breathed into the statics of the archaeological record.

I would rather take the view that these patterns in the data are a route to understanding the problems which adaptive systems had to solve. These included variation in population densities and the need to devise intricate labour schedules in space and time if certain resources were to be exploited. These problems existed all through the pleistocene. What we have finally come to is a consideration of *change* in adaptive systems such that options, e.g. salmon fishing and painting caves, which could contribute to the solution of such problems and were always available as options (Gamble 1983a), then became part of the adaptive repertoire of palaeolithic groups. The use of material culture in either open access of relatively closed interaction and demographic systems is therefore a variable operating within the long term process of social change. With this perspective we must also consider population growth and effective population pressure as other variables contributing to the same process. We must constantly keep in mind that models of mating network closure and social group closure must be clearly separated. A model using demographic principles such as the mating network cannot be used directly as a means of reconstructing the degree of access or closure for a socially, rather than demographically, constituted unit. Until we have examined how we can investigate such variables and the process of change they contributed towards in the archaeological record, we should be cautious about committing ethnography with a shovel.

CHAPTER 8

SOCIETY, SEDIMENTS AND SETTLEMENT

'Yes, but not in the South', with slight adjustments, will do for any argument about any place, if not about any person. It is an impossible comment to answer.

Stephen Potter, *Lifemanship* (1954:43)

Introduction

Palaeolithic societies were much more than adaptive mechanisms designed to secure food and marriage partners at the least possible cost. They not only *responded* to the cards in the constantly changing hand held by the physical environment but they *changed* the ground rules which governed the game.

We must not forget in the analysis of repeated regional patterns that the human systems which produced them were dynamic and subject to change. While acquiring subsistence and mates was absolutely essential to survival, the mode by which these ends were achieved formed the very essence of social evolution. The set of social relations which give significance to all human action forms the dominant element in directing subsistence strategies and mating networks (Chapter 2, fig. 2.1). Archaeologists have moreover documented and inferred qualitative and quantitative changes in past human societies, and the liveliest debates in the subject have always been about *why* such changes took place (Pfeiffer 1977, 1978, 1982).

In this chapter, I will follow the procedure that is now familiar from the preceding two chapters. I will first look at those aspects of the archaeological record which can provide a measure of changed social circumstances (Chapter 2, table 2.6). Once again the regional model of palaeolithic Europe will be used to structure the investigation. Secondly I will draw on some case studies to explore both the spatial and temporal implications of changes in palaeolithic society. The temporal factor is emphasised in this chapter as I begin to work towards an integration of the spatial and demographic signatures contained in the palaeolithic period.

Monitoring social change

If we are to investigate change in palaeolithic social systems, then it is imperative that an unambiguous measure be found. It might be tempting to assume that, once we have chains of connection in the upper palaeolithic, the 'rich' burials of the EUP, or the painted caves of the LUP, we are witnessing massive changes in palaeolithic society (Bender 1978). Indeed, the contrasts between the so-called burials associated with Neanderthals and *Homo sapiens sapiens* are repeatedly used as evidence for increased status differentiation (S. Binford 1968), or for a greater number of social distinctions being reflected in the burials of anatomical' - modern humans (Harrold 1980). While such interpretations are highly plausible, there are problems if we take them at face value as a direct indication of social developments (Gamble 1983a:206). It would be equally possible to argue that differentiated status was displayed at earlier times in perishable mediums such as body painting and tattooing and that the evidence from the upper palaeolithic is therefore of a change in the mediums used rather than in the underlying premises upon which society was based. Since this could very plausibly have been the case, we would find ourselves caught in another circular argument, where we assume that social changes will be reflected in burial data, we examine the burial data and find this to be the case, and so prove our assumption correct without having put up a satisfactory test of these initial assumptions!

The approach I favour here uses as a starting point the prosaic evidence of settlement archaeology and site histories. The model I am employing is very simple. Changes in palaeolithic society resulted in changes in the dominant relations which controlled survival strategies. The major impact of such changes would therefore be on the determinant features of the environment which under existing conditions exerted constraints on such strategies, with the result that settlement ceased in particular areas under particular environmental and resource conditions. I have already argued in Chapter 3 (p. 114) that the availability of energy was never in itself a limiting factor on palaeolithic strategies in the regions of pleistocene Europe. The effect of changes in society resulted in the overthrow of some of the environmental hurdles to long term continuous occupation of the regions of pleistocene Europe.

In the first instance, I am not therefore asking very much from the settlement histories of the various regions. A simple measure of presence/absence is all that is required. As we have seen in Chapter 5, a great deal of information exists on this very question, although there is a need for more precise and detailed chronologies. This should be welcomed, for here is a reason to refine our chronologies and develop new dating techniques that can bridge the gaps between conventional C14 and other isotope systems of measurement. We shall see later in this chapter just how different this chronological precision will be in interpreting the past from a behavioural perspective rather than from the standpoint of the culture historian. Both paradigms want more and better absolute dates. It is what is done with them once they are available that is the point at issue.

The measurements provided by settlement histories also link in closely with the space/energy framework that led to the construction of the regional model for studying palaeolithic Europe. The carnivore data in the last chapter provided a measure of variation in selection pressure for aspects of behaviour, and in this chapter the settlement histories will be used in a similar manner. However, before we move to a consideration of the presence/absence of human occupation, I shall first look in more detail at the nature of the evidence, and the subtleties for more detailed analysis that it undoubtedly possesses.

Depositional environments

Palaeolithic materials are found in three major depositional contexts: (a) within caves and rock shelters, (b) interstratified in water-laid (fluvial) deposits such as travertines, river terrace gravels, alluvial red beds, lake muds and marine beach deposits, and (c) interbedded in aeolian sediments such as loess.

(a) caves and rock shelters

While all three contexts will be taken into consideration when regional settlement histories are discussed, I shall concentrate here upon cave deposits. The reasons for this are quite simple. They represent constrained locations in terms of the organisation of activities. They form facilities in the landscape that are available for many millennia, and under a wide array of different climatic conditions present relative advantages when compared one with another in terms of light, heat retention, panoramic views and shelter from prevailing winds. Moreover, such facilities are found throughout much of Europe due to the distribution of suitable parent geology. Since in many cases this is limestone, the possibility exists of comparing the differential build up of deposits resulting from regional climates operating on local factors of weathering within the rock shelters. While such studies are still in their infancy (Farrand 1975), the aim is that by understanding how the depositional envelope is constructed and varies between regions, we can then turn our attention to a more objective comparison of its archaeological content. This could not be said of fluvial deposits or of loess deposits. The latter do not extend over all the nine regions of Europe, while the variations in river regimes are difficult to characterise to their geographical position in the regional model. Our best chance for tracing the operation of the 'intellectual anchors' (Chapter 3) which led to the construction of this model is, in the case of depositional environments, cave and rock shelter deposits, though I would not underestimate for a moment the problems involved with such data if they are to be used in this manner.

A very basic reason for employing caution in such an approach is the simple observation that *no* European cave contains a complete record of pleistocene sediments. Some caves such as Castilló (Butzer 1981), Kůlna (Valoch *et al.* 1969), La Cotte (McBurney and Callow 1971) or Hunas (Brunnacker 1982) have impressively long sequences accompanied in part by industrial assemblages. However, both sedimentologically and culturally these are discontinuous records, and it is often difficult to assign the *floating* slices of pleistocene history they contain to schemes of regional climatic events (see Chapter 3). Farrand (1975) warns against jumping to generalisations concerning rock shelter chrono-stratigraphies based on a limited range of observations.

A further reason for caution is raised by the discontinuous nature of sediment and occupational lenses (Bordes 1975a) as revealed by the excavation of horizontally extensive rock shelters such as Laugerie-Haute (Smith 1966). At this site, the stratigraphic layers are remarkably horizontal and yet cannot be traced across the distance of 180 m from the excavated east to west parts of the shelter. Moreover, human occupation was not necessarily continuous across the areas protected by the rock shelters. This can be seen at the Abri Caminade (fig. 8.1) where there is only partial overlap in those areas used by aurignacian and mousterian 'occupations'. A detailed study of the sediments from this site can be found in Laville *et al.* (1980:chapter 5).

With this cautionary note in mind, it is clearly not possible to make hard and fast rules about how cave and rock shelter sediments will vary between the regions of palaeolithic Europe. However, some impressions can be offered. The sediment studies by Butzer (1981) on caves from Cantabria reveal clear evidence for frost activity in the accumulating sediments. This can be seen in his description of the profile from the Cueva Morín. These observations are of interest, since according to reconstructions of pleistocene Europe (e.g. Kaiser 1960), this area lay on the border of the permafrost/non-permafrost regions. The Dordogne sites studied by Laville *et al.* (1980) also show in their stratigraphic profiles the contorting effects of frozen ground phenomenon on the distortion of

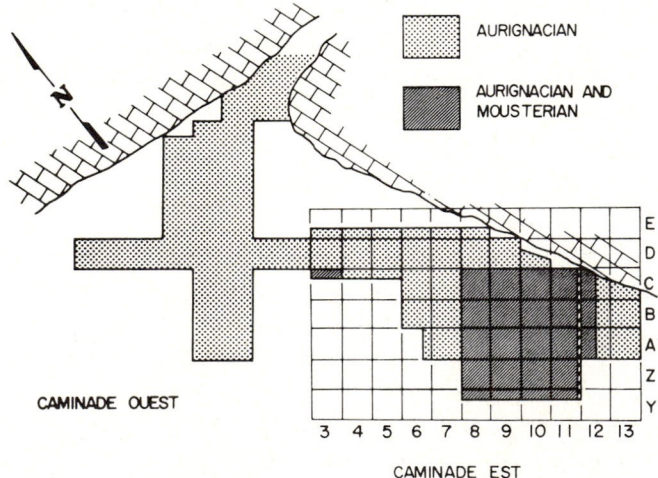

8.1 Site plan of Abri Caminade (Laville and de Sonneville-Bordes 1967; Laville *et al* 1980:107, fig. 5.1).

deposited sediments. The sites of La Ferrassie, Pech de l'Azé II and Le Flageolet provide such examples. However, other rock shelter profiles reveal very little subsequent frost action displacing the sediments, even though the analysis of the sediments themselves indicates that the weathering of the cave walls and roof took place under glacial conditions. Among this group of sites would be the classic horizontal stratigraphies of Le Moustier and Laugerie-Haute (Laville *et al.* 1980:figs. 7.9, 9.4, 9.5). My impression from the sections of sites in the French part of the MW region is that post-depositional distortion is generally low (Miscovsky 1976), as shown for example in the Hortus deposits of Würm II age. However, if we want to find stratigraphies which bear no traces of such frozen ground disturbance, we would probably have to look at sections outside Europe such as the cave of the Haua Fteah in Libya (McBurney 1967).

At the other extreme are cave sites in the NW and NC regions where sediments distorted by frost heaving, mud flows and other localised permafrost features are very common. The sediments at Pontnewydd (Green *et al.* 1981), La Cotte (McBurney and Callow 1971), Kůlna (Valoch 1970) and the Bockstein (Wetzel and Bosinski 1969) serve as examples. Some sites in the Alpine region such as Broion (Leonardi and Broglio 1962) reveal comparable post-depositional movement of sediments and materials.

The depositional envelopes into which palaeolithic materials were sealed are not therefore constant across the regions of the continent. There is a suspicion that the intensity of post-depositional processes can be linked to the space/energy framework of the regional model. One test could be supplied by plotting the frequency of cryoturbated flint artifacts. These have been noted in the Lonetal of southern Germany (Hahn *et al.* 1973) and in the lower levels of the Szeleta cave, NC region (Allsworth-Jones 1975). Tayacian implements from La Micoque, SW region, are also regarded as frost rolled, but I would expect as we move from the northern and into the southern and mediterranean provinces that the incidence of such altered pieces becomes much less and finally disappears altogether. A much larger sample is needed to confirm this intuitive impression.

(b) rates of deposition in caves and rock shelters

An example of the potential that is offered by the study of cave sediments for measuring aspects of the palaeolithic record is provided by recent work on the excavated sites of Kastritsa and Asprochaliko in Epirus, ME region (Bailey *et al.* 1983a, b). The analysis compares the occupational densities for the upper palaeolithic levels from a number of the trenches in the two sites. This can be done in two ways. The first simply compares the geometric density of material per excavated column of sediment and where the rate of sedimentation is assumed to be constant. This could be calculated as N/m^3. However the C14 dates for these two sites allow a more subtle time density measure to be made.

Table 8.1. *Densities of cultural materials in selected excavated rectangles (R) at Asprochaliko and Kastritsa*

Excavation area[a]	Asprochaliko			Kastritsa			
	R2	R3	R42	R2	R3	R11	R12
Excavation layers	4, 7, 10			1–15		11–15	
Time span (Kyr)[b]	12.7	12.7	12.7	7.0	7.0	3.0	3.0
Mean layer area (m^2)	1.12	1.29	1.67	1.97	1.80	3.00	3.00
Total finished tools	215	54	14	1907	2261	287	595
Total waste	5071	1499	427	17,714	21,646	2625	8119
Total manufacture	5286	1553	441	19,621	23,907	2912	8714
Finished tools: waste	1/24	1/28	1/30	1/9	1/10	1/9	1/14
Time density (manufacture/m^2/kyr)	371	95	81	1423	1897	323	968
Adjusted for shelter size ($\times$ 120/75)[c]	594	152	33	1423	1897	323	968
Mean time density		260			1153		
Identified bones	15	2	2	204	522	157	352
Identified teeth	10	6	3	143	365	85	250
Total fauna	25	8	5	347	887	242	602
Tooth: bone	1/1.5	1/0.33	1/0.67	1/1.4	1/1.4	1/1.9	1/1.4
Mean tooth: bone		1/0.83			1/1.5		
Time density (fauna/m^2/kyr)	1.76	0.94	0.24	25.2	70.4	26.9	66.9
Adjusted shelter size ($\times$ 120/75)[c]	2.81	0.78	0.38	25.2	70.4	26.9	66.9
Mean time density		1.32			50.8		

Source: Bailey *et al.* 1983a: table 7.4

Notes: [a] Estimates have been adjusted to take account of rockfalls and areas of disturbed or collapsed deposit.

[b] From 26.1 to 13.4 at Asprochaliko; 20.4 to 13.4 at Kastritsa.

[c] Shelter size adjustment is in proportion to the available living area and assumes that the Asprochaliko shelter was not occupied to capacity.

Table 8.2. *A summary of time density figures for Kastritsa and Asprochaliko*

Accumulation per annum

	Kastritsa	Asprochaliko
Total chipped stone	87	19
Retouched tools	63	0.4
Identified bone specimens	3.5	0.096
Average rate of sediment accumulation	1.3 mm	0.12 mm

Source: Bailey *et al.* 1983a, b

This measures the number of specimens per unit area per unit time ($N/m^2/Kyr$). Moreover, the following formula can be applied to allow for boulders or other objects in the column which may distort the calculation of time density estimates:

Aa = Au − (a x h/H) where
Aa = adjusted area of column (allowing for intrusions)
Au = unadjusted area of column
a = mean cross section of intrusion
h = depth of intrusion
H = total depth of column.

A constant rate of sedimentation within that unit of the column being studied is assumed.

The Asprochaliko column represents almost 13 Kyr during the EUP and LUP while at Kastritsa Rectangles 2 and 3 have a time span of 7 Kyr and Rectangles 11 and 12 some 3 Kyr. All four rectangles contain LUP (table 8.1). A further consideration that has been taken into account is the difference in shelter size. The estimated potential area at Kastritsa is 75 m^2 while at Asprochaliko this increases to at least 120 m^2. At the latter site there is therefore some potential for the greater dispersal of activity, and hence possibly lower density of residues.

The time density figures (tables 8.1, 8.2) reveal very different relative rates of accumulation for the two sites. The density of total chipped stone at Kastritsa is almost 247% higher than at Asprochaliko, while for bone the figure increases to 3332%! Furthermore, the much higher ratio of debitage to retouched tools at Kastritsa points to further differences in the sorts of residues which were deposited. It is tools rather than waste which form the Kastritsa sample and which make its higher accumulation rates even more striking.

These figures could be indicating variation in the number of people and the length of time the two sites were used, not to mention the activities being performed. The figures are not however intended to answer such questions but to provide a basis for comparison by discovering something about the *rates* at which the palaeolithic record was formed. One casualty however is the earlier model of Higgs *et al.* (1967) that was developed for these two sites and which classified them both as home bases (Chapter 5). It would be difficult, given the time density data, to maintain a similar description for both sites. The evidence suggests that we should regard them as different components in a long term settlement system.

However, the figures might have much greater importance for assessing the two sites. To what extent are the faster rates of sediment accumulation at Kastritsa, almost 130 cm per 1000 years, responsible for the better preservation of bone material due to quicker burial and hence the avoidance of trampling? Furthermore, if materials are being buried quicker, then lumps of raw material and cores left behind on the surface of the site for use at another time will be lost. At Asprochaliko, the very slow rate of sediment accumulation means that tools and raw material that were left behind could be easily relocated and re-used. A factor such as this may help explain the great discrepancies in tools: waste between the two sites has to be considered along with other behavioural possibilities discussed in Chapter 6.

These basic measures of the depositional envelopes in which palaeolithic materials are found have not been applied to many other sites. As a result, it is not possible to see whether the stone and bone assemblages from Kastritsa are typical of a site from the ME region or how they compare with other 'rich' cave occupations from the other regions and provinces. However, with the advent of detailed sedimentological work and C14 dated sections, such data, which would provide a truly objective comparative framework between sites in the different regions, could be produced.

Sediment accumulation studies have been published from a few sites. At La Riera, SW region, Straus *et al.* (1981) calculated that the sediments accumulated at a rate of 25 cm per 1000 years, while at La Madeleine (Bouvier 1977) between archaeological levels 7 and 14 almost 2.5 m of sediment matrix was deposited in 800 C14 years. These figures emphasise how very large amounts of cryoclastic sediments can be deposited in comparatively short periods of time. At the Abri Pataud, Farrand (1975) has distinguished two main weathering horizons or breaks in the depositional sequence (fig. 8.2). A mean figure for deposition at the site is 55 cm per 1000 years but of course the model of uniform sedimentation is not applicable. The two main depositional episodes indicate much higher figures of 1 m and 1.82 m per 1000 years.

In the mediterranean province, there is evidence for uniform and continuous sedimentation at the Grotta Paglicci (Palma di Cesnola 1975) where a figure of 63 cm per 1000 years can be calculated. The most detailed study has been conducted by Bofinger and Davidson (1977) on the MW region caves of Parpalló and Les Mallaetes. It is perhaps worth noting that the site with abundant artifacts and engraved plaques, Parpalló, has a high sedimentation rate of 71 cm per 1000 years for the period 20–14 Kyr, while at the nearby site of Les Mallaetes, the figure is only 13 cm for the period 30–16 Kyr. (Davidson 1980:table 10.1).

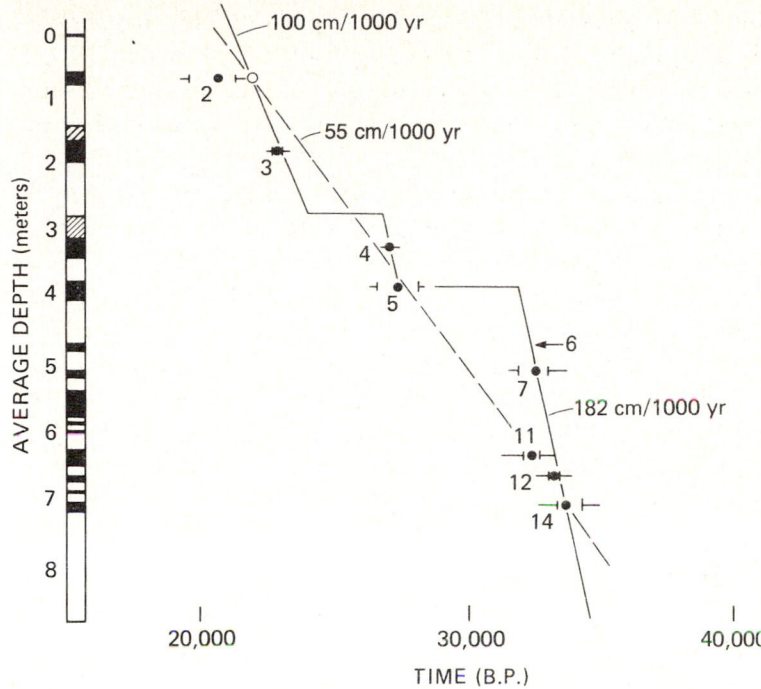

8.2 A curve showing the changing sedimentation rates in the Abri Pataud sediments. The curve is based on C14 dates for habitation levels, as numbered, and the average thickness of sedimentation units (Farrand 1975:51, fig. 10).

The similarity to the relative accumulation rates and artifact densities at Kastritsa and Asprochaliko may be more than mere coincidence. The rates of accumulation for chipped stone and engraved plaques at Parpalló are presented in table 8.3.

The Parpalló study is particularly important due to the statistical rigour with which the model of uniform sedimentation was tested (fig. 8.3). This should not however be taken as an indicator that all sites in the Mediterranean province will follow such uniform sedimentation. In a pioneering study at the Haua Fteah, McBurney used a well dated C14 profile to show changes in sedimentation rates. Sedimentation in this huge cave was rapid from the present day to 11 Kyr, and measured 48 cm per 1000 years. Between 18 and 33 Kyr sedimentation rates were only 5 cm per 1000 years.

An important point that sediment studies could establish is the degree to which sites from the different regions have continuous sediment accumulation. It appears that those sites from the mediterranean province – Kastritsa, Asprochaliko, Grotta Paglicci, Haua Fteah, Parpalló and Les Mallaetes – which all span the last glacial maximum at 18 Kyr, have such a pattern of sedimentation. In the SW region there are clear breaks in the sedimentation profiles at the Abri Pataud and in the Cantabrian sites (Butzer 1981). This process was

Table 8.3. *Accumulation rates for chipped stone and engraved plaques at Parpalló*

Depth m	'Culture'	Age Kyr	Chipped stone per annum	Retouched tools per annum	Bone tools per annum	Engraved slabs per annum
2.3 –3.5	Magdalenian II	15.2	34.2	1.7	0.65	0.32
3.5 –4	Magdalenian I	16.5	36.6	2.5	0.38	0.43
4 –4.5	Solutrean/ Gravettian	17.2	22.2	2.8	0.21	0.89
4.5 –5.25	Upper Solutrean	17.9	18.0	2.2	0.08	0.77
5.25–6.25	Middle Solutrean	18.9	4.2	0.8	0.06	0.6
6.25–7.25	Lower Solutrean	20.2	0.7	0.1	0.02	0.13
Totals			109,541	8,333	1,459	3,058
Geometric density			438 per m^3	33 per m^3	5.8 per m^3	12 per m^3

Source: Data from Davidson n.d., 1980:table 6.5; stone counts from Fullola 1979

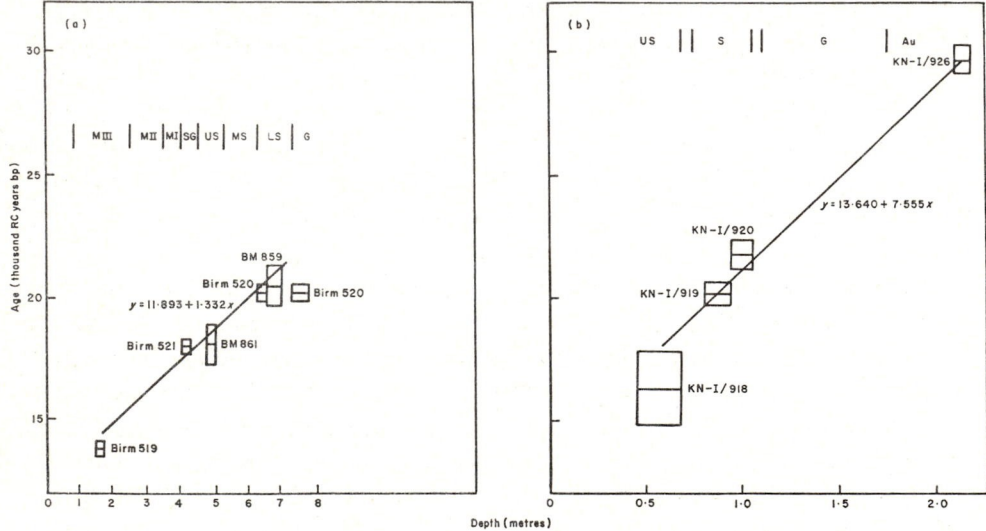

8.3 Graphs of age against depth for (a) Parpalló and (b) Les Mallaetes. Also shown are the regression lines and the stratigraphic divisions recorded by the excavations (MI–III, magdalenian I–III; SG, solutreo-gravettian; US, upper solutrean; MS, middle solutrean; LS, lower solutrean; G, gravettian; Au, aurignacian). C14 ages are shown with one standard deviation. (Bofinger and Davidson 1977:233, fig. 1)

intensified in the northern province as cycles of erosion scoured the caves and sedimentation responded to smaller changes in the prevailing climatic regimes.

The formation of the depositional envelopes in caves and rock shelters and in the regions of palaeolithic Europe is therefore of great importance for understanding *what* we are comparing, in terms of the archaeological materials they contain. The envelopes are more than just a route to climatic reconstruction or chronological ordering, but form the all important matrix for investigating the variable settlement histories of the regions. Our archaeological materials are rather like bees trapped in amber, and it is time the amber was investigated by taphonomists since it could provide a means to calibrate aspects of the past behaviour which led to materials being intentionally included (Gifford 1981).

Lithic assemblages

We are not yet in a position to utilise the subtleties that a comparative study of the depositional envelopes could provide for the analysis of lithic assemblages. We can begin to examine some of the properties of the excavated materials, but this will have to be, of necessity, divorced from their depositional matrix.

(a) assemblage size

The majority of assemblages recovered from the caves and rock shelters of Europe must be regarded as *collections*. They are biased towards the collection of typologically distinct items rather than a representative sample of all aspects of the lithic assemblage.

These collections reflect the interests of the culture history paradigm. Once out of the ground they have been treated accordingly. Bouvier (1977:79) has traced substantial collections from La Madeleine, first dug between 1863 and 1865, to no less than twenty-eight museums in France and a further fourteen in nine other countries. As a result, it is in most cases impossible to use the size of the extant collections to make even a rough estimate of the sampled population of artifacts that could potentially have been recovered from a site. These sampled populations were in some cases enormous. At the magdalenian site of Gare de Couze (Bordes *et al.* 1972:27) a sample of some 7000 artifacts came from an excavated area of 6 m². The deposits from these shelters, which had been quarried by earlier archaeologists, were probably 100 m in length by 20 m in width. Bordes estimates a sampled population from the site, on the basis of the 6 m² excavation, of between one and two million artifacts. Moreover, the use of fine screening recovery techniques has dramatically increased the size of artifact collections for the LUP with the retrieval of microlithic elements (Albrecht 1979; Bouvier 1977).

A selection of assemblages from both cave and open sites is presented in Appendix 5. The chronological divisions are intended to draw attention to the problem of retrieving the small elements mentioned above. While compiling the appendix, it proved impossible to apply systematic selection procedures. The sample is best described as the most readily available, but I have tried to select assemblages from the three provinces during the three chronological periods.

Perhaps the strongest conclusion that can be drawn from these lists is the

Table 8.4. *Pech de l'Azé IV, The Mousterian industries*

| Level | Total chipped stone | Chronology | Tools (included in total) | | Variant |
			real count	essential count	
Z	3851		271	126	Typical Mousterian
Y	1756		214	93	''
X	13,703		857	391	''
J3c	3330		222	55	Asinipodien
J3b	9674		941	194	''
J3a	9548	WÜRM I	601	102	''
J3	2323		305	76	''
J2	835		90	42	Typical Mousterian
J1	597		68	27	''
I2	10,890		1010	464	''
I1	1074		116	72	''
H2	326		46	34	''
H1	225		24	14	''
G	839		56	39	Mousterian
F4	22,698	WÜRM II	953	567	MTA A
F3?	3540		252	141	MTA A–B
F2	5297		356	219	
F1	3259		215	141	MTA B

Source: Bordes 1975b

great degree of consistency in assemblage/collection size for all three periods and provinces. The range for retouched tools is comparatively small when we consider all the possible sources of variation that are involved. These would include the size of the excavation, recovery efficiency, the location of the trench relative to the density of material, the interests of the excavator, and so on. For all these reasons I was surprised when drawing up the lists that few assemblages of any age or place contained more than 5000 retouched tools. Variation in total chipped stone is much greater, as table 8.4 for Pech de l'Azé IV shows. Moreover, it comes as no surprise that m^2 densities of chipped stone and retouched tools are consistently higher in rock shelters than in open sites, but it is worth pointing out again that in terms of absolute numbers of retouched tools recovered in excavation these different depositional environments do not vary all that much.

The main purpose of the lists in Appendix 5 is to provide some quantitative data that may help replace the qualitative labels of 'rich' and 'poor' site (Chapter 5). This approach is examined in greater detail in figs. 8.4 and 8.5, where the data 'rich' area of the Périgord (de Sonneville-Bordes 1960) is contrasted with a data 'poor' area, England (Campbell 1977), for the upper palaeolithic. While the shape of the histograms is very different, we can see that 82% of the 143 assemblages from the Périgord contain less than 1000 retouched implements in the 92 type list. No collection from England exceeds 1000 retouched tools. If we remember the haphazard way many of these assemblages were excavated, it seems to me all the more surprising that the range of absolute assemblage size should be so limited. In terms of long term human behaviour compared on a regional basis, is

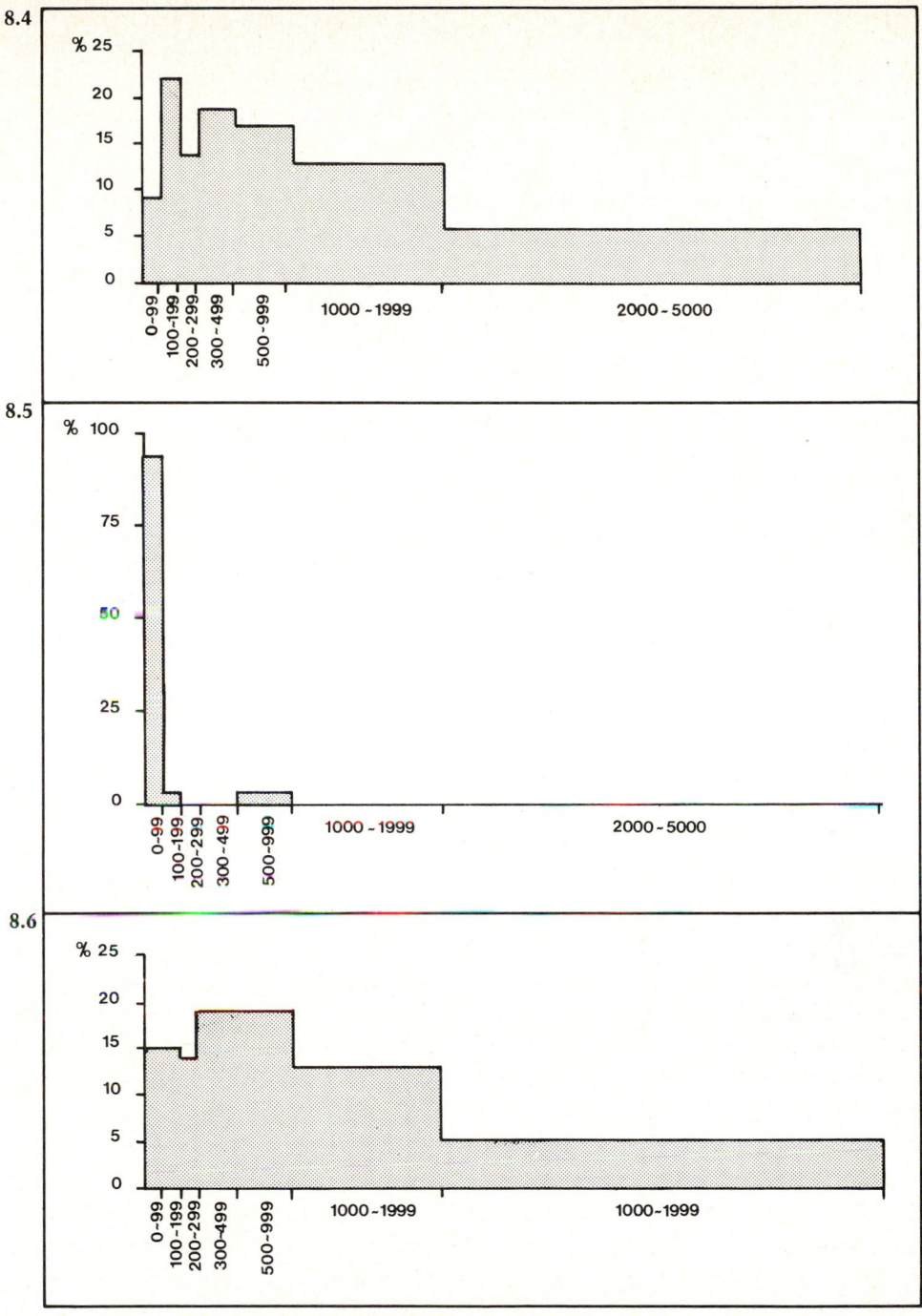

8.4 Upper palaeolithic assemblage size for retouched tools (type list 1–92) in 143 assemblages from Périgord, SW region (de Sonneville-Bordes 1960; P. Smith 1966).

8.5 Upper palaeolithic assemblage size for retouched tools in 55 collections from England, NW region (Campbell 1977).

8.6 Upper palaeolithic assemblage size for retouched tools in 259 collections (MW, MC, ME, SW, NC and Alpine regions) (Laplace 1966).

there any great significance in an extra 3000 retouched tools in a very few sites? The answer to this face-value assessment has to be no.

A further check to these figures is provided by Laplace's rival typological scheme (fig. 8.6). His material is drawn from a much wider geographical area than the Périgord and includes a number of open sites. From his lists, 81% of all leptolithic assemblages have less than 1000 retouched tools.

A final analysis points to the robustness of this pattern. In fig. 8.7, the number of types in the 92 type list are plotted against the number of retouched tools. This has been done for the EUP and LUP assemblages from the SW, NC and Alpine regions. A very clear relationship can be seen, irrespective of culture group, between increasing numbers of tools and the number of types represented in the 92 element list. As a point of comparison, Rolland's (1977, 1981) study of middle palaeolithic material from the Périgord showed that increased implement frequencies were instead associated with specific artifact types, side scrapers, rather than with the overall sample size for retouched implements.

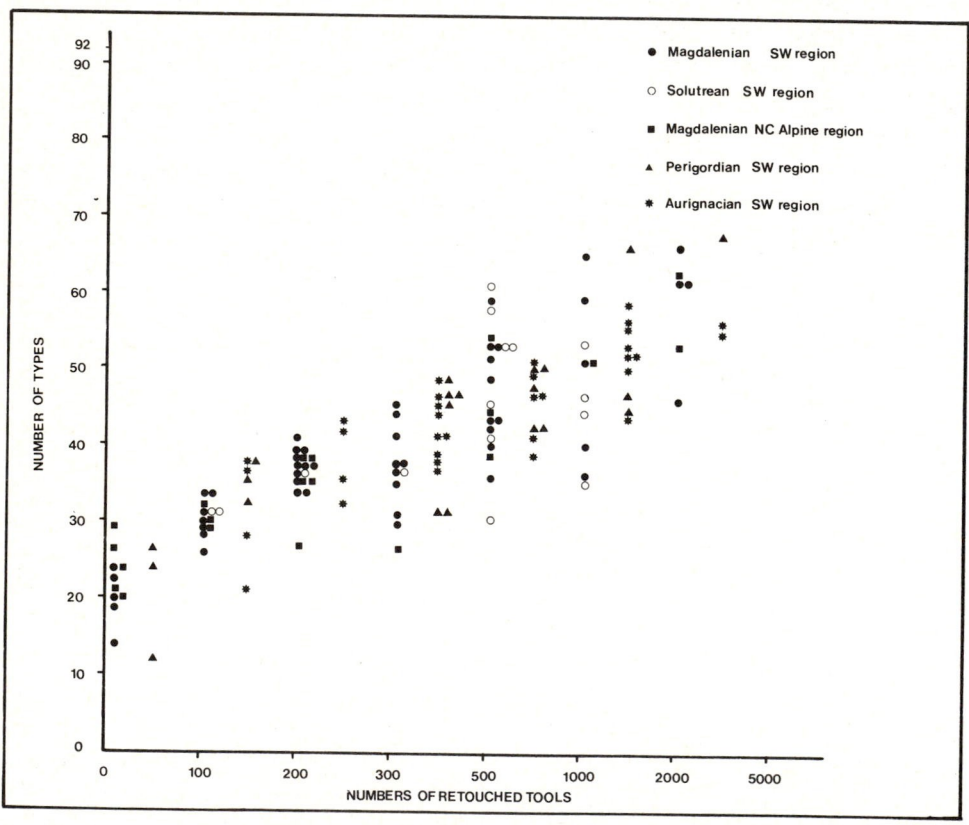

8.7 Numbers of retouched tools compared with numbers of artifact types in the 92 element list for the EUP and LUP of the Périgord, SW region, and magdalenian assemblages from the NC and Alpine regions (de Sonneville-Bordes 1960, 1961, 1963a, 1965, 1968, 1969; Valoch 1960; Klima 1974).

On the basis of these lists I can see no reason for expecting 'rich' sites, as measured by the conventional methods of numbers of retouched tools, to occur in particular regions of palaeolithic Europe. Caves such as La Cotte, Spy and the Petersfels demonstrate the ability of site assemblages in the northern province to more than hold their own against the so-called classic 'rich' sites of southern and mediterranean Europe.

However, the next question we must ask is whether the number of retouched tools per assemblage is a useful measure of past adaptations at a regional scale? The rich site/poor site investigation adds some understanding of the dimensions and character of the palaeolithic record but does not interpret it. We have yet to consider that assemblage size is determined not by palaeolithic behaviour but by the requirements of typological analysis. Indeed the dominance of assemblages containing less than 1000 retouched tools is most probably a result of the typological analysis of assemblages and the effect these procedures have had on research into different depositional environments that may very well be highly differentiated between regions.

The procedure can be described in terms of a triangle (fig. 8.8) that expresses the relationship between size of excavated area, recovery standards and typological requirements. The latter factor in this example is crucial, since an assemblage analysis requires at least 100 retouched tools (de Sonneville-Bordes 1974–5:17). If the aim of the excavation is to recover samples in order to conduct such analyses within a culture history framework, then the returns rapidly diminish once this quantity of material has been recovered. In sites with high

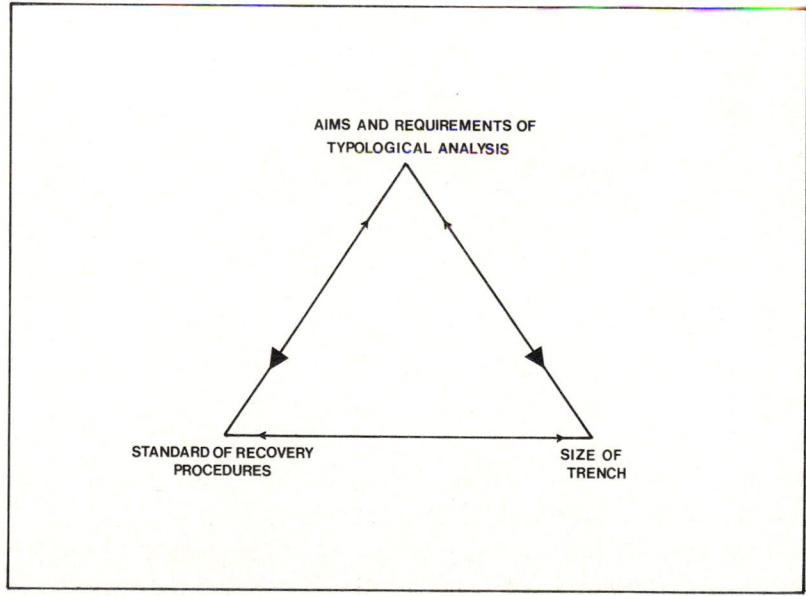

8.8 The relationship between research design and sampling procedures in palaeolithic cave and rock shelter archaeology.

Table 8.5. *La Ferrassie, grand abri. A comparison of stratigraphic observations and assemblage counts for the aurignacian levels in this site*

Peyrony		Delporte and Mazière			
1934	tools[a]	1977	tools		
H″	482	E1 F Gf G0s	88 84 115 94	381	Aurignacian IV
H′	371	G1s H I1f I2s I2	285 120 228 95 171	899	Aurignacian III
H	4050	J K2 K3 K3a K3b K3c K4	185 496 77 113 301 195 407	1774	Aurignacian II
F	2460	K5 K6	211 221	432	Aurignacian I

Note: [a] artifact counts from de Sonneville-Bordes 1960

artifact densities and uniform sedimentation rates, excavation trenches can be small and yet recover a 'meaningful' sample for typological analysis. Conversely, a large area will need to be dug in sites with a low density of artifacts in the soil. The size of excavated area is also dependent upon recovery standards. Sieving will produce the desired number of retouched tools from a smaller area than that dug by hand. An example is provided in table 8.5, comparing the two excavations at La Ferrassie. The improved recovery standards in the later excavation from a smaller dug area resulted in more closely observed stratigraphic relationships between ever more finely defined assemblages. Of course, other research objectives such as the recovery of bone material would need a very different strategy. However, few sites have been dug with this as the prime aim. The recovery of *enough* artifacts has dominated the research designs of the past 130 years of palaeolithic endeavour.

The model (fig. 8.8) emphasises that we need at the very least geometric density figures, and preferably time density estimates, if we are to compare and understand variation in assemblage size. For example, at the Kůlna cave, NC region, Valoch (1980b) had to excavate some 900 m^2 or a cubic volume of 3000 m^3 in order to recover what preliminary reports (Valoch 1968–9) describe as average size collections of middle and upper palaeolithic industries. The Hungarian cave site of Istállöskö, also in the NC region, is some 45 m long by 8–10 m wide. This was excavated over a surface area of 460 m^2 to depths of between 2.5 and 8 m (Bhattacharya 1977:251). When this labour is compared against the small artifact collections of stone and bone (Chapter 5) then they do seem a meagre return.

By comparison, the re-excavation of La Riera (Straus *et al.* 1981), SW region, investigated a mere 16 m² of intact sediments and a depth of deposit of 2–2.5 m. This column produced 2795 retouched tools from 24 separate levels, an average of 116.5 tools per level (*ibid.*: 661). Similar results came from excavations at Kastritsa (table 8.2) in the ME region.

The pay-off in terms of small trenches and a high artifact return explains the sort of approach to the study of lithic assemblages advocated by Laplace (1966). Indeed, he draws his samples from those areas of Europe where small trenches yield assemblages of sufficient size to apply the Typologie Analytique and where constant rates of sedimentation have parcelled them up into distinctive stratigraphic units. If there is insufficient stratigraphic distinction then analysis by dug spits of arbitrary but equal depth is apparently acceptable, as is shown at both Palidoro (Bietti 1976–7) and Polesini (Radmilli 1974) in the MC region.

If it was possible to plot area excavated against number of artifacts recovered then I would expect a very marked increase in the former as we moved from the mediterranean to the northern province. An indication of this may be contained in the greater use of type fossil approaches in the northern regions, since very often large excavations have failed to produce enough artifacts, i.e. more than 100, to conduct a typological analysis (fig. 8.5). For this reason, the finding of handaxes, leaf points and bone points has been seized on (Chapter 5). They often occur as components of very small assemblages, as the data from the Ilsenhöhle, NC region, shows (table 8.6).

Of course generalisations such as these invite the comment 'Yes, but not in the south' which opened this chapter. There are always some data which reveal the flaws in making generalisations from empirical observations. An example in this context would be the finds from the Sesselfelsgrotte in the Altmühltal of southern Germany, NC region (Freund 1968), where individual m² have yielded high densities of flints (table 8.7). However, the generalisations I am offering here derive their significance from the principles embodied in the regional model and not from trying to find a conclusion that accounts for every bit of palaeolithic data.

(b) assemblage frequency

A major distinction can be drawn between cave sites in the northern province and those elsewhere in Europe on the basis of the frequency with which the minimum assemblage size of 100 tools occurs in a single sequence. We have seen at the Ilsenhöhle (table 8.6) that although there are several artifact horizons defined stratigraphically, four of the five assemblages fall below the minimum requirement. It is very common to find in the northern province sites such as the Bockstein (Wetzel and Bosinski 1969), Vogelherd (Riek 1934) or Klaussenische

Table 8.6. *Composite profile and artifact assemblages from the Ilsenhöhle at Ranis*

The profile is over 6 m in depth and represents an ideal profile made up from excavations in various parts of the cave. Due to the presence of leaf-points in Ranis 1 and 2 this site is often regarded as possessing critical information on the development of upper palaeolithic industries in Central Europe (Müller-Beck 1968a)

	Profile		Chipped stone total
I	made ground	medieval	
II	black/grey		
	humus level	prehistoric pottery	
III	grey/brown level		
IV	black/grey level		
Va	coloured rodent	Ranis 5	
	bone level	(late upper	48
		palaeolithic)	
V	rodent bone level		
VI	yellow level with		
	burnt zone in the	Ranis 4	
	middle	(magdalenian)	62
VII	upper brown level		
VIII	black level	Ranis 3	
		(transition to upper	
		palaeolithic)	140
IX	middle brown level	Ranis 2	
X	grey level	(late middle	
		palaeolithic)	63
XI	lower brown level	Ranis 1	
		(middle palaeolithic)	17
XII	bedrock		

Source: Hülle 1977

Table 8.7. *Artifact densities in the Sesselfelsgrotte, lower Altmühltal*

The material in this table came from a single m^2 (square A7) excavated in level G during 1966. In 1965 excavations in the same level produced 450 retouched tools, 2550 flakes and 18,500 pieces of chipped stone debris.

	Tools	Flakes	Debris	Total
G1	53	270	1750	2073
G2	58	279	1030	1367
G3	3	81	330	414
G4	30	127	430	587
G5	25	121	410	556
Totals	169	878	3950	4997

Source: Freund 1968

Table 8.8. *Grotte de l'Hyène at Arcy-sur-Cure: the mousterian industries*

Real count	Levels	IVb6	IVb5	IVb4	IVb3	IVb2	IVb1	IVa
		146	80	108	411	78	2052	819

Source: Girard 1978

(Bosinski 1967) which have a single, or at most two, numerically important assemblages and a number of much smaller stratified assemblages which can be assigned a cultural status only if they contain distinctive type fossils. This, as we have seen above, is not due to small excavations. Sites such as La Cotte, the Brillenhöhle (Riek 1973), Sesselfelsgrotte or Grotte de l'Hyène at Arcy sur Cure, where there are several stratified assemblages with more than 100 tools, must be counted as exceptions in this area (table 8.8; Appendix 5).

When we compare this with rock shelters in the southern and mediterranean provinces, the contrast is dramatic. The site of Combe-Grenal contains 55 separate mousterian assemblages, many of which are reported to contain over 100 retouched tools (Bordes 1972). The site of Pech de l'Azé IV has 18 artifact horizons of which no fewer than 13 have sufficient quantities of retouched tools to conduct a typological analysis (table 8.4). Upper palaeolithic examples would include Piage (Champagne and Espitalié 1981), Abri Pataud (Movius (ed.) 1977), and the classic stations of La Ferrassie and Laugerie-Haute (de Sonneville-Bordes 1960). Also in the SW region we find La Riera (Straus *et al.* 1981) and Cueva Morín (González-Echegaray and Freeman 1971, 1973), shown in table 8.9. The Bacho Kiro cave in the SE region (Kozlowski 1975, 1982) has a number of stratified assemblages but these are small in quantities of retouched tools (table 8.10).

The mediterranean province has many caves with multiple industrial sequences of large numerical size. These would include Kastritsa (Bailey *et al.* 1983b) and Crvena Stijena (Brodar 1958/9) where 12.5 m of deposit contains 14 archaeological assemblages. In Italy, the Grotta Paglicci (Palma di Cesnola 1975), Grotta Cala, with 12 artifact assemblages, and the Uluzzo and Cavallo caves all demonstrate this pattern of large, multiple archaeological assemblages (Palma di Cesnola 1976). The MW region of southern France has many such sites including Hortus (H. de Lumley 1972) and Salpêtrière (Escalon de Fonton 1966, and Bazile 1976; Bazile 1980). These French examples can be set in context by examining the regional surveys provided by H. de Lumley ((ed.) 1976a). In the Iberian peninsula both Parpalló and Gorham's Cave (Waechter 1964) conform to the same pattern.

It is quite clearly not assemblage size which distinguishes the palaeolithic record between the various provinces and regions of Europe, but rather the frequency with which such assemblages occur within single stratigraphic sequences. Once this is appreciated we can begin to see that great differences must exist between the quantities of palaeolithic artifacts deposited in the caves

Table 8.9. *Cueva Morín, middle and upper palaeolithic assemblages*

			Middle Palaeolithic							
		lower								
levels	22	17	17	16	15	14	13 & 14	12	11	10
tools types 1–62	8	124	506	372	124	16	97	316	226	484
bifaces types 1–20		276	20	18	4					
other chipped stone[a]			1691	1429	753		1563	1541	1446	3101

			Upper Palaeolithic						
levels	9	8	7	6	5	4	3	2	1
tools types 1–92	206	669	346	345	310	217	119	310	359
other chipped stone[a]	2864	13342	9594	7783	6498	3546	1684	3757	2853

Source: González-Echegaray and Freeman 1971, 1973

[a] includes cores

Table 8.10. *Artifact counts from Bacho Kiro cave, SE region*

	14	13/14	13 humus	13	12/13	12	11/12	11a
					Middle Palaeolithic levels			
Tools	2	1	33	68	61	7	17	12
Cores	0	1	3	20	17	3	0	1
Flakes/blades	1	9	297	624	464	29	37	28
Hammer-stones, Pebbles, sandstone			40	74	37	13	12	10

	11	9	6c	8	6b/8	7/6b	7	6a/7	4b/6a	4b	4a	3a	3b	5	4
						Upper Palaeolithic levels									
Tools	667	15				15	40	61		15	3	1		1	1
Cores	18	2				3	4	3		2					
Blades and waste from blade cores	270	17				5	30	52	2	6	6				9
Waste from retouching tools	54	4					1	4							
Flakes	1874	201	1	2	2	51	577	401		142	20	1	4		10
<1.5cm chips	16,889														

Source: Kozlowski 1982

and rock shelters of the various regions and provinces. This is most marked between the NW and NC regions and the well researched data base of the SW, MC and MW regions. Confirmation for this pattern is beginning to appear in the ME region, while the SE may well show more similarities in this aspect of its palaeolithic record with the northern province. This may reflect the extreme continental conditions experienced in this region.

The conclusion from this survey is that rates of accumulation of palaeolithic materials were both more constant and more continuous in the SW region and throughout the mediterranean province of the continent. The significance of this finding will become apparent later when we discuss the bearing that settlement histories have upon understanding changes in regional adaptations and social change.

(c) open, or spatially unconstrained locations

I have so far made little mention of either the NE region or of the depositional envelopes associated with open sites. The loess localities of the NE, NC and SE regions are of considerable interest in the light of the previous discussion about assemblage size and frequency in cave deposits.

The distribution of loess in Europe forms a wedge with the thin end placed on the Paris Basin and the thick end covering the open continental plains of the Ukraine. We have seen in Chapter 3 that continuous sequences of loess deposition and soil formation can be traced at exposures such as Červený Kopec and Krems Schiestätte. These loess 'heartlands' of Austria, Moravia, Roumania and the Ukraine have also produced evidence for multiple archaeological horizons in restricted locations. One classic example is the site of Molodova V (Chapter 5) where in excavations between 1951 and 1960 a maximum of 774 m^2 were dug, revealing twelve major archaeological horizons and in places reaching a depth of 14 m. The lowest levels, XII and XI, could be reached only by deep sondages, and so were observed over a smaller area of 169 m^2. Later excavations (Ivanova and Chernysh 1965) increased the total area to 935 m^2 of which 256 m^2 was to a depth of 11–12 m.

A similar impressive excavation took place at Ripiceni-Izvor, located on the Prut river to the west of the Dniestr (Păunescu 1965). Two main areas were excavated. In surface I, 492 m^2 were dug and a depth of 8.5 m was reached in a succession of large steps. The adjacent surface II covered 1919 m^2, stepped to depths of 8.5–10 m, with further sondages down to 11.5–12.5 m. Fifteen middle and upper palaeolithic assemblages were recovered throughout this sequence. However, the assemblages are often very small; a fact emphasised by the size of the areas excavated. This is a pattern repeated at the Ceahlău sites, Appendix 5 (Nicolăescu-Plopşor et al. 1966) in the SE region. By comparison, the upper palaeolithic assemblages at Molodova are numerically large although they too were recovered from large area excavations (table 8.11). The open sites at

Table 8.11. *Artifact counts from the upper palaeolithic levels at Molodova V, NE region*

Level	X	IX	VIII	VII	VI	V	IV	III	II	Ia	I
Area m² excavated	510	510	510	750	750	750	750	750	774	750	750
Debitage/waste	454	1000	1200	41,500	4888	2900	3900	2910	3930	6027	3950
Cores	17	32	64	1475	91	88	128	73	150	115	171
Blades	105	180	275	10,710	760	573	726	556	1059	1573	905
Retouched tools	41	70	116	1262	230	182	230	169	212	239	298
Total chipped stone	617	1282	1655	54,947	5969	3743	4984	3708	5351	7954	5324
Tools: waste, blades	1:14	1:17	1:13	1:41	1:26	1:19	1:20	1:23	1:24	1:32	1:28
Cores: waste, blades	1:33	1:37	1:23	1:35	1:62	1:39	1:37	1:54	1:33	1:66	1:16
Total chipped stone per m²	1.2	2.5	3	73	8	5	7	5	7	11	7
Tools per m²	0.08	0.1	0.2	1.7	0.3	0.2	0.3	0.2	0.3	0.3	0.4

Source: Chernysh 1961: table 2

Table 8.12. *The quantities of retouched tools at Willendorf II, Lower Austria, NC region*

	Aurignacian			Gravettian				
Level	2	3	4	5	6	7	8	9
Retouched tools	30	24	155	129	70	146	450	857

Source: Hahn 1977; Otte 1981

Kostenki have also produced large collections of chipped stone but among these the quantities of retouched tools are generally less than 1000 (Klein 1969a). This finding is of interest since the aims of these area excavations at Kostenki were not only to recover artifacts but also to investigate settlement plans. The low quantities of retouched material highlight the findings in the open site data in Appendix 5 that artifact densities are generally low, an observation also documented by Isaac and Crader (1981) for earlier East African material.

Willendorf II on the Danube in Lower Austria has eight major archaeological levels of which five contain relatively large artifact assemblages (table 8.12). Multiple occupations were also discovered at the Moravian site of Předmost, although stratigraphic information is difficult to reconstruct and most of the artifact collections have been destroyed. The 20 m thick loess deposits were first investigated by Maska in 1893/4 and at a later date by Absolon (Absolon and Klima 1977). The site contained assemblages of mousterian, szeletian, aurignacian and gravettian material (Zebera (ed.) 1954; Freund 1952). Multiple occupations are also known from the Rhine sites of Lommersum (Hahn 1970, 1977) and Rheindahlen (Bosinski 1973a).

The open loess sites mentioned here do show some similarities as a group with the rock shelter and cave deposits. The numerical size of assemblages is the obvious point of comparison. However, it is difficult to generalise further from such a small sample. It might be tempting to see an increase in the frequency of assemblages of more than 100 retouched tools in sections from the NE region, but at present the data do not exist to confirm or negate such an impression. Moreover, the conditions which led to the reoccupation of rock shelters and loess bluffs were no doubt rather different, and we are not necessarily comparing like with like just because we have several archaeological assemblages in a stratified sequence!

A similar objection can be raised if fluvial deposits are considered. For example, the large time spans covered by a site such as Swanscombe (Roe 1981:67) make any considerations of the various archaeological occupations of a different order from those of the rather more restricted time spans covered by the cave and loess contexts. This is even before we have ruled out any such comparison due to the nature of the depositional envelope, which, in the case of a river terrace site such as Swanscombe, may well have had a great influence on bringing material together, as the rivers harvested the artifacts and redeposited them in 'sites'. This did not always occur (Wymer 1976), although when it did the results are often spectacular. An example from the Tagus gravel pits at El Almendro (Freeman 1975) records 8000 lower and middle palaeolithic tools coming from a single pit in a single year. A great deal more investigation needs to be carried out into the depositional environments of rivers and aeolian sediments, so that any variation in the frequency and rates of accumulation of the palaeolithic materials they contain can be ascertained. The study of caves and rock shelters, which is slightly more advanced from a taphonomic point of view, at least shows that we should expect regional variation. The precise form that these regional signatures will take is as yet unclear for the loess and river sites.

Settlement histories

The evidence from these various depositional environments can be combined in the ebb and flow settlement model that was mentioned at the beginning of this chapter. This exploits the temporal information from the sites, irrespective of whether they are rock shelters or open locations. The questions being asked are very simple – when do we have evidence for human occupation in a region? – and the answers require only a presence/absence indication from the data. The potential of the archaeological record to inform us about the past is hardly being explored, but as we saw in Chapters 2 and 3, if we can answer these simple questions using the space/energy framework of our regional model then an important first step has been made in achieving more sophisticated measures of variation and change in past human adaptive behaviour.

The ebb and flow model outlined in Chapters 2 and 3 was based on a very general assessment of the suitability of particular environments for exploitation. I shall now examine the archaeological record against this model at selected points in the last interglacial/glacial cycle and in a number of regions.

(a) 128 Kyr: was the last interglacial a 'Garden of Eden'?

The last interglacial is now firmly associated with sub-stage 5e in the deep sea cores and lasted for some 10 Kyr. During this period the forests of northern Europe were highly productive environments with many arboreal species. The pollen diagrams also indicate relatively greater proportions of arboreal to non-arboreal pollen for this period than for the succeeding sub-stages 5c and a, which now seem to correlate with the early last glacial or Würm I (Woillard and Mook 1982; Dennell 1983 a, b). This climax, oak-mixed forest during stage 5e accords well with the evidence from the deep sea cores which indicates very small ice cap size and consequently high sea levels (see Chapter 3).

Indeed, if we compare sub-stage 5e in the deep sea core record with other possible interglacials (fig. 3.3) it stands out as the most significant 'warm' peak

Table 8.13. *A comparison of the large mammal faunas attributed to the last interglacial (Ipswichian stages II and III) and post-glacial (Flandrian) in the British Isles*

	Ipswichian	Present in the Victoria Cave at 120±6 Kyr	Flandrian
Carnivora			
Canis lupus (wolf)	+		+
Ursus sp. (bear)	+	+	+
Meles meles (badger)	+		+
Crocuta crocuta (hyena)	+	+	
Panthera leo (lion)	+	+	
Vulpes vulpes (red fox)	+		+
Felis sylvestris (wild cat)	+		+
Proboscidea			
Palaeoloxodon antiquus (straight tusked elephant)	+	+	
Mammuthus primigenius (mammoth)	+		
Perissodactyla			
Equus sp. (horse)	+		+
Dicerorhinus hemitoechus (narrow nosed steppe rhino)	+	+	
Dicerorhinus kirchbergensis (Merck's rhino)	+		
Artiodactyla			
Hippopotamus amphibius (hippo)	+	+	
Megaloceros sp. (giant deer)	+	+	
Dama dama (fallow deer)	+		
Cervus elaphus (red deer)	+	+	+
Bos primigenius (aurochs)	+	+	+
Bison priscus (steppe bison)	+		
Sus scrofa (wild pig)	+		+
Alces alces (elk)			+
Capreolus capreolus (roe deer)	+		+

Source: Stuart 1982; Gascoyne *et al.* 1981; Gamble 1984a

in the last 700 Kyr. In the NW region it is also possible to tie in a very distinctive animal community with this brief interglacial phase. The most distinctive member of this community is the hippopotamus, which was a member of the faunal community in England at this time. A hippo fauna has recently been dated by 230Th/234U on flowstone in the Victoria Cave, Yorkshire (Gascoyne *et al.* 1981). The date of 120±6 Kyr places this firmly within sub-stage 5e. While it is not possible to be quite so precise with many of the other faunas from England (and moreover opinions still differ as to the duration and timing of the last Ipswichian interglacial in this area (e.g. Stuart 1982)), we can nonetheless appreciate the range of animal species which were most probably associated with this climatic episode (table 8.13). This list is impressive, although of course we learn nothing from it about numbers and density of the animals represented.

A review of the evidence makes it difficult to escape the conclusion that an extremely equable set of conditions existed in northern Europe during the 10 Kyr period of the last interglacial. The model that palaeolithic populations were in a constant state of struggle with the cold of the ice ages has for this brief moment to be relaxed (Gamble 1984a). Hippos wallowed in the Thames and straight-tusked elephants roamed the forests, stalked by hyenas and lions. If palaeolithic man was a Big Game Hunter, as many contend (e.g. Freeman 1981), then here existed ideal conditions for following this chosen lifestyle. The settlement evidence from pre-stage 5 Europe overwhelmingly indicates that human populations had colonised the northern province, although it was most probably not on a continuous basis (Chapter 5). According to the models which see human existence in the palaeolithic as a battle to keep warm, and keep the larder stocked with mammoth steaks, the advent of the last interglacial would have seemed like winning a free holiday to the Serengeti. In relative terms this might have been the moment for the 'original affluent societies' of north-western Europe to appear.

The settlement history evidence from the NW and SW regions at once throws doubt on these models. The evidence for human occupation during sub-stage 5e was reviewed in Chapter 5 and found to be entirely lacking for these two regions. There may be evidence in the NC region at Hunas (Brunnacker 1982) but there is as yet no overwhelming case for frequent and dense settlement. In the NE region there may well be sub-stage 5e occupation, but we lack chronological precision in tying together the Mikulino interglacial, recognised through pollen studies, with the deep sea record (Quaternary Sistema 1982). This is also the case with the mediterranean province.

The interglacial forests of northern Europe and in particular those of the SW and NW regions appear to be human deserts even though they were warm, well stocked larders. How significant for the model of Big Game Hunters that not one hippo fauna from England is associated with any stone tools! Indeed Ipswichian dated artifacts, which may of course be associated with any part of stage 5, are noted as rare/absent in England (Wymer 1981:67; Evans 1975:33; Stuart 1982:176).

Other parts of Europe were no doubt still occupied during this period. I would expect many parts of the mediterranean province to produce sites of last interglacial age. In this respect the excavations at Klasies River Mouth (Singer and Wymer 1982) in the mediterranean environment of southern Africa is a possible pointer to the human occupation of such habitats during sub-stage 5e.

The archaeological signature of settlement histories in the NW and SW regions can be compared with that associated with the post-glacial for these regions. The contrast could hardly be greater. The plains of northern France and southern England are covered in a carpet of mesolithic sites (Rozoy 1978; Wymer (ed.) 1977) that date to open conditions as well as full forest environments. This pattern of settlement evidence is repeated throughout the other regions of the continent.

However, the environments available to mesolithic populations were not as equable as their nearest counterparts some 110 Kyr previously. The deep sea cores show a less pronounced peak while the animal community that was available has had all the megafaunal, and many of the large, elements winnowed from it.

The purpose of this case study is to show how similar, but not equivalent, environments are capable of carrying very different archaeological signatures. I would interpret the differences in settlement histories between 128 and 8 Kyr in the NW and SW regions according to the structure of social and ecological relations discussed in Chapter 2 (fig. 2.1). In both cases we can consider the environment as determinant. However, in only one case, the last interglacial example, was this a barrier to settlement. If we were to apply the simple interpretative model that more animal species and large ^{18}O peaks represent 'better' environments for prehistoric hunters and gatherers, then the post-glacial environment should obviously be 'worse' for potential settlement than its interglacial counterpart. Even more surprising, then, that we find such overwhelming evidence at this time for settlement.

Something obviously happened in the intervening 110 Kyr which changed the groundrules. The outcome, as measured by a settlement history signature, led to the breaking of the determining hold of the environment on human adaptations. Instead the fresh groundrules specified alternative ways for coping with these environmental problems, and by so doing settlement was assured. The problems of harvesting the forest storehouses (Clarke 1976) have been discussed at length in Chapter 3. The interglacial forests contained a great amount of usable energy. It came however in very costly packages. It is inescapable that the settlement histories of the regional model are measuring between these two periods a process of social change that led to intensification, one outcome of which was to tap for the first time the vast potential in these resources.

(b) The big surprise of the upper palaeolithic

The 110 Kyr that separated the two case studies discussed above can be divided into four climatic periods on the basis of deep sea core stratigraphy and terrestrial based events (Chapter 3). It is during this same period that we see at c.35 Kyr one of archaeology's Big Surprises in the form of the pan-European replacement of middle palaeolithic flake industries with upper palaeolithic blade based assemblages. This event is regarded as a watershed transition since it is at this time that anatomically modern man appears in the fossil record of Europe. The changes in technology and additions to material culture in the form of art and ornament (Collins and Onians 1978) are regarded as positive indications of the appearance, at least after 35 Kyr, of fully 'modern' human behaviour (Dennell 1983a:102).

This transition has received considerable attention. Mellars (1973) discusses changes in south-west France during the transition under three main behavioural headings (see also White 1982):

Material technology   A greater range and complexity of tool forms and a replacement of *stability* in middle palaeolithic tool forms with rapid change during the upper palaeolithic; a development in bone, ivory and antler working; the appearance of personal ornaments.

Subsistence activities   A greater emphasis on a single species (often reindeer); a broadening of the subsistence base to include small game; the possible development of large scale co-operative hunting and a greater efficiency in hunting due to the invention of the bow and arrow; very possibly these changes were accompanied by improvements in food storage and preservation techniques.

Demography and social organisation   A substantial increase in population density and the maximum size of the co-residential group as inferred from the number of sites and the dimensions of settlements; group aggregation occurs to participate in co-operative hunting of migratory herd animals such as reindeer; increase in corporate awareness.

A similar list of traits is outlined by Klein (1973:121–2) using a data base from the Ukraine. A through-time comparison reveals that:

(1)   upper palaeolithic populations in the Ukraine made a greater variety of stone tools than the mousterians;
(2)   they transported raw materials over several hundred km;
(3)   they worked bone;
(4)   they produced art;
(5)   their range of settlement increased from 54° N to above the Arctic circle; and a further two inferences are deduced from the data:
(6)   the greater number of sites known for the upper palaeolithic points to an increase in population;
(7)   if anything they were less nomadic in the upper palaeolithic, and occupied semi-permanent structures.

Comparable changes could be found in all the regions of Europe. There are also the same inferences that the upper palaeolithic witnessed an increase in population, and that the changes we can see in the archaeological record represent a 'quantum advance' (Klein 1973:122) over the earlier mousterian. These changes were furthermore felt not only in technology (Dennell 1983a:chapter 5) but also in aspects of social organisation (White 1982; Bender 1978; Harrold 1980; S. Binford 1968).

How well this 'surprise' fits in with our earlier interglacial case study! You will remember how the differences between the archaeological record of northern Europe at 118 and 8 Kyr needed something dramatic to account for such discrepancies in the signatures. It would be difficult to imagine anything more dramatic than the upper palaeolithic, and the ready-made inferences about changes in social organisation also seem very pertinent in accounting for variation in settlement histories in comparable environments. The case for social change seems proven.

However, before we get too carried away with this scenario we should examine more closely the impact of the upper palaeolithic transition on the archaeological records in the regional model. It is all too easy, as I have tried to show in the preceding paragraph, to explain the archaeological record by using another part of the archaeological record as an explanation. The logic is as follows:

Q. What explains a change between two points in time?
A. A dramatic looking change that occurred after the first event but before the second!

The regional model with its embodied space/energy principles provides an independent framework for measuring such changes. Instead of accepting the appearance of the elements in the upper palaeolithic package as the keys to socio-cultural evolution, we should see if the advances detailed by Mellars, Klein and others are always encountered.

The only way to do this is to use the measure provided by settlement histories. The reason for using this measure in preference to any other is as follows. If a region lacks ornaments, art or rich burials in the EUP we cannot use this negative evidence to argue that they were not part of the upper palaeolithic package in that area. There are for example many parts of mesolithic Europe where such material evidence is lacking; and yet it would be unreasonable to infer from this that the potential for such behaviour did not exist. It was simply not required. The settlement history evidence, the presence/absence of human occupation in an area, is however entirely unambiguous. We are in less danger with such data of reading into them what we want to see; for example that the appearance of rich burials signifies the development of status and ranked behaviour. This lack of ambiguity does not however free us from the responsibility of interpreting the settlement evidence.

The upper palaeolithic data presented by Mellars (1973) and Klein (1973) reveal differences of scale, even though the conclusions they reach are very similar. The Ukraine study area measures some 1.5 million km^2 (1973:map 2 – the area north of Odessa) while the Périgord area covers some 12,500 km^2 (de Sonneville-Bordes 1960:fig. 1), or 0.8% of the Ukrainian region. Klein considers a much longer period of time, while Mellars focuses on the transition period between 35 and 30 Kyr.

A finer scale of resolution begins to cast doubts on a universal set of traits that characterises the impact of upper palaeolithic lifestyles on the regional archaeological record. In tables 8.14 and 8.15 the settlement histories of two limestone areas of approximately equivalent size are compared. The data come from the SW and NC region and reveal that, while there is indeed an increase in the number of sites for the Périgord in the EUP, this is definitely not the case in the Swabian limestone alb. A further breakdown is provided in table 5.15, where we can also see that the rate of increase in known sites is much less between the middle and EUP in Cantabria than it is in the Périgord area of the SW region. It would not for example be possible in the light of this data to infer

Table 8.14. *Findspot frequency for southern Germany and south-west France*

Period	Swabian and Franconian limestone albs		Périgord	
	sites	%	sites	%
Middle Palaeolithic (mousterian, micoquian) 80–35 Kyr	42	34	32	13
Early Upper Palaeolithic (chatelperronian aurignacian upper perigordian/ gravettian) 35–20 Kyr	21	17	98	40
Late Upper Palaeolithic (solutrean magdalenian) 20–10 Kyr	60	49	113	47

Sources: (After Gamble 1983a:table 18.1); Mellars 1973, Peyrony 1949 and Gamble 1978a, b

Table 8.15. *Number of sites per km² in southern Germany and south-west France*

Périgord area calculated from de Sonneville-Bordes (1960, fig. 1).

	Swabian and Franconian limestone albs 15,000 km²	Périgord 12,600 km²
Middle Palaeolithic	0.0028	0.0025
Early Upper Palaeolithic	0.0014	0.0078
Late Upper Palaeolithic	0.004	0.0089

Source: After Gamble 1983a:table 18.2

an across-the-continent increase in population as a standard upper palaeolithic trait.

A more constructive question would be to ask if it is possible to infer population increase from an increase in the number of findspots? At hunter-gatherer population densities, the answer is most certainly negative. This problem has been encountered with other prehistoric settlement data (Renfrew 1972; Bintliff 1977; Cherry 1982), where alternative explanations, such as the shift from nucleated to dispersed settlement patterns by the same number of people, need to be considered before population increase can be accepted.

Of equal importance in the palaeolithic case are variations in settlement histories that the immense time spans might possibly mask. The middle palaeolithic data in table 8.14 cover the period between 118 and 35 Kyr in the last glacial cycle. If we look more closely at the settlement histories for both areas we find that in the Périgord occupation was continuous throughout Würm I and II (Laville *et al.* 1980), while in southern Germany the archaeological occupations are generally interstadial in age (Müller-Beck 1957). For example, several of the important micoquian assemblages are correlated with the Brørup interstadial as recognised in northern Europe (Mania and Toepfer 1973). It is possible, as greater resolution in dating for these assemblages becomes available, that assemblages dated to the period 75–35 Kyr were associated only with interstadial deposits, while the period between 118 and 75 Kyr will be represented by evidence for longer, perhaps continuous spans of settlement occupation.

This variation in the early last glacial is also found when we compare evidence within regions. The Cantabrian data analysed by Butzer (1981) show very little occupation in Würm I (118–75 Kyr), but continuous evidence for settlement in this part of the SW region during Würm II. As might be expected, the analysis of sediments in the southern French area of the MW region indicates continuous occupation during Würm I and Würm II (H. de Lumley 1969b, 1971) which I would interpret as the period between 118 and 35 Kyr.

The regional model once again shows, via the measurements provided by settlement histories, that no monothetic set of traits (Clarke 1978:fig. 3) characterises the appearance of the upper palaeolithic. It is very likely that in many regions the upper palaeolithic colonised empty territory, while elsewhere Neanderthal populations were present. Variation in inter-regional demographic patterns would have had a great effect on the formation of regional archaeological signatures.

The contrasted settlement histories between the NC and SW regions are set out in diagrammatic form in fig. 8.9. The patchy nature of the settlement histories in southern Germany is emphasised and it is possible that the earliest upper palaeolithic, as defined by technology, encountered empty territory. The C14 date of 36.5±5 Kyr for an aurignacian assemblage in level III/8 at the Geissenklösterle (Hahn 1983) is at present 2 Kyr older than the earliest EUP dates from the SW region. The important finding indicated in fig. 8.9 is that occupation existed at all in southern Germany during the polar desert conditions which followed the Denekamp interstadial. Comparable conditions during the period 75–30 Kyr led to the ebb of settlement, with the resettlement of these areas taking place only during the interstadials. Here is a measure of the difference between upper palaeolithic and earlier adaptations within a single region.

However, we have already seen in Chapter 5 that most of the NC and NW regions were unoccupied during the height of the glacial advance, 20–17 Kyr. The evidence for palaeolithic occupation in the mediterranean province at 18 Kyr is very strong (Davidson 1980; Bartolomei *et al.* 1979; Higgs *et al.* 1967; Bailey *et al.* 1983a) and moreover it may well be that this was the first time under

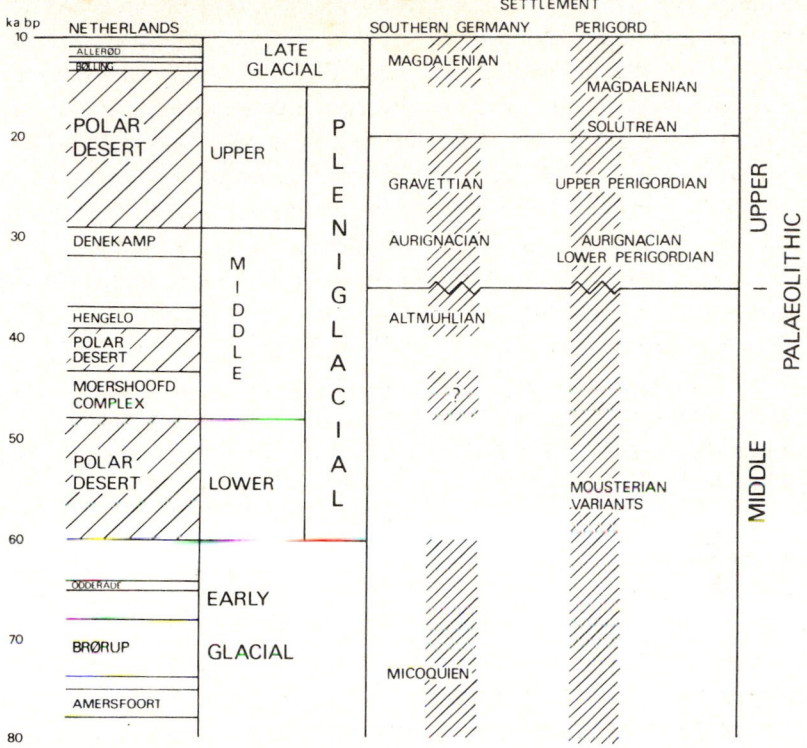

8.9 Climatic sequences and settlement histories in southern Germany, NC region and the Périgord, SW region (Gamble 1983a:207, fig. 18.1).

stage 3 climatic conditions (Chapter 3) that palaeolithic settlement was present in the SW and NE regions.

The settlement history data are giving us an insight into the complexities and variation in adaptive patterns to the different environments at different times in upper pleistocene Europe. We can begin to see very different settlement signatures between regions as well as quantitative changes in these signatures, even though many aspects of the environments, for example the appearance of polar desert conditions, were recurrent. If we can begin to see such variation in a very simple measure such as the presence/absence of settlement, we must also expect both synchronic and diachronic variation in other items of the upper palaeolithic 'package'.

The simple presence/absence measure is also masking significant variation. It might for example be argued, using the data from southern Germany, NC region, that fewer sites in the EUP than the MP, and no sites between 20 and c.15 Kyr, are evidence that argues against any significant adaptive changes associated with the upper palaeolithic package. The ensemble of traits appears to be well adjusted only to the 'better' environments of the SW region at 18 Kyr (Chapter 7). It could here be said, with good reason, that the changes that distinguish the middle from the upper palaeolithic can be explained as the outcome of richer environmental conditions.

The reason that the evidence does not support such a view lies in the scales of analysis that are involved. The argument makes sense only if we approach the study of regional settlement evidence with a model of *complete* settlement systems (Gamble 1983a). In other words, wherever we find a few sites, the largest is designated a home base and the rest are analysed as satellite stations around this hub. This is very common practice (table 6.12) but as we have seen in the earlier sections of this chapter, the settlement histories are sufficiently different between regions to suggest that such models cannot be indiscriminately applied to all bodies of settlement data. Instead we should consider the possibility that some regions contained *partial* settlement records (fig. 8.10). They formed, in Binford's (1980, 1983) terms, the outer ring of the territory exploited by a logistically organised system (Chapter 2). Into such areas small hunting parties would occasionally move if pressure on resources in the core areas had to be reduced. As a result, no residential camps or home bases would be created and instead the evidence would be overwhelmingly for special purpose field camps and procurement locations. The settlement traces in this area of a group's lifetime territory would be very different in terms of density and frequency of occupation from those in the core area of operations. I have suggested elsewhere (1983a:211) that the EUP of Germany represents such a partial settlement record. At this time the area was caught between two advancing ice sheets and came to form the outer logistic ring of the exploitation zone of groups whose main centre of operations lay outside this area. The small artifact collections, the broken bone and antler points and the female figurines, indicative of open systems of interaction and information sharing, are all elements of the archaeological signature of the past survival strategy.

The size of the territories exploited by palaeolithic groups changed as a function of the structure of resources (Chapter 2). They also changed due to the development of social solutions to the high cost tariffs involved in exploiting either r selected resources or large mammals at low densities and hence high risk. Combined with this were the equally important costs that resulted either from increased conflict (Jochim 1983) as groups became packed into territories and dependent upon r selected resources such as fish, or from the costs and uncertainties involved with exploiting very large annual territories and maintaining mating networks (Gamble 1982; Wobst 1976). These problems could be

---

8.10 Settlement record in an arbitrarily defined region of 120,000 km²: (a) *complete*, which includes the seasonal movements of a residential base; and (b) *partial*, where only sites concerned with exploitation in the logistical radius are present and the residential bases lie outside the study region. The region of 120,000 km² is roughly equivalent to the unglaciated area of upper pleniglacial Germany. The model situation demonstrates how patterns of regional exploitation condition the formation of the archaeological record between two contrasted areas within the SW and NC regions (Gamble 1983a:210, fig. 18.2).

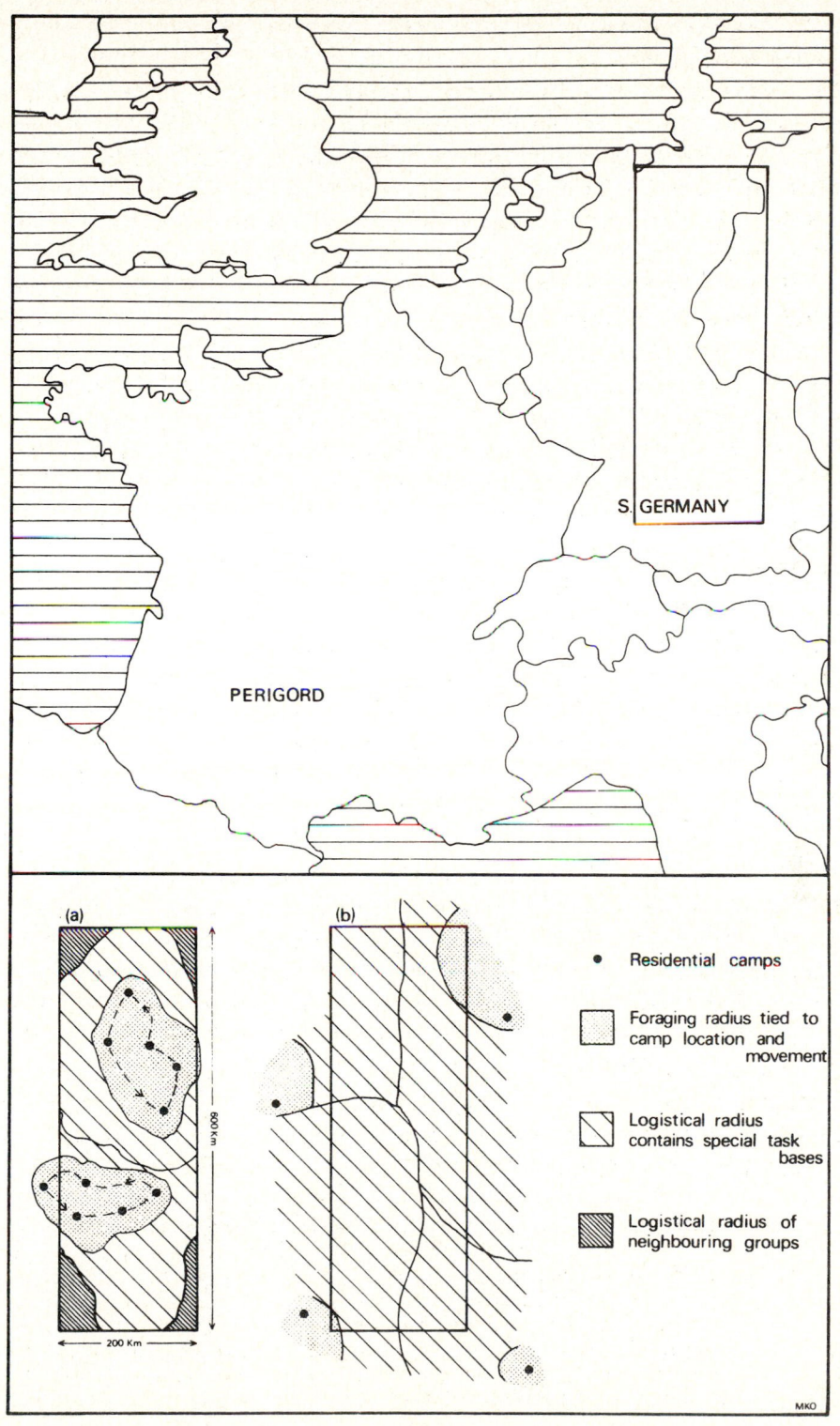

(a)

600 Km

200 Km

(b)

- • Residential camps

- Foraging radius tied to camp location and movement

- Logistical radius contains special task bases

- Logistical radius of neighbouring groups

PERIGORD

S. GERMANY

MKO

alleviated by developing more efficient technologies or unleashing the information messaging potential in material culture (Chapter 7). But these developments that are so closely linked to the upper palaeolithic package were not prime movers for change by themselves. They must instead be viewed as instruments used in the production and appropriation of resources. They are tactical options to be utilised in the pursuit of a social strategy. The determinant features of the environment require first and foremost social solutions rather than technological innovations. Change occurs through new demands on production and appropriation of resources so that obligations, positions, and statuses can be reproduced (Bender 1978). Changes in these demands create changes in technology, settlement systems, the distribution of personnel and the role of material culture in signalling social distinctions, and set new levels of acceptable costs for exploitation strategies. These can be modelled as changes in the networks of alliances which determined relative levels of resource appropriation and use. Such networks provided the framework whereby individuals and groups were articulated into the local and regional processes of social reproduction. In this sense the model of alliance networks (Gamble 1983a; Gilman 1984) serves to identify the intricate web of interactions that now needs both theoretical and empirical investigation if palaeolithic archaeology is to move beyond description to explanation.

Another way to view the process is as an intensification strategy. Exploiting r selected resources on any scale, investing material culture with stylistic rules, surviving in high risk environments and maintaining low density mating networks all involve an increase in effort and the acceptance of higher costs as measured by inputs of energy and time. This involves intensification at a regional scale irrespective of the size of that region. The repercussions will be felt at the local level. The example used here of the development of logistic based settlement systems in the NC region during the EUP shows how changes at the local or site level need to be interpreted in the context of processes operating at a regional scale of adaptation. This throws our settlement history data into much sharper relief and should stop us from counting up sites within arbitrarily defined regions and then passing judgments on the success or failure of a palaeolithic system. What I am advocating here is that at every site we should use the space/energy principles implicit in the regional model as a sounding board for examining the character of the variable archaeological signatures that have been recovered. This contributes to an understanding about *how* the intensification strategies altered the regional palaeolithic signatures, even if there is still no answer about *why* such strategies were set in train.

(c) world systems

The last section has provided us with a more detailed understanding of the variable archaeological record associated with the upper palaeolithic, and where the elements in this package are seen as the outcome of changes that involved the intensification of survival strategies. The different archaeological records during the last interglacial and early post-glacial can now be examined from the perspective of this model.

The contrast between middle palaeolithic tools employing large hafted projectile points and the microlithic components in the mesolithic assemblages is shown in figs. 8.11 and 8.12. This represents a change not only in manufac-

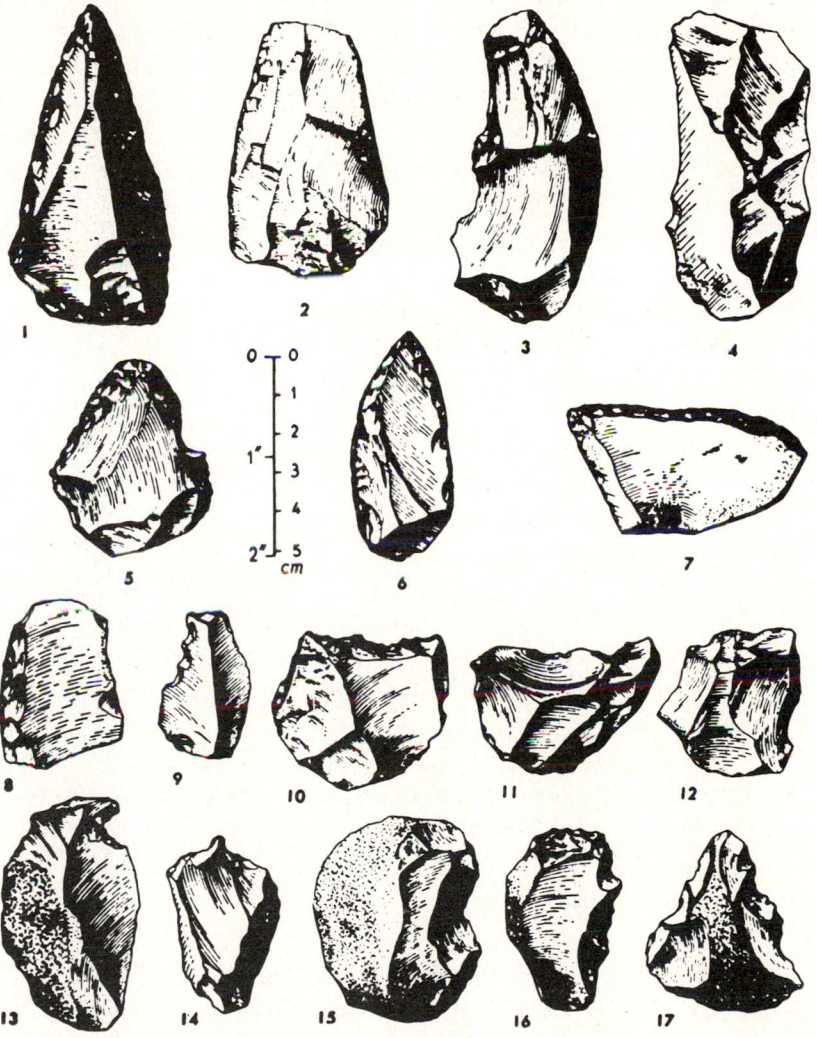

8.11 Possible technology at 128 Kyr. Characteristic flake artifact types for the typical mousterian: points (1, 6), scrapers (2, 3, 5, 7), unretouched flakes (4); and denticulate mousterian: scraper (8), denticulates and notches (9–13, 15–17), and borer (14).

The large size and generally low investment of effort in tool manufacture would have been a feature of such a technology (Bordes 1961b:805, fig. 20).

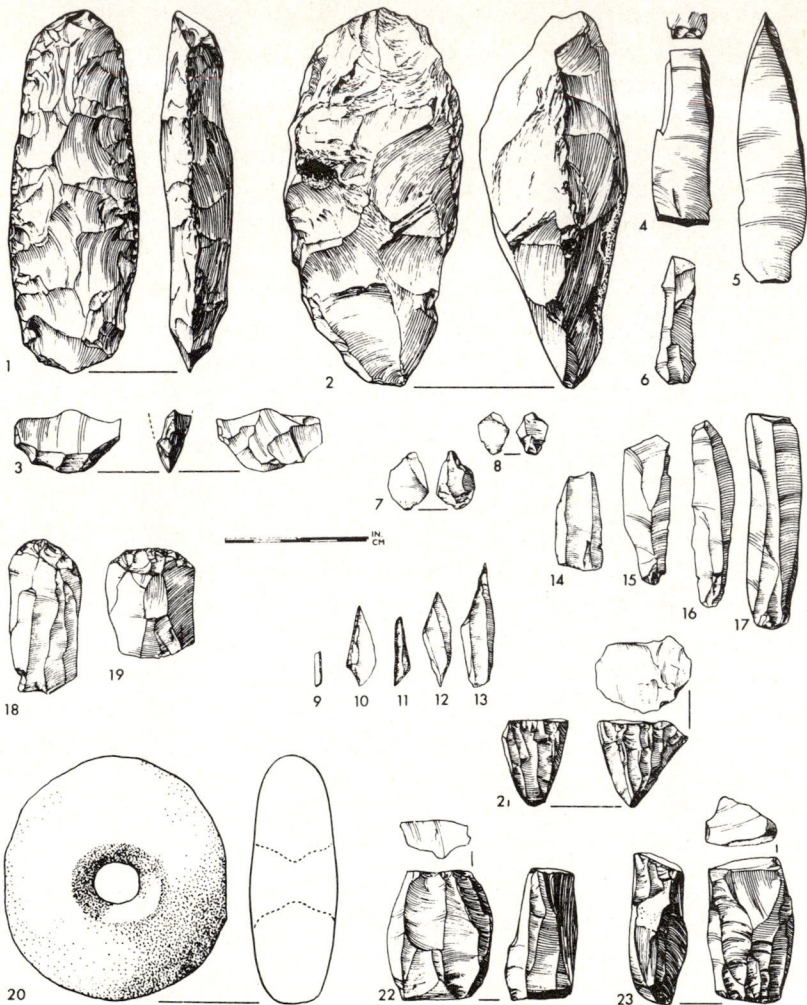

8.12 Representative technology at 8 Kyr. Characteristic blade, microblade and core implements from the mesolithic of the NW region.

(1) tranchet axe; (2) pick; (3) tranchet axe sharpening flake; (4–5) burins; (6) saw; (7–8) micro-burins; (9–13) microliths; (14–17) blades; (18–19) scrapers; (20) digging stick weight; (21–23) cores. The small size, standardised production and high investment of effort in making complex tools is the dominant feature of such a technology (Wymer (ed.) 1977:xiii, fig. 2).

turing technology but also in the manner in which it was organised (Chapter 2). The time stress that faced the mesolithic population in obtaining food from the forests of northern Europe is here directly reflected in more costly and efficient tools that help to relieve some of the acute scheduling problems in allocating segments of the time budget to particular tasks (Torrence 1983).

Changes in technology are also paralleled by physical differences between Neanderthals and anatomically modern humans. Studies of Neanderthal skeletons conclusively show massive and robust individuals (Trinkaus and Howells 1979). Evidence for stress fractures on the limbs can often be seen. The skeletons of anatomically modern man are by comparison very gracile. Skeletal proportions are very different, with the lower half of the body forming a much greater percentage of total body size. While many aspects of the short, robust features of the Neanderthal body can be explained as cold adaptations, these same features were also well suited to close quarter impact hunting using spears. Later populations are not anatomically suited to this kind of bruising approach to the hunt.

Other features of the package include the development of 'chains of connection' and the expansion of contacts in geographical space. This implies much larger societies between 128 and 8 Kyr in both a social, demographic and spatial sense, and as a result increased requirements for integration would select for the use of material culture as part of an information processing strategy.

The limitations on Neanderthal society were therefore set at low threshold values by environmental conditions. The social relations governing levels of appropriation and production required that groups were attached to locally abundant resources. The density of these animal resources determined to a large degree the viability of society. If resources became more dispersed and human territory size had to increase, then problems of integrating group members ensued. The social relations only specified that such costs were unacceptable. One result was for populations in these changing environments to contract and become locally extinct. Hence the ebb and flow model, where occupation of an area is determined by the impact that environmental conditions have upon human survival strategies.

The environment still had a great impact on later societies, including those at 8 Kyr, but the addition of intensive labour and information systems not only helped to procure resources but also permitted social interaction and population maintenance to take place. A final example of the intensification process in the mesolithic case study is provided by the appearance of cemeteries (Albrethsen and Petersen 1976) and other archaeological evidence for organisationally complex hunters (Rowley-Conwy 1983). Under such systems adaptive strategies often involved a close association with a defined, defended territory, a longer working day and an intensive level of exploitation to fulfil a new level of demand arising from changes in society, possibly brought about by the appearance in the post-glacial of agricultural formations in the world system.

I have been careful in this interpretative sketch to avoid letting one single element have more importance than any other in trying to understand the upper palaeolithic package. It would be tempting to put the overall changes down to developments in storage techniques or embedded procurement strategies. However, not only is there at present a lack of evidence for such developments but to dwell on these unknown quantities would be as misleading as trying to pin all the changes on the importance of the bone needle or the super-efficiency of the raclette. Neither, as Conkey (1983) has proposed, am I arguing that someone had the bright idea of sending messages in material culture code and that this allowed society to expand. Instead, it is during this period that a change occurred in the dominant relations between social and ecological systems. The ceilings which environments imposed in terms of exploitation costs were dramatically raised. One consequence of this rise in acceptable cost tariffs is seen directly in the increased attendance records as shown by the settlement histories from the ecologically specialised regions. A consequence of raising the stakes was a rapid transformation of the way *all* aspects of technology were organised. For example, every item of material culture suddenly carried additional information in the form of stylistic messaging once one item was explicitly used for this purpose (Wobst 1977:326). This increased dramatically the scale and range of information that could be processed and which was now required (Pfeiffer 1982).

This sketch does not answer the question *why* changes in the dominant social relations took place. I cannot pretend to have an answer or a model showing why or how this happened. I am however quite sure about one thing in identifying this relation as the nexus for change: explaining the process is not necessarily a relevant problem for the data from palaeolithic Europe. This continent can provide comparative information to define the problem, as I have tried to do in the last three chapters. One reason for a closer look at palaeolithic data has been to provide measurements which eventually can be compared with other palaeolithic data sets in order to provide quantitative information on the archaeological signatures of core and peripheral areas. While Europe may have on occasion a dramatic palaeolithic record, e.g. the earliest cave art, I would still maintain that, when judged by the late timing of initial colonisation and its proximity to the harsh ice age environments, the continent forms a periphery to core areas in Africa and Asia. However, due to a long history of research the European data base is both well known and abundant and it is at the moment difficult to compare in the same regional detail with these probable core areas.

One theme I would investigate in relation to the general problem of change and the appropriate scales at which to analyse it is the link between anatomically modern humans and the major colonisation of new habitats. This involved human populations colonising Australia at 40 Kyr (Jones 1979) and inhabiting areas in Tasmania at 18 Kyr which, at Western contact, were uninhabited (Kiernan *et al.* 1983). During the period 35–10 Kyr, anatomically modern man colonised eastern Siberia above the Arctic Circle (Tseitlin 1979) and at some hotly contested date (I favour 12 Kyr) entered the New World. This colonisation is also part of social change leading to intensification in the human use of the earth and shows at a global scale how the determinant obstacles for so long offered by environments were being overturned. The European data also have information on the colonisation of empty space by anatomically modern populations and in microcosm provide a series of regional case studies that document the process, even if the explanation of the process remains elusive. This raises a final intriguing question: is the biological form of human populations a response to social relations or is society created by biology? The short answer has to be that biology does not establish a deterministic programme for social formations. Otherwise we would still live in a world of hunters and gatherers. What is now an issue for future research is how many different types of hunter-gatherer society were associated with a single biological population.

CHAPTER 9

THE PALAEOLITHIC SETTLEMENT OF EUROPE

> General views, whatever other interest they may have, are chiefly useful as suggesting the way to fresh enquiry.
>
> W. J. Sollas, *Ancient Hunters and their Modern Representatives*
> (1911:viii)

Introduction

At the beginning of this book I raised the question, why study the European palaeolithic? In particular why study it once the rationale supplied by the pursuit of culture history for the earliest human representatives of the various regional traditions has been abandoned?

I hope to have shown in the preceding pages that by using an alternative framework which regards culture as part of an adaptive process it is possible to investigate complex behaviour, and the changes it underwent, via a study of the European archaeological record. Moreover, this can be done without recourse to imagination and unwarranted speculation. I also asked readers to judge as the book proceeded the relative information return from the two approaches. This can be done by contrasting Chapter 5 with Chapters 6–8, where the regional traditions have to some extent been relaced by alternative patterns based on an attempt to understand variation in the archaeological record. In order to complete the process I will now offer in summary my interpretative sketch of the palaeolithic settlement of Europe in order to suggest further applications of the regional model to the investigation of past behaviour. A guideline to the evidence needed to test such a model is provided in table 9.1.

What happened?

Viewed from the perspective of world prehistory the colonisation of Europe was a late affair that involved a grade within the classification of *Homo sapiens* (table 5.6). The middle pleistocene geographical expansion associated with early forms of *Homo sapiens* occurred as part of a broader set of ecological processes. The first of these saw the simultaneous radiation of modern ungulate grazing forms into Europe and other northerly latitudes of the Old World such as north China. This expansion of a novel animal community, of which humans were a part, was also linked with vegetational communities that had, by the onset of the middle pleistocene, been severely disrupted by the interglacial/glacial cycles of the lower pleistocene (Luchterhand 1978:411).

Table 9.1. *Some implications for the archaeological signatures from the three interpretative models*

	Model 1	Model 2	Model 3
Settlement system	continuous in small geographical areas	less continuous across landscapes and a greater degree of residue aggregation, but in larger geographical areas	pinpointed, dense clusters of material, very large geographical areas
Food management strategy	foraging for meat, marrow and fat from frozen carcasses; some summer hunting and scavenging	intercept hunting of large herd animals, scavenging, tactical use of storage; variable strategies between regions	planning ahead and a considerable use of storage after successful intercept hunting
Organisation of technology	tools to make tools, especially wooden implements; time stress results in a greater investment in some flake production	some degree of investment in hunting equipment but still many expedient and ad hoc tools; very little use of caches	curated, with high investment in raw material selection, multi-component implements, caches
Lifespace layouts	accumulative, rarely based around a repeatedly used facility such as a hearth	use of fixed facilities such as rock shelters and river bluffs by fords; some formal layout	regularities in organisation and repeated use of fixed facilities, such as hearths, lead to very formal patterning and are part of the planning ahead
Raw material transfers	local only	predominantly local	high grade transfers over considerable distances, use of quarries
Stylistic messaging	no use outside local group requirements	very limited use, if any, outside local group requirements	use in a range of contexts and mediums in both open and closed systems at local and regional scales
Interaction	closed systems irrespective of the ecological conditions	closed systems irrespective of the ecological conditions	open/closed depending on ecological constraints
Alliance networks	does not extend outside local group	strangers rarely encountered; insurance against failure not needed	basis for complex differentiation of individuals and groups
Settlement histories	periodic: occupation of area shifts with ecological balance of biomass and animal community organisation	longer in duration at sub-region and keyed to climatic stage 2 open conditions with large biomass	intensification of exploitation, tactical use of poor resource areas within and between regions; strategic use of expensive *r* selected resources leads to greater settlement duration

The long term success of *Homo sapiens* has been to ride with the periodic perturbations in biome changes that are such a feature of the pleistocene. The deep sea core stratigraphies have revealed the repeated frequency and standard temporal wavelengths of these cycles (fig. 3.3), while terrestrial investigations of faunal and floral communities all point to their progressive simplification within these restless habitats. Early hominids matched their long term survival strategies with the environmental rhythms of the pleistocene, and a direct measure of their evolutionary success is provided by the foundation of the European palaeolithic record at 0.73 Myr.

Butzer (1982:299) has made some powerful arguments that the appearance of early *Homo sapiens* depended on an unequal distribution of resources at the sub-continental scale. In other words large regional populations existed which were keyed in to dense, abundant and predictable resources and yet isolated from other such regional populations by areas where resources could not maintain population at such densities and hence no population was to be found. He also argues that the effect of the predictable, long term shifts in habitat organisation and resource structure that happened during the pleistocene would have been vital for bringing these isolated populations together and then pushing them apart. In this way gene flow and genetic drift would have taken place as well as directional selection for novel adaptive traits.

Three models of what they did when they got to Europe

Model 1: meat management strategies

The initial colonisation of Europe by early *Homo sapiens* was therefore not a case of an opportunistic species seizing the first favourable set of environmental circumstances that just happened to turn up at 0.73 Myr. Instead at this time hominids had evolved the necessary long term strategies, measured here in millennia, which allowed for the successful colonisation of alternative habitats. There had at all times since the appearance of the australopithecines been sufficient energy and resources within all the regions of Europe for colonisation to have taken place. However, significant colonisation required evolutionary long term survival solutions to both periodic shifts (time) and the geographical distribution (space) of environments and resources, including other hominids, at both a regional and a continental scale.

As absolute dates for human settlement become available for the middle pleistocene we shall see that they fall predominantly at times when the environments of climatic stage 2 were present (Chapter 3, fig. 3.12), since these account for the majority of time during the past 700 Kyr. Human strategies, both reproductive and social, were therefore matched to the structure and temporal duration of these environmental circumstances. As suggested earlier, the other two environmental stages (interglacial and full glacial) were of a brief duration that would have placed a species such as early *Homo sapiens* at a disadvantage, since no sooner was the door opened than it was slammed in their faces by the pleistocene bouncer. The human species appears, on this evidence, to be adapted to the long term settlement (i.e. a minimum of 50 Kyr cycles) of environments at the regional scale as used throughout this book. This does not mean however that such regions were solidly packed with human populations or that settlement in the regions was uninterrupted during such cycles. At any particular moment most of a region was probably lying fallow. From a European perspective the evolutionary history of human adaptations to the varied pleistocene environments of this continent has been to occupy for a greater proportion of time a greater number of regions, and sub-regions within them, during successive pleistocene cycles of 90 Kyr duration.

This scenario sees long term evolutionary advantages for the human species in adapting to those environmental conditions with a sustained temporal wavelength (fig. 3.3), as indicated by the deep sea cores. One reason for this view considers the different types of resources available for exploitation. The successful, as measured by the evolutionary long term history of the species, colonisers of northern latitudes would be hominids which could exploit a variety of economic niches provided by the large ungulate biomass associated with climatic stage 2 conditions. These herds fulfilled the necessary requirements of locally dense and abundant resources. In the northern latitudes the alternative plant and marine resources presented a very costly set of foods which were utilised for the first time in an intensive manner only in the LUP and the postglacial. For the reasons already given in Chapters 2 and 3 I could not support a model which maintained that the colonisation of Europe was achieved by using a wide spectrum of resources, including significant proportions of plant foods, shellfish and fish. This does not imply however that the meat based strategies were simple and involved only a single pattern of procurement behaviour. There were always several ways to acquire the all important meat resources through foraging, scavenging and hunting. However, the critical limiting factor that faced the early colonisers would have been the long period of winter dearth when large herds dispersed and migrated such that the mobility of the potential prey far exceeded the potential of the human predator to keep in contact.

One solution to this problem would have been the niche, uncontested by other carnivores, that was provided by frozen animal carcasses. These were the result of natural mortalities during late autumn and winter. An important aspect of these winter strategies would have been systematic and intensive searching in order to locate frozen animal carcasses, a seach for which a mobile species was well adapted.

The suitability of this niche for human exploitation would have been dependent upon technology. For example, such items as long wooden probes (or spears, as the Lehringen and Clacton examples are often called) would have been essential for discovering potential food hidden under the snow or trapped down fissures in the ice of frozen lakes and rivers. Once located, the frozen carcasses would become the subject of defrosting strategies in which the management of fire would have played an important role.

This foraging strategy for frozen food resources in the long hard winters of climatic stage 2 would moreover be adapted to a foraging group of large size rather than the support of individual foragers. This would be due to the size of the animal carcasses recovered, and the immediate consumption (Dennell 1983a:190) that was involved. Large group size would make foraging a more secure strategy in terms of organising the search for food hidden under the snow and utilising it once located. The alternative strategy of using such resources on a chance encounter basis by either individuals or small groups would carry too many risks, since accurately matching group size to the resources recovered in such a chance manner would be impossible. Large foraging groups would also provide additional protection from the neighbourhood carnivores.

The predictable and substantial winter mortalities among the European herds would, with the appropriate food management strategy, have provided a means of solving the problem of the long period of no-growth in the northern winters and the movement of herd animals away from the local territories of hominids. It would also have provided an opportunity to use the vast food potential of a megafaunal carcass – mammoth, woolly rhino and adult male bison – which were both hazardous and uneconomical (Chapter 3) to hunt as live animals (see Müller-Beck 1982 for an alternative interpretation). Many of the stone tools in this winter foraging strategy were therefore designed to make other tools, and in particular wooden implements such as shovels, scoops, digging sticks and snow probes that were needed to locate and dig out the vital resources. Individual wooden implements would have had a low technounit score (Chapter 2). A feature of the lithic materials would be their unstandardised nature and their deposition at wood procurement and manufacturing sites rather than at the foraging rendezvous.

In the spring and summer such simple wooden implements would not have been needed. During these seasons some hunting was possible as the large migratory herds of bison, horse, red deer and reindeer formed suitably large aggregated resources. Moreover, additional food could be scavenged down at the riverside, as discussed in Chapter 7, sometimes with fatal consequences for some of the hominids. At such seasons of the year the defrosting strategies would have been unnecessary, and rather speed in acquiring the all important meat, fat and marrow resources from fresh kills would have been selected for. The implications for the organisation and variation in technology under differing selection pressure from the environment have already been dealt with in Chapter 7. At this time it is possible to see variation between the regional palaeolithic records that reflects differences in ecology and selection pressure across the continent, while the few absolute dates also point to the appropriateness of the ebb and flow settlement model at an inter- and intra-regional scale.

These foraging groups were keyed to predictable and abundant meat, fat and marrow resources. As a result they were spatially and socially compact systems. The foraging, snow searching winter strategies and the summer strategies with some hunting and scavenging would have been possible only so long as the annual territories were compact in size. These home ranges were regularly patrolled by the entire group and absolute mobility over the year would have been high, as indeed is the case with present day plant foragers (table 2.3). However, although the spatial areas patrolled by groups of early *Homo sapiens* were small in area, they were stocked with comparatively high human population densities. Mobility served to reduce conflict, while the social forum for competitive status resulting from the differential appropriation of resources was weakly, if at all, developed. As Butzer maintains in his interpretative model, there would have been a number of these regional populations within the provinces of Europe, and, equally, areas surrounding these foci of human activity where for considerable periods of time, no settlement took place.

The model presented here (table 9.1) would not look for home bases or special purpose logistic camps in the archaeological record. It is very much an off-site model where I would expect a clear relation between the density of food resources, in this case carcasses as well as live animals, and the density of findspots. As a result I am not surprised to find an overwhelming recovery in the earliest palaeolithic for artifacts from rivers and lakes, and far fewer sites from the intervening territory. This seems to apply to all the provinces, but obviously requires closer checking with the geomorphological evidence for erosion and destruction of archaeological evidence. These sites would not only be food procurement locations of live and dead animals but also places along the rivers where wood could be obtained from the surviving gallery woods during climatic stage 2b, and where the all important fuel for defrosting could also be found. A further implication would be that such groups rarely moved into seasonally different areas but that their centre of operations was anchored in the winter range, since here the major limiting factors were confronted. In terms of assemblage grain, the residues left behind in clumps should be relatively fine grained. The only curated items would be the wooden tools, and hence if we ever find them we should expect them to show a large degree of ancient breaks that resulted in their discard as is the case with the Clacton spearpoint/probe (Oakley *et al.* 1977).

The knowledge needed to pursue a successful survival strategy depended upon a very general set of skills (e.g. how to locate carcasses). The most important of these was mobility, by which information crucial to survival was gathered. These tactics could be readily applied in other areas within a region as environmental changes buffeted local populations around. Over time this would have the effect of smoothing the archaeological signatures left behind on the surface of the regions and eliminating some of the patchiness in the spacing between groups that would have been apparent at any one point in time. The extinction of population at a sub- or local regional level was compensated by the rapid colonisation of other areas within the same region. In that sense the early *Homo sapiens* grades were opportunistic, since their investment in an environment, as measured by knowledge and planning, was low and could be mapped on to any suitable set of rich resource conditions. Survival took place during the long acts in the regional theatres rather than among the attractions of the crush bars in the intervals.

Model 2: meat storage and self-sufficiency

The palaeolithic record associated principally with fossil grades 3a and 2 of *Homo sapiens* (table 5.6) presents some significant variation on this first model (table 9.1). To begin with, there is more evidence for planning ahead rather than encounter strategies of the foraging kind. The single most important aspect of these more logistically based strategies was an increase in the spatial scale of society, and the consequent reduction of whole group foraging activities and a greater incidence of individual and smaller group ventures. The planning ahead is indicated by a change in the settlement system evidence, with the use of cave facilities and repeatedly used open locations (e.g. Molodova V) as temporary halts by task groups operating away from the main group. One result of this is seen in the recurrent assemblage patterning from the SW region, a feature lacking in the off-site scatters associated with model 1. It is also seen in the programming of camp sites in terms of the layout of hearths and the zonation of activities. The planning ahead in turn places a selective hone on technology, since these strategies will be based upon the acquisition of live resources through hunting rather than of dead ones obtained by foraging and scavenging. The organisation of technology to allow for a degree of forward planning provided one set of tactics for reducing risks. At this time the *Homo sapiens* grades were moving to food management strategies based upon the four main herd species – bison, horse, red deer and reindeer – throughout the nine regions. Associated with this shift in emphasis of food management strategies were developments in the tactical use of storage to cope with those times of the year, primarily the long winters, when migratory resources were not available. As a result, overall population density would have been higher in the nine regions, although at the scale of the local region/annual territory, it would have been lower than the earlier, model 1, strategy where groups were keyed in to very dense, local resources. In other words, more of the local regions within a region were used, albeit at lower population densities. According to this second model, human groups were able to exploit environments within regions for greater periods of time than was possible under model 1 conditions. A model 2 strategy was better adapted to climatic stage 2 of the interglacial/glacial cycle, and particularly suited to the four large herd ungulates which formed the central core of the large mammal communities.

In this respect planning and the tactical use of storage led to a greater degree of population stability and hence adaptive security. The likelihood of populations at the local or sub-regional scale becoming extinct as a result of short wavelength periodicities in pleistocene environments (Butzer 1982:table 2.2) would have been minimised to some extent by the greater degree of investment in knowledge about the environment and in planning to meet its temporal and spatial problems. Only the longer wavelengths associated with extreme environmental perturbations, stages 1 and 3, would place the adaptive systems, at a province scale, under extreme stress. The model 2 strategy required a set of skills where environmental knowledge was a key to planning and hence to successful adaptation, and these were closely tied to particular community attributes of biomass density, predictability, mobility and prey size. In that sense the adaptive strategies worked within well defined and relatively narrow limits imposed by the structure and organisation of resources. Moreover, this form of involvement with a home range suggests a very different mating network, where the pattern of marriages helped restrict groups to particular areas and where rapid migration to unpopulated areas when resources became available was a rarely taken option, since the guiding information about how to exploit the particular configuration of a territory would not exist.

These social and demographic units were also relatively closed in terms of their patterns of interaction. They did not require the potential offered by open regional behaviour for insuring against the problems of a risky resource base (Chapter 2).

What distinguishes them from model 3 strategies that in Europe are associated with anatomically modern humans, grade 3b (table 5.6), is their reluctance to intensify their food management strategies in the face of worsening resource exploitation costs, even though during the interglacials resource availability and abundance were increasing.

At this time there existed considerable inter-regional differences within Europe. The archaeological records from both caves and open sites provide very different signatures between the SW and NE regions and almost all other parts of the continent. Due to closer chronological control, the evidence from settlement histories for the differential ebb and flow of population in regions is also apparent. At a continental scale these two regions stand out as *core areas*. Unfortunately it is still difficult to contrast the mediterranean province with the southern and northern provinces in terms of their archaeological signatures at this time, and yet I suspect that a snapshot view of continental adaptations would have looked rather like a meat sandwich. The areas of more constant settlement were located in the oceanic climates of the SW region and in the southern parts, especially along the river valleys, of the NE region. Above and below these regions were areas occupied on an ebb and flow basis as shorter wavelengths of the pleistocene took their toll on resources. However, it is very possible that during interglacials these same core area populations became established in northern Scandinavia and even more continental areas where a large mammal biomass was to be found and where of course the destruction of the archaeological record has subsequently been totally due to the reappearance of continental ice sheets based on such areas.

Model 3: planned competition

The final model deals with the upper palaeolithic (Chapter 8) and does not need to be repeated here (table 9.1, Gamble 1984b). Suffice it to say that changes in social relations within the context of alliance networks led to an intensification in logistic based strategies that resulted in a massive increase in both spatial and social systems, as the resource conditions worsened. The settlement signature now becomes extremely coarse grained, and evidence appears for task specific sites. Moreover, we must consider local groups operating between the regions of our model (fig. 8.10). Once again continuity in settlement occurs in the SW and NE regions as well as in the mediterranean province, as measured against the height of the last glaciation at 18 Kyr. This intensification can be seen in the first systematic exploitation of r selected resources as well as in patterns of inter-regional contact. Moreover, it also resulted in the dense packing of population into small geographical areas where these r selected resources formed the basis for food management strategies with consequent changes in technology. The need to resolve conflict in such competitive systems led to changes in information exchange. These are not so much surprises as necessary developments, given the new form of social organisation. Within Europe at this time there would have been a varied mosaic of societies, variable densities of population, exchange networks, competition and subsistence strategies.

One challenge that now faces palaeolithic archaeologists involves the investigation of these changes and the implications they hold for the relative intensity of exploitation strategies. Is there a single *change* in overall strategy at 35 Kyr with subsequent *variation* in regional adaptations reflecting nothing more than differential pummelling of such a strategy by changing environments and the resources they contained? According to this view any further intensification, unrelated to the costs involved in exploiting particular resources, only occurred when mesolithic populations of hunters and gatherers formed part of a world system that now included distant agricultural neighbours. An alternative approach might still acknowledge the fundamental restructuring in social relations and alliance networks at 35 Kyr but would characterise subsequent developments as multiple independent trajectories where social formations were dynamic, and therefore variable, rather than passive to the environment. This debate is already under way amongst studies of prehistoric hunters and gatherers in Australia (Lourandos 1983; Beaton 1983). Many of the issues raised in this book are pertinent in this context. In particular are those concerned with the need for independent checks and measurement of the archaeological record in order to avoid imposing our view of the past on the data. I would subscribe to the first model and advocate a research strategy, into the archaeological record associated with anatomically modern humans, based upon models and concepts designed to understand variation rather than continually argue for change in the groundrules of the survival strategies operating in prehistory. However I can appreciate the appeal of the second model, particularly since it warns us against falling into the tyrannical traps set by a blinkered reading of the ethnographic record. It is now up to the proponents of such a view to argue their case in detail by tracing the links between the dynamics they favour and the static residues.

The palaeolithic settlement of Europe provides an opportunity to observe the intensification of a long term evolutionary strategy by a mobile species in a part of its geographical range. The mode of production now known as hunting and gathering is compounded of many aspects dealing with individual and group selection. The changing rates of selection on the species can be assessed via an investigation of the archaeological record, and within a regional framework the European evidence allows us to measure these processes.

The palaeolithic settlement of Europe is of interest since it combines the register of rates of change in an evolutionary trajectory with the record of adaptive solutions to ecological and social process. But so does any palaeolithic record. The European data provide no answers to the question why change took place. That requires an altogether larger analytical frame, using the data in conjunction with other such data sets, if we are to have any chance of answering it. The problem has always been to find a common basis to compare such different archaeological records, and some pointers have been given in the preceding pages. However, the European data do at least magnify, through their peripheral position, the long term evolutionary success of *Homo sapiens*, and by so doing give us some hope that what today is merely the measurement of adaptation in the past will one day provide a base for answering the question why change happened.

APPENDICES

Appendix 1 *Moments in the early history of European Palaeolithic studies*

1717	The publication of observations made over a century earlier by Michaelis Mercatus (1541–93) who was the superintendent of the Botanical Gardens at the Vatican. He recognised distinctively chipped stones as human artifacts.
1797	John Frere wrote to the Society of Antiquaries, London, about his discoveries at Hoxne of stone artifacts. These would now be classified as acheulean handaxes. He referred them to 'a very remote period indeed, even beyond that of the present world'. His letter together with illustrations of the handaxes was published in the journal *Archaeologia* for 1800.
1830–3	Lyell's classic work in three volumes, *Principles of Geology, being an attempt to explain the former changes of the earth's surface by reference to causes now in action*. This established that the route to understanding the past lay in applying the principle of uniformitarianism.
1836	C. J. Thomsen developed the Three Age System of classification based upon a technological succession from stone to bronze to iron. This system gained universal acceptance and was used to organise the many discoveries being made in Europe. His scheme was translated into English in 1848.
1838	Boucher de Perthes, a customs official, claimed that the stone tools from the gravel terraces of the Somme river were made by antediluvian man and were hence of very great antiquity. His work was ignored.
1859	Prestwich and Evans visited Boucher de Perthes, and the significance of his observations was at last widely recognised. The association of stone tools with the bones of extinct animals demonstrated the High Antiquity of Man.
	The Origin of Species by Charles Darwin was published.
1860–1	Lartet began his excavations at the caves of Massat and Aurignac.
1865	Lubbock first used the terms palaeolithic and neolithic (old and new stone age) to subdivide Thomsen's scheme in his book *Prehistoric Times*.
1872	G. de Mortillet subdivided the palaeolithic into three stages and a number of cultural groupings.
1865–75	Lartet and Christy published the results of their excavations, *Reliquiae Aquitanicae, being contributions to the archaeology and palaeontology of Périgord and the adjoining provinces of southern France*.
1877	Lewis Henry Morgan took de Mortillet's division of the palaeolithic into a lower, middle and upper stage and transformed these into three stages of social evolution – lower, middle and upper savagery – in his book *Ancient Society*.

Appendix 1 – *continued*

1881	The de Mortillets published a five-stage scheme (chellean, acheulean, mousterian, solutrean and magdalenian) for the palaeolithic in their guide to the Musée Préhistorique.
1895	Authenticity of cave art established.
1901	Discovery of Font de Gaume and Les Combarelles cave art sites at Les Eyzies.
1912	Breuil subdivided the upper palaeolithic and inserted an aurignacian phase between the mousterian and solutrean.
	R. R. Schmidt used the French scheme to classify the results from cave excavations in Germany in his book *Die Diluviale Vorzeit Deutschlands*.

Appendix 2 *Some finds of fossil humans in Europe*
The table concentrates upon pre *Homo sapiens sapiens*

1823	Red 'Lady' of Paviland (Wales)
1848	Forbes Quarry (Gibraltar)
1856	Neander Valley (West Germany)
1868	Crô Magnon (France) anatomically modern man
1872	Earliest finds at Grimaldi/Menton (French/Italian Riviera)
1886	Neanderthalers from Spy cave (Belgium)
1899–1905	Krapina (Yugoslavia), claims of cannibalism amongst Neanderthalers
1907	Mauer (Heidelberg, West Germany)
1908	Old man of Chapelle-aux-Saints (France)
1909	La Ferrassie I (France), Combe-Capelle (France)
1910	La Ferrassie II (France)
1911	La Quina (France); Piltdown forgeries found in southern England
1912	La Ferrassie 3 and 4 (France)
1920	La Ferrassie 5
1921	La Ferrassie 6
1924–6	Kiik-Koba (Crimea)
1925	Ehringsdorf (East Germany)
1926	Gánovce (Slovakia)
1929	Saccopastore (Italy)
1929–34	Tabun I and II; Skūhl (Mt Carmel, Israel)
1933	Steinheim (West Germany)
1935–6	Swanscombe (England), occipital and left parietal
1947	Fontéchevade (France)
1949	Montmaurin (France)
1949	La Chaise (France)
1953	Piltdown hoax unmasked; Starosel'e (Crimea)
1955	Swanscombe (England), right parietal
1959–60?	Petralona (Greece)
1960–4	Hortus (France)
1964–71	Tautavel finds at Caune de l'Arago (France)
1965	Vértesszöllös (Hungary)
1967–9	La Chaise (France)

Appendix 2 – *continued*

1972–5	Bilzingsleben (East Germany)
1972–5	La Chaise (France)
1973	Hahnöfersand (West Germany)
1976	Atapuerca (Spain)
1980	St Césaire (France)
1981–3	Pontnewydd (Wales)

Appendix 3 *Lower and middle palaeolithic 63 element type list*

1	éclat levallois typique	typical levallois flake
2	éclat levallois atypique	atypical levallois flake
3	pointe levallois	levallois point
4	pointe levallois retouchée	retouched levallois point
5	pointe pseudo-levallois	pseudo levallois point
6	pointe moustérienne	mousterian point
7	pointe moustérienne allongée	elongated mousterian point
8	limace	limace (thick 'slug' like tool)
9	racloir simple droit	single straight side scraper
10	racloir simple convexe	single convex side scraper
11	racloir simple concave	single concave side scraper
12	racloir double droit	double straight side scraper
13	racloir double droit/convexe	double straight/convex side scraper
14	racloir double droit/concave	double straight/concave side scraper
15	racloir double biconvexe	double convex side scraper
16	racloir double biconcave	double concave side scraper
17	racloir double concave/convexe	double concave/convex side scraper
18	racloir convergent droit	convergent straight side scraper
19	racloir convergent convexe	convergent convex side scraper
20	racloir convergent concave	convergent concave side scraper
21	racloir déjeté	offset side scraper
22	racloir transversal droit	straight transverse scraper
23	racloir transversal convexe	convex transversal scraper
24	racloir transversal concave	concave transversal scraper
25	racloir sur face plane	side scraper on the ventral surface
26	racloir à retouche abrupte	abrupt retouched side scraper
27	racloir à dos aminci	side scraper with thinned back
28	racloir à retouche biface	side scraper with bifacial retouch
29	racloir à retouche alterne	alternate retouched side scraper
30	grattoir typique	typical end scraper
31	grattoir atypique	atypical end scraper
32	burin typique	typical burin
33	burin atypique	atypical burin
34	perçoir typique	typical borer
35	perçoir atypique	atypical borer
36	couteau à dos typique	typical backed knife
37	couteau à dos atypique	atypical backed knife
38	couteau à dos naturel	naturally backed knife

Appendix 3 – *continued*

39	raclette	raclette (fine continuous retouch on flat flakes)
40	éclat ou lame tronquée	truncated blade or flake
41	tranchet moustérien	mousterian tranchet
42	encoche	notch
43	denticulé	denticulate
44	bec burinant alterne	alternate retouched beaks
45	retouche sur face plane	piece retouched on the ventral surface
46	retouche abrupte (épaisse)	abrupt retouched piece (thick)
47	retouche alterne (épaisse)	alternate retouched piece (thick)
48	retouche abrupte (mince)	abrupt retouched piece (thin)
49	retouche alterne (mince)	alternate retouched piece (thin)
50	retouche biface	bifacially retouched piece
51	pointe de Tayac	Tayac point
52	triangle à encoche	notched triangle
53	pseudo microburin	pseudo microburin
54	encoche en bout	end notched piece
55	hachoir	hachoir
56	rabot	push plane
57	pointe pédonculée	tanged point
58	outil pédonculé	tanged tool
59	chopper	chopper
60	chopper inverse	inverse chopper
61	chopping tool	chopping tool
62	divers	miscellaneous
63	pièce foliacée biface	leaf shaped bifacial piece

	Bifaces	*Handaxes*
1	lancéolé	lanceolate
2	ficron	ficron
3	micoquien	micoquian
4	biface triangulaire	triangular
5	biface triangulaire allongée	elongated triangular
6	cordiforme	cordiform
7	cordiforme allongé	elongated cordiform
8	subcordiformes	sub-cordiform
9	ovalaire	oval
10	amygdaloide	amygdaloid
11	discoide	discoids
12	limande	limandes
13	hachereau bifacial	bifacial cleaver
14	hachereau sur éclats	flake cleaver
15	lagéniforme	lageniform (bottle shaped)
16	lozengique	lozenge shaped
17	naviforme	naviform
18	nucléiforme	nucleiform
19	divers	miscellaneous
20	partiel	partial
21	abbevillien	abbevillian

(*Source:* Bordes 1961a, 1972)

Appendix 4. *The 105 upper palaeolithic type list*
This is a modification of the list using 92 elements developed by de Sonneville-Bordes and Perrot (1954–6)

1	Grattoir simple sur lame	Single end scraper
1bis	Grattoir sur bout rétréci	End scraper on thinned end
2	Grattoir double	Double end scraper
3	Grattoir sur éclat	End scraper on flake
4	Grattoir 'Gravette'	Gravette end scraper
5	Grattoir circulaire	Circular end scraper
6	Grattoir unguiforme	Unguiform end scraper
7	Grattoir Caminade	Caminade end scraper
8	Grattoir en éventail	Fan end scraper
9	Grattoir sur lame retouchée	End scraper on retouched blade
10	Grattoir sur lame aurignacienne	End scraper on Aurignacian blade
11	Grattoir caréné	Carinated end scraper
12	Grattoir caréné atypique	Atypical carinated end scraper
13	Grattoir caréné à museau ou épaulement	Nosed/shouldered carinated end scraper
14	Grattoir caréné à museau ou épaulement atypique	Atypical nosed/shouldered carinated endscraper
15	Grattoir à museau plat	Flat nosed end scraper
16	Grattoir à épaulement plat	Flat shouldered end scraper
17	Grattoir-burin-dièdre	End scraper-dihedral burin
17bis	Grattoir-burin sur troncature	End scraper-burin on retouched truncation
18	Grattoir-troncature	Endscraper-truncated piece
19	Burin-troncature	Burin-truncated piece
20	Perçoir-troncature	Perçoir-truncated piece
20bis	Bec-troncature	Bec-truncated piece
21	Perçoir-grattoir	Perçoir-end scraper
21bis	Bec-grattoir	Bec-end scraper
22	Perçoir-burin	Perçoir-burin
22bis	Bec-burin	Bec-burin
23	Perçoir simple	Perçoir
23bis	Perçoir double	Double perçoir
24	Microperçoir	Microperçoir
25	Perçoir en étoile	Multiple perçoir
26	Zinken	Zinken
27	Bec simple	Bec
27bis	Bec double etc	Multiple bec
28	Épine	Spine
29	Bec burinant alterne	Bec burinant alterne
30	Burin dièdre d'axe médian	Straight dihedral burin
30bis	Burin dièdre d'axe déjeté	Déjeté dihedral burin
31	Burin dièdre d'angle	Angle dihedral burin
32	Burin d'angle sur cassure	Angle on break burin
33	Burin caréné	Carinated burin
34	Burin de Corbiac	Corbiac burin
35	Burin busqué simple ou double	Busked burin
35bis	Burin busqué mixte (?)	Multiple heterogeneous busked burin
36	Burin dièdre multiple	Multiple dihedral burin

Appendix 4 – *continued*

37	Burin d'axe sur troncature retouchée	Burin d'axe on retouched truncation
38	Burin d'angle sur troncature retouchée normale	Angle burin on retouched truncation
38bis	Burin d'angle sur troncature retouchée oblique	Angle burin on oblique retouched truncation
39	Burin de Lacan	Lacan burin
40	Burin 'bec de perroquet'	Parrot beak burin
41	Burin transversale sur retouche latérale	Transverse burin on lateral retouch
41a	Burin transversale/ret. lat. multiple homogène	Multiple homogeneous transverse burin on lateral retouch
41b	Burin transversale/ret. lat. multiple hétérogène	Multiple heterogeneous transverse burin on lateral retouch
41bis	Burin transversal sur encoche	Transverse burin on notch
41bis a	Burin transversal/encoche multiple homogène	Multiple homogeneous transverse burin on notch
41bis b	Burin transversal/encoche multiple héterogène	Multiple heterogeneous transverse burin on notch
42	Burin multiple sur troncature retouchée	Multiple burin on retouched truncation
43	Burin de Noailles	Noailles burin
44	Burin de Bassaler	Bassaler burin
45	Burin de Bassaler atypique	Atypical Bassaler burin
46	Burin multiple mixte	Multiple mixed burin
47	Pièce à chanfrein	Chanfrein
48	Couteau à dos	Backed knife
49	Châtelperron (couteau)	Châtelperron knife
49bis	Châtelperron (pointe)	Châtelperron point
50	Pointe des Cottés	Cottés point
51	Pointe de la Gravette	Gravette point
52	Microgravette	Microgravette
53	Eléments tronqués	Truncated elements
54	Fléchette périgordienne	Flechette
55	Pointe de la Font-Robert	Font-Robert point
56	Pointe à cran périgordienne	Perigordian shouldered point
57	Pièce à troncature retouchée normale	Truncated piece
58	Pièce à troncature retouchée oblique	Oblique truncated piece
59	Pièce à troncature retouchée partielle	Piece with partial retouched truncation
59bis	Pièce à troncature retouchée en coin	Piece with partial retouched truncation on corner
60	Pièce bitronquée	Bitruncated piece
63	Lame aurignacienne	Aurignacian blade
64	Lame étranglée	Strangulated blade
64bis	Lame à large encoche	Blade with wide notch
65 à 69	Outils solutréens	Solutrean pieces
70	Armature méditerranéenne	Mediterranean point

Appendix 4 – *continued*

72	Pièce à encoche	Notch
73	Lame à coche(s) proximale ou distále	Piece with proximal/distal notch
74	Denticulé	Denticulate
74bis	Denticulé à microdenticulation	Denticulate made with micro-denticulation
75	Racloir	Sidescraper
76	Raclette	Raclette
77	Triangle	Triangle
78	Lamelle scalène	Scalene bladelet
79	Rectangle	Rectangle
80	Trapèze	Trapeze
81	Segment de cercle microlithique	Microlithic segment
82	Microlithe divers	Other microlith
83	Lamelle tronquée	Truncated bladelet
83bis	Lamelle bitronquée	Bitruncated bladelet
84	Lamelle à dos pointu	Pointed backed bladelet
85	Lamelle à dos	Backed bladelet
86	Fragment de petite pièce à dos	Fragment of backed piece
87	Lamelle à dos tronquée	Truncated backed bladelet
87bis	Lamelle à dos bitronquée	Bitruncated backed bladelet
88	Lamelle à dos denticulée	Denticulated backed bladelet
89	Dard	Dart
90	Lamelle denticulée	Denticulated bladelet
91	Lamelle à encoche	Notched bladelet
92	Font-Yves	Font-Yves point
92bis	Para-Font-Yves (Krems etc.)	
93	Lamelle Dufour	Dufour bladelet
94	Lamelle à fine retouche directe	Bladelet with fine direct retouch
95	Lamelle à retouche inverse	Inversely retouched bladelet
96	Pointe azilienne 'ordinaire'	Azilian point
96bis	Grand segment de cercle	Large segment
96ter	'Malaurie'	Malaurie point
97	Pointe de Laugerie-Basse	Laugerie-Basse point
98	Pointe de Teyjat	Teyjat point
99	Pointe à cran magdalénienne	Magdalenian shouldered point
100	Pointe de Hambourg	Hamburgian point
100bis	Pointe de Ahrensbourg	Ahrensburgian point
101	Lame appointée	Pointed blade
102	Pointe 'arénienne'	Arenian point
103	Lame magdalénienne appointée ou bipointée	Magdalenian point/bipointed blade
104	Lame magdalénienne à coche sur talon	Magdalenian blade with basal notch
105	Divers	Diverse
105a	Encoche sous cassure	Notch beneath break
105b	Pièce à retouche inverse	Inversely retouched piece

Appendix 4 – *continued*

Excluded from list

61	Pièce à retouche continue sur 1 bord	Piece with continuous retouch – 1 edge
61bis	Pièce à retouche continue sur 2 bords	Piece with continuous retouch – 2 edges
62	Pièce à ret. continue partielle	Piece with partial continuous retouch
71	Pic	Pick

Additional 'type' classes

Lame/éclat machurée	Hammered or chewed piece
Pièce esquillée	Splintered piece
Pièce à retouche anormale ou pièce de La Bertonne	Bertonne retouched piece

Source: Bietti 1976–7; Bordes 1978; Hemingway 1980.

Appendix 5 *Quantitative information for cave/rock shelter and open sites*

The data are arranged according to region and three time periods: pre-35 Kyr, 35–20 Kyr, and post-20 Kyr. Where possible, information is presented on area excavated, retouched tools, cores and unretouched flakes and blades. These are then compared in a simple set of ratios and density figures to enable comparisons to be made between sites in terms of the quantity of their contents.

The data are far from complete or systematically collected. The purpose of the appendix is to point to the basic minimum level of recording that is necessary if excavated assemblages of artifacts are to be compared in a manner that might serve as a basis for supporting behavioural interpretations, based on an understanding of variation in the material record at our disposal.

Cave and rock shelter assemblages

Site	m² dug	Tools	Cores	Flakes and chips	Chipped stone total	Tools: waste	Cores: waste	Total stone per m²	Tools per m²	References
Pre-35 Kyr										
NW region										
La Cotte de St Brelade										
upper 6/5/4/3		380	50	1146	1576	1:3	1:23			McBurney and Callow 1971
lower 3/2/1		98	22	505	625	1:5	1:23			
A		207	37	1253	1497	1:6	1:34			
B		494	107	3853	4454	1:8	1:36			
C/D1		162	36	1254	1452	1:8	1:35			
D1/D2		129	27	678	834	1:5	1:25			
D2		119	22	679	820	1:6	1:31			
E		275	122	2249	2646	1:8	1:18			
F		478	211	6343	7032	1:13	1:30			
F/G		89	33	922	1044	1:10	1:30			
G		112	71	2189	2372	1:19	1:31			
H		313	174	3983	4470	1:13	1:23			
NC region										
Bockstein III		576	21	2194	2791	1:4	1:104			Wetzel and Bosinski 1969
Sipkǎ		431	89	479	999	1:1.1	1:5			Valoch 1965
Mauern 5		89	56	463	608	1:5	1:8			von Koenigswald *et al.* 1974
Mauern 4		111	17	269	397	1:2	1:16			
Sesselfelsgrotte G	1	169		532	5497	1:31		5497	169	Freund 1968
G	4	450		21050	21500	1:46		5375	112	
SW region										
Cueva Morín lower 17	2	124	1	275	400	1:2	1:275	200	62	González-Echegaray and Freeman 1973
17	7	526	18	1673	2217	1:3	1:93			
16	3.5	390	13	1416	1819	1:4	1:109	260	56	

15	2	128	6	733	881	1:6		231	36		
13 & 14		97	2	1561	1660	1:16	1:780	830	48		
12		316	10	1429	1857	1:5	1:153				
11	19	226	17		1672	1:6	1:84				
Caminade east M3	19	193							10	De Sonneville-Bordes 1969	
M2	19	162							8		
M1	19	169							9		
Pech de l'Azé		4112	275	29411	33798	1:7	1:107			Bordes 1972	

Alpine region

Cotencher		70		350	420	1:5				Dubois and Stehlin 1933	

SE region

Bacho Kiro humus 13	45	33	3	297	333	1:9	1:99	7	0.7	J. Kozlowski 1982	
13	45	68	20	624	712	1:9	1:31	16	1.5		
12/13		61	17	464	542	1:8	1:27				

MW region

Lazaret	35	125	5	707	837	1:6	1:141	24	3	H. de Lumley 1969c	
Hortus würm II		486	133	3636	4255	1:7	1:27			H. de Lumley 1972	

MC region

Torre dell Alto A	4.8	199	33	1436	1668	1:7	1:51	347	41	Borzatti von Löwenstern 1966	
B	4.8	97	33	1045	1175	1:11	1:32	244	20		
upper C	4.8	127	6	591	724	1:5	1:99	151	26		
lower C	4.8	115	19	535	669	1:5	1:28	139	24		
D	4.8	735	87	6470	7292	1:9	1:74	1519	153		
E	4.8	111	14	666	791	1:6	1:47	165	23		
Uluzzo C G		1139	129	2338	3606	1:2	1:18			Borzatti von Löwenstern 1966	
H		11	6	86	103	1:8	1:14				
I		8	7	42	57	1:5	1:6				
Torre Nave 13		660	106	2204	2970	1:3	1:21			Bulgarelli 1972	
Gosto D		2202	84	237						Tozzi 1974	
Guattari 1		69	14	29	112	1:0.4	1:2			Taschini and Bietti 1979	
2		158	45	239	442	1:1.5	1:5				
4		247	39	511	797	1:2	1:13				
5		125	42	272	439	1:2	1:6				

35–20 Kyr

NW region

Paviland		554	138	3676	4368	1:7	1:27			Campbell 1977	
Kents Cavern		112	3	319	434	1:3	1:106			Campbell 1977	
Wookey Hole		4	2	18	24	1:4.5	1:9			Campbell 1977	

NC region

Geissenklösterle	17	67	17	333	417	1:5	1:19	25	4	Hahn et al. 1977; Otte 1981	

Cave and rock shelter assemblages—*continued*

Site	m² dug	Tools	Cores	Flakes and chips	Chipped stone total	Tools: waste	Cores: waste	Total stone per m²	Tools per m²	References
Brillenhöhle VII	255	583	122	4041	4746	1:7	1:33	19	2	Riek 1973; Otte 1981
VI	255	81	53	1156	1290	1:14	1:22	5	0.3	
V	255	25	11	443	479	1:18	1:40	2	0.1	
Mauern C		234	48	1228	1510	1:5	1:25	25		Otte 1981
Vogelherd V		909	33	1190	2132	1:1.3	1:36	19		Hahn 1977
IV		1729	89	1569	3387	1:0.9	1:18	5		
Bockstein Törle VII		88	2	305	395	1:3	1:153	2		Hahn 1977
VI		71	10	329	410	1:5	1:33			
Stadel IV		68	23	290	381	1:4	1:13			Hahn 1977
SW region										
Cueva Morín 9	3	206		2864*	3070	1:14		1023	69	González-Echegaray and Freeman 1973
8	4	669		13342*	14011	1:20		3503	167	* = includes cores in total
7	c.7	346		9594*	9940	1:28		1420	49	
6	6.5	345		7783*	8128	1:23		1250	53	
5	6.5	310		6498*	6808	1:21		1047	48	
4	6.5	217		3546*	3763	1:16		579	33	
Caminade east D2 upper	38	686							18	De Sonneville-Bordes 1970
D2 lower	38	782							21	
F	38	752							20	
G	38	348							9	
Cueva Morín 10		484	59	3042	3585	1:6	1:51			González-Echegaray and Freeman 1973
Laugerie Haute 36		412	46	5715	6173	1:14	1:124			Bordes 1978
Piage F	84	235							3	Champagne and Espitalié 1981
F1	84	127							1.5	
G—I	84	2286							27	
J	84	405							5	
K	84	672							8	
SE region										
Bacho Kiro 11	41	667	18	19149	19834	1:30	1:1101	483	16	J. Kozlowski 1982
9		15	2	222	239	1:15	1:111			
7		40	4	608	652	1:15	1:152			
6a/7		61	3	457	521	1:7	1:152			

NW region

Mother Grundy's Parlour		117	5	236	358	1:2	1:47		Campbell 1977
Robin Hood's cave		63	3	266	332	1:4	1:89		Campbell 1977
Kents Cavern		50	3	102	155	1:2	1:34		Campbell 1977
King Arthur's cave		29	1	74	104	1:2	1:74		Campbell 1977
Cathole		18	—	107	125	1:6	—		Campbell 1977
Gough's cave		799	19	3673	4491	1:5	1:193		Campbell 1977

NC region

Petersfels P3 AH2	16	251	20	3055	3326	1:12	1:152	207	16	Albrecht 1979
Teufelsbrücke	120	2492	252	21376	24120	1:9	1:85	201	21	Feustel 1980
Kniegrotte		1610	137	4415	6162	1:3	1:32			Feustel 1974
Brillenhöhle IV upper	290	300	53	1392	1745	1:5	1:26	6	1	Riek 1973; Weniger 1982
IV lower	290	282	26	737	1045	1:3	1:28	4	0.9	
Kesslerloch II	200	271	207	3266	3744	1:12	1:16	19	1	Weniger 1982
III	200	739	293	5157	6189	1:7	1:18	31	4	
Schweizersbild	207	646	262	7564	8472	1:12	1:29	41	3	Weniger 1982
Teufelsküchen	15	445	46	3001	3492	1:7	1:65	233	30	Weniger 1982
Bärensfelsgrotte	20	56	5	484	545	1:9	1:97	27	3	Weniger 1982
Bildstockfels	5	37	12	95	144	1:3	1:8	29	7	Weniger 1982
Geissenklösterle	10	7	—	31	38	1:4	—	4	1	Weniger 1982
Hütten (grau)	20	17	—	22	39	1:1.2	—	2	1	Weniger 1982
(gelb)	20	30	6	228	264	1:8	1:38	13	1.5	Weniger 1982
Stadel III	?	90	19	254	363	1:3	1:13			Weniger 1982
Schmiechenfels	20	34	2	94	130	1:3	1:47	7	2	Weniger 1982
Sirgenstein I	80	72	8	318	398	1:4	1:40	5	0.9	Weniger 1982
Spitalhöhle VII	10	10	1	65	76	1:7	1:65	8	1	Weniger 1982

SW region

Balmori		218	59	1185	1462	1:5	1:20			Clark 1974–5
Altamira magdalenian		215	82	818	1115	1:4	1:10			Straus 1977a
solutrean		522	56	543		1:1.04	1:10			
Cueva Morín 3	4	119		1684*	1803	1:14		450	30	González-Echegaray and Freeman 1973
2	7	310		3757*	4067	1:12		581	44	(* = includes cores in total)
Piage C–E	84	1215							14	Champagne and Espitalié 1981

Alpine region

Rislisberghöhle	20	c.2000		18000		1:9		900	100	Barr 1977

MC region

Polesini	114	26889	2888	363125	392902	1:13	1:126	3446	236	Radmilli 1976–7
Palidoro 1–4	0.5	1077	98	7335	8510	1:7	1:75	17020	2154	Bietti 1974
5–8	1	1099	251	5860	7210	1:5	1:23	5860	1099	

Open, unconstrained location assemblages

Site	m² dug	Tools	Cores	Flakes and chips	Chipped stone total	Tools: waste	Cores: waste	Total stone per m²	Tools per m²	References
ME region										
Kastritsa rectangle 2		1907		17714	19621	1:9				Bailey *et al.* 1983b
rectangle 3		2261		21646	23907	1:10				
rectangle 11		287		2625	2912	1:9				
rectangle 12		595		8119	8714	1:14				

Open, unconstrained location assemblages

Pre-35 Kyr

Site	m² dug	Tools	Cores	Flakes and chips	Chipped stone total	Tools: waste	Cores: waste	Total stone per m²	Tools per m²	References
NW region										
Swanscombe		368	9	8212	8589	1:23	1:954			Howell 1966
Hoxne		158	3	299	460	1:2	1:100			Howell 1966
Blanzy		1124	188	1023						Desbrosse and Tavoso 1970 (surface coll.)
Botany Pit		109	273	3445	3837	1:32	1:13			Roe 1981
Clacton gravel	c.375				762			2		Singer *et al.* 1973
marl	c.375				103			0.3		
NC region										
Bilzingsleben	2.25	297		2189	2486	1:7		1105	132	Mania 1975
Jezeřany I		737	321	1877	2935	1:2.5	1:6			Oliva 1979
II		574	370	1568	2512	1:3	1:4			
Bohunice Ziegelei		147	35	995	1177	1:7	1:28			Valoch 1976b
Bohunice Kejbaly I		500	102	5462	6064	1:11	1:53			Valoch 1976b
II		150	81	2822	3053	1:19	1:35			
III		4	7	97	108	1:24	1:14			
Königsaue A		90	38	1357	1485	1:15	1:36			Mania and Toepfer 1973
B		116	163	3693	3972	1:32	1:23			
C		23	9	264	296	1:11	1:29			
Rheindhalen	c.200	30		1360	1390	1:45		7	0.1	Bosinski 1966, 1976
NE region										
Molodova V/XII	c.170	118							0.7	Klein 1969b
V/XI	c.170	123							0.7	
SE region										
Érd upper a	214	212		710	922	1:3		4	0.9	Gábori-Csánk 1968

d	214	91		110	201	1:1			0.9	0.4	
e	214	113		426	529	1:4			2	0.5	
lower	214	19		38	57	1:2			0.3	0.08	
Tata	34	2035	64							60	Vértes 1964
Vértesszöllös		479	19		500						Kretzoi and Vértes 1965; Howell 1966
Vértesszöllös		196		312	508	1:1.5					

MW region

Torralba B4a	300	327	47	387	761	1:1.1	1:8		2	1.09	Freeman 1975; Howell 1966
Ambrona lower	1047	326	16	677	1020	1:2	1:20		0.9	0.3	Santonja *et al.* 1980
Aridos 1	30	49	8	276	333	1:6	1:35		11	1.6	
2	7.5	14	4	16	34	1:1	1:4		4.5	1.8	

MC region

Torre in Pietra d	40	322	92	329	743	1:1	1:3		18	8	Piperno and Biddittu 1978
m	200	150	17	211	378	1:1.4	1:12		2	0.75	
Inforchìa		120	74	400	594	1:3	1:5				Borzatti von Löwenstern and Stoduti 1974

35–20 Kyr

NC region

Tvarožná		1524	132	6227	7883	1:4	1:47				Valoch 1976c
Podstránská		603	61	3682	4346	1:6	1:60				Valoch 1974
Neslovice		883	246	5609	6738	1:6	1:23				Valoch 1973
Ořechov I		651	183	4172	5006	1:6	1:23				
II		198	54	894	1146	1:4	1:17				
Zělešice		476	63	1824	2363	1:4	1:29				
Ondratice III		24	9	102	135	1:4	1:11				Valoch 1967b
IV		70	12	146	228	1:2	1:12				
V		52	3	113	168	1:2	1:38				
VII		98	35	342	475	1:3	1:10				
Zoitzberg		240	101	7771	8112	1:32	1:77				Feustel 1974
Cracow Spadzista B	91	240	49	1090	1379	1:4	1:22		15	3	Kozlowski 1974
Mainz-Linsenberg		115	4	624	743	1:5	1:156				Otte 1981
Bilzingsleben		154	20	694	868	1:4	1:35				Otte 1981
Lubna 1–4		306	17	2701	3024	1:9	1:159				Otte 1981
Dolní Věstonice		301	25	386	712	1:1.3	1:15				Otte 1981
Pavlov II		299	29	443	771	1:5	1:15				Otte 1981
Petřkovice		448	133	8360	8941	1:19	1:63				Otte 1981
Cejkov		202	149	1783	2134	1:9	1:12				Otte 1981
Lommersum	62	158	2	1068	1228	1:7	1:534		20	2.5	Hahn 1977
Langmannersdorf		458	124	1652	2234	1:4	1:13				Hahn 1977
Barca I, 1–2		103	16	764	883	1:7	1:48				Hahn 1977
I, 3		186	45	1258	1489	1:7	1:28				Hahn 1977
Barca II		188	47	1454	1689	1:8	1:31				Hahn 1977

Open, unconstrained location assemblages – *continued*

Site	m² dug	Tools	Cores	Flakes and chips	Chipped stone total	Tools: waste	Cores: waste	Total stone per m²	Tools per m²	References
Tibava		89	32	490	611	1:6	1:15			Hahn 1977
Breitenbach		675	72	4376	5123	1:6	1:61			Hahn 1977
NE region										
Bistricioara-Lutarie	210	291	30	1058	1379	1:4	1:35	6	1.4	Nicolăescu-Plopşor *et al.* 1966
Ceahlău-Bofu Mic	688	436	20	344	810	1:0.8	1:17	1	0.6	
Ceahlău-Cetătica I	220	53	15	84	152	1:1.6	1:6	0.7	0.2	
Ceahlău-Dîrtu	461	555	68	782	1405	1:1.4	1:11	3	1.2	
Ceahlău-Podis	505	597	74	2864	3535	1:5	1:39	7	1	
Molodova V/X	774	41	17	559	617	1:14	1:33	0.8	0.05	Chernysh 1961
Molodova V/IX	774	70	32	1180	1282	1:17	1:37	2.7	0.09	Chernysh 1961
V/VIII	774	116	64	1475	1655	1:13	1:23	2	0.1	
V/VII	774	1262	1475	42210	44947	1:33	1:29	58	2	
SW region										
Creysse	67	200+								Bordes 1970
Corbiac	150	481	49	9278	9808	1:19	1:189	63	3	Bordes 1968b
Tambourets	8	122	35	385	542	1:3	1:11	68	15	Bricker and Laville 1977
SE region										
Remetea-Somos I	302	448	119	1489	2056	1:3	1:12	7	1.5	Bitiri 1972
MC region										
Armailo		79	98	2179	2356	1:27	1:22			Magi 1973
San Romano		984	355	2384	3723	1:2	1:7			
Maroccone		1439	560	3818	5817	1:3	1:7			
Post-20 Kyr										
NW region										
Verberie	56	248							4	Audouze *et al.* 1981
Les Tarterets I	57	79	26	1043	1148	1:13	1:40	20	1.4	Schmider 1975
II	176	95	50	3686	4007	1:39	1:74	23	0.5	
Pincevent I	56	332							6	Leroi-Gourhan and Brézillon 1966
Obourg 'St Macaire'	111	105	351	27897	28353	1:266	1:79	255	0.9	Letocart 1970
NC region										

Barbing	30	132	28	1508	1961					
Smolín A	150	264	171	4580	5015	1:17	1:27	33	2	Valoch 1978
B	120	256	136	4654	5046	1:18	1:34	42	2	
C	151	516	364	18623	19503	1:36	1:53	129	3	
D	100	199	114	4888	5201	1:24	1:46	52	2	
Voletiny	32	90	32	1911	2033	1:21	1:60	63	3	Vencl 1978
Tišnov I	2.3	20	9	232	261	1:12	1:26	113	9	Kos 1971
II	24.5	13	6	124	143	1:9	1:21	6	0.5	
III	20.9	20	9	265	294	1:13	1:29	14	1	
IV	11.9	25	44	470	519	1:19	1:11	44	2	
Saaleck	70	650	120	10320	11090	1:16	1:86	147	9	Toepfer 1970
Olknitz		1296	57	7632	8985	1:6	1:129			Feustel 1974
Kahla-Löbschutz		982	22	10482	11486	1:11	1:476			Feustel 1974
Groitzsch A		310	113	9687	10110	1:31	1:85			Feustel 1974
Gera Binsenacker		471	57	2461	2989	1:5	1:43			Feustel 1974
Gojśc	100	127	124	4136	4387	1:32	1:33	41	1.2	Ginter 1974
Olbrachcice	250	456	51	4990	5497	1:11	1:98	22	2	Burdukiewicz 1980
Gönnersdorf	96	1350							14	Bosinski 1969; Albrecht 1979
Borneck hamburgian	192	490	53	3400	3943	1:7	1:64	20	2.5	Rust 1958
magdalenian	104	70	10	900	980	1:13	1:90	9	0.7	
Borneck mitte	54	42		200+					0.7	
west	91	96	25	1380	1501	1:14	1:55	16	1	
Borneck Bornwisch	151	230	30	1900	2160	1:8	1:63	14	1.5	
ost	110	80	29	1650	1759	1:20	1:57	16	0.7	
nord	48	27	9	550	586	1:20	1:61	12	0.5	
Poggenwisch	110	490	20	2330	2840	1:5	1:116	26	4	Rust 1958
Hasewisch	112	711	20	3025	3756	1:4	1:151	33	6	Rust 1958
Meiendorf		879	46	1430	2355	1:2	1:31			Rust 1958
Munzingen	300	648	292	4065	5005	1:6	1:14	17	2	Weniger 1982
NE region										
Ceahlău-Cetăţiça I, III, IV	220	27	3	44	74	1:2	1:15	0.3	0.1	Nicolǎescu-Plopşor *et al.* 1966
Scaune	710	268	105	13627	14000	1:51	1:130	20	0.4	Nicolǎescu-Plopşor *et al.* 1966
Molodova V/VI	774	230	91	5648	5969	1:25	1:62	7	0.3	Chernysh 1961
V/V	774	182	88	3473	3742	1:19	1:39	5	0.2	
V/IV	774	230	128	4626	4984	1:20	1:36	6	0.3	
V/III	774	169	73	3466	3708	1:21	1:47	5	0.2	
V/II	774	212	150	4989	5351	1:24	1:33	7	0.3	
V/Ia	774	239	115	7600	7954	1:32	1:66	10	0.3	
V/I	774	298	171	4855	5324	1:16	1:28	7	0.4	

Open, unconstrained location assemblages – *continued*

Site	m² dug	Tools	Cores	Flakes and chips	Chipped stone total	Tools: waste	Cores: waste	Total stone per m²	Tools per m²	References
SW region										
Solvieux sud	16	502	22	34	558	9:1	1:1.5	35	31	Gaussen 1980
Grillasou	27	142	48	1240	1430	1:9	1:26	53	5	Gaussen 1980
Cerisier	c.25	45	16	399	460	1:9	1:25	18	2	Gaussen 1980
Le Breuil	c.12	11	1	7	19	1:4.1	1:7	2	0.9	Gaussen 1980
Le Mas 1	14	44	8	260	312	1:6	1:32	22	3	Gaussen 1980
Le Mas 2	33	85	19	740	844	1:9	1:39	26	3	Gaussen 1980
Plateau Parrain	49	335	67	1522	1924	1:5	1:23	39	7	Gaussen 1980
SE region										
Kadar		195	35	2810	3040	1:14	1:80			Montet-White and Basler 1977
Arka	97.5	1159	242						12	Vértes 1964/5

BIBLIOGRAPHY

Abramova, Z. A. (1967). Palaeolithic art in the U.S.S.R. *Arctic Anthropology*, 4: 1–179.

Absolon, K. (1935–1936). *Über grossformen des quartzitischen Aurignaciens der palaeolithischen station Ondratice in Mähren*. Brno, Barvič & Novotný.

Absolon, K. (1938–45). Die erforschung die diluvialen mammut-jager station von Unterwisternitz an der Pollauer Bergen in Mähren, 1924–6. *Mitteilungen aus der paläolithischen abteilung am Mährischen Landesmuseum*, C. Pal. Serie, Nos. 5, 6, 7.

Absolon, K., and Klíma, B. (1977). Předmostí, ein mammutjägerplatz in Mähren. *Fontes Archaeologiae Moraviae*, VIII, Prague.

Agassiz, L. (1840). *Études sur les glaciers*. Neuchâtel.

Aguirre, E., and de Lumley, M.-A. (1977). Fossil men from Atapuerca, Spain: their bearing on human evolution in the middle pleistocene. *Journal of Human Evolution*, 6: 681–8.

Albrecht, G. (1979). *Magdalénien-inventare von Petersfels*. Tübingen, Archaeologica Venatoria, 6.

Albrecht, G., Hahn, J., and Torke, W. G. (1972). *Merkmalanalyse von Geschoßspitzen des mittleren Jungpleistozäns in Mittel- und Osteuropa*. Tübingen, Archaeologica Venatoria, 2.

Albrethsen, S. E., and Petersen, E. B. (1976). Excavation of a Mesolithic cemetery at Vedbaek, Denmark. *Acta Archaeologica*, 47: 1–28.

Allsworth-Jones, P. (1975). The palaeolithic 'leafpoint' assemblages in central and south-eastern Europe. Cambridge, Ph.D. dissertation.

Altuna, J. (1972). Fauna de mamíferos de los yacimientos prehistóricas de Guipúzcoa con catálogo de los mamíferos cuaternarios del Cantabrico y del Pirineo Occidental. *Munibe*, 24.

Altuna, J. (1979). La faune des ongulés du Tardiglaciaire en Pays Basque et dans le reste de la région Cantabrique. In D. de Sonneville-Bordes (ed.), *La Fin des Temps Glaciaires*, Paris, CNRS, 85–95.

Ammerman, A. J., and Feldman, M. W. (1974). On the 'making' of an assemblage of stone tools. *American Antiquity*, 39: 610–16.

van Andel, T. H., and Shackleton, J. C. (1982). Late palaeolithic and mesolithic coastlines of Greece and the Aegean. *Journal of Field Archaeology* 9: 445–54.

Anderson, P. C. (1980). A testimony of prehistoric tasks: diagnostic residues on stone tool working edges. *World Archaeology*, 12: 181–94.

Andree, J. (1928). *Das Paläolithikum der Höhlen des Hönnetals in Westfalen*. Leipzig. Mannus-Bibliothek, 42.

Andree, J. (1939). *Der Eiszeitliche Mensch in Deutschland und seine Kulturen*. Stuttgart.

Aparicio, J., and Fletcher, D. (1971). La cueva paleolítica del 'Volcán del Faro', Cullera, Valencia. *Congreso Nacional de Arqueología*, 11: 175–83.

ApSimon, A. M., Gamble, C. S., and Shackley, M. L. (1977). Pleistocene raised beaches on Portsdown, Hampshire. *Proceedings of the Hampshire Field Club*, 33: 17–32.

Audouze, F., Cahen, D., Keeley, L. H. and Schmider, B. (1981). Le site magdalénien du Buisson Campin à Verberie (Oise). *Gallia Préhistoire*, 24: 99–143.

Bächler, E. (1940). *Das Alpine Paläolithikum der Schweiz*. Basel.

Bader, O. N. (1967). Eine ungewöhnliche paläolithische bestattung in Mittelrussland. *Quartär* 18: 191–4.

Bader, O. N. (1978). *Sunghir* (in Russian). Moscow, Nauka.

Bagolini, B. (1968). Ricerche sulle dimensioni dei manufatti litici preistorici non ritoccati. *Annali dell'Università di Ferrara* 10: 195–219.

Bahn, P. G. (1977). Seasonal migration in south-west France during the late glacial period. *Journal of Archaeological Science*, 4: 245–57.

Bahn, P. G. (1982). Inter-site and inter-regional links during the upper palaeolithic: the Pyrenean evidence. *Oxford Journal of Archaeology*, 1: 247–68.

Bahn, P. G. (1983). Late pleistocene economies of the French Pyrenees. In G. N. Bailey (ed.), *Hunter-Gatherer Economy in Prehistory*, 168–86. Cambridge, Cambridge University Press.

Bailey, G. N. (1975). The role of molluscs in coastal economies: the results of midden analysis in Australia. *Journal of Archaeological Science*, 2: 45–62.

Bailey, G. N. (1978). Shell middens as indicators of postglacial economies: a territorial perspective. In P. Mellars (ed.), *The Early Postglacial Settlement of Northern Europe*, 37–64. London: Duckworth.

Bailey, G. N. (1983a). Economic change in late pleistocene Cantabria. In G. N. Bailey (ed.). *Hunter-Gatherer Economy in Prehistory*, 149–65. Cambridge, Cambridge University Press.

Bailey, G. N. (ed.) (1983b). *Hunter-Gatherer Economy in Prehistory*. Cambridge, Cambridge University Press.

Bailey, G. N., Carter, P. L., Gamble, C. S. and Higgs, H. P. (1983a). Epirus revisited: seasonality and inter-site variation in the upper palaeolithic of north-west Greece. In G. N. Bailey (ed.) *Hunter-Gatherer Economy in Prehistory*, 64–78, Cambridge, Cambridge University Press.

Bailey, G. N., Carter, P. L., Gamble, C. S., and Higgs, H. P. (1983b). Asprochaliko and Kastritsa: further investigations of palaeolithic settlement and economy in Epirus (north-west Greece). *Proceedings of the Prehistoric Society*, 49: 15–42.

Bailey, G. N., and Davidson, I. (1983). Site exploitation territory and topography: two case studies from palaeolithic Spain. *Journal of Archaeological Science*, 10: 87–115.

Bailey, H. P. (1960). A method of determining the warmth and temperateness of climate. *Geografiska Annaler*, 43: 1–16.

Bandi, H.-G. (1969). Le paléolithique supérieur en Suisse. *Préhistoire Spéléologique d'Ariège*, 24: 55–71.

Bánesz, L. (1960). Die problematik der paläolithischen Besiedlung in Tibava. *Slovenská Archaeológia*, 8: 7–58.

Bánesz, L. (1967). Die altsteinzeitlichen Funde der Ostslowakei. *Quartär* 18: 81–98.

Bánesz, L. (1968). *Barca bei Košice*. Bratislava, Vydavateľstvo Slovenskej Akadémie Vied.

Bánesz, L. (1976). Prírodné Prostredie Hospodárska základňa a Materiálna Kultúra Aurignacienu Strednej Európy. *Slovenská Archaeológia*, 24: 5–82.

Barker, G. W. W. (1973). Cultural and economic change in the prehistory of central Italy. In C. Renfrew (ed.) *The Explanation of Culture Change: Models in Prehistory*, 359–70. London, Duckworth.

Barker, G. W. W. (1975). Prehistoric territories and economies in central Italy. In E. Higgs (ed.) *Palaeoeconomy*, 111–75. Cambridge, Cambridge University Press.

Barker, G. W. W. (1981). *Landscape and Society: Prehistoric Central Italy*. London, Academic Press.

Barr, J. H. (1977). Die Rislisberghöhle, ein neuer magdalénienfundplatz im Schweizer Jura. *Archäologisches Korrespondenzblatt*, 7: 85–7.

Bárta, J. (1965). *Slovénsko v Staršej a Strednej Dobe Kammenj*. Bratislava.

Bárta, J. (1967). Stratigraphische Übersicht der paläolithischen funde in der Westslowakei. *Quartär*, 18: 57–80.

Bárta, J. (1974). Kniektorým historicko-spoločenským otázkam paleolitu na Slovensku. *Slovenská Archaeologiá*, 22: 9–32.

Bárta, J. and Bánesz, L. (1981). The palaeolithic and mesolithic. In *Archaeological Research in Slovakia*, 11–29. Nitra, Institute of Archaeology of the Slovak Academy of Sciences.

Bartolomei, G., and Broglio, A. (1972). Riparo Tagliente. *Guida alla escursione nel Veronese e. nel Trentino, XV Riunione Scientifica Instituto Italiana Preistoriche e Protostorica*, 73–7.

Bartolomei, G., Broglio, A., Guerreschi, A., Leonardi, P., Peretto, C., and Sala, B. (1974). Una sepoltura epigravettiana nel deposito pleistocenico del Riparo Tagliente in Valpantena. *Rivista Scienze Preistoriche*, 29: 101–52.

Bartolomei, G., Broglio, A., and Palma di Cesnola, A. (1979). Chronostratigraphie et écologie de l'Epigravettien en Italie, in D. de Sonneville-Bordes (ed.) *La Fin des Temps Glaciaires en Europe*, 297–324. Paris, CNRS.

Basler, D. (1979). Le paléolithique final en Herzégovine. In D. de Sonneville-Bordes (ed.) *La Fin des Temps Glaciaires en Europe*, 345–57, Paris, CNRS.

Baumann, F. (1949). *Die Freilebenden Säugetiere der Schweiz*, Bern.

Bazile, F. (1974). Nouvelles données sur le paléolithique supérieur ancien en Languedoc oriental. *Congrès Préhistorique de France*, 24–8. Châteauneuf-les-Martigues.

Bazile, F. (1976). Datations absolues sur les niveaux paléolithiques supérieurs anciens de la grotte de l'Esquicho-Grapaou (Ste. Anastasie, Gard). *Bulletin de la Société Préhistorique Française*, 73: 207–17.

Bazile, F. (1980). Précisions chronologiques sur le Salpêtrien, ses relations avec le solutréen et le magdalénien en Languedoc oriental, *Bulletin de la Société Préhistorique Française*, 77: 50–6.

Bazile, F. (1981). Languedoc Oriental. In R. Desbrosse and J. K. Kozlowski (eds.) *Resumen de las Investigaciones de 1976 a 1981*, 45–8. Mexico City, U.I.S.P.P. X Congreso, Comision X.

Beaton, J. (1983). Does intensification account for changes in the Australian holocene archaeological record? *Archaeology in Oceania*, 18:94–7.

Behm-Blancke, G. (1958). Umwelt, Kultur und Morphologie des eeminterglazialen menschen von Ehringsdorf bei Weimar. In *Hundert Jahre Neanderthaler*, 141–50, Köln, Böhlau.

Behm-Blancke, G. (1960). Altsteinzeitliche Rastplätze im Travertingebiet von Taubach, Weimar, Ehringsdorf. *Alt-Thüringen*, 4: 1–246.

Behrensmeyer, A. K. and Hill, A. P. (eds.) (1980). *Fossils in the Making: Vertebrate Taphonomy and Paleoecology*. Chicago, University of Chicago Press.

Bell, R. H. V. (1970). The use of the herb layer by grazing ungulates in the Serengeti. In A. Watson (ed.) *Animal Populations in Relation to Their Food Resources*, 111–24. Oxford, Oxford University Press.

Bender, B. (1978). Gatherer-hunter to farmer: a social perspective. *World Archaeology*, 10: 204–22.

Bender, B. (1981). Gatherer-hunter, intensification. In A. Sheridan and G. Bailey (eds.)

414 Bibliography

Economic Archaeology, 149–57. Oxford, British Archaeological Reports, International Series, 96.

Bernaldo de Quiros, F. (1981). L'aurignacien et le périgordien sur la façade atlantique de l'Espagne. In R. Desbrosse and J. K. Kozlowski (eds.) *Resumen de las Investigaciones de 1976 a 1981*, 23–6. Mexico City, U.I.S.P.P., X Congreso, Comision X.

Berndt, R. M. (1976). Territoriality and the problem of demarcating socio-cultural space. In N. Peterson (ed.) *Tribes and Boundaries in Australia*, 133–61. Canberra, Australian Institute of Aboriginal Studies.

Bettinger, R. L. (1980). Explanatory/predictive models of hunter-gatherer adaptation. In M. B. Schiffer (ed.) *Advances in Archaeological Method and Theory*, 3: 189–255. New York, Academic Press.

Bhattacharya, D. K. (1977). *Palaeolithic Europe*. New Jersey, Humanities Press.

Bicchieri, M. G. (ed.) (1972). *Hunters and Gatherers Today*. New York, Holt, Rinehart and Winston.

Biddittu, I., Cassoli, P. F., Radicati di Brozolo, F., Segre, A. G., Segre Naldini, E., and Villa, I. (1979). Anagni, a K-Ar dated lower and middle pleistocene site, central Italy: preliminary report. *Quaternaria*, 21: 53–71.

Bietti, A. (1976–7). Analysis and investigation of the epigravettian industry collected during the 1955 excavations at Palidoro (Rome, Italy). *Quaternaria*, 19: 197–387.

Binford, L. R. (1962). Archaeology as anthropology. *American Antiquity*, 28: 217–25.

Binford, L. R. (1965). Archaeological systematics and the study of cultural process. *American Antiquity*, 31: 203–10.

Binford, L. R. (1969). Comment on D. Collins 'Culture traditions and environment of early man'. *Current Anthropology*, 10: 297–9.

Binford, L. R. (1972). Contemporary model building: paradigms and the current state of palaeolithic research. In D. L. Clarke (ed.) *Models in Archaeology*, 109–66, London, Methuen.

Binford, L. R. (1973). Interassemblage variability – the Mousterian and the 'functional' argument, in C. Renfrew (ed.) *The Explanation of Culture Change: models in prehistory*, 227–54. London, Duckworth.

Binford, L. R. (1977a). General introduction. In L. R. Binford (ed.) *For Theory Building in Archaeology*, 1–10. New York, Academic Press.

Binford, L. R. (1977b). Forty-seven trips. In R. V. S. Wright (ed.) *Stone Tools as Cultural Markers*, 24–36. Canberra, Australian Institute of Aboriginal Studies.

Binford, L. R. (1978a). *Nunamiut Ethnoarchaeology*. New York, Academic Press.

Binford, L. R. (1978b). Dimensional analysis of behaviour and site structure: learning from an eskimo hunting stand. *American Antiquity*, 43: 330–61.

Binford, L. R. (1979). Organization and formation processes: looking at curated technologies. *Journal of Anthropological Research*, 35: 255–73.

Binford, L. R. (1980). Willow smoke and dogs tails: hunter-gatherer settlement systems and archaeological site formation. *American Antiquity*, 45: 4–20.

Binford, L. R. (1981). *Bones: Ancient Men and Modern Myths*. New York, Academic Press.

Binford, L. R. (1982). Meaning, inference and the material record. In C. Renfrew and S. J. Shennan (eds.) *Ranking Resource and Exchange*, 160–3. Cambridge, Cambridge University Press.

Binford, L. R. (1983). *In Pursuit of the Past*. London, Thames and Hudson.

Binford, L. R., and Bertram, J. B. (1977). Bone frequencies and attritional processes. In L. R. Binford (ed.) *For Theory Building in Archaeology*, 77–153. New York, Academic Press.

Binford, L. R., and Binford, S. R. (1966). A preliminary analysis of functional variability in the Mousterian of Levallois facies. *American Anthropologist*, 68(2): 238–95.

Binford, S. R. (1968). A structural comparison of disposal of the dead in the mousterian and the upper palaeolithic. *Southwestern Journal of Anthropology*, 24: 139–54.

Binford, S. R. (1969). Comment on D. Collins 'Culture traditions and environment of early man'. *Current Anthropology*, 10: 299–301.

Binford, S. R. and Binford, L. R. (eds.) (1968). *New Perspectives in Archaeology*. Chicago, Aldine.

Binford, S. R., and Binford, L. R. (1969). Stone tools and human behaviour. *Scientific American*, 220: 70–84.

Bintliff, J. L. (1977). New approaches to human geography: prehistoric Greece, a case study. In F. Carter (ed.) *An Historical Geography of the Balkans*, 59–114. London, Academic Press.

Birdsell, J. B. (1953). Some environmental and cultural factors influencing the structuring of Australian Aboriginal populations. *American Naturalist*, 87: 171–207.

Birdsell, J. B. (1958). On population structure in generalized hunting and collecting populations. *Evolution*, 12: 189–205.

Birdsell, J. B. (1968). Some predictions for the pleistocene based on equilibrium systems among recent hunter-gatherers. In R. B. Lee and I. DeVore (eds.) *Man the Hunter*, 229–40. Chicago, Aldine.

Birdsell, J. B. (1976). Realities and transformations: the tribes of the Western Desert of Australia. In N. Peterson (ed.), *Tribes and Boundaries in Australia*, 95–120. Canberra, Australian Institute of Aboriginal Studies.

Bitiri, M. (1972). *Paleoliticul in Țara Oașului*. București, Institul de Archeologie.

Bitiri, M. (1976). La culture aurignacienne dans le Nord de la Roumanie. In J. K. Kozlowski (ed.) *L'Aurignacien en Europe*, 51–74. Nice, U.I.S.P.P. IX Congrès, Colloque XVI.

Blanc, A. C. (1942). I paleantropi di Saccopastore e del Circeo. *Quartär*, 4: 1–37.

Blanc, A. C. (1957). On the pleistocene sequence of Rome. Paleoecologic and archaeologic correlations. *Quaternaria*, 4: 95–109.

Blanc, A. C. (1958). Torre in Pietra, Saccopastore e Monte Circeo. La chronologia dei giacimenti e la paleogeografia quaternaria del Lazio. *Bolletino della Società Geografica Italiana*, 8: 196–214.

Blanc, A. C., and Segre, A. G. (1953). Le Quaternaire du Mont Circé, in *Rome–Pisa. INQUA 4ᵉ Congrès Guides*, 23–107.

Blanchard, R., Peyrony, D., and Vallois, H.-V. (1972). Le gisement et le squelette de Saint-Germain-La-Rivière, *Archives de l'Institut de Paléontologie Humaine*, Mémoire 34.

Blurton-Jones, N., and Konner, M. J. (1976). !Kung knowledge of animal behaviour (or: the proper study of mankind is animals). In R. B. Lee and I. DeVore (eds.) *Kalahari Hunter-Gatherers*, 325–48. Cambridge, Mass., Harvard University Press.

Boessneck, J., and Von den Driesch, A. (1973). Die jungpleistozänen Tierknochenfunde aus der Brillenhöhle. In G. Riek (ed.) *Das Paläolithikum der Brillenhöhle bei Blaubeuren Teil II*, Stuttgart, Forschungen und Berichte zur vor- und frühgeschichte in Baden-Württemberg, 4/II.

Bofinger, E., and Davidson, I. (1977). Radiocarbon age and depth: a statistical treatment of two sequences of dates from Spain. *Journal of Archaeological Science*, 4: 231–43.

Bohmers, A. (1951). Die Höhlen von Mauern. *Palaeohistoria*, 1.

Boismier, W. A. (1981). Human behaviour and spatial analysis. Southampton University, Unpublished MA dissertation.

Bonifay, E., Bonifay, M. F., Panattoni, R., and Tiercelin, J.-J. (1976). Soleihac (Blanzac,

Haute Loire), nouveau site préhistorique au début du Pléistocène moyen. *Bulletin de la Société Préhistorique Française*, 73: 293–304.

Bordaz, J. (1970). *Tools of the Old and New Stone Age*. New York, Natural History Press.

Bordes, F. (1950). L'évolution buissonnante des industries en Europe occidentale. Considérations théoretiques sur le paléolithique ancien et moyen. *L'Anthropologie*, 54: 393–420.

Bordes, F. (1953a). Essai de classification des industries 'Moustériennes'. *Bulletin de la Société Préhistorique Française*, 50: 457–66.

Bordes, F. (1953b). Levalloisien et Moustérien. *Bulletin de la Société Préhistorique Française*, 50: 226–35.

Bordes, F. (1953c). Le dernier interglaciaire et la place du Micoquien et du 'Tayacien'. *L'Anthropologie*, 57: 172–7.

Bordes, F. (1954). *Les limons quaternaires du bassin de la Seine*. Paris, Archives Institut du Paléontologie Humaine, Mémoire 26.

Bordes, F. (1956). Some observations on the Pleistocene succession in the Somme valley. *Proceedings of the Prehistoric Society*, 22: 1–5.

Bordes, F. (1959). Evolution in the palaeolithic cultures. In S. Tax (ed.) *The Evolution of Man*, 99–110. Chicago, University of Chicago Press.

Bordes, F. (1961a). Typologie du Paléolithique Ancien et Moyen. *Publications de l'Institut de Préhistoire de l'Université de Bordeaux*, Mémoire No. 1, 2 vols.

Bordes, F. (1961b). Mousterian cultures in France. *Science*, 134: 803–10.

Bordes, F. (1968a). *The Old Stone Age*. London, Weidenfeld and Nicolson.

Bordes, F. (1968b). Emplacements de tentes du Périgordien supérieur évolué à Corbiac (près Bergerac, Dordogne). *Quartär*, 19: 251–62.

Bordes, F. (1969). Reflections on typology and technology in the Palaeolithic. *Arctic Anthropology*, 6: 1–29.

Bordes, F. (1970). Compte rendu des activités de la circonscription préhistorique d'Aquitaine. *Gallia Préhistoire*, 13: 485–511.

Bordes, F. (1971). Observations sur l'acheuléen des grottes de Dordogne. *Munibe*, 23: 5–23.

Bordes, F. (1972). *A Tale of Two Caves*. New York, Harper and Row.

Bordes, F. (1973). On the chronology and contemporaneity of different palaeolithic cultures in France. In C. Renfrew (ed.) *The Explanation of Culture Change: Models in Prehistory*, 217–26. London, Duckworth.

Bordes, F. (1975a). Sur la notion de sol d'habitat en préhistoire paléolithique. *Bulletin de la Société Préhistorique Française*, 72:139–44.

Bordes, F. (1975b). Le gisement du Pech-de-l'Azé IV: note préliminaire. *Bulletin de la Société Préhistorique Française*, 72: 293–308.

Bordes, F. (1978). Le protomagdalénien de Laugerie-Haute Est (fouilles F. Bordes). *Bulletin de la Société Préhistorique Française*, 75: 501–21.

Bordes, F. (1980). Le débitage Levallois et ses variants. *Bulletin de la Société Préhistorique Française*, 77: 45–49.

Bordes, F. (1981). Vingt-cinq ans après: le complexe Moustérien revisité. *Bulletin de la Société Préhistorique Française*, 78: 77–87.

Bordes, F. and Bourgon, M. (1951). Le complexe Moustérien: Moustérien, Levalloisien, et Tayacien. *L'Anthropologie*, 55: 1–23.

Bordes, F. and Fitte, P. (1953). L'Atelier Commont. *L'Anthropologie*, 57: 1–44.

Bordes, F. and Gaussen, J. (1970). Un fond de tente Magdalénien près de Mussidan (Dordogne). In *Frühe Menschheit und Umwelt*, 312–29. Köln, Fundamenta Reihe A/2.

Bordes, F., and Labrot, J. (1967). La stratigraphie du gisement de Roc de Combe (Lot) et ses implications. *Bulletin de la Société Préhistorique Française*, 64: 15–28.

Bordes, F., and Prat, F. (1965). Observations sur les faunes de Riss et du Würm I en Dordogne. *L'Anthropologie*, 69: 31–45.

Bordes, F., Rigaud, J. P. and de Sonneville-Bordes, D. (1972). Des buts, problèmes et limites de l'archéologie paléolithique. *Quaternaria*, 15: 15–34.

Bordes, F., and de Sonneville-Bordes, D. (1966). Proto-magdalénien ou périgordien VII? *L'Anthropologie*, 70: 113–22.

Bordes, F., and de Sonneville-Bordes, D. (1970). The significance of variability in palaeolithic assemblages. *World Archaeology*, 2: 61–73.

Borzatti von Löwenstern, E. (1966). Alcuni aspetti del musteriano nel Salento. *Rivista Scienze Preistoriche*, 21: 203–87.

Borzatti von Löwenstern, E., and Stoduti, P. (1974). Industria del paleolitico inferiore rinvenuta in località Inforchià (Potenza). *Rivista Scienze Preistoriche*, 29: 73–99.

Bosinski, G. (1966). Der paläolithische Fundplatz Rheindahlen, Stadtkreis Mönchengladbach. *Prähistorische Zeitschrift*, 43/4: 312–16.

Bosinski, G. (1967). *Die Mittelpaläolithischen Funde im Westlichen Mitteleuropa*. Köln, Fundamenta Reihe A/4.

Bosinski, G. (1969). Der Magdalénien-Fundplatz Feldkirchen-Gönnersdorf, Kr. Neuwied. *Germania*, 47: 1–38.

Bosinski, G. (1973a). Der paläolithische Fundplatz Rheindahlen, Stadtkreis Mönchengladbach (Nordrhein-Westfalen). In H.-J. Müller-Beck (ed.) *Neue paläolithische und mesolithische Ausgrabungen in der Bundesrepublik Deutschland*, 11–14. Tübingen, Zum 9 INQUA-Congress.

Bosinski, G. (1973b). Der Mittelpaläolithische Fundplatz Rörshain, Stadtkreis Schwalmstadt (Hessen). In H. Müller-Beck (ed.) *Neue paläolithische und mesolithische Ausgrabungen in der Bundesrepublik Deutschland*, 27–8. Tübingen, Zum 9 INQUA-Kongress.

Bosinski, G. (1976). Middle paleolithic structural remains from western central Europe. In L. G. Freeman (ed.) *Les Structures d'Habitat au Paléolithique Moyen*, 64–77. Nice, U.I.S.P.P. IX Congrès, Colloque XI.

Bosinski, G. (1979a). Ein Fundplatz des mittleren jungpaläolithikums bei Sprendlingen, Kreis Mainz-Bingen. *Archäologisches Korrespondenzblatt*, 9: 147–53.

Bosinski, G. (1979b). *Die Ausgrabungen in Gönnersdorf 1968–1976 und die Siedlungsbefunde der Grabung 1968*. Gönnersdorf Band 3, Wiesbaden, Franz Steiner GMBH.

Bosinski, G. (1979c). Stratigraphie du paléolithique supérieur récent et du paléolithique final dans le bassin de Neuwied (Vallée du Rhin moyen, R.F.A.). in D. de Sonneville-Bordes (ed.) *La Fin des Temps Glaciaires en Europe*, 193–202. Paris, CNRS.

Bosinski, G. (1982a). The transition lower/middle palaeolithic in north-west Germany. In A. Ronen (ed.) *The Transition from Lower to Middle Palaeolithic and the Origin of Modern Man*, 165–75. Oxford, British Archaeological Reports, International Series S151.

Bosinski, G. (1982b). *Die Kunst der Eiszeit in Deutschland und in der Schweiz*. Bonn, Habelt.

Bosinski, G., and Brunnacker, K. (1973). Eine neue fundschicht in Rheindahlen. *Archäologisches Korrespondenzblatt*, 3: 1–6.

Bosinski, G., and Fischer, G. (1974). *Die Menschdarstellungen von Gönnersdorf der Ausgrabung von 1968*. Gönnersdorf Band 1, Wiesbaden, Franz Steiner GMBH.

Bosinski, G., and Hahn, J. (1973). Der Magdalénien-Fundplaz Andernach (Martinsberg). *Rheinische Ausgrabungen*, 11: 81–257.

Bottema, S. (1974). *Late Quaternary Vegetation History of Northwestern Greece.* Groeningen, Groeningen University Press.

Bouchud, J. (1966). *Essai sur le Renne et la Climatologie du Paléolithique Moyen et Supérieur.* Périgueux, Mague.

Bouchud, J. (1975). Étude de la faune de l'Abri Pataud. In H. L. Movius (ed.) Excavation of the Abri Pataud, Les Eyzies (Dordogne), 69–153. *American School of Prehistoric Research Bulletin*, 30. Cambridge, Mass., Peabody Museum Press.

Bourdier, F. (1976). Les industries paléolithiques anté-würmiennes dans le Nord-Ouest. In H. de Lumley (ed.) *La Préhistoire Française*, 956–63. Paris, CNRS.

Bourgon, M. (1957). Les industries Moustériennes et pré-Moustériennes du Périgord. *Archives de l'Institut de Paléontologie Humaine*, 27.

Bouvier, J.-M. (1977). *Un gisement préhistorique: La Madeleine.* Périgueux, Pierre Fanlac.

Bouvier, J.-M. (1979). La Madeleine: acquis récents. In D. de Sonneville-Bordes (ed.) *La Fin des Temps Glaciaires en Europe*, 435–42. Paris, CNRS.

Bouyssonie, J. (1954). Les sépultures moustériennes, *Quaternaria*, 1: 107–15.

Bowen, D. Q. (1978). *Quaternary Geology.* Oxford, Pergamon Press.

Bowen, D. Q. (1979). Quaternary Correlations. *Nature*, 277: 171–2.

Bradley, B. (1977). Experimental lithic technology with special reference to the middle palaeolithic. Cambridge University, Ph.D. dissertation.

Brain, C. K. (1967). Hottentot food remains and their meaning in the interpretation of fossil bone assemblages. *Scientific Papers of the Namib Desert Research Station*, 32: 1–11.

Brain, C. K. (1976). Some principles in the interpretation of bone accumulations associated with man. In G. L. Isaac, and E. R. McCown (eds.) *Human Origins*, 97–116. Menlo Park, Benjamin.

Brain, C. K. (1981). *The Hunters or the Hunted? An Introduction to African Cave Taphonomy.* Chicago, University of Chicago Press.

Brancaccio, L., Capaldi, G., Cinque, A., Pece, R., and Sgrosso, I. (1978). $^{230}Th - ^{238}U$ dating of corals from a Tyrrhenian beach in Sorrentine Peninsula (Southern Italy). *Quaternaria*, 20: 175–83.

Bräuer, G. (1981). New evidence on the transitional period between neanderthal and modern man. *Journal of Human Evolution*, 10: 467–74.

Breuil, H. (1912). Les subdivisions du paléolithique supérieur et leur signification. *Comptes Rendus du 14ᵉ Congrès International d'Anthropologie et d'Archéologie Préhistorique, Genève*, 165–238.

Breuil, H. (1932). Les industries à éclat du paléolithique ancien, I. Le Clactonien. *Préhistoire*, 1: 125–90.

Breuil, H. (1939). The pleistocene succession in the Somme valley. *Proceedings of the Prehistoric Society*, 5: 33–8.

Breuil, H. (1945). The discovery of the antiquity of man. *Journal of the Royal Anthropological Institute*, 75: 21–31.

Breuil, H. (1952). *Quatre cents siècles d'art pariétal.* Montignac, Centre d'études et de documentation préhistoriques.

Breuil, H., and Kozlowski, L. (1932). Études de stratigraphie paléolithique dans le nord de la France, la Belgique et l'Angleterre. *L'Anthropologie*, 42: 27–47, 291–314.

Brézillon, M. (1968). Le dénomination des objets de pierre tailleé. *Gallia Préhistoire*, supplément 4. Paris, CNRS.

Bricker, H. M., and Laville, H. (1977). Le gisement châtelperronien de plein air des Tambourets (Commune de Cou!ardère, Haute-Garonne). *Bulletin de la Société Préhistorique Française*, 74: 505–17.

Brodar, M. (1958–9). Crvena Stijena, eine neue paläolithstation aus dem Balkan in Jugoslavien. *Quartär*, 10/11: 227–36.

Brodar, M. (1979). 50 years of palaeolithic research in Slovenia. *Arheološki Vestnik*, 30: 21–8.

Broglio, A., and Laplace, G. (1966). Études de typologie analytique des complexes leptolithiques de l'Europe centrale. I: Les complexes aurignacoïdes de la Basse Autriche, II: Les complexes gravettiens de la Basse Autriche: Willendorf II. *Rivista di Scienze Preistoriche*, 21: 61–121, 303–64.

Brunnacker, K. (1975). The mid-pleistocene of the Rhine basin. In K. W. Butzer and G. L. Isaac (eds.) *After the Australopithecines*, 189–229. The Hague, Mouton.

Brunnacker, K. (ed.) (1978). *Geowissenschaftliche untersuchungen in Gönnersdorf*. Gönnersdorf, Band 4. Wiesbaden, Franz Steiner GMBH.

Brunnacker, K. (1980). Stand der Quartar-stratigraphie in der Bundesrepublik Deutschland. In J. Chaline (ed.) *Problèmes de stratigraphie Quaternaire en France et dans les Pays Limitrophes*, 135–40. Dijon, Association Française pour l'Étude de Quaternaire.

Brunnacker, K. (1982). Environmental conditions in Middle Europe during the lower/middle palaeolithic transition. In A. Ronen (ed.) *The Transition from Lower to Middle Palaeolithic and the Origin of Modern Man*, 123–9. Oxford, British Archaeological Reports, International Series S151.

Brunnacker, K., and Streit, R. (1966). Neuere Gesichtspunkte zur Untersuchung von Höhlensedimenten. *Jahresheft für Karst und Höhlenkunde*, 7: 29–44.

Büdel, J. (1951). Die Klimazonen des Eiszeitalters. *Eiszeitalter und Gegenwart*, 1: 16–28.

Bulgarelli, G. M. (1972). Il paleolitico della grotta di Torre Nave (Pavia a Mare-Cosenza). *Quaternaria*, 16: 149–88.

Bunn, H. T. (1981). Archaeological evidence for meat-eating by Plio-Pleistocene hominids from Koobi Fora and Olduvai Gorge. *Nature*, 291: 574-7.

Burch, E. S. (1972). The caribou/wild reindeer as a human resource. *American Antiquity*, 37: 339–68.

Burch, E. S. (1975). *Eskimo Kinsmen: Changing Family Relationships in Northwest Alaska*. American Ethnological Society Monograph 59. New York, West Publishing.

Burch, E. S., and Correll, T. C. (1972). Alliance and conflict: inter-regional relations in North Alaska. In D. L. Guemple (ed.) Alliance in Eskimo Society. *Proceedings of the American Ethnological Society, 1971, Supplement*, 17–39. Seattle, University of Washington Press.

Burdukiewicz, J. M. (1980). The flint technology of the hamburgian culture (Olbrachcice, S.W. Poland). *Third International Symposium on Flint, 1979, Maastricht, Staringia*, 6: 67–70.

Butzer, K. W. (1971). *Environment and Archaeology*. 2nd edn. London, Methuen.

Butzer, K. W. (1975). Pleistocene littoral-sedimentary cycles of the Mediterranean basin: a Mallorquin view. In K. W. Butzer and G. Ll. Isaac (eds.). *After the Australopithecines*, 25–71. The Hague, Mouton.

Butzer, K. W. (1981). Cave sediments, upper pleistocene stratigraphy and mousterian facies in Cantabrian Spain. *Journal of Archaeological Science*, 8: 133–83.

Butzer, K. W. (1982). *Archaeology as Human Ecology*. Cambridge, Cambridge University Press.

Butzer, K. W., and Isaac, G. L. (eds.) (1975). *After the Australopithecines*. The Hague, Mouton.

Cacho, C. (1981). Espagne Mediterranéenne. In R. Desbrosse and J. K. Kozlowski (eds.) *Resumen de las Investigaciones de 1976 a 1981*, 36–8. Mexico City, U.I.S.P.P. X Congreso, Comision X.

Cahen, D., Keeley, L. H., and Van Noten, F. (1979). Stone tools, toolkits and human behaviour in prehistory. *Current Anthropology*, 20: 661–83.

Callow, P. (1976). The lower and middle palaeolithic of Britain and adjacent areas of Europe. Cambridge University, Ph.D. dissertation.

Callow, P. (1981). *La Cotte de Saint-Brélade, 1881–1981*. Cambridge, Jersey Heritage Trust.

Campbell, J. B. (1977). *The Upper Palaeolithic of Britain*, 2 vols. Oxford, Oxford University Press.

Campbell, J. B. and Sampson, G. (1971). A new analysis of Kent's Cavern, Devonshire, England. *University of Oregon Anthropological Papers*, 3.

Campbell, J. K. (1964). *Honour, Family and Patronage*. Oxford, Clarendon Press.

Campbell, J. M. (1968). Territoriality among ancient hunters: interpretations from ethnography and nature. In B. J. Meggars (ed.) *Anthropological Archaeology in the Americas*, 1–21. Washington, Anthropological Society of Washington.

Campen, I., and Hahn, J. (1977). Die vierte Untersuchung des mittelpaläolithischen Fundplatzes Rörshain, Gemeinde Schwalmstadt, Schwalm-Eder-Kreis. *Fundberichte aus Hessen*, 15: 9–20.

Camps-Fabrer, H. (ed.) (1974). *L'Industrie de l'os dans la préhistoire*. University of Provence, CNRS.

Capitan, L., and Bouyssonie, J. (1924). *Limeuil: son gisement à gravures sur pierres de l'age du renne*. Paris, Libraire Emile Nourry.

Capitan, L., Breuil, H., and Peyrony, D. (1910). *La caverne de Font-de-Gaume aux Eyzies (Dordogne)*. Monaco.

Capitan, L., Breuil, H., and Peyrony, D. (1924). *Les Combarelles aux Eyzies (Dordogne)*. Monaco.

Capitan, L., and Peyrony, D. (1928). La Madeleine, son gisement – son industrie, ses oeuvres d'art. *Publications de l'Institut International d'Anthropologie*, 2. Paris.

Cârciumaru, M. (1980). *Mediul Geografic în Pleistocenul Superior şi Culturile Paleolitice din România*. Bucareşti, Editura Academiei Republicii Socialiste România.

Cârciumaru, M. (1982). Cîteva datări C14 în contextual schemei paleoclimatice a pleistocenului superior din România. *Studii şi Cercetări Istorie Veche şi Archeologie*, 33: 395–401.

Cardini, L. (1946). Gli strati paleolitici e mesolitici delle Arene Candide. *Rivista Studia Liguri*, 12: 3–11.

Carlstein, T. (1982). *Time Resources, Society and Ecology: Vol. I: Pre-Industrial Societies*. London, George Allen and Unwin.

Chagnon, N.A. (1977). *Yąnomamö: The Fierce People*, 2nd ed. New York, Holt, Rinehart and Winston.

Champagne, F., and Espitalié, R. (1981). *Le Piage, site préhistorique du Lot*. Paris, Société Préhistorique Française.

Champion, T. C., Gamble, C. S., Shennan, S. J. and Whittle, A. W., (1984). *Prehistoric Europe*. Academic Press, London.

Chang, K. C. (1962). A typology of settlement and community patterns in some circumpolar societies. *Arctic Anthropology*, 1: 28–41.

Cheetham, G. H. (1976). Palaeohydrological investigations of river terrace gravels. In D. A. Davidson and M. L. Shackley (eds.) *Geoarchaeology*, 335–44. London, Duckworth.

Chernysh, A. P. (1961). *Palaeolitiginia Stoanka Molodóva V*. Kiev, An. Ukr. SSR.

Cherry, J. F. (1982). A preliminary definition of site distribution on Melos. In C. Renfrew and J. M. Wagstaff (eds.) *An Island Polity: The Archaeology of Exploitation in Melos*, 10–23. Cambridge, Cambridge University Press.

Cherry, J. F., Gamble, C. S., and Shennan, S. J. (eds.) (1978). *Sampling in Contemporary British Archaeology*. Oxford, British Archaeological Reports, British Series, 50.

Cherry, J. F., and Shennan, S. J. (1978). Sampling cultural systems. In J. F. Cherry, C. S. Gamble and S. J. Shennan (eds.) *Sampling in Contemporary British Archaeology*, 17–48, Oxford, British Archaeological Reports, British Series, 50.

Cheynier, A. (1949). Badegoule, station solutréenne et proto-magdalénienne. *Archives de l'Institut de Paléontologie Humaine*, 23.

Childe, V. G. (1951). *Social Evolution*. London, Watts.

Chmielewska, M. (1961). Huttes d'habitation épipaléolithiques de Witów, Distr. de Lęczyca. Lodz, *Acta Archaeologica Universitatis Lodziensis*, No. 10.

Chmielewski, W. (1961). *Civilisation de Jerzmanovice*. Wroclaw–Warzawa–Krakow, Institut Historicae Kultury Materialnej Polskiej Akademii NAUK.

Cioni, O., Gambassini, P., and Torre, D. (1979). Grotta di Castelcivita: risultati delle ricerche negli anni 1975–77. *Atti Società Toscana di Scienze Naturali Memorie, Serie A*, 86: 275–96.

Clark, G. A. (1974–5). Excavations in the late pleistocene cave site of Balmori, Asturias (Spain). *Quaternaria*, 18: 383–426.

Clark, G. A., and Straus, L. G. (1983). Late pleistocene hunter-gatherer adaptations in Cantabrian Spain. In G. N. Bailey (ed.) *Hunter-Gatherer Economy in Prehistory*, 131–48. Cambridge, Cambridge University Press.

Clark, J. D. (1975). Africa in prehistory: peripheral or paramount. *Man*, 10: 175–98.

Clark, J. D., and Walton, J. (1962). A late stone age site in the Erongo Mountains, Southwest Africa. *Proceedings of the Prehistoric Society*, 28: 1–16.

Clark, J. G. D. (1946). *From Savagery to Civilization*. London, Cobbetts Press.

Clark, J. G. D. (1957). *Archaeology and Society*. London, Methuen.

Clark, J. G. D. (1975). *The Earlier Stone Age Settlement of Scandinavia*. Cambridge, Cambridge University Press.

Clarke, D. L. (1972). A provisional model of an Iron Age society and its settlement system. In D. L. Clarke (ed.) *Models in Archaeology*, 801–70. London, Methuen.

Clarke, D. L. (1976). Mesolithic Europe: the economic basis. In G. de G. Sieveking, I. H. Longworth and K. E. Wilson (eds.) *Problems in Economic and Social Archaeology*, 449–82. London, Duckworth.

Clarke, D. L. (1978). *Analytical Archaeology*, 2nd ed. London, Methuen.

CLIMAP (1976). The surface of ice age earth. *Science* 191: 1131–37.

Close, A. E. (1978). The identification of style in lithic artifacts. *World Archaeology*, 10: 223–37.

Clottes, J. (1976). Les civilisations du paléolithique supérieur dans les Pyrénées. In H. de Lumley (ed.) *La Préhistoire Française*, 1214–31. Paris, CNRS.

Clottes, J., and de Begouen, C. (1981). Apports mobiliers dans les cavernes du Volp (Enlène, Les Trois-Frères, Le Tuc d'Audoubert). In *Altamira Symposium*, 157–88. Madrid, Ministry of Culture.

Clottes, J., and Simonnet, R. (1972). Le réseau René Clastres de la caverne de Niaux, *Bulletin de la Société Préhistorique Française*, 69: 293–323.

Coles, J. M., and Higgs, E. S. (1969). *The Archaeology of Early Man*. London, Faber and Faber.

Collie, G. L. (1928). *The Aurignacians and their Culture*. Wisconsin Logan Museum, Beloit.

Collins, D. (1969). Culture traditions and environment of early man. *Current Anthropology*, 10: 267–316.

Collins, D. (1970). Stone artefact analysis and the recognition of culture traditions. *World Archaeology*, 2: 17–27.

Collins, D., and Onians, J. (1978). The origins of art. *Art History*, 1: 1–25.

Collins, M. B. (1973). Observations on thermal treatment of chert in the solutrean of Laugerie-Haute, France. *Proceedings of the Prehistoric Society*, 39: 461–6.

Coltorti, M., Cremaschi, M., Delitala, M. C., Esu, D., Fornaseri, M., McPherron, A., Nicoletti, M., van Otterloo, R., Peretto, C., Sala, B., Schmidt, V., and Sevink, J. (1982). Reversed magnetic polarity at an early lower palaeolithic site in central Italy. *Nature*, 300: 173–6.

Combier, J. (1967). *Le paléolithique de l'Ardèche, dans son cadre paléoclimatique.* Bordeaux, Delmas.

Combier, J. (ed.) (1976). L'Evolution de l'Acheuléen en Europe. Nice, U.I.S.P.P. Congrès IX, Colloque X.

Conkey, M. W. (1978). Style and information in cultural evolution: toward a predictive model for the palaeolithic. In C. L. Redman *et al.* (eds.) *Social Archaeology*, 61–85. Academic Press, New York.

Conkey, M. W. (1980). The identification of prehistoric hunter-gatherer aggregation sites: the case of Altamira. *Current Anthropology*, 21: 609–30.

Conkey, M. W. (1983). On the origins of palaeolithic art: a review and some critical thoughts. In E. Trinkaus (ed.) *The Mousterian Legacy*, 201–27. Oxford, British Archaeological Reports, International Series, 164.

Cook, J., Stringer, C. B., Currant, A. P., Schwartz, H. P., and Wintle, A. G. (1982). A review of the chronology of the European middle pleistocene hominids. *Yearbook of Physical Anthropology*, 25: 19–65.

Cook, S. F., and Heizer, R. F. (1965). Relationships among houses, settlement areas and populations in aboriginal California. In K. C. Chang (ed.) *Settlement Archaeology*, 79–106. Palo Alto, National Press.

Coope, G. R. (1977). Fossil coleopteran assemblages as sensitive indicators of climatic changes during the Devensian (Last) cold stage. *Philosophical Transactions of the Royal Society of London*, B. 280: 313–40.

Coope, G. R., Morgan, A., and Osborne, P. J. (1971). Fossil coleoptera as indicators of climatic fluctuations during the last glaciation in Britain. *Palaeogeography, Palaeoclimatology, Palaeoecology*, 10: 87–101.

Crabtree, D. E. (1970). Flaking stone with wooden implements. *Science*, 169: 146–53.

Crabtree, D. E., and Butler, R. (1964). Notes on experiments in flint knapping: heat treatment of silica materials. *TEBIWA, the Journal of the Idaho State Museum*, 7: 1–6.

Cronin, J. E., Boaz, N. T., Stringer, C. B., and Rak, Y. (1981). Tempo and mode in hominid evolution. *Nature*, 292: 113–21.

Cubuk, G. A. (1976). Erste Altpaläolithische Funde in Greichenland bei Nea Skala, Kephallinia. In K. Valoch (ed.) *Les Premières Industries de l'Europe*, 152–77. Nice, U.I.S.P.P. Congrès IX, Colloque VIII.

Dakaris, S. I., Higgs, E. S., and Hey, R. (1964). The climate, environment and industries of stone age Greece, Part I. *Proceedings of the Prehistoric Society*, 30: 199–244.

Damas, D. (ed.) (1969a). Contributions to Anthropology: Band Societies. *National Museum of Canada Bulletin*, 228.

Damas, D. (1969b). Characteristics of Central Eskimo band structure. In D. Damas (ed.), Contributions to Anthropology: Band Societies. *National Museum of Canada Bulletin*, 228: 116–38.

Dams, L. (1978). *L'Art Paléolithique de la Caverne de la Pileta*. Graz, Akademische Druck und Verlagsanstalt.

Daniel, G. (1964). *The Idea of Prehistory*. Harmondsworth, Pelican Books.

Dansgaard, W., Johnsen, S. J., Clausen, H. B., and Langway, C. C. (1970). Ice cores and paleoclimatology. In I. U. Olsson (ed.) *Radiocarbon Variations and Absolute Chronology* (Uppsala 1969), 337–51. Stockholm, Almquist and Wiksell.

Dansgaard, W., Johnsen, S. J., Clausen, H. B., and Langway, C. C. (1971). Climatic record revealed by the Camp Century ice core. In K. K. Turekian (ed.) *The Late Cenozoic Glacial Ages*, 37–56. New Haven, Yale University Press.

Darling, F. F. (1937). *A Herd of Red Deer: A Study in Animal Behaviour*. Oxford, Oxford University Press.

David, N. (1973). On upper palaeolithic society, ecology, and technological change: the Noaillian case. In C. Renfrew (ed.) *The Explanation of Culture Change: Models in Prehistory*, 277–303. London, Duckworth.

Davidson, I. (1974). Radiocarbon dates for the Spanish solutrean. *Antiquity*, 48: 63–5.

Davidson, I. (1976). Les Mallaetes and Mondúver: the economy of a human group in prehistoric Spain. In G. de G. Sieveking, I. H. Longworth and K. E. Wilson (eds.) *Problems in Economic and Social Archaeology*, 483–99. London, Duckworth.

Davidson, I. (1980). Late palaeolithic economy in Eastern Spain, Cambridge University, Ph.D. dissertation.

Davidson, I. (1981). Can we study prehistoric economy for fisher-gatherer-hunters? In A. Sheridan and G. N. Bailey (eds.) *Economic Archaeology*, 17–33. Oxford, British Archaeological Reports, International Series, 96.

Davidson, I. (1983). Site variability and prehistoric economy in Levante. In G. N. Bailey (ed.) *Hunter-Gatherer Economy in Prehistory*, 79–95. Cambridge, Cambridge University Press.

Davidson, I. (n.d.). The Magnificent Seven: a stingy view of fisher/gatherer/hunters in the late Pleistocene of western Europe, and their economy. Unpublished manuscript.

Davis, D. D. (1978). Lithic assemblage variability in relation to early hominid subsistence strategies at Olduvai Gorge. In D. D. Davis (ed.) *Lithics and Subsistence*, 35–86. Nashville, Vanderbilt University Publications in Anthropology, 20.

Dawkins, W. D. (1869). British postglacial mammals. *Proceedings of the Geological Society*, 25.

Day, M. H. (1977). *Guide to Fossil Man*, 3rd ed. London, Cassell.

Debenath, A. (1976). Les civilisations du paléolithique inférieur en Charente. In H. de Lumley (ed.) *La Préhistoire Française*, 929–35. Paris, CNRS.

Deetz, J. (1968). Discussions, Part IV. In R. B. Lee and I. DeVore (eds.) *Man the Hunter*, 281–5. Chicago, Aldine.

Deevey, E. (1968). Discussions, Part II. In R. B. Lee and I. DeVore (eds.) *Man the Hunter*, 94–5. Chicago, Aldine.

Dehm, R. (1966). The cave of Erpfingen as a bear's cave. In G. Wagner (ed.) *The Bear's Cave of Erpfingen*, 21–3. Erpfingen.

Delibrias, G., and Evin, J. (1980). Sommaire des datations 14C concernant la préhistoire en France. *Bulletin de la Société Préhistorique Française*, 77: 216–24.

Delibrias, G., Guillier, M.-T., Evin, J., Thommeret, J., and Thommeret, Y. (1976). Datations absolues des dépôts quaternaires et des sites préhistoriques par la méthode du carbone 14. In H. de Lumley (ed.) *La Préhistoire Française*, 1499–1513. Paris, CNRS.

Delluc, B., and Delluc, G. (1978). Les manifestations graphiques aurignaciennes sur support rocheux des environs des Eyzies (Dordogne). *Gallia Préhistoire*, 21: 213–438.

424 Bibliography

Delpech, F. (1970). L'abri magdalénien du Flageolet II – Paléontologie (Bézenac-Dordogne). *Bulletin de la Société Préhistorique Française*, 67: 494–9.

Delpech, F. (1976). *Les Faunes du Paléolithique Supérieur dans le Sud-Ouest de la France*, 3 vols. Thèse, Doctorat d'Etat, Université de Bordeaux.

Delpech, F., and Rigaud, J.-P. (1974). Étude de la fragmentation et de la répartition des restes osseux dans un niveau d'habitat paléolithique. In H. Camps-Fabrer (ed.) *l'Industrie de l'os dans la Préhistoire*, 47–55. Aix-en-Provence, Editions de L'Université de Provence.

Delporte, H. (1976). Les premières industries humaines en Auvergne. In H. de Lumley (ed.) *La Préhistoire Française*, 801–3. Paris, CNRS.

Delporte, H. (1979). *L'Image de la femme dans l'art préhistorique*. Paris, Picard.

Delporte, H. (1981). Preface. In F. Champagne and R. Espitalié, *Le Piage, Site Préhistorique du Lot*, 5–10. Paris, Société Préhistorique Française, 15.

Delporte, H., and Mazière, G. (1977). L'aurignacien de la Ferrassie: observations préliminaires à la suite des fouilles récentes. *Bulletin de la Société Préhistorique Française*, 74: 343–61.

Dennell, R. (1983a). *European Economic Prehistory*. London, Academic Press.

Dennell, R. (1983b). A new chronology for the mousterian. *Nature*, 301: 199–200.

Desbrosse, R., and Kozlowski, J. K. (eds.) (1981). *Resumen de las investigaciones de 1976 à 1981*. Mexico City, U.I.S.P.P. X Congreso, Comision X.

Desbrosse, R., and Tavoso, A. (1970). Un gisement moustérien à Blanzy (Saône et Loire). *Quartär*, 21: 21–45.

Dixon, R. M. W. (1976). Tribes, languages and other boundaries in northeast Queensland. In N. Peterson (ed.) *Tribes and Boundaries in Australia*, 207–38. Canberra, Australian Institute of Aboriginal Studies.

Dolukhanov, M. (1979). Evolution des systèmes éco-sociaux en Europe durant le pléistocène récent et le début de l'holocène. In D. de Sonneville-Bordes (ed.) *La Fin des Temps Glaciaires en Europe*, 869–76. Paris, CNRS.

von den Driesch, A., and Boessneck, J. (1975). Schnittspuren an neolithischen Tierknochen. *Germania*, 53: 1–23.

Dubois, A., and Stehlin, H. G. (1933). La grotte de Cotencher: station moustérienne. *Mémoires de la Société Paléontologique Suisse*, LII/LIII.

Dunnell, R. C. (1971). *Systematics in Prehistory*, New York, Free Press.

Dunnell, R. C. (1978). Style and function: a fundamental dichotomy. *American Antiquity*, 43: 192–202.

Duport, L. (1976). La grotte de Montgaudier, commune de Montbron, Charente. In *Livret-Guide de l'excursion* A4, 151–8. Nice, U.I.S.P.P. IX Congrès.

Durham, W. H. (1981). Overview: optimal foraging analysis in human ecology. In B. Winterhalder and E. A. Smith (eds.) *Hunter-Gatherer Foraging Strategies*, 218–31. Chicago, University of Chicago Press.

Ebert, J. I. (1979). An ethnographical approach to reassessing the meaning of variability in stone tool assemblages. In C. Kramer (ed.) *Ethnoarchaeology*, 59–74. New York, Columbia University Press.

Efimenko, P. P. (1958). *Kostenki, I* (in Russian). Moscow–Leningrad, NAUKA.

Efimenko, P. P., and Boriskovskij, P. I. (1953). The palaeolithic site of Borshevo II (in Russian). *Materialy vsesoyuznogo soveschchaniya po izucheniyu chetvertichnogo perioda*, 39: 56–110.

Efremov, I. A. (1940). Taphonomy: a new branch of palaeontology. *Pan-American Geologist*, 74: 81–93.

Egloff, M. (1979). La transition du tardiglaciaire au postglaciaire en Suisse. In D. de Sonneville-Bordes (ed.) *La Fin des Temps Glaciaires en Europe*, 231–8. Paris, CNRS.

Ehrenberg, K. (1951). 30 Jahre paläobiologischer Forschung in Österreichischen Höhlen. *Quartär*, 5.

Eisenberg, J. F. (1966). The social organisation of mammals. *Handbuch der Zoologie*, 8: 1–92.

Escalon de Fonton, M. (1966). Du paléolithique supérieur au mésolithique dans le midi mediterranéen. *Bulletin de la Société Préhistorique Française*, 63: 66–180.

Escalon de Fonton, M., and Bazile, F. (1976). Les civilisations du paléolithique supérieur en Languedoc oriental. In H. de Lumley (ed.) *La Préhistoire Française*, 1163–73. Paris, CNRS.

Escalon de Fonton, M., and Onoratini, G. (1976). Les civilisations du paléolithique supérieur en Provence littorale. In H. de Lumley (ed.) *La Préhistoire Française*, 1145–56. Paris, CNRS.

Evans, J. G. (1975). *The Environment of Early Man in the British Isles*. London, Elek.

Ewer, R. F. (1973). *The Carnivores*. London, Weidenfeld and Nicolson.

Fagerstrom, J. A. (1964). Fossil communities in palaeoecology: their recognition and significance. *Geological Society of America Bulletin*, 75: 1197–216.

Farrand, W. (1975). Analysis of the Abri Pataud sediments. In H. L. Movius (ed.) *Excavation of the Abri Pataud, Les Eyzies (Dordogne)*, 27–68, Cambridge, Mass., American School of Prehistoric Research, Bulletin 30, Peabody Museum Press.

Fedele, F. G. (1978). Man in the Italian Alps: a study of the pleistocene and post-glacial evidence. In L. G. Freeman (ed.) *Views of the Past*, 317–55. The Hague, Mouton.

Fedele, F. G. (1981). Il popolamento delle Alpi nel paleolitico. *Le Scienze*, 160: 56–73.

Felgenhauer, F. (1956–9). *Willendorf in der Wachau*. Wien, Mitteilungen Prähistorisches Kommission 8/9.

Felgenhauer, F. (1962). *Das Niederösterreichische Freilandpaläolithikum*. Wien, Mitteilung Österreich, Arbeitsgemeinschaft für Urgeschichte.

Fentum, T. (1983). Site structure at Molodova V. Southampton University, unpublished MA dissertation.

Feustel, R. (1973). *Technik der Steinzeit*. Weimar, Hermann Böhlaus.

Feustel, R. (1974). *Die Kniegrotte*. Wiemar, Hermann Böhlaus.

Feustel, R. (1979). Le Magdalénien final en Thuringe (R.D.A.). In D. de Sonneville-Bordes (ed.) *La Fin des Temps Glaciaires en Europe*, 877–88. Paris, CNRS.

Feustel, R. (1980). *Magdalenienstation Teufelsbrücke*, Weimar, Museum für Ur und Fruhgeschichte Thüringens.

Filip, J. (ed.) (1966). *Investigations Archéologiques en Tchécoslovaquie*, Prague, U.I.S.P.P. VII Congrès.

Fink, J. (1976). Exkursion durch ein Österreichischen Teil des nordlichen Alpenvorlandes und den Donauraum zwischen Krems und Wiener Pforte. *Mitteilung Kommission Quartärforschungen Österreichischen Akademie die Wissenschaft*, Band 1.

Firbas, J. (1949–52). *Spät- und nacheiszeitliche Waldgeschichte Mitteleuropas nordlich der Alpen*. Jena, G. Fisher.

Fish, P. R. (1979). The interpretative potential of mousterian debitage. *Arizona State University, Anthropological Research Papers*, No. 16.

Flannery, K. V. (1967). Culture history versus cultural process: a debate in American archaeology. *Scientific American*, 217: 119–22.

Flannery, K. V. (ed.) (1976). *The Early Mesoamerican Village*, New York, Academic Press.

Flint, R. F. (1971). *Glacial and Quaternary Geology*. New York, Wiley.

Flohn, H. (1978). On time-scales and causes of abrupt palaeo-climatic events. *Quaternary Research*, 12: 135–49.

Florschütz, F., Amor, J. M., and Wijmstra, T. A. (1971). Palynology of a thick quaternary succession in southern Spain. *Palaeogeography, Palaeoclimatology, Palaeoecology*, 10: 233–64.

Foley, R. (1978). Incorporating sampling into initial research design: some aspects of relation to archaeological sites. In D. L. Clarke (ed.) *Spatial Archaeology*, 163–87. London, Academic Press.

Foley, R. (1978). Incorporating sampling into initial research design: some aspects of spatial archaeology. In J. F. Cherry, C. S. Gamble, and S. J. Shennan (eds.) *Sampling in Contemporary British Archaeology*, 49–66. Oxford, British Archaeological Reports, British series, 50.

Foley, R. (1981a). *Off-site Archaeology and Human Adaptation in Eastern Africa*. Oxford, British Archaeological Reports, International Series, 97.

Foley, R. (1981b). Off-site archaeology: an alternative approach for the short-sited. In I. Hodder, G. L. Isaac, and N. Hammond (eds.) *Pattern of the Past: Studies in Honour of David Clarke*, 157–83. Cambridge, Cambridge University Press.

Foley, R. (1981c). A model of regional archaeological structure. *Proceedings of the Prehistoric Society*, 47: 1–17.

Foley, R. (1982). A reconsideration of the role of predation on large mammals in tropical hunter-gatherer adaptation. *Man*, 17: 393–402.

Foley, R. (ed.) (1984). *Hominid Evolution and Community Ecology: Prehistoric Human Adaptation in Biological Perspective*. London, Academic Press.

Formozov, A. N. (1970). Écologie des plus importantes espèces de la faune subartique. In *Ecology of the Subarctic Regions*, 257–72. Proceedings of the Helsinki Symposium, Paris, UNESCO.

Fortea, J. (1973). *Los complejos Microlaminares y Geométricos del Epipaleolítico Mediterráneo Español*. Salamanca, Facultad de Filosofía y Letras, Universidad de Salamanca.

Fortea, J., and Jordá Cerdá, F. (1976). La cueva de Les Mallaetes y los problemas del paleolítico superior del mediterráneo Español. *Zephyrus*, 26–7: 129–66.

Frank, A. H. E. (1969). Pollen stratigraphy of the Lake of Vico (Central Italy). *Palaeogeography, Palaeoclimatology, Palaeoecology*, 6: 67–85.

Freeman, L. G. (1973). The significance of mammalian faunas from palaeolithic occupations in Cantabrian Spain. *American Antiquity*, 38: 3–44.

Freeman, L. G. (1975). Acheulean sites and stratigraphy in Iberia and the Maghreb. In K. W. Butzer and G. Ll. Isaac (eds.) *After the Australopithecines*, 661–743. The Hague, Mouton.

Freeman, L. G. (1978a). The analysis of some occupation floor distributions from earlier and middle palaeolithic sites in Spain. In L. G. Freeman (ed.) *Views of the Past*, 57–116. The Hague, Mouton.

Freeman, L. G. (1978b). Mousterian worked bone from Cueva Morín (Santander, Spain): a preliminary description. In L. G. Freeman (ed.) *Views of the Past*, 29–51. The Hague, Mouton.

Freeman, L. G. (1981). The fat of the land: notes on palaeolithic diet in Iberia. In R.S.O. Harding and G. Teleki (eds.) *Omnivorous Primates*, 104–65. New York, Columbia University Press.

Freeman, L. G. (1983). More on the mousterian: flaked bone from Cueva Morín, *Current Anthropology*, 24: 366–77.

Freeman, L. G., and Butzer, K. W. (1966). The acheulean station of Torralba (Spain). A progress report. *Quaternaria*, 8: 9–21.

Freeman, L. G., and González-Echegaray, J. (1970). Aurignacian structural features and burials at Cueva Morín (Santander, Spain), *Nature*, 226: 722–6.

Frenzel, B. (1967). *Die Klimaschwankungen des Eiszeitalters*. Braunschweig.

Frenzel, B. (1968a). *Grundzüge der Pleistozänen Vegetationsgeschichte NordEurasiens.* Wiesbaden, Steiner.

Frenzel, B. (1968b). The Pleistocene vegetation of northern Eurasia. *Science*, 161: 637–49.

Frenzel, B. (1973). *Climatic Fluctuations of the Ice Age.* Cleveland, Case Western Reserve University.

Freund, G. (1952). *Die Blattspitzen des Paläolithikums in Europa.* Bonn, Quartär-Bibliothek, l.

Freund, G. (1963). *Die ältere und die mittlere Steinzeit in Bayern.* Jahresberichte der Bayerischen Bodendenkmalpflege, 4.

Freund, G. (1968). Mikrolithen aus dem mittelpaläolithikum der Sesselfelsgrotte in unteren Altmühltal, Ldkr. Kelheim. *Quartär*, 19: 133–54.

Freund, G. (1978). Zum paläolithikum aus der Höhlenruine von Hunas in der nördlichen Fränkischen Alb. *Archäologisches Korrespondenzblatt*, 8: 259–63.

Fridrich, J. (1976). The first industries from eastern and south-eastern central Europe. In K. Valoch (ed.) *Les Premières Industries de l'Europe*, 8–23. Nice, U.I.S.P.P. IX Congrès, Colloque VIII.

Frison, G. C. (ed.) (1975). *The Casper Site.* New York, Academic Press.

Fullola, J. M. (1979). Las industrias líticas de palcolítico superior Ibérico. *Trabajo Vario del Servicio de Investigación Prehistórica*, 60.

Gábori, M. (1976). *Les Civilisations du Paléolithique Moyen entre les Alpes et L'Oural.* Budapest, Akadémiai Kiadó.

Gábori-Csánk, V. (1968). *La Station du Paléolithique Moyen d'Érd, Hongrie.* Budapest, Akadémiai Kiadó.

Gábori-Csánk, V. (1970). C14 Dates of the Hungarian Palaeolithic. *Acta Archaeologica Academiae Scientarúm Hungarica*, 22: 3–11.

Gamble, A. M. (1981). *An Introduction to Modern Social and Political Thought.* London, Macmillan.

Gamble, C. S. (1978a). Resource exploitation and the spatial patterning of hunter-gatherers: a case study. In D. Green, C. Haselgrove and M. Spriggs (eds.) *Social Organisation and Settlement*, 153–85. Oxford, British Archaeological Reports, International Series, 47(i).

Gamble, C. S. (1978b). Animal communities and their relationship to prehistoric economies in Western Europe. Cambridge University, Ph.D. dissertation.

Gamble, C. S. (1979). Hunting strategies in the central European palaeolithic. *Proceedings of the Prehistoric Society*, 45: 35–52.

Gamble, C. S. (1982). Interaction and alliance in palaeolithic society. *Man*, 17: 92–107.

Gamble, C. S. (1983a). Culture and society in the upper palaeolithic of Europe. In G. N. Bailey (ed.) *Hunter-Gatherer Economy in Prehistory*, 201–11. Cambridge, Cambridge University Press.

Gamble, C. S. (1983b). Caves and faunas from last glacial Europe. In J. Clutton-Brock and C. Grigson (eds.) *Animals and Archaeology: 1. Hunters and their Prey*, 163–72. Oxford, British Archaeological Reports, International Series, 163.

Gamble, C. S. (1984a). Regional variation in hunter-gatherer strategy in the upper pleistocene of Europe. In R. Foley (ed.) *Hominid Evolution and Community Ecology*, London, Academic Press.

Gamble, C. S. (1984b). Earliest humans in Europe *and* Subsistence and society in palaeolithic Europe. In T. C. Champion, C. S. Gamble, S. J. Shennan, and A. W. Whittle, *Prehistoric Europe*, 16–87. London, Academic Press.

Gardin, J.-C. (1980). *Archaeological Constructs.* Cambridge, Cambridge University Press.

Gascoyne, M., Currant, A. P., and Lord T. C. (1981). Ipswichian fauna of Victoria Cave and the marine palaeoclimatic record. *Nature*, 294: 652–4.

Gates, W. L. (1976). Modelling the ice-age climate. *Science*, 191: 1138–44.

Gaussen, J. (1980). Le paléolithique supérieur de plein air en Périgord. *Gallia Préhistoire*, Supplément 14.

Gifford, D. P. (1981). Taphonomy and paleoecology: a critical review of archaeology's sister disciplines. In M. B. Schiffer (ed.) *Advances in Archaeological Method and Theory*, 4: 365–438. New York, Academic Press.

Gifford, E. W. (1936). Californian Balanophagy. In R. H. Lowie (ed.) *Essays in Anthropology presented to A. L. Kroeber*, 87–98. Berkeley, University of California Press.

Gilman, A. (1984). Explaining the upper palaeolithic revolution. In M. Spriggs (ed.) *Marxist Perspectives in Archaeology*, 115–26. Cambridge, Cambridge University Press.

Ginter, B. (1974). The extraction, production and distribution of raw material and flint products at the late palaeolithic in the northern part of central Europe (in Polish). *Przegląd Archeologiczny*, 22: 5–122.

Girard, C. (1976). Les civilisations du paléolithique moyen en Basse-Bourgogne (Yonne). In H. de Lumley (ed.) *La Préhistoire Française*, 1115–19. Paris, CNRS.

Girard, C. (1978). Les industries moustériennes de la grotte de l'Hyène à Arcy-sur-Cure (Yonne). *Gallia Préhistoire*, Supplement XI.

Gladfelter, B. G. (1975). Middle pleistocene sedimentary sequences in East Anglia (United Kingdom). In K. W. Butzer and G. L. Isaac (eds.) *After the Australopithecines*, 225–58. The Hague, Mouton.

Gomez-Tabanera, J. M. (1978). *Les Statuettes Féminines Paléolithiques dites 'Vénus'*. Asturias, Love-Gijon.

González-Echegaray, J. (1960). El magdaleniense III de la costa Cantábrica, *Boletín del Seminario de Estudios de Arte y Arqueologiá* (Valladolid), 26: 69–100.

González-Echegaray, J. (1971). Apreciaciones cuantitativas sobre el magdaleniense III de la costa Cantábrica. *Munibe*, 23: 323–7.

González-Echegaray, J., and Freeman, L. G. (1971). *Cueva Morín, Excavaciones 1966–8.* Santander, Publicaciones del patronato de las cuevas prehistóricas de la provincia de Santander, VI.

González-Echegaray, J., and Freeman, L. G. (1973). *Cueva Morín Excavaciones 1969.* Santander, Publicaciones del patronato de las cuevas prehistóricas de la provincia de Santander, X.

González-Echegaray, J., and Freeman, L. G. (1981). La máscara del santuario de la cueva del Juyo. In *Altamira Symposium*, 251–64. Madrid, Ministry of Culture.

Gordon, B. H. C. (1982). Tooth sectioning as an archaeological tool. *National Museum of Man, Canadian Studies Report*, 14e.

Goretsky, G. I., and Ivanova, I. K. (eds.) (1982). *Molodova I. Unique Mousterian Settlement in the middle Dniestr region* (in Russian). Moscow, NAUKA.

Goretsky, G. I., and Tseitlin, S. (eds.) (1977). *The multilayer palaeolithic site Korman IV on the middle Dniestr* (in Russian). Moscow, NAUKA.

Gorjanovic-Kramberger, K. (1906). *Der diluviale Mensch von Krapina in Kroatien.* Wiesbaden.

Gould, R. A. (1967). Notes on hunting, butchering and snaring of game among Ngatatjara and their neighbours in the west Australian desert. *Kroeber Anthropological Society Papers*, 36.

Gould, R. A. (1968). Living archaeology: the Ngatatjara of Western Australia. *Southwestern Journal of Anthropology*, 24: 101–22.

Gould, R. A. (1977). Ethno-archaeology; or, where do models come from? In R. V. S.

Gould, R. A. (1971). The archaeologist as ethnographer: a case from the Western Desert of Australia. *World Archaeology*, 3: 143–77.
Wright (ed.) *Stone Tools as Cultural Markers*, 162–8. Canberra, Australian Institute of Aboriginal Studies.

Gould, R. A. (1980). *Living Archaeology*, Cambridge, Cambridge University Press.

Gould, R. A., Koster, D., and Sontz, A. (1971). The lithic assemblage of the Western Desert Aborigines of Australia. *American Antiquity*, 36: 149–69.

Gould, S. J., and Eldredge, N. (1977). Punctuated equilibria: the tempo and mode of evolution reconsidered. *Paleobiology*, 3: 115–51.

Grahmann, R. (1955). The lower palaeolithic site of Markkleeberg and other comparable localities near Leipzig. *Transactions of the American Philosophical Society*, 45: 509–687.

Grayson, D. K. (1978). Minimum numbers and sample size in vertebrate faunal analysis, *American Antiquity*, 43: 53–65.

Graziosi, P. (1960). *Palaeolithic Art*. London, Faber.

Graziosi, P. (1966). Riparo del Romito (Papasidero, prov. di Cosenza). *Rivista Scienze Preistoriche*, 21: 442.

Green, H. S. (1981). The first Welshman: excavations at Pontnewydd, *Antiquity*, 55: 184–95.

Green, H. S. (ed.) (1984). *Pontnewydd Cave*. Cardiff, National Museum of Wales.

Green, H. S., Stringer, C. B., Collcutt, S. N., Currant, A. P., Huxtable, J., Schwarcz, H. P., Debenham, N., Embleton, C., Bull, P., Molleson, T. I., and Bevins, R. E. (1981). Pontnewydd cave Wales – a new middle pleistocene hominid site. *Nature*, 294: 707–13.

Grichuk, V. P. (1973). Vegetation (in Russian). In *The Palaeogeography of Europe During the Late Pleistocene, Reconstruction and Models*, 182–219. Moscow, NAUK.

Grime, J. P. (1977). Evidence for the existence of three primary strategies in plants and its relevance to ecological and evolutionary theory. *The American Naturalist*, 111: 1169–94.

Grote, K. (1978). Die Grabung 1977 in der mittelpaläolithischen Freilandstation Salzgitter-Lebenstedt. *Archäologisches Korrespondenzblatt*, 8: 155–62.

Guemple, D. L. (1972). Kinship and alliance in Belcher Island Eskimo society. In D. L. Guemple (ed.) Alliance in Eskimo Society, *Proceedings of the American Ethnological Society*, 1971, Supplement, 56–78. Seattle, University of Washington Press.

Günther, K. (1964). *die Altsteinzeitlichen Funde der Balver Höhle*. Bodenaltertümer Westfalens 8.

Guichard, G. (1976). Les civilisations du paléolithique inférieur en Périgord. In H. de Lumley (ed.) *La Préhistoire Française*, 909–28. Paris, CNRS.

Guichard, J. (1976). Les civilisations du paléolithique moyen en Périgord. In H. de Lumley (ed.) *La Préhistoire Française*, 1053–69. Paris, CNRS.

Guth, C. (1974). Découverte dans le Villafranchien d'Auvergne de galets aménagés. *Comptes Rendus de l'Académie des Sciences*, 1071–3.

Guthrie, R. D. (1968). Palaeoecology of the large mammal community in interior Alaska during the late pleistocene. *American Midland Naturalist*, 79: 346–63.

Guthrie, R. D. (1982). Mammals of the mammoth steppe as palaeoenvironmental indicators. In D. M. Hopkins *et al.* (eds.) *Paleoecology of Beringia*, 307–26, New York, Academic Press.

Hahn, J. (1969). Gravettien-Freilandstationen im Rheinland. *Bonner Jahrbücher*, 169: 44–87.

Hahn, J. (1970). Die stellung der männlichen statuette aus dem Hohlenstein-Stadel in der jungpaläolithischen Kunst. *Germania*, 48: 1–2.

Hahn, J. (1972a). Das aurignacien in Mittel- und Osteuropa. *Acta Praehistorica et Archaeologica*, 3: 77–107.

Hahn, J. (1972b). Aurignacian signs, pendants and art objects in central and eastern Europe. *World Archaeology*, 3: 252–66.

Hahn, J. (1974). Die jungpaläolithische station Lommersum, Gemeinde Weilerswist, Kreis Euskirchen. *Rheinische Ausgrabungen*, 15: 1–49.

Hahn, J. (1976a). Das Gravettien im westlichen Mitteleuropa. In B. Klíma (ed.) *Périgordien et Gravettien en Europe*, 100–20. Nice, U.I.S.P.P. Congrès IX, Colloque XV.

Hahn, J. (1976b). Les industries aurignaciennes dans le Bassin du Haut-Danube. In J. Kozlowski (ed.) *L'Aurignacien en Europe*, 10–29. Nice, U.I.S.P.P., Congrès IX, Colloque XVI.

Hahn, J. (1976c). Bericht über die Grabungen 1973 und 1974 in Lommersum, Gemeinde Weilerswist, Kreis Euskirchen. *Bonner Jahrbücher*, 176: 285–98.

Hahn, J. (1976d). Ein Eskimo-Werkzeug-Cache von Banks Island, N.W.T., Kanada. *Polarforschung*, 46: 95–105.

Hahn, J. (1977). *Aurignacien: das ältere Jungpaläolithikum in Mittel-und Osteuropa.* Köln, Fundamenta Reihe A 9.

Hahn, J. (1979a). Elfenbeinplastiken des Aurignacien aus dem Geissenklösterle, Gem. Blaubeuren-Weiler, Alb-Donau-Kreis. *Archäologisches Korrespondenzblatt*, 9: 135–42.

Hahn, J. (1979b). Essai sur l'écologie du Magdalénien dans le Jura souabe. In D. de Sonneville-Bordes (ed.) *La Fin des Temps Glaciaires en Europe*, 203–14. Paris, CNRS.

Hahn, J. (1981a). Abfolge und umwelt der jüngeren altsteinzeit in südwestdeutschland. *Fundberichte aus Baden-Württemberg*, 6: 1–27.

Hahn, J. (1981b). Recherches sur l'art paléolithique depuis 1976. In R. Desbrosse and J. K. Kozlowski (eds.) *Resumen de las Investigaciones de 1976 a 1981*, 77–80. Mexico City, U.I.S.P.P. X Congreso, Comision X.

Hahn, J. (1983). Eiszeitliche Jäger zwischen 35000 und 15000 Jahren vor heute. In H.-J. Müller-Beck (ed.) *Urgeschichte in Baden-Württemberg*, 273-330. Stuttgart, Konrad Theiss.

Hahn, J., von Koenigswald, W., Wagner, E., and Wille, W. (1977). Das Geissenklösterle bei Blaubeuren, Alb-Donau-Kreis. Eine altsteinzeitliche Höhlenstation der mittleren Alb. *Fundberichte aus Baden-Württemberg*, 3: 14–37.

Hahn, J., Müller-Beck, H.-J., and Taute, W. (1973). *Eiszeithöhlen im Lonetal*. Stuttgart, Müller & Gräff.

Hanitzsch, H. (1972). Groitzsch bei Eilenburg. Schlag- und siedlungsplätze der späten Altsteinzeit. Berlin, *Veröffentlichungen der Landesmuseums für Vorgeschichte Dresden*, 12.

Haq, B. U., Berggren, W. A., and van Couvering, J. A. (1977). Corrected age of the Pliocene boundary. *Nature*, 269: 483–8.

Harmon, R. S., Glazek, J., and Nowak, K. (1980). ^{230}Th/^{234}U dating of travertine from the Bilzingsleben archaeological site. *Nature*, 284: 132–5.

Harpending, H. C., and Davis, H. (1977). Some implications for hunter-gatherer ecology derived from the spatial structure of resources. *World Archaeology*, 8: 275–86.

Harris, D. R. (1969). Agricultural systems, ecosystems and the origins of agriculture. In P. J. Ucko and G. W. Dimbleby (eds.) *The Domestication and Exploitation of Plants and Animals*, 3–16. London, Duckworth.

Harrold, F. B. (1980). A comparative analysis of Eurasian palaeolithic burials. *World Archaeology*, 12: 196–211.

Hassan, F. (1975). Determination of the size, density and growth rate of hunting-gathering populations. In S. Polgar (ed.) *Population, Ecology and Social Evolution* 27–53. The Hague, Mouton.

Hawkes, K., and O'Connell, J. F. (1981). Affluent hunters? Some comments in light of the Alyawara case. *American Anthropologist*, 83: 622–6.

Hayden, B. (1979a). *Palaeolithic Reflections*. Canberra, Australian Institute of Aboriginal Studies.

Hayden, B. (ed.) (1979b). *Lithic Use-Wear Analysis*. New York, Academic Press.

Hayden, B. (1980). Comment. *Current Anthropology*, 21: 623–4.

Hayden, B. (1981a). Subsistence and ecological adaptations of modern hunter/gatherers. In R. S. O. Harding and G. Teleki (eds.) *Omnivorous Primates*, 344–421. New York, Columbia University Press.

Hayden, B. (1981b). Research and development in the stone age: technological transitions among hunter-gatherers. *Current Anthropology*, 22: 519–48.

Hayden, B., and Cannon, A. (1982). The corporate group as an archaeological unit. *Journal of Anthropological Archaeology*, 1: 132–58.

Hays, J. D., Imbrie, J., and Shackleton, N. J. (1976). Variations in the Earth's orbit: pacemaker of the ice ages. *Science*, 194: 1121–32.

Heffley, S. (1981). The relationship between northern Athapaskan settlement patterns and resource distribution: an application of Horn's model. In B. Winterhalder and E. A. Smith (eds.) *Hunter-Gatherer Foraging Strategies*, 126–47. Chicago, University of Chicago Press.

Heizer, R. F. (1958). Aboriginal California and Great Basic Cartography, *University of California Archaeology Survey Report*, 41.

Heller, Fl. (1955). Die Fauna. In L. Zotz (ed.) *Das Paläolithikum in den Weinberghöhlen bei Mauern*, 220–307. Bonn, Quartär-Bibliothek, 2.

Heller, Fl. (1972). *Die Zoolithenhöhle bei Burggaillenreuth/Ofr.* Erlangen, Erlangen Forschungen Reihe B – Naturwissenschaften, Band 5.

Helm, J. (1969). Discussion. In D. Damas (ed.) Contributions to anthropology: band societies. *National Museum of Canada Bulletin*, 228: 52.

Hemingway, M. F. (1980). *The Initial Magdelenian in France*. Oxford, British Archaeological Reports, International Series, 90.

Hennig, G. J., Herr, W., Weber, E., Xirotiris, N. I. (1981). ESR-dating of the fossil hominid cranium from Petralona Cave, Greece. *Nature*, 292: 533–6.

Hennig, G. J., Herr, W., Weber, E., and Xirotiris, N.I. (1982). Petralona Cave dating controversy. *Nature*, 299: 280–2.

Henri-Martin, G. (1928). La frise sculptée de l'atelier solutréen du Roc (Charente). *Archives de l'Institut de Paléontologie Humaine*, Mémoire, 5.

Henri-Martin, G. (1957). La Grotte de Fontéchevade. Paris, *Annales Institut Paléontologie Humaine*, Mémoire, 28.

Heptner, V. G., Nasimovič, A. A., and Bannikov, A. G. (1966). *Die Säugetiere der Sowjetunion, Band I, Paarhufer und Unpaarhufer*. Jena, Gustav Fischer.

Hescheler, K., and Kuhn, E. (1949). Die Tierwelt der prähistorischen Siedlungen der Schweiz. In O. Tschumi (ed.) *Urgeschichte der Schweiz*, 1, 121-368. Frauenfeld.

Hiatt, L. R. (1962). Local organization among the Australian aborigines. *Oceania*, 32: 276–86.

Higgs, E. S. (ed.) (1972). *Papers in Economic Prehistory*. Cambridge, Cambridge University Press.

Higgs, E. S. (ed.) (1975). *Palaeoeconomy*. Cambridge, Cambridge University Press.

Higgs, E. S., and Vita-Finzi, C. (1966). The climate, environment and industries of stone age Greece: Part II. *Proceedings of the Prehistoric Society*, 32: 1–29.

Higgs, E. S., Vita-Finzi, C., Harris, D. R., and Fagg, A. E. (1967). The climate, environment and industries of stone age Greece: Part III. *Proceedings of the Prehistoric Society*, 33: 1–29.

Higgs, E. S., and Webley, D. P. (1971). Further information concerning the environment of palaeolithic man in Epirus. *Proceedings of the Prehistoric Society*, 37: 367–80.

Hill, A. (1983). Hyaenas and early hominids. In J. Clutton-Brock and C. Grigson (eds.) *Animals and Archaeology: 1. Hunters and their Prey*, 87–92. Oxford, British Archaeological Reports, International Series, 163.

Hill, J. H. (1978). Language contact systems and human adaptations. *Journal of Anthropological Research*, 34: 1–26.

Hodder, I. (1978). The maintenance of group identities in the Baringo district, Western Kenya. In D. Green, C. Haselgrove and M. Spriggs (eds.) *Social Organisation and Settlement*, 47–73. Oxford, British Archaeological Reports, International Series 47(i).

Hodson, F. R. (1971). Numerical typology and prehistoric archaeology. In F. R. Hodson, D. G. Kendall and P. Tăutu (eds.) *Mathematics in the Archaeological and Historical Sciences*, 30–45. Edinburgh, Edinburgh University Press.

Hole, F., and Flannery, K. V. (1967). The prehistory of south-western Iran: a preliminary report. *Proceedings of the Prehistoric Society*, 33: 147–206.

Holley, G. A., and del Bene, T. A. (1981). An evaluation of Keeley's microwear approach. *Journal of Archaeological Science*, 8: 337–52.

Hookyaas, R. (1963). *The Principle of Uniformity in Geology, Biology and Theology: Natural Law and Divine Miracle*. Leiden, Brill.

Hopkins, D. M., Matthews, J. V., Schweger, C. E., and Young, S. B. (eds.) (1982). *Paleoecology of Beringia*. New York, Academic Press.

Hörmann, K. (1923). Die Petershöhle bei Velden in Mittelfranken. *Abhandlungen der Naturhistorische Gesellschaft zu Nürnberg*, 21: 123–54.

Horn, H. S. (1968). The adaptive significance of colonial nesting in the Brewer's blackbird (*Euphagus cyanocephalus*). *Ecology*, 49: 682–94.

Howell, F. C. (1966). Observations on the earlier phases of the European lower palaeolithic. *American Anthropologist*, 68(2): 88–201.

Hülle, W. (1977). *Die Ilsenhöhle unter Burg Ranis*. New York, Gustav Fischer.

Imbrie, J., and Newell, N. (1964). *Approaches to Paleoecology*, New York, Wiley.

Ingold, T. (1980). *Hunters, Pastoralists and Ranchers*. Cambridge, Cambridge University Press.

Ingold, T. (1981). The hunter and his spear: notes on the cultural mediation of social and ecological systems. In A. Sheridan and G. N. Bailey (eds.) *Economic Archaeology*, 119–30. Oxford, British Archaeological Reports, International Series, 96.

Isaac, G. L. (1971). The diet of early man. *World Archaeology*, 2: 279–98.

Isaac, G. L. (1972). Early phases of human behaviour: models in lower palaeolithic archaeology. In D. L. Clarke (ed.) *Models in Archaeology*, 167–200. London, Methuen.

Isaac, G. L. (1977). Squeezing blood from stones. In R. V. S. Wright (ed.) *Stone Tools as Cultural Markers*, 5–12. Canberra, Australian Institute of Aboriginal Studies.

Isaac, G. L. (1978). The food-sharing behaviour of protohuman hominids. *Scientific American*, 238: 90–118.

Isaac, G. L. (1981a). Stone age visiting cards; approaches to the study of early land use patterns. In I. Hodder, G. L. Isaac, and N. Hammond (eds.) *Pattern of the Past: Studies in Honour of David Clarke*, 131–55. Cambridge, Cambridge University Press.

Isaac, G. L. (1981b). Archaeological tests of alternative models of early hominid behaviour: excavation and experiments. *Philosophical Transactions of the Royal Society of London*, B, 292: 177–88.

Isaac, G. L., and Crader, D. C. (1981). To what extent were early hominids carnivorous? In R. S. O. Harding, and G. Teleki (eds.) *Omnivorous Primates*, 37–103. New York, Columbia University Press.

Ivanova, I. K. (1982). Geology and palaeogeography of Molodova I mousterian settlement (in Russian). In G. I. Goretsky and I. K. Ivanova (eds.) *Molodova I*, 188–235. Moscow, NAUK.

Ivanova, I. K., Bolihovskaja, N. S., and Rengarten, N. V. (1982). Geological age and natural environments of the mousterian site Ketrosy (in Russian). In N. D. Praslov (ed.) *Ketrosy*, 152–61. Moscow, NAUK.

Ivanova, I. K., and Chernysh, A. P. (1965). The palaeolithic site of Molodova V on the middle Dniestr (USSR). *Quaternaria*, 7: 197–217.

Iwanowa, S. (1979). Differentiation of middle palaeolithic cultures in the Balkan peninsula (in Russian). *Arkheologiya*, 21: 1–12

Jacob-Friesen, K. H. (1956). Eiszeitliche Elephantenjäger in der Lüneburger Heide. *Jarbüch des Römisch-Germanischen Zentralmuseums Mainz*, 3: 1–22.

Jacobi, R. M. (1980). The upper palaeolithic in Britain, with special reference to Wales. In J. A. Taylor (ed.) *Culture and Environment in Prehistoric Wales*, 15–99. Oxford, British Archaeological Reports, British Series, 76.

Jacobsen, T. W. (1976). 17,000 years of Greek prehistory. *Scientific American*, 234: 76–87.

Jánossy, D. (1955). Die Vogel- und Säugetierreste der spätpleistozänen Schichten der Höhle von Istállöskö. *Acta Archaeologica Academiae Scientiarúm Hungarica*, 5: 149–81.

Jánossy, D. (1963–4). Letztinterglaciale vertebraten-fauna aus der Kálmán Lambrecht-Höhle (Bükk-Gebirge, Nordost-Ungarn), 2 pts. *Acta Zoologica Academiae Scientifica Hungarica*, 9: 293–331, 10: 139–197.

Janssens, P., González-Echegaray, J., and Azpeitia, P. (1958). *Memoria de las Excavaciones de la Cueva del Juyo (1955–1956)*. Santander, Patronato de las Cuevas Prehistóricas.

Jarman, M. R. (1972). A territorial model for archaeology: a behavioural and geographical approach. In D. L. Clarke (ed.) *Models in Archaeology*, 705–34. London, Methuen.

Jarman, M. R., Bailey, G. N., and Jarman, H. N. (eds.) (1982). *Early European Agriculture*. Cambridge, Cambridge University Press.

Jelinek, A. J. (1977). The lower palaeolithic: current evidence and interpretations. *Annual Review of Anthropology*, 6: 11–32.

Jéquier, J. P. (1975). *Le Moustérien Alpin*. Yverdon, Eburodunum, 2.

Jochim, M. A. (1976). *Hunter-Gatherer Settlement and Subsistence*. New York, Academic Press.

Jochim, M. A. (1981). *Strategies for Survival*. New York, Academic Press.

Jochim, M A. (1983). Palaeolithic cave art in ecological perspective. In G. N. Bailey (ed.) *Hunter-Gatherer Economy in Prehistory*, 212–19. Cambridge, Cambridge University Press.

Johnsen, S. J., Dansgaard, W., Clausen, H. B., and Langway, C. C. (1972). Oxygen isotope profiles through the Antarctic and Greenland ice sheets. *Nature*, 235: 429–34.

Johnson, G. A. (1982). Monitoring complex system integration and boundary phenomena with settlement size data. In S. E. van der Leeuw (ed.) *Archaeological Approaches to the Study of Complexity*, 142–88; comments in discussion, pp. 87–90. Amsterdam, Cingvla 6, University of Amsterdam.

Johnson, R. G. (1960). Models and methods for analysis of the mode of formation of fossil assemblages. *Geological Society of America Bulletin*, 71: 1075–86.

Jones, G. (1979). *Vegetation Productivity*. London, Longman.

Jones, R. (1971). The demography of hunters and farmers in Tasmania. In D. J. Mulvaney and J. Golson (eds.) *Aboriginal Man and Environment in Australia*, 271–87. Canberra, Australian National University Press.

Jones, R. (1977). The Tasmanian paradox. In R.V.S. Wright (ed.) *Stone Tools as Cultural Markers*, 189–204. Canberra, Australian Institute of Aboriginal Studies.

Jones, R. (1979). The fifth continent: problems concerning the human colonization of Australia. *Annual Review of Anthropology*, 8: 445–66.

Judge, W. J. (1973). *Paleoindian Occupation*. Albuquerque, University of New Mexico Press.

Julien, M. (1982). Les harpons magdaléniens. *Gallia Préhistoire*, supplément 17.

Kahlke, H. D. (1975). The macro-faunas of continental Europe during the middle pleistocene: stratigraphic sequence and problems of inter-correlation. In K. W. Butzer and G. L. Isaac (eds.) *After the Australopithecines*, 309–74. The Hague, Mouton.

Kaiser, K. (1960). Klimazeugen des periglazialen Dauerfrostbodens in Mittel- und West Europa. *Eiszeitalter und Gegenwart*, 11: 121–41.

Kantmann, S. (1969). Essai sur la formation du concept du 'type' dans l'étude du paléolithique. *Quartär*, 20: 69–77.

Keeley, L. H. (1974). Technique and methodology in microwear studies: a critical review. *World Archaeology*, 5: 323–36.

Keeley, L. H. (1980). *Experimental Determination of Stone Tool Uses: A Microwear Analysis*. Chicago, University of Chicago Press.

Keeley, L. H. (1981). Reply to Holley and Del Bene. *Journal of Archaeological Science*, 8: 348–52.

Keeley, L. H. (1982). Hafting and retooling: effects on the archaeological record. *American Antiquity*, 47: 798–809.

Keeley, L. H., and Newcomer, M. H. (1977). Microwear analysis of experimental flint tools: a test case. *Journal of Archaeological Science*, 4: 29–62.

Keene, A. S. (1979). Economic optimization models and the study of hunter-gatherer subsistence settlement systems. In C. Renfrew and K. L. Cooke (eds.) *Transformations: Mathematical Approaches to Culture Change*, 369–404. New York, Academic Press.

Keene, A. S. (1981). Optimal foraging in a non-marginal environment: a model of prehistoric subsistence strategies in Michigan. In B. Winterhalder and E. A. Smith (eds.) *Hunter-Gatherer Foraging Strategies*, 171–93. Chicago, University of Chicago Press.

Kelsall, J. P. (1968). *The Migratory Barren-ground Caribou of Canada*. Ottawa: Department of Indian Affairs and Northern Development, Canadian Wildlife Service.

Kiernan, K., Jones, R., and Ranson, D. (1983). New evidence from Fraser Cave for glacial age man in south-west Tasmania. *Nature*, 301: 28–32.

Kintigh, K. W., and Ammerman, A. H. (1982). Heuristic approaches to spatial analysis in archaeology. *American Antiquity*, 47: 31–63.

Kirch, K. V. (1980). The archaeological study of adaptation: theoretical and methodological issues. In M. B. Schiffer (ed.) *Advances in Archaeological Method and Theory*, 3: 101–56.

Kitching, J. W. (1963). *Bone, Tooth and Horn Tools of Palaeolithic Man: An Account of the Osteodontokeratic Discoveries in Pin Hole Cave, Derbyshire*. Manchester, Manchester University Press.

Klein, R. G. (1965). The middle palaeolithic of the Crimea. *Arctic Anthropology*, 3: 34–68.

Klein, R. G. (1969a). *Man and Culture in the Late Pleistocene: A Case Study*. San Francisco, Chandler Publishing Company.

Klein, R. G. (1969b). Mousterian cultures in European Russia. *Science*, 165: 257–65.

Klein, R. G. (1970). The mousterian of European Russia. *Proceedings of the Prehistoric Society*, 25: 77–112.

Klein, R. G. (1973). *Ice-Age Hunters of the Ukraine*. Chicago, University of Chicago Press.

Klein, R. G., Wolf, C., Freeman, L. G., and Allwarden, A. (1981). The use of dental crown heights for constructing age profiles of red deer and similar species in archaeological samples. *Journal of Archaeological Science*, 8: 1–31.

Kleinschmidt, A. (1953). Die zoologischen Funde der Grabung Salzgitter-Lebenstedt, 1952. *Eiszeitalter und Gegenwart*, 3: 166–88.

Klíma, B. (1954). Pavlov, nové paleolitické sídliště na jžní Moravě, *Archeologické Rozhledy* 6: 721–8.

Klíma, B. (1957). Übersicht über die jüngsten paläolithischen Forschungen in Mähren. *Quartär*, 9: 85–130.

Klíma, B. (1959). Výzkum paleolitického sídliště u Pavlova v roce 1956. *Archeologické Rozhledy*, 11: 3–15, 33–7.

Klíma, B. (1963). *Dolní Věstonice*. Prague, Czechoslovak Academy of Sciences.

Klíma, B. (1966). Exploration archéologique de la grotte de Pekárna (Mokrá) près de Brno (Moravie). In J. Filip (ed.). *Investigations Archéologiques en Tchécoslovaquie*. Prague, U.I.S.P.P., VII Congrès.

Klíma, B. (1974). Archeologicky výzkum plošiny přéd jeskyni Pekárnou. *Studie Archeologického ústava ČSAV v Brně*, 2: 3–78.

Klíma, B. (ed.) (1976a). *Périgordien et Gravettien en Europe*. Nice, U.I.S.P.P., IX Congrès, Colloque XV.

Klíma, B. (1976b). Le Pavlovien. In B. Klíma (ed.) *Périgordien et Gravettien en Europe* 128–141. Nice, U.I.S.P.P., IX Congrès, Colloque XV.

Klíma, B. (1981). Der mittlere teil der paläolithischen station bei Dolní Věstonice. *Památky Archeologické*, 62: 5–92.

von Koenigswald, W. (1975). Das pleistozän der Weinberghöhlen bei Mauern (Bayern). *Quartär*, 26: 107–18.

von Koenigswald, W., Müller-Beck, H.-J., and Pressmar, E. (1974). *Die Archäologie und Paläontologie in der Weinberghöhlen bei Mauern (Bayern)*. Tübingen, Archaeologica Venatoria, 3.

Kos, O. (1971). Die Grabung auf dem spätpaläolithischen Station Tisnov in den Jahren 1966 und 1977. *Casopis Moravského Muzea* 56: 9–52.

Kowalski, K. (1959). *Katalog ssaków plejstocenu polski*. Wroclaw, Polska Akademie Nauk.

Kozlowski, J. K. (1961). Bemerkungen über den Stand der paläolithforschung in Polen. *Archaeologia Austriaca*, 30: 118–43.

Kozlowski, J. K. (1971). Les problèmes du magdalénien en Europe centre-est. *Congrès VIII, U.I.S.P.P.*, vol. I, 53–72. Budapest, U.I.S.P.P.

Kozlowski, J. K. (1974). Upper palaeolithic site with dwellings of mammoth bone – Cracow, Spadzista Street B. *Folia Quaternaria*, 44: 1–110.

Kozlowski, J. K. (1975). Studies on the transition from the middle to the upper palaeolithic in the Balkans (in Polish). *Przegląd Archeologiczny*, 23: 5–48.

Kozlowski, J. K. (ed.) (1976a). *L'Aurignacien en Europe*. Nice, U.I.S.P.P., IX Congrès, Colloque XVI.

Kozlowski, J. K. (1976b). Les industries à pointes à cran en Europe Centre-Est. In B. Klíma (ed.) *Périgordien et Gravettien en Europe*, 121–7. Nice, U.I.S.P.P., IX Congrès, Colloque XV.

Kozlowski, J. K. (1979). La fin des temps glaciaires dans le bassin du Danube moyen et inférieur. In D. de Sonneville-Bordes (ed.) *La Fin des Temps Glaciaires en Europe*, 821–36. Paris, CNRS.

Kozlowski, J. K. (ed.) (1982). *Excavation in the Bacho Kiro cave, Bulgaria (Final Report)*. Warsaw, Paristwowe Wydarunictwo, Naukowe.

Kozlowski, J. K., and Kozlowski, S. K. (1979). *Upper Palaeolithic and Mesolithic in Europe: Taxonomy and Palaeohistory*. Warsaw, Polska Akademia Nauk, Prace Komisji, Archeologicznej, 18.

Kozlowski, S. K. (1979). Le paléolithique final entre les Carpartes et l'Oural. In D. de Sonneville-Bordes (ed.) *La Fin des Temps Glaciaires en Europe*, 387–45. Paris, CNRS.

Kozlowski, S. K., and Sachse-Kozlowska, E. (1976). The system of providing flint raw materials in the late palaeolithic in Poland. In *Second International Symposium on Flint, 1975, Maastricht, Staringia*, 3: 66–9.

Kozlowski, S. K., and Sachse-Kozlowska, E. (1980). Slovakian radiolorite in palaeolithic and mesolithic cultures in Poland. In *Third International Symposium on Flint, 1979, Maastricht, Staringia*, 6: 126–9.

Krause, W., and Kollau, W. (1943). Die steinzeitlichen Wirbeltierfaunen von Stellmoor in Holstein. In A. L. Rust, *Die Alt- und Mittelsteinzeitlichen Funde von Stellmoor*, 49–59. Neumünster, Karl Wachholz.

Kretzoi, M. (1968). Zoologie archéologique. In V. Gábori-Csánk (ed.), *La Station du Paléolithique moyen d'Érd*, 230. Budapest, Kiadó.

Kretzoi, M., and Vértes, L. (1965). Upper Biharian (intermindel) pebble-industry site in western Hungary. *Current Anthropology*, 6: 74–87.

Kristiansen, K. (1981). A social history of Danish archaeology. In G. Daniel (ed.) *Towards a History of Archaeology*, 20–44. London, Thames and Hudson.

Kroeber, A. L. (1922). Elements of culture in native California. *University of California Publications in American Archaeology and Ethnology*, 13: 260–328.

Kroeber, A. L. (1925). *Handbook of the Indians of California*, Washington, D.C., U.S. Government Printing Office.

Kruuk, H. (1972). *The Spotted Hyena*. Chicago, Aldine.

Kruuk, H., and Turner, M. (1967). Comparative notes on predation by lion, leopard, cheetah and wild dog in the Serengeti area, East Africa. *Mammalia*, 31: 1–27.

Kukla, G. J. (1975). Loess stratigraphy of central Europe. In K. W. Butzer and G. L. Isaac, (eds.), *After the Australopithecines*, 99–188. The Hague, Mouton.

Kukla, G. J. (1977). Pleistocene land-sea correlations, 1. Europe. *Earth Science Review*, 13: 307–74.

Kukla, G., and Briskin, M. (1983). The age of the 4/5 isotopic stage boundary on land and in the oceans. *Palaeogeography, Palaeoclimatology, Palaeoecology*, 42: 35–45.

Kurtén, B. (1968). *Pleistocene Mammals of Europe*. London, Weidenfeld and Nicolson.

Kuznetsova, L. V. (1982). Early palaeolithic of the Russian plains. Moscow, paper delivered at the XI INQUA Congres.

Lais, R. (1941). Uber Höhlensedimente. *Quartär*, 3: 56–108.

Lalanne, G., and Breuil, H. (1911). L'abri sculpté du Cap-Blanc à Laussel (Dordogne). *L'Anthropologie*, 22: 385–402.

Lalanne, J. G., and Bouyssonie, J. (1941–6). Le gisement paléolithique de Laussel. *L'Anthropologie*, 50: 1–163.

Lamb, H. H., and Woodruffe, A. (1970). Atmospheric circulation during the last ice age. *Quaternary Research*, 1: 29–58.

Laming-Emperaire, A. (1962). *La signification de l'art rupestre paléolithique*. Paris.

Laplace, G. (1961). Recherches sur l'origine et l'évolution des complexes leptolithiques. *Quaternaria*, 5: 153–240.

Laplace, G. (1964). Les subdivisions du leptolithique italien (étude de typologie analytique). *Bulletino di Paletnologia Italiana*, 15: 25–63.

Laplace, G. (1966). Recherches sur l'origine et l'évolution des complexes leptolithiques. *Ecole Française de Rome, Mélanges d'Archéologie et d'Histoire*, 4.

Laplace, G. (1970). L'industrie de Krems Hundssteig et le problème de l'origine des complexes aurignaciens. In *Frühe Menschheit und Umwelt*, 242–97. Köln, Fundamenta Reihe, A2.

Laplace, G., and Merino, J. M. (1979). Application de la typologie analytique et structurale à étude du 'Processus d'Azilianisation': la série phylétique de la grotte Urtiaga en Pays Basque. In D. de Sonneville-Bordes (ed.) *La Fin des Temps Glaciaires en Europe*, 693–709. Paris, CNRS.

Lartet, E., and Christy, H. (1865–75). *Reliquiae Aquitanicae, being contributions to the archaeology and palaeontology of Périgord and the adjoining provinces of Southern France*. London.

Laville, H. (1975). *Climatologie et chronologie du Paléolithique en Périgord: Étude sédimentologique de dépots en grottes et sous abris*. Université de Provence, Mémoire No. 4, Études Quaternaires.

Laville, H. (1976). Les remplissages de grottes et abris sous roche dans le Sud-Ouest. In H. de Lumley (ed.), *La Préhistoire Française*, 250–70. Paris, CNRS.

Laville, H. (1982). On the transition from 'lower' to 'middle' palaeolithic in south-west France. In A. Ronen (ed.) *The Transition from Lower to Middle Palaeolithic and the Origin of Modern Man*, 131–5. Oxford, British Archaeological Reports, International Series, 151.

Laville, H., and Renault-Miskovsky, J. (eds.) (1977). *Approche écologique de l'homme fossile*. Paris, Supplément au Bulletin de l'Association Française.

Laville, H. and Rigaud, J.-P. (1973). The Perigordian V industries in Périgord. Typological variations, stratigraphy and relative chronology. *World Archaeology* 4: 330–38.

Laville, H., Rigaud, J.-P., and Sackett, J. R. (1980). *Rock Shelters of the Périgord*, New York, Academic Press.

Laville, H., and de Sonneville-Bordes, D. (1967). Sédimentologie des niveaux moustériens et aurignaciens de Caminade-Est (Dordogne). *Bulletin de la Société Préhistorique Française*, 64: 35–52.

Leacock, E. (1954). The Montagnais 'hunting territory' and the fur trade, *Memoirs of the American Anthropological Association*, 78.

Leacock, E. (1969). The Montagnais-Naskapi band. In D. Damas (ed.) Contributions to anthropology: band societies. *National Museums of Canada Bulletin*, 228: 1–17.

Leacock, E., and Lee, R. B. (eds.) (1982). *Politics and History in Band Societies,.* Cambridge, Cambridge University Press.

Lee, R. B. (1968). What hunters do for a living, or how to make out on scarce resources. In R. B. Lee and I. DeVore (eds.) *Man the Hunter*, 30–48. Chicago, Aldine.

Lee, R. B. (1969). !Kung bushmen subsistence: an input-output analysis. In A. P. Vayda (ed.) *Environment and Cultural Behaviour*, 47–79. New York, Natural History Press.

Lee, R. B. (1972). The !Kung bushmen of Botswana. In M. G. Bicchieri (ed.) *Hunters and Gatherers Today*, 327–68. New York, Holt, Rinehart and Winston.

Lee, R. B. (1976). !Kung spatial organisation. In R. B. Lee, and I. DeVore (eds.) *Kalahari Hunter-Gatherers*, 73–97. Cambridge, Mass., Harvard University Press.

Lee, R. B. (1979). *The !Kung San: Men, Women and Work in a Foraging Society*. Cambridge, Cambridge University Press.

Lee, R. B., and DeVore, I. (eds.) (1968a). *Man the Hunter*. Chicago, Aldine.

Lee, R. B., and DeVore, I. (1968b). Problems in the study of hunter-gatherers. In R. B. Lee and I. DeVore (eds.) *Man the Hunter*, 3–12. Chicago, Aldine.

Lee, R. B., and DeVore, I. (eds.) (1976). *Kalahari Hunter-Gatherers*. Cambridge, Mass., Harvard University Press.

Legge, A. J. (1972). Cave climates. In E. S. Higgs (ed.) *Papers in Economic Prehistory*, 97–103. Cambridge, Cambridge University Press.

Lenoir, M. (1975). Style et technologie lithique. *Bulletin de la Société Préhistorique Française*, 74: 46–9.

Leonardi, P. (1976). Acheuléen et industries apparentées de la côte adriatique italienne (Vénétie, Romagne, Marches). In J. Combier (ed.) *L'Évolution de l'Acheuléen en Europe*, 66–85. Nice, U.I.S.P.P., Congrès IX, Colloque X.

Leonardi, P., and Broglio, A. (1962). *Le paléolithique de la Vénétie*. Ferrara, Annali dell'Universita di Ferrara.

Leroi-Gourhan, A. (1961). Les fouilles d'Arcy-sur-Cure (Yonne). *Gallia Préhistoire*, 4: 1–16.

Leroi-Gourhan, A. (1968). *The Art of Prehistoric Man in Western Europe*. London, Thames and Hudson.

Leroi-Gourhan, A. (1982). *The Dawn of European Art*. Cambridge, Cambridge University Press.

Leroi-Gourhan, A. and Arl. (1964). Chronologie des grottes d'Arcy-sur-Cure (Yonne). *Gallia Préhistoire*, 7: 1–64.

Leroi-Gourhan, A., and Brézillon, M. (1966). L'habitation magdalénienne No. I de Pincevent (Seine-et-Marne). *Gallia Préhistoire*, 9: 263–385.

Leroi-Gourhan, A., and Brézillon, M. (1972). Fouilles de Pincevent: essai d'analyse ethnographique d'un habitat magdalénien. *Gallia Préhistoire*, supplément 7.

Leroi-Gourhan, A., Brézillon, M., and Schmider, B. (1976). Les civilisations du paléolithique supérieur dans le centre et le sud-est du Bassin parisien. In H. de Lumley (ed.) *La Préhistoire Française*, 1321–38. Paris, CNRS.

Leroi-Gourhan, Arl. (1980). Les interstades du Würm supérieur. In J. Chaline (ed.) *Problèmes de Stratigraphie Quaternaire en France et dans les Pays Limitrophes*, 192–4. Dijon, Association Française pour l'Etude du Quaternaire.

Leroi-Gourhan, Arl, and Allain, J. (1979). Lascaux Inconnu. *Gallia Préhistoire*, supplément 12.

Leroy-Prost, C. (1974). Les pointes en matière osseuse de l'Aurignacien. *Bulletin de la Société Préhistorique Française*, 71: 449–58.

Letocart, L. (1970). Un gisement du paléolithique final à Obourg 'St Macaire' Hainault. In *Frühe Menschheit und Umwelt*, 352–61. Köln, Fundamenta Reihe, A/2.

Lévêque, F., and Vandermeersch, B. (1980). Les découvertes de restes humains dans un horizon castelperronien de Saint-Césaire (Charente-Maritime). *Bulletin de la Société Préhistorique Française*, 77: 35.

Lieberman, P. (1976). Interactive models for evolution: neural mechanisms, anatomy, and behaviour. In S. Harnad, H. D. Steklis, J. Lancaster (eds.) Origins and evolution of language and speech. *Annals of the New York Academy of Sciences*, 280: 660–72.

Lieberman, P., and Crelin, E. S. (1971). On the speech of Neanderthal man. *Linguistic Inquiry*, 11: 203–22.

Lieth, H., and Whittaker, R. H. (1975). *Primary Productivity of the Biosphere*. Berlin, Springer.

Lockwood, J. G. (1974). *World Climatology*. London, Edward Arnold.

Loubine, V. P. (1980). *Kudaro* (in Russian). Moscow, NAUK.

Loubine, V. P. (1981). L'Acheuléen de la partie Européenne de l'U.R.S.S. et du Caucase (matériaux et quelques problèmes). *Anthropologie*, 19: 33–46.

Lourandos, H. (1983). Intensification: a late pleistocene–holocene archaeological sequence from south-western Victoria. *Archaeology in Oceania* 18: 81–94.

Luchterhand, K. (1978). Late cenozoic climate, mammalia, evolutionary patterns, and middle pleistocene human adaptation in Eastern Asia. In L. G. Freeman (ed.) *Views of the Past*. The Hague, Mouton.

de Lumley, H. (1965). La grande révolution raciale et culturelle de l'Inter-Würmien II-III. *Cahiers Ligures de Préhistoire et d'Archéologie*, 14 (2 ème partie).

de Lumley, H. (1969a). A paleolithic camp site at Nice. *Scientific American*, 220: 42–50.

de Lumley, H. (1969b). Le paléolithique inférieur et moyen du Midi méditerranéen dans son cadre géologique, 1. Ligurie-Provence. *Gallia Préhistoire*, supplément 5.

de Lumley, H. (1969c). *Une cabane acheuléenne dans la Grotte du Lazaret*. Paris, Mémoires de la Société Préhistorique Française, 7.

de Lumley, H. (1971). Le paléolithique inférieur et moyen du Midi méditerranéen dans son cadre géologique, 2. Bas Languedoc Roussillon-Catalogne. *Gallia Préhistoire*, supplément 5.

de Lumley, H. (1972). *La Grotte Moustérienne de l'Hortus*. Marseille, Études Quaternaires, 1.

de Lumley, H. (1975). Cultural evolution in France in its palaeoecological setting during the middle pleistocene. In K. W. Butzer and G. L. Isaac (eds.) *After the Australopithecines*, 745–808. The Hague, Mouton.

de Lumley, H. (ed.) (1976a). *La Préhistoire Française*, 1. Paris, CNRS.

de Lumley, H. (1976b). Introduction. In H. de Lumley (ed.) *La Préhistoire Française*, 1: xv-xvi. Paris, CNRS.

de Lumley, H. (1976c). Les civilisations du paléolithique moyen en Languedoc méditerranéen et en Roussillon. In H. de Lumley (ed.) *La Préhistoire Française*, 1: 1005–26. Paris, CNRS.

de Lumley, H. (1976d). Les premières industries humaines en Provence. In H. de Lumley (ed.) *La Préhistoire Française*, 1: 765–76. Paris, CNRS.

de Lumley, H. (1976e). Les civilisations du paléolithique inférieur en Provence. In H. de Lumley (ed.) *La Préhistoire Française*, 1: 819–51. Paris, CNRS.

de Lumley, H. (1976f). Les civilisations du paléolithique inférieur en Languedoc méditerranéen et en Roussillon. In H. de Lumley (ed.) *La Préhistoire Française*, 1: 852–74. Paris, CNRS.

de Lumley, H. and Boone, Y. (1976a). Les structures d'habitat au paléolithique moyen. In H. de Lumley (ed.) *La Préhistoire Française*, 1: 644–55. Paris, CNRS.

de Lumley, H., and Boone, Y. (1976b). Les structures d'habitat au paléolithique inférieur. In H. de Lumley (ed.) *La Préhistoire Française*, 1: 625–43. Paris, CNRS.

de Lumley, H., and Bottet, B. (1961). Pointes foliacées moustériennes dans le Midi de la France (Baume Bonne, Quinson, Basses-Alpes). *Gallia Préhistoire*, 4: 165–74.

de Lumley, M.-A. (1973). Anténéandertaliens et néandertaliens du bassin méditerranéen occidental, *Études Quaternaires*, 2. Paris, CNRS.

de Lumley, M.-A. (1976a). Les anténéandertaliens dans le Sud. In H. de Lumley (ed.) *La Préhistoire Française*, 1: 547–60. Paris, CNRS.

de Lumley, M.-A. (1976b). Les néandertaliens dans le Midi méditerranéen. In H. de Lumley (ed.) *La Préhistoire Française*, 1: 567–77. Paris, CNRS.

Luttropp, A., and Bosinski, G. (1971). *Der altsteinzeitliche Fundplatz Reutersruh bei Ziegenhain in Hessen*. Köln, Fundamenta Reihe, A/6.

Lynch, T. F. (1966). The 'Lower Perigordian' in French archaeology. *Proceedings of the Prehistoric Society*, 32: 156–98.

Mace, A. (1959). An upper palaeolithic open-site at Hengistbury Head, Christchurch, Hants. *Proceedings of the Prehistoric Society*, 25: 233–59.

Magi, M. (1973). Industria di 'facies' aurignaziana rinvenuta a nord di Armailo (Rapolano-Terme-Siena). *Rivista Scienze Preistoriche*, 28: 377–408.

Maglio, V. J. (1975). Pleistocene faunal evolution in Africa and Eurasia. In K. W. Butzer and G. L. Isaac (eds.) *After the Australopithecines*, 419–76. The Hague, Mouton.

Malez, M. (1958–9). Das paläolithikum der Veternicahöhle und der Bärenkult. *Quartär*, 10/11: 171–88.

Malez, M. (1976). Excavation of the villafranchian site Sandalja I near Pula (Yugoslavia). In K. Valoch (ed.) *Les Premières Industries de l'Europe*, 104–23. Nice, U.I.S.P.P., Congrès IX, Colloque VIII.

Malez, M. (1979). Position des couches de la grotte Vindija dans la séquence du quaternaire du Piémont alpin (in Serbo-Croat). *RAD Jugoslavenske Akademije Znanosti i Umjetnosti*, 383: 187–218.

Malina, J. (1970). Die jungpaläolithische steinindustrie aus Mähren, ihre Rohstoffe und ihre Patina. *Acta Praehistorica et Archaeologica*, 1: 157–73.

Mangerud, J., Sønstegaard, E., and Sejrup, H.-P. (1979). Correlation of the Eemian (interglacial) stage and the deep-sea oxygen-isotope stratigraphy. *Nature*, 277: 189–92.

Mania, D. (1975). Bilzingsleben (Thüringen): eine neue altpaläolithische fundstelle mit knochenreste des *Homo erectus*. *Archäologisches Korrespondenzblatt*, 5: 263–72.

Mania, D. (1978). *Homo erectus* von Bilzingsleben, Kreis Arten, und seine kultur. *Jahreschrift Mitteldeutsches Vorgeschichte*, 62: 51–86.

Mania, D., and Baumann, W. (1980). Neufunde des acheuléen von Markkleeberg bei Leipzig (DDR). *Anthropologie*, 18: 237–48.

Mania, D., and Dietzel, A. (1980). *Begegnung mit dem Urmensch*. Leipzig, Urania.

Mania, D., and Toepfer, V. (1973). *Königsaue*. Berlin, Veröffentlichungen des Landesmuseums für Vorgeschichte in Halle, Band 26.

Mania, D., Toepfer, V., and Vlček, E. (1980). *Bilzingsleben* I. Berlin, Veröffentlichungen des Landesmuseums für Vorgeschichte in Halle, Band 32.

Mankinen, E. A., and Dalrymple, G. B. (1979). Revised geomagnetic polarity time scale for the interval 0–5 m.y. BP. *Journal of Geophysical Research*, 84: 615–26.

Marks, A. E. (ed.) (1977). *Prehistory and Paleoenvironments in the Central Negev, Israel*, vol. 2. Dallas, Southern Methodist University.

Marks, S. A. (1976). *Large Mammals and a Brave People*. Seattle, University of Washington.

Marquet, J.-C. (1975). Un atelier magdalénien à Bénagu, commune de Chaumussay (Indre-et-Loire). *Bulletin de la Société Préhistorique Française*, 72: 309–18.

Marr, J. E., Moir, J. R., and Smith, R. A. (1921). Excavations at High Lodge, Mildenhall, in 1920 A.D. *Proceedings of the Prehistoric Society of East Anglia*, 3: 353–79.

Marshack, A. (1972). *The Roots of Civilisation*. New York, McGraw-Hill.

Mauss, M. (1906). Essai sur les variations saisonnières des sociétés Eskimos: étude de morphologie sociale. *L'Année Sociologique*, 9: 39–132 (English translation, 1979, London, Routledge and Kegan Paul).

Maviglia, C. (1940). Scheletri umani del paleolitico superiore rinvenuti nella Grotta di San Teodoro (Messina). *Archeologica Antropologica Etnologica*, 70: 94–104.

Mech, L. D. (1970). *The Wolf*. New York, Natural History Press.

Meillassoux, C. (1972). From reproduction to production: Marxist approach to economic anthropology. *Economy and Society*, 1: 93–105.

Meillassoux, C. (1973). On the mode of production of the hunting band. In P. Alexandre (ed.) *French Perspectives in African Studies*, 187–203. London, Oxford University Press.

Meldgaard, M. (1983). Resource fluctuation and human subsistence: a zoo-archaeological and ethnographical investigation of a West Greenland caribou hunting group. In J. Clutton-Brock and C. Grigson (eds.) *Animals and Archaeology: 1. Hunters and their Prey*, 259–72. Oxford, British Archaeological Reports, International Series, 163.

Mellars, P. (1964). The middle palaeolithic surface artifacts at Kokkinopilos. In S. I. Dakaris (*et al.*) The climate, environment and industries of stone age Greece, Part 1, 229–35. *Proceedings of the Prehistoric Society*, 30: 199–244.

Mellars, P. A. (1967). The mousterian succession in S.-W. France. Cambridge University, Ph.D. dissertation.

Mellars, P. A. (1969). The chronology of mousterian industries in the Périgord region of south-west France. *Proceedings of the Prehistoric Society*, 35: 134–71.

Mellars, P. A. (1970). Some comments on the notion of 'functional variability' in stone-tool assemblages. *World Archaeology*, 2: 74–89.

Mellars, P. A. (1973). The character of the middle-upper palaeolithic transition in south-west France. In C. Renfrew (ed.) *The Explanation of Culture Change: Models in Prehistory*, 255–76. London, Duckworth.

Mészáros, G. Y., and Vértes, L. (1955). A point mine from the early upper palaeolithic age near Lovas (Hungary, county Veszprém). *Acta Archaeologica Academiae Scientiarúm Hungarica*, 5: 1–34.

Mezzena, F., and Palma di Cesnola, A. (1972). Scoperta di una sepoltura gravettiana nella Grotta Paglicci (Rignano Garganico). *Rivista Scienze Preistoriche*, 27: 27–50.

Milisauskas, S. (1978). *European Prehistory*. London, Academic Press.

Miscovsky, J.-C. (1976). Le pléistocène du midi méditerranéen (Provence et Languedoc), d'après les remplissages de grottes et abris sous roche. In H. de Lumley (ed.) *La Préhistoire Française*, 201–24. Paris, CNRS.

Mogoşanu, F. (1976). L'aurignacien du Banat. In J. K. Kozlowski (ed.) *L'Aurignacien en Europe*, 75–97. Nice, U.I.S.P.P., Congrès IX, colloque XVI.

Mogoşanu, F. (1978). *Paleoliticul din Banat*. Bucureşti, Academei Republicae Socialae Rômâniei.

Mohr, E. (1971). *The Asiatic Wild Horse: Equus Przevalskii* (Poliakoff, 1881). London, J. A. Allen.

Monnier, J.-L. (1980). *Le Paléolithique de la Bretagne dans son cadre géologique*. Rennes, Travail Laboratoire Anthropologie-Préhistoire-Protohistoire et Quaternaire Armoricains.

Monnier, J.-L. (1982). Le gisement paléolithique supérieur de Plassen-al-Lomm, Ile de Bréhat (Côtes-du-Nord). *Gallia Préhistoire*, 25: 131–65.

Montet-White, A. (1979). Ensembles d'outils et structures latentes dans un site gravettien en Yougoslavie. In D. de Sonneville-Bordes (ed.) *La Fin des Temps Glaciaires en Europe*, 357–64. Paris, CNRS.

Montet-White, A. (1981). Yugoslavie. In R. Desbrosse and J. K. Kozlowski (eds.) *Resumen de las Investigaciones de 1976 a 1981*, 39–41. Mexico City, U.I.S.P.P., X Congreso, Comision X.

Montet-White, A., and Basler, D. (1977). L'industrie gravettienne de Kadar en Bosnie du Nord (Yugoslavie). *Bulletin de la Société Préhistorique*, 74: 531–44.

Moore, J. A. (1981). The effects of information networks in hunter-gatherer societies. In B. Winterhalder and E. A. Smith (eds.) *Hunter-Gatherer Foraging Strategies*, 194–217, Chicago, University of Chicago Press.

Morgan, L. H. (1877). *Ancient Society*. New York, World Publishing.

Morgan, L. H. (1965). *Houses and House-Life of the American Aborigines* (first published 1881). Chicago, University of Chicago Press.

Morphy, H. (1977). Schematisation, meaning and communication in *toas*. In P. J. Ucko (ed.) *Form in Indigenous Art*, 77–89. London, Duckworth.

Morrison, A. (1980). *Early Man in Britain and Ireland*. London, Croom Helm.

Mottl, M. (1941). Die interglacial and interstadial-zeiten im lichte der Ungarischen Säugetierfaunas. *Mitteilungen aus dem Jahrbüche der Kgl. Ungar, Geologischen Anstalt*, 35: 1–33.

Moure-Romanillo, J. A. (1975). *Excavaciones en la cueva de 'Tito Bustillo' (Asturias): Campañas de 1972 y 1974*. Oviedo, Instituto de Estudios Asturianos.

Moure-Romanillo, J. A., and Cano Herrera, M. (1976). *Excavaciones en la Cueva de 'Tito Bustillo' (Asturias): Trabajos de 1975*. Oviedo, Instituto de Estudios Asturianos.

Movius, H. L. (1966). The hearths of the upper perigordian and aurignacian horizons at the Abri Pataud, Les Eyzies (Dordogne), and their possible significance. *American Anthropologist*, 68(2): 296–325.

Movius, H. L. (1969). The châtelperronien in French archaeology: the evidence of Arcy-sur-Cure. *Antiquity*, 43: 111–23.

Movius, H. L. (1973). Quelques commentaires supplémentaires sur les sagaies d'Isturitz: données de l'Abri Pataud, Les Eyzies (Dordogne). *Bulletin de la Société Préhistorique Française*, 70: 85–9.

Movius, H. L. (1974). The Abri Pataud program of the French upper palaeolithic in retrospect. In G. R. Willey (ed.) *Archaeological Researches in Retrospect*, 87–116, Cambridge, Winthrop.

Movius, H. L. (ed.) (1975). *Excavation of the Abri Pataud, Les Eyzies (Dordogne)*. American School of Prehistoric Research, Bulletin 30. Cambridge, Peabody Museum Press.

Movius, H. L. (ed.) (1977). *Excavation of the Abri Pataud, Les Eyzies (Dordogne): Stratigraphy*. American School of Prehistoric Research, Bulletin 31. Cambridge, Peabody Museum Press.

Mueller, J. W. (ed.) (1975). *Sampling in Archaeology*. Tucson, University of Arizona Press.

Müller-Beck, H.-J. (1957). *Das Obere Altpaläolithikum in Suddeutschland*, 1. Bonn, Habelt.

Müller-Beck, H.-J. (1968a). A possible source for the Vogelherd aurignacian. *Arctic Anthropology*, 5: 48–61.

Müller-Beck, H.-J. (1968b). *Die Ältere und Mittlere Steinzeit*. Basel, Ur- und Frühgeschichtliche Archäologie der Schweiz, Band 1.

Müller-Beck, H.-J. (1973a). Weinberghöhlen (Mauern) und Speckberg (Meilenhofen), 1964–1972. In H. Müller-Beck (ed.) *Neue paläolithische und mesolithische Ausgrabungen in der Bundesrepublik Deutschland*, 29–36. Tübingen, zum 9, INQUA-Kongress.

Müller-Beck, H.-J. (ed.) (1973b). *Neue paläolithische und mesolithische Ausgrabungen in der Bundesrepublik Deutschland*. Tübingen, zum 9, INQUA-Kongress.

Müller-Beck, H-J. (1974). Die pleistozänen Sedimente und ihre archäologischen Einschlüsse in dem Weinberghöhlen bei Mauern. In W. von Koenigswald, H.-J. Müller-Beck and E. Pressmar, *Die Archäologie und Paläontologie in der Weinberghöhlen bei Mauern (Bayern)*, 17–51. Tübingen, Archaeologica Venatoria, 3.

Müller-Beck, H.-J. (1982). Late pleistocene man in northern Alaska and the mammoth-steppe biome. In D. M. Hopkins *et al.* (eds.), *Palaeoecology of Beringia*, 329–52. New York, Academic Press.

Müller-Karpe, H. (1966). *Handbuch der Vorgeschichte*, Band I. München, C. H. Beck'sche.

Mulvaney, D. J. (1976). 'The chain of connection': the material evidence. In N. Peterson (ed.) *Tribes and Boundaries in Australia*, 72–94. Canberra, Australian Institute of Aboriginal Studies.

Murdock, G. P. (1967). Ethnographic atlas; a summary. *Ethnology*, 6: 109–236.

Murphy, R. F., and Steward, J. H. (1956). Tappers and trappers: parallel processes in acculturation. *Economic Development and Culture Change*, 4: 335–55.

Musil, R. (1965). Die Barenhöhle Pod hradem. Die Entwicklung des Höhlenbären in Letzen Glazial. *Anthropos*, 18: 8–92.

Musil, R. (1980–1). *Ursus spelaeus. Der Höhlenbär*, 3 vols. Weimar, Museum für Ur- und Frühgeschichte Thüringens.

Musil, R., and Valoch, K. (1968). Stránská skála: its meaning for pleistocene studies. *Current Anthropology*, 9: 534–9.

McBurney, C. B. M. (1950). The geographical study of the older palaeolithic stages in Europe. *Proceedings of the Prehistoric Society*, 16: 163–83.

McBurney, C. B. M. (1967). *The Haua Fteah (Cyrenaica) and the Stone Age of the South-East Mediterranean*. Cambridge, Cambridge University Press.

McBurney, C. B. M. (1968). The cave of Ali Tappeh and the epi-palaeolithic of Iran. *Proceedings of the Prehistoric Society*, 23: 385–413.

McBurney, C. B. M. (1973). Measurable long term variations in some old stone age sequences. In C. Renfrew (ed.) *The Explanation of Culture Change: Models in Prehistory*, 305–15. London, Duckworth.

McBurney, C. B. M. (1976). *Early Man in the Soviet Union*. London, British Academy, Oxford University Press.

McBurney, C. B. M., and Callow, P. (1971). The Cambridge excavations at La Cotte de St Brelade, Jersey – a preliminary report. *Proceedings of the Prehistoric Society*, 37: 167–207.

McCartney, A. P., and Scholtz, S. C. (1977). Silmiut houses: to cluster or not to cluster. *Arctic Anthropology*, 21: 109–19.

McCoy, F. W. (1980). Climatic change in the Eastern Mediterranean area during the past 240,000 years. In C. Doumas (ed) *Thera and the Aegean World*, 2: 79–100. London, Thera and the Aegean World.

McNaughton, S. J., and Wolf, L. L. (1970). Dominance and niche in ecological systems. *Science*, 167: 131–9.

Naroll, R. S. (1962). Floor area and settlement populations. *American Antiquity*, 27: 587–9.

Nelson, R. K. (1969). *Hunters of the Northern Ice*. Chicago, University of Chicago Press.

Nelson, R. K. (1973). *Hunters of the Northern Forest*. Chicago, University of Chicago Press.

Newcomer, M. H. (1971). Some quantitative experiments in handaxe manufacture. *World Archaeology*, 3: 85–94.

Newcomer, M. H. (1974). Study and replication of bone tools from Ksar Akil (Lebanon). *World Archaeology*, 6: 138–53.

Newcomer, M. H. (1976). Spontaneous retouch. In *Second International Symposium on Flint*, 1975, Maastricht. *Staringia*, 3: 62–4.

Newcomer, M. H., and Sieveking, G. de G. (1980). Experimental flake scatter-patterns: a new interpretative technique. *Journal of Field Archaeology*, 7: 345–52.

Newell, R. R., and Dekin, A. A. (1978). An integrative strategy for the definition of behaviourally meaningful archaeological units. *Palaeohistoria*, 20: 7–38.

Nicolăescu-Plopşor, C. S., Păunescu, A. L., and Mogoşanu, F. (1966). Paléolithique du Ceahlău. *Dacia*, 10: 5–116.

Ninkovitch, D., and Shackleton, N. J. (1975). Distribution, stratigraphic position and age of ash layer 'L' in the Panama basin region. *Earth Planet Science Letter*, 27: 20–34.

Nougier, L.-R., and Robert, R. (1958). *The Cave of Rouffignac*. London, George Newnes.

Oakley, K. P. (1969). *Frameworks for Dating Fossil Man*, 3rd edn. London, Weidenfeld and Nicolson.

Oakley, K. P., Andrews, P., Keeley, L. H., and Clark, J. D. (1977). A reappraisal of the Clacton spearpoint. *Proceedings of the Prehistoric Society*, 43: 13–30.

Oakley, K. P., Campbell, B. G., and Molleson, T. I. (1971). *Catalogue of Fossil Hominids: 2. Europe*. London, British Museum (Natural History).

Oberg, K. (1973). *The Social Economy of the Tlingit Indians*. Seattle, University of Washington Press, American Ethnological Society Monograph 55.

Obermaier, H. (1924). *Fossil Man in Spain*. New Haven, Yale University Press.

Odell, G. H. (1975). Micro-wear in perspective: a sympathetic response to Lawrence H. Keeley, *World Archaeology*, 7: 226–40.

Odell, G. H., and Odell-Vereecken, F. (1980). Verifying the relationship of lithic use-wear assessments by 'blind tests': the low-power approach. *Journal of Field Archaeology*, 7: 87–120.

Ohel, M. Y. (1977). On the clactonian: reexamined, redefined and reinterpreted. *Current Anthropology*, 18: 329–31.

Ohel, M. Y. (1979). The clactonian: an independent complex or an integral part of the acheulian? *Current Anthropology*, 20: 685–726.

Ohel, M. Y., and Lechevalier, C. (1979). The 'clactonian' of Le Havre and its bearing on the English clactonian. *Quartär*, 29/30: 85–103.

Okladnikov, A. P. (ed.) (1957). *Paléolithique et néolithique de l'U.R.S.S.* Gap, Louis Jean.

Oliva, M. (1979). Die Herkunft des szeletian im Lichte neuer funde von Jezeřany. *Casopis Moravského Musea*, 64: 45–78.

Onoratini, G. (1978). Un nouveau type de pointe à cran: la pointe de la Bouverie dans le complexe général des pointes à cran. *Bulletin de la Société Préhistorique Française*, 75: 522–42.

Osborn, A. J. (1977). Strandloopers, mermaids and other fairy tales: ecological determinants of marine resource utilization – the Peruvian case. In L. R. Binford (ed.) *For Theory Building in Archaeology*, 157–205. New York, Academic Press.

Osgood, C. (1940). *Ingalik Material Culture*. New Haven, Yale University Press.

Osole, F. (1962–3). Mlajši paleolitik iz Ovče jame. *Arheološki Vestnik*, 13–14.

Oswalt, W. H. (1973). *Habitat and Technology*. New York, Holt, Rinehart and Winston.

Oswalt, W. H. (1976). *An Anthropological Analysis of Food-getting Technology*. New York, Wiley.

Oswalt, W. H., and Vanstone, J. W. (1967). *The Ethnoarchaeology of Crow Village, Alsaka*. Smithsonian Institution, Bureau of American Ethnology, Bulletin 199.

Otte, M. (1976a). L'Aurignacien en Belgique. In J. K. Kozlowski (ed.) *L'Aurignacien en Europe*, 144–63. Nice, U.I.S.P.P., Congrès IX, Colloque XVI.

Otte, M. (1976b). Le Périgordien en Belgique. In B. Klíma (ed.) *Périgordien et Gravettien en Europe*, 142–54. Nice, U.I.S.P.P., Congrès IX, Colloque XV.

Otte, M. (1977). Deux coquilles, probablement d'origine anglaise, découvertes à Spy, Belgique. In J. B. Campbell *The Upper Palaeolithic in Britain*, 211–12. Oxford, Oxford University Press.

Otte, M. (1979). *Le paléolithique supérieur ancien en Belgique*. Bruxelles, Musées Royaux d'art et d'histoire, Monographies d'Archéologie Nationale 5.

Otte, M. (1981). *Le Gravettien en Europe Centrale*. Brugge, Dissertationes Archaeologi-cae Gandenses, 20, de Tempel.

Ovey, C. D. (ed.) (1964). *The Swanscombe Skull*. London, Royal Anthropological Institute, Occasional Paper 20.

Pales, L. (1976). *Les gravures de la Marche II – Les Humains*. Paris, Ophrys.

Palma di Cesnola, A. (1965–6). Il paleolitico superiore arcaico (facies uluzziana) della grotta del Cavallo (Lecce). *Rivista di Scienze Preistoriche*, 20: 33–62; 21: 3–59.

Palma di Cesnola, A. (1969). Datazione assoluta dell'Uluzziano col metodo del C14. *Rivista Scienze Preistoriche*, 24.

Palma di Cesnola, A. (1971). Il gravettiano evoluto della Grotta della Cala a Marina di Camerota (Salerno). *Rivista Scienze Preistoriche*, 26: 259–324.

Palma di Cesnola, A. (1975). Il gravettiano della Grotta Paglicci nel Gargano. *Rivista Scienze Preistoriche*, 30: 3–177.

Palma di Cesnola, A. (1976). Le leptolithique archaique en Italie. In B. Klíma (ed.) *Périgordien et Gravettien en Europe*, 66–99. Nice, U.I.S.P.P., Congrès IX, Colloque XV.

Palma di Cesnola, A. (1981). Italie. In R. Desbrosse and J. K. Kozlowski (eds.) *Resumen de las Investigaciones de 1976 a 1981*, 31–5. Mexico City, U.I.S.P.P., X Congreso, Comision X.

Paquereau, M.-M. (1974–5). Le Würm ancien en Périgord. Etude palynologique. Première partie; Les diagrammes palynologiques – la zonation climatique. Deuxième partie: L'évolution des climats et des flores. *Quaternaria*, 18: 67–160.

Păunescu, AL. (1965). Sur la succession des habitats paléolithiques et postpaléolithiques de Ripiceni-Izvor. *Dacia*, 9: 1–32.

Păunescu, AL. (1970). *Evolutia Uneltelor și Armelor de Piatră cioplită Descoperite pe Territoriul României*. București, Academi Republicae Socialae României.

Penck, A., and Brückner, E. (1909). *Die Alpen in Eiszeitalter*. Leipzig.

Pérez, J. A. (1974). El yacimiento de 'Las Fuentes' Navarrés-Valencia y el musteriense en la región Valenciana (Éspana). *Quartär*, 25: 25–52.

Pericot, L. G. (1942). *La Cueva des Parpalló*. Madrid, Consejo superior de Investigaciones Científicas, Instituto Diego Velázquez.

Perlès, C. (1976). Le feu. In H. de Lumley (ed.) *La Préhistoire Française*, 679–83. Paris, CNRS.

Perlman, S. M. (1980). An optimum diet model, coastal variability, and hunter-gatherer behaviour. In M. B. Schiffer (ed.) *Advances in Archaeological Method and Theory*, 3: 257–310. New York, Academic Press.

Peters, E. (1930). *Die Altsteinzeitliche Kulturstätte Petersfels*. Augsburg, Dr Benno Filser Verlag.

Peterson, G. M., Webb, T., Kutzbach, J. E., Van der Hammen, T., Wijmstra, T. A., and Street, F. A. (1979). The continental record of environmental conditions at 18,000 yr. B.P.: an initial evaluation. *Quaternary Research*, 12: 47–82.

Peterson, N. (1975). Hunter-gatherer territoriality: the perspective from Australia. *American Anthropologist*, 77: 53–68.

Peterson, N. (1976a). The natural and cultural areas of Aboriginal Australia. In N. Peterson (ed.) *Tribes and Boundaries in Australia*, 50–71. Canberra, Australian Institute of Aboriginal Studies.

Peterson, N. (ed.) (1976b). *Tribes and Boundaries in Australia*. Canberra, Australian Institute of Aboriginal Studies.

Peyrony, D. (1930). Le Moustier: ses gisements, ses industries, ses couches géologiques. *Revue Anthropologique*, 40: 48–76, 155–76.

Peyrony, D. (1932). Les gisements préhistoriques de Bourdeilles. *Archives de l'Institut de Paléontologie Humaine*, Mémoire, 10.

Peyrony, D. (1933). Les industries aurignaciennes dans le bassin de la Vézère. Aurignacien et Périgordien. *Bulletin de la Société Préhistorique Française*, 30: 543–59.

Peyrony, D. (1934). La Ferrassie – Moustérien, Périgordien, Aurignacien. *Préhistoire*, 3: 1–92.

Peyrony, D. (1938). La Micoque, les fouilles récentes, leurs significations. *Bulletin de la Société Préhistorique Française*, 6: 257–88.

Peyrony, D. (1949). *Le Périgord préhistorique: essai de géographie humaine*. Périgueux, Société Historique et Archéologique du Périgord.

Peyrony, D., and Peyrony, E. (1938). Laugerie-Haute, près des Eyzies (Dordogne). *Archives de l'Institut de Paléontologie Humaine*, Mémoire 19.

Pfeiffer, J. E. (1977). *The Emergence of Society*. New York, McGraw-Hill.

Pfeiffer, J. E. (1978). *The Emergence of Man*, 3rd edn. New York, Harper and Row.

Pfeiffer, J. E. (1982). *The Creative Explosion*. New York, Harper and Row.

Phillipson, J. (1973). The biological efficiency of protein production by grazing and other land-based systems. In J. G. W. Jones (ed.) *The Biological Efficiency of Protein Production*, 217–36. Cambridge, Cambridge University Press.

Pianese, S. P. (1968). Rassegna storica della richerche sul paleolitico in Sicilia. *Quaternaria*, 10: 213–50.

Pianka, E. R. (1970). On r and K selection or b and d selection? *American Naturalist*, 106: 581–8.

Pianka, E. R. (1978). *Evolutionary Ecology*, 2nd edn. New York, Harper and Row.

Pidoplichko, I. G. (1969). *Upper Palaeolithic Mammoth Bone Dwellings in the Ukraine*, (in Russian). Kiev, Mukova Dumka.

Piette, E. (1895). La station de Brassempouy et les statuettes humaines de la période glyptique. *L'Anthropologie*, 6: 129–51.

Pillard, B. (1972). La faune des grands mammifères du Würmien II. In H. de Lumley (ed.) *La Grotte de l'Hortus*, 163–205. Marseille, Études Quaternaires, 1.

Piperno, M. (1976–7). Analyse du sol moustérien de la Grotte Guattari au Mont Circé. *Quaternaria*, 19: 71–92.

Piperno, M., and Biddittu, I. (1978). Studio tipologico ed interpretazione dell'industria acheuleana e pre-musteriana dei livelli m e d di Torre in Pietra (Roma). *Quaternaria*, 20: 441–536.

Piperno, M., and Segre, A. G. (1982). The transition from lower to middle palaeolithic in central Italy: an example from Latium. In A. Ronen (ed.) *The Transition from Lower to Middle Palaeolithic and the Origin of Modern Man*, 203–22. Oxford, British Archaeological Reports, International Series, 151.

Poser, H. (1948). Boden- und Klimaverhältnisse in Mittel-und Westeuropa während der Würmeiszeit. *Erdkunde*, 2: 53–68.

Potter, S. (1954). *Lifemanship*. London, Rupert Hart-Davis.

Potts, R., and Shipman, P. (1981). Cutmarks made by stone tools on bones from Olduvai Gorge, Tanzania. *Nature*, 291: 577–80.

Pradel, L. (1961). La grotte des Cottés, commune de Saint-Pierre-de-Maillé (Vienne). *L'Anthropologie*, 65: 229–58.

Pradel, L. (1972/3). Nomenclature de l'outillage en pierre du paléolithique en France. *Quartär*, 23/4: 37–51.

Praslov, N. D., and Rogachev, A. N. (eds.) (1982). *Palaeolithic of the Kostenki-Borshevo area on the Don river, 1879–1979* (in Russian). Leningrad, NAUKA.

Price, T. D. (1978). Mesolithic settlement systems in the Netherlands. In P. Mellars (ed.) *The Early Postglacial Settlement of Northern Europe*, 81–113. London, Duckworth.

Price, T. D., Chappell, S., and Ives, D. J. (1982). Thermal alteration in mesolithic assemblages. *Proceedings of the Prehistoric Society*, 48: 467–85.

Prošek, F. (1961). Die jungpaläolithische Wohnstätte in der Tschechoslowakei. *Památky Archeologické*, 521: 57–75.

Pruitt, W. O. (1970). Some ecological aspects of snow. In *Ecology of the Subarctic Regions*, 83–99. Proceedings of the Helsinki Symposium 1966, Paris, UNESCO.

Quaternary Sistema (1982). *The Quaternary System of the U.S.S.R.* Moscow, NEDRA.

Quéchon, G. (1976). Les sépultures des hommes du paléolithique supérieur. In H. de Lumley (ed.) *La Préhistoire Française*, 728–33. Paris, CNRS.

Querol, M. A., and Santonja, M. (1979). El yacimento achelense de Pinedo (Toledo). *Excavaciones Arqueológicas en España*, 106.

Radcliffe-Brown, A. (1930). The social organisation of Australian tribes, part 1. *Oceania*, 1: 34–63.

Radmilli, A. M. (1963). Il paleolitico superiore nel Riparo Maurizio. *Atti Societa Toscana di Scienze Naturali*, 70: 220–43.

Radmilli, A. M. (1974). *Gli scavi nella grotta Polesini a Ponte Lucano di Tivoli e le più antiche arte nel Lazio*. Firenze, Sansoni.

Radmilli, A. M. (1976). The first industries of Italy. In K. Valoch (ed.) *Les Premières Industries de l'Europe*, 35–74. Nice, U.I.S.P.P., Congrès IX, Colloque VIII.

Radmilli, A. M. (1977). *Storia dell'Abruzzo dalle origini all'Età del Bronzo*. Pisa, Giardini.

Raynal, J. P. (1977). Influence du milieu physique sur l'habitat préhistorique au Würm dans le bassin de Brive (Corrèze). In H. Laville and J. Renault-Miscovsky (eds.) *Approche Écologique de l'Homme Fossile*, 111–15. Paris, Supplement au Bulletin de l'Association Française pour l'étude du quaternaire, Université Pierre et Marie Curie, Laboratoire de Géologie, 1.

Redmann, R. E. (1982). Production and diversity in contemporary grasslands. In D. M. Hopkins, J. V. Matthews, C. E. Schweger and S. B Young (eds.) *Paleoecology of Beringia*, 223–39. New York, Academic Press.

Reher, C. A. (1977). Adaptive process on the short grass plains. In L. R. Binford (ed.) *For Theory Building in Archaeology*, 13–40. New York, Academic Press.

Reidhead, V. A. (1979). Linear programming models in archaeology. *Annual Review of Anthropology*, 8: 543–78.

Reidhead, V. A. (1980). The economics of subsistence change: a test of an optimization model. In T. K. Earle and A. L. Christenson (eds.) *Modelling Change in Prehistoric Subsistence Economies*, 141–86. New York, Academic Press.

Reisch, L. (1974). Eine spät jungpaläolithische Freilandstation in Donautal bei Barbing, Ldkr. Regensburg. *Quartär*, 25: 53–71.

Reisch, L. (1982). The transition from lower to middle palaeolithic in Greece and the southern Balkans. In A. Ronen (ed.) *The Transition from Lower to Middle Palaeolithic and the Origin of Modern Man*, 223–32. Oxford, British Archaeological Reports, International Series, 151.

Renfrew, C. (1972). *The Emergence of Civilisation: The Cyclades and the Aegean in the Third Millennium B.C.* London, Methuen.

Renfrew, C. (1973). Monuments, mobilization and social organization in neolithic Wessex. In C. Renfrew (ed.) *The Explanation of Culture Change: Models in Prehistory*, 539–58, London, Duckworth.

Renfrew, C., and Wagstaff, J. M. (eds.) (1982). *An Island Polity: The Archaeology of Exploitation in Melos*. Cambridge, Cambridge University Press.

Rick, J. W. (1976). Downslope movement and archaeological intrasite spatial analysis. *American Antiquity*, 41: 133–44.

Riek, G. (1934). *Die Eiszeitjägerstation am Vogelherd, Band 1: Die Kulturen*. Tübingen, Heine.

Riek, G. (1970). Steinere Einbauten in jungpaläolithisch besidelten Höhle der Schwäbischen Alb. In *Frühe Menschheit und Umwelt*, 298–305. Köln, Fundamenta Reihe, A/2.

Riek, G. (1973). *Das Paläolithikum der Brillenhöhle bei Blaubeuren, Schwäbische Alb*. Stuttgart, Forschung Berichte vor-Frühgeschichte Baden-Württemberg 4/1, Müller und Gräff.

Rigaud, J.-P. (1976). Les civilisations du Paléolithique supérieur en Périgord. in H. De Lumley (ed.) *La Préhistoire Française*, 1257–70. Paris, CNRS.

Rigaud, J.-P. (1978). The significance of variability among lithic artifacts: a specific case from southwestern France. *Journal of Anthropological Research*, 34: 299–310.

Robins, G. V., Seeley, N. J., McNeil, D. A. C., and Symons, M. R. C. (1978). Identification of ancient heat treatment in flint artefacts by ESR spectroscopy. *Nature*, 276: 703–4.

Roe, D. A. (1964). The British lower and middle palaeolithic: some problems, methods of study and preliminary results. *Proceedings of the Prehistoric Society*, 30: 245–67.

Roe, D. A. (1968a). British lower and middle palaeolithic handaxe groups. *Proceedings of the Prehistoric Society*, 34: 1–82.

Roe, D. A. (1968b). *A Gazetteer of British Lower and Middle Palaeolithic Sites*. London, Council for British Archaeology, Research Report 8.

Roe, D. A. (1976). Typology and the trouble with hand-axes. In G. de G. Sieveking, I. H. Longworth and K. E. Wilson (eds.) *Problems in Economic and Social Archaeology*, 61–70. London, Duckworth.

Roe, D. A. (1981). *The Lower and Middle Palaeolithic Periods in Britain*. London, Routledge and Kegan Paul.

Rogachev, A. N. (1961). The relative antiquity of the upper palaeolithic sites of the central Russian upland (in Russian). *Materialy vsesoyuznogo soveshchaniya po izucheniyu chetvertichnogo perioda*, 1: 397–404.

Rogers, E. S. (1963). The hunting group territory among the Mistassini Indians. *National Museum of Canada Bulletin*, 195.

Rogers, E. S. (1969). Band organization among the Indians of Eastern Subarctic Canada. In D. Damas (ed.) Contributions to Anthropology: Band Societies. *National Museum of Canada Bulletin*, 228: 21–50.

Rogers, E. S., and Black, M. B. (1976). Subsistence strategy in the Fish and Hare period, Northern Ontario: the Weagamow Ojibwa, 1880–1920. *Journal of Anthropological Research*, 32: 1–43.

Rolland, N. (1977). New aspects of middle palaeolithic variability in western Europe. *Nature*, 266: 251–2.

Rolland, N. (1981). The interpretation of middle palaeolithic variability. *Man*, 16: 15–42.

Ronen, A. (ed.) (1982). *The Transition from Lower to Middle Palaeolithic and the Origin of Modern Man*. Oxford, British Archaeological Reports, International Series, 151.

Rosenfeld, A. (1971). The examination of use marks on some magdalenian endscrapers. *British Museum Quarterly*, 35: 176–82.

Rosenfeld, A. (1977). Profile figures: schematisation of the human figure in the magdalenian culture of Europe. In P. J. Ucko (ed.) *Form in Indigenous Art*, 90–109, London, Duckworth.

Rowlett, R. M., and Schneider, M. J. (1974). The material expression of Neanderthal child care. In M. Richardson (ed.) *The Human Mirror*, 41–58. Bâton Rouge, Louisiana State University Press.

Rowley-Conwy, P. (1983). Sedentary hunters: the Ertebølle example. In G. N. Bailey (ed.)

Hunter-Gatherer Economy in Prehistory, 111–26. Cambridge, Cambridge University Press.

Rozoy, J. G. (1978). *Les Derniers Chasseurs*. Reims, Imprimerie de Compiègne.

Ruddiman, W. F., and McIntyre, A. (1976). Northeast Atlantic palaeoclimatic changes over the past 600,000 years. *Geological Society of America Memoir*, 145: 11–146.

Ruddiman, W. F., Sancetta, C. D., and McIntyre, A. (1977). Glacial/interglacial response rate of subpolar North Atlantic waters to climatic change: the record in ocean sediments. *Philosophical Transactions of the Royal Society of London*, B, 280: 119–42.

Rust, A. (1943). *Die Alt- und Mittelsteinzeitlichen Funde von Stellmoor*. Neumünster, Karl Wachholtz.

Rust, A. (1958). *Die Jungpaläolithischen Zeltanlagen von Ahrensburg*. Neumünster, Karl Wachholtz.

Sacchi, D. (1976). Les civilisations du paléolithique supérieur en Languedoc occidental (Bassin de L'Aude). In H. de Lumley (ed.) *La Préhistoire Française*, 1174–88. Paris, CNRS.

Sackett, J. R. (1968). Method and theory of upper palaeolithic archaeology in southwestern France. In S. R. Binford and L. R. Binford (eds.) *New Perspectives in Archaeology*, 61–83. Chicago, Aldine.

Sackett, J. R. (1977). The meaning of style in archaeology: a general model. *American Antiquity*, 42: 369–80.

Sackett, J. R. (1981). From de Mortillet to Bordes: a century of French palaeolithic research. In G. Daniel (ed.) *Towards a History of Archaeology*, 85–99. London, Thames and Hudson.

Sackett, J. R. (1982). Approaches to style in lithic archaeology. *Journal of Anthropological Archaeology*, 1: 59–112.

Sahlins, M. D. (1968). Notes on the original affluent society. In R. B. Lee and I. DeVore (eds.) *Man the Hunter*, 85–9. Chicago, Aldine.

de Saint-Périer, R. (1930). *La Grotte d'Isturitz I: Le Magdalénien de la Salle de St Martin*. Archives de l'Institut de Paléontologie Humaine, 7. Paris, Masson.

de Saint-Périer, R. (1936). *La Grotte d'Isturitz II: Le Magdalénien de la Grande Salle*. Archives de l'Institut de Paléontologie Humaine, 17. Paris, Masson.

de Saint-Périer, R., and de Saint-Périer, S. (1952). *La Grotte d'Isturitz III: Les Solutréens, les Aurignaciens et les Moustériens*. Archives de l'Institut de Paléontologie Humaine, 25. Paris, Masson.

Santonja, M., López-Martínez, N., and Pérez-González, A. (1980). Ocupaciones Achelenses en el Valle del Jarama (Arganda, Madrid). *Arqueologia y Paleoecologia*, 1: 1–352.

Schafer, D. (1981). Taubach. *Ethnographische-Archäologisches Zeitschrift*, 22: 369–96.

Schalk, R. F. (1977). The structure of an anadromous fish resource. In L. R. Binford (ed.) *For Theory Building in Archaeology*, 207–50. New York, Academic Press.

Schaller, G. B. (1972). *The Serengeti Lion*. Chicago, University of Chicago Press.

Schiffer, M. B. (1972). Archaeological context and systemic context. *American Antiquity*, 37: 156–65.

Schiffer, M. B. (1976). *Behavioral Archaeology*. New York, Academic Press.

Schild, R. (1971). Location of the so-called chocolate flint extraction sites on the northeastern footslopes of the Holy Cross mountains (in Polish). *Folia Quaternaria*, 39: 1–61.

Schild, R. (1975). Późny paleolit. In W. Chmielewski, R. Schild, and H. Więckowska, *Paleolit im Mezolit, Prahistoria ziem Polskich*, 1: 159–338. Warsaw, Polish Academy.

Schild, R. (1976). The final palaeolithic settlements of the European Plain. *Scientific American*, 234: 88–99.

Schild, R. (1979). Chronostratigraphie et environnement du paléolithique final en Pologne. In D. de Sonneville-Bordes (ed.) *La Fin des Temps Glaciaires en Europe*, 799–820. Paris, CNRS.

Schmid, E. (1969). Cave sediments and prehistory. In D. R. Brothwell and E. S. Higgs (eds.) *Science in Archaeology*, 151–66. London, Thames and Hudson.

Schmid, E. (1976). Beobachtungen an Würmeiszeitlichen Hyänenkoprolithen und zerbissenen Knochen. In F. Poplin (ed.) *Problèmes Ethnographiques des Vestiges Osseux*, Thème Spécialisé B, 143–9. Nice, U.I.S.P.P., IX Congrès.

Schmider, B. (1975). Le gisement paléolithique supérieur des Tarterets 1 à Corbeil-Essonnes (Essonne). *Gallia Préhistoire*, 18: 315–40.

Schwabedissen, H. (1954). *Die Federmesser-Gruppen des Nordwesteuropäischen Flachlandes*. Neumünster, Karl Wachholtz.

Schwabedissen, G. (1970). Zur Verbreitung der Faustkeile in Mitteleuropa. In *Frühe Menschheit und Umwelt*, 61–98. Köln, Fundamenta Reihe, A/2.

Schwarz, H. P., and Blackwell, B. (1983). ^{230}Th/^{234}U age of a mousterian site in France. *Nature*, 301: 236–7.

Schwarz, H. P., and Skoflek, I. (1982). New dates for the Tata, Hungary, archaeological site. *Nature*, 295: 590–1.

Scott, K. (1980). Two hunting episodes of middle palaeolithic age at La Cotte de Saint-Brelade, Jersey (Channel Islands). *World Archaeology*, 12: 137–52.

Semenov, S. A. (1964). *Prehistoric Technology*. London, Cory, Adams & Mackay.

Semmel, A. (1973). Periglacial sediments and their stratigraphy. *Eiszeitalter und Gegenwart*, 23/4: 293–305.

Service, E. R. (1962). *Primitive Social Organization: An Evolutionary Perspective*. New York, Random House.

Service, E. R. (1966). *The Hunters*. Englewood Cliffs, N.J. Prentice-Hall.

Shackleton, N. J. (1969). The last interglacial in the marine and terrestrial record. *Proceedings of the Royal Society of London*, B, 174: 135–54.

Shackleton, N. J., and Opdyke, N. D. (1973). Oxygen isotope and palaeomagnetic stratigraphy of equatorial Pacific core, V28–238. *Quaternary Research*, 3: 39–55.

Shennan, S. J. (1981). Settlement history in east Hampshire. In S. J. Shennan and R. T. Schadla-Hall (eds.) *The Archaeology of Hampshire*, 106–21. Hampshire Field Club and Archaeological Society, Monograph 1.

Shimkin, E. M. (1978). The upper palaeolithic in north-central Eurasia: evidence and problems. In L. G. Freeman (ed.) *Views of the Past*, 193–315. The Hague, Mouton.

Shotton, F. W. (1977). The Devensian stage: its development, limits and substages. *Philosophical Transactions of the Royal Society*, B, 280: 107–18.

Shovkoplyas, I. G. (1965). *The Mezin Site* (in Russian). Kiev, Naukova dumka.

Sieveking, A. (1976). Settlement patterns of the later magdalenian in the central Pyrenees. In G. de G. Sieveking, I. H. Longworth and K. E. Wilson (eds.) *Problems in Economic and Social Archaeology*, 583–603. London, Duckworth.

Siiriainen, A. (1977). Pieces in vertical movement: a model for rock shelter archaeology. *Proceedings of the Prehistoric Society*, 43: 349–54.

Silberbauer, G. B. (1972). The G/wi Bushmen. In M. G. Bicchieri (ed.) *Hunters and Gatherers Today*, 271–326. New York, Holt, Rinehart and Winston.

Silberbauer, G. B. (1981). *Hunter and Habitat in the Central Kalahari Desert*. Cambridge, Cambridge University Press.

Simek, J. F., and Larick, R. R. (1983). The recognition of multiple spatial patterns: a case study from the French upper palaeolithic. *Journal of Archaeological Science*, 10: 165–80.

Singer, R., and Wymer, J. J. (1976). The sequence of acheulian industries at Hoxne, Suffolk. In J. Combier (ed) *L'Évolution de l'Acheuléen en Europe*, 14–30. Nice, U.I.S.P.P., IX Congrès, Colloque X.

Singer, R., and Wymer, J. J. (1982). *The Middle Stone Age at Klasies River Mouth in South Africa*. Chicago, University of Chicago Press.

Singer, R., Wymer, J. J., Gladfelter, B. G., and Wolff, R. G. (1973). Excavation of the clactonian industry at the golf course, Clacton-on-Sea, Essex. *Proceedings of the Prehistoric Society*, 39: 6–74.

Sivertsen, B. J. (1980). A site activity model for kill and butchering activities at hunter-gatherer sites. *Journal of Field Archaeology*, 7: 423–41.

Sklenář, K. (1975). Palaeolithic and mesolithic dwellings: problems of interpretation. *Památky Archeologické*, 67: 266–304.

Sklenář, K. (1976). Palaeolithic and mesolithic dwellings: an essay in classification. *Památky Archeologické*, 68: 249–340.

Smiley, F. E., Sinopoli, C. M., Jackson, H., Wills, W. H., and Gregg, S. A. (eds.) (1980). *The Archaeological Correlates of Hunter-Gatherer Societies: Studies from the Ethnographic Record*. Michigan Discussions in Anthropology, 5.

Smith, E. A. (1979). Human adaptation and energetic efficiency. *Human Ecology*, 7: 53–74.

Smith, J. G. E. (1978). Economic uncertainty in an 'original affluent society': Caribou and Caribou Eater Chipewyan adaptive strategies. *Arctic Anthropology*, 15: 68–88.

Smith, P. E. L. (1964). The solutrean culture. *Scientific American*, 211: 86–94.

Smith, P. E. L. (1966). Le solutréen en France. *Publications de l'Institut de Préhistoire de l'Université de Bordeaux*, Mémoire 5.

Soergel, W. (1943). *Der Klimacharakter der als Nordisch geltenden Säugetiere des Eiszeitalters*. Heidelberg, Heidelberger Akademie der Wissenschaften.

Sollas, W. J. (1911). *Ancient Hunters and Their Modern Representatives*. London, Macmillan.

de Sonneville-Bordes, D. (1960). *Le paléolithique supérieur en Périgord*, 2 vols. Bordeaux, Delmas.

de Sonneville-Bordes, D. (1961). Le paléolithique supérieur en Belgique. *L'Anthropologie*, 65: 421–43.

de Sonneville-Bordes, D. (1963a). Le paléolithique supérieur en Suisse. *L'Anthropologie*, 67: 205–68.

de Sonneville-Bordes, D. (1963b). Upper palaeolithic cultures of western Europe. *Science*, 143: 347–55.

de Sonneville-Bordes, D. (1965). Observations statistiques sur l'aurignacien du Vogelherd, Lonetal, Württemberg, fouilles G. Riek. *Fundberichte aus Schwaben*, 17: 69–75.

de Sonneville-Bordes, D. (1968). Remarques statistiques sur le magdalénien des sites de Münzingen et Oelberg près de Freiburg-en-Breisgau, Allemagne. *Quartär*, 19: 125–32.

de Sonneville-Bordes, D. (1969). Pointes à cran (Kerbspitzen) du magdalénien supérieur du Petersfels. *Quartär*, 20: 175–82.

de Sonneville-Bordes, D. (1970). Les industries aurignaciennes de l'abri de Caminade-Est, commune de la Canéda (Dordogne). *Quaternaria*, 13: 77–131.

de Sonneville-Bordes, D. (1973). The upper palaeolithic: c.33,000–10,000 B.C. In S.

Piggot, G. Daniel and C. McBurney (eds.) *France Before the Romans*, 30–60. London, Thames and Hudson.

de Sonneville-Bordes, D. (1974–5). Les listes types. Observations de méthode. *Quaternaria*, 18: 9–43.

de Sonneville-Bordes, D. (ed.) (1979). *La Fin des Temps Glaciaires en Europe: Chronostratigraphies et écologie des cultures du paléolithique final*. Paris, CNRS.

de Sonneville-Bordes, D., and Perrot, J. (1953). Essai d'adaptation des méthodes statistiques au paléolithique supérieur. *Bulletin de la Société Préhistorique Française*, 50: 323–33.

de Sonneville-Bordes, D., and Perrot, J. (1954–6). Lexique typologique du paléolithique supérieur. Outillage lithique. *Bulletin de la Société Préhistorique Française*, 51: 327–35, 52: 76–9, 53: 408–12, 547–59.

Spaulding, A. C. (1968). Explanation in archaeology. In S. R. Binford and L. R. Binford (eds.) *New Perspectives in Archaeology*, 33–9. Chicago, Aldine.

Spencer, R. F. (1959). *The North Alaskan Eskimo*. New York, Dover Publications.

Speth, J. D. (1983). *Bison Kills and Bone Counts*. Chicago, University of Chicago Press.

Spiess, A. E. (1979). *Reindeer and Caribou Hunters: An Archaeological Study*. New York, Academic Press.

Stanley, V. (1980). Paleoecology of the arctic-steppe mammoth biome. *Current Anthropology*, 21: 663–6.

Stanner, W. E. H. (1965). Aboriginal territorial organization: estate, range, domain and regime. *Oceania*, 36: 1–26.

Starkel, L. (1977). The palaeogeography of mid- and east-Europe during the last cold stage, with west European comparisons. *Philosophical Transactions of the Royal Society of London*, B, 290: 351–72.

Steel, T. (1975). *The Life and Death of St Kilda*. Glasgow, Fontana.

Steiner, W., and Wagenbreth, O. (1971). Zur geologischen situation der altsteinzeitlichen Rastplätze in unteren travertin von Ehringsdorf bei Weimar. *Alt Thüringen*, 11: 47–75.

Steward, J. H. (1936). The economic and social basis of primitive bands. In R. H. Lowie (ed.) *Essays in Anthropology Presented to A. L. Kroeber*, 331–50. Berkeley, University of California Press.

Steward, J. H. (1938). *Basin-Plateau Aboriginal Sociopolitical Groups*. Washington, Smithsonian Institute Bureau of American Ethnology, Bulletin 120.

Stordeur-Yedid, D. (1979). Les aiguilles à chas au paléolithique. *Gallia Préhistoire*, Supplement 13.

Straus, L. G. (1976–7). The upper palaeolithic cave site of Altamira (Santander, Spain). *Quaternaria*, 19: 135–48.

Straus, L. G. (1977a). Of deerslayers and mountain men: palaeolithic faunal exploitation in Cantabrian Spain. In L. R. Binford (ed.) *For Theory Building in Archaeology*, 41–76. New York, Academic Press.

Straus, L. G. (1977b). Pointes solutréennes et l'hypothèse de territorialisme. *Bulletin de la Société Préhistorique Française*, 74: 206–12.

Straus, L. G. (1982). Carnivores and cave sites in Cantabrian Spain. *Journal of Anthropological Research*, 38: 75–96.

Straus, L. G., Altuna, J., Clark, G. A., González, M., Laville, H., Leroi-Gourhan, Arl., Menéndez, M., and Ortea, J. A. (1981). Paleoecology at La Riera (Asturias, Spain). *Current Anthropology*, 22: 655–74.

Strehlow, T. G. H. (1970). Geography and the totemic landscape in central Australia: a functional study. In R. M. Berndt (ed.) *Australian Aboriginal Anthropology*, 92–140. Perth, University of Western Australia Press.

Stringer, C. B. (1974). A multivariate study of the Petralona skull. *Journal of Human Evolution*, 3: 397–404.

Stringer, C. B., Howell, F. C., and Melentis, J. K. (1979). The significance of the fossil hominid skull from Petralona, Greece. *Journal of Archaeological Science*, 6: 235–53.

Stuart, A. J. (1982). *Pleistocene Vertebrates in the British Isles*. London, Longman.

Sturdy, D. A. (1972). The exploitation patterns of a modern reindeer economy in west Greenland. In E. S. Higgs (ed.) *Papers in Economic Prehistory*, 161–8. Cambridge, Cambridge University Press.

Sturdy, D. A. (1975). Some reindeer economies in prehistoric Europe. In E. S. Higgs (ed.) *Palaeoeconomy*, 55–95. Cambridge, Cambridge University Press.

Sturdy, D. A. (ms.). Notes on the Kastelhöhle fauna. Unpublished manuscript.

Sutcliffe, A. J. (1970). Spotted hyena: crusher, gnawer, digester and collector of bones. *Nature*, 227: 1110–13.

Szabo, B. J., and Collins, D. M. (1975). Ages of fossil bone from British interglacial sites. *Nature*, 254: 680–2.

Taborin, Y., Olive, M., and Pigeot, N. (1979). Les habitats paléolithiques des bords de Seine: Etiolles (Essonne, France). In D. de Sonneville-Bordes (ed.) *La Fin des Temps Glaciaires en Europe*, 773–82. Paris, CNRS.

Taschini, M. (1972). Sur le paléolithique de la Plaine Pontine (Latium). *Quaternaria*, 16: 203–23.

Taschini, M., Bietti, A. (1979). L'industrie lithique de Grotta Guattari au Mont Circé (Latium): définition culturelle, typologique et chronologique du Pontinien. *Quaternaria*, 21: 179–247.

Taute, W. (1968). *Die Stielspitzen-Gruppen im Nördlichen Mitteleuropa*. Köln, Fundamenta Reihe, A/5.

Thévenin, A. (1976). Les civilisations du paléolithique inférieur en Alsace. In H. de Lumley (ed.) *La Préhistoire Française*, 984–6. Paris, CNRS.

Thévenin, A., and Sainty, J. (1974). Une aire de dépeçage préhistorique à Achenheim. *Archeologia*, 74: 68–9.

Thiede, J. (1978). A glacial mediterranean. *Nature*, 276: 680–3.

Thompson, H. V., and Armour, C. J. (1951). Control of the European rabbit (*Oryctolagus cuniculus* L.). An experiment to compare the efficiency of gin trapping, ferreting and cyanide gassing. *Annals of Applied Biology*, 38: 464–71.

Thomson, D. F. (1962). The Bindibu Expedition. *Geographical Journal*, 128: 1–14, 143–57, 262–78.

Tindale, N. B. (1940). Results of the Harvard–Adelaide Universities anthropological expedition, 1938–1939. Distribution of Australian Aboriginal tribes: a field survey. *Transactions of the Royal Society of South Australia*, 64: 140–231.

Tindale, N. B. (1953). Tribal and intertribal marriage among the Australian Aborigines. *Human Biology*, 25: 169–90.

Tindale, N. B. (1974). *Aboriginal Tribes of Australia*. Los Angeles, University of California Press.

Tixier, J. (1963). Typologie de l'épipaléolithique du Maghreb. *Mémoires du Centre de Recherches Anthropologiques, Préhistoriques et Ethnographiques*, 2.

Tode, A. (ed.) (1953). Die untersuchung der paläolithischen Freilandstation von Salzgitter-Lebenstedt. *Eiszeitalter und Gegenwart*, 3: 144–220.

Toepfer, V. (1957). *Die Mammutfunde von Pfännerhall in Geisetal*. Halle, Veröffentlichungen des Landesmuseum für Vorgeschichte.

Toepfer, V. (1963). *Tierwelt des Eiszeitalters*. Leipzig, Geest and Portig.

Toepfer, V. (1968). Das clactonien im Saale-Mittelelbgebiet. *Jahresschrift für Mitteldeutsche Vorgeschichte*, 52: 1–26.

Toepfer, V. (1970). Stratigraphie und Ökologie des Paläolithikums. In *Periglazial-Löss-Paläolithikum im Jungpleistozän der Deutschen Demokratischen Republik*, 329–422. Leipzig, Gotha.

Toepfer, V. (1976). Alt-, Mittel- und Jungpaläolithikum, 25 Jahre archäoligische forschungen der Deutschen Demokratischen Republik. *Ausgrabungen und Funde*, 21: 17–24.

Torrence, R. (1983). Time budgeting and hunter-gatherer technology. In G. N. Bailey (ed.) *Hunter-Gatherer Economy in Prehistory*, 11–22. Cambridge, Cambridge University Press.

Tozzi, C. (1974). L'industria musteriana della Grotta di Gosto sulla montagna di Cetona (Siena). *Rivista Scienze Preistoriche*, 29: 271–304.

Trigger, B. (1981). Anglo-American archaeology. *World Archaeology*, 13: 138–15.

Tringham, R., Cooper, G., Odell, G., Voytek, B., and Whitman, A. (1974). Experimentation in the formation of edge damage: a new approach to lithic analysis. *Journal of Field Archaeology*, 1: 171–96.

Trinkaus, E. (1982). Evolutionary continuity among archaic *Homo sapiens*. In A. Ronen (ed.) *The Transition from Lower to Middle Palaeolithic and the Origin of Modern Man*, 301–20. Oxford, British Archaeological Reports, International Series, 151.

Trinkaus, E., and Howells, W. W. (1979). The Neanderthals. *Scientific American*, 241: 94–105.

Tromnau, G. (1973). Neue ausgrabungen von jungpaläolithischen wohnplätzen auf der Teltwisch bei Ahrensburg, Kreis Stormarn (Schleswig-Holstein). In H. J. Müller-Beck (ed.) *Neue Paläolithische und Mesolithische Ausgrabungen in der Bundesrepublik Deutschland*, 49–54. Tübingen, Zum 9 INQUA-Kongress.

Tseitlin, S. M. (1979). *Geology of the Palaeolithic of Northern Asia* (in Russian). Moscow, NAUK.

Tuffreau, A. (1976a). Les civilisations du paléolithique inférieur dans la région Parisienne et en Normandie. In H. de Lumley (ed.) *La Préhistoire Française*, 947–55. Paris, CNRS.

Tuffreau, A. (1976b). Les civilisations du paléolithique moyen dans le bassin de la Somme et en Picardie. In H. de Lumley (ed.) *La Préhistoire Française*, 1105–9. Paris, CNRS.

Tuffreau, A. (1976c). Les civilisations du paléolithique moyen dans la région Parisienne et en Normandie. In H. de Lumley (ed.) *La Préhistoire Française*, 1098–104. Paris, CNRS.

Tuffreau, A. (1982). The transition lower/middle palaeolithic in northern France. In A. Ronen (ed.) *The Transition from Lower to Middle Palaeolithic and the Origin of Modern Man*, 137–49. Oxford, British Archaeological Reports, International Series, 151.

Tuffreau, A., Sommé, J., Cháline, J., Munaut, A. V., Piningre, J. F., Puisségur, J. J., and Vandermeersch, B. (1977). Der altpaläolithische Fundplatz Biache-Saint-Vaast (Nordfrankreich). *Archäologisches Korrespondenzblatt*, 7: 1–7.

Turnbull, C. M. (1966). *Wayward Servants. The Two Worlds of the African Pygmies*. London, Eyre and Spottiswoode.

Turner, C., and West, R. G. (1968). The subdivision and zonation of interglacial periods. *Eiszeitalter und Gegenwart*, 19: 93–101.

Turq, A. (1978). Note préliminaire sur l'outillage en quartzite entre Dordogne et Lot. *Bulletin de la Société Préhistorique Française*, 75: 136–9.

Ucko, P. J., and Rosenfeld, A. (1967). *Palaeolithic Cave Art*. London, World University Library.

Ulrix-Closset, M. (1975). *Le paléolithique moyen dans le bassin Mosan en Belgique*. Wetteren, Bibliothèque de la Faculté de Philosophie et Lettres de l'Université de Liège, Publications Exceptionélles No. 3, Éditions Universa.

Valoch, K. (1957). Étude statistique du szélétien. *L'Anthroplogie*, 61: 83–9.

Valoch, K. (1960). Magdalénien na Moravĕ. *Anthropos*, 12 (N.S.4).

Valoch, K. (1965). Die Höhlen Sipka und Certova Dira bei Stramberk. *Anthropos* 17 NS 9.

Valoch, K. (1967a). Le paléolithique moyen en Tchecoslovaquie. *L'Anthropologie*, 71: 135–44.

Valoch, K. (1967b). Die altstenzeitlichen Stationen im Raum von Ondratice in Mähren. *Casopis Moravského Muzea*, 52: 5–46.

Valoch, K. (1968). Evolution of the palaeolithic in central and eastern Europe. *Current Anthropology*, 9: 351–68.

Valoch, K. (1968–9). Das Mittelpaläolithikum mit Blattspitzen (Schicht, 9b), aus der Höhle Kůlna bei Sloup in Mähren. *Casopis Moravského Muzea*, 53/4: 5–30.

Valoch, K. (1970). Erster Bericht über die Grabungen in der Höhle Kůlna (Mähren). In *Frühe Menschheit und Umwelt*, 239–41. Köln, Fundamenta Reihe, A/2.

Valoch, K. (1973). Neslovice, eine bedeutende Oberflächenfundstelle des Szeletiens in Mähren. *Casopis Moravského Muzea*, 58: 5–76.

Valoch, K. (1974). Die jungsteinzeitlichen Station Podstranská in Mähren. *Casopis Moravského Muzea*, 59.

Valoch, K. (ed.) (1976a). *Les Premières Industries de L'Europe*. Nice, U.I.S.P.P., IX Congrès, Colloque VIII.

Valoch, K. (1976b). Die Altsteinzeitliche Fundstelle in Brno-Bohunice. *Studie Archeologického ústava Československé Akademie věd v Brně*, 4: 3–120.

Valoch, K. (1976c). Das Entwickelte aurignacien von Tvarožná bei Brno. *Casopis Moravského Muzea*, 61: 7–30.

Valoch, K. (1978). Die endpaläolithische Siedlung in Smolin. In *Studie Archeologického ústava ČSAV v Brně*, 6: 3–117.

Valoch, K. (1980a). Knochenartefakte aus dem Micoquien (Schicht, 7c) in der Kůlna-Höhle in Mährischen Karst. *Casopis Moravského Muzea*, 65: 7–18.

Valoch, K. (1980b). Vorläufiger komplexer Bericht über die Erforschung der Kůlna Höhle bei Sloup/Bez. Blansko/in den jahren, 1961–1976. *Přehled Výzkumů 1977*, Brno, 11–22.

Valoch, K. (1982a). The lower/middle palaeolithic transition in Czechoslovakia. In A. Ronen (ed.) *The Transition from Lower to Middle Palaeolithic and the Origin of Modern Man*, 193–201. Oxford, British Archaeological Reports, International Series, 151.

Valoch, K. (1982b). Die Beingeräte von Předmostí in Mähren (Tschechoslovakei). *Anthropologie*, 20: 57–69.

Valoch, K., Pelisek, J., Musil, R., Kovanda, I., and Opravil, E. (1969). Die Erforschung der Kůlna Höhle bei Sloup in Mährischen Karst (Czech). *Quartär*, 20: 1–45.

Van den Brink, F. H. (1967). *A Field Guide to the Mammals of Britain and Europe*. London, Collins.

Van der Hammen, T., Wijmstra, T. A., and Zagwijn, W. H. (1971). The floral record of the late cenozoic of Europe. In K. K. Turekian (ed.) *The Late Cenozoic Glacial Ages*, 391–424. New Haven, Yale University Press.

Vandermeersch, B. (1976). Les sépultures néanderthaliennes. In H. de Lumley (ed.) *La Préhistoire Française*, 725–7. Paris, CNRS.

Velichko, A. A., and Berdnikov, V. V. (1973). Forms and phases of the old cryogenesis (in Russian). In *The Paleogeography of Europe during the Late Pleistocene, Reconstruction and Models*, 146–61. Moscow, NAUK.

Vencl, S. V. (1978). Voletiny – une nouvelle industrie du paléolithique final en Bohême. *Památky Archeologické*, 69: 1–44.

Vencl, S. (1979). Le paléolithique tardif en Tchécoslovaquie. In D. de Sonneville-Bordes (ed.) *La Fin des Temps Glaciaires en Europe*, 847–58. Paris, CNRS.

Vereshschagin, N. K. (1974). The mammoth 'cemeteries' of north-east Siberia. *Polar Record*, 17: 3–13.

Vereshschagin, N. K., and Baryshnikov, G. F. (1982). Paleoecology of the mammoth fauna in the Eurasian Arctic. In D. M. Hopkins *et al.* (eds.) *Paleoecology of Beringia*, 267–80. New York, Academic Press.

Vermeersch, P. M. (1982). Magdalenien open air sites in Belgium. In *Abstracts*, 2: 343. Moscow, 9 INQUA-Congress.

Vértes, L. (1955a). Paläolithische Kulturen des Würm I/II Interstadials in Ungarn. *Acta Archaeologica Academiae Scientiarúm Hungaricae*, 5: 261–77.

Vértes, L. (1955b). Neuere Ausgrabungen und paläolithische funde in der Höhle von Istállöskö. *Acta Archaeologica Academiae Scientiarúm Hungaricae*, 5: 111–31.

Vértes, L. (1960). Die Altsteinzeit der südlichen Donaugebiete. *Quartär*, 12: 53–105.

Vértes, L. (1964). *Tata – eine Mittelpaläolithische Travertinsiedlung in Ungarn*. Budapest, Akadémiai Kiado.

Vértes, L. (1964–5). Das jungpäläolithikum von Arka in Nord-Ungarn. *Quartär*, 15/16: 79–132.

Vértes, L. (1965). Typology of the Buda industry: a pebble-tool industry from the Hungarian lower palaeolithic. *Quaternaria*, 7: 185–95.

Vértes, L. (1975). The lower palaeolithic site of Vértesszöllös, Hungary. In R. Bruce-Mitford (ed.) *Recent Archaeological Excavations in Europe*, 287–301. London, RKP.

Vialou, D. (1976). *Guide des Grottes Ornées Paléolithiques*. Paris, Masson.

Villa, P. (1976–7). Sols et niveaux d'habitat du paléolithique inférieur en Europe et du Proche Orient. *Quaternaria*, 19: 107–34.

Villa, P. (1982). Conjoinable pieces and site formation processes. *American Antiquity*, 47: 276–90.

Vita-Finzi, C. (1969). *The Mediterranean Valleys*. Cambridge, Cambridge University Press.

Vita-Finzi, C. (1978). *Archaeological Sites in their Setting*. London, Thames and Hudson.

Vita-Finzi, C., and Higgs, E. S. (1970). Prehistoric economy in the Mount Carmel area of Palestine, site catchment analysis. *Proceedings of the Prehistoric Society*, 36: 1–37.

Vlček, E. (1978). A new discovery of *Homo erectus* in central Europe. *Journal of Human Evolution*, 7: 239–251.

Vörös, I. (1982). Faunal remains from the gravettian reindeer hunters' campsite at Ságvár. *Folia Archaeologica*, 33: 43–69.

Waddington, C. H. (1978). *Tools for Thought*. Frogmore, Granada.

Waechter, J. d'A (1964). Excavation at Gorham's Cave, Gibraltar. *Proceedings of the Prehistoric Society*, 17: 83–92.

Waechter, J. d'A., Hubbard, R.N.L.B., and Conwy, B. W. (1971). Swanscombe, 1971. *Proceedings of the Royal Anthropological Institute*: 73–85.

Wagner, E. (1981). Eine Löwenkopfplastik aus Elfenbein von der Vogelherdhöhle. *Fundbericht aus Baden-Württemberg*, 6: 29–57.

Weniger, G.-C. (1982). *Wildbeuter und ihre Umwelt*. Tübingen, Archaeologica Venatoria, 5.

Wernert, P. (1957). Stratigraphie paléontologique et préhistorique des sédiments quaternaires d'Alsace, Achenheim. *Mémoires Service Carte Géologique Alsace Lorraine*, 14.

West, R. G. (1970). Pollen zones in the pleistocene of Great Britain and their correlation. *New Phytologist*, 69: 1179–83.

West, R. G. (1977a). *Pleistocene Geology and Biology with Especial Reference to the British Isles*. London, Longman.

West, R. G. (1977b). Early and Middle Devensian flora and vegetation. *Philosophical Transactions of the Royal Society of London* B, 280: 229–46.

Wetzel, R. (1958). *Die Bocksteinschmiede mit dem Bocksteinloch der Brandplatte und dem Abhang sowie der Bocksteingrotte*. Stuttgart.

Wetzel, R., and Bosinski, G. (eds.) (1969). *Die Bocksteinschmiede im Lonetal (Markung Rammingen, Kr, Ulm)*. Stuttgart, Veröffentlichen der Staatliche Amtes für Denkmalpflege, A.15.

Whallon, R. (1978). The spatial analysis of mesolithic occupation floors: a reappraisal. In P. A. Mellars (ed.) *The Early Postglacial Settlement of Northern Europe*, 27–35. London, Duckworth.

White, L. A. (1959). *The Evolution of Culture*. New York, McGraw-Hill.

White, R. (1982). Rethinking the middle/upper palaeolithic transition. *Current Anthropology*, 23: 169–192.

White, T. E. (1953). A method of calculating the dietary percentage of various food animals utilized by aboriginal people. *American Antiquity*, 18: 396–8.

Whitelaw, T. M. (n.d.). People and space in hunter-gatherer camps: a generalising approach in ethnoarchaeology. Unpublished manuscript.

Wiegers, F. (1949/50). Rohstoffversorgung im paläolithikum. *Prähistorisches Zeitschrift*, 34/5: 225–30.

Wiessner, P. (1974). A functional estimator of population from floor area. *American Antiquity*, 39: 343–50.

Wiessner, P. (1982). Risk, reciprocity and social influences on !Kung San economics. In E. Leacock and R. B. Lee (eds.) *Politics and History in Band Societies*, 61–84. Cambridge, Cambridge University Press.

Wiessner, P. (1983). Style and social information in Kalahari San projectile points. *American Antiquity*, 48: 253–76.

Wildman, M. (1982). Handaxes: an energetic approach. Southampton University, unpublished B.A. dissertation.

Wilkinson, P. F. (1975). The relevance of musk ox exploitation to the study of prehistoric animal economies. In E. S. Higgs (ed.) *Palaeoeconomy*, 9–53. Cambridge, Cambridge University Press.

Williams, B. J. (1974). A model of band society. *Society for American Archaeology*, Memoir 29.

Wilmsen, E. N. (1970). Lithic analysis and cultural inference: a palaeo-indian case. *Anthropological Papers of the University of Arizona*, 16.

Wilmsen, E. N. (1973). Interaction, spacing behaviour, and the organization of hunting bands. *Journal of Anthropological Research*, 29: 1–31.

Wilson, E. O. (1975). *Sociobiology: The New Synthesis*. Cambridge, Belknap.

Winterhalder, B. P. (1981). Foraging strategies in the boreal forest: an analysis of Cree hunting and gathering. In B. Winterhalder and E. A. Smith (eds.) *Hunter-Gatherer Foraging Strategies*, 66–98. Chicago, University of Chicago Press.

Winterhalder, B. P., and Smith, E. A. (eds.) (1981). *Hunter-Gatherer Foraging Strategies*. Chicago, University of Chicago Press.

Winters, H. D. (1963). An archaeological survey of the Wabash valley in Illinois. *Illinois State Museum, Reports of Investigations*, No. 10.

Wobst, H. M. (1974). Boundary conditions for palaeolithic social systems: a simulation approach. *American Antiquity*, 39: 147–78.

Wobst, H. M. (1976). Locational relationships in palaeolithic society. *Journal of Human Evolution*, 5: 49–58.

Wobst, H. M. (1977). Stylistic behaviour and information exhange. In C. E. Cleland (ed.) *Papers for the Director: Research Essays in Honour of James B. Griffin*, 317–42. Anthropological Papers, Museum of Anthropology, University of Michigan, No. 61.

Wobst, H. M. (1978). The archaeo-ethnology of hunter-gatherers or the tyranny of the ethnographic record in archaeology. *American Antiquity*, 43: 303–9.

Woillard, G. M. (1978). Grande Pile Peat Bog: a continuous pollen record for the last 140,000 years. *Quaternary Research*, 9: 1–21.

Woillard, G. M. (1980). The pollen record of Grande Pile (N.E. France) and the climatic chronology through the last interglacial-glacial cycle. In J. Chaline (ed.) *Problèmes de Stratigraphie Quaternaire en France et dans les Pays Limitrophes*, 95–103. Dijon, Association Française pour l'Étude du Quaternaire.

Woillard, G., and Mook, W. G. (1982). Carbon-14 dates at Grande Pile: correlation of land and sea chronologies. *Science*, 215: 159–61.

Woldstedt, P. (1958). *Das Eiszeitalter, Grundlinien einer Geologie des Quartärs*. Stuttgart.

Wolpoff, M. H. (1975). Discussion. In R. H. Tuttle (ed.) *Palaeoanthropology, Morphology and Paleoecology*, 15. The Hague, Mouton.

Wolpoff, M. H., Smith, F. H., Malez, M., Radovčić, J., and Rukavina, D. (1980). Upper pleistocene human remains from Vindija Cave. *American Journal of Physical Anthropology*, 54: 499–545.

Wood, W. R., and Johnson, D. L. (1978). A survey of disturbance processes in archaeological site formation. In M. B. Schiffer (ed.) *Advances in Archaeological Method and Theory*, 1: 315–81. New York, Academic Press.

Woodcock, A. (1981). *The Lower and Middle Paleolithic Periods in Sussex*. Oxford, British Archaeological Reports, British Series, 94.

Wymer, J. J. (1968). *Lower Palaeolithic Archaeology in Britain, as Represented by the Thames Valley*. London, John Baker.

Wymer, J. J. (1976). The interpretation of palaeolithic cultural and faunal material found in pleistocene sediments. In D. A. Davidson and M. L. Shackley (eds.) *Geoarchaeology*, 327–34. London, Duckworth.

Wymer, J. J. (1977). The archaeology of man in the British Quaternary. In F. W. Shotton (ed.) *British Quaternary Studies: Recent Advances*, 93–106, Oxford, Clarendon Press.

Wymer, J. J. (ed.) (1977). *Gazetteer of Mesolithic Sites in England and Wales*. London, Council for British Archaeology, Research Report 20.

Wymer, J. J. (1981). The palaeolithic. In I. G. Simmons and M. J. Tooley (eds.) *The Environment in British Prehistory*, 49–81. London, Duckworth.

Wymer, J. J. (1982). *The Palaeolithic Age*. London, Croom Helm.

Yellen, J. E. (1977a). *Archaeological Approaches to the Present*. New York, Academic Press.

Yellen, J. E. (1977b). Cultural patterning in faunal remains: evidence from the !Kung Bushmen. In D. Ingersoll, J. E. Yellen and W. Macdonald (eds.) *Experimental Archaeology*, 271–331. New York, Columbia University Press.

Yellen, J. E., and Harpending, H. C. (1972). Hunter-gatherer populations and archaeological inference. *World Archaeology*, 4: 244–53.

Yengoyan, A. A. (1968). Demographic and ecological influence in Aboriginal Australian marriage sections. In R. B. Lee and I. DeVore (eds.) *Man the Hunter*, 185–99. Chicago, Aldine.

Yengoyan, A. A. (1972). Ritual and exchange in aboriginal Australia: an adaptive interpretation of male initiation rites. In E. N. Wilmsen (ed.) *Social Exchange and Interaction*, 5–9. Anthropological Papers, Museum of Anthropology, University of Michigan, 46.

Yengoyan, A. A. (1976). Structure, event and ecology in Aboriginal Australia: a comparative viewpoint. In N. Peterson (ed.) *Tribes and Boundaries in Australia*, 121–32. Canberra, Australian Institute of Aboriginal Studies.

Zaverniaev, F. M. (1978a). *Chotylevskoe paleolititcheskoe mestonachozhdenie*. Leningrad, NAUK.

Zaverniaev, F. M. (1978b). Antropomorfnaja skul'ptura chotylevskoj verchnepaleolitičeskoj stojanki. *Sovetskaja Archaeologica*, 4: 145–61.

Zebera, K. (ed.) (1954). Compte rendue de la IIe étape de recherches géologiques quaternaires à Předmost. *Anthropozoikum*, 4: 291–362.

Zeuner, F. E. (1959). *The Pleistocene Period*, 2nd edn. London, Hutchinson.

Zotz, L. F. (1941). Eine Karte der ürgeschichtlichen Höhlenrastplätze Gross-Deutschlands. *Quartär*, 3: 132–55.

Zotz, L. F. (1951). *Altsteinzeitkunde Mitteleuropas*. Stuttgart.

Zotz, L. F. (1955). *Das Paläolithikum in den Weinberghöhlen bei Mauern*. Bonn, Quartär-Bibliothek, 2.

Zotz, L. F. (1968). Die Venusstatuette von Moravany nad Váhom. *Slovenská Archeologiá*, 16: 5–17.

SITE INDEX

Abri Blanchard 198
Abri Bourgeois-Delaunay 149, 153
Abri Caminade 346
Abri Cap Blanc 232
Abri Castanet 198
Abri Facteur 192–3
Abri Fritsch 218
Abri Laussel 198
Abri Messena 171
Abri Olha 169
Abri Pataud 192, 195, 197, 263, 285, 289, 295–6, 313, 350, 361
Abri Suard 153
Abri Vaufrey 149
Achenheim 146, 270, 309
Altamira 221–2, 228, 232–3, 340, 342
Altmühl Valley 166
Ambrona 156–8
Anagni 156–7
Andernach 205
Anoskova II 185
Arago 157, 309
Arcy-sur-Cure 165, 167, 187
Ardèche 157
Arene Candide 238–9
Aridos 156, 270
Arka 219, 221
Aschersleben See 160
Asprochaliko 175, 200, 239, 347, 349, 351
Atapuerca 158, 309
Atelier Commont 141
Avdeevo 185, 327

Bacho Kiro 169, 194, 196, 281, 331, 361
Badanj 237, 244
Badegoule 226
Bakers Hole 144
Balve Cave 163, 165
Banat 196
Banks Island 289
Banolas 309
Barca I 268
Barca II 268
Barranc Blanc 239
Baume Bonne 157, 286

Baume Latronne 245
Bayol Cave 245
Bedeilhac 232
Benagu 252
Bergeraçois 153
Biache-St-Vaast 140–1, 309
Bilzingsleben 141, 144, 147, 149, 303, 309–10
Bockstein 161, 163, 347, 359
Bohunice 161
Brassempouy 198
Breitenbach 183, 185
Brillenhöhle 183, 263, 319, 361
Broion Cave 171, 347
Bruniquel 228
Buda-Dealul Viei 212
Buda-Lespezi 205, 212

Ca 'Verde 173
Cala della Ossa 200, 237
Calinesti 221
Calowanie 207, 212
Camp Century 83, 85, 88
Canaule I 194
Canecaude I 244
Cariguela 173
Castelcivita Cave 199
Castillo 150, 193, 196, 345
Cavallo Cave 201, 361
Ceahlau 186
Cerveny Kopec 77, 79, 81, 364
Chatelperron 189
Cheddar Gorge 210
Chillac 149
Clacton 120, 129, 141, 147, 153, 268, 278, 303, 310, 387
Combe-Grenal 14, 126, 149–50, 172, 281, 297, 312, 361
Combe-Capelle 197
Corbiac 262
Cotencher 171
Cougnac 232
Cova Negra 158, 309
Creswell Crags 210
Crvena Stijena 175, 200, 201, 237, 361

Cro Magnon 197
Cueta de la Mina 342
Cueva del Niño 244
Cueva Morín 193–4, 196, 346, 361
Cueva Volcán 242

D27b Negev Desert 255
Dniestr 161
Dobranichevka 216, 265
Dolní Vestonice 181, 186, 265, 299, 324
Drachenhöhle bei Mixnitz 318
Drachenloch 150

Ebbou 245
Ederheim Hohlenstein 217
Ehringsdorf 140, 146–7, 149, 272, 309
El Almendro 367
El Juyo 221, 235
El Pendo 193
Enlene Cave 226, 232
Erd 169, 318
Erpfingen Barenhöhle 312
Esquicho-Grapaou 200–1

Font de Gaume 232
Fontanet 232, 234
Fontéchevade 149–50, 153, 309
Fourneau de Diable 232
Franchthi Cave 239

Gare de Couze 218, 353
Gargas 187, 232
Garnsey Site 296
Geissenklosterle 180, 186, 245, 374
Geldrop 216
Gönnersdorf 205, 216, 226, 265, 289, 329, 336–7
Gontsy 265
Gorham's Cave 174–5, 199, 361
Gough's Cave 210
Grand Pile 83, 85, 87
Grimadli Caves 202
Groitzsch 207

Grotta della Cala 202, 361
Grotta Guattari 176, 270
Grotta Paglicci 200, 202,
 237–8, 350–1, 361
Grotta Polesini 239, 242, 244,
 319, 359
Grotte de l'Adaouste 236
Grotte de l'Hyène 165, 361
Grotte de la Betche 180
Grotte de la Bouverie 236,
 238
Grotte des Enfants 201
Grotte du Cheval 216
Grotte du Pape 198
Grotte du Prince 309
Grotte de Renne 180, 187,
 189, 262–3
Gudenushöhle 212
Guillassou 268

Hahnofersand 167
Haua Fteah 347, 351
Hengistbury Head 207, 210,
 260
High Lodge 141, 147
Holy Cross Mountains 120
Hortus 174–5, 314, 347, 361
Hoxne 129, 140–1, 278
Hunas 141, 160, 345, 369

Ilsenhöhle 166, 188, 359
Isernia la Pineta 150, 155–7,
 177
Istállösko Cave 180, 183, 284,
 318, 358
Isturitz 196, 219, 222, 226,
 228, 336

Jarama gravels 157
Jerzmanowice 163, 166, 180,
 245, 286

Kadar 221
Kálmán-Lambrecht Cave 161
Kapovaya 216
Karlich 77
Kartstein 165
Kastelhöhle 219
Kastritsa 237, 239, 347, 349,
 351, 359, 361
Kents Cavern 163, 167, 179,
 245, 205
Kephallinia 156
Kesslerloch 205, 208, 214,
 216
Ketrosy 161
Khotylevo 147, 187
Kiik-koba 163, 168
Klasies River Mouth 369
Klaussenische 163, 167, 359
Kniegrotte 207
Kokkinopilos 174–5

Konigsaue 160, 163, 167
Korman IV 161, 205, 211
Kosice 186
Kosten 286
Kostenki 180–1, 183, 185,
 187, 188, 212, 260–2,
 265, 287–90, 299, 327,
 377, 366
Krakow-Zwierzyniec 333
Krapina 171–3
Krems Hundsteig 183
Kudaro 147
Kůlna Cave 161, 163,
 212, 345, 347, 358

L'Hermitage 165
La Calmette 174
La Chaise 309
La Chaix 309
La Chapelle aux Saints 172
La Cotte 141, 288–9, 345,
 357, 361
La Ferrassie 172, 189, 192–5,
 198, 347, 358, 361
La Madeleine 135, 208, 218,
 220, 222, 228, 350, 353
La Marche 226
La Micoque 149–50, 152,
 347
La Pasiega 233
La Pileta 244
La Riera 218, 222, 350, 259,
 361
La Salpêtrière 200, 236, 262,
 361
Labastide 228
Lake Onega 289
Lake Vico 102
Lascaux 232
Lassac 236
Laugerie-Basse 228
Laugerie-Haute 7, 195, 218–
 20, 346,–7, 361
Laussel 324
Lazaret 157–8, 260, 263, 309
Le Breuil 268
Le Cerisier 268
Le Figuier 245
Le Flageolet 195, 218, 274,
 347
Le Moustier 172, 189, 347
Le Portel 219, 232
Le Tillet 140, 165
Le Tuc d'Audoubert 232
Le Verberie 290
Lehringen 120, 387
Les Combarelles 232
Les Cottés 180
Les Eglises 219
Les Etiolles 207, 255, 260
Les Eyzies 6, 189
Les Jambes 193

Les Mallaetes 199–210, 236,
 239, 242, 244, 350, 351
Les Tarterets 207, 255
Les Trois Frères 232
Lespugue 198
Levallois 119
Levanzo 244
Lezetxiki 314, 321
Limeuil 226
Lipa 212
Lommersum 180, 185, 262,
 366
Lonetal 347
Lovas 289
Lubna 260

Madonna del Freddo 158
Mainz Linsenberg 187
Maisières canal 181, 183
Manzanares 157
Markkleeberg 140, 146–7,
 158
Mas d'Azil 218–19, 222, 228,
 336
Maszycka Cave 212
Mauer 147, 272, 309
Mauern 161, 166, 183, 187,
 255, 286, 293, 318
Meer 279
Meiendorf 205, 210
Mezhirich 216, 265, 289
Mezin 207, 212, 216, 265,
 289, 299
Mikaelovska 147
Molodova 161, 180–1, 185,
 205, 207, 212, 258, 282,
 265, 364
Monfenera 150
Monte Castillo 233
Monte Circeo 175
Montgaudier Cave 289
Montmaurin 153
Moravany nad Vahom 183,
 327
Moravany Podkovica 185,
 187
Mosbach 308
Moskva River 147
Mother Grundy's Parlour 210
Munzingen 214, 335
Muselievo 171, 175

Neander Valley 167
Nebra 217
Negev 279
Niaux 232
Nitra 185
Northfleet 303
Noviny 185

Odderade 88
Oelknitz 217

Ojcow 163
Oka river 147
Olbrachiche 120
Orgnac 157–8, 174, 309
Ovca 221
Ovcja 219

Padul 102
Pair non Pair 232
Palaiokastron 157
Palidoro 237, 359
Parpalló 200, 226, 236, 242, 244, 350–1, 361
Paviland 188
Pavlov 181, 260, 299
Pech de l'Azé 149–50, 168–9, 281, 347, 361
Pech Merle 232, 234
Pégourié Cave 218
Pekarna 212, 216
Petersfels 205, 208, 210, 214, 217, 220, 252, 335, 357
Petralona 309
Piage 192, 361
Pilisszanto 297
Pincevent 210, 255, 260, 279, 289–90
Pinedo 157
Plassen-al-Lomm 181
Plateau Parrain 268
Pod Hradem 318
Poggenwisch 205
Pont d'Ambon 218
Ponte di Veia 219, 221
Pontnewydd 140–1, 147, 309, 347
Predmost 185, 188, 366
Prezletice 140

Quinzano 173

Remenham 152
Remetea Somos 221, 331
René Clastres 234
Repoulst 150
Reutersruh 144
Rheindhalen 146, 165, 366
Rigabe 174
Riparo Maurizo 241
Riparo Tagliente 219, 221, 235
Ripiceni Izvor 163, 169, 183, 256, 364

Rissen 207
Robin Hood's Cave 207
Roc de Combe 192
Roc de Sers 232
Roche Lalinde 217
Romanesti Dumbravita 196
Romanelli 237, 239
Romito 237, 245
Rorshain 163, 286
Rouffinac 232
Rozdrojovice 335

Saccopastore 176
Sagvar 219, 221, 225, 297
Salleles Cabarades 245
Salzgitter Lebenstedt 146–7, 270
Samuilitsa Cave 169
San Teodoro 245
Sandalja 157–8, 237
Schambach 163
Schussenquelle 205, 214
Schweizersbild 205, 214
Sesselfelsgrotte 359, 361
Soleihac 149
Solutré 219, 238
Spadzista Street 181, 185, 265, 287, 289–90, 327
Speckberg 163
Sprendlingen 183, 337
Spy 165, 167, 357
St Acheul 141
St Brais 219
St Césaire 172
St Germaine la Rivière 235
St Isidro 157
Stadel 161, 167, 180, 186, 318
Starosel'e 163, 168, 318
Ste Anne d'Evenos 157
Steinheim 309
Stellmoor 207, 210, 295
Stranska Skala 141
Streletskaya 185
Sun Hole 205
Sunghir 181, 185, 188
Sussenborn 308
Swabian Alb 180, 214
Swanscombe 139–41, 144, 303, 309, 366
Swidry 207, 212
Szeleta Cave 180, 347

Tara Oaşului 196

Tata 169
Taubach 141, 144, 147, 152, 272
Taurisano 237
Tel'manskaya 265
Tenaghi Phillipon 77, 83
Terme Piliat 198
Terra Amata 157, 269
Thurrock 303
Tibava 288
Tito Bustillo 221
Torralba 120, 156–8, 270, 272, 284
Torre del Alto 286
Torre in Pietra 156–7, 175, 270
Trecassats 174, 299

Uluzzo 361
Upton Warren 88

Valencia 174
Valle Guimenta 158
Vallonnet 156–7
Velika Pecina 194
Venosa 158
Verberie 258, 260, 289
Vértesszöllös 149–50, 152–4, 303, 310
Veternica 171, 260
Victoria Cave 82–3, 160, 368
Vindija 171–2, 194
Vogelherd 180, 183, 186, 284, 359

Wallendorf 144, 303
Wangen 144, 303, 310
Westbury-sub-Mendip 139, 141
Wildkirchli 150
Wildemannlissloch 150
Wildscheuer 167
Willendorf II 181, 183, 185, 187, 327
Witow 207, 212, 268
Wylotne 163

Yeliseyevichi 205, 212, 265
Yudinovo 216

Zhitomir 147
Zoolithenhöhle 318
Zupanov 221

GENERAL INDEX

acheulean (*see* micoquian)
  tools and assemblages 141,
    150, 153, 156, 158, 310
  geographical distribution
    147, 167
  Cantabria 150
  Caucasus 147
  Italy 157
  Jungacheuléen 146
  Sicily 157
  Spain 157
activity area
  differential distribution 16
  concept 273
adaptation 16, 375, 387
adaptedness 16
adaptive
  behaviour 249
  strategies 32, 56, 250
Adriatic 91
Africa
  Amboseli basin 21, 64
  grasslands 36
aggression 104
ahrensburgian points 210
alliance
  changes in networks 378
  closure 56
  environmental constraints
    58
  information 55
  North Alaska 54
  redistribution 54
Alpine glaciation 74, 75
Alpine region 150, 197
Alyawara 43
animal species
  behaviour 112
  changing proportions 297
  diversity 297
annual territory 69, 376
antler 210
  groove and splinter 284
anvil technique 117
arc patterns, lithics 252
archaeological record
  constraints on formation
    249
  debate on formation 15
  over-simplification of 12

  visibility 20
archaeological signatures 176,
    369–70, 391
Arctic fauna 161
Arctic fox (*Alopex lagopus*)
  103, 110
Arctic tundra 40
arrowheads
  barbed and tanged 122, 236
art (*see* cave art, engraving)
  associated with
    magdalenian 226, 228
  general 139
  mediterranean province
    202
  mobiliary 248
  northern province 186–9,
    216–17
  representational 216
  southern France 197
  southern province 197–9,
    226–35
artifact
  antler 121
  bone 121
  carved 228
  contemporary residues 310
  cryoturbated 181, 347
  decorated 216, 228
  density, open sites 366
  flint 202
  ideational 17
  ivory 121
  material 17
  recycling 275
  replacement rates 284
  societal 17
  types 144
  unit of observation 62
  use life 284
  wood 120
assemblage
  analysis 10
  as collection 353
  characterisation 279
  coarse grained 23
  consistent size 354
  contemporaneity 248
  creation of assemblage 214
  date 147

  definition 9
  diachronic variation 152
  equals human group 12
  fine grained 24
  flake 144, 147
  frequency 359, 361
  interstratification 192–3,
    246, 248
  leaf point 165, 180–3
  links with northern
    province 152
  lower palaeolithic 149
  LUP 7, 239
  middle palaeolithic 163
  minimum 359
  non-handaxe 158
  non-projectile point
    element 286
  Périgord 356–7
  quantitative data 354
  recurrent patterning 390
  regional variation 201
  scraper dominated 171, 174
  similarity 133
  synchronic variation 152
  variants 146
asinipodien 169
arenien 236, 238
aurignacian 7, 180, 183, 186,
    189, 192, 195, 199, 201,
    245, 246
Artemisia steppe 101
Athapaskan 48, 56
aurochs (*Bos primigenius*)
  103, 110
Australia
  aboriginal 47
  Arnhem Land 34
  colonisation 384
  dialect tribes 51
  environmental impact on
    local groups 34
  local organisation 34
  raw material networks 331
  Western Desert 34
awls 121

bachokirian 194
backed blade assemblages
  210, 245

base camp 171, 299
baton de commandement
　　210
beads 187, 198
bear (*Ursus* sp.) 104, 307,
　　311, 314, 319
　brown 110
　cave (*Ursus spelaeus*) 110,
　　171, 314, 318
beech (*Fagus* sp.) 100
beetles
　habitat tolerance 88
behaviour 16, 249, 263
　repetitive 260
　seasonal 176
behavioural realm
　non-utilitarian 17
　utilitarian 17
behavioural perspective 344
Belgium 165
bifaces 157
bifacial
　implements 167
　knives 163
　tools 165
Bihor 33
biological constant 18
biology
　non-deterministic 383
biomass
　animal 111
　density 104
birch (*Betula* sp.) 88, 101
bison (*Bison* sp.) 81, 104, 106,
　　110
blades
　preparation 120
　standard blanks 120
Blake magnetic excursion 83
Bocksteinmesser 163
Bohemia 335
bone
　antler tools, geographical
　　pattern 225
　fragmentation 293
　groove and splinter 284
　manufacture 284
　utilitarian objects 210
　worked 244
Bordes analysis 125–6 (*see*
　　typology)
boundaries 33, 52, 71
bow 122, 181, 239
bracelets 187
breakage rates
　projectile points 287
　relative 286
breccia 168
Brittany 165
Bromme/Lyngby point 210
Brunhes epoch 75
Buda industry 152

burials 168, 172, 246, 248,
　　343
　double 245
　early aurignacian 197
　flexed 235
　magdalenian 235
　mediterranean province
　　202, 245
　missed 197
　northern province 186–9,
　　216–17
　southern province 197–9,
　　235
　Sunghir 188
budgeting 114
buffer zone 213

caches 289
camp (*see* site)
　overnight 299
　sites 251, 264
cannibalism 173
Cantabria 171, 196, 199, 202,
　　222, 223
carnivores
　change through time 319
　competition 309, 320
　coping strategy 307
　denning behaviour 307, 320
　independent measure 307
　large 311
　last glacial 311
　proportions 312, 313, 314
　regional variation 318
　residues 309, 320
Caspian Sea 69, 91
Caucasus 69
cave art 216, 228–34, 248 (*see*
　　art; engraving)
　animal 232
　Cantabria 233
　Dordogne 232
　engraving 232, 244
　explanation 338–9
　Gironde 232
　hand signs 232
　interpretation 233
　Lot 232
　measure of competition
　　340
　painting 244–5
　patterning 233
　polychrome 232
　sculpture 232
　styles 228–32
　sub regions 232
cave sediments
　accumulation 85, 347, 351
　Cantabria 85, 87
　cryoclastic 350
　deposits 345
　frost activity 346–7

mud flows 347
　origin 85
　preservation of
　　archaeological material
　　350
　southern Germany 87
cave sites 149, 153, 186
　artifact numbers 353
　carnivore variation 321
　discontinuous occupation
　　346
　discontinuous sediment
　　346
　mousterian 171
　Northern Province 161
　orientation 222
　parent geology 345
　pleistocene sediments 345
　tactical appreciation 320
　time sharing 321
central Europe 91
chamois (*Rupicapra
　　rupicapra*) 104, 109–10
Channel river 207
Charentian 165, 174 (*see*
　　Mousterian)
chatelperronian/Lower
　　perigordian 180, 194, 200
chert 121
Chipewyan 54
chopping tools 117, 147, 152,
　　303 (*see* pebble tools)
chronology 139, 149–50, 155–
　　6, 160–3, 165–9, 173–5,
　　179–81, 189, 192, 199,
　　205, 212–19, 236–7, 246
　dating anomalies 205
chronostratigraphy 192
civilisation 10
Clactonian 141, 144, 158
　geographical distribution
　　147
clams 113
clean-up strategies 264
CLIMAP 95
climate 74, 87, 174, 222
closed system 332
clusters 272–3
coastal lowlands 175
cockles (*Cardium edule*) 113
cold climate (*see* pleistocene)
　conditions 160
　episodes 85
　sediments 161
collector system 47
　settlement types 47
colonisation 177
communication
　density 51
　verbal 322
comparative approach 32, 40
conceptual framework 26

constraint
  ecological 23
cooking 292
core reduction strategies 120,
  336
core tools 117
Cree 45
Creswell point 210
Crow village 265
cryoturbation 171, 270
cultural
  material 263
  tradition 5, 12
culture 10, 13, 310
  normative view 12
  particularisation of hunters
  32
culture history 9–12, 116 (*see
  also* paradigm)
  'straight' archaeology 9
  groupings 248
curation 275, 177–9, 389
cut marks 293

data
  monothetic and polythetic
  sets 250
deciduous forest 100–1
debitage 281
deep sea cores 8, 75, 386
  V28–238 76
deglaciation 204, 247
deme 51
demography 40, 61
  change 371
  domain 65
  imbalance 310
dens 307 (*see* carnivores)
density figures 358
depositional envelopes 353,
  364
discard 20, 251, 257–8
disturbance 139
Dogger Bank 92
domain 34, 65 (*see* spatial)
Dordogne 189
dwarf shrubs 102
dwellings 268 (*see* houses,
  huts, tents)
drainage
  basins 71
  divisions 71
Dryas octopetala 94
Dryas
  older 205
  phases 94
drop zone 257 (*see* spatial)

ecofactual data 18
ecological principles 32
economic anatomy 295
ecotone 171

effective temperature 37
efficiency 45, 288
electron spin resonance 160
elk (*Alces alces*) 110
Elster glaciation 80
embedded strategy 275
encounter strategy 388, 390
endogamy 52
energy 45, 279 289
England 92, 94, 102, 165
engraving 197, 216–17, 244
  (*see* art; cave art)
  antler rods 340
  objects 216
  plaques 329
  plaquettes 217
  slabs 226, 244
environment
  brittle 41
  complex 40–2
  determinant 30, 370
  general 45
  high risk 324
  limiting factors 109
  selection pressures on
  strategies 22, 46
  simple 40–2
  variation 17
  zonation 17
epigravettian
  Alpine region 221
  assemblages 219, 221, 230
  early 237
  final 221, 237
  mediterranean province
  238
Epirus 240
erosion 87
Eskimo 32, 48, 51, 56
estate 34 (*see* spatial)
ethnicity 172
ethnoarchaeology 28, 59–62,
  290, 305
ethnographic record 26, 59
Eurasia 69
Europe 66
  climatic patterns 71
  demarcation 69
  division into regions 70
  environmental variation 69
  latitude/longitude 70
  regions/provinces 71
  relief 70
European century 1
European palaeolithic
  changing relevance 8
evenosien 157
evergreen oak (*Quercus ilex*)
  100
evolution
  goal oriented 4
  industrial 169

'many-headed' 169
  socio-cultural 372
  strategy 393
  theory 2
excavation 357
exchange system 58
exogamy 33, 50
exploitation
  cost 42
  frozen carcasses 387
  human 110
  magdalenian 214
  pattern 262
  seasonal 172
extraction site 120 (*see* raw
  material)

family 32
fauna
  British pleistocene 308
  cave 311
  mesolithic 370
faunal assemblage
  composition 293
  integrity and resolution
  296
  preservation 293
Faunal
  date 312, 320
  exploitation studies 196
  record 307
  remains 139, 171
Feddermesser assemblage
  207, 218
figurines 121, 217
  absence 202
  baked clay 186
  distribution 329
  eastern gravettian 186–7
  female 198
  ivory 186
  Kniegrotte 216
  locality 389
  Venus 187, 202, 324
fine grained assemblage 24
fir (*Abies*) 88
fire 11
fishing 35, 213
fission and fusion 32, 44
flake
  assemblages 144, 147
  implements 157
  production 177
  refitting 268
  tools 117
flexibility 44, 63
flint 120 (*see* raw material)
  blades 121
  fracture 119–20
  heat treatment 120
  Holy Cross Mountains 281
  production techniques 181

flora 213
fluvial
  deposition 270
  deposits 366
food
  frozen resources 387–8
  marine 222
  nutrients 43
  parcels 291
  resources 101
  supply 112
  unearned 112
  winter 109
food management
  signature 65
  strategies 290, 292, 296, 390
footprints 234
Font Robert tanged points 181
forager system 46, 47
foraging
  optimal behaviour 45
  strategy 388
  technology 388
foraminifera 75, 82
forest elephant (*see* straight tusked elephant)
forest
  exploitation costs 370
  genial conditions 310
  oak mixed 367
  regeneration 83
  steppe 161
fox (*Vulpes vulpes*) 319
France 92
  effect of palaeolithic studies 7
  human remains 158
  mediterranean littoral 174
  regional tradition 5–7
frozen carcasses
  exploitation 387
functional argument 14

'Garden of Eden' 7
gear
  personal 277
  situational 277
gene flow 386
General Utility Index (GUI) 291
genetic drift 386
genotype 26
geographical variation in Palaeolithic Europe
  provinces 152–3, 158, 166, 171–2, 175–6, 185, 196–7, 212, 221–6, 239–43
geomorphology 74
Germany
  middle palaeolithic 126

interstadials 88
giant deer (*Megaloceros giganteus*) 104, 110
glaciation 79, 85
glacial
  cycles 8
  full 204
gnawing 293
gravel terrace 87, 156
gravettian 7, 181, 183, 201, 246 (*see* perigordian)
  eastern 181, 185–6, 205, 212
  evolved 207
  gravettian/upper perigordian 245
  later 200
  lower perigordian 194
  noaillian 238
  post noaillian 238
  solutreo 2–36, 238
  type fossil 183
  Yeliseyevichian 212
group
  organisation 32
  participation 235
G/wi San 54

habitat
  diversity 171
  resilience 41
habitation pits 265
hafting 247
hammers
  hard 117
  soft 117
handaxes 117, 123, 152–3, 163, 310
  bout coupé 165
  distribution 146, 331
  England 123
  finishing 118
  intermediate 141
  ovate 141
  pointed 141
  replication experiment 117
  roughing out 117
  source of flakes 288
  southern England 141
  thinning and shaping 117
  Ukraine 147
harpoons 220
  antler 208
hazel (*Corylus* sp.) 100
heat treatment 120
Helicigona banatica 83
hematite 202
herb pollen 101
herbivores 97, 103, 312
herd
  following 225
  species 110, 297, 396

hearth 207, 255, 260
  arc patterns 252
  central 258
  drop zone 257
  ethnographic examples 262
  lithic processing 262
  multiple user 262
  outside working 260
  re-use 289
  sleeping 262
  toss zone 257
hippopotamus (*Hippopotamus amphibius*) 83, 109–11, 368
Holland 88
hollow based points 185
holocene 74
Holy Cross Mountain 336
home base 241
home range 47–9, 69, 391 (*see* spatial)
Homo
  erectus 26, 178
  sapiens neanderthalensis 167
  sapiens sapiens 178
horse 104, 106, 110
houses (*see* dwellings; huts; tents)
  archaeological remains 260
  Dolní Věstonice 265
  Gönnersdorf 216
  implications of size 264
  mammoth bone 216, 289
  permanent 213
  winter 265
human
  adaptation 96
  behaviour 251, 304, 306
  diet 320
  material 139
  strategies 35, 386–7
human remains 178–9, 272
  by province 147–9, 153–4, 158–60, 167–8, 172–3, 176, 308–9
hunting 35, 107, 111, 214, 388
  and gathering 393
  behaviour 158
  camp 291, 299
  stand 291
hunter-gatherers 20
  Africa 36
  alliance 54
  analogy with past 28
  Australia 392
  breeding unit 50
  Chipewyan 54
  ecological exploitation 30
  equilibrium models 50

group size 50
G/wi 54
impact of world systems 66
Ingalik 265
insurance strategies 54
!Kung San 28, 36, 43, 45–6, 258, 291, 324
language dialects 51
latitudinal transect 35
local group 50
maximum band 50
mesolithic 392
Nunamiut 28, 256, 263, 265
organisation and ecological structure 39
patterns of exploitation 29
Pintupi 20, 57
population density 49
regional systems 54ff, 69
social relations 29
Tlingit 43, 113
visibility in the archaeological record 20
huts (*see* dwellings; houses; tents)
hyena (*Crocuta* sp.) 103, 106, 110, 293, 307, 311, 314, 319, 369
    activity 272
    den 176, 270
hydrological regimes 270

Iberia 92, 174–5
ibex (*Capra ibex*) 104, 109–10
ice
    caps 87, 91
    cores 83
    sheets 306
    wedges 87, 160
industry and industrial groupings
    definition 9
    evolutionary groupings 177
    geographical treatment 7
    middle palaeolithic 7
    provinces 144–6, 150–2, 157, 163–6, 169–71, 174–5, 181–5, 194, 200–1, 208–12, 219–22, 237–9, 246–7
    upper palaeolithic 246–7
    variation 174
information
    Aboriginal Australia 58
    cost of communication 57
    culture as 56
    exchange 58, 392
    flow 61
    language differences 58
    links 322
    material culture 57

mediums 330
    Kalahari San 57
    social system dominant strategy 56–9
    tribal encyclopedia 56
    verbal and visual 56
Ingalik 265
initiation ceremonies 235
intensification strategy 340, 378
interglacial 139
    faunal communities 83, 111
    Ipswichian 368
    last cycle 82–97, 368
    Mikulino 161
    use of plants 100
interstadial
    Allerød 94, 205
    Amersfoort 161
    Bølling 94, 205
    Brørup 160–1
    Chelford 88
    correlation 92–4
    Denekamp 90
    episodes 161
    Hengelo 161
    Moershoofd/Upton Warren complex 161
Iran 69
isotope (*see* deep sea cores)
    ^{16}O, ^{18}O 76
    record 94
Italy 174–5

Jaramillo event 156
Jungacheuléen 146

K selection 41
K-Ar dating 75, 177
karst 311
Kashgee 265
kill site 291
knapping techniques 117 (*see* lithics)
Kostenki shouldered knives/points 185, 330
!Kung San 28, 36, 43, 45–6, 258, 291, 324

lacustrine sediments 155
Lagomorphs 112
    /bird horizon 320
Lamarckian principles 40
lamelles Dufour 183, 195
land use
    palaeolithic 239
    studies 186, 196
    reconstruction 147
language 264
    phonetic differences 58
Languedoc 200–1
Laplace typology (*see* typology)

as organic model 135
    dialectic method 135
    polymorphic base 135
large mammals
    exploitation costs 376
latitude
    changes in productivity 35
    global 17
    subsistence 35
    transects 97
Laugerian 196
leaf points 171, 175, 179
    assemblages 165, 180, 181–3
    earlier palaeolithic 286
    laurel 219
    willow 219
Leopard (*Panthera pardus*) 103, 110, 161
leptolithic 121
Les Cottés point 194
levallois
    blades 119
    flakes 118
    points 119
    raw material 144
    technique 119, 144, 157, 165, 169, 175, 201
    tortoise core 119
lichens 100
limpet (*Patella vulgata*) 113
lion (*Felix leo*) 103, 106, 110, 293, 311, 314, 319, 369
Lithic
    artifacts 330
    industries 238
    knapping techniques 117
    manufacture 117, 178
    material 139, 181, 195
    reduction sequences 178
    reduction strategies 120, 246–7, 336
    technique 201
    traditions 7
local group
    32
location
    intercept 223
    lakeside 156
loess
    accumulation 87
    cycle 96
    deposits 160
    glacial cycle 83
    localities 364
    profiles 83
    sequences 79
lynx (*Felis lynx*) 104

magdalenian
    antler harpoons 328

magdalenian – cont.
  asemblage 207, 212, 218–
    21, 238
  Cantabria 221
  distribution 208, 239
  early 220
  initial 218
  later 220
  microlithic elements 220
  proto- 192, 195
  Pyrenees 220
  regional comparisons 216
  spear throwers 328
  Switzerland 221
mammoth (*Mammonteus
  primigenius*) 81, 104,
  109, 147, 319
  'cemeteries' 272
Man the Hunter symposium
  32
marine
  food 222
  molluscs 175
  productivity 35
  transgression 79
marriage network 53
Mask Site study 256–7
material culture 382
  adaptive strategy 323
  behavioural realms,
    material, societal,
    ideational 17
  communication 322
  information content 321
  meaning 323
  messages 330
  visible messages in 322
mating network 52, 339, 391
  central groups 52
  cost 53
  peripheral groups 52
  maintenance 376
  strategies 61
Matuyama epoch 75, 156
meat
  acquisition 97
  based strategies 387
Mediterranean 69, 87, 92
megafauna 106, 109, 297
  carcass exploitation 388
mesolithic
  cemeteries 381
  hunting organisation 381
methodology
  constructs 21
  middle range theory 21
  problems 23
  transformational
    procedures 21
micoquian 163, 165 (*see*
  acheulean)
  Belgium 163

distribution 167
  Germany 163
  Poland 163
  Russia 163
microlith
  backed blades 122
  bladelets 122
  blade production 120
  element 208, 353
  -isation 221
microwear analysis 126, 135
  high power 129
  low power 129
  studies 278
middle class
  ascendancy of 1
  class identity 2
  Danish 2
minimum number of
  individuals (MNI) 290
mobile
  adaptation 297
  resources 202
mobility 19, 60, 104, 389–90
mode of production 29
model
  adaptation 15
  alliance networks 376
  alternative models of
    exploitation 214
  aquatic 5
  big game hunter 369
  bilateral 32–3
  complete settlement
    system 376
  crude/fine 249
  diet 42–6
  foraging 42–6
  formation of archaeological
    record 274
  'Garden of Eden' 192
  home base 299
  hunter 293
  hunter gatherer mobility
    242
  ice age 8
  intercept hunting 225
  meat management
    strategies 386
  meat storage and self
    sufficiency 390
  multi-dimensional 15–16
  nomadic style 33
  off-site 20, 63, 389
  organic 10, 12
  parallel phylum 152
  patrilocal band 32
  phylogenetic 10
  Pincevent 260
  planned competition 392
  population, ebb and flow
    367, 381

  regional 71–4, 374
  seating plan 256
  self-fulfilling 306
  settlement system 299
  Stanner 33
  three interpretative models
    of the European
    palaeolithic 386–93
  workings of social
    formation 30
modern humans
  arrival of 370
  physical appearance 381
  society 381
Modified General Utility
  Index (MGUI) 291
Molodovian group 211
Moravia
  karst 212
  settlement 185
  varying use of lithic
    resources 333
morphoclines 179
mousterian
  acheulean tradition (MTA)
    153, 165
  Alpine region 171
  charentian 165, 174
  debate 13
  denticulate 171, 174
  micro 175
  pre- 157
  Quina 169, 175
  type sites, 165
  typical 165, 169, 174
  variants 171
musk ox (*Ovibos moschatos*)
  81, 103, 109, 110
multi-disciplinary studies
  221

nationalism 2
natural selection 16
neanderthals
  cold adaptations 381
  physical appearance 380
  population 374
  pre- 158
  remains 176
  society 381
  spear hunting 381
necklace 202
needles 121, 220, 247
Netherlands 80, 88, 102,
  161
network (*see* mating
  network)
  demographic 321
  maintenance 322
  marriage 53
  regional 321
New World colonisation 382

non-food
  products 111
  yield 42
north European plain 91, 167,
    205, 247
northern Europe
  abandonment 339
  forests 85, 367
Nunamiut 28, 256, 263, 265
nutrients 43

oak (*Quercus* sp.) 100
obsidian 121
occupation 161, 169, 213, 247
ocean productivity 35
off site
  archaeology 20, 63
  home range concept 20
olive 100
open sites 140, 150, 153, 171,
    268, 366
open systems 322
opposite platform cores 120
ornaments 121, 187–8
  necklace 202
  pendants 187
over-wintering 197
oyster (*Ostrea edulis*) 113

palaeoeconomic studies 247
palaeolithic
  behaviour 30
  caves 382
  change in personnel 365
  earlier lithic technology
    117–18
  exploitation strategies 106
  global perspective 3
  groups 243
  industries 6
  material 345, 364
  record 16, 17, 19ff, 63, 306
  'yard' 264
  palaeolithic Europe (*see*
    geographical variation)
  interpretative sketch 384
  peripheral area 382
  recolonisation 213, 329
palaeomagnetic
  dating 177
  studies 75
palaeontological records 21
paradigm
  culture as adaptation 8, 13
  culture history 8, 12, 24
pastoralists
  Africa 36
patterns
  covariation 272
  data 116
  partitioning exercises 27
  statistically robust 272

patrilocal band 32–3 (*see*
    social)
pebble tools 117, 157, 303
    (*see* chopping tools)
pendants 187
periglacial 87–8, 92
Périgord 87, 172, 218
perigordian 189, 194–5 (*see*
    gravettian)
permafrost 97, 307
phenotype 26
phylum 144
pig (*Sus scrofa*) 103
pine (*Pinus sylvestris*) 88, 92,
    101
pingos 87
Pintupi 20, 57
plant
  growth 92
  productivity 97
  r selected 98
  resources 98, 101–2
  species 100
  strategies 98, 100
pleistocene 8, 74–5, 80, 82,
    85, 88, 95, 103, 139, 156,
    310 (*see* Quaternary)
  late glacial 94
  maximum 92
  middle 156, 310
points (*see* projectile)
  antler 285
  antler/bone 181
  arrowheads 122, 236
  Brømme/Lyngby 210
  Creswell 210
  Font Robert 181
  hollow based 185
  Kostenki 185, 330
  leaf 171, 175, 179
  Les Cottés 194
  levallois 119
  puntas de muesca 236
  shouldered 210
  tanged 7, 207, 212
pollen analysis 83, 88, 90, 92,
    94, 102, 161, 367
pontinian 174
population
  density 390
  distribution 305
  expansion 213
  explosion 222
  growth and decline 305
  increase 247
  inference of increase 373
  in the landscape 249
  low 324
  refuge zone 339
  regional 32
porcupine (*Hystrix* sp.) 161,
    293

post-depositional factors 290
Pradnik 163
preciptation 71, 91, 102
predictive frameworks 311
prehistoric past 2
pressure flaking 262
primitiveness 29
principle of least effort 42
procurement
  direct 275
  embedded 275
projectile points 120–1, 247,
    286, 379
protomagdalenian 192, 195
Provence 201
Prut valley 331
pseudomorphs 197
puntas de muesca 236
Pyrenees 219–19, 262, 335

quartzite 120, 171
Quaternary 74 (*see*
    pleistocene; periglacial;
    permafrost)
  studies 77, 306

r selection 41, 43, 112, 376,
    392
rabbit (*Oryctalagus
    cuniculus*) 112
raised beaches 82, 85, 140–1,
    156
range 34, 389 (*see* spatial)
raw material 194, 331 (*see*
    chert; flint; obsidian;
    quartzite)
  curation 284
  distribution 331, 337
  dumps 290
  energy input 281
  extraction 120
  imports 331
  local 331
  movement 222, 332, 335
  Slovakian radiolarite 333,
    336
recovery
  standards 358
  technique 353
recycling 19
red deer (*Cervus elaphus*)
    103, 106, 110, 222, 312
'red lady' of Paviland 188
regional
  analysis 16, 26, 39ff
  case studies 167, 199–212,
    212–16, 239–43
  catchment 242
  criteria 69–71
  environment 242
  model 71–4, 239–42, 372
  perspective 32

regional – cont.
  sampling unit 67
  scale 31
  test for behaviour 306
  traditions 3, 116
reindeer (*Rangifer tarandus*)
    80, 103, 106, 110, 196,
    214, 312
  exploitation 223
research design 62–8
resharpening 288
resources
  animal 103ff, 109
  availability 44
  exploitation costs 43
  key 97
  localised 112
  mobile 186
  spatial exploitation 44
  structure 376
  sub-continental
    distribution 386
resource base 222
resource use schedule 42
retouch
  artifacts 126
  heat treatment 120
  natural 126
  pressure 120
  resharpening 288
  secondary 178
  tools 196, 354, 357
risk 14
Riss 149
ritual 171, 338, 339
rock shelters 174, 263, 285
roe deer (*Capreolus
    capreolus*) 103
Roumania 194

Sagaies d'Isturitz 285
saiga antelope (*Saiga
    tartarica*) 109
Sagvarian assemblage 221
salmon 113, 339
Salpetrien assemblage 236
sampling 66
scales 376
scavenging 111
scheduling 43, 112, 114, 339
sea birds 113–14
sea
  level 92, 222
  temperature 339
seals 255
seasonal movement 176, 214
sedentism 339
sediments 168
  particle movement 270
  rates 199
  studies 168
selection pressure 16

settlement 185
  central Italy 202
  coarse grained signature
    392
  coastal plain 171
  continuity 392
  effective temperature 38
  history 66, 177, 247, 353,
    372, 374
  human 369, 386
  mesolithic 369
  off site 299
  partial record 376
  patterns 196
  sedentary strategies 38
  signatures 375
  site 251
  systems 37, 251, 297–304,
    390
shell 337
  traffic 337
shellfish 113, 196
shoreline deposits 156
Sicily 92
signs 186
signature
  archaeological 178, 369–70,
    391
  coarse grained 275
  definition 22
  food management 65
  spatial 297
site
  arc patterns 252
  camp 251, 264, 299
  catchment 201, 241
  contemporaneity 303
  extraction 120
  furniture 277, 289
  group ceremony 234–5
  high integrity 269
  increase in numbers 222
  living 251
  open 140, 150, 153, 171,
    268, 366
  principal unit of analysis
    62
  seasonal aggregation 222
  shelters 256
  survival 247
  transit 299
  type 156, 299
  workshop 120
skeletal material 172
Snow
  cover 109
  probes 387, 389
  ptarmigan (*Lagopus albus*)
    319
social
  behaviour 61
  change 343–4, 371

definition 40
domain 65
evolution 66, 343
geography 61
knowledge 57
organisation 371
relations 30
strategy 378
solar radiation 71, 91
solifluction 150, 181, 270
solutreo-gravettian
    assemblages 236, 238
solutrean 218–26
  distribution 239
  division 219
  expansion 238
  final 220
  Languedoc 238
  lower 219
  mediterranean 236
  middle 219
  proto- 219
  Spanish 238
spacing principle 258, 260
Spain 113, 201
spatial 40ff
  arc patterns 252
  behaviour 60–1
  definition 40
  distribution 252
  domain 34, 65
  drop zone 257
  estate 34
  home range 47–9, 69, 391
  individual 252–5
  lithic material 252
  Mask site 256–7
  patterning 270, 272
  range 34, 389
  signatures 304
  toss zone 257
Spear 122
  throwers 121
spruce (*Picea*) 88
St Kilda 113
status 344
stone artifacts (*ss* lithics)
  function 129
  manufacture 117
  morphology 129
  raw material 120
  stylistic variation 12
storage 37, 107, 214, 390–1
straight tusked elephant
    (*Elephas antiquus*) 104,
    111, 156, 369
strategy
  animal dependent 97
  clean up 264
  early hominid 386
  embedded 275
  encounter 388, 390

food management 46, 290, 292, 296, 390
foraging 388
human coping 322
intensification 340, 378
scavenging 310
settlement system 320
storage 37, 107, 214
subsistence 42
survival 390
stratigraphic
    relationship 125
    succession 139
style
    definition 323
    open systems 324
    problems 338
    selection 330
stylistic variation 12
subsistant 38
subsistence
    change 371
    choice 114
    diversification 213
    economy 175
    reconstruction 147
    shift 196
    strategy 42
    studies 166
Switzerland 223
symbolling 338
system
    closed 332
    collector 47
    exchange 58
    forager 46–7
    open 322
    transformation 34

tally sticks 244
tanged point 7, 207, 212
taphonomy 21
Tarnovian 210
Taubachian 144
Tayacian 150
technological
    division 135
    groupings 248
technology 116, 194, 387
    bone and antler 121
    change 370
    curated 275

efficient 378
expedient 275
latitude 38
manufacturing 380
selection pressure 38
selective hone 38, 390
tactical variable 279
variation and global energy 38
technocomplex 9, 204, 208, 210, 212
technounit 38, 280
temperate oscillation 200
tents 260, 265–6 (*see* dwellings; houses; huts)
territoriality 339
territory
    annual 69, 376
    foraging groups 389
    size 47–9, 376
thermodynamics
    laws 17
time density estimates 358
Tjongerian 210
Tlingit 43, 113
Toas 323
topography 311
toolkit 273–4, 290
tools
    ancillary 141
    antler 185
    bone 183–5
    flake bone 293
    flint 289
    ivory 185
    manufacture 126
toss zone 257 (*see* spatial)
tradition 9
transit camp 299
travertine 141, 169
trophic level 35
tropical rainforest 36, 40
tundra 147
Turkey 69
type fossils 126, 132, 163, 195, 212, 248, 359, 361
typologie analytique 319
typology 194
    analysis 116, 139
    approaches 123, 135
    Bordes 125–6

division 135
Laplace 135, 319
problems 126
procedure 124
research objectives 357
scheme 130, 133, 316

uluzzian 199–200
uniformitarianism 18
upper palaeolithic 4, 90, 120, 179, 248, 268, 371–2, 374
Urals 69

variants 166
variation 60
varves 94
varying hare (*Lepus timidus*) 112
vasconien 169
vegetation 79, 88, 103–4
Venus figurines 187, 202, 324, 326–7
Villafranchian 156

water 53
    sorting 270
watershed 53
Weagamow Ojibwa 114
weathering
    frost 85
    solifluction 85
    water action 85
willow (*Salix*) 88, 92, 102
wolf (*Canis lupus*) 104, 106, 110, 293, 307, 311, 314, 319
wolverine (*Gulo gulo*) 103, 110
woolly rhino (*Coelodonta antiquitatis*) 104, 109, 319
wormwood (*Artemisia*) 92
worked bone 244
world
    ecosystem 35
    prehistory 384
    systems 378
Würm 168, 174, 179, 189

Zinken 210